THE SOUTH AFRICAN DICTIONARY OF FINANCE

RUDY WUITE

Edited by
Prof. Mthuli Ncube of the Wits Business School

© Rudy Wuite

All rights reserved. No part of this book may be reproduced or transmitted in any form or by any means, electronic or mechanical, including photocopying, recording or any information storage or retrieval system, without permission from the copyright holder.

ISBN: 978-1920334024

First edition, first impression 2009

Published by Rollerbird Press
PO Box 4532
Northcliff
2115
South Africa

Edited by Jeannie van den Heever
Proofread by Pat Botes
Cover design by René de Wet
Typeset by Lebone Publishing Services, Cape Town
Printed by ABC Press, Cape Town

Disclaimer

Absa Capital, a division of Absa Bank Limited ("Absa Capital") has sponsored this dictionary only and not provided the information in this dictionary and has not verified for correctness or audited any of the information contained in the various definitions herein. No part of this dictionary in any way constitutes advice by Absa Capital (whether professional, technical or of any other nature).

Any party that uses the dictionary or any of the information contained herein accepts by doing so that he/she/it uses it at his/her/its own risk and without any recourse against any person involved in the preparation or dissemination of the dictionary or the information, and accepts that he/she/it is responsible for obtaining his/her/its own advice on all applicable laws and regulations in any jurisdiction.

ABSA Capital expressly disclaims any liability for any loss or damage (whether direct, indirect or consequential) arising from the use of any information in this dictionary.

To Megan, Nicholas and Ross

Foreword

The origins of investment banks, or merchant banks as they were known as for centuries, date back to the Italian grain merchants of Lombardy during the Middle Ages. Since then, the industry has constantly been redefining itself. The language of investment bankers has become more peculiar to their craft and conversations between practitioners have become increasingly complex.

This situation is not limited to investment banking. Everything from medical terms to plumbing jargon can be intimidating and alienating unless one is able to decode the terminology. *The South African Dictionary of Finance* has been compiled to unlock the language of investment banking and the wider world of finance. Not only does it act as a key to unlocking industry terms, but it does so in a way that is accessible to new entrants to the financial industry.

The South African Dictionary of Finance has been penned by an uncharacteristic source and adopts a non-academic style, resulting in an easily digestible reference guide. The author, Rudy Wuite, a physicist by profession, was drawn to the challenges that investment banking offered. The first challenge facing Rudy was to understand the language used in his MBA classes. A 20-page glossary of terms, handed out by a lecturer, became his compass as he explored this new and unfamiliar world.

As Rudy's understanding of financial and investment banking terms grew, the original glossary of terms became increasingly deficient. More terms were added and adjustments made during the course of his studies and entrance into the financial industry. After completing his MBA studies, Rudy continued this practice at Absa Capital – first at its affiliate in London, Barclays Capital, and then at Absa Capital in Johannesburg.

Ultimately, the 20-page glossary evolved into a 408 page reference work with over 5 500 definitions that were verified and rechecked when the book neared publication. The book took over three years to compile – a relentless pursuit of knowledge, teamwork and collaboration that Absa Capital espouses and admires.

In so many ways, this dictionary not only reflects our business ethos, but more importantly, it also provides a platform to share financial and investment banking terminology in a non-threatening manner with relevant local input and illustrations.

John Vitalo
Chief Executive
Absa Capital

144A See *Rule 144A*.

364 day A loan that is given to a client by a bank for less than a full year. These loans were done for this period of time because less regulatory capital had to be put aside under Basel I banking capital adequacy requirements. Due to the implementation of Basel II, there are no longer any advantages to this type of loan. Also see *Basel; capital adequacy*.

419 fraud scheme A fraud scheme whereby a target is persuaded to advance small amounts of money with the aim of realising large gains in the future. Many of these schemes are Nigerian in origin.

A A credit rating that indicates a company of reasonable quality with a higher risk than AA and possibly susceptible to changes in economic cycles. The A rating is used in the S&P, Fitch and Moody's credit rating scales. Also see *credit rating*.

AA/Aa A credit rating that indicates a quality company with a higher credit or business risk than AAA. The AA rating is used in the S&P and Fitch credit rating scales and Aa is used by Moody's. Also see *credit rating*.

AAA/Aaa The best quality company credit rating. AAA is used by S&P and Fitch and Aaa is used by Moody's. Also see *credit rating*.

AAGR See *average annual growth rate*.

abandonment
1. Not settling an option on delivery date.
2. The forfeiture of title rights on an asset. Also see *title*.

abandon option An American-style put option that affords the holder the right, but not the obligation, to dispose of a fixed asset at a predetermined price. Also see *American style; fixed asset; option; put option*.

ABC See *activity-based costing*.

ABI
1. See *absolute breath index*.
2. Association of British Insurers.

ABM Activity-based management. Also see *activity-based budgeting*.

abnormal return A return in excess of what the market anticipated. Excess returns are usually measured against those derived using the capital asset pricing model and other sophisticated models. Also see *capital asset pricing model*.

above par The price of an asset, usually a bond, that is currently trading above par value. Also see *bond; par value*.

above the line A gain or loss indicated in the income statement that has a material effect on the balance sheet. Also see *balance sheet*.

ABP Approved business partner.

abridged Shortened.

ABS
1. See *asset-backed security*.
2. See *absolute value*.
3. Automated bond system.

absolute breath index (ABI) A measure of the difference between advancing and declining share prices. By differencing and obtaining the absolute value, the user gains an indication of which direction the market is moving in. The ABI is calculated by:

$$\text{absolute breath index (ABI)} = \frac{|\text{advancing issues} - \text{declining issues}|}{\text{advancing issues} + \text{declining issues} + \text{unchanged prices}} \times \frac{100}{1}$$

The denominator in the equation is introduced to normalise the indicator and make values comparable over time.

If the value of the index is high, then there is activity in the market and price movements are coming. Also see *absolute value; standard deviation*.

absolute rate An interest rate expressed as a percentage and not against a reference rate such as LIBOR. Also see *interest rate; LIBOR; reference rate*.

absolute recovery See *liquidation preference*.

absolute return The return of an asset measured against that asset and not a benchmark index or the broader market.

absolute return fund (ARF) An absolute return fund aims to make positive returns in upward bull and downward bear markets. Trading strategies and investments of ARFs include selling short, leverage, programme trading, swaps, arbitrage, derivatives, shares, bonds, currencies, options, futures, commodities, real estate securities and other financial instruments. ARFs are sometimes called hedge funds. Also see *arbitrage; bear; bond; bull; derivative; futures contract; hedge fund; option; short position; swap*.

absolute value (ABS) The value of a number ignoring the sign. The formal mathematical definition of the absolute value of a number is:

$$|x| = \begin{cases} x, \text{ if } x \geq 0 \\ -x, \text{ if } x < 0 \end{cases}$$

abusive squeeze See *corner the market*.

ABX index An index based on a basket of credit default swaps written against high-risk assets such as prime rate or subprime mortgages and home equity loans. Also see *credit default swap; mortgage; prime rate; subprime loan*.

ACCA Associate of the Association of Chartered Certified Accountants.

acceleration The process of a lender calling for early payment of outstanding monies due in an event of default or other breach of terms and conditions. Lenders may often have the right to accelerate but for various reasons choose not to do so. Also see *event of default*.

acceptance
1. An agreement between two parties that accepts the terms and conditions associated with a financial transaction.
2. The legal commitment on a bill of exchange that commits the signatory. Also see *bill of exchange*.
3. A bill of exchange that has been accepted. Also see *bill of exchange*.

acceptance credit A letter of credit type instrument with which an investment bank extends finance to importers by promising to pay the holder a specified sum of money at a specified date. The issuing bank effectively guarantees payment. An acceptance credit is opened whereby an exporter can draw a bill of exchange from the investment bank. The bill is accepted by a bank and can then be traded at a discount as a money market instrument thereby realising cash early for the exporter. Also see *bill of exchange; investment bank; letter of credit; money market*.

acceptance house An institution that specialises in issuing and trading in acceptance credits and bills of exchange. Investment banks are sometimes called acceptance houses. Also see *acceptance credit; bill of exchange; investment bank*.

acceptance region When testing a hypothesis, there is a sample space or region of possible values of the test statistic that will result in the null hypothesis being accepted. Also see *hypothesis testing; null hypothesis; p-value*.

acceptor The drawee of a bill of exchange after acceptance of the bill. Also see *bill of exchange*.

accommodation Central banks lend to deposit-taking institutions, usually commercial banks, to accommodate additional liquidity. The accommodation operations inject liquidity into the market. The central banks do the lending through the accommodation, discount or emergency window. Also see *central bank; deposit-taking institution*.

accommodation window See *accommodation*.

accordion feature An option that a company may exercise to extend or reduce its line of credit. Companies use this feature to maintain flexibility and to access finance in the future if any unanticipated opportunities occur. Also see *credit line*.

account
1. A place in the financial books of a company (ledger) where transactions are recorded.
2. A statement of a purchase on credit, sometimes called an invoice. Also see *invoice*.

accountability The obligation of a person afforded the responsibility to justify his/her actions and performance. A board of directors is accountable to the shareholders of a company. Also see *board of directors*.

accounting equation assets = owners equity + liabilities (A = O + L)

Also see *liability; owners equity*.

accounting package Software such as AccPac and SAP that is used to manage the accounts and financial aspects of the operations of companies.

accounting period The period for which businesses prepare their accounts. The frequency can be monthly, quarterly, semi-annually or yearly. For tax purposes an accounting period is defined as 12 months and all transactions after the beginning and before the end of the period are recorded in financial statements according to accrual-based accounting. Also see *accrual*.

accounting policies The specific principles, bases, conventions, rules and practices applied by an entity when preparing and presenting financial statements. Public companies are required under stock exchange provisions to state accounting policies in the first note to annual financial statements. Also see *financial statements*.

accounting profit The profit or loss for a period before deducting tax expense as indicated by various accounting policies. Also see *accounting policies*.

accounting rate of return (ARR) A ratio that compares the average accounting profits made by a company with the average book value over the same period. It can be calculated according to the following formula:

$$\text{accounting rate of return (ARR)} = \frac{\frac{1}{n}\sum_{\text{all } n}\text{net profit}}{\frac{1}{n}\sum_{\text{all } n}\text{book value}}$$

where n = number of time periods.

If ARR is greater than the hurdle rate, the ratio indicates a possible good investment opportunity.

If ARR is less than the hurdle rate, the ratio indicates a possible bad investment opportunity.

If ARR is equal to the hurdle rate, the ratio does not indicate whether the investment opportunity is expected to be profitable.

The ARR method of determining the performance of an investment does not discount cash flows to account for the time value of money and furthermore uses only accounting cash flows which are susceptible to different accounting treatments. ARR also does not take risk into account and measures of profit are often not comparable to projected cash flows. Using ARR as a performance measure will not necessarily lead to the maximisation of shareholder wealth and must be used with considerable caution. Sometimes called an average accounting return. Also see *book value; cash flow; hurdle rate; time value of money*.

accounts payable (AP) See *creditor*.

accounts receivable See *debtor*.

accounts receivable collection period See *debtors days*.

accreditation The process of giving an entity a rating or membership of a controlling or industry body.

accreting The increase in value of an asset over its life. For example, if a bond is bought at a discount, the accounting treatment is to accredit the value of the capital gains as it approaches par value at maturity. Accretation is the opposite of amortisation. Also see *amortisation; bond; capital gains*.

accreting cap An interest rate cap on increasing principal. Also see *interest rate cap*.

accreting swap A swap with an increasing notional principal over the life of the swap. An accreting swap can be used in conjunction with construction projects or on loans with gradual drawdown profiles to match the swap with the project cash flows. Also see *drawdown; notional principal; swap*.

accretion See *accreting*.

accrual Recognition and reporting of financial events in the period in which they occur. Also see *accrual basis of accounting*.

accrual basis of accounting The effects of transactions and other events are recognised when they occur and not when cash or its equivalent is received or paid. Transactions are recorded in the accounting records and reported in the financial statements of the periods in which they occur. For example, if an asset is sold just before financial year end and the cash is only received in the next financial year, the sale is recorded in the period in which the sale occurred and not when the actual cash was received. Also see *financial statements*.

accrued benefits Under a pension scheme the accrued benefits are the benefits to which a contributor is entitled according to contributions that were made and the period for which those contributions were made.

accrued expenses See *accrued liability*.

accrued income or revenue Income earned in a financial period that has not been settled in cash by the counterparty. Accrued income appears as a current asset in the balance sheet of a company's accounts. The accrued income account is used as a mechanism for satisfying the principles of the accrual basis of accounting. Also see *accrual basis of accounting; accrued liability; balance sheet*.

accrued interest The coupon earned on a bond from the date of the last coupon payment to the present point in time. The accrued interest is effectively the coupon payments that have up until the present point in time not been made. The accrued interest is calculated by taking the face value of the bond, multiplying by the coupon rate and adjusting for the number of days between coupon payments or the day count fraction. Also see *bond; cum interest; ex interest; face value*.

accrued liability/expense An item, usually an expense, that can sometimes appear in the current liabilities section of a company's balance sheet. The line item accounts for expenses such as electricity bills where services have been provided for the reporting period in question and no cash has actually been paid for that consumption. Accrued expenses are included in companies' reports due to the underlying principles of the accrual basis of accounting. Also see *accrual basis of accounting; balance sheet; current liability*.

accrued market discount Zero coupon bonds and treasury bills are issued at a discount to face value because investors that hold the instruments are rewarded as the value increases or accrues from the discounted value over time. Investors in discount bonds obtain their returns from appreciation in the value of the bond (pull to par) and not through the receipt of coupons. The accrued market discount is thus the gain made from the date the instrument was acquired to the present point in time. Also see *pull to par; treasury bill; zero coupon bond*.

accumulated depreciation The amount that an asset has been depreciated by since the asset was brought into the company's records. The purchase price less the accumulated depreciation is considered to be the book value of the asset. Also see *book value*.

accumulated dividend When dividends are not paid on preference shares, the payments are accumulated and considered to be a liability to the company until they are ultimately settled. Some classes of preference shares give holders additional rights should the payments of dividends not occur. Also see *dividend; preference share*.

accumulated profits See *retained earnings*.

accumulating shares Additional shares issued to the current holders of ordinary shares instead of a dividend payment. These shares are usually subject to capital gains tax. The value of the shares exceeds the value of the dividends declared by a small premium to entice the shareholders to take them. Also see *capital gains tax; dividend; dividend in specie*.

accumulation
1. When the price of a share begins to increase or when it remains at constant levels as the volume of shares traded increases. This is known as the accumulation phase

and indicates that the share is perhaps becoming stronger and entering a bull market. Also see *bull*.
2. The process whereby a shareholder gradually increases shareholdings in a company driving the share price up in the process.

accumulation area A price range below which purchasers of a security are willing to purchase. Analysts detect these when securities do not fall below certain prices over time. Also see *resistance*.

accumulation unit An investment fund that reinvests dividends or coupons in the fund. Shareholders benefit in the long term through accumulated capital gains. Also see *dividend*.

ACD Authorised corporate director.

ACE Accelerated change enablement.

ACH Automated clearing house.

acid test (quick) ratio A ratio that measures the liquidity of a company. It is defined by:

$$\text{acid test ratio} = \frac{\text{current assets} - \text{inventory}}{\text{current liabilities}}$$

The acid test ratio is used rather than the current ratio because inventory is often less liquid than other current assets such as the debtors book. The acid test ratio is sometimes called the liquidity ratio. Also see *cash ratio; current asset; current ratio; debtor; inventory; liquid*.

ACP Average collection period.

acquisition
1. The process of gaining a controlling stake in a company. A company, the holding company, acquires more than 50% share of or significant control of a second company, the subsidiary. Also see *holding company; subsidiary*.
2. The purchase of an asset.
    Also see *agreed bid; hostile takeover bid; merger*.

acquisition loan A loan used specifically for the acquisition of an asset. Acquisition loans have a finite tenor and may only be used for the purchase of specific assets.

across the board A trend in an industry or the stock market as a whole.

ACRS Accelerated cost recovery system.

acting in concert Investors or speculators that act collectively to drive prices in directions from which they can profit. These activities are almost always illegal.

active bond A bond that is well traded and liquid on an exchange.

active delivery month The most frequently quoted delivery month for futures contracts. Spot prices are determined by the contract price for the delivery month. Also see *contract month; futures contract; option; spot price*.

active management A fund or person who manages shareholders funds by selecting stocks and financial assets that give returns greater than the market average or outperform a chosen benchmark. Also see *shareholders capital*.

active market A market in which all the following conditions exist:
- The items traded in the market are homogeneous.

- Willing buyers and sellers can normally be found at any time.
- Prices are freely available to the public.

active member A member of a benefit scheme who is presently contributing to and accruing benefits in the scheme.

active partner A person or entity that has a portion of ownership in a business and significant management control.

active stocks or bonds Stocks or bonds that are actively traded in the market and are liquid. Also see *overactive*.

activity-based budgeting The process of planning and controlling expected activities of an organisation. Activity-based budgeting links work input or activity with strategic cost, time and quality objectives.

activity-based costing (ABC) The principle of activity-based costing is that the production of goods and services consumes activities and these activities in turn consume resources. Consumption of resources then drives costs.

activity-based management (ABM) See *activity-based budgeting*.

activity indicator An indicator that shows the state of an economy or where it currently is in the business cycle. Variables such as vehicle sales and industrial production are often used in the composition of such indicators. Also see *business cycle; indicator; leading indicator*.

activity ratios Financial ratios such as debtors days and inventory turnover that are used to measure the efficiency with which a company uses its working capital. Also see *debtors days; inventory turnover; working capital*.

act of God Natural disasters and unforeseen events.

act of God bond A bond that has coupons. Sometimes the principal is linked to losses associated with an act of God. Also see *act of God*.

actuals
1. Physical commodities available for delivery.
2. The actual for futures or options is the underlying asset.
3. Expenses that have actually been incurred.

actuarial gain In pension fund provisions, usually defined benefit funds, there can be a difference in the liability provision and the fund valuation. The actuarial liability/surplus is often calculated using a discounted future cash flow model that uses high-quality corporate debt (AA). Also see *liability; pension fund; surplus*.

actuarial liability A liability that results in a pension fund due to an actuary valuing the assets of the pension fund less than its liabilities. Also see *defined benefit fund*.

actuarial loss Opposite of actuarial gain. Also see *actuarial gain*.

actuarial surplus A surplus that results in a pension fund where an actuary has valued the assets of the pension fund as greater than the liabilities of the fund. Also see *defined benefit fund*.

actuarial value of assets The value of assets in an investment portfolio as calculated by an actuary. Also see *defined benefit fund*.

actuaries index Indices, both sector specific and overall, on the JSE that indicate the performance of the market as a whole or a specific sector. Also see *JSE*.

actuary A professional trained in the mathematics and statistics of the management of insurance and other funds.

adaptive expectations Expectations of future prices or trends often based on past values. A good example is inflation. If inflation has been high in the past, the market often expects it to be high in the future. Also see *inflation; path dependent*.

ADB See *Asian Development Bank*.

additional paid-in capital See *share premium*.

additional voluntary contributions Extra voluntary contributions to a retirement or pension fund by an employee to gain increased benefits on retirement.

add-on certificate of deposit A certificate of deposit (COD) that allows the holder to deposit additional funds after the purchase of the certificate at the same interest rate. The holder of such a security is advantaged by being in a position to access future interest rates that could be above the prevailing market rates at that point in time. Also see *certificate of deposit; interest rate; negotiable certificate of deposit*.

adhocracy A term used for organisations that produce individual or custom-made products.

ADI Authorised deposit-taking institution.

adjudication The process of examining the facts and providing judgement.

adjustable peg See *crawling peg*.

adjustable rate mortgage (ARM) A mortgage with a floating or variable interest rate. In South Africa these mortgages are linked to the prime rate. Also see *floating interest rate; mortgage; prime rate; variable interest rate*.

adjustable rate preference share A preference share whose dividend payments are linked to a variable rate debt security such as a treasury bill. These instruments allow investors to invest in equity-type instruments with cash flows that are the same as debt instruments. They are often issued if there is an advantage to be gained from differing accounting and tax treatments for equity and debt. Also see *dividend; preference share; treasury bill*.

adjusted beta An adjusted beta value is calculated by:

$$\beta_{adjusted} = \frac{2}{3}\beta_{raw} + \frac{1}{3}\beta_{market}$$

where β_{market} is typically set to 1.

It effectively adds more market beta to the raw beta. This adjustment is made because empirical studies have shown that over time the beta of a company trends towards the market beta (mean reversion). Sometimes called a Blume adjustment. Also see *adjusted beta; beta; mean reversion*.

adjusted hybrid capital asset pricing model This is an approach used to determine the cost of equity in a foreign market by investors. The model proposes the following relationship:

Cost of equity = $(Rf_{world} + CRP) + \beta_1 \beta_2 (Rm_{world} - Rf_{world})(1 - R^2)$

where CRP = country risk premium; Rf_{world} = risk-free rate in the world market; Rm_{world} = rate of return in the world market; β_1 = beta value of local country index versus world index; β_2 = average beta of comparable global companies; R^2 = volatility of local market's returns explained by country risk (avoiding double counting of CRP and β_1).

The approach assumes stability of cross-border betas. Also see *beta approach; Bludgeon approach; country risk premium; Estrata downside risk model; global capital asset pricing model; Godfrey and Espinosa cost of equity model; Goldman Sachs model; lambda approach; Lessard's model; Pereiro's adjusted CAPM model.*

adjusted present value (APV) The net present value (NPV) of a project if financed solely by equity plus the present value (PV) of any debt financing benefits (the additional effects of debt). There is a benefit gained through debt financing as interest payments are usually tax deductible. Also see *all equity net present value; net present value; present value.*

adjusted R^2 Adjusted R^2 is a variation of the R^2 (R-squared) statistic in a linear regression that accounts for the number of parameters in the regression model. The adjustment is essentially a penalty for increasing the number of parameters in the model. Also see *analysis of variance; linear regression; R^2.*

adjusted strike price A strike price in an option contract that is adjusted due to an unforeseen event such as a share split in the underlying security. Also see *option; share split; strike price.*

adjustment bond A bond issued where interest is payable only if the company has sufficient earnings. Non-payment of the coupon therefore does not constitute a default under the bond contract. These bonds are subordinate to other senior debt. Adjustment bonds are flexible in nature and are often used when it is likely that earnings will not fully meet debt service obligations for companies that experience significant economic cyclicality or are expecting substantial future growth. Also see *senior debt; subordinate; toggle note.*

adjustment credit An advance made by central banks to commercial banks to satisfy short-term loan obligations. Also see *accommodation; repo rate; South African Reserve Bank.*

adjustment interval The regularity with which interest rates can be changed or adjusted. Also see *interest rate; monetary policy committee.*

administration See *administration order.*

administration order An order by a court to administer the payments of debt by individuals. Court orders can also involve the appointment of an administrator to manage the assets and operations of a business. Also see *Chapter 11.*

administrative agent An agent that handles all the administration of a syndicated loan or any other financial arrangements. Also see *syndicated loan.*

administrative agent fee A fee charged annually by the administrative agent. Also see *commitment fee; facility fee; participation fee; prepayment fee; syndicated loan; upfront fee; usage fee.*

administrator A person appointed to administer the assets or business of another person or company. Administrators are often appointed in the case of bankruptcy or death. Also see *bankruptcy.*

ADR See *American depository receipt.*

ADR ratio The number of ordinary shares for an individual American depository receipt (ADR). Also see *American depository receipt*.

ADS American depository shares. Also see *American depository receipt*.

ADSCR See *annual debt service cover ratio*.

ad valorem duty A duty levied on certain commodities, assets and services in proportion to their value.

advance A drawing under a loan facility.

advance payment A payment made in advance for services or goods to be delivered at a future date. Also see *option*.

advance ratio (decline ratio) The ratio of advancing (increasing in price) over declining (decreasing in price) shares or, in the case of a decline ratio, the ratio of declining over advancing shares. Investors use the ratio to understand the direction of movement of the market. A ratio of greater than one implies a bull market and less than one a bear market. Sometimes called the net advance or net decline ratio. Also see *absolute breath index; bear market; bull market*.

advance refunding Issuing a new bond to settle an outstanding bond early. This is often undertaken when interest rates in the current market are lower than the coupon payment obligations on the outstanding bond to be repaid. Also see *arbitrage bond; bond; interest rate*.

adverse balance A negative balance on an account. The term is often used with reference to the balance of payments. Also see *balance of payments*.

adverse opinion A statement by the auditor of a company that the company's accounts are not a fair representation of its business dealings. Also see *auditor*.

advice of acceptance A notification from one bank to another detailing funds transferred and any associated charges.

advisory broker A broker who advises customers on share purchases. Also see *broker*.

advisory funds Funds placed with an intermediary where the intermediary has full discretion over investments made. Also see *non-discretionary account*.

AED Currency of the United Arab Emirates, the dirham.

AER See *annual effective rate*.

AF Ancillary facility.

AFDB See *African Development Bank*.

Affarsvarlden General Index An overall index of funds on the Stockholm Stock Exchange. Also see *index*.

affiliate A company in whom another company has a minority interest and has no substantial management control. Also see *associate; division; joint venture; minority interest; subsidiary*.

affirmation
1. The agreement of the terms of trade of a transaction.
2. If credit ratings are affirmed, they remain the same. Also see *credit rating*.

affirmative action A form of discrimination with respect to employment based on the ethnicity of the applicant.

affirmative covenant A standard covenant that requires the borrower of money to pay interest, to maintain corporate income and insurance and to pay tax. Also see *covenant; financial covenant; negative covenant*.

afghani The unit of currency of Afghanistan divided into 100 puls.

afloat Goods that are currently en route to their destination.

African Development Bank (AFDB) 'The African Development Bank is the premier financial development institution of Africa, dedicated to combating poverty and improving the lives of people of the continent and engaged in the task of mobilising resources towards the economic and social progress of its Regional Member Countries.' (*Source*: www.afdb.org)

after date The date specified on a bill of exchange that denotes the date after which the bill is a valid financial instrument. Also see *bill of exchange*.

after-hours trading Trading after a stock market has closed. The gains or losses made in after-hours trading are realised when the market opens the next day.

after market See *secondary market*.

afternoon fix The gold price fix in London by bullion dealers. The fix price is agreed by consensus and guided by market trading that day. Also see *bullion*.

after-tax profit The profit that a company has made less tax payable.

AG Aktiengesellschaf. AG is an indication that the company is a limited liability company with shareholders that can sell shares. This is the German, Swiss and Austrian equivalent of the British PLC. Also see *GmbH; PLC; shareholders*.

against the box See *short position*.

agency
  1. An arrangement between a customer and an agent. Also see *agent*.
  2. A business or organisation providing an intermediary service.

agency agreement A legally binding agreement between a group of lenders and a borrower that states the rights and responsibilities of the agent.

agency bond A bond issued by US government backed agencies such as Freddie Mac and Fannie Mae. Also see *Fannie Mae; Freddie Mac*.

agency cross transaction A transaction that is brokered by a member of a stock exchange and that matches a buy and sell from non-members.

agency fee
  1. An annual fee paid to an agent for work done.
  2. The fee that a bank charges for being the agent in a syndicated loan. Also see *agent; syndicated loan*.

agency problem Conflict of interest between shareholders and management. Also see *shareholders*.

agency relationship The relationship between shareholders and management of a company. Also see *shareholders*.

agency security See *agency bond*.

agent
1. An entity that acts on behalf of another entity in a transaction and has no underlying financial interest in the transaction.
2. In loan syndications, the agent handles the administration of a syndicated loan. The agent acts as an intermediary between the borrower and the syndication banks. He/she handles the disimbursement of funds and sees that conditions precedent are met as well as all aspects of notification and communication associated with the mechanics of the loan. Also see *conditions precedent; syndicated loan*.

agent bank The bank that acts as an agent in a financial transaction. In the US the term agent bank is often used to describe a lead or book runner bank. Also see *agent; book runner*.

agent de change French word for stockbroker or securities house. Also see *stockbroker*.

agent trader A trader that simply matches buy and sell orders and does not take a position in the market. Also see *dual capacity; position; principal trader*.

aggregate The process of combining a set of numbers into a single number. For an example see *aggregate demand*.

aggregate demand The value of the total expenditure in an economy. The expenditure includes individual, business and government expenditure.

aggregate risk The total exposure that a bank has for spot and forward contracts. Also see *forward contract dealing; spot market*.

aggregate supply The value of the total goods and services produced in an economy by individuals, businesses and government. Also see *aggregate demand; gross domestic product*.

aggregate value See *enterprise value*.

aggregation Lumping assets and liabilities together.

aggressive growth fund A fund focused on capital growth and not income. These funds invest in smaller companies, possibly out of the top 100 on the stock exchange, but with significant expected growth potential.

aging schedule Breakdown of the debtors (accounts receivable) book by time. Also see *debtor*.

agio
1. The difference between the rate at which a bank borrows and lends. Also see *spread*.
2. A charge levied for the exchange of currency.

AGM See *annual general meeting*.

agora Monetary unit of Israel divided into 100 shekels.

agreed bid A takeover bid that is supported by the shareholders and management of a company as opposed to a hostile takeover bid. Sometimes called a friendly bid. Also see *hostile takeover bid; shareholders*.

agreement value The value of a swap if the swap is terminated early. Also see *swap*.

agribusiness The business of farming and related activities such as the provision of farming equipment and processing of agricultural products.

Agricultural Bank See *Land Bank*.

AIM See *Alternative Investment Market*.

Aktb Abbreviation that appears after the name of a Swedish joint stock company. Also see *joint stock*.

ALBI See *All Bond Index*.

ALCO Asset and liabilities committee.

All Bond Index (ALBI) A bond index on the Bond Exchange of South Africa (BESA) that contains 19 of the most liquid government, utility and corporate bonds listed on BESA. The ALBI is split into the GOVI Index which contains only government bonds in which dealers make a market and the OTHI Index containing another 14 bonds. Also see *GOVI Index; OTHI Index*.

all equity net present value The net present value (NPV) of a company if it was funded with equity capital alone. Debt funding often has a positive benefit and the introduction of debt will typically enhance the NPV of a company. Also see *adjusted present value; equity capital; net present value*.

All Gold Index A gold index on the JSE that contains only gold mining shares. The All Gold Index is a market capitalisation index. Also see *JSE; market capitalisation index*.

allied markets These are markets such as the foreign exchange and commodities markets that are closely related to the equity and debt markets. Also see *foreign exchange*.

alligator spread A spread in an options market that cannot be realised due to commission charges and transaction expenses. Also see *arbitrage channel*.

all-in discount rate The total cost of a discount security expressed as a discount interest rate. The total cost includes interest, commission and stamp duties. Also see *commission; discount security; interest rate; stamp duty; transaction cost*.

all-in price
1. The price of a bond including interest accrued. To calculate the all-in price, add the accrued interest to the clean price:

$$\text{all-in price} = C\left[\frac{1-\frac{1}{(1+r)^t}}{r}\right] + \frac{FV_t}{(1+r)^t} + (r \times FV_t)\left(\frac{n}{\text{days}}\right)$$

where FV_t = future value after t whole periods; t = number of whole periods until redemption; r = interest rate or discount rate; C = annuity or coupon payment; n = number of days from the last whole period to the redemption date or register close date; $days$ = number of days in a year (typically 365 or sometimes 360).

Sometimes called the dirty price. Also see *bond; clean price; cum interest; dirty price; ex interest; future value; total price; yield to maturity*.

2. The rate on a loan including the margin, commitment fee, utilisation fees and other upfront fees. Also see *commitment fee; margin; upfront fee; usage fee*.

allocation
1. The number of shares or bonds that is allocated to an applicant in a new issue.

2. The amount allocated to members of a syndicated loan. Allocations can be predefined, negotiated or in line with commitments made.

All Ordinaries Share Index An Australian stock market index that is calculated as a weighted average of the top 500 companies by market capitalisation on the Australian Stock Market. Also see *ALSI*.

all or nothing option See *binary option*.

allotment The allocation of securities during an auction. Also see *auction*.

allotted shares Shares distributed to shareholders during an allotment (auction). Often accounted for with a balance sheet line item called allotted share capital. Also see *allotment; balance sheet; line item*.

all-risks insurance An insurance contract that covers all risks.

All Share Index (ALSI) See *ALSI*.

A-loan
1. The most senior loan in a debt structure. This is usually the part of a deal sold to high-grade banks who do not have significant appetite for risky assets. A-loans often have a short tenor. Also see *B-loan; C-loan; D-loan*.
2. A loan from a multilateral agency such as the International Finance Corporation. Also see *International Finance Corporation*.

alpha coefficient The alpha coefficient measures the degree to which stock prices are affected by the internal workings of a company. The beta of a share measures the responsiveness of the shares to the market as a whole. The alpha coefficient is often calculated by determining the intercept of the security market line. Also see *beta; security market line*.

ALSI An index of all the companies on the JSE. The index is weighted by market capitalisation. The index can be traded as a derivative instrument on SAFEX. Also see *FINDI; index; INDI; JSE; market capitalisation; RESI; South African Futures Exchange*.

ALSI 40 An index composed of the top 40 companies by market capitalisation on the JSE. Also see *index; JSE; market capitalisation*.

Alt-A loan A loan given to a person of good credit quality but furnished with alternative documentation because the borrower does not have proof of income from a traditional employer. Alt-A loans lessen the challenges associated with due diligence and verification processes but attract higher interest rates as they are more risky to the loan providers. Also see *due diligence; interest rate; subprime loan*.

alternate director A person who can stand in for an absent director if the articles of association of a company permit. Also see *board of directors*.

alternative currency option An option where the underlying asset is priced in a different currency to the option itself. Also see *option*.

alternative hypothesis When testing a hypothesis, two hypotheses are made, namely the null hypothesis and the alternative hypothesis. The alternative hypothesis is the alternative not being tested for. Also see *null hypothesis*.

alternative interest rate clause A clause in a loan agreement that allows for the base rate to be changed. This is often present to account for the unlikely event that the original base rate such as LIBOR or JIBAR cannot be determined. The alternative interest rate clause is contained in the market disruption clauses. Also see *base rate; LIBOR; market disruption.*

alternative investment An investment where monetary gains are expected and the investment has a pleasurable use. Vintage sports cars, artworks and jewellery are common examples of an alternative investment.

Alternative Investment Market/Index (AIM) A market in the UK aimed at smaller companies that do not qualify for listings on the main exchange. South Africa has a similar market called the AltX. Also see *AltX.*

AltX A division of the JSE dedicated to smaller companies and start-ups. The AltX has more relaxed listing requirements than the main board. Also see *Alternative Investment Index (AIM); JSE; main board.*

amalgamation The process of two companies forming a new entity. Amalgamation can occur through a merger or an acquisition. Also see *acquisition; merger.*

amendment The mutual change of conditions in a contract without having to draft a new agreement. Amendments are evidenced by signed documents reflecting the effective changes to the original contract.

amendment fee A fee charged to amend the conditions of a contract. Amendment fees are sometimes charged when a borrower makes changes to a bond or loan contract. Also see *bond.*

American callable bond A callable bond that can be called at any time over the life of the bond. Also see *American option; callable bond.*

American depository receipt (ADR) An instrument whereby foreign shares are traded in the USA. Foreign companies are required to list on the US stock markets through ADRs. ADRs usually settle within T+3 days and are defined in terms of a ratio to ordinary shares. Also see *global depository receipt.*

American option An option that may be exercised at any time up to and including its expiration date. American options are often useful to hold just before or after the underlying share goes ex dividend and the underlying price subsequently drops. Also see *ex dividend; option.*

American Stock Exchange (AMEX) A stock exchange based in New York that specialises in options and exchange traded funds. Small to medium companies are also listed on this exchange. Also see *exchange traded fund; option.*

American style An option that may be exercised at any time up to and including its expiration date. Also see *American option.*

American-style FX A foreign exchange currency quote where the US dollar is listed as the variable leg, for example US$1.3 = €1. Also see *European-style FX.*

American terms The process of quoting a currency in the number of US dollars the currency in question can buy, for example ZAR1 = US$0.14.

American warrant See *American option; warrant.*

AMEX See *American Stock Exchange.*

amortisation (depreciation)

1. The systematic allocation of the depreciable amount of an asset over its useful life. In the case of an intangible asset or goodwill, the term amortisation is generally used instead of depreciation. Both terms have the same meaning. Goodwill is not amortised under IFRS. Also see *asset; depreciation; goodwill; intangible asset; International Financial Reporting Standards*.
2. The repayment of debt using a system of instalments over time.
3. Spreading the fees of a financial transaction such as raising a loan over time.

amortisation schedule A specification of the dates and timeline by which the capital on a loan will be repaid or an asset depreciated.

amortised cost method The process of distributing or amortising the cost of raising debt over the term of the loan. For example, if an investment bank charges a client 10 units to issue a bond, a proportion of the upfront 10-unit cost would be allocated to the client's liability over each year of the bond's lifetime. Also see *bond; investment bank*.

amortised loan A loan where the borrower has to pay the interest each period in addition to a capital portion. The capital reduction can be tailored to suit the borrower's requirements although amortised loan capital balances are usually reduced using the straight line method.

amortising cap An interest rate cap on a principal amount that is reducing. Also see *interest rate cap*.

amortising collar A collar on a principal amount that is reducing. Also see *collar*.

amortising option An option that has the principal amount amortised or reduced over time.

amortising swap A swap where the principal amount reduces or is amortised over time. These swaps are used in situations where risk decreases over time. A start-up project may use these where business risk decreases over time or on loans where capital is reduced or amortised over time. Also see *swap*.

amortising term loan A term loan with a progressive repayment schedule that runs six or fewer years. Sometimes called an A-term loan. Also see *repayment schedule*.

Amsterdam Stock Exchange Stock exchange in the Netherlands. It merged with the Brussels and Paris Stock Exchange to form Euronext. Also see *CBS Index*.

analysis of variance (ANOVA) Used to determine a linear relationship between variables. The ANOVA method assumes that there is a linear relationship between the variables and the deviations from a linear trend are normally distributed and random. Total variability in an ANOVA is given by the sum of squares. ANOVA is characterised by the following parameters:

- The F statistic given in an ANOVA is the $\frac{\text{mean sum of squares of the regression}}{\text{mean sum of squares of residual}}$.
- The higher the value of the F statistic is, the more the regression counts in explaining the relationship between the two variables.
- The statistic multiple R is the correlation coefficient of the linear regression.
- The R-squared statistic is the correlation coefficient squared. This gives an indication as to what proportion of the variation in the dependent variable is explained by the independent variables.

analyst | annual financial statement

- The adjusted R^2 statistic is a variation of the R^2 statistic that accounts for the number of parameters in the regression model.

- The standard error is the standard deviation from the regression line, i.e. the standard deviation of $f(x, y)$ gives an indication of the spread of the data off the regression line. The standard error should be compared with the mean of the dependent variable. Also see *adjusted R^2; correlation coefficient; linear regression; linear; P-value; standard deviation.*

analyst A person trained in the analysis of companies, financial markets and financial products.

analytic study A study where sample statistics are used to infer results for the entire population.

ancillary business See *ancillary credit business.*

ancillary credit business Extra business obtained by the offering of credit facilities to a client. Banks often lend key clients funds at lower interest rates in anticipation of ancillary business.

anergy The opposite of synergy. Also see *synergy.*

angel An investor, usually an individual, who supplies capital to high-risk start-up companies. Also see *venture capital market.*

angel bond An investment grade bond. The terminology comes from the opposite of fallen angels, i.e. an angel is a company that has not fallen from investment grade grace yet. Also see *fallen angel; investment grade bond.*

annual accounts See *financial statements.*

annual compounding Interest that is compounded annually. Also see *compound interest.*

annual debt service cover ratio (ADSCR) A debt service cover ratio calculated for a 12-month period, typically the reporting period. Also see *debt service cover ratio.*

annual depreciation allowance The amount by which assets are legally allowed to be depreciated per year for tax purposes. These allowances are set by a country's tax authorities. Also see *deferred taxation; depreciation; South African Revenue Service.*

annual dividend The total of all dividends paid during the course of a financial year. Also see *dividend; financial year.*

annual effective rate (AER) The effective rate of interest per annum adjusted for a series of compounding operations during the year. The rate is given by:

$$\text{annual effective rate (AER)} = \left(1 + \frac{r}{n}\right)^n - 1$$

where n = the number of compounding periods; r = the quoted rate of interest.

annual financial statement A document produced by companies under a requirement of the Companies Act. The annual financial statements are presented at the company's annual general meeting. The annual statements must contain, among other things, an income statement, balance sheet, cash flow statement, changes in equity, a directors' and an auditor's report. Also see *annual general meeting; balance sheet; Companies Act; income statement.*

17

annual general meeting (AGM) A meeting of shareholders of a company that is usually held within six months of a company's year end. Shareholders vote on various issues affecting the company at these meetings. The minimum requirements for these meetings are set out in the Companies Act. Also see *Companies Act*.

annualise Make adjustments to returns or interest rates for periods of less than a year to represent them as an annual number. Also see *effective annual return; interest rate*.

annualised profit The process of taking a profit for a period shorter than a year and upscaling or downscaling it for analysis purposes to obtain an indication of a full year number. For example, one would double half-year results to obtain annualised numbers.

annual percentage rate (APR) The APR is an interest rate or rate of return expressed as an annual rate of interest. The following formula details the calculation of APR:

annual percentage rate (APR) = $\sqrt[n]{i_{eff} + 1} - 1$

APR = interest rate per period = i_{nom}

where n = the number of compounding operations; i_{eff} = the effective annual return.

Also see *effective annual return; effective rate per period; interest rate*.

annual percentage yield See *annual percentage rate*.

annual report An audited financial report compiled (and published for public companies) that presents the financial dealings of the company to its shareholders.

annuitant A person or entity that receives an annuity.

annuity A level stream of cash flows received for a fixed period of time. A person would invest in an annuity using a series of premiums and, on a specific date, usually at retirement, a level stream of cash flows will be paid over the life of the annuity. See *annuity present value* for details on the calculation of the present value of an annuity. Also see *annuity due; cash flow; ordinary annuity*.

annuity due An annuity whose payment is to be made immediately rather than at the end of the payment period. For example, in many lease arrangements, the first payment is due immediately and each successive payment must be made at the beginning of the month.

The value of an APV in today's terms of the future cash flow generated by an annuity due is calculated by:

annuity present value (APV) = $C(1+r)\left[\dfrac{1 - \dfrac{1}{(1+r)^t}}{r}\right]$

where C = coupon payment; r = discount rate; t = the number of time periods.

Note that this formula is not for an ordinary annuity. Also see *annuity; cash flow; discount rate; ordinary annuity*.

annuity present value (APV) The value in today's terms of the future cash flow generated by an ordinary annuity:

annuity present value (APV) = $C\left[\dfrac{1 - \dfrac{1}{(1+r)^t}}{r}\right]$

where C = coupon payment; r = discount rate; t = the number of time periods.

Also see *cash flow; discount rate; ordinary annuity*.

anomaly An opportunity to gain returns in excess of what the wider market is yielding.

anticipatory hedge A hedge for a financial transaction that is expected to take place in the future.

anti-dilution clause A clause in the articles of association of a company that protects current shareholders from ownership dilution by allowing them to buy an appropriate proportion of shares on a new issue so that their portion of ownership remains the same. Also see *dilution; rights issue offer*.

anti-layering Clauses in loan documents that ensure that the borrower does not insert debt between existing senior and senior subordinated debt. There may be requirements in existing debt contracts that force borrowers to bring any new debt into an existing intercreditor agreement. Also see *intercreditor agreement; subordinate*.

anti-trust legislation Laws enacted to create free market competition and to ensure that monopolistic organisations do not use their dominant positions to take advantage of consumers. Also see *monopoly*.

AP
  1. Accounts payable. Also see *creditor*
  2. Authority to purchase.
  3. Authority to pay.

APEC See *Asia Pacific Economic Cooperation*.

API gravity A unit of measure that expresses the specific gravity of oils. The higher the API gravity numbers are, the richer the yield is in the product refined from the oil.

appreciation
  1. The rise in value of an asset.
  2. The increase in value of a currency in a floating exchange rate market.

appropriation
  1. Funds that are set aside for specific purposes. These funds are allocated in reserve accounts such as non-distributable reserves. Also see *non-distributable reserves*.
  2. The setting aside of land for public use.

approved list A list of investors that are deemed appropriate for subscription to a particular financial transaction or instrument.

APR See *annual percentage rate*.

APT See *arbitrage pricing theory*.

aquaculture An industry that raises sea creatures in captivity for human consumption. The abalone industry is a well-developed example of this in South Africa.

ARA Amsterdam, Rotterdam and Antwerp.

Arb A short term used for arbitrage or an entity that takes advantage of arbitrage opportunities. Also see *arbitrage*.

arbitrage A financial transaction that returns a profit without taking on any risk.

arbitrage bond A bond issued to take advantage of a lower interest rate environment. The bond is issued prior to calling an existing bond that has a higher interest rate. Also see *advance refunding; interest rate*.

arbitrage channel A set of bands about the fair value price of an asset where arbitrage opportunities are not capitalised on due to transaction costs exceeding the profit attainable through the arbitrage opportunity. Also see *alligator spread*.

arbitrage free condition Due to market participants rapidly capitalising on arbitrage opportunities, the opportunities themselves vanish in the process as supply and demand dynamics adjust price differentials. The arbitrage free condition postulates that sophisticated markets are sufficiently efficient so that there are no opportunities for risk-free returns. Sometimes called the no-arbitrage condition. Also see *arbitrage free pricing; efficient capital market; law of one price*.

arbitrage free pricing Prices are determined relative to other prices quoted in the market in such a manner as to preclude any arbitrage opportunities. For example, if two equivalent assets are priced differently, the demand for the cheaper asset will ultimately bring its price in line with the more expensive asset.

arbitrage pricing theory (APT) A theory that the expected return of an asset is a linear combination of macroeconomic factors and market indices where sensitivities are factored by coefficients called beta coefficients. If the model correctly derives the price of the asset, arbitrage operations will bring the price back into line.

The return on a portfolio is given by:

$$\text{return} = a + b_2 (r_{\text{factor 2}}) + b_3 (r_{\text{factor 3}}) + b_4 (r_{\text{factor 4}}) + b_5 (r_{\text{factor 5}}) + \ldots + \text{noise}$$

where the factors can be anything such as gross domestic product (GDP) or oil prices.

This reduces to a risk premium approach:

$$r - r_f = a + b_2 (r_{\text{factor 2}} - r_f) + b_3 (r_{\text{factor 3}} - r_f) + b_4 (r_{\text{factor 4}} - r_f) + b_5 (r_{\text{factor 5}} - r_f) + \ldots + \text{noise}$$

If a portfolio has zero sensitivity to these factors, then it is risk free and must therefore offer the risk-free rate and the value of all the b's should be zero. If the rate is higher than that of the risk-free rate, an arbitrage opportunity exists. Also see *arbitrage; gross domestic product*.

arbitration A manner of settling disputes outside the legal framework of the courts. An arbitrator is appointed to hear the case and can make a judgement that may be indicative or binding.

arithmetic mean This is a simple average. In a series $a_1; a_2; a_3 \ldots a_n$ the arithmetic mean is defined as:

$$\text{arithmetic mean} = \frac{a_1 + a_2 + a_3 + \ldots + a_n}{n} = \frac{1}{n} \sum_{i=1}^{n} a_i$$

Also see *geometric mean; median; mode*.

ARM See *adjustable rate mortgage*.

arms length Transactions between two parties that are related, but undertaken on a basis as if they were unrelated. There should be no conflict of interest. Chinese walls are often used to maintain the no-conflict condition. Transactions between two completely unrelated parties are also called arms-length transactions. Also see *Chinese wall*.

around par Terminology used in quotes of bond instruments where points are quoted around the instruments' par value, i.e. the number of points above and below par value. Also see *par value*.

ARP Adjustable rate preference shares. ARPs are preference shares with varying dividend payment rates. Also see *preference share*.

ARPU See *average revenue per user*.

ARR See *accounting rate of return*.

arrangement The process of lenders entering into agreements with borrowers to repay outstanding principal and interest without going through formal bankruptcy proceedings. The arrangement may involve the selling of assets and the payment of creditors with the proceeds. Also see *liquidation*.

arrangement fee An upfront fee charged by a bank for structuring, arranging and selling down of syndicated loans and other financial transactions such as the issue of a bond. Sometimes the arrangement fee is aggregated into a single upfront fee and can include fees such as underwriting fees. Also see *commitment fee; margin; participation fee; underwriting fee; upfront fee; usage fee*.

arranger An entity that participates in putting together a financial transaction such as a syndicated loan, bond or equity issue.

arranger group A group of banks or financial institutions that put together a financial transaction such as a syndicated loan, bond or equity issue.

arrears Outstanding debt that results from payments not being made.

ARS The currency of Argentina, the Argentine peso.

articles of association Rules required by the Companies Act that are adopted by a company in the governance of its internal affairs. The information provided in the articles of association may include the proceedings of general meetings, voting rights, borrowing power and the power and authority of directors. Also see *annual general meeting; Companies Act; extraordinary general meeting; memorandum; special general meeting*.

ascending tops A series of peaks in the price history of a security that is increasing.

ASE See *Athens Stock Exchange*.

ASEAN Association of South East Asian Nations. ASEAN members include Brunei, Cambodia, Indonesia, Laos, Malaysia, Myanmar, Philippines, Singapore, Thailand and Vietnam.

AsgiSA A South African government objective called the Accelerated and Shared Growth Initiative. The initiative details plans to accelerate the growth of the South African economy through infrastructure and skills development.

A-share An equity share issued with voting rights equal to or exceeding the voting rights of any existing equity shares. Commonly referred to as an ordinary share. Also see *B-share; N-share; ordinary share*.

Asian Development Bank (ADB) 'ADB is an international development finance institution whose mission is to help its developing member countries reduce poverty and improve the quality of life of their people.

Headquartered in Manila, and established in 1966, ADB is owned and financed by its 67 members, of which 48 are from the region and 19 are from other parts of the globe.' (*Source*: www.adb.org)

Asian option See *average price option*.

Asian tigers The countries of Taiwan, South Korea, Hong Kong and Singapore. The name has come about due to the rapid economic growth these countries have experienced since the 1960s.

Asia Pacific Economic Cooperation (APEC) An organisation that works towards free and open trade and investment in the Asia Pacific region. Members strive to pool resources and achieve efficiencies in the region. Members of APEC in 2008 included Australia, Brunei, Canada, Chile, China, Hong Kong, Indonesia, Japan, Korea, Malaysia, Mexico, New Zealand, Papua New Guinea, Peru, Philippines, Russia, Singapore, Taipei, Thailand, United States and Vietnam.

ASIC Australian Securities and Investments Commission.

ask See *ask price*.

ask price (offer price) The price at which a trader will sell the investor securities as opposed to the bid price which is the price the trader will sell at. The difference between the bid and ask price is the profit the trader makes. The ask price is sometimes called the offer price. Also see *bid price; spread*.

assay A test indicating the purity of a precious metal. Also see *precious metals*.

assented share A share whose owner has agreed (assented) to the terms of a takeover bid. Takeover bids may involve differential pricing for assented and non-assented shares. Also see *takeover*.

assessed loss A loss that has accrued in the past and that is used to offset tax liabilities for the current profitable year. An example of an assessed loss is a company making a loss of R100 in year one and a profit of R200 in year two. The loss in year one can be offset against the profit in year two so tax will be calculated on R200 – R100.

Companies that are near profitable and have large assessed losses are often acquisition targets for cash-generative profitable companies as the assessed losses can be written off against current profits and tax liabilities reduced. Also see *acquisition*.

assessment The process of a tax authority determining the total tax bill payable by a company.

asset A resource that is controlled by an entity as a result of past events and from which future economic benefits are expected to flow. Examples of assets are shares and securities, property, plant and equipment and debtors. Assets may be tangible assets or intangible assets. Assets often have capital gains taxes levied against them when sold for a profit. Also see *capital gains tax; intangible asset; tangible asset*.

asset allocation Spreading the risk of a portfolio by using a range of varying assets. The range of assets may span equities, bonds and cash. The asset allocation may be defined in a portfolio manager's mandate.

asset allocation fund A collective investment scheme that uses a range of different assets such as equities, bonds and cash to diversify risk. Managers usually seek assets whose returns are not highly correlated. Also see *collective investment scheme; correlation*.

asset-backed fund A fund that is invested in tangible assets such as property and corporate shares.

asset-backed security/credit (ABS) Companies use this structure to liquefy their non-tradable assets on their balance sheets. They effectively borrow money and secure those borrowings against cash-generating assets. ABSs are used by financial institutions where securitised debt is raised against mortgage, credit cards and vehicle finance books. The advantage of ABSs for the banks is that they can reduce the amount of capital they would otherwise have to maintain under stringent capital guidelines mandated by the bank regulators. The cash payments due on the securities are covered by the cash flows of the backing asset. Also see *balance sheet; collateralised debt obligation; mortgage; securitisation.*

asset backing
1. See *asset-backed security.*
2. A company that has considerable assets on its balance sheet has strong asset backing. Also see *balance sheet.*

asset base Share capital raised by a company along with reserves that have not been distributed (retained income), effectively the shareholders' interest in the company. Also see *share capital.*

asset class An investment such as a share, bond, property or cash. A share in a company is of the equity asset class. Also see *bond.*

asset constraint The limits imposed by the rules of an investment fund as to what assets may or may not be included. May be called a mandate.

asset conversion cycle See *cash conversion cycle.*

asset conversion loan A short-term loan whose repayment is made from the proceeds of the sale of an asset. Bridging finance is often an asset conversion loan. Also see *bridging finance.*

asset correlation Assets that have returns that are mathematically correlated. Also see *correlation.*

asset cover A ratio that indicates the solvency position of a company, calculated by the following equation:

$$\text{asset cover} = \frac{\text{net assets}}{\text{total debt}}$$

The larger the asset cover ratio is, the more solvent the company is. Also see *net assets.*

asset financing Funding provided by a lender to a borrower to purchase a specific asset with the asset being used as collateral for the finance. Also see *collateral.*

asset liability management Techniques used by banks to match their assets and liabilities. Banks manage risk in such a manner that assets must always exceed liabilities and tenors should ideally be matched.

asset management The management of a set of assets by a company or individual. Asset management usually aims to give returns to investors in excess of the wider market.

asset management ratios See *collection period; fixed asset turnover; inventory turnover; net working capital turnover; receivables turnover; total asset turnover.*

asset play A company that has a net asset value that is higher than the market value of the firm. These companies are often susceptible to private equity takeovers and stripping where the new owner of the company sells off its assets. Also see *asset stripping.*

asset sales prepayment Prepayment of loans and other obligations with the proceeds of the sales of assets. Also see *bridging finance*.

asset securitisation See *collateralised debt obligation; securitisation*.

asset sensitive A term used to describe a situation where banks have assets that are renewed sooner than their liabilities. This may make the bank sensitive to changes in interest rates and the yield curve. Also see *interest rate; yield curve*.

asset stripping The process of purchasing a company for less than the sum of its assets and selling off the assets individually, thereby realising a profit. The company is effectively bought to realise cash from the sale of assets and not to realise future income. Also see *asset play; break-up value*.

asset structure The analysis of a company's assets. Ratios like fixed to total assets, current to total assets, inventory to total assets and debtors to total assets are used in the analysis.

assets under management The total assets that are contained in a fund.

asset swap Combining an interest-bearing instrument with an interest rate swap. The reason for entering these swaps is to change the basis of payments. For example, if investors seek a floating interest rate investment, but have only fixed rate investments in their portfolios, they can swap the fixed rate for the floating rate asset and collect the floating rate cash flows. Also see *floating interest rate; interest rate swap*.

asset swap margin The amount above a reference rate such as LIBOR, EURIBOR or JIBAR that is paid on the floating interest rate leg of an asset swap. Asset swaps strip out interest rate characteristics of a bond and express it as a value over an interbank rate. For example, if the asset swap margin on a bond is quoted at 60 bp, then the asset swap investor is prepared to swap the fixed coupon cash flows for a floating rate that is 60 bp over a reference rate such as LIBOR or the relevant swap rate. Asset swap margins provide a unified measure of credit spreads. Also see *asset swap; bond; credit spread; EURIBOR; floating interest rate; interest rate; JIBAR; LIBOR; reference rate*.

asset turnover See *fixed asset turnover*.

asset valuation The process of assigning a value to an asset. There are many valuation methods such as discounted cash flow valuation and the multiple valuation method. Asset valuation is a wide field with a variety of different methods, approaches and research available. Also see *discounted cash flow valuation; multiple valuation*.

asset value per share See *net asset value*.

assignable cause The portion of variability in a observation set that is attributable to specific causes.

assignment In the assignment sale of a loan the buyer is set up as the legal lender on record. The rights, but not the obligations, are transferred to the purchaser. Also see *encumbrance*.

associate An entity, including an unincorporated entity such as a partnership, over which the investor has significant influence but not control. The investment is not classed as a subsidiary or a joint venture. The ownership in an associate is usually between 20% and 50%. Also see *affiliate; division; joint venture; subsidiary*.

associated company See *associate*.

associated cost When used in the context of a corporate loan, this term often refers to costs associated with compliance with central bank regulations. Sometimes called statutory cost. Also see *statutory cost*.

assurance (life) An insurance policy that pays a lump sum to the nominated beneficiary on the death of the policy holder.

ASX Australian Stock Exchange.

asymmetric information See *asymmetry of information*.

asymmetric margining The application of different margins to different entities in a deal. This may be reflective of the creditworthiness or strategic worth of the entity.

asymmetric payoff The return profile on a particular financial instrument is variable.

asymmetry of information Any situation where a party enters into a deal with a counter-party armed with information that is not publicly available. For example, management may have access to information that shareholders do not. Trading on asymmetric information is often illegal and considered to be insider trading. Also see *insider trading*.

at best A buy or sell order that is executed at the best price available.

at call Money that has been lent in the short term and must be repaid immediately on demand. Loans that are on call are called revocable loans.

A-term loan See *amortising term loan*.

Athens Stock Exchange (ASE/ATHEX) Stock Exchange in Greece.

ATHEX See *Athens Stock Exchange*.

at limit See *limit order*.

ATM
1. See *automated teller machine*.
2. See *at the money*.

ATOI After-tax operating income which is defined as operating income less taxes.

at par A security that is currently trading at par value. For example, if a bond was issued at a par value of R1 million and a year later that bond trades at R1 million, it is said to trade at par. Also see *par value*.

ATS
1. Automated trading system.
2. Austrian shilling.

attachment The legal process by which lenders use the courts to secure obligations payable. In personal finance this may take the form of a judgement being passed where direct deductions can be made from salaries.

attachment point The minimum level of losses that a tranche in a collateralised debt obligation is exposed to. Also see *collateralised debt obligation; detachment point; tranche*.

attest Certification by means of a signature or an oath. Also see *notary*.

at the money (ATM) The exercise price of an option is exactly equal to the current market price of the underlying asset. Also see *in the money; option; out the money*.

attributable earnings Earnings attributable to shareholders after servicing of debt (interest payments) and after any extraordinary items. Also see *extraordinary item*.

attributable profit Profits attributable to shareholders after taxation, servicing of debt (interest payments) and any extraordinary items. Some of the profit is retained and the balance is declared as dividends. Also see *attributable earnings; dividend; extraordinary item; retained earnings/income*.

ATX See *Austrian Traded Index*.

auction The sale of an asset where parties are invited to bid for the purchase of the asset. For securities the auction continues until all the securities available are sold. Two types of auction systems are generally used in financial markets, English auctions and Dutch auctions. The term open auction is used when bidders are aware of the offers made by all other bidders. Also see *Dutch auction; English auction*.

auction period At the start and end of day trading on certain exchanges, there is an auction period where no automatic execution occurs. Orders only are captured during these periods. Also see *automatic execution; housekeeping period*.

auction rate security A security whose interest rate is set through a Dutch auction. The interest rates on securities such as corporate and government bonds and even dividend rates on preference shares can be determined by this process. In the security auction, potential investors enter a competitive bidding process through an auction agent. Investors detail how many securities they wish to subscribe to and the rate at which they are willing to subscribe. The auction agent collects the bids and determines the rate at which all the securities will clear, defining the clearing rate. The determined clearing rate is paid on the entire issue and investors whose bids were at or above the clearing rate are granted the securities at the clearing rate. Also see *clearing rate; Dutch auction; interest rate*.

AUD Australian dollar.

audit Independent analysis of a company's financial statements and accounts. An audit is undertaken by an independent auditor who signs off the financial statements as a fair reflection of the company's operations and accounts. Audits are often legislated by companies acts and stock market listing requirements. Internal audits are conducted by companies themselves to ensure that their businesses are being conducted in a proper manner. Also see *adverse opinion; Companies Act*.

audit fee The fee charged by an auditor or audit firm for the work done in processing an audit. Also see *audit*.

auditor The person or company that performs an audit. Also see *audit*.

auditors report The section of the financial statements where an independent auditor states that in their opinion the financial statements presented are a fair reflection of the company's financial activities over the period. The use and format of an auditors report vary according to the purpose of the audit and the intended report audience. Also see *adverse opinion; financial statements*.

audit trail The process and transaction log involved in a particular business activity. The trail gives an investigator the ability to trace all aspects of the business transaction. Companies have procedures and technology in place to ensure that audit trails are left and are easily navigable. Sometimes called a paper trail.

Australian All Ordinaries Index A market capitalisation index of the top 500 companies by market capitalisation on the Australian Stock Exchange (ASX). Also see *market capitalisation index*.

Austrian Traded Index (ATX) A market capitalisation index of stocks on the Vienna Stock Exchange in Austria. Also see *market capitalisation index*.

AUT Authorised unit trust.

authorised auditor A person fit and qualified to undertake an independent audit. To audit a company, auditors are usually required to be authorised by the relevant financial supervisory authority.

authorised capital See *authorised share capital*.

authorised share capital The amount of share capital a company is permitted to issue under its articles of association. The authorised share capital must be stated in the company's financial statements. Companies do not issue all the authorised share capital at once but leave some share capital as reserve unissued shares. Also see *articles of association; financial statements; share capital; shares in issue*.

autocorrelation The degree to which a variable is dependent on the previous values of itself. In statistics, the autocorrelation function (ACF) of a discrete time series or a process X_t describes the correlation between the processes at different points in time. If X_t has mean μ and variance σ^2 then the definition of ACF is:

$$R(t, s) = \frac{E[(X_t - \mu)(X_s - \mu)]}{\sigma^2}$$

where E is the expected value.

Note that this is not well-defined for all time series or processes since the variance may be zero for a constant process or infinity. If the function is well defined, then this definition has the attractive property of being in the range [−1, 1] with 1 indicating perfect correlation and −1 indicating perfect anti-correlation. A method of testing for the presence of first-order correlation is the Durbin-Watson test. Also see *autoregressive; Durbin-Watson test; unit root; variance; vector autoregression*.

autocovariance The *j-th* autocovariance of a stochastic process y_t is the covariance between its time t value and the value at time $t-j$. It is denoted gamma below and $E[]$ indicates expectation or mean:

$\text{gamma}_{jt} = E[(y_t - Ey)(y_{t-j} - Ey)]$.

Also see *covariance; stochastic process*.

autocrat A leadership structure in government where a single self-appointed ruler holds political power.

automated teller machine (ATM) A machine that banking customers can use independently to draw cash, make deposits and do many other financial transactions. Sometimes called a cash machine or hole in the wall in the UK. Also see *SASWITCH*.

automatic execution When trading on stock exchanges, an automatic execution is the matching of a buy and sell automatically by trading technology.

autonomous expenditure Expenditure from past savings.

autoregressive (AR) A stochastic process (denoted here as e_t) that can be described by a weighted sum of its previous values and a white noise error term. An *AR(1)* process is a first-order process, meaning that only the immediately previous value has a direct effect on the current value:

$e_t = re_{t-1} + u_t$

where r is a constant that has an absolute value less than one and u_t is drawn from a distribution with mean zero and finite variance, often a normal distribution.

An *AR(2)* would have the form:

$$e_t = r_1 e_{t-1} + r_2 e_{t-2} + u_t$$

The value of r in the model is closely related to the autocorrelation function and the concept of non-stationarity. Also see *non-stationary process; stochastic process; unit root; vector autoregression.*

autoregressive distributed lag (ADL)

$$Y_t = \alpha + \delta t + \phi_1 Y_{t-1} + \ldots + \phi_p Y_{t-p} + \beta_0 X_t + \ldots + \beta_q X_{t-q} + e_t$$

In this model the dependent variable Y depends on how p lags of itself, the current value of the explanatory variable, X as well as q lags of X. This is denoted by $ADL(p, q)$.

availability factor A measure of efficiency of a power station. It is defined by:

$$\text{availability factor} = \frac{\text{power produced in the period}}{\text{theoretical maximum power production for a period}}$$

availability period The period in which borrowers may make drawings on loans.

available cash flow The total cash flow available to service debt.

available earnings Earnings in a company attributable to ordinary shareholders. Also see *attributable profit*.

available ore reserve Mineral-bearing ore in a mine that is available for future mining. Even though there may be significant ore reserves in a mine, not all the ore may be available to mine due to various technicalities.

average accounting return (AAR) See *accounting rate of return*.

average annual growth rate (AAGR) The arithmetic mean or average of the returns on an asset portfolio over time. Also see *arithmetic mean*.

average cost
1. The average price adjusted for trading volume of a set of shares traded over a specified time period.
2. A method of accounting for the value of inventory. All units are expected to have a cost equal to the cost of goods available for sale divided by the number of physical units for sale. Also see *FIFO; inventory; LIFO*.

average effective maturity A measure of the maturity for a bond that statistically accounts for the possibility that the bond may be called by the issuer. Also see *bond; call option*.

average life The average life of a loan is a measure of the amount of time that the loan principal is outstanding. It is defined by the following formula:

$$\text{average life (AL)} = \sum_{i=1}^{n} \frac{C_i}{P} t_i$$

where C_i = the principal payment at point in time i; P = the principal; t_i = the time passed from the start of the loan.

For example, for a loan with a principal value of 40 units and where the outstanding amount is amortised by 10 units each year, i.e. from 40 down to 30, 20 and 10, then the average life is calculated as follows:

$$AL = \frac{10}{40} \times 1 + \frac{10}{40} \times 2 + \frac{10}{40} \times 3 + \frac{10}{40} \times 4 = 2.5$$

The average life measure is used to calculate the annualised rate of the upfront fees. Also see *amortisation; half life*.

average loan life See *average life*.

average number of employees The average of the monthly number of employees of a company, usually calculated over a 12-month period. The calculation is detailed below where n is usually set to 12:

$$\frac{\sum_{i=1}^{n} Employees_{Month\ i}}{n}$$

average price option An option whose value is determined by the strike price and the average price of the underlying asset over the life of the option. Sometimes called an Asian option or a path-dependent option. Also see *option*.

average rate option See *average price option*.

average revenue per user (ARPU) A measure used for the analysis of telecommunications companies that measures increases in profit margins. The calculation is given by:

$$\text{average revenue per user (ARPU)} = \frac{\text{total revenue}}{\text{total number of users}}$$

The measure effectively spreads revenue over all users. Analysts use this number to compare and rank telecoms companies. The measure gives an indication of the quality of the subscriber base.

average shareholders equity The equity of a company can change over the course of a financial year. Public companies have various changes in shareholders equity that are associated with raising capital and issuing shares used to incentivise management through share options. When doing return on equity (ROE) calculations, the average shareholders equity is calculated by adding the shareholders equity at the beginning of a period to the shareholders equity at the period's end and dividing the result by two. Also see *financial year; return on equity; share option*.

average tax rate The tax bill divided by taxable income expressed as a percentage of a company's or a person's income that goes to taxes.

average weighted maturity A weighting of the maturity of instruments in a fund. This is effectively the average maturity of instruments in the fund. The higher the average weighted maturity is, the greater the sensitivity of the fund is to changes in economic variables such as interest rates. Also see *interest rate*.

avo Currency of Macao divided into 100 pataca.

away from the market
1. A purchase order that is lower than current market prices. Also see *limit order*.
2. An option that is not in the money. The term is used in the bond market where the rise or fall in interest rates for the option to be at the money is quoted. Also see *at the money; interest rate; in the money; limit order; out the money*.

AWG The currency of Aruba, the Aruba guilder.

axe Indication of price.

axe sheet A list from dealers with indicative secondary prices for loans.

B A credit rating used by S&P and Fitch that indicates that the company's credit risk is high and varies substantially with economic cycles. A B-rating is sub-investment grade. Also see *credit rating; credit risk; sub-investment grade*.

B2B Business to business.

BA/Ba
1. See *bankers acceptance*.
2. A Moody's credit rating band that is approximately equivalent to the S&P BB band. The rating is divided into Ba1, Ba2 and Ba3. The band is sub-investment grade with Ba1 being the most creditworthy of the three. Also see *BB; credit rating; sub-investment grade*.

Baa A Moody's credit rating band that is approximately equivalent to the S&P BBB band. The rating is divided into Baa1, Baa2 and Baa3, all of which are considered to be investment grade. Also see *BBB; credit rating; sub-investment grade*.

baby bond
1. A bond with a small nominal value.
2. A tax-free savings scheme for children in the UK.

baccalaureate bond A bond issued by governmental organisations that has favourable returns and tax treatment and is used to encourage parents to save for the tertiary education of their children.

backcast Using historical information for financial modelling instead of using forecast information.

backdate To change the date on a document or contract to a date that occurred earlier.

back door
1. Gaining access via an unconventional method.
2. The central bank adjusts money supply by purchasing government debt on the open market rather than through banking lending rates. Also see *open market operations*.
3. See *back-door listing*.

back-door listing A method of achieving a stock market listing by taking over a listed company. This is usually done to avoid the complications and costs associated with listing a new company.

back of a fag packet A rough and quick calculation to obtain a general feel for what is being calculated rather than doing a detailed, highly accurate calculation. The reference comes from the days when people often used to write notes and do rough calculations on cigarette boxes (fag packets). Sometimes called a back of an envelope calculation.

back office Work areas that are not client facing where financial transactions are executed, delivered and settled.

backpricing A contract, usually on commodities and common on the London Metals Exchange, whereby the price of the deliverable asset in the contract will be determined at a date in the future. For example, a purchaser may enter a contract today stating that he/she will purchase 1 000 oz of gold in six months' time at a price to be determined by the spot gold price in five months' time. Purchasers may enter these contracts to ensure a supply of commodities. Also see *London Metals Exchange; spot market*.

back spread A trading strategy that involves selling an option near the strike price and purchasing an option out the money. The strategy benefits from high volatility or a big move in price. Put or call options can be used depending on the direction of the anticipated price movement. Also see *call option; out the money*.

backstop date The date at which a final decision on a transaction will take place.

backstop facility A line of credit given by a bank to a client to be used in the event of an unfavourable event. The event or range of events is usually defined in the terms and conditions of the backstop facility. Backstop facilities are often used as a Plan B if the initial financing options do not work. Sometimes called a back-up facility. Also see *back-up facility; credit line; standby liquidity facility*.

back-to-back loan A loan given by party A to party B which B then lends to C.

back-up facility A loan facility that can be drawn on if an unlikely and usually predefined event occurs. For example, a back-up facility may be required in a bond issue to provide insurance against all bonds not being taken up by the wider market. Sometimes called a standby liquidity facility or backstop facility. Also see *backstop facility; bond*.

backwardation

1. This occurs when the spot price of an asset is higher than the future price. This may occur as a result of interest rates on finance being less than lease rates on the particular asset. The graph shows a yield curve that is in backwardation (inverted). Also see *asset; contango; forward differential; future price; interest rate; spot price*.

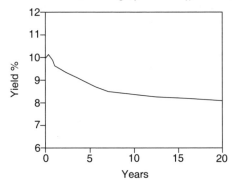

2. The bid price is higher than the ask price on an asset.

backwardation swap A yield curve swap where the yield curve is in backwardation. Also see *backwardation; swap; yield curve; yield curve swap*.

backward elimination A variable selection technique in linear regressions that eliminates the least significant variables first, leaving the most significant. Also see *linear regression*.

backward integration Businesses entering into operations whereby they manufacture earlier stage goods that are generally components of their later inputs. Companies often do this to secure supply. Also see *forward integration; horizontal integration; vertical integration*.

bad debt Debt that cannot be recovered. The debt is written off against the company's profits. Provisions are typically made for bad debt. Companies that extend significant amounts of debt such as credit retailers and banks are particularly sensitive to bad debt.

bad debt recovered Bad debt that is ultimately recovered. Also see *bad debt*.

bad delivery The registrar of shares rejects a transfer of ownership of a share.

baht Currency of Thailand.

baiza Currency of Oman.

balanced budget multiplier The effect on national income (GNP) by an increase in government expenditure and the offsetting of a change in taxation.

balanced fund A fund that consists of a range of securities, equities, bonds and cash both on and offshore. There are limitations imposed on these funds. They are set up to give investors an income together with capital appreciation at low risk levels.

balanced portfolio A portfolio of shares that is well diversified and carries little concentration risk. These portfolios usually track overall stock market indices and do not give excessive returns over the market. To gain returns in excess of the market, investors need to take on a degree of concentration risk. Also see *ALSI; concentrated portfolio, Satrix 40*.

balanced scorecard A means of measuring financial and non-financial performance against the strategy set by a company. The balanced scorecard often helps translate high-level long-term strategy into short-term objectives.

balance of cost scheme See *defined benefit fund*.

balance of payments (BoP) A measure of the flow of money in and out of a country. The BoP is effectively a measure of a country's accounts with the outside world. The balance of payments is divided into the capital account and current account. The BoP is represented in nominal and not real terms because the currency and inflation mixes are difficult to determine in real terms. The BoP is a widely used economic indicator of the value of a country. The aim is to have a positive balance of payments. Also see *capital account; current account; inflation; trade balance*.

balance of payments identity The net financial flows and changes in foreign exchange must sum to zero in a country's current account. Also see *current account; foreign exchange*.

balance of public finance The net foreign assets of a country are the net national savings and constitute the balance of public finance. Also see *net foreign assets*.

balance of trade See *trade balance*.

balance sheet An accounting representation of the assets, liabilities and owners holdings of a business at a particular point in time. The balance sheet is therefore always a snapshot. Balance sheets detail the sources of funds (shares, reserves and deferred taxation) against the employment of that capital (assets, debtors, inventory less creditors and current liabilities). Also see *current liability*.

balance sheet credit-linked note (CLO) A synthetic credit-linked note or CLO that is issued by a bank to adjust the risk of its balance sheet loan assets. The bank effectively sells the risks associated with assets on its balance sheet without legal transfer of title of the assets. Also see *balance sheet; credit-linked note; synthetic CLO*.

balance sheet insolvency A financial position where a company's liabilities exceed its assets. Also see *cash flow insolvency; insolvency*.

balancing charge Tax charged on the disposal of an asset when the taxable book value of that asset is less than the proceeds of the disposal. The balancing charge can be deducted from allowances such as an assessed loss. However, when the allowances

balancing item | **bank bill**

are effectively used up, cash will have to be paid to the tax receiver. Also see *assessed loss; book value*.

balancing item A variable that adjusts to maintain the consistency in a financial plan. For example, dividends are often used as a balancing item to maintain debt to equity ratios. Also see *dividend*.

Balassa-Samuelson effect The real exchange rate is defined as the nominal bilateral exchange rate for two countries adjusted by the relative prices of goods in those countries. This is called the purchasing power parity approach. The model is based on work by Balassa (1964) and Samuelson (1964). The assumption of purchasing power parity is relaxed and allowance is made for the real exchange rate to depend on the relative price of tradables and non-tradables, itself a function of productivity differentials. Also see *bilateral real exchange rate; purchasing power parity; real exchange rate*.

balboa The currency of Panama.

balloon See *balloon loan*.

balloon loan A loan that consists of monthly payments to cover interest and often a small capital portion, and a large capital payment at the date of maturity. The large final payment is sometimes called a bullet payment. A bullet loan, on the other hand, technically requires repayment of all the capital on the date of maturity. In South Africa, vehicle financing is often in the form of a balloon loan where the consumer pays a significant residual at the end of the contract period. Also see *bullet loan; maturity*.

balloon maturity A bond issuance profile that has the bulk of the maturities in a single year.

BAN See *bond anticipation note*.

band
1. A range in which a price will be made.
2. A range of dates.

bandwidth contract A capacity swap linked to the purchase or sale of telecommunications bandwidth. Telecom companies may use these contracts to cover themselves for variable operational bandwidth requirements. They are often sold in the form of options. Also see *capacity swap; option*.

bandwidth option See *bandwidth contract*.

bank A financial institution whose principal activities are to take deposits and borrow with the objective of lending and investing. Banks match surplus and deficit units in an economy. Banks have diversified their range of product offerings to include foreign exchange, share trading, financial advice and many others. The scope of activities a bank may undertake must be in line with banking legislation. Also see *deficit unit*.

bankable Suitable to be financed. A project is said to be bankable when enough due diligence has been done to verify that the project is viable and can be successfully financed. Also see *bankable feasibility study*.

bankable feasibility study A term often used in the mining industry to indicate that a project has gone past exploration and mining feasibility studies and is currently in a phase of financial feasibility studies to determine how to finance the project adequately.

bank assurance A term used with reference to banks that offer insurance products.

bank bill A bill of exchange issued by a bank. Also see *bill of exchange*.

bank certificate A certificate by a bank confirming the status of a transaction or account.

bank draft A cheque drawn by a financial institution against funds deposited into its account at another institution. These are effectively cheques that are guaranteed by a bank.

bankers acceptance (BA) A negotiable time draft or bill of exchange that has been accepted by a bank. By accepting, the bank is obliged to pay the holder the face value of the amount associated with the instrument on the maturity date specified. BAs give the holder a degree of safety as they are guaranteed by a bank that has a good credit rating. Due to the safety of these investments they are usually used to finance exports, imports or storage of goods where counterparties do not fully trust one another for payment. BAs are conceptually similar to post-dated cash-guaranteed cheques. They are issued by banks after due consideration and analysis of the issuer. The holder of the BA then has a claim on maturity. Banks sell the BAs to the market upon issuing them so the market therefore effectively finances the company requiring the credit. BAs can be traded on secondary markets in a similar fashion to treasury bills and are usually of bearer form. Also see *bearer; bill of exchange; credit rating; documentary letter of credit; face value; secondary market; treasury bill.*

bankers acceptance rate (BA rate) The rate at which a bankers acceptance is issued. The rate is quoted as a discount rate. BA rates are published by banking supervisors and are an important measure of credit tightening and credit cycles. BA rates are often used as the underlying index in various options. Also see *bankers acceptance; discount rate; option.*

bankers bank
1. See *central bank*.
2. A bank set up to provide clearing and trading services to a consortium of banks. Also see *clearing*.

bankers reference A report of the creditworthiness of a client published by a bank.

bank failure When a bank cannot satisfy its obligations to its creditors and depositors and subsequently goes out of business.

bank financial strength rating (BFSR) A risk measure used by the Moody's credit rating agency to indicate the financial strength of banks. The measure is used to derive an overall credit rating metric for banks. The rating indicator takes into account financial fundamentals, franchise value, risk positioning, regulatory environment and economic insolvency. The rankings for BFSR are:
- **A:** Superior intrinsic financial strength. Predictable and stable economic environment.
- **B:** Strong financial strength, valuable and defensible franchise and predictable operating environment.
- **C:** Adequate financial strength with a more limited but adequate franchise.
- **D:** Modest financial strength requiring outside support at times. There may be limiting factors such as the franchise and financial fundamentals.
- **E:** Modest intrinsic financial strength, higher probability of needing outside support. Limited by one or more factors including limited financial profiles and franchises.

+ or – modifiers are used to indicate split ranking. Also see *credit rating; credit rating agency.*

Bank for International Settlements (BIS) 'The Bank for International Settlements (BIS) is an international organisation which fosters international monetary and financial cooperation and serves as a bank for central banks.' (*Source:* www.bis.org)

bank guarantee A guarantee issued by a bank.

bank holiday A public holiday in the UK.

bank investment contract (BIC) An investment whose interest rate is guaranteed by a bank. Fixed deposits are examples of bank investment contracts. These types of investments are usually safe if the bank in question has a good credit rating and so usually yield a lower rate of interest. Also see *credit rating; interest rate*.

bank loan The lending of money by a bank to a customer. The loan will carry a series of terms and conditions such as interest payments, dates, maturity and covenants. Bank loans often require a guarantee or form of security. Also see *covenant*.

bank note Paper money or currency issued by a central bank. Central banks are usually the only entities authorised to issue hard currency. Also see *hard currency*.

Bank of England (BOE) The central bank of the UK. Also see *central bank*.

Bank of Japan (BOJ) The central bank of Japan. Also see *central bank*.

bank rate The interest rate at which central banks lend to commercial banks. Sometimes called the repo rate in South Africa, the marginal lending rate or the central bank discount rate. Also see *base rate; central bank discount rate; interest rate; marginal lending rate; repo rate*.

bank reconciliation statement A statement produced by an accountant of a company that reconciles the company's books with the balance in their bank account. There are many adjustments that need to be made due to the accrual basis of accounting. Cheques not cashed, funds clearing as well as other transactions may not appear on the bank statement at the date the reconciliation is done. Also see *accrual basis of accounting; clearing*.

bankruptcy When a company can no longer service its debt obligations, it is placed in liquidation. The company is effectively out of business if bankrupt. The liabilities of a bankrupt company typically exceed the assets. Also see *liquidation*.

bankruptcy remote A special-purpose entity set up to move credit risk off a balance sheet and minimise the risk of bankruptcy. Also see *balance sheet; credit risk*.

bank statement A statement issued by a bank at periodic intervals that shows all the transactions, debits and credits, as well as the remaining balance for that period.

bank supervision The process of organisations such as central banks and other regulators supervising banks and other financial institutions. This supervision is in place to ensure that:
- banks have adequate shareholders capital and are not excessively leveraged
- adequate risk management strategies are in place in the banks
- management of the banks is accountable for the actions of their institutions
- banks respond correctly to and cooperate with central banks in the implementation of monetary policy such as reserve requirements.

Also see *central bank; leverage; reserve requirement*.

bank transfer The transfer of monies from one account directly into another bank account.

Banque de France The central bank of France. Also see *central bank*.

bar One million.

BA rate See *bankers acceptance rate*.

bargain
1. A sale at a price significantly lower than the rest of the market or often less than the purchaser expected or was willing to pay.
2. Transaction on the London Stock Exchange.

barometer A variable or specific share price that gives a good indication of the overall trend. Also see *leading indicator*.

barrel (bbl) The unit used to measure oil. A barrel of crude oil is 42 US gallons which is about 35 imperial gallons or 159 litres. The abbreviations bbl or bl are used to indicate a barrel. Also see *crude oil*.

barrier option An option contract that is activated by coming into existence or ceasing to exist if the price of the underlying asset reaches a certain predefined level before the maturity of the option. Sometimes called a trigger option or a knock in/out option. Also see *asset*.

barrier to entry The hurdles that outsiders to an industry must face to establish themselves in that industry. For example, a barrier of entry into the banking industry is a banking licence.

Barron's Confidence Index An index that divides the yield of high-grade bonds by the yield of lower grade bonds. The index captures market sentiment because an increasing ratio indicates that the market is more risk averse and is purchasing higher grade bonds while a decreasing ratio indicates that the market is willing to take on more risk in the form of higher yield bonds.

barter The mutual exchange of goods with no exchange of money. Sometimes called a countertrade.

barter revenue Revenue recognised for the mutual exchange of goods with no exchange of physical cash.

base case A financial model that uses the expected values as inputs. More optimistic and pessimistic variables are then used to model the up and downside cases or sensitivity.

base currency The currency that is used as the basis for the exchange rate. The base currency used is usually US dollars. For example, if the exchange rate is quoted as R7.5 per dollar, the dollar is the base currency and the rand is the pricing currency. Also see *American-style FX*.

base date The year which is chosen for a particular data set to equal 100 units. A base year can be chosen arbitrarily and can significantly influence the appearance of any trends in the data set. Also see *base year*.

Basel A committee in Europe that sets standards and guidelines for the banking industry and its supervision. The recommendations are then implemented by the national authorities of individual nations. The committee's aim is to converge approaches and

baseline credit assessment (BCA) | base year

standards for risk management across Europe. Basel is based on the three pillars, namely:

- capital requirements
- supervisory review
- market discipline.

The original Basel accord, commonly referred to as Basel I, was replaced by Basel II in 2008.

baseline credit assessment (BCA) One of the four rating inputs to the Moody's credit rating methodology. BCA is expressed on a scale of 1 to 21 where 1 is the lowest credit risk. Also see *credit rating*.

base load plant A power plant that runs at a constant output throughout the day and is not used in periods of peak demand.

base metal Any non-precious metal that oxidises or corrodes easily. Base metals include copper, lead, tin, aluminium and zinc. The London Metals Exchange is a leading exchange where base metals are traded in the spot and futures market. Also see *futures contract; London Metals Exchange; spot market*.

base price The initial price of an asset before the addition of a margin or additional charges. Also see *margin*.

base rate The rate at which banks benchmark lending. This is most often the relevant interbank rate and banks lend at a margin over this rate to their customers. LIBOR and JIBAR are examples of base rates used in London and in South Africa. Sometimes called a reference rate. Also see *bank rate; JIBAR; LIBOR; margin*.

base rate agreement When banks lend money, their cost of lending may move higher than the stipulated base rate. A base rate agreement is often introduced into loan documents that gives the lender the ability to construct rates based on other alternatives should this be required and reasonable. Also see *prime rate*.

base requirement A capital adequacy requirement that indicates how much liquidity in the form of cash that financial services companies need to set aside to remain solvent. Also see *capital adequacy; liquidity*.

base weighted index An index which is constructed against the values of a set of variables from a base year. Also see *base year*.

base year Base year calculations are usually used in the analysis of variables such as GDP that have the effects of inflationary growth included in them. Because analysts are usually interested in the real changes, the effects of inflation are removed. GDP is then recalculated with respect to prices in a set base year. If the CPI in 1995 = 30 and in 2000 the CPI = 40, then the increase in prices is $(40 - 30)/30 = 33\%$. To adjust the GDP in 2000, discount by 33%:

$$\text{GDP} \times \frac{1}{1 + 33\%}$$

In general the calculation is defined by:

$$\text{GDP}_{@t=x \text{ in } t=0 \text{ prices}} = \frac{\text{GDP}_{@t=x}}{\left[1 + \frac{\text{CPI}_{t=x} - \text{CPI}_{t=0}}{\text{CPI}_{t=0}}\right]}$$

where CPI = consumer price index which is a measure of inflation.

Also see *capital adequacy; consumer price index; gross domestic product; inflation.*

basic charge A fee in addition to a brokerage charge that is applicable to shares bought and sold on the same day.

basic custody The safekeeping and administration of securities on behalf of others.

basic earnings per share Profit for the period that is attributable to ordinary shareholders divided by the weighted average number of ordinary shares outstanding during the period:

$$\text{basic earnings per share} = \frac{\text{profit after taxation}}{\text{average number outstanding shares}}$$

Also see *ordinary share; weighted average.*

basis The difference between the cash and futures prices of the next delivery month. As the futures contract approaches expiry, the basis should shrink to zero. If the basis is negative, then the contract is in contango. If it is positive, it is in backwardation. Also see *backwardation; contango; contract month.*

basis point A single basis point is 1/100th of a per cent. For example, if interest rates are expected to rise by 50 basis points, then they are set to be raised 0.5%. Basis points are usually used in the context of interest rates. Also see *interest rate.*

basis price See *yield price.*

basis risk The risk associated with hedging activities that arises from changes in the difference between the spot and futures price of an asset. Also see *asset; hedge; spot market.*

basis swap An interest rate swap or currency swap where both sides float but according to a different basis. The basis may be in the same or different currencies. For example, a one-month LIBOR can be swapped for a six-month LIBOR or in the case of a cross-currency swap, a three-month LIBOR can be swapped for a three-month JIBAR. Basis swaps can be used to manage risk where assets and liabilities depend on different reference rates. Basis swaps are quoted as spreads to one of the basis rates. If one leg of the swap is against LIBOR, the spread is quoted against the other reference rate. For example, LIBOR+0 swaps into JIBAR+25.

The rates at which basis swaps are concluded are determined by market supply and demand dynamics. Also see *currency swap; interest rate swap; JIBAR; LIBOR; reference rate.*

basis trading A trading strategy that involves the sale and purchase of a similar asset. Often this type of trading is done on a spot asset and its futures price or the trading of shares in the same company listed on different exchanges. Also see *future price; negative basis trade, positive basis trade; spot market.*

basket of shares A portfolio of shares comprising a number of shares of each constituent company in an index. Also see *index.*

basket option An option written on more than one underlying security or asset. Also see *asset; security.*

basket pegging An exchange rate fixed against a basket of currencies. Also see *trade weighted exchange rate.*

basket price The price of a selected set or basket of items. These are often shares when used in the context of investments or physical goods in the context of consumer prices and inflation. Also see *consumer price index; inflation; Satrix 40*.

Baxter's Index or adjustment A formula used to adjust inflation indices to produce an index more relevant to the building, waste disposal and specialist engineering sectors. It takes more significant account of fuel, labour and maintenance costs. Also known as NEDO and Osborne indices. Also see *inflation*.

Bay Street The Toronto Stock Exchange.

BB
1. A credit rating band used by S&P and Fitch. The credit rating is further divided by the + and − indicators. The BB rating band indicates poorer credit quality than the investment grade BBB band. Also see *credit rating*.
2. Business bank.

BBA British Bankers' Association.

BBB A credit rating that indicates the company is a satisfactory credit risk and is investment grade. A BBB rating is worse than an A rating and is used by S&P and Fitch. The band is further divided by the + and − indicators. Also see *credit rating; credit risk*.

BBD The currency of Barbados, the Barbados dollar, divided into 100 cents.

bbl See *barrel*.

BBR See *BBSW*.

BBSW The Australian market bank bill reference rate. The abbreviation is often used for the interbank rate for the Australian bank market. This is effectively the Australian equivalent of LIBOR. Also see *interbank rate; LIBOR; reference rate*.

BBSY Bank bill swap bid rate. This is a screen on the Reuters information system that gives reference interest rates against which floating interest rate loans in the Australian market are set. Also see *BBSW; floating interest rate; interest rate*.

BCA See *baseline credit assessment*.

BCP Books closed period.

BDA Broker deal accounting system.

BDT The currency of Bangladesh, the Bangladesh taka divided into 100 paisa.

bear A dealer or trader who is expecting the market to fall. Also see *bull*.

bear call spread A strategy that involves selling a call option at a lower strike price and buying a call at a higher strike price with the same maturity. Profit will be made when the lower price option generates revenue greater than the cost of the higher price option. The bet is then that the market price goes down. The higher option is out the money and is not exercised. Also see *call option; out the money; strike price*.

bear closing The closing of a bear or short position. Also see *short position*.

bearer A person in possession of an investment certificate or cheque. A bearer instrument does not require identification or endorsement of the owner and is a risky asset. There is no record of ownership and the current holder is considered to be the owner. There is a trend worldwide against the issuing of bearer bonds. Also see *asset; bearer bond*.

bearer bond A bond issued without the owner's name. Payment is made to the person in possession of or the bearer of the bond. Also see *bearer; bond.*

bearer form See *bearer.*

bearer instrument See *bearer.*

bearer security See *bearer.*

bear market Share prices that are on a downward trend, usually evidenced as a random walk with downward drift. Also see *bull market; drift; random walk with drift.*

bear position See *short position.*

bear put spread A strategy similar to a bear call spread that involves the purchase and sale of put options instead of call options. Also see *bear call spread.*

bear raid Investors with a bear position (sold short) who try to cover the position by further short selling to depress the price. Such a trading strategy can result in huge losses. Also see *sell short; short position.*

bear sale The sale of a list of shares that the seller does not own. The seller does this expecting the price to drop. Before delivery of the shares, the seller attempts to pick up the shares in the market at the lower price, thereby profiting from the difference. Investors are usually legally required to declare bear sales. The requirement of conducting such a sale is that the investor has to borrow a scrip of shares from a financial institution. The investor then purchases those shares in the market at an anticipated lower price in the future and returns the shares. Also see *short position.*

bear spread See *bear call spread; bear put spread.*

bear squeeze When a series of bear investors short sell securities in anticipation of prices trending downwards and the price actually trends upwards. To cover their positions, the bear investors are forced to purchase the securities in an upward trending market, thereby boosting market prices further and ultimately losing the bear investors even more money.

bear trend A long downward trend in the price of a security or index. Also see *index; security.*

bed and breakfast deal The sale of shares at a financial year end with a corresponding purchase at the beginning of the next financial year with the objective of showing a capital profit and loss for taxation purposes. Also see *financial year.*

BEE See *black economic empowerment.*

BEF Former currency of Belgium, the frank. Also see *euro.*

behavioural equilibrium exchange rate (BEER) An exchange rate modelling approach that focuses on the dynamic behaviour of the exchange rate, including short-run movements and deviations and taking broader macroeconomic conditions into account. The choice of fundamental variables may differ according to the theoretical model being used.

behind the fence An operation or project that relies on revenues from a local customer. The operation that is behind the fence is an integral part of a manufacturing process of the single customer. Sometimes the term inside the fence is used. Also see *toll manufacturing concern.*

beige book Information compiled by the Fed and used when setting interest rates. Also see *Federal Reserve; interest rate*.

bells and whistles Unusual or exotic features in a financial transaction. Also see *vanilla*.

bellwether
1. See *leading indicator*.
2. Shares that typically indicate the trend of the market. They will have beta values at or near 1. Also see *beta*.

below the line Items in an income statement that detail how profit is distributed.

benchmark A point of reference against which progress can be measured. Fund managers' performance is measured against a set of defined benchmarks which are measured in the form of an index. Also see *index*.

benchmark bond A bond that is used as a key indicator of the overall bond market. These are usually key government ten-year bonds. Also see *bond*.

benchmarking Comparing an asset against a similar asset to gauge performance.

beneficial owner The owner of a security or asset even though the security is not registered in his/her name. These securities may be held by a nominee or trustee. Also see *security*.

beneficiary
1. The entity that receives the proceeds of an estate or a trust.
2. The person receiving payment in a transaction.

benefit distribution A distribution made to shareholders in a company. Usually in the form of regular dividends, special dividends or securities and in proportion to their shareholding. Also see *dividend; special dividend*.

benefit in kind Payment in a form other than cash. Also see *payment in kind*.

Benelux Belgium, Netherlands and Luxembourg.

Bermuda option An option that can be exercised on specified dates before the expiration date. Also see *option*.

Berne Union An international organisation that facilitates 'cross-border trade and investments by fostering international acceptance of sound principles in export credits and investments insurance, and by providing a forum for professional exchanges among its members'. (*Source*: www.berneunion.org) Sometimes called the International Union of Credit & Investment Insurers.

Bernoulli distribution A discrete probability distribution that takes the value 1 with probability p and the value 0 with probability $q = 1 - p$. An example of a Bernoulli distribution is the tossing of a coin where heads is assigned a score of 1 and tails a score of 0. The probability of scoring a 1 is 50% (p) and the probability of scoring a 0 is 50%, i.e. $1 - 50\%$. Also see *normal or Gaussian distribution*.

Bernoulli trials A sequence of events that has two outcomes, either success or failure. The process itself does not change the probability of success or failure at the next attempt, i.e. it is not path dependent. A simple sequence of the tossing of a coin is a good example. Each toss has success or failure and the previous toss has no influence over the current toss. Also see *path dependent*.

BESA See *Bond Exchange of South Africa*.

bespoke | beta approach

bespoke Custom-built.

best and final offer A bid made in a second round of a public procurement process.

best efforts A syndicated loan or bond issuance arrangement whereby the arranger group commits to underwrite some, or usually none, of the entire quantum sought. The full amount is therefore left to the wider credit market. If the transaction is undersubscribed, the credit may not close or may need to be adjusted to clear the market. Also see *club deal; credit market; syndicated loan; underwrite.*

best price A buy or sell order on an exchange that implies that the transaction must be done at the best available price when the order is given.

beta The beta of a share measures the share's responsiveness to the market as a whole, i.e. the level of systematic risk. The slope of the best fit of the excess return on the company over the risk-free rate (y-axis) versus the return of the market over the risk-free rate (x-axis) constitutes the beta of a share. The beta is effectively the amount of systematic or market risk present in a particular risky asset relative to an average market asset. This linear relationship is known as the security market line.

To obtain beta a linear regression of the data as indicated by the security market line is required. The reliability of the relationship is given by the standard error of the beta estimate. In the linear regression the R^2 (R-squared) statistic measures the proportion of the total risk that is systematic.

Be careful when comparing betas. Adjustments for capital structure differences using the Hamada equation are needed as well as comparisons with companies with similar financial and business risk profiles.

Beta is also measured as the ratio of covariance to variance:

$$\beta = \frac{\text{covariance }(i, m)}{\sigma_m^2} = \frac{\rho_{i,m} \sigma_i \sigma_m}{\sigma_m^2} = \frac{\rho_{i,m} \sigma_i}{\sigma_m}$$

where i = investment; m = market; ρ = correlation coefficient; σ = variance.

Aggressive stocks have high betas that are greater than 1.0, meaning that their returns tend to respond more than one-for-one to changes in the return of the overall market. The betas of defensive stocks are less than 1.0. A beta of 1 implies that the share is a market tracker. The returns of these stocks vary less than one-for-one with market returns. The average beta of all stocks is 1.0 exactly. Also see *adjusted beta; alpha coefficient; asset; capital structure; capital asset pricing model; covariance; Hamada equation; linear regression; market risk premium; R^2; security market line; total risk; variance.*

beta approach A method of determining the cost of capital in foreign markets. It is an extension of the Bludgeon approach, with the country risk premium being adjusted by beta. The project itself, which may not be exposed to full market risk, now has an adjustment for market risk through beta. Investors may want this type of approach when valuing a mining company such as AngloGold, where its beta value is low because it is exposed primarily to international gold prices and exchange rates.

For a South African investor investing in Nigeria, then local = SA and foreign = Nigeria:

cost of equity = $(Rf_{\text{local market}}) + \beta(Rm_{\text{local market}} - Rf_{\text{local market}} + CRP)$

where CRP = country risk premium; $Rf_{\text{local market}}$ = risk-free rate in the local market; $Rm_{\text{local market}}$ = rate of return in the local market; β = beta value of the project with respect to the project's market returns.

Also see *adjusted hybrid capital asset pricing model; beta; Bludgeon approach; cost of capital; country risk premium; Erb-Harvey approach; Estrata downside risk model; global capital asset pricing model; Godfrey and Espinosa cost of equity model; Goldman Sachs model; lambda approach; Lessard's model; Pereiro's adjusted CAPM model.*

beta play An investment with high betas that gives good or excessive returns when the market does well and vice versa.

better price A price that is lower than the offer price or higher than the bid price.

BFSR See *bank financial strength rating*.

BGL The currency of Bulgaria, the Bulgarian lev divided into 100 stotinki.

BGN See *BGL*.

BHD The currency of Bahrain, the Bahrain dinar divided into 100 fils.

bias Distortion of results or unfair favouring of an entity in a financial transaction.

bible A complete set of documents that details a particular transaction. Typically used in project finance. Also see *project finance*.

BIC
1. Bank identifier code. Also see *Society for Worldwide Interbank Financial Transactions*.
2. See *bank investment contract*.

bid See *bid price*.

bidco A company set up by a sponsor to be used to acquire an asset or company. Also see *sponsor*.

bidding group Banks that are bidding for finance on the same project.

bid price The price at which traders or market makers buy shares. The difference between the bid and ask price equates to the profit the trader makes on the transaction. Also see *ask price; market maker; spread*.

bid spread See *spread*.

bid to cover ratio The ratio is often used to quantify how much market demand exists for a security.

$$\text{bid to cover ratio} = \frac{\text{total value of bids}}{\text{the total size of auction}}$$

A failed auction will have a value less than 1. Also see *auction*.

Big Blue The information technology company IBM.

big board A name sometimes used for the New York Stock Exchange. Also see *main board*.

bilateral A loan between a corporate customer and a single bank. A bilateral differs from a syndicated loan where the loan transaction is between a single borrower and a range of banks. Also see *syndicated loan*.

bilateral agency An organisation usually established by governments to promote international trade. An export credit agency (ECA) falls into this category. Also see *export credit agency*.

bilateral loan See *bilateral*.

bilateral real exchange rate The real exchange rate when considering only two countries. When formulating a compound exchange rate with multiple countries, it is called a multilateral real exchange rate. Also see *multilateral real exchange rate; real exchange rate; trade weighted exchange rate*.

bill See *bill of exchange*.

billion 1 000 000 000 = one thousand million = 10^9.

bill of exchange A negotiable security signed and dated by the issuer. It contains an unconditional order or instruction for the drawee to pay a fixed sum of money to a certain entity on maturity. Bills of exchange are used by exporters to obtain cash as soon as the goods have been dispatched and by importers to delay payment of goods until they have arrived. Sometimes called commercial bills. Also see *acceptance credit; negotiable certificate of deposit; security*.

bill of lading A contract or document issued by cargo carriers detailing the terms and conditions of haulage. A bill of lading indicates that the carrier has taken charge on behalf of the shipper. They are used when the ship is carrying cargo for many customers.

bill pass The process of central banks purchasing discount securities, i.e. non-coupon bearing securities, in open-market operations. When the banks purchase coupon-earning instruments the term coupon pass is used. Also see *central bank; discount security; open market operations*.

bill rate The discount rate at which a bill of exchange is traded in the market. Also see *discount rate*.

bimodal distribution Distribution with two nodes, i.e. two peaks. A distribution with a single peak is termed uni-modal. Also see *normal or Gaussian distribution; unimodal*.

binary credit default swap See *binary settlement*.

binary option An option whose payoff is a fixed asset, a fixed amount of cash or nothing at all. Also see *option*.

binary settlement A payout for a credit default swap after a credit event that is fixed and not dependent on a recovery rate. Also see *credit default swap*.

binomial distribution In probability theory and statistics, the binomial distribution is the discrete probability distribution of the number of successes in a sequence of n independent (so no autocorrelation) yes/no experiments, each of which yields success with probability p. Such a success/failure experiment is also called a Bernoulli distribution or Bernoulli trial. For example, a coin flip for heads or tails will yield a discrete set of results with a mean of about 50 and a particular standard deviation. Also see *Bernoulli distribution; standard deviation*.

binomial tree A binomial or binary tree is a tree data structure in which each node has at most two possible options.

biological assets Livestock. These appear on the balance sheet at fair value. Also see *balance sheet*.

bips See *basis point*.

birr The currency of Ethiopia divided into 100 cents.

BIS See *Bank for International Settlements*.

bivariate See *multivariate distribution*.

bl See *barrel*.

black box A process that is used to derive an answer or result where understanding of the process itself is limited. Many mathematical computer models are considered to be black box.

black box transaction A derivative asset that has an underlying pool of assets. The derivative investor is unable to tell exactly what the underlying assets are and relies on the agreed industry, geographic and credit rating mix. Also see *credit rating*.

black chip A term used in South Africa that indicates a highly rated black-owned company. Also see *black economic empowerment*.

black diamonds The elite and wealthy black individuals who have benefited economically from empowerment transactions in South Africa.

black economic empowerment (BEE) The process of the transformation of the South African economy to include individuals who were previously disadvantaged under apartheid. There are various pieces of legislation and charters that govern the process including the BEE and Employment Equity Acts.

black knight The entity that is leading an unwelcome or hostile takeover bid. Also see *hostile takeover bid; white knight*.

black market
1. Business transactions that are not officially recorded to avoid prosecution and taxation. Black markets often emerge in environments where prices are fixed and demand-supply dynamics create significant real price differentials. Black-market transactions are generally illegal and black markets generally have no formal rights to property ownership and enforceable contracts. Black markets bring few benefits to society at large as the protection that is required by investors to take on risk is not affordable. Black markets are subject to dubious traders, dealers and mobsters.
2. In South Africa the term is sometimes used to refer to a body of consumers who are predominantly ethnically black.

black money Money earned illegally.

Black-Scholes options pricing model A mathematical options pricing model that is based on the following assumptions:
- The option being valued is a European option
- Only one source of uncertainty (no rainbow options)
- Only one underlying asset
- Underlying asset pays no dividends
- Current market price and stochastic processes are observable
- Variance of return is constant through time, i.e. a stationary process
- Exercise price is known and constant
- Log normally distributed asset prices
- Constant volatility and drift

- Constant interest rates.

The mathematical representation for a call option value (C_0) is given by:

$$C_0 = SN(d_1) - Xe^{-r_fT}N(d_2)$$

and for a put option:

$$P_0 = Xe^{-r_fT}N(-d_2) - SN(-d_1)$$

where

$$d_1 = \frac{\ln\left(\frac{S}{X}\right) + \left(r_f + \frac{\sigma^2}{2}\right)T}{\sigma\sqrt{T}}$$

$$d_2 = \frac{\ln\left(\frac{S}{X}\right) + \left(r_f - \frac{\sigma^2}{2}\right)T}{\sigma\sqrt{T}}$$

where S = price of underlying asset; $N(d_1)$ and $N(d_2)$ = cumulative normal probability of unit normal variable d_1 and d_2 where probability tables are needed to obtain these numbers; X = exercise price; T = time to maturity; r_f = risk-free rate.

The e^{-r_fT} term continuously discounts the future revenue.

The above call option equation can be broken down as follows:

option value = expected revenue from sale of stock discounted − exercise price × probability of exercise × discount factor

Also see *asset; call option; dividend; drift; European option; interest rate; log normal; put option; rainbow option; stationary process; stochastic process; strike price; variance; volatility*.

blank cheque A cheque that does not have an amount specified on it. This gives the holder the ability to choose the amount of monies to be transferred or cashed. Also see *cheque*.

blind auction An auction process where bidders cannot see the terms, conditions and pricing being proposed by the other bidders in the process. Also see *auction*.

blind trust A trust that administers the assets of an individual who cannot have any business interests, usually for political reasons. The trust does not receive instructions from the beneficial holder of the assets and is meant to ensure that the person in question is not subject to any conflicts of interest.

B-loan A loan that has less seniority than an A-loan and subsequently has slightly higher margins and potentially longer tenors. Also see *A-loan; C-loan; D-loan; margin; seniority*.

block A large number of securities sold as a single unit. These are usually 1 000 or more shares. Also see *block trade*.

blocked account

1. An account that is frozen by a bank for technical reasons.
2. See *blocked funds*.

blocked funds Funds usually held by non-residents that are blocked by exchange control regulations and may not be repatriated to the non-residents' home countries. This is sometimes done by desperate governments that are short of foreign exchange reserves.

block sale See *block trade*.

block trade The sale of a large number of shares. This is often done by institutional investors and can be associated with changes in share prices. Sometimes brokers break up the blocks and sell them off as smaller units. Also see *institutional investor*.

Bloomberg
1. The Bloomberg Terminal is an information system and service that supplies the financial market with real-time data on markets and trades.
2. A TV channel dedicated to business news and market reports.

Also see *Reuters; secondary information provider.*

Bludgeon approach This is an approach used to determine the cost of equity in a foreign market by investors. For a South African investor investing in Nigeria, then local = SA and foreign = Nigeria:

Cost of equity = $(Rf_{\text{local market}} + CRP) + \beta(Rm_{\text{local market}} - Rf_{\text{local market}})$

where CRP = country risk premium; $Rf_{\text{local market}}$ = risk-free rate in the local market; $Rm_{\text{local market}}$ = rate of return in the local market; β = beta value of the project with respect to the project's market returns.

This approach uses the same country risk for all projects. Also see *adjusted hybrid capital asset pricing model; beta approach; country risk premium; Erb-Harvey approach; Estrata downside risk model; global capital asset pricing model; Godfrey and Espinosa cost of equity model; Goldman Sachs model; lambda approach; Lessard's model; Pereiro's adjusted CAPM model.*

blue book A set of guidelines or rules imposed on companies for merger and acquisition transactions in the UK. Also see *acquisition.*

blue chip A company or share traded on the stock markets that is a consistently strong performer. Blue chips are well known, have an excellent reputation and a considerable track record. Also see *black chip.*

blue month The month in which a derivative trade is the highest. This may be related to the price volatility of the underlying asset.

blue ocean The ocean refers to the market or industry. Blue oceans are untapped and uncontested markets which provide little or no competition for anyone who dives in since the market is not crowded.
- Create uncontested marketplace.
- Make the competition irrelevant.
- Create and capture new demand.
- Break the value/cost trade off.
- Align activities to differentiate and make cost low.

blue sky value The premium (goodwill) paid by a buyer in the expectation of profits in excess of the required return on invested capital. Also see *goodwill.*

Blume adjustment See *adjusted beta.*

BMD The currency of Bermuda, the Bermudan dollar divided into 100 cents.

BME See *TBMA.*

board lot See *marketable parcel.*

board of directors (BOD) Individuals elected by the shareholders of a company to carry out certain tasks in the interest of shareholders. The board appoints senior management and approves or disapproves the issuance of shares and declaration of dividends. Directors can be internal and external and have a fiduciary duty to the company. Directors are accountable for the overall performance of the company. Also see *dividend; fiduciary duty*.

board order See *market if touched*.

board resolution A resolution passed by the board of directors of a company making a key decision. For example, the approval of acquisitions and financing strategies are passed as board resolutions. Also see *acquisition; board of directors; resolution; special resolution*.

bobl A three- to five-year German government bond. Also see *bund; government bond; schatz*.

BOD See *board of directors*.

BOE See *Bank of England*.

boiler plate document A standard document or template. Boiler plate documentation usually enables the user to change a few minor details to obtain a standard contract. Also see *Loan Market Association*.

boiler room A company that purchases and sells securities on a short-term basis, typically over the phone. The company is probably not a member of a financial regulatory authority and sometimes has questionable motives. Sometimes called a bucket shop.

boiling the frog A frog can be boiled alive if the water is heated slowly enough. The temperature changes are so slow that the frog's heat detection system is incapable of detecting the changes and it eventually dies without attempting to jump out of the pot. This phrase is often used in economics when talking about central banks moving interest rates slowly so as not to hurt the economy but ultimately killing it by not obtaining appropriate timely feedback. Also see *interest rate*.

BOJ The Bank of Japan which is the country's central bank. Also see *central bank*.

bolivar The currency of Venezuela divided into 100 centimos.

boliviano The currency of Bolivia divided into 100 centavos.

Bollinger bands Lines on a graph of share closing prices that indicate one standard deviation above and below a moving average. When volatility is low, the bands narrow. When prices break out of the bands, a significant movement has occurred and may signal the start of a new trend.

bolsa A Spanish term for stock exchange, similar to the German word bourse. Also see *bourse*.

Bombay Stock Exchange (BSE) The stock exchange in Mumbai, India.

bona fide Acting in good faith. For example, a purchaser of an asset buys the asset in good faith believing that the seller is entitled to sell.

bond A bond is usually a form of secured debt. Bonds conceptually take the form of an IOU issued by the government or a private company. The issuer of a bond pays the investor interest and at the end of the term repays the principal amount invested.

The term is often used to describe debt that is secured or unsecured but a promise exists that the obligation will be honoured. Also see *bond; secured; secured loan; treasury bill; unsecured debt*.

bond anticipation note (BAN) A short-term security that can be used for bridge-type financing that companies and governments issue before issuing a full bond. Also see *bond; commercial paper.*

bond basis The calculation of accrued interest on a bond. Also see *accrued interest; bond.*

bond conversion Conversion from one bond to another. This is important to the bond futures market. Also see *bond; cheapest to deliver.*

bond duration (Macaulay duration) The weighted average maturity of a bond's cash flows. The duration of a zero coupon bond with a maturity period of n is n. When coupon payments are introduced, the duration decreases. Duration effectively measures the price sensitivity of a bond to a change in its yield. The duration is defined as:

$$\text{duration} = \frac{\text{cash flows (discounted)} \times \text{time}}{\text{price of bond today}} = \sum_{i=1}^{n} \frac{P(i)t(i)}{V}$$

where $P(i)$ = the discounted value of the coupon cash flows of coupon i; $t(i)$ = the future payment date; V = the bond price.

The Macaulay duration is a rough calculation. The modified duration is often used as a more accurate number. The drivers of duration are the maturity, coupon size and discounting factor (yield).

Also see *bond; dollar duration; effective duration; modified duration; portfolio duration; zero coupon bond.*

bond equivalent The restatement of the yields from bonds whose coupon payments are made in intervals that are not annual. The calculation is given by the following equation:

$$\text{yield} = \frac{\text{par value} - \text{purchase price}}{\text{purchase price}} \times \frac{365}{\text{time to maturity}}$$

bond exchange A market where bonds are traded between investors. Also see *Bond Exchange of South Africa; Yield-X Bond Exchange.*

Bond Exchange of South Africa (BESA) The South African exchange where fixed income securities and associated derivatives are traded. Also see *derivative; fixed income.*

bond fees When issuing a bond, issuers are charged the following fees by the issuing investment bank:
- Upfront fees associated with legal and documentation costs, road shows, work fees and other miscellaneous expenses
- An underwriting fee for underwritten deals.

bond floor For convertible debt, the floor is the lower of the value of the debt itself and the current market value of the shares into which it can be converted. The bond floor is the present value, calculated by discounting the bullet payment on redemption and the bond coupons. The bond floor is usually below issue price due to the fact that there is an embedded option. Investors with a focus on the debt component of a convertible bond look closely at the bond floor. The bond floor can be used to price the embedded option. Also see *bond; convertible debt bond; embedded option.*

bond fund A collective investment scheme that invests in bonds. Bond funds usually have the objective of preserving capital and giving constant income streams. Also see *collective investment scheme; widow and orphans fund.*

bond future A legally binding futures contract to buy or sell a given amount of face value of a specific bond, at an agreed price on a specific date or at a range of dates in the future. Bond futures are generally quoted in points and 1/64th of a point. 1/64th of a point is often referred to as a tick. Also see *bond; face value; future contract; tick*.

bond indenture See *indenture*.

bonding facility A commitment by a bank or insurer for a fee to provide surety bonds up to a predefined limit. This facility does not usually affect any working capital or other borrowing facilities. When obtained from a bank, the bank regards bonding facilities as part of the overall banking facilities and often insists on full tangible collateral. An alternative to a bonding facility is to draw against a revolving credit facility, deposit the cash and collateralise any contracts against the cash deposit. Also see *collateral; revolving credit facility; surety bond; working capital*.

bond ladder An investment strategy that involves making equal investments into fixed income securities (bonds) that mature on different dates. As the bonds mature, the money is reinvested at the prevailing rate. The strategy minimises reinvestment risk because not all bonds become due at the same time and the risk of reinvestment of the entire portfolio at lower market rates is reduced.

bond option The option to buy a bond with a maturity greater than the expiration date of the option.

bond ordinance Authorisation of a bond issue. Also see *bond*.

bond quote The statement of the price of a bond.

bond rating A measure of the risk of default of the issuer of a bond. Also see *credit rating*.

bond ratio A measure of how much of the capital employed of a business is in the form of bonds.

$$\text{bond ratio} = \frac{\text{value of outstanding bonds}}{\text{total capital employed}}$$

bond risk The risk to the holder of a bond that interest rates will change, the bond will lose value and that the issuer may potentially default. Also see *bond; bond value; event of default; interest rate*.

bond swap The simultaneous purchase and sale of a bond. Also see *bond; swap*.

bond value Bond value = present value of all coupon payments + present value of redemption amount (terminal value):

$$\text{bond value} = \frac{C}{1+r} + \frac{C}{(1+r)^2} + \frac{C}{(1+r)^3} + \dots + \frac{C}{(1+r)^n} + \frac{FV}{(1+r)^n}$$

Simplified using the sum of a geometric series:

$$\text{bond value} = C \left[\frac{1 - \frac{1}{(1+r)^t}}{r} \right] + \frac{FV_t}{(1+r)^t}$$

where FV_t = future value after t periods; t = number of periods; r = interest rate or discount rate; C = annuity or coupon payment.

The bond value calculation works for a whole number of periods only and constitutes the clean price. If there are a fraction of days outstanding, then the accrued interest needs to be added to the clean price to obtain the all-in or dirty price.

Also see *current yield; clean price; future value; geometric series; terminal value; yield to maturity*.

bond washing Selling a bond cum interest and purchasing more when the bond goes ex interest. This has the effect of converting the interest payment on the bond into a capital gain. Also see *bond; cum interest; ex interest*.

bond with warrants A bond with an embedded warrant. These are a form of convertible debt and are often considered to be a hybrid form of capital. The warrant is included as an incentive to lower the overall debt finance costs. The warrant also implies that equity capital flows will occur when the warrant is exercised. Also see *bond; convertible debt/bond; equity capital; hybrid; warrant*.

bond yield See *current yield*.

bonus An additional payment to employees by a company in recognition of good work. These payments are often a share in the profit of a company and are designed to motivate employees.

bonus dividend See *special dividend*.

bonus issue The distribution of shares to existing shareholders in proportion to the shares they already hold. A bonus issue has the effect of reducing the share price in the market and has a similar effect to a share split. Sometimes called a capitalisation or scrip issue. Also see *dividend in specie; share split*.

bonus share See *bonus issue*.

book builder An activity undertaken by an investment bank managing an issue of a new security, loan or share where the bank polls the market and determines demand for the new issue. These steps are used to price the new issue and minimise the risk that the issue is undersubscribed or oversubscribed. Also see *investment bank*.

book entry security Securities and shares that do not have issued physical certificates but are simply entries in computer systems. Also see *dematerialisation*.

book entry system A system that manages financial securities on computer systems and not through physical certificates. The system allows for easy transfer of securities between counterparties. Also see *dematerialisation*.

book equity See *book value*.

book over When a single broker matches a purchase and sell order of two of his/her own clients, the trade is put through an independent broker to ensure that the transaction is fair to all parties. Also see *arms length*.

book reserve Provision for a future liability. Also see *contingent liability*.

book runner
1. The lead entity that controls the syndication of a loan or the issue of bonds or equity shares. Book runners are responsible for coordinating and managing the book building, sales and distribution in the issue process. The book runner is usually one of the mandated lead arrangers in the case of a syndicated loan. Also see *book builder; mandated lead arranger; syndicated loan*.
2. For share (equity) issues, the book runner is the underwriter who controls the securities to be sold. Also see *equity*.

books close date See *record date*.

book to bill ratio A ratio used in the analysis of the technology industry (usually chip and semiconductor) that relates demand to supply. The orders on the company's books represent demand and the sales on the company's books represent the supply capacity.

book value
1. The value of an asset as indicated on a company's balance sheet. This is the purchase value less the accumulated depreciation. The book value of an asset may differ considerably from the actual market value. There is a range of accounting procedures used to adjust the values of assets that appear on a company's balance sheet. Also see *balance sheet; depreciation*.
2. Total assets – total liabilities, i.e. shareholders equity A – L = O. This is often compared to the share price to see if the company trades at a premium to the net value of its assets. Also see *market value*.

boom A sustained period of strong economic performance.

bootstrapping
1. The process of deriving zero coupon yields from a set of coupon-bearing instruments. Also see *stripping bonds*.
2. Making a cash offer for shares in a company to acquire control of the company and then making an offer for the remaining shares at a later stage.

BoP See *balance of payments*.

borrowers swap An interest rate swap where a floating interest rate is converted into a fixed rate by the borrower. Also see *floating interest rate; interest rate swap; swap*.

borrowing cost cover See *interest cover*.

borrowing requirement The amount of money needed by a business or government to finance a budget deficit and maturing debt obligations. Also see *budget deficit*.

borrowings The long-term debt of a company. Short-term debt is usually termed creditors debt or accounts payable or is indicated as a separate line item in a company's financial reports. Also see *creditor; line item; long-term debt; short-term debt*.

borsa Italian term used for stock exchange. Also see *bourse*.

borse See *bourse*.

bosberaad A South African term for an offsite meeting. Also see *offsite*.

Boston matrix An analytical plotting tool as illustrated below used to analyse business units or products.

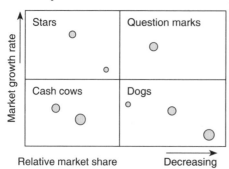

- Stars are the products or business units with high market shares in growing industries. These are the products that will carry a firm's profitability into the future.
- Cash cows are the products or business units with high market shares in slow growth industries and produce more cash than is consumed to maintain the business. Cash cows generally supply the funds to develop the stars and ensure a future for the business.
- Question marks are products or business units with low market shares in growing industries that are net consumers of cash. These products will ultimately become stars or dogs.
- Dogs are products or business units with low market shares in low growth industries. Dogs only break even or make a marginal profit. Sometimes they are kept for social or ancillary business issues but are most often sold.

Boston option See *break forward*.

BOT Balance of trade. Also see *trade balance*.

bottom The lowest value in an economic, business or pricing cycle variable.

bottom fishing
1. Acquiring companies to break them up and sell or to acquire their assets. Also see *asset stripping*.
2. Purchasing shares when they are at historical lows and unlikely to fall further.

bottom line Net profit after tax. Also see *net profit*.

bottom up (cash flow) Known as the indirect method of determining cash flow. Cash flow is calculated off the income statement by:

operating cash flow = net profit after tax + depreciation + change in net working capital.

Also see *cash flow; depreciation; indirect method of reporting cash flows; net profit; net working capital*.

bought deal When an issue of shares is underwritten, the underwriter essentially agrees to purchase all the shares in the event of the issue being undersubscribed. The risk of undersubscription is therefore transferred to the underwriter. Also see *underwriter*.

boundary condition A strategy used in mathematics that involves using a finite space to solve a problem with an infinite domain and using conditions at the boundaries of the finite space that are reasonable approximates or assumptions to assist in the solution of the overall problem.

bourse Alternative term used for a stock or foreign currency market. Used in Europe and typically referring to the German (borse) or Paris (bourse) stock exchange.

boutique A niche market provider of financial or investment products. They usually deliver investment banking services and cover only specific products or sectors.

box spread An option trading strategy that is risk free and that involves two pairs of puts and calls with the same time to expiry. One will go long and short on a call at different strike prices and long and short on a put at different strike prices. In efficient markets these strategies carry little profit and are often called alligator spreads due to trading charges eliminating profits. Also see *alligator spread*.

BPN British pence.

bracket
1. A category.
2. A term used to describe the category of investor. For example, a major bracket investor is a large investor.
3. The level of commitment and titles offered to banks participating in a syndicated loan. Also see *syndicated loan; ticket*.

bracket creep See *fiscal drag*.

bracket indexation The indexation of tax charges to ensure that inflation-related increases in salaries do not place taxpayers into higher tax brackets as their real income has remained unchanged. Also see *fiscal drag; indexation; inflation*.

Brady bond A bond issued by developing countries with guarantees or collateral issued by the World Bank. These bonds were designed to create liquidity for developing country bonds. Brady bonds allowed commercial banks to remove emerging market debt from their balance sheets through tradable instruments. Also see *collateral; concentration risk; World Bank*.

Brazilian real (BRL) The currency of Brazil.

break A sharp fall in prices.

breakage cost A fee that can be charged by banks if prepayment of a loan is initiated without prior proper notice. The fee is charged because banks have costs associated with lending in the interbank market and not notifying them in due time often implies that they incur costs associated with breaking their funding.

break even
1. Point at which net profit = 0, i.e. revenue equals expenses. Also see *net profit*.
2. Net differential cash flow = 0 when doing relevant costing. Also see *cash flow*.

break-even contribution margin per unit The contribution required from each unit to cover fixed costs. It is defined by:

$$\text{break-even contribution margin per unit} = \frac{\text{total fixed costs}}{\text{number produced}}$$

Also see *break-even number of units; fixed expense*.

break-even number of units The number of units to be sold so that fixed costs are covered. It is defined by:

$$\text{break-even number of units} = \frac{\text{fixed costs}}{\text{contributed margin per unit}}$$

Also see *break-even contribution margin per unit*.

break-even volume See *break-even number of units*.

break fee See *termination fee*.

break forward A forward contract, usually on a currency, where one party has the right and not the obligation (i.e. has an option) to terminate or break the contract at predetermined dates in the future. For example, an entity seeking dollars may be able to enter a five-year forward exchange rate contract at R7 per US dollar. They are now locked into the contract for five years, during which time the rate may become unfavourable.

A break forward contract could be used instead where the rate is quoted at R7.5 per US dollar which is a less favourable rate but has the flexibility to be terminated if forex market conditions should change. Sometimes called a Boston option. Also see *forward contract/dealing; option*.

break out When the price of a security rises or falls after a period of stagnation, it is said to break out of its price band. Break-outs can be buy or sell signals. Also see *Bollinger bands; security*.

break-up fee See *termination fee*.

break-up value
1. The value of a company once it has been liquidated and sold, usually as a series of separate assets. Also see *asset stripping; liquidation*.
2. The net asset value of a share. Also see *net asset value*.

Brent North Sea crude oil Crude oil found in the Brent Oilfield in the North Sea off the coast of Scotland. Also see *crude oil*.

Bretton Woods See *gold standard*.

BRIC Brazil, Russia, India and China.

bricks and clicks See *clicks and mortar*.

bridge loan See *bridging finance*.

bridging finance A short-term loan that is used to bridge the gap between the purchase and sale of an asset or to smooth timing between redemption and issuance of a bond. The interest rates or margins on bridge facilities often increase over time to encourage the borrower to refinance the facility. Also see *interest rate*.

Britannia Coin The British equivalent of the Kruger Rand.

BRL The currency of Brazil, the real divided into 100 centavos.

broad money A measure of money supply in an economy with broad coverage. Broad money usually includes all monies held by residents in deposit-taking institutions and physical cash. It is measured by M3. Also see *deposit-taking institution; M3; money supply; narrow money*.

broken date The date outside the usual dates on which a trade may occur.

broker A person or company that does not buy and sell for their own account, but rather matches buyers and sellers and makes profits through brokerage fees or commissions. Also see *agent; intermediary*.

brokerage A fee that a broker charges for undertaking a transaction. For example, when an investor trades shares through a stockbroker, he/she pays a brokerage fee based on the size of the trade. Also see *broker; stockbroker*.

brokerage house A firm that acts as a broker in financial markets. Also see *broker*.

broker code A numerical code given to brokers who trade on stock exchanges.

brokered deposit
1. A deposit that was attained with the assistance of a broker.
2. A deposit that is sold by a bank to a broker. The broker then sells off portions of the deposit to his/her client base. Also see *negotiable certificate of deposit*.

brokers note
1. A publication issued by a broker offering purchase and sale advice on assets. Brokers notes often analyse companies in detail and are useful sources of information about the finances of a company.
2. A note issued by a broker to a buyer or seller of a security to verify that the purchase or sale has occurred.

brownfield Take over or further develop a project or site that has previously been fully or partially developed. In the mining industry, this refers to a company buying a mine already in or near production and developing it further. A greenfield project, on the other hand, is a project that is started from scratch. Also see *greenfield*.

Brownian motion A random motion or random walk. Mathematically, a Brownian motion is a Wiener process in which the conditional probability distribution of a variable at time $t + dt$, given that its position at time t is p, is a normal distribution with a mean of $p + \mu dt$ and a variance of $\sigma^2 dt$. The parameter μ is the drift velocity and the parameter σ^2 is the power of the noise. These properties clearly establish that Brownian motion is Markovian, i.e. it satisfies the Markov property. Brownian motion is related to the random walk problem. It is generic in the sense that many different stochastic processes reduce to Brownian motion in suitable limits. Also see *drift; geometric Brownian motion; random walk with drift; stochastic process; variance*.

BS See *balance sheet*.

BSD
1. Bond security deposit.
2. Bahamas dollar.

BSE See *Bombay Stock Exchange*.

BSE 30 A market capitalisation index of the top 30 companies on the Bombay Stock Exchange. The base year when the index was set to 100 is 1979. Sometimes called the SENSEX. Also see *base year; market capitalisation index*.

bsh See *bushel*.

B-share A share in a company that has fewer voting rights than ordinary shares. Often called an N-share in South Africa. Also see *A-share; N-share; ordinary share*.

BTAN Type of French government bond of two- to five-year maturity. Also see *government bond; OAT*.

BTP Long-term Italian government bond that pays semi-annually. Also see *government bond; semi-annual*.

Btu British thermal unit. A unit of measure used for the sale of natural gas. One Btu is approximately 1 060 joules.

bu See *bushel*.

bubble A trend in market pricing where prices become inflated through speculative activity and not underlying market fundamentals. Also see *fundamentals*.

bucket shop See *boiler room*.

budget A financial plan for an upcoming financial period. Budgets are quantitative and specify a host of parameters including things like revenue and cost targets. An organisation normally has budgets drawn up for each of its business units. Also see *budget deficit*.

budget deficit When government or corporate spending is greater than taxes collected or income received. A deficit is financed on the financial markets through the issue of bonds or through other forms of debt.

buffer stock
1. Stock that is used to balance production and cyclic demand.
2. A stock of commodities used to buy and sell to manage prices and supplies in the market. Diamond mining companies often use buffer stock to control market prices.

builders all-in risk An insurance policy used on construction projects. Also see *bonding facility*.

building society An organisation that accepts deposits and lends to people for mortgages on residential and light commercial properties. Building societies are mutual organisations that are effectively owned by their customers. In the US, savings and loans associations are classed as similar organisations. Also see *mortgage; mutual*.

bulge bracket The top investment banks.

bulking An illegal practice that involves investment management companies negotiating favourable interest rates and not passing the benefit on to their clients. Also see *interest rate*.

bull An investor who is expecting the prices of assets in the market to increase. Also see *bear*.

bulldog bond A form of foreign bond issued in the UK by a company outside the UK. Also see *Eurobond; foreign bond*.

bullet See *bullet loan*.

bullet bond A bond that is not callable and is redeemable in full at maturity. They generally pay a fixed rate of interest and have no special features. Also see *treasury bill*.

bullet GIC A guarantee investment contract or certificate (GIC) with a single payment at maturity. Also see *guarantee investment contract certificate*.

bullet loan A loan where interest only is paid over the term of the loan and the entire principal is paid on the date of maturity. Bullet loans are usually fixed interest rate loans. Sometimes referred to as a balloon loan although balloon loans are technically different because they often pay off some of the capital before the final date of maturity. Also see *balloon loan; fixed interest rate*.

bullion This often refers to precious metals, usually gold, that are sold in bulk. A standard gold bullion bar is 400 troy ounces. Also see *precious metals; troy ounce*.

bull market Share prices that are on the up, typically modelled as a random walk with upward drift. Also see *bear market; drift; random walk with drift*.

bull position See *long position*.

bull spread A combination of buying a call option with a lower price than another call option sold. The effect is a cap on the up and down side forming a band between the two different strike prices with a positively sloped line joining them. The same effect can be achieved using a combination of put options. Also see *bear call spread; bear put spread; call option; vertical spread*.

bull trend Long periods of consistently rising share prices.

bund Ten- to 30-year German government bond. The term can be generic in nature, but more specifically a bund is a federal government bond. They are considered to be the top Eurozone bonds and credit spreads in the wider European markets are often measured relative to these. Also see *bobl; credit spread; Eurozone; government bond; schatz*.

Bundesbank The central bank of Germany. The Bundesbank regulates German banks, publishes research and statistics and represents the German banking system at the European Central Bank (ECB). The Bundesbank no longer controls interest rates in Germany as this role has been taken over by the ECB under the European monetary union. Also see *central bank; European Central Bank; interest rate*.

bundling Combining financial instruments or assets together to sell at better prices or attain more favourable funding.

bunny bond A form of bond stripping where the coupons are converted into identical bonds. In some bunny bond instruments the issuer has the option of issuing a separate bond as an interest payment or by paying in cash. Sometimes called a multiplier bond. Also see *stripping bonds; toggle note; zero coupon bond*.

burn rate The speed at which cash is used in an organisation, measured against the speed at which it is coming in. Technology companies are often measured by a burn rate metric.

bushel A unit of measure for dry commodities such as maize and wheat.

1 US bushel = 35.23907017 litres = 8 corn/dry gallons = 9.309177489 wine/liquid gallons

1 imperial bushel = 36.36872 litres = 8 imperial gallons

Sometimes abbreviated to bsh or bu.

Bushveld Complex Platinum group metal ore body in the northern parts of South Africa that holds a significant portion (about 79%) of the world's proven platinum reserves. Also see *platinum group metals*.

business An integrated set of activities and assets conducted and managed for the purpose of providing:
- a return to investors or
- lower costs or other economic benefits directly and proportionately to policy holders or participants.

A business generally consists of inputs, processes applied to these inputs and resulting outputs that are, or will be, used to generate revenues. If goodwill is present in a transferred set of activities and assets, the transferred set is presumed to be a business. Also see *goodwill*.

business combination The bringing together of separate entities or businesses into one reporting entity.

business costs Total expenses as determined by accounting practice.

business cycle Upswings (expansions) and downswings (contractions) in business activity. Measured by variables such as the fluctuations in GDP, employment numbers, money supply and vehicle sales. Also see *coinciding indicator; gross domestic product; hard number; leading indicator.*

business day
1. Day on which businesses are open for trade. Also see *calendar day.*
2. A leading South African business and financial newspaper.

business interruption policy or insurance An insurance policy designed to cater for an event that causes a financial loss due to a company having to reduce significantly or discontinue operations. Events such as fires and natural disasters usually fall within the broad category of events. Sometimes called a consequential loss policy or a loss of profits policy.

business plan A plan that sets out the objectives and strategy of a business for a future or series of future periods. Business plans are useful for new operations to raise capital in the form of equity and debt. Business plans usually include market and product overviews, pro forma statements and a range of other relevant materials and analysis. Also see *debt; equity; pro forma statement.*

business profit Total revenue (as recognised by accounting practice) less business costs.

business risk The risk of a firm being unable to cover its operating costs. In general, the higher the degree of operating leverage is, the higher the business risk is.

$$\text{operating leverage} = \frac{\text{NPAT}}{\text{sales}}$$

where NPAT = net profit after tax.

Also see *financial risk; firm; net profit; operating leverage; total risk.*

business segment A distinguishable component of an entity that is engaged in providing an individual product or service or a group of related products or services and that is subject to risks and returns that are different from those of other business segments.

business sentiment Expectation of business for the expansion of profits and productive capacity. Business sentiment ultimately depends on the optimism of business managers.

busted convertible security A convertible debt instrument that has the convert option so far out the money that it trades as a simple debt only instrument. Also see *convertible debt/bond.*

butterfly spread A spread of trading strategies created using options with limited risk and profit and that profits from prices going up and down.

buy and hold An investment strategy that involves the purchase of securities and holding them for a long period of time. The buy and hold strategy ignores short-term fluctuations in the market and investors invest with the view that in the long term the market will rise. Also see *long position.*

buy back The repurchasing of financial obligations. Usually referred to in the context of share buy-backs, where companies purchase their own shares on the open market. Also see *share buy-back.*

buy-down The process of the seller of an asset, usually property, subsidising the initial financing repayment profile. The buy-down may take the form of the asset seller taking responsibility for initially servicing the loan and thereby achieving a better interest rate or the seller placing funds into an escrow account to subsidise the initial payments. Also see *escrow; interest rate*.

buy-in
1. The purchase of a security from a buyer on the open market which the seller failed to deliver. Under these circumstances a buy-in is a failed trade and has severe consequences.
2. The process of an entity acquiring more than 50% of a company to gain control of that company.
3. Closing out of a position by matching a long position with an existing short. Also see *close out; long position; short position*.

buying forward Buying an asset at a price specified today for delivery at a future date.

buying pressure When demand for an asset exceeds supply, this is almost always followed by a subsequent rise in prices as there are more buyers than sellers. Also see *selling pressure*.

buy line A line plotted on a graph through which a momentum indicator intersects that constitutes a buy signal. The line indicates whether a share is overbought or oversold. Also see *momentum indicator*.

buyout The process of acquiring the listed shares in a company to make the company a private company. Also see *leverage buyout; management buyout*.

buy the spread Buy a near-dated futures contract and sell a far-dated contract to take advantage of the futures price narrowing.

BV Besloten vennootschap, which implies that a Netherlands registered company is a private limited liability company. The shares in these companies are registered and are not freely transferable. Also see *limited liability; GmbH; NV; PLC*.

BWP Botswana pula divided into 100 thebe.

C | calendar spread

C A credit rating used by credit rating agencies such as S&P, Moody's and Fitch that is the lowest achievable before a company goes into default. S&P, Moody's and Fitch all use the C rating. Also see *credit rating*.

Ca A credit rating from the credit rating agency, Moody's, that indicates that the company is near default on its debt obligations. Also see *credit rating*.
1. Chartered accountant.
2. Candidate attorney.

Caa A credit rating band from the credit rating agency, Moody's, that indicates that the company is near default on its debt obligations. The Caa rating band is divided into Caa1, Caa2 and Caa3 with Caa1 being the best credit quality rating in the band. Also see *credit rating*.

cable data A historic term used for the price of British pounds in US dollars.

CAC 40 The top 40 market capitalisation index on the French Stock Exchange. Also see *market capitalisation index*.

CAC Index The top 14 companies by market capitalisation on the French Stock Exchange. Also see *market capitalisation index*.

CAD
1. Canadian dollar.
2. Capital adequacy directive. Also see *capital adequacy*.
3. Cash against documents.
4. Computer-aided design.

calculated intangible value (CIV) A methodology used to value intangible assets. Intangible assets may be assets such as brand names and intellectual property. A quick calculation for this value is to subtract the market value of a company from its book value. Also see *book value; intangible asset*.

calculation agent An agent responsible for calculating the amounts due under a credit derivative contract when a specified credit event occurs. Also see *credit derivative*.

calendar day Any day on the calendar including Saturdays, Sundays and public holidays. Also see *business day*.

calendar spread A trade position created by combining options of different maturities with the same exercise price. The near-term option is usually purchased and the far-term option sold. The following diagram shows a calendar call spread. Sometimes called a horizontal spread or delta spread. Also see *delta spread; horizontal spread*.

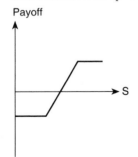

call
1. See *call option*.
2. Notification that redeemable or callable debt or shares have been redeemed.
3. A demand made by creditors for debt to be repaid after an event of default. Also see *event of default*.

callable See *callable bond*.

callable bond A bond where the principal is redeemable at the discretion of the issuer, often with limitations. There is effectively a call option written into the bond contract that is exercisable by the issuer of the bond under the written circumstances. Some bonds are call protected debt and others have periods during which the bonds may not be called. Also see *bond; call option; call protected debt*.

callability risk The risk associated with the variability of the return of an investment due to the possibility that bonds or preference shares may be called. Also see *convertible debt/bond; preference share*.

call date The date at which a call option can be exercised. Also see *call option*.

called away A callable bond that has had the call option exercised. Also see *callable bond; call option*.

called up share capital See *share capital*.

call money The price paid for a call option. Also see *call option*.

call option A financial contract where the holder has the right, but not the obligation, to buy a quantity of shares or assets at a price specified today at or until a given future date. When a call option is exercised, the buyer of the option pays the previously agreed price and the seller delivers the underlying asset.

Investors use call options when expecting the price of an asset to increase. The investor purchases a call option at a low strike price today and when the future price is higher, the call option can be used to buy the asset at a cheaper rate than the prevailing market price. The price of puts and calls is linked through put-call parity. The payoff relationships of purchasing and selling a call option are illustrated below. Also see *asset; option; put-call parity; put option*.

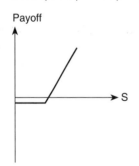
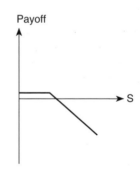

Purchasing a call (long)   *Selling a call (short)*

call premium The cost of purchasing a call option on the market. The call premium is composed of the time premium and the intrinsic value of the option. Also see *call option; intrinsic value; time premium*.

call protected debt Debt that cannot be redeemed before the date of maturity or before the end of the stipulated protection period. Also see *callable bond*.

call provision An agreement that gives the entity that issued the bond the ability to repurchase that bond at a premium prior to the maturity of the bond. Also see *bond*.

call risk The risk of the call option on callable debt being exercised. The risk is contained in the fact that the investor will not be able to find an investment that will generate equivalent returns. Also see *call option; call protected debt; reinvestment risk*.

call schedule When convertible debt is issued, the schedule according to which the bond can be converted is stated. For example, the period during which a call cannot be exercised is specifically stated as well as the exact dates or range of dates the call option can be exercised. Also see *bond; convertible debt/bond*.

call spread The creation of a spread with the use of two call options. Also see *call option; spread*.

call warrant See *call option; warrant*.

Canada premium bond A Canadian savings bond with a high rate of interest and cashable only once a year. Also see *bond; premium bond*.

Canada savings bond A bond issued by the Canadian government to the general public resident in Canada. The bond can be cashed by the holder at any time. Also see *bond*.

cannibalise The process of a new product entering the market and reducing the market share of an existing product.

cap An option that provides protection against interest rate increases. Interest rate guarantees are used for these. Also see *floor; interest rate; interest rate guarantee*.

CAP See *Common Agricultural Policy*.

capacity swap A swap contract that producers can use to fill unused production capacity or gain extra capacity from another producer when market conditions require them to do so. Also see *bandwidth contract*.

capacity utilisation An economic measure of the total possible industrial output being used in a country. Changes in this measure are indicators of the movement and cycles in the economy. A higher capacity utilisation indicates a strong manufacturing sector and possible inflationary pressures. Capacity utilisation is measured by surveying goods-producing industries at plant level. Also see *leading indicator*.

CAPE Cyclically adjusted price earnings.

capex See *capital expenditure*.

capital
1. The total value of an asset.
2. Money supplied for the purchase of factors of production. This can be raised in the form of both equity and debt. Non-distributed reserves are considered to be part of the capital of a business. Also see *non-distributable reserves*.
3. The money contributed by investors to start a business.

Also see *debt capital; equity capital; share capital*.

capital account The account that records the flow of money into and out of a country related to that portion of the balance of payments associated with financial investments and related transactions rather than the trade in goods and services. Both long- and short-term capital flows are included. The capital account is a standard component of the balance of payments accounts. Capital account data is available from central banks. Also see *balance of payments; central bank; current account*.

capital adequacy To maintain a stable financial system, banks are required to remain solvent and have enough cash to service demands for short-term deposits. Central banks set capital adequacy requirements under international guidelines (Basel) that force banks to maintain proper liquidity provisions and ensure they do not become overextended. The capital requirement is defined by capital ratios under the Basel guidelines for international banks. Also see *Basel; capital ratio; central bank*.

capital adequacy ratio See *capital ratio*.

capital allowance The capital or depreciation allowance given by a tax authority that specifies how much companies can deduct from profits before calculation of tax. Tax authorities allow the deductions in recognition of the loss of the capital value of assets through use and over time. Also see *capital gains; capital loss; depreciation*.

capital amount The value of the outstanding amount of a loan. The amount usually excludes any accrued interest.

capital appreciation The increase in the capital value of an asset or security. Sometimes called a capital gain. Also see *security*.

capital asset pricing model (CAPM) An equation of the security market line (SML) showing the relationship between expected return and beta (systematic risk). The CAPM is defined by the following linear relationship:

$$E(R_i) = R_f + [E(R_m) - R_f] \times \beta$$

where $[E(R_m) - R_f]$ = the risk premium of the market; β = systematic risk; $E(R_m)$ = expected return of the market; R_f = risk-free rate; $E(R_i)$ = expected return on i.

The capital asset pricing model takes into account:

- the time value of money through the risk-free rate
- the reward for bearing systematic risk as measured by the market risk premium
- the amount of systematic risk measured through beta.

Also see *beta; expected return; market risk premium; security market line; systematic risk; time value of money*.

capital at risk product A structured product where not all the capital invested is guaranteed to be preserved at the maturity or redemption date. An investment in an ordinary share constitutes 100% capital at risk as all the money invested could potentially be lost. Also see *capital secure product; structured product*.

capital balance The balance of the original loan amount that is still due to the lender. The capital balance declines as a loan is paid off over time (amortisation). Also see *amortisation; balloon loan; bullet loan*.

capital bond A savings bond in the UK that gives fixed returns over a number of years. Also see *bond*.

capital budgeting The process of planning and managing a firm's long-term investments. Evaluating size, timing and risk associated with future cash flow is the essence of capital budgeting. Also see *cash flow; firm*.

capital commitment A commitment, usually approved by the board of a company, to spend a predefined amount of money on new assets (capital goods).

capital consumption A macroeconomic measure of the amount of capital assets consumed in an economy during the period in question. This measure equates to the total depreciation of all productive assets in an economy. Economic analysts compare capital consumption with capital expenditure to gauge whether an economy is expanding or contracting. Also see *capital expenditure; depreciation; gross fixed capital formation*.

capital conversion A product or strategy that converts capital in an investment into an income. This is often done to circumvent capital gains tax and to fund the retirement of the investors. Also see *capital gains tax*.

capital depreciation The decrease in the capital value of an asset or security. Also see *security*.

capital employed The sum of a company's fixed assets and its working capital, i.e. operating working capital and non-operating working capital. It is therefore equal to the sum of the net amounts devoted by a business to the operating and investment cycle. Capital employed is financed by two main sources of funds, namely shareholders equity and net debt, sometimes grouped under the heading of invested capital. Sometimes called operating assets. Also see *debt to net capital employed ratio; fixed asset; net debt; working capital*.

capital expenditure (capex) The amount paid for the acquisition, improvement, development or restoration of an asset. Capital expenditure is not always confined to physical assets but may be money spent on the maintenance and development of income or on benefiting trade. Examples of capital expenditure include:
- land and buildings
- alterations to business assets such as property, plant and equipment
- the cost of installation of assets
- goodwill
- expenditure to gain market share
- expenditure to protect capital assets
- legal expenses with direct reference to capital assets.

Also see *acquisition; goodwill*.

capital flight Money that leaves the borders of a country or market in large volumes because investors feel that the risk associated with that market is too high and they wish to invest their money in more stable markets. In South Africa, capital flight has previously been associated with political unrest. Capital flight has severe adverse effects on the exchange rate and the economy. Also see *capital movement*.

capital formation See *gross fixed capital formation*.

capital gains The gain in value in the price of an asset. Capital gains are often taxed. Sometimes called capital appreciation. Also see *asset; capital allowance; capital loss*.

capital gains tax (CGT) A tax levied by the government on the profits associated with the buying and selling of assets such as securities and property.

capital gains yield (CGY) The gain in value of an investment is the sum of the capital and dividend gains yield. The capital gains yield is the gain the asset holder accrues from the appreciation in price of the asset and is given by the following equation:

capital gains yield (CGY) = $\frac{(P_{t+1} - P_t)}{P_t} \times \frac{100}{1}$

where P_t = price at time t.

Also see *dividend*.

capital goods Fixed assets used as factors of production in an economy. Examples of capital goods include factories, infrastructure and equipment. Also see *factors of production*.

capital growth See *capital gains*.

capital inflow The receipt of money in one country from another. Capital inflows are the monies that come into a country under normal trade and investment. Also see *capital outflow*.

capital intensity ratio The ratio that defines how many assets are needed to generate sales:

capital intensity ratio = $\frac{\text{net assets}}{\text{sales}}$

The higher the ratio is, the more capital intensive the business is.

capital intensive A business that requires large amounts of capital to operate.

capitalisation
1. Recognising a cost incurred as part of the total cost of an asset. Also see *asset*.
2. The total capital employed by a business. Also see *capital employed*.
3. The capital structure of a business. Also see *capital structure; gearing*.
4. The market value of a company, calculated by multiplying the price per share by the number of outstanding shares. Also see *market capitalisation*.
5. The capital provided to a business or organisation.
6. The conversion of a company's reserves into capital through a bonus issue. Also see *bonus issue*.

capitalisation issue See *bonus issue*.

capitalisation of interest Interest payable on a loan that is rolled into the principal value of the loan. This is often done on projects that have weak or negative cash flows in the early part of their life cycle. Also see *payment in kind; toggle note*.

capitalised earnings Determining the current value of future earnings of a business through discounting cash flows. Also see *discounting*.

capitalism An economic system whereby participants are in business to make a profit and ownership of assets is attributable to the private sector. Also see *communism*.

capital lease A lease agreement that normally lasts the life of the asset where the present value of the lease obligation covers more than 90% of the purchase price of the asset. A capital lease is accounted for with borrow and buy accounting mechanics, i.e. a liability and asset in the balance sheet as follows:
- An asset held under a capital lease is generally capitalised at the estimated present value of the underlying lease payments at the date of acquisition. The corresponding liability to the lessor, net of finance charges, is usually included in the balance sheet as a finance lease obligation.

- Finance costs, which usually represent the difference between the total leasing commitment and fair value of the asset acquired, are charged to the income statement over the term of the relevant lease to produce a constant periodic rate of interest on the remaining balance of the obligation for each accounting period.

With capital leases the lessee is usually responsible for the maintenance of the asset.

Be careful when analysing these leases and be mindful of the terms in the lease agreement as the lease obligations may rank pari passu or be subordinate to other debt on the balance sheet.

A capital lease is sometimes called a financial lease. Also see *lease; net lease; operating lease; pari passu; present value; subordinate; synthetic lease.*

capital loss The loss made when an asset is sold for less than its book value. Capital losses are often offset against capital gains for the calculation of tax. Also see *book value; capital allowance; capital gains; capital gains tax.*

capital maintenance concept
1. A concept used in accounting that indicates that the profit for a period is the profit left over after the starting value of the capital of the business has been restored.
2. The physical capital is maintained if the productive capacity of a business is equal to or greater than that at the beginning of the accounting period.

capital market A financial market where long-term debt and equity securities are traded. The debt in this type of market is of longer maturity than the debt issued in money markets. Capital market instruments include shares, debentures, government and quasi-government bonds. Also see *debenture; government bond; long-term debt; money market.*

capital movement The movement of capital between countries. Capital invested in a country may be long term, which is usually termed foreign direct investment, or can be shorter term and speculative in nature. Capital markets have historically had restrictions imposed on capital movement through exchange controls which have now been liberalised or are in the process of being liberalised globally. Also see *capital flight; capital market; foreign direct investment.*

capital note A form of commercial paper issued by corporations. Also see *commercial paper.*

capital outflow The net payment of money from one country to another under normal trade and investment conditions. Also see *capital inflow.*

capital profit See *capital gains.*

capital project A project that requires substantial investment. Examples of capital projects include the building of roads, factories, dams and power stations. Capital projects are project financed. Also see *project finance.*

capital ratio A ratio that measures the capital adequacy of financial institutions. Capital adequacy ratios are often used as financial covenants when lending money to financial institutions and are used by banking regulators to set liquidity requirements for banks. The capital ratio is usually expressed as a percentage of a bank's capital to its risk weighted credit exposure:

$$\text{capital ratio (CR)} = \frac{\text{core tier 1 capital} + \text{eligible tier 2 capital} + \text{eligible tier 3 capital}}{\sum \text{exposure indicator} \times \text{probability of default} \times \text{loss given default}} \times \frac{100}{1}$$

Also see *capital adequacy; credit risk; financial covenant.*

capital ratio covenant A minimum capital ratio is often specified as a covenant when lending to financial institutions. The tangible net worth covenant is sometimes used in conjunction with the capital ratio covenant. Also see *capital ratio; covenant; tangible net worth covenant*.

capital rationing The process of limiting the capital investment of a company. This can be done by lowering the pool of available investment capital or adjusting the hurdle rate for project returns. Also see *hurdle rate; internal rate of return; net present value; return on capital employed*.

capital recovery The recovery of monies spent on property, plant and equipment including carrying costs. Also see *property, plant and equipment*.

capital reduction Excess capital in a company is distributed to shareholders and capital is thereby reduced. Distributions are in the form of share buy-backs or special dividends. Also see *share buy-back; shareholders; special dividend*.

capital repayment
1. The return to a shareholder of any portion of the issued capital of a company.
2. The repayment of the principal portion of a loan. Also see *principal*.

capital reserves Include ordinary shares, share capital, retained income, treasury shares and currency reserves. The capital reserves of a company are accounted for in the balance sheet. A reserve account is used to set aside resources for long-term projects and investments. It is, in essence, a savings account. Also see *balance sheet; economic capital; ordinary share; share capital*.

capital secure product A structured product of fixed term with a guaranteed return of invested capital. Also see *capital at risk product; structured product*.

capital share A share in a company or fund that does not offer cash flows such as dividends or interest payments but rewards investors through capital appreciation.

capital stock An American term for an equity share in a company. Both ordinary and preference shares are classed as capital stock. Also see *equity; preference share*.

capital structure A firm may use a variety of different types of long-term capital such as debt and equity capital to finance its operations. The capital structure of a business gives an indication of how the total capital employed is made up. Ratios such as the debt to total capital and debt equity ratio are used to indicate the capital structure of a business. Also see *debt capital; debt to equity ratio; debt to total capital ratio; equity capital; firm; gearing; weighted average cost of capital*.

capital surplus See *share premium*.

capital transfer tax See *inheritance tax*.

capital turnover A ratio that measures how capital intensive a business is against revenue/sales:

$$\text{capital turnover ratio} = \frac{\text{sales}}{\text{capital employed}}$$

The higher a company's capital turnover ratio relative to its peers is, the more efficiently the business is using its assets. Also see *capital intensity ratio; capital intensive*.

caplets See *interest rate cap*.

CAPM See *capital asset pricing model*.

capped The limitation on the total gain on a financial instrument. For example, a capped interest rate is a floating interest rate that is not allowed to exceed a predetermined level. Also see *floating interest rate; interest rate.*

capped option An option which has a maximum payout value.

capped quote A quote that is binding on the indicated price. Capped quotes do not include terms that allow for additional charges should they arise.

caps and floors When referring to options, these are the upper and lower boundary conditions that determine the underlying value. For example, mortgage rates may have a cap that prevents them going above a predefined level. Also see *interest rate cap; mortgage.*

caption An option on a cap. Also see *cap.*

captive finance company A company that has been set up as a subsidiary of a manufacturing operation to lease or finance the products that the parent produces. Motor companies are good examples as they often have vehicle financing subsidiaries.

captive insurer A company that has been set up as a subsidiary to insure the assets of other companies in the group. SABMiller is an example with a subsidiary called SABSure.

CAR Compound annual return.

carat (ct or kt)
1. A unit of measure of mass equal to 0.2 grams. Gemstones such as diamonds are measured in carats.
2. A measure of the purity of gold. The purity of gold is calculated by the following equation:

$$ct = 24 \times \frac{mass_{pure\ gold}}{mass_{total\ material}}$$

From this equation it follows that 18 carat gold is 18 parts pure gold and 6 parts base metal so it is 75% pure.

carbon sequestration The capture and storage of carbon dioxide from manufacturing processes. The storage is usually in underground caverns.

carried interest The percentage of profits that private equity houses keep when exiting a deal or selling a company. Also see *private equity.*

carrier An entity that transports goods, usually a third party to the buyer and seller. Carriers are usually shippers and airlines.

carrier against shares The process of securing debt against shares.

carry back The process of carrying taxation benefits from one financial year to another. Sometimes called a carry forward.

carry cost The cost of holding or financing the purchase of an asset over a period of time. The difference between the futures value of an asset and its current spot price is the carry cost of the asset. Also see *asset; spot price.*

carry fee See *cost of carry model.*

carry forward See *carry back.*

69

carrying
1. A term used on the London Metals Exchange that describes the process of lending. Also see *London Metals Exchange*.
2. The lending of money against listed shares posted as security.

carrying amount The value of an asset on the books of a company after deducting any accumulated depreciation (amortisation) and accumulated impairment losses from the cost of the asset:

carrying amount = cost price − depreciation − impairment

Also see *amortisation; asset; book value; depreciation; impairment*.

carrying market The market for goods that are not perishable and can be held in warehouses for some time before they are sold.

carrying value See *carrying amount*.

carry over
1. To delay the payment of an obligation, such as an interest payment, from one period to the next.
2. Goods or products offered for sale in the market produced in a previous period.

carry revenue The revenue made from holding assets. Banks make this form of revenue as well as revenue from fees.

carry trade A strategy that involves borrowing at a low interest rate and investing the proceeds in a different market at a higher interest rate. The profit is made through the differential in the interest rates. Exchange rate risks need to be considered when undertaking carry trades. Also see *covered interest arbitrage; interest rate*.

cartel An association of independent organisations that control a particular market by controlling the supply and hence the prices. OPEC is a well-known cartel that attempts to control the prices and supply of oil. Also see *OPEC*.

carve out A generic term used to describe the process of excluding particular terms in standard loan agreements and covenants. For example, there may be a carve out in the restriction on disposals clause that allows a business to dispose of certain assets in a manner classed as being in the ordinary course of trade. Also see *covenant*.

cascade shareholdings The process of a holding company acquiring a stake in another company that holds an interest in yet another company. Also see *holding company*.

cash Cash on hand, physical notes and coins. Cash notes are effectively the non-interest bearing debt of the government. Also see *M1; M2; M3*.

cash accounting A system of accounting that records cash transactions as and when they occur rather than as and when they are earned in a way similar to the accrual basis of accounting. Also see *accrual basis of accounting*.

cash advance See *short-term loan*.

cash and carry strategy A strategy that involves borrowing cash in the money markets, purchasing an asset, selling a futures contract on that asset and then delivering the asset into the futures contract. This strategy is undertaken in the hope that the money collected on the futures contract is more than the money market interest rate paid. Cash and carry trades create close links between bond prices, the future bond prices and repo rates. Also see *bond; interest rate; money market*.

cash call See *margin call*.

cash collateralised debt obligation (CDO) A special-purpose vehicle set up for a collateralised debt obligation that owns physical securities and does not sell credit default swaps as is done in a synthetic CLO. Also see *collateralised debt obligation; credit default swap; special-purpose vehicle; synthetic collateralised loan obligation*.

cash confirm letter A letter to a regulatory authority that confirms that a company making an acquisition has certain funds. Also see *acquisition; certain funds*.

cash conversion cycle (CCC) The number of days between paying for raw materials and receiving the cash from the sale of the goods made from those raw materials.

cash conversion cycle (CCC) = debtors days + inventory days − creditors days

$$= \frac{\text{accounts receivable}}{\frac{\text{sales}}{365}} + \frac{\text{invoices}}{\frac{\text{cost of sales}}{365}} - \frac{\text{accounts payable}}{\frac{\text{purchases}}{365}}$$

where purchases = opening inventory + closing inventory + variable costs.

The higher the CCC measure is, the longer a firm's money is tied up in operations of the business and is unavailable for other activities. Also called the asset conversion cycle. Also see *creditor settlement; debtors days; firm; inventory days*.

cash coverage ratio A ratio that shows the ability of a company to generate cash and how that cash covers the service of its debt:

$$\text{cash coverage ratio} = \frac{\text{EBITDA}}{\text{interest paid}}$$

where EBITDA = earnings before interest, tax, depreciation and amortisation.

Sometimes adjustments are made to EBITDA for items that are not cash flow in nature. Also called the interest cover ratio or times interest earned. Also see *EBITDA; times interest earned*.

cash cow See *Boston matrix*.

cash cycle See *cash conversion cycle*.

cash deficiency guarantee A guarantee that project sponsors provide in the event that the project becomes short of cash (deficient). Also see *deficiency agreement; sponsor*.

cash discount A reduction in cost associated with the settlement of an invoice.

cash dividend See *dividend*.

cash equivalent A short-term, highly liquid investment that is readily convertible to known amounts of cash and is subject to an insignificant risk of changes in value. They are usually money market type instruments. Also see *liquid; money market*.

cash flow The inflow and outflow of cash and cash equivalents. Cash inflows usually arise from financing, operations or investments and cash outflows result from expenses or investments. Cash flow is calculated by taking EBITDA for the period and:

1. adding changes in working capital
2. adding cash receipts and deducting cash payments in respect of any exceptional items not already taken into account when calculating EBITDA
3. adding the amount of any cash receipts for tax rebates or credits and deducting the amount actually paid or due and payable in respect of taxes

4. to the extent not already taken into account when determining EBITDA, adding the amount of any dividends or other profit distributions received in cash and deducting the amount of any dividends paid in cash to minority shareholders in members of the group
5. adding cash paid to a member of the group that represents repayment of any loan made to a joint venture
6. adding any increase in provisions, other non-cash debits and charges (which are not current assets or current liabilities) and deducting non-cash credits (which are not current assets or current liabilities) in each case to the extent not taken into account when calculating EBITDA
7. deducting cash costs of pension items to the extent not taken into account when calculating EBITDA
8. deducting capital expenditure and the aggregate of any cash consideration or cost paid for any business acquisitions and joint venture investments in cash except in each case to the extent funded from:
   a) proceeds of disposals or insurance claims
   b) retained excess cash flow (this inclusion may need to be carefully considered)
   c) any capex facility
   d) new shareholder injections.

Also see *acquisition; cash equivalent; current asset; current liability; EBITDA*.

cash flow cascade See *cash waterfall*.

cash flow cover A measure of the ability of the free cash flows of a company to service debt obligations. Cash flow cover is defined by:

$$\text{cash flow cover} = \frac{\text{free cash flows}}{\text{debt service}} \text{ or } \frac{\text{NPBT} + \text{depreciation} + \text{amortisation}}{\text{total debt payments}}$$

where NPBT = net profit before tax.

Banks often use cash flow coverage ratios to specify covenants in loan agreements. Also see *cash coverage ratio; covenant; debt service; free cash flow; interest cover*.

cash flow insolvency When the cash flow generated by a business cannot meet debt service obligations. Also see *balance sheet insolvency; insolvency*.

cash flow statement The financial statement required by law to be published for a company. It tracks cash inflows and outflows for the reporting period in question. The cash flow statement tracks or reconciles the cash assets between the opening and closing balances on the balance sheet. A great advantage of cash flow statements is that they can balance different accounting treatments as they track the actual transfer of cash.

The cash flow statement is constructed using direct and indirect methods. Sometimes called a source and application of funds statement. Also see *balance sheet; direct method of reporting cash flows; income statement; indirect method of reporting cash flows*.

cash flow to total debt ratio A ratio used to give an indication of the ability of a company to service its debt obligations:

$$\text{cash flow to total debt ratio} = \frac{\text{cash flow from operations}}{\text{total debt}}$$

Also see *cash flow cover; debt service cover ratio*.

cash instrument A financial instrument sold for cash.

cash management bill (CMB) A short-term security sold by the US Treasury. The maturity on these bills is variable and issues are made as and when the treasury needs cash to meet shortfalls. These bills tend to have greater yields than regular treasury bills to attract the required liquidity at short notice.

cash market A market for goods and trades that settles immediately.

cash on cash return (COC) A quick and easy financial measure often used in the property market to ascertain if the equity value of an asset is under- or overvalued. It is defined as:

$$\text{cash on cash return (COC)} = \frac{\text{annual cash flow from asset} - \text{tax due or paid}}{\text{total cash invested}}$$

For example, if a house is purchased for R800 000 with a R200 000 deposit, collects R6 000 in rent, pays R4 000 in finance charges and R400 in tax, then this gives:

$$\text{COC} = \frac{(\text{R6 000} - \text{R4 000}) - \text{R400}}{\text{R200 000}} = 0.8\%$$

cash or nothing option See *binary option*.

cash ratio A ratio used to give an indication of the short-term liquidity of the business:

$$\text{cash ratio} = \frac{\text{cash}}{\text{current liabilities}}$$

The cash ratio is a useful ratio for lenders to see if the company has enough cash to finance short-term debt obligations. Cash ratios are often set for banks by regulators. Sometimes called the liquidity ratio. Also see *capital adequacy; cash ratio; short-term debt*.

cash reserve ratio See *reserve requirement*.

cash reserves
1. With reference to general corporates, see *cash equivalent*.
2. With reference to banks, see *reserve requirement*.

cash settlement
1. Payment for a financial instrument, usually a derivative, that is made in cash.
2. In the event of default on an underlying debt instrument covered by a credit default swap, the required cash settlement is made by calculating the difference between the par value of the reference obligation and its recovery rate. Also see *credit default swap; par value; recovery rate*.

cash shell A company listed on a stock exchange that contains no significant assets or operations. Its principal assets are cash, cash equivalents and the listing itself. It is often advantageous to acquire such a shell company, reverse assets into it and thereby reduce the cost of a public listing. Sometimes called a shell operation. Also see *cash equivalent*.

cash sweep A clause in a loan agreement that forces a company to service debt with available cash. Cash sweeps are defined by an inequality on the total debt to EBITDA ratio. Cash sweeps kick in after a lockup and are in place to ensure that companies do not distribute funds to equity over debt shareholders. Cash sweeps are sometimes included in the later phase of a loan tenor to incentivise borrowers to refinance the debt. Cash sweep tests are usually applied semi-annually. Also see *lockup; sweep*.

cash waterfall The assignment of cash proceeds to a set of creditors by a pre-assigned agreement.

casting vote A deciding vote. When a voting process has come to a deadlock, a single member, often the chairman, is given the deciding or casting vote. Also see *golden shares*.

CAT
1. See *catastrophe bond*.
2. Central African Time.
3. Computer-assisted trading.

catalyst A factor that brings about more rapid change.

catastrophe bond (CAT) A bond whose coupon is reduced in the event of a catastrophe. These instruments effectively allow the market the opportunity to underwrite some of the risks faced by the insurance industry. Also see *bond; underwrite*.

CAT bond See *catastrophe bond*.

catching bargain A contract that is unfair and where one party has been taken advantage of.

category 1 transaction A Johannesburg Stock Exchange (JSE) rule governing acquisitions, disposals and reverse takeovers of listed companies. A category 1 transaction indicates that the transaction value is 25% or more of the market capitalisation of the company or the voting rights of the shareholders are reduced by more than 25%. Also see *acquisition; JSE; reverse takeover*.

category 2 transaction A Johannesburg Stock Exchange (JSE) rule governing acquisitions, disposals and reverse takeovers of listed companies. A category 2 transaction indicates that the transaction value is between 5 and 25% of the market capitalisation of the company or the voting rights of the shareholders are reduced by between 5 and 25%. Also see *acquisition; JSE; reverse takeover*.

causality When the movement in one variable causes changes in another variable. Also see *Granger causality*.

causal variable When a variable, for example x, is considered to cause y, then x is referred to as the causal variable. Also see *causality; Granger causality*.

cautionary announcement An announcement made by a publicly listed company to inform the market that its shares must be traded with caution. For example, the company may be selling or acquiring an asset or may be in merger or sale negotiations. Cautionaries are made to protect investors and usually appear in leading daily financial publications.

CBO
1. See *collateralised bond obligation*.
2. See *competitive bid option*.

CBOE See *Chicago Board Options Exchange*.

CBOT See *Chicago Board of Trade*.

CBS Index An index of stocks on the Amsterdam Stock Exchange.

CC A credit rating used by S&P and Fitch that indicates a highly risky company that is at or near bankruptcy. A CC rating is worse than a CCC rating and is approximately equal to the Moody's Ca rating. Also see *credit rating*.

CCA Current cost accounting.

CCC
1. A credit rating band used by S&P and Fitch with + and − operators that indicates a highly risky company with variable cash flows that is highly dependent on economic cycles. A CCC rating band is worse than the B rating band. Also see *credit rating*.
2. See *cash conversion cycle*.

CCF See *credit conversion factor*.

CD
1. Central depository.
2. See *certificate of deposit*.

CDB China Development Bank.

CDO See *collateralised debt obligation*.

CDO squared A collateralised debt obligation with a pool of assets that consist of other collateralised debt obligations. Also see *collateralised debt obligation*.

CDS See *credit default swap*.

CDX See *credit default swap index*.

cedi The currency of Ghana divided into 100 pesewas.

CEF See *credit enhancement facility*.

central bank A government-affiliated organisation that controls the money supply, foreign reserves and interest rates in a country or monetary union. The main functions of a central bank are to set commercial bank reserve levels, store money safely for banks, regulate banks and financial institutions, act as a lender of last resort to the banks, control money supply and inflation and be a banker to the government and nation. The South African Reserve Bank (SARB) is the central bank of South Africa. Sometimes called a reserve bank. Also see *European Central Bank; Federal Reserve; foreign reserves; inflation; interest rate; lender of last resort; money supply; South African Reserve Bank*.

central bank discount rate The rate at which central banks lend to financial institutions on a short-term basis. Central banks lend on a secured basis against specified security such as treasury bills. The lending against security is in the form of a repurchase agreement (repo). The term discount rate is used in the US while marginal lending rate is used elsewhere. Also see *central bank; Fed funds rate; marginal lending rate; treasury bill*.

Central Energy Fund (CEF) A company owned by the government of South Africa that has been established to finance and promote the exploitation of energy resources and conduct energy research. It has a number of subsidiaries that span the South African energy landscape and administers a number of related funds such as the Equalisation Fund and the Road Accident Fund. Also see *Equalisation Fund*.

central funds Funds held by Lloyds of London to pay claims in the event of an underwriting member's failure to pay. Also see *initial margin*.

central limit theorem The sampling distribution of the mean of a random sample drawn from any population is approximately normal for any sample size. The theorem is sometimes alternately stated as the sum of n independent random variables will tend to be randomly distributed as n becomes larger. Also see *normal random variable*.

central securities depository (CSD) A computer-based custodial entity or system for securities that is used to facilitate their transfer between counterparties buying and selling. The CSD is used for immobilisation and is key to facilitating the transfer of ownership of shares. CSD systems have facilities to move cash in parallel to the transfer of securities. Also see *immobilisation*.

central tendency The tendency of financial data to cluster around a particular value. Also see *mean reversion*.

central treasury See *treasury*.

CER See *coupon equivalent rate*.

certain annuity See *annuity*.

certain funds When assets or companies are purchased, the bidder must have certain funds, i.e. they need guaranteed finance for the price at which they are bidding to be considered a valid purchaser. Also see *underwrite*.

certainty equivalent The process of turning risky future cash flows into certain equivalents. This is effectively the value of the risk-free or less risky assets that the decision maker will accept in exchange for the risk. These cash flows are discounted at the risk-free rate to take into account the time value of money. For example, R1.2 million of corporate bonds could be exchanged for R1 million of government bonds. Also see *time value of money*.

certificate A physical piece of paper proving that the holder is the beneficial owner of a financial instrument such as a share or a bond. Certificates can be bearer or registered in nature. Also see *bearer*.

certificate of authorisation See *certificate of good standing*.

certificate of deposit (COD/CD) A certificate from a bank stating that a named party has a sum of money deposited with the bank. A COD holder usually receives a fixed interest rate for a fixed period of time. CODs often offer higher interest rates than most comparable investments. They are often tradable, usually in bearer form. An add-on certificate of deposit allows the holder of the COD to deposit additional funds after the purchase of the certificate at the same interest rate. Also see *add-on certificate of deposit; fixed interest rate; interest rate; negotiable certificate of deposit*.

certificate of existence See *certificate of good standing*.

certificate of good standing A certificate issued by a governmental regulatory authority indicating that a particular entity is incorporated or authorised to conduct business in that particular country and that the company is in compliance with all required formalities. Sometimes called a certificate of existence or authorisation, or a good standing certificate.

certificate of government receipt A US government bond that has been stripped of its coupon payments and is sold as a discount security. These instruments are synthetic and are issued by financial institutions such as investment banks rather than the US government. Also see *discount security*.

certificate of incorporation A certificate issued by the relevant government department, usually the registrar of companies, that brings a company into existence. Many submissions are made in the incorporation process including that of the articles of association.

certificate of indebtedness A short-term instrument issued by the government with a coupon. This is effectively a treasury bill with coupon payments. Also see *treasury bill*.

certificate of participation (COP) An investment where the investor purchases revenue associated with a bond but not the actual underlying bond.

certificated transaction A transaction accompanied by a physical certificate. Most transactions and records of ownership are now accounted for electronically.

certified cheque A cheque guaranteed by a bank.

cession The ceding or surrendering of an asset. Cession is the act of relinquishing one's rights to the beneficial use of an asset. In the credit environment a creditor can cede their rights and claims against the debtor in question so that the cessionary becomes the ultimate creditor. Also see *encumbrance; factor debtors; invoice discounting facility*.

CET
1. Central European Time.
2. Common external tariff.

ceteris paribus All other things remain unchanged, i.e. consider one variable and hold all the others fixed.

CEY Coupon equivalent yield. Also see *coupon equivalent rate*.

CFA
1. Certified financial analyst.
2. See *CFA franc*.

CFA franc The currency of the West African countries of Benin, Burkina Faso, Côte d'Ivoire, Guinea-Bissau, Mali, Niger, Senegal and Togo. The central bank of West African states, the Banque Centrale des États de l'Afrique de l'Ouest or BCEAO, located in Dakar, issues and manages the currency.

CFD See *contract for difference*.

CFF Cash flow from financing.

CFI Cash flow from investments.

CFO
1. Cash flow from operations.
2. Chief financial officer.

CFTC Commodity Futures Trading Commission.

CGT See *capital gains tax*.

CGY See *capital gains yield*.

chairman's report A report by the chairman of the board of directors of a company published in the annual financial statements. A chairman's report is not compulsory but has become customary, especially for the larger blue-chip companies. The report details aspects of policy and strategy. Also see *board of directors*.

chamber of commerce An organisation that represents the joint interests of business to government.

change in accounting estimate An adjustment of the carrying amount of an asset or a liability, or the amount of the periodic consumption of an asset that results from the assessment of the present status of, and expected future benefits and obligations associated with, assets and liabilities. Changes in accounting estimates result from new information or new developments and, accordingly, are not normally corrections of errors. Also see *asset; liability*.

changes in working capital Changes in debtors, creditors and inventory. If inventory goes up, cash flow goes down and a negative number will result. Working capital is cash tied up in operating activities. Also see *cash flow; creditor; inventory; working capital*.

chaos theory A mathematical theory used to describe non-linear dynamic systems that are sensitive to initial conditions. Due to the sensitivity of the initial conditions and the exponential growth of errors, the systems appear chaotic.

CHAPS Clearing house automated trading system. This is a Bank of England foreign exchange clearing system.

Chapter 7 When a company in the US is in Chapter 7 bankruptcy proceedings, it is under liquidation and legal authorities have appointed a trustee to take over management control, secure funding and prevent further losses. Also see *Chapter 11*.

Chapter 11 In the US, when a company that is in financial difficulties is reorganised but remains in control of the debtors, it is said to be in Chapter 11. Under Chapter 11, companies are protected from creditors seeking to wind the company up and creditors therefore cannot effect security. Called administration in English law or judicial management in South Africa. Also see *Chapter 7*.

Chapter 13 When a company in the US is in Chapter 13, it is having its debt obligations restructured.

charge The appropriation of assets to satisfy debt obligations. A charge does not transfer the legal ownership of an asset but creates certain rights to the property in the event of default on a debt obligation. There are two types of charges over assets, namely fixed charges and floating charges. The term is often used loosely for a generic form of security such as a mortgage or lien. It is not a term commonly used in South Africa where a notarial bond over assets is used. Also see *event of default; fixed charge; floating charge; lien; mortgage*.

chargeable asset An asset that is subject to capital gains tax. Also see *capital gains tax*.

chargeable gain A profit associated with the sale of an asset that is subject to capital gains tax. Also see *capital gains tax*.

charge card A card similar to a credit card in nature, where the settlement of debt is required in full at the end of a specified period. The drawn credit cannot be rolled over as with credit cards. Store cards are often in the form of charge cards.

charting The graphical representation of a security's price over time. The charts are used to interpret trends. Charting is sometimes known as technical analysis. Also see *technical analysis*.

chastity bond A form of poison pill employed by companies that involves issuing bonds that mature if a takeover or any other specific event occurs. Parties wishing to take over a company that has issued chastity bonds will be saddled with maturing debt obligations immediately after takeover. Change of control prepayment clauses in loan documents have a similar poison-pill effect. Also see *poison pill*.

cheapest to deliver (CTD) The least expensive underlying asset that can be delivered into a futures contract. This is prevalent in the bond futures market where different underlying bonds can be used with conversion factors to deliver into particular contracts. Cheaper bonds arise because conversion factors are calculated with fixed yield at the nominal coupon rate in the delivery month. These can differ from market-related yields. The cheapest to deliver bond maximises the expression:

$F \times C - P$

where F = the futures price; C = the conversion factor; P = the price of the underlying bond.

The CTD bond is the bond with the highest implied rate. Also see *bond; contract month*.

cheap money Money lent at low interest rates. Under special circumstances governments may lower the cost of borrowing and thereby encourage economic development.

check American spelling of cheque. Also see *cheque*.

checking account American spelling of cheque account. Also see *cheque*.

cheque A paper form that bears instructions to pay monies to the holder of the cheque from the bank account of the cheque issuer. Cheques are money transfer instruments that are steadily losing popularity due to fraud. Alternative methods of money transfer over the Internet are gaining in popularity. Also see *blank cheque; crossed cheque; money transfer; open cheque; order cheque; rubber cheque*.

cheque account A bank account from which cheques can be drawn. Also see *cheque*.

cheque clearing The process whereby a cheque makes its way from the institution where it was deposited to the institution from which it was written while funds move in the opposite direction. The process takes some time before funds are available to the depositor.

cherry picking The process of choosing the most profitable items. Parties asset stripping companies often cherry pick the most prized assets. Also see *asset stripping*.

CHF The Swiss frank divided into 100 rappen.

Chicago Board of Trade (CBOT) 'The Chicago Board of Trade (CBOT®), established in 1848, is a leading futures and futures-options exchange. More than 3,600 CBOT member/stockholders trade 50 different futures and options products at the CBOT by open auction and electronically.' (*Source*: www.cbot.com 2007) Also see *auction*.

Chicago Board Options Exchange (CBOE) A large US options exchange. Also see *option*.

Chicago Mercantile Exchange (CME) The CME is the largest futures exchange in the US and operates the largest futures house in the world.

Chinese wall Internal barriers set up in an institution to prevent the unauthorised transfer of information that could constitute a conflict of interest. Also see *arms length*.

chip card A banking card with an embedded microchip. The microchip is used to store information on the cardholder and provide additional security.

CHIPS Clearing house and interbank payment system.

chi-squared distribution The chi-squared distribution is widely used in inferential statistics (statistical significance tests). Easily calculated quantities can often be proven to have distributions that approximate to the chi-square distribution if the null hypothesis is true. If X_i are k independent, normally distributed random variables with means μ_i and variances σ_i^2, then the random variable Q is distributed according to the chi-squared distribution:

$$Q = \sum_{i=1}^{k}\left(\frac{X_i - \mu_i}{\sigma_i}\right)^2$$

A graph of various chi-squared distributions is shown below. Also see *log normal; normal or Gaussian distribution; null hypothesis; variance*.

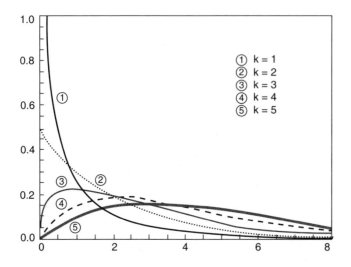

choice price The price of an asset when the bid price and ask price are the same. Also see *ask price; backwardation; bid price*.

chooser option An option where the holder can choose at defined points whether the option is a call option or a put option. Also see *call option; put option*.

churning
1. The practice of dealing with the purpose of collecting commission on an excessive number of trades. For example, brokers may frequently issue buy and sell recommendations in the hope that customers will buy and sell and they will thus collect commissions on the buy and sell orders.
2. The process of a company such as a cellular phone or pay TV operator losing subscribers.

circuit breaker A procedure put in place by exchanges that suspends trading if a predefined event occurs. For example, if massive price fluctuations occur, trading may be suspended. Also see *suspension of trading; trading halt*.

circular transaction A transaction between companies in a group used to boost or inflate the turnover of one or both companies.

circulation notes Money in circulation outside the banking system. The reserves that banks hold in safes and cash machines are not included. Also see *M1; M2; M3*.

CIS See *collective investment scheme*.

CITIC China International Trust and Investment Corporation.

city code A code used in the UK that manages and controls the merger and acquisition process.

CIV See *calculated intangible value*.

claim
1. The right an entity has to the assets or cash flows of another entity. The term is often used in the context of a holder of a security (lender) having claim to the assets or cash of the issuer (borrower). Also see *lien; security*.
2. The process of seeking compensation for losses associated with a loss event covered by an insurance policy.

claims ratio A ratio used in the analysis of insurance companies. The ratio calculates the total value of claims to premiums received:

$$\text{claims ratio (CR)} = \frac{\text{claims paid}}{\text{premiums received}}$$

Insurance companies seek to minimise this ratio. Also see *credit loss ratio; expense ratio*.

class 1 transaction A transaction that requires shareholder approval. These are usually large or business-altering transactions. Also see *cash sweep; lockup; special general meeting*.

class action A legal suit in the US where a representative of a class of entities such as shareholders seeks a claim.

class of assets The grouping of assets of a similar nature and used in company operations.

clawback
1. The process of government claiming taxes from the public after extra concessions or spending has occurred. The money is often not clawed back from the beneficiaries of the public spending or concessions.
2. A clause in a financial agreement that enables a party to retrieve money already paid out.

clawback clause A clause used in a loan agreement that allows the lender to recover any cash distributed to the project sponsor. Also see *cash sweep; lockup; sponsor*.

clean float The foreign exchange rate of a country is termed a free float when it is allowed to fluctuate without excessive intervention by the monetary authorities. With a clean float, monetary authorities may manipulate the exchange rate but do so infrequently and only in special circumstances. Also see *crawling peg; dirty float; fixed exchange rate; foreign exchange rate; free float; managed float*.

clean price The price of a bond excluding accrued interest. This is generally the price quoted in the market. To calculate the clean price, use the bond value formula:

$$\text{bond value} = C \left[\frac{1 - \frac{1}{(1+r)^t}}{r} \right] + \frac{FV_t}{(1+r)^t}$$

where FV_t = future value after t whole periods; t = number of whole periods until redemption; r = interest rate or discount rate; C = annuity or coupon payment.

To calculate the all-in price, add the interest that will accrue after the last whole period till the date of redemption or the date of the register closing. Also see *accrued interest; all-in price; bond; bond value; cum interest; ex interest; future value; total price; yield to maturity*.

clean-up call A call option on a collateralised debt obligation bond that can be exercised if the value of the pool of assets falls below a predetermined threshold. Also see *call option; collateralised debt obligation*.

clear days The number of days under which a contract is held excluding the start and end days.

clearing The processes involved between the conclusion of a financial transaction and the settling of the transaction, i.e. between the handshake and the money changing hands. Clearing involves reporting, managing risk, netting of trades and the handling of failed transactions. Clearing is needed because trading is more rapid than transaction settlement.

clearing agent A clearing agent ensures that when goods are imported and exported all the appropriate forms, procedures and means of product and party identification are completed properly.

clearing bank A bank that can clear cheques and various other interbank payments. For example, when writing a cheque to the client of another bank, a deposit of funds can be made into the cheque bearer's account through an interbank cheque clearing system. Banks that have access to these clearing systems are called clearing banks. Also see *clearing; Society for Worldwide Interbank Transactions*.

clearing cycle The process or cycle that involves the transfer of funds from one account to another when a cheque is used as the form of payment. Also see *clearing*.

clearing fee A fee charged by clearing houses for providing a clearing service. Also see *clearing; clearing house*.

clearing house A clearing house on a futures exchange provides guarantees that two parties entering into a futures contract will perform the conditions set out in the contract. The clearing house also ensures that contracts are settled, margin monies are maintained and collected and that delivery of the underlying asset takes place. The existence of the clearing house effectively abstracts counterparties, there is minimised counterparty risk and the relationship is like dealing with a single counterparty. Dealing with a clearing house also enables transactions to be anonymous. Clearing houses manage exposure to counterparties using a margining system whereby variation margins and initial margins are posted. Also see *counterparty risk; futures exchange; initial margin; margin; South African Futures Exchange; variation margin*.

clearing margin Brokers who are members of clearing exchanges or houses are required to maintain margin accounts with the clearing houses. These margin accounts have initial margins but no maintenance margins. Brokers must top up or draw down on their margin accounts at the end of every trading day to ensure that the original margin levels are maintained. Also see *clearing house; initial margin; maintenance margin*.

clearing rate The rate at which all securities clear in an auction process. Also see *auction; auction rate security*.

clear market Clauses that book runners and arrangers use in debt market agreements (typically mandate) that restrict the ability of the issuer of the instrument to raise debt in the international and domestic markets. These provisions are included to ensure that when bonds or syndicated loans are being placed in the market, the borrower does not attempt any parallel processes that may jeopardise the issue and hence affect the success of the placement. Clear market restrictions are especially important to book runners when transactions are underwritten. Also see *book runner; facility agreement; mandate; underwrite*.

clicks and mortar A company that has a significant online retail business coupled with physical stores. Sometimes called bricks and clicks.

client account An account operated by an authorised person and transacted on behalf of the client of a broker. Sometimes called a discretionary account. Also see *discretionary account; non-discretionary account*.

client money Money held by an authorised person in a trust fund or account. Also see *client account*.

CLN
1. See *construction loan note*.
2. See *credit-linked note*.

CLO Collateralised loan obligation. Also see *collateralised debt obligation*.

C-loan A loan that has less seniority than a B-loan and subsequently has higher margins and often longer tenors. C-loans are aimed at participation from investment funds and lower grade banks. Also see *A-loan; B-loan; D-loan; margin; seniority*.

close In published share tables the close price is the last cash sale price of the day.

close corporation A legal form of corporate entity designed for small business. There is usually a maximum of ten equity shareholders.

closed economy An economy that does not trade substantially with the outside world. Also see *openness of market*.

closed end fund A collective investment scheme that has a limited number of shares in issue. No new shares are issued and shares are not redeemable for cash or assets until the fund liquidates. Shares in these funds can usually be obtained in secondary markets.

Closed end funds are sponsored by investment management companies who control the investment of funds. Closed end funds can be geared with debt to enhance returns and often trade at values higher than their net asset values. Also see *collective investment scheme*.

closed-ended indenture Terms in a bond contract that ensure that certain collateral can only be used on the contract in question and cannot be used against the issue of other bonds. Also see *collateral; negative pledge; open-ended indenture*.

closed period The period during which directors may not pass information to the markets about their companies' annual, semi-annual or quarterly financial results or deal in the companies' shares.

closed position A position that leaves the investor with no net exposure to the market. Also see *close out*.

close link Businesses that have significant shareholdings in one another are classed as close-linked businesses. Sometimes called a related party.

close of trade The time of day at which trade on an exchange stops.

close out The termination of a position in a market by employing an equal and opposite position. Also see *closed position; position*.

closing balance The balance on an account, usually in accounts on the balance sheet, that will be carried through to the next accounting period. Also see *balance sheet*.

closing deal The transaction that creates a closed out position or pays off a liability. Also see *close out*.

closing price The price of an asset on a traded market at the close of the day's trading. Also see *asset*.

closing purchase A purchase made to close out an investment position.

closing sale A sale made to close out an investment position. Also see *position*.

closing transaction The selling or exercising of an option.

CLP The Chilean peso divided into 100 centavos.

CLS Continuous linked settlement.

CLS Bank A bank in London whose objective is to minimise counterparty risk in foreign exchange (FX) transactions. The bank's existence was brought about as a result of different world market opening times. Also see *CLS; counterparty risk; foreign exchange*.

club deal A syndicated loan agreement in which the participants in the syndicate are treated equally and usually contribute equally. No titles such as book runner or mandated lead arranger (MLA) are awarded. A coordinator is usually appointed and paid a work fee to manage the syndication process. Also see *best efforts; book runner; mandated lead arranger; syndicated loan*.

CMB See *cash management bill*.

CMBS See *commercial mortgage-backed security*.

CMCDS See *constant maturity credit default swap*.

CME See *Chicago Mercantile Exchange*.

CMO See *collateralised mortgage obligation*.

CMS See *constant maturity swap*.

CMT See *constant maturity treasury rate*.

C-note A cash note of nominal value of 100. Also see *nominal value*.

CNY The Chinese yuan divided into 10 jiao or 100 fen.

co-agent A title awarded to a bank for a large commitment in a syndicated loan. Sometimes also called a managing agent. Also see *syndicated loan*.

COB Close of business.

COC

1. See *cash on cash return*.
2. Change of control.

CoCo See *contingent convertible*.

COD See *certificate of deposit*.

COE See *cost of equity*.

coefficient of variation (*CV*) Variation adjusted for the mean or expected value. *CV* is a useful measure when comparing the riskiness of stocks with different expected returns.

$$CV = \frac{\sigma}{\mu}$$

where σ = the standard deviation; μ = expected value or mean.

Also see *expected return; expected value; arithmetic mean; standard deviation*.

coefficient variability of earnings per share

$$CV = \frac{\sigma_{EPS}}{\text{expected EPS}}$$

As a firm is leveraged, the standard deviation of earnings per share (EPS) increases and therefore increases the coefficient of variability. Also see *firm; earnings per share; leverage*.

coemption The purchase of all the shares of a company. Also see *mandatory offer*.

cogeneration The production of electricity as a by-product of an industrial process.

coinciding indicator An indicator that is used to define business and economic trends. The South African Reserve Bank publishes a business cycle indicator which can be found in the SARB Quarterly Bulletin. This indicator gives a good indication of the trend in SA business cycles. Also see *hard number*.

coinsurance The process of a series of insurers insuring for a single risk exposure. Insurers often do this if potential losses may exceed the funds available to settle claims. The insured entity deals only with a single insurer who acts as an agent. Coinsurance is conceptually similar to a syndicated loan. Also see *Lloyds of London; syndicated loan*.

cointegration An econometric technique for testing the correlation between non-stationary combined linear time series variables. If two or more series are themselves non-stationary, but a linear combination of them is stationary, then the series are said to be cointegrated. The linear combination is specified by the cointegration vector.

For example, prices of goods in a local market and prices of goods in a foreign market may be non-stationary. Purchasing power parity places restrictions on the movement of exchange rates and price levels. A linear combination of the prices and exchange rates is a stationary process and the variables are thus cointegrated.

In some cases, even though two series have a unit root and follow a random walk individually, they move together in the long run. If $Y_t = Y_{t+1} + \varepsilon_{Y_t}$ and $X_t = X_{t+1} + \varepsilon_{X_t}$ it can be seen that Y and X each have a unit root. If there is no unit root in the error term from the regression $Y_t = b_0 + b_1 X_t + u_t$, then Y and X are cointegrated.

Johansen tests are used to test for cointegration. Cointegration techniques help identify persistent patterns of co-movements or co-trending among variables. Also see *cointegration vector; Johansen test; non-stationary process; purchasing power parity; stationary process; unit root*.

cointegration vector If two time series are cointegrated, a linear combination exists that is stationary. The components of the vector $x_t = (x_{1t}, x_{2t}, x_{3t} \ldots x_{nt})$ are said to be cointegrated of order d, b if:

- all components of x_t are integrated of order d
- a vector $\beta = (\beta_1, \beta_2 \ldots \beta_n)$ exists such that a linear combination $\beta x = \beta_1 x_{t_1} + \beta_2 x_{t_2} + \ldots + \beta_n x_{nt}$ is integrated of order (d, b).

The vector β is called the cointegrating vector. Also see *cointegration*.

cold call An unsolicited call to a potential customer with the objective of selling him/her a product or service.

collar
1. A strategy of buying and selling options that protects investors against wide fluctuations in interest rates. A cap option protects against interest rates going over a threshold value and a floor option protects against interest rates going below a particular value. Also see *interest rate; zero cost collar*.
2. The lowest rate of return for a bond investor or lowest price that a bond issuer is willing to accept. Also see *bond*.

collateral An asset that is offered to secure a loan and that will be liquidated if payments are not honoured or if the company defaults on its debt obligations. Collateral is usually offered to reduce interest expense and gain access to a wider range of funding and quanta. Also see *asset; liquidation*.

collateral asset A financial asset or security that central banks accept as collateral when illiquid banks are accommodated. Central banks lend through the accommodation window and accept a narrow range of low-risk securities such as treasury bills. A policy tool that central banks can use when banking markets are illiquid is to accept a wider range of securities as collateral assets. Also see *asset; accommodation; central bank; collateral; illiquid; security*.

collateralisation A system adopted in over-the-counter markets whereby one party pays funds to another using a pre-agreed valuation approach when they are counterparties to derivative contracts. This is the over-the-counter equivalent to the posting of margins in transactions where clearing houses are intermediaries. Collateralisation reduces the counterparty risk. Also see *clearing house; counterparty risk; over the counter; variation margin*.

collateralised bond obligation (CBO) A form of collateralised debt obligation (CDO) where a series of sub-investment grade bonds are packaged into a CDO and sold by issuing new bonds with varying levels of subordination in different tranches. Also see *CDO squared; collateralised debt obligation; sub-investment grade; subordinate*.

collateralised debt/loan obligation (CDO/CLO) A security that is backed by a pool of assets. Securitisation is the process by which debt is collateralised and CDOs are engineered. For example, a bank may wrap up its home loan book, syndicated loan book or credit card book and sell the loans to a special-purpose vehicle (SPV). The SPV then issues bonds of various degrees of creditworthiness (levels of subordination) as CDOs to investors. The holder of a CDO exchanges a set of interest payments for bearing the credit risk of the CDO issuer.

CDOs are set in a series of tranches with differing maturities, levels of subordination and with different risk characteristics. The subordinate tranches carry more risk and

collateralised loan obligation (CLO) | combined market risk premium approach

hence higher returns. Institutional investors are often purchasers of these kinds of investments.

A raft of poorly constructed CDOs on the back of underlying subprime loan assets caused a credit market crisis called the subprime crisis in 2007/8.

Also see *companion bond; credit risk; institutional investor; pfandbrief; securitisation; special-purpose vehicle; subordinate; subprime loan.*

collateralised loan obligation (CLO) A collateralised debt obligation constructed on an underlying portfolio of loan assets. Also see *collateralised debt obligation.*

collateralised mortgage obligation (CMO) A collateralised debt obligation constructed on an underlying portfolio of mortgage backed loans. Also see *collateralised debt obligation.*

collateral margin See *haircut.*

collateral trust bond A bond that has securities such as treasury bills put up as collateral. The loss given default of the bond is minimised by doing this and hence the returns on these bonds are low. Also see *bond; collateral; loss given default; treasury bill.*

collateral warranty The entity responsible for the development and construction of a project accepts liability for performance to the lenders. Also see *surety bond.*

collection The process of sending a cheque or other money transfer instrument or request to the bank of the account holder. Also see *clearing; money transfer.*

collection period A financial ratio that measures the average period it takes clients to pay their accounts:

$$\text{collection period} = \frac{\text{accounts receivable}}{\left[\frac{\text{sales}}{365}\right]}$$

A low collection period number implies that the company in question is efficient at managing its debtors book and money in the form of working capital is not tied up for excessively lengthy periods. Benchmark ratios vary from industry to industry. Also see *asset management ratios.*

collective investment scheme (CIS) A term used in the UK for investment schemes where investors pool assets in funds that are generally actively managed and that invest in a range of different securities. In South Africa they are called unit trusts and in the US they are called mutual funds. Also see *mutual fund; unit trust.*

collusive oligopoly See *cartel; oligopoly.*

colon The currency of Costa Rica and El Salvador divided into 100 centimos.

combination An options trading strategy that involves using both call options and put options on the same underlying assets. Also see *call option; option; put option; straddle; strangle.*

combination bond A bond which has coupon cash flows derived from an underlying asset and a guarantee from a parent company or government. Also see *bond.*

combined market risk premium approach A method by which the market risk premium (MRP) is adjusted for volatility in the bond and equity markets:

$$CRP_{\text{country X}} = MRP_{\text{home country}} + ARP_{\text{country X}}$$

where $\text{ARP}_{\text{country X}}$ = default spread$_{\text{country X}} \times \dfrac{\sigma_{\text{country X equity}}}{\sigma_{\text{country X bond}}}$; ARP = additional risk premium.

This approach uses historical data and is often biased by a lack of liquidity in developing markets. This results in artificially low risk measures. The validity of being able to combine equity and bond market returns is also questionable. Also see *bond; country risk premium; market risk premium; relative equity market standard deviation; volatility.*

COMEX The Commodity Exchange of New York. COMEX is a significant platform for the trade of silver, gold and copper and options on these commodities.

comfort letter A letter that supports a financial transaction and that is effectively like a guarantee although not a formal guarantee. It is not legally enforceable like a guarantee and is given when guarantors are unable to guarantee debt legally. Also called a letter of comfort.

command economy An economy in which government centrally plans production, spending and prices. Communist countries have command economies. Also see *market economy.*

commercial bank A bank operated for profit and owned by the private sector. Commercial banks usually provide a range of retail and investment banking services to the general public and corporate clients. They receive a large portion of their funds from depositors. The funds received from depositors are then lent on to borrowers.

commercial bill See *bill of exchange.*

commercial credit company A company that provides credit exclusively to businesses. Investment and business banks are classed as commercial credit companies.

commercial loan selling A process used principally in the US where a bank grants a loan to a customer and then sells the loan to another bank. The loan is sold at a profit and the purchasing bank obtains a loan on its books that it would otherwise not have been able to originate on its own. Sometimes called warehouse lending. Also see *syndicated loan.*

commercial mortgage-backed security (CMBS) A mortgage backed security (collateralised debt obligation) that is secured against commercial property. Also see *collateralised debt obligation; securitisation.*

commercial paper (CP) Money market securities, usually bonds and treasury bills, that are issued by commercial companies and governments and that have short maturities, usually of less than one year. Instruments such as promissory notes, drafts, cheques and certificates of deposit are often included in the definition. Commercial paper is usually issued by low credit risk corporations. They are unsecured and at maturity the entity holding the paper is paid the principal value. Commercial paper is widely traded on secondary markets. It does not usually carry coupon payments and is thereby considered to be a discount security. Commercial paper is not a form of bank debt (unless issued by a bank) even though banks are involved in issuing and trading in it. Formal credit ratings are not an absolute requirement for CP programmes but margins and liquidity are improved with official credit ratings. Also see *certificate of deposit; cheque; credit rating; credit risk; margin; money market; principal; promissory note; secondary market; treasury bill; unsecured debt.*

commingled property Property or assets that are mixed with the assets of a third party. For example, oil in a pipeline can be a commingled asset.

commission A fee charged by an agent or broker, i.e. an intermediary, for facilitating a transaction.

commission ratio (CR) A ratio used in the analysis of the insurance industry that analyses the cost of commission-earning brokers:

$$\text{commission ratio (CR)} = \frac{\text{commissions paid}}{\text{premiums received}}$$

Insurance companies seek to minimise this ratio.

Commit Index An index of shares on the Milan Stock Exchange.

commitment
1. The amount that participants invited to a syndicated loan are willing to pledge or lend. The commitment may exceed the final hold. Also see *final hold*.
2. The maximum guaranteed amount a bank will lend to a client.

commitment fee When committing to a loan facility such as a revolving credit facility that is not fully drawn, a bank is usually paid an annual fee for making the commitment. The commitment fee is specified as a percentage of the applicable margin and is charged on the undrawn portion of the facility for the term of the availability period. In general, the undrawn portion of a loan is cancelled at the end of the availability period and hence the commitment fee terminates. Banks charge a commitment fee for the cost of having to put regulatory capital aside and to compensate for the opportunity cost of the lending activities that could otherwise have been undertaken.

Commitment fees are usually charged on revolving credit facilities and can be charged on term loans with long draw down or availability periods. Corporates are often sensitive to commitment fees. Also see *administrative agent fee; availability period; facility fee; margin; opportunity cost; prepayment fee; capital adequacy; revolving credit facility; term loan; upfront fee; usage fee.*

committed facility A line of credit extended to a borrower that is guaranteed to be available for a specified period. The lender is obliged to lend the predetermined amount for the defined period under the terms of the facility. A commitment fee is usually paid for this facility because banks need to be compensated for the cost of having to put regulatory capital aside. Committed facilities are typically revolving credit facilities and are committed at margins over floating interest rates such as LIBOR or JIBAR. Also see *commitment fee; floating interest rate; JIBAR; LIBOR; credit line; capital adequacy; revolving credit facility; uncommitted facility.*

committed principal See *market maker.*

commodity A physical good traded on a market. These goods are primary goods such as metals, grain, oil, meat and a range of others. Commodities are usually bought and sold on exchanges and are priced by supply and demand dynamics. Also see *primary goods.*

commodity based A financial trend or obligation that is based on the price of commodities. An example is the use of the term commodity-based economy when referring to a country that relies heavily on the export of commodities such as oil or other minerals. The South African economy can be considered to be commodity based as it is heavily reliant on the export of minerals.

commodity broker A broker who trades in commodities. Also see *broker.*

commodity swap In a commodity swap, the exchange of payments by counterparties is based on the value of a particular physical commodity. Also see *currency swap; interest rate swap; swap*.

Common Agricultural Policy (CAP) A policy set out by the European Union (EU) that supports free trade in agricultural commodities and uses a system of tariffs and quotas to ensure stable prices and supply of food in the EU. The EU sets a series of threshold prices, intervention prices and appropriate import duties to manage supply, demand and price stability. The CAP also enables the payment of subsidies to farmers in the EU.

common base year financial statement A standardised financial statement presenting all items relative to a certain base year amount. Also known as an indexed statement. Also see *base year; like for like sales*.

common budget A fund into which levies and customs duties in the EU are paid. The common budget is used to provide subsidies under the Common Agricultural Policy. Also see *Common Agricultural Policy; European Union*.

common external tariff (CET) The import tariff charged on goods entering the EU from non-member states that is used to bolster the common budget and provide subsidies under the Common Agricultural Policy. Also see *Common Agricultural Policy; common budget; European Union*.

common law The part of South African and English law that is derived from custom and judicial precedent rather than statutes.

common size statement A standardised financial statement presenting all items in percentage points. Balance sheets are shown as percentages of assets and income statements as percentages of sales. It eliminates the effects of growth and focuses on margins. Also see *balance sheet; income statement; margin*.

common stock A term generally used in the US for an ordinary share. Also see *ordinary share*.

common terms agreement An agreement between creditors of a company that specifies the terms and conditions of a debt package. The terms specified are common to all creditors. A common terms agreement is sometimes called an intercreditor agreement.

common trends Two time series that move together are described as common trends or more formally as cointegrated. Also see *cointegration*.

communism An economic system where assets are not owned by individuals and businesses are not in existence to make a profit attributable to private individuals. A communist system strives to be classless and the means of production belong to the greater society. A communist economy is classed as a command economy. Also see *capitalism; command economy*.

commutation The exchange of an upfront payment for reduced future payments from an annuity. This is often done for pensions where the beneficiary takes a lump sum on retirement and reduced payments over the life of the annuity.

Companies Act A government act in the UK and other countries such as South Africa that governs the activities of companies. In South Africa, the Companies Act does not apply to close corporations. The Companies Act dictates what financial statements need to be prepared by companies, what duties directors have and a range of other legal and administrative issues.

Companies House The registration authority in the UK with which all companies must register.

companion bond A bond issued through securitisations such as collateralised mortgage obligations (CMOs) that are paid off before other bondholders as the underlying debt obligations are prepaid. Companion bonds absorb most of the prepayment risk in a CMO-type structure. Also see *collateralised mortgage obligation; prepayment risk*.

company A business created as a distinct legal entity comprising one or more owners called equity holders. Often known as a corporation. Private companies must have less than 50 shareholder members.

company doctor A consultant charged with rectifying problems in ailing companies. These consultants may be given management authority to implement significant changes.

company limited by guarantee A company structure in the UK that is used by non-profit organisations. These companies do not have issued share capital but have members who are guarantors in the event of the company winding up. Companies limited by guarantee cannot distribute profits to their members. In South Africa, Section 21 companies are used to set up non-profit organisations. Also see *section 21; winding up*.

company limited by shares A company that has issued shares held by shareholders. The shareholders' liabilities extend as far as the original amount invested.

company risk See *unsystematic risk*.

company tax The tax levied on the net profit of corporates. Typically, company tax is levied at or near 30% in many countries and is levied at a rate of 28% (2008) in South Africa.

compensation for loss of office Compensation paid to senior management of a company if their contract is terminated before date of expiry due to activities such as mergers or acquisitions. Also see *acquisition*.

Compensation Scheme A scheme run by the Financial Services Authority (FSA) in the UK to compensate an investor in the event of default of an FSA authorised person in a financial transaction. Also see *Financial Services Authority*.

Competition Board A board appointed by the government of South Africa that investigates unfair and uncompetitive business practices. The Competition Board in South Africa has the authority to hand down fines and judgements.

competitive bid option (CBO) A specific type of syndicated loan where borrowers are allowed to solicit the best bids from the syndicate group. The agent for the loan conducts an auction to raise funds for the borrower and the best bids are accepted. This type of syndicated loan is in general only available to investment-grade borrowers. Also see *auction; syndicated loan*.

competitive tender A bidding process where many different parties are encouraged to submit tenders. The objective is to lower overall costs and solicit highly competitive bids. Also see *tender*.

completion The date on which cash flows from a project are strong enough to cover finance repayment obligations. Before completion, interest on debt is capitalised or covered by the project sponsors. Sometimes called technical completion. Also see *sponsor*.

completion guarantee A guarantee used for real estate and project finance. If a project is not completed on time, the guarantee may be used to cover losses incurred as a result of the delay. Also see *project finance*.

compliance The satisfaction of legal or conditional requirements. Banks have compliance departments that check that transactions comply with legal regulators and ethical considerations.

compliance certificate A certificate that indicates that an entity (company or individual) meets a set of requirements. Compliance certificates for loans indicate that all the covenants and conditions precedent have been met. Also see *conditions precedent; covenant*.

compliance risk The risk that a company may not comply with particular laws or rules. These laws and rules are set by central banks, financial regulators and stock exchanges. Also see *central bank*.

compound accreted value (CAV) The value of a zero coupon bond based on the accrued interest expressed at a rate that is compounded and reinvested in the bond. The reason for calculating CAV is because the zero coupon bond is callable and the call option provisions are usually linked to the CAV and principal. Also see *accrued interest; callable bond; call option; zero coupon bond*.

compound interest Interest earned on initial principal invested and the interest received from the prior periods, i.e. interest on capital and interest on interest. With compounding interest calculations, the interest payments are considered to be reinvested at the same rate of return. Also see *present value; simple interest*.

compound multiple times per year A formula used to calculate the value of an investment that has multiple compounding periods in a single year, defined by:

$$FV = PV\left(1 + \frac{r}{m}\right)^{t \times m}$$

where r = interest rate per annum; t = number of years; PV = present value of the investment; m = the number of compounding periods per annum.

compound option An option on an option. An example of a real option that is a compound option is an option to exit and re-enter an industry. Also see *option; real option*.

compulsory purchase annuity Certain investments, usually pension fund investments, require that at maturity an annuity be purchased to provide an income stream for the balance of the natural life of the investor. In certain legislative environments a portion of the pension fund investment may be cashed.

concentrated portfolio A portfolio that seeks to gain returns in excess of what the wider market or a balanced portfolio can return. To do this, portfolio managers have to assume a degree of concentration risk and invest in industries that they predict will outperform the market. Also see *balanced portfolio; concentration risk*.

concentration The degree to which a market, industry or portfolio is dominated by a single or select group of companies. A portfolio's concentration is measured by the concentration ratio. Also see *concentration ratio*.

concentration ratio (CR) The concentration risk of a single debtor or investment expressed as a percentage of the whole portfolio or loan book:

concentration risk | conditional sale agreement

concentration ratio (CR) = $\dfrac{\text{value of outstanding balances of individual loan or investment}}{\text{total value of debtors/investment book}} \times \dfrac{100}{1}$

Also see *concentration risk*.

concentration risk The risk that a portfolio of assets faces due to a lack of diversification. Concentration risk is the risk that investors face when putting many or all their eggs in a single basket. Concentration risk for a bank is the debt exposure that it has to a particular entity or industry. For portfolio managers it may be the exposure to specific shares in their portfolio. The concentration risk is often expressed using the concentration ratio. Also see *concentration ratio*.

concert party A group of individuals that have a link to one another and act as a collective to profit.

concession A licence or permission for a private sector entity to operate a piece of infrastructure such as a toll road or a mine for a period of time and then return the asset to the public sector in a predefined condition.

concession agreement An agreement that governs the rights and obligations under a concession. Also see *concession*.

concurrent creditor An unsecured creditor who receives proceeds under liquidation only after all secured creditors have been paid in full. Also see *structural subordination*.

conditional bid See *conditional offer*.

conditional offer An offer made for an asset that is conditional on the occurrence of an event. For example, in takeovers a condition is often imposed that more than 50% of shareholders must accept the offer before it becomes binding.

conditional order An order to buy or sell an asset given to a broker that should only be executed when a triggering condition or event occurs. A stop loss order is considered to be a conditional order. Also see *stop loss*.

conditional prepayment rate (CPR) For asset-backed securities such as collateralised debt obligations (CDOs), the investor in CDOs incurs the risk associated with debt obligations in the underlying pool of assets being repaid early. The conditional payment rate measure gives investors a measure of the risk of repayment and is defined by:

conditional prepayment rate (CPR) = $\dfrac{\text{prepayments made}}{\text{outstanding loan balance}}$

A CPR of 30% indicates that it is likely that 30% of the underlying assets will be prepaid in the next measurement period, usually a year. Also see *collateralised debt obligation*.

conditional probability The probability of the occurrence of an event given that the random experiment produces an outcome from another event, i.e. what is the probability of X given the occurrence of Y. Also see *path dependent*.

conditional probability distribution The distribution of a random variable given that the random experiment produces an outcome in an event. For example, if an event X occurs, what is the probability distribution of an event Y occurring? The given event may specify values for one or more other random variables.

conditional sale agreement A sale agreement that is bound by particular conditions being met. The legal title of the asset being sold is not conveyed until all conditions have been met. Mergers and takeovers are often concluded on this basis as various analyses and due diligence processes are required. Similar concepts are employed in loans under conditions precedent terms. Also see *conditions precedent; due diligence; merger.*

conditional variance The variance of the conditional probability distribution of a random variable. Also see *conditional probability distribution; variance.*

conditions precedent Before parties enter into financial transactions such as the provision of debt or purchase of an asset such as a business, they may need to satisfy a series of conditions precedent before cash changes hands. The borrower in a loan agreement or the seller of an asset needs to provide the respective counterparties with evidence that they have the capacity and all the necessary authorisations to enter into financial agreements. The conditions precedent clauses normally contain points of commercial and legal importance. Sometimes conditions precedent are called the suspensive conditions.

conduit
1. The institution through which payments are channelled with a view to avoiding payment of withholding tax. One important consideration for borrowers consenting to their loans being traded on a secondary market is avoiding withholding tax in the country where the acquirer of the loan is domiciled. Also see *domicile; withholding tax.*
2. A special-purpose vehicle created by financial institutions to move credit assets off their books. They are most often created in securitisation-type structures and issued bonds or commercial paper to provide funds. Most South African banks have conduits in which they place assets such as loans. Also see *commercial paper; securitisation; special-purpose vehicle.*

conference board A business membership and research organisation best known for consumer confidence indices and other economic indicators. See www.conference-board.org.

confi See *confidentiality agreement.*

confidence interval A range between two numbers with an associated probability. For example, instead of estimating a population parameter as a single number, a statistician would express a range of numbers and the level of probability that the number lies within that range.

confidentiality agreement A legally enforceable document that binds parties to keep information confidential within defined parameters.

confirmation Documentation that sets out the terms of a derivative contract. The equivalent of a term sheet for loans. Also see *term sheet.*

confirmation note A note which outlines the conditions of a financial trade just undertaken.

conflict of interest A situation that can arise if an entity is acting in more than one separate capacity. For example, a stockbroker may be trading in stocks and giving financial advice to companies whose stocks he/she is trading in. Organisations such as investment banks have Chinese walls to avoid such conflicts of interest. Also see *Chinese wall; stockbroker.*

conformed copy A copy of a set of financial documents that is in final form and ready for signature after final legal review.

conforming loan A loan that meets criteria set by the lender.

congestion After periods of rising prices in a bull market, profit-taking by market participants can cause prices to dip slightly before resuming their upward trend.

conglomerate A large company that is typically a multinational and is involved in a range of different industries. Also see *multinational*.

connected person A person that has a relationship with a powerful, influential person such as a director of a company. Connected persons may include family, partners, body corporates and trusts. Sometimes called related parties. Also see *related party*.

consents
1. A series of approvals that may need to be gained so that a financial transaction may proceed.
2. In loan agreements, consents usually refer to the process of one or more parties giving consent before a loan asset can be sold.

consequential loss policy See *business interruption policy*.

consideration
1. The price paid for a bond, calculated by discounting the future cash flows of the bond. Also see *bond*.
2. The fee that a bank is given in return for providing a guarantee.

consignee The term used by a goods carrier to describe a party who will apply for the release of cargo at a destination. The consignee is not necessarily the buyer or seller and can be a clearing agent. Also see *carrier; clearing agent*.

consistency concept An accounting concept whereby company accounts are prepared on a like basis from one year to the next. If changes are made to the accounting policy, firms often report in dual formats or highlight the differences in notes to the financial statements. Also see *like for like sales*.

consol A UK government gilt that is a form of consolidated stock. They usually pay coupons quarterly. Also see *consolidated stock; gilt*.

console Another word for an annuity. Also see *annuity*.

consolidated The process of combining results and analysing all a company's subsidiaries and associates. Also see *consolidated accounts*.

consolidated accounts A company that has a subsidiary is required by law to consolidate the financial accounts of the subsidiary into its own accounts. There are line items such as income attributable to outside shareholders in consolidated accounts that show the effects of the consolidation process. Also see *subsidiary*.

consolidated borrowings The aggregate outstanding principal, capital or nominal amount of borrowings of an entire group of companies, i.e. all the borrowings of all the subsidiaries have been combined into a single number. Also see *aggregate*.

consolidated financial statements See *consolidated accounts*.

consolidated stock Illiquid bonds or shares that are bought on the market and repackaged into a new financial instrument that will hopefully be traded more widely than the underlying asset and will therefore be more liquid. Also see *consol; illiquid; liquid*.

consolidation of control In the UK, when an entity controls between 30% and 50% of a company and it acquires more than another 1% in a year, it must make a mandatory offer for the remaining shares in the company. Also see *blue book; mandatory offer*.

consolidation of shares Combining a number of shares into a single share thereby raising the price of the remaining shares. This is the opposite of a share split. Also see *share split*.

consortium A group of entities that work together on a project. Consortiums are often set up in the form of joint ventures and are held in special-purpose vehicles. They are also set up to eliminate competition or to take advantage of complementary resources. Also see *joint venture; special-purpose vehicle*.

constant auction See *instant auction*.

constant dollar Adjustments made to prices to remove the effects of inflation. Also see *inflation; real price*.

constant maturity Calculation adjustments made to an interest-bearing instrument such as a treasury bill to give equivalent maturities. The Fed quotes constant maturity yields on a number of treasury bills so that they can be compared to other fixed-income instruments. Also see *treasury bill*.

constant maturity credit default swap (CMCDS) A credit default swap in which protection costs float according to changes in the credit environment and follow prevailing credit spreads. For example, in a two-year CMCDS the rate is set each month or quarter to the reference rate which is the CDS rate prevailing in the market at that point in time. Also see *credit default swap; reference rate*.

constant maturity swap (CMS) An interest rate swap where a floating interest rate is linked to a long-term rate. The fixed rate is fixed at inception of the deal and at reset dates and the floating interest rate leg is reset to the prevailing interest rate. Also see *floating interest rate; interbank rate; interest rate; interest rate swap; swap*.

constant maturity treasury rate (CMT) An index that is calculated by averaging the yield on US treasury bills adjusted to a constant maturity of one year. Also see *treasury bill; yield*.

constant proportion debt obligation (CPDO) A derivative-based instrument that borrows up to 15 times invested capital to sell credit default swaps against corporate debt indices such as the CDX and iTraxx Indices. For example, a special-purpose vehicle (SPV) issues commercial paper to an investor for $100. The $100 is invested in high-quality collateral assets such as government bonds and the SPV sells $1 500 of credit default swaps against a selected index such as CDX or iTraxx. The SPV is thus 15× geared. As with any geared product, CPDOs are highly susceptible to downturns in economic cycles. Also see *collateral; special-purpose vehicle*.

construction loan note (CLN) A short-term form of finance similar in nature to commercial paper that is used to fund construction projects. The notes are refinanced using longer term debt such as bonds and bank loans. Also see *commercial paper; project finance*.

consumer confidence index A survey of consumers detailing their attitudes to their present and future economic expectations.

consumer credit Short-term credit extended to the general public. Consumer credit is extended to the public through hire purchase agreements, store and credit cards. Also see *hire purchase*.

consumer instalment loan An American term for hire purchase.

consumer price index (CPI) The weighted price of a basket of goods and services purchased by an average household. CPI is usually expressed as a percentage with respect to a set base year. CPI data is released monthly in most countries and is used to quantify inflation. Monetary policy authorities use the CPI measure among others to set interest rates. In general, if the CPI goes up, then interest rates will follow. Because CPI is a measure of inflation, it can be used to calculate real price changes.

In the UK another measure called the retail price index or RPI is used more widely than the CPI. The RPI generally includes owner-occupied living costs and local property taxes while the CPI does not.

CPI data for South Africa is obtainable from Statistics South Africa (www.statssa.gov.za). CPI data for the US is obtainable from the US Bureau of Labour Statistics. Also see *base year; harmonised index of consumer prices; inflation; interest rate; real price; retail price index.*

consumption expenditure Expenditure by households on goods and services.

consumption theory A theory that postulates that the richer a person is, the more the person will save. This is generally true for the populations in countries like Germany and Japan. On average, the US does not conform to this theory as the richer Americans get, the more they tend to spend. This is evidenced by the expanding US current account deficit with simultaneous conditions of GDP growth. Also see *current account; gross domestic product.*

contagion The cross-country or cross-market transmission of economic shocks or trends. The transmission often goes beyond market fundamentals. Also see *correlation; fundamentals.*

contango A situation where a difference is possible between the future value and the current spot price of a commodity. The prices in succeeding delivery months are progressively higher than the nearer delivery months. For gold, the contango differential is usually close to the money market interest rate. A contango is the opposite of backwardation and is sometimes called forwardation.

The liquidity preference theory describes how yield curves are theoretically meant to be in contango by default. The graph below illustrates a normal yield curve that is in contango.

Also see *backwardation; forward differential; liquidity preference theory; normal yield curve; spot price.*

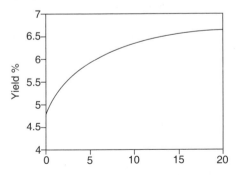

contango swap A yield curve swap entered into when the yield curve is in contango. Also see *contango; yield curve swap.*

contemporaneous effect Occurring in the same period of time. For example, a rise in interest rates is often contemporaneous with an increase in inflation. Also see *inflation; interest rate*.

contingency reserve Monies set aside and not allocated in advance to accommodate possible shortfalls in future years.

contingent A term used to indicate that an accounting provision needs to be made in case an income or loss event occurs in the future.

contingent annuity An annuity that starts payments only after a specific event. These may be used to cover the financial needs of dependents on the death of a breadwinner. Also see *life insurance*.

contingent convertible (CoCo) A convertible bond that can be converted only when the underlying share price reaches a predefined target. These securities are often used because dilutive effects are not reported under accounting rules until the share price hits the defined level. Also see *convertible debt bond*.

contingent equity A standby equity commitment that is made in the event that a project incurs cost overruns or anticipated debt-based finance cannot be raised for the project. Also see *backstop facility*.

contingent immunisation The process where a manager of a portfolio of assets is afforded the power to move assets into and out of a portfolio while making a profit. If losses are incurred, a point will be reached where the manager must halt his/her current strategy and lock in returns at the minimum level. The process of locking in the minimum return is called immunisation or hedging.

contingent liability
1. A possible obligation that arises from past events and whose existence will be confirmed only by the occurrence or non-occurrence of one or more uncertain future events not wholly within the control of the entity.
2. A present obligation that arises from past events but is not recognised because:
   - it is improbable that an outflow of resources embodying economic benefits will be required to settle the obligation
   - the amount of the obligation cannot be measured with sufficient reliability.

Contingent liabilities are not put on the balance sheet but appear as notes in the financial statements. Also see *balance sheet; financial statements*.

contingent value right (CVR) A CVR provides investors with the right to sell stocks for a fixed price and thus derive profits from volatility. A CVR also provides investors with the ability to hedge their losses. Typically used when the market undervalues a firm and management wants to take advantage of this belief. Under these conditions they may give a signal of undervaluation. Also see *hedge; put option; volatility*.

continuous auction See *instant auction*.

continuous compounding When money is compounded continuously in time and not at discrete points in time. Instead of using the formula:

$$FV = PV(1 + r)^t$$

derived mathematically from a geometric series compounding model, the time periods are made increasingly small and the following continuous compounding mathematical expression results:

$$FV = PVe^{rt}$$

where t = time; r = discount rate quoted for a single time period; FV = future value at time t_1; PV = present value at t_0 (the beginning).

Also see *discount rate; effective annual return; formula; future value; logarithmic return*.

continuous discounting When money is discounted continuously in time. Instead of using the discrete geometric series based formula given mathematically by:

$$PV = \frac{FV}{(1+r)^t}$$

the time periods are made increasingly small and the following equation results:

$$PV = FVe^{-rt}$$

where t = time; r = the discount rate quoted for a single time period; FV = value at time t_1 (the end point); PV = value at t_0 (the beginning).

Also see *discount rate; effective annual return; geometric series*.

continuous distribution A probability distribution for a continuous random variable. Also see *continuous random variable*.

continuous net settlement See *variation margin*.

continuous random variable A random variable with an interval, either finite or infinite, of a real number.

contract A voluntary agreement between two or more parties with clear economic consequences that parties have little, if any, discretion to avoid. Parties accept rights and obligations against one another under contracts. Contracts are usually enforceable by law. Contracts may take a variety of forms and need not always be in writing.

contract for difference (CFD) A financial contract whereby the seller (or writer) of the contract pays the difference between the current value of an asset and the value of the asset at a contracted future date. Settlements on CFDs are made in cash and not by physical delivery of an asset. CFDs allow traders to speculate on price movements without having full ownership and costs associated with the underlying assets. Also see *asset; non-deliverable forward; physical delivery; single stock future*.

contract grade The purity (grade) and quality of the physical commodity to be delivered into a futures contract.

contract guarantee insurance Financial instruments such a surety bond that are used to guarantee performance of a contract. Also see *surety bond*.

contraction risk The risk of the cash flows of a security being brought forward in time. This process will effectively shorten the duration. Also see *duration; reinvestment risk*.

contract month The month in which delivery of the asset under a futures contract is scheduled. Also called the delivery month.

contract note See *brokers note*.

contract option The option to scale back a project for a fixed price. It is a type of American-style put option. Also see *American style; option; put option*.

contract price The price at which a deal is struck or executed.

contract size The quantity of the underlying asset in an options contract. Also see *option*.

contract specification A document that specifies the conditions of a derivatives or futures contract. These documents are usually derived from standard templates

contractual obligation | control premium

developed by associations such as the International Swaps and Derivatives Association (ISDA) to ensure they are easily understood and traded. Also see *International Swaps and Derivatives Association*.

contractual obligation An act or course of action to which someone is legally bound by a contract.

contrary opinion An investor who feels that a view that is contrary to the current market view is a potentially profitable one.

contributed margin Revenue generated from sales of a particular product less variable costs required to produce the product. The contributed margin is effectively the amount by which profit increases if one more unit is sold.

contributed margin per unit See *contributed margin*.

contributed margin ratio A ratio that defines what proportion of sales is contributed by the product in question:

$$\text{contributed margin ratio} = \frac{\text{contributed margin}}{\text{sales}}$$

Also see *contributed margin*.

contribution arrears Monies owed to a pension or retirement fund that are a result of an employee or employer not making payments.

contribution holiday The term is usually used with reference to pension funds and describes a period when employers' and members' contributions are temporarily suspended. This usually occurs when the fund is in surplus. Also see *pension fund*.

contribution rate The percentage of an employee's salary that is contributed to a pension, retirement or medical aid fund. The rate varies from scheme to scheme and may be a flat rate.

contributory A person or entity that is liable for claims against a company in liquidation. Equity holders that own fully paid-up shares are not usually contributories.

contributory fund A pension fund where both the employer and employee contribute. Also see *pension fund*.

control The power to govern the financial and operating policies of an entity to obtain benefits from its activities. Control usually entails owning more than 50% of the voting rights associated with the shares in the company. One does not always need a minimum of 50% to have effective control.

controlling interest A controlling shareholder has a controlling interest in a company. A controlling interest is typically more than 35% of the share capital of listed companies or 50% of the share capital of unlisted firms. Also see *controlling shareholder*.

controlling shareholder A shareholder that has a significant degree of control over a company through voting rights. A controlling shareholder owns 50% or more of the voting rights. For listed companies with a diverse investor base, a controlling stake is considered to be a 35% or more holding of the voting rights. Also see *Securities Regulation Panel*.

control premium When a controlling stake is bought in a company, a control premium is usually factored into the price. The theory behind the control premium is that once control of the company has been gained, the controlling shareholders can run the business in any way they choose, including declaring special dividends, and initiate a range of activities that may advance their own cause.

convenience yield The price that a market will pay for the convenience of supply or cash flow certainty. For example, one may select a certain service provider at an increased cost knowing that the service provider will be extremely reliable.

convergence
1. The process of a futures contract price approaching the spot price of an asset as the delivery date approaches. Also see *spot price*.
2. The process of the current price of a bond approaching the par value of the bond as time approaches the date of maturity. Sometimes called the pull-to-par. Also see *bond*.

conversion See *conversion arbitrage*.

conversion arbitrage
1. An arbitrage transaction that involves buying a put and call option at the same strike price. The opportunity comes about due to mispricing of the puts and calls. The arbitrage condition leads to the theory of put call parity. Also see *arbitrage; call option; put-call parity*.
2. See *convertible arbitrage*.

conversion cycle See *cash conversion cycle*.

conversion discount See *conversion premium*.

conversion exposure The risk of adverse fluctuations in foreign exchange transactions.

conversion option The option written into some bonds and preference shares that gives the instrument holder the right to convert the instrument into equity. Also see *convertible debt/bond*.

conversion parity price The price that is paid for a convertible bond which is bought solely to exercise the conversion option and acquire the underlying asset. Also see *convertible debt/bond*.

conversion premium (CP) The amount by which the price of the underlying equity component of a convertible debt instrument has to increase for the embedded option to be in the money. The conversion premium is defined by:

$$\text{conversion premium (CP)} = \frac{X - S}{S}$$

where X = the exercise price; S = the current share price.

Also see *convertible debt/bond; embedded option*.

conversion price The price per share at which convertible debt can be exchanged for equity. This is effectively the strike price of the embedded conversion option. The conversion price will be stipulated in the original bond contract. To calculate the number of shares that will be received on conversion, the nominal value of the bond is divided by the conversion price. Also see *bond*.

conversion ratio (CR) The number of shares that can be bought with a single convertible bond. The CR is defined by:

$$\text{conversion ratio (CR)} = \frac{\text{principal}}{\text{conversion price}}$$

Also see *conversion price; convertible debt/bond*.

conversion value The value of a convertible security if it were to be converted into equity immediately.

convertibility The ability of residents to exchange a currency freely in the international foreign exchange markets. Also see *convertible currency*.

convertibility risk An investment risk that is associated with conversion options on convertible bonds and preference shares being exercised. Also see *convertible debt/bond; option; preference share*.

convertible arbitrage Options embedded in convertible debt embedded options are often cheaper than options available in the derivative market. Traders combine long positions in convertible bonds and positions in the underlying assets. The mismatch between embedded option pricing and regular market traded options presents an opportunity to make arbitrage profits. Also see *convertible debt/bond; long position*.

convertible bond See *convertible debt/bond*.

convertible currency A currency that is easily convertible to another in the international foreign exchange markets.

convertible debt/bond Debt that is convertible to equity. The holder has the right and not the obligation to convert the debt (usually a bond) into equity shares and there is effectively an embedded option in the debt contract. Convertibles are often issued when the market does not have an appetite for equity business risk but would like exposure to the upside benefits that the equity component has to offer. Conversion ratios are predefined before entering into the contract.

The parity of convertible debt is defined as the value of the equity component of the debt. This can be higher or lower than the current price of the bond. It is calculated by multiplying the conversion ratio by the underlying equity price. To calculate the number of shares that will be received on conversion, the nominal value of the bond is divided by the conversion price.

Convertible bonds are often subordinated to existing bonds and are normally unsecured. Issuers usually use call and put options to protect themselves from abnormal rises in equity prices and to cap the potential upside of the equity component.

Hedge funds often purchase convertible debt because embedded options are cheaper than other options available resulting in arbitrage opportunities. Convertible bonds become attractive options for raising money when volatility in the market creates more valuable embedded options.

Convertible bonds are traded over the counter and investors sometimes have some concerns about their liquidity. Also see *conversion parity price; conversion premium; conversion price; conversion ratio; convertible arbitrage; bond with warrants; embedded option; hedge fund; over the counter; subordinate; unsecured*.

convertible preference share A preference share where the holder has the right to exchange the share for other forms of security, usually ordinary shares, by a predetermined formula. Convertible preference shares may be convertible on election by the holder or may automatically convert at a predefined date. Also see *convertible debt; participating preference share; preference share; redeemable preference share; security*.

convertible subordinate note Convertible debt that is subordinate to other debt. Also see *convertible debt/bond; subordinate*.

convexity Bond duration is a measure of how bond prices change in response to interest rate changes. As interest rates change, the price response is not linear but rather a non-linear or convex function. Duration is classed as the first derivative and convexity the second derivative of the bond price function. It is better to use convexity when there are large changes in the yield of bonds and simple linear approximation is inaccurate. Convexity also gives an indication of the spread of future cash flows. Also see *bond; duration; interest rate*.

COO Chief operating officer.

cookie jarring The process where a company uses reserve accounts to smooth earnings. In good years extra funds are allocated to reserves and in bad years funds in the reserve accounts are used to smooth earnings. Companies may undertake these operations to post consistent dividends and meet expectations of investors. One method of achieving this is to purchase substantial levels of stock at year end and not account for that stock on the balance sheet. Also see *income smoothing; off balance sheet reserve*.

Cook's distance In regression, Cook's distance is a measure of the influence of each individual observation on the estimates of the regression model parameters. It expresses the distance that the vector of model parameter estimates with the *ith* observation removed lies from the vector of model parameter estimates based on all observations. Large values of Cook's distance indicate that the observation is influential.

cooling-off period A period after the close of a transaction when an investor is entitled to change his/her mind. Cooling-off periods in contracts are often legislated for products sold in an unsolicited manner to unsophisticated clients.

cooperative A business that is owned by members who each have the same voting rights irrespective of what share they own in the business. Cooperative businesses are run democratically and are usually used to further the group's social, economic or cultural needs.

co-opetition Two competing companies that cooperate to achieve cost or revenue benefits for both.

coordinator The coordinator of a syndicated loan is responsible for:

- advising the borrower on appropriate pricing and role allocation in the mandated lead arranger group
- drawing up a transaction timetable and ensuring that all banks adhere to it
- assisting the borrower and drafting a term sheet to distribute to the lead bank group for further negotiation
- coordinating the syndication process and providing regular updates to the borrower
- acting as a single point of contact for the borrower and providing guidance on the syndication process
- press management.

Also see *mandated lead arranger; term sheet*.

COP The Columbian peso divided into 100 centavos.

copyright A set of rights enabling the holder to retain the exclusivity to use information, a particular expression or a unique idea.

core earnings Earnings from operations that have been adjusted for one-off expenses or revenue items. For example, if a subsidiary was sold and a profit made, the core earnings number would not include the profit attributable to the sale.

core inflation A measure of inflation that excludes certain items subject to volatile price movements. Energy and food prices are usually the excluded variables in this measure. Core inflation eliminates products that are prone to temporary price shocks because these shocks can diverge from the overall trend of inflation and give false measures. Also see *consumer price index; CPIX; headline inflation; inflation*.

corner the market Purchasing enough of a particular asset to allow the price of the asset to be manipulated. This can be done more easily in the futures market where the cost of entry is lower. Cornering the market is an illegal practice. Sometimes called rigging the market. Also see *position limit*.

corporate bond A form of debt instrument issued by a company that is usually listed on an exchange. Often called a debenture. South African corporates list corporate bonds on the Bond Exchange of South Africa. Also see *debenture*.

corporate inflation-linked security An inflation-linked bond issued by a corporate. Also see *inflation-linked bond; treasury inflation-protected security*.

Corporation for Public Deposits (CPD) A wholly-owned subsidiary of the South African Reserve Bank that intermediates mainly between government, the foreign sector and public sector borrowers. These institutions include pension funds, insurance companies and the Public Investment Corporation. From time to time the CPD lends to other institutions such as the Land Bank. Also see *Public Investment Corporation; South African Reserve Bank*.

corporatisation The transfer of state-owned businesses to private companies. Sometimes called privatisation. Also see *privatisation*.

correction When the price of a security in the market has been unsustainably high, the price may correct downwards to the fair value price. A correction is the opposite of a rally. Also see *rally*.

correlation The interdependence of variables or data. The data may include more than one variable and is often described quantitatively by the correlation coefficient. Also see *correlation coefficient*.

correlation coefficient (Pearson product-moment correlation coefficient) A dimensionless measure of the interdependence of two variables. The correlation coefficient lies in the interval from −1 to +1, with zero indicating the absence of correlation but not necessarily the independence of the two variables. The most common mathematical form of the correlation coefficient used in practice is:

$$r = \frac{\text{covariance}(x, y)}{\sigma_x \sigma_y}$$

where σ = standard deviation.

corridor There is a corridor in which adjustments are not made when calculating the losses or gains for pension and other investment funds. Also see *pension fund; unrealised actuarial loss/gain*.

cost The amount of cash or cash equivalent paid or the fair value of a consideration given to acquire an asset. The amount attributed to that asset when initially recognised is in accordance with the specific requirements of accounting standards. Also see *asset; cash equivalent; fair value; International Financial Reporting Standards*.

cost accounting An accounting practice where inputs are measured at cost. Cost accounting focuses companies on driving the costs of production down and hence increasing profitability.

Cost accounting is an accounting form that is not used to publish financial data but is used internally for management purposes in a form called management accounting.

cost basis The purchase price of an asset including all commissions and other acquisition costs. The cost basis is used to determine capital gains tax. Also see *acquisition; capital gains tax*.

cost centre A division or subsidiary of a company that does not generate revenue directly. Cost centres may provide internal support or beneficiate products before revenue is collected from the sale of goods or a service.

cost method A method of accounting for an investment whereby the investment is recognised at cost. The investor recognises income from the investment only to the extent that the investor receives distributions from accumulated profits arising after the date of acquisition. Distributions received in excess of such profits are regarded as a recovery of investment and are recognised as a reduction of the cost of the investment. Also see *acquisition*.

cost model of impairment Used for property, plant and equipment (PPE), the asset is carried at cost. This model gives a better return on equity (ROE) than carrying the asset at revolved amounts. Also see *asset; property, plant and equipment; return on equity*.

cost of capital The rate of return required to compensate investors, both shareholders and providers of debt, for bearing risk when providing capital. There are many methods used to calculate the costs of capital with the most widely used being the weighted average cost of capital (WACC). Also see *weighted average cost of capital*.

cost of carry The cost of holding an asset, financial instrument or position. For example, if an investor borrows money at a rate of 10% to invest in shares that return 12%, he/she would have a 10% cost of carry and would make a 2% profit. Also see *cost of carry model*.

cost of carry model The cost of carry is the cost of holding any asset for a defined period of time while entering a financial transaction. The concept is illustrated below with a forward commodity pricing model. The forward price of any commodity is defined by:

$F = Se^{(r+s-c)t}$

where F = the forward price; S = the spot price; e = the base of the natural logarithms; r = the risk-free interest rate; s = the storage cost; c = the convenience yield; t = the time to delivery of the forward contract expressed as a fraction of one year.

For currencies there is no storage cost and c is interpreted as the foreign interest rate. Currency prices should be quoted as domestic units per foreign units in the above expression. Also see *convenience yield; forward contract dealing; interest rate parity; spot price*.

cost of conversion Costs directly related to the units of production, such as direct labour, together with a systematic allocation of fixed and variable production overheads that are incurred in converting materials into finished goods.

cost of debt The return that lenders require on a borrower's debt. Cost of debt is measured by the interest rate that lenders must pay on any new borrowings in which case it is sometimes called the marginal or incremental cost of debt. Also see *cost of equity; weighted average cost of capital*.

cost of equity (COE) The return that equity investors require on their investments in a company. COE can be calculated by using the dividend growth model or the security market line (capital asset pricing model) approach.

If $P_0 = \dfrac{D_1}{COE - g}$ then $COE = \dfrac{D_1}{P_0} + g$

There are other methods of calculating the cost of equity capital such as the beta and Bludgeon approach. Also see *beta approach; Bludgeon approach; capital asset pricing model; cost of debt; dividend growth model; security market line; weighted average cost of capital.*

cost of funds
1. The interest charges that financial institutions must pay for the use of money. For banks these are often the interbank rates such as JIBAR or LIBOR for shorter term transactions. Also see *interbank rate.*
2. The total cost of funds to a company. Also see *weighted average cost of capital.*

cost of inventory All costs of purchase, costs of conversion and other costs incurred in bringing the inventory to its present location and current condition.

cost of purchase The purchase price, import duties and other taxes (other than those subsequently recoverable by the entity from the taxing authorities), transport, handling and other costs directly attributable to the acquisition of an asset. Trade discounts, rebates and other similar items are deducted in determining the cost of purchase.

cost of risk The costs associated with an event that may cause a loss. These costs may be quantified in the form of insurance premiums.

cost of sales The cost of producing an item for sale. The cost of sales may be the inputs required to produce a product or the cost of purchasing a finished product for resale. Sales less cost of sales gives the gross profit of a business. Also see *variable cost expense.*

cost push See *cost push inflation theory.*

cost push inflation theory If aggregate demand exceeds aggregate supply because the supply has been reduced, then the general level of prices in an economy will rise to accommodate the effective excess demand. Factors such as limitations on raw materials and increases in the costs of production such as wage hikes or strike action may influence supply. Also see *aggregate demand; aggregate supply; consumer price index; demand pull inflation theory.*

costs to sell The incremental costs directly attributable to the disposal of an asset (or disposal group), excluding finance costs and income tax expense.

cost to company (CTC) The total cost to a company to employ a person. Pension and medical fund contributions as well as other perks are included in the cost to company.

cost to income ratio An efficiency measure widely used in the financial industry. The ratio is defined as:

$$\text{cost to income ratio} = \dfrac{\text{operating expenses}}{\text{operating income}}$$

The ratio gives a good indication of how costs are changing compared to income. The lower the ratio is, the more profitable the company is. Absa Bank's cost to income ratio in 2007 was 51.8% and Standard Bank's for the same period was 51.6%. The cost to income ratio is sometimes also called the efficiency ratio or expense ratio. Also see *claims ratio; credit loss ratio; operating margin.*

cost volume profit A tool to analyse the impact of volatility. Also see *volatility*.

co-trending See *common trends*.

countercyclical Firms or investments that do well when other firms and the economy in general are doing poorly. Gold as an investment often falls into this class as investors invest in gold as an asset class if there is a worldwide economic downturn, significant world inflation or worldwide political uncertainty. Also see *cyclical company*.

counterparty The party to a financial transaction.

counterparty limit The maximum exposure a bank is willing to take against a single client.

counterparty risk The risk that a participant in a financial transaction will default on an obligation. Clearing houses have been established to manage these risks for the trading of derivative instruments. Banks and other lending institutions spend considerable time and effort quantifying and managing counterparty risk. Also see *clearing house; derivative; Herstatt risk*.

countertrade See *barter*.

countervailing duty A duty levied on imports to provide subsidies for exports of particular goods or services.

country limit The exposure limit a bank is willing to take for all combined public and private enterprises in a specific country.

country risk Country risk usually arises from international and domestic political risk. Investors face risks such as changes in expropriation of funds and assets and war. The risk profile of a country may have the effect that investors seek additional premiums to their local market. Also see *country risk premium*.

country risk premium (CRP) When investing in a foreign market, the risk profile of that market may have the effect that investors seek an additional premium to their local market. There are various methods used to determine this premium:
- default risk spreads or credit spreads
- relative equity market standard deviations
- combined market risk premium approach.

The CRP is used to determine the cost of equity in foreign markets. Also see *beta approach; combined market risk premium approach; default risk spread; market risk premium; relative equity market standard deviation*.

coupon The stated interest payment on a bond. It is usually quoted as a percentage of the principal. Long dated bonds in South Africa pay coupons on a semi-annual basis. Also see *bond; principal; semi-annual*.

coupon bond Another term used for bearer bond. Also see *bearer bond*.

coupon equivalent rate (CER) The effective yield on a zero coupon bond if it were to pay a coupon. Calculated with the following formula:

$$\text{coupon equivalent rate (CER)} = \frac{\text{current price} - \text{principal value}}{\text{current price}} \times \frac{365}{\text{time to maturity}}$$

Sometimes called the coupon equivalent yield.

coupon equivalent yield (CEY) See *coupon equivalent rate*.

coupon pass The process where central banks purchase coupon bearing instead of discount securities in the market through open market operations. When central banks purchase discount securities the term used is bill pass. Also see *central bank; open market operations*.

coupon rate The coupon of a bond divided by the principal, face or par value of the bond.

$$\text{coupon rate} = \frac{\text{annual total coupon}}{\text{principal value}}$$

Also see *bond; principal*.

coupon yield See *coupon rate*.

covariance Covariance describes how two variables vary relative to one another. For example, the covariance on the returns of two shares A and B is given by:

$$\text{Covar}(R_A; R_B) = \sum_{i=1}^{S}(R_{Ai} - \overline{R}_A)(R_{Bi} - \overline{R}_B)$$

$$\text{Covar}(R_A; R_B) = \rho_{A,B}\,\sigma_A\,\sigma_B$$

where R_A = return on share A; R_B = return on share B; $\overline{R}$ = mean; $\rho_{A,B}$ = correlation coefficient.

Also see *correlation coefficient; arithmetic mean; variance*.

covenant Terms and conditions imposed by lenders on borrowers. A covenant usually governs how indebted the company is allowed to become and how it should maintain earnings to cover debt interest obligations. Lenders do not have voting rights in the companies they lend to like equity holders do and hence need covenants to provide some level of control over their investment. Covenants are usually associated with banks rather than bond debt. Also see *affirmative covenant; bond; capital structure; financial covenant; negative covenant*.

covenant light/lite A debt or loan agreement with few covenants that are not too restrictive. It has bond-like incurrence covenants and fewer maintenance covenants than normal loans. These instruments are bought by non-banking institutions such as hedge funds that do not have the manpower or inclination to monitor all the covenants. Also see *covenant; hedge fund; incurrence covenant; maintenance covenant*.

cover
1. The degree to which insurance payouts will cover a loss event.
2. In project finance, cover is the degree to which the debt service cover ratio exceeds 1.0×. Also see *debt service cover ratio; project finance*.
3. The value of securities or shares used as collateral for loans in excess of the value borrowed. For example, if lenders seek 2× cover they require R2 worth of shares for every R1 advanced.

coverage covenant A financial covenant on a loan that requires the borrower to maintain a minimum level of cash flow or earnings relative to expenses and more often debt and interest expense. The covenant may also require that the borrower maintain sufficient cash flow for fixed charges and capital expenditure. Often measured as the interest cover ratio or debt service coverage ratio (DSCR). Also see *cure right; debt service cover ratio; financial covenant; interest cover*.

covered bond A bond backed by cash flows from mortgages or other cash-generating portfolios. Covered bonds are effectively a form of securitisation where ownership of the debt is not transferred to a special-purpose vehicle (SPV) and the debt remains on the balance sheet of the issuer. Also see *balance sheet; pfandbrief; securitisation; special-purpose vehicle.*

covered call When an underlying asset is purchased and combined with selling a call option. If the option expires out the money, the writer keeps the premium and therefore can have enhanced returns in stable markets. The downside is that because the underlying assets are held, large losses can accrue. Sometimes called a portfolio enhancement. Also see *call option; out the money.*

covered interest arbitrage An arbitrage or carry trade opportunity that exists when a risk-free profit can be made by investing in a foreign market with a higher interest rate and covering exchange rate risk by buying currency forward. Also see *arbitrage; carry trade; exchange rate risk; interest rate.*

covered interest rate parity The covered interest rate parity proposition states that the interest rate difference between two countries' currencies is equal to the percentage difference between the forward exchange rate and the spot exchange rate. Simply put, one can cover oneself against interest rate differences by buying currency forward.

$$(1 + i_0) = \frac{F}{S} (1 + i_C)$$

where i_0 = the domestic interest rate; i_C = the interest rate in the foreign country; F = the forward exchange rate between domestic currency (0) and foreign currency (c).

One can derive the above by solving the following problem. If a person invests $1 in South Africa at a 1:10 exchange rate expecting the future exchange rate to go to 1:12, he/she needs 32% interest in South Africa to obtain a return of 10% in dollar terms.

Covered interest rate parity explains why currency exchange rates are prone to significant movements in the event of interest rate changes. Also see *cost of carry model; interest rate; spot market; uncovered interest rate parity.*

covered option See *covered call; covered put.*

covered put Selling or shorting a put option while taking a short position in the underlying asset. This is effectively the same strategy as selling a call option. Also see *call option; put option; short position.*

covered warrant A call option or put option. Also see *call option; put option.*

CP See *commercial paper.*

CPD See *Corporation for Public Deposits.*

CPDO See *constant proportion debt obligation.*

CPI See *consumer price index.*

CPIX CPIX = consumer price index (CPI) – volatile food elements – interest rates. Interest rates are removed so that the CPIX can be used to measure the effect of interest rates on inflation. Also see *consumer price index; core inflation; inflation; interest rate.*

CPR See *conditional prepayment rate.*

CPS Clearing processing system.

CR See *conversion ratio.*

crack spread The profit that an oil refinery can earn by refining crude oil into other products. The term crack is used to describe the process of separating chemical components from crude oil.

crawling peg A currency system adopted by a country where exchange rates are fixed for small intervals of time. Changes are made gradually and in a transparent manner. This fixes market expectations and maintains a degree of exchange rate flexibility. It involves establishing a par value around which the rate can vary up to a given per cent. The par value is revised regularly according to a formula determined by the authorities. Crawling pegs are adopted to address the need for exchange rates to adjust and are better than fixed rates which are often prone to serious misalignments. Crawling pegs can minimise the potentially negative effects associated with speculative flows of capital. Fixed and crawling pegs have the downside of being considered an inefficient alternative to the free play of market forces. Sometimes called a sliding peg. Also see *clean float; fixed exchange rate; free float; managed float*.

creative destruction A concept in economics popularised by Joseph Schumpeter whereby it is postulated that in capitalist economic systems the processes of change and revolution of the economy comes from within. New companies and competitors emerge that challenge the dominance of the existing players and ensure that the old and inefficient are replaced by the innovative and new.

credit The acceptance of cash or an asset today along with the promise to make payment for that asset or cash at a date in the future. Also see *asset*.

credit agreement An agreement between banks participating in a syndicated loan that governs how much each bank in the syndication is willing to lend. Also see *common terms agreement; intercreditor agreement; syndicated loan*.

credit arbitrage When the credit spread of a debt instrument differs in two markets, interest rate swaps can be used to profit and the credit spreads will converge. Also see *interest rate swap*.

credit ceiling A legislative limit on commercial banks to govern money supply by restricting the quantity of loans they can issue. Also see *money supply*.

credit cliff A set of circumstances related to credit extended to a company that can cause an already underperforming company to get into even more financial trouble. A ratings downgrade may constitute the triggering event that in turn triggers covenants or redemptions and puts the 'squeeze' on the lender. Also see *covenant*.

credit committee A committee in a bank that must approve all transactions with nominal values larger than a given threshold. Lending conditions and pricing quoted to the prospective borrower are firm only after a credit committee has passed approval.

credit conversion factor (CCF) Under Basel II, credit conversion factors are applied to off balance sheet commitments and are used to adjust the exposure at default (EAD). The conversion factors used depend on the Basel II implementation approach adopted by the relevant bank. Under the standardised approach of Basel II, the credit conversion factors are prescribed values and under the advanced approach, banks may use internal ratings based methods of determining the CCFs. Also see *Basel; exposure at default*.

credit crunch A situation where lenders are excessively cautious and not keen to lend even to the most creditworthy of borrowers. In a credit crunch, banks are often not prepared to lend to one another in the interbank market.

credit default swap (CDS) An agreement where one party promises to compensate the other party if a bond or lender defaults on a debt obligation. A CDS protects a buyer against a credit-related event and is quoted as a spread. For example, to purchase credit protection against a $10 million exposure at a spread of 0.20%, the purchaser of the CDS will pay $20 000 per annum.

A CDS is effectively an insurance premium but is termed a swap as counterparties exchange payments. One party pays a premium and the other pays up in the event of a defined default.

CDSs are settled by cash or by deliverable obligation in the event of the underlying credit defaulting. If a predefined credit event occurs, then a payment in cash will be made to the purchaser of the swap. The event usually relates to a predefined asset or lender and includes bankruptcy, insolvency, receivership, winding up, material adverse restructuring of debt or failure to meet payment obligations when due.

CDSs are used to manage credit risk. Parties use them to diversify market risk, country risk and exposure to particular financial assets. Instruments such as credit spread options which are not defined in terms of specific credit events are also used to manage credit risk.

CDSs have become more widely traded than their underlying debt obligations as they are standardised, flexible and more frequently traded. Underlying cash bonds are often difficult to sell short and supply is finite and often limited. Credit default swaps are over-the-counter instruments.

Due to being defined as a swap and having the economic effect of being an insurance premium, the market for CDS instruments is not subject to the same regulations that the insurance industry is. Also see *credit risk; credit spread option; deliverable obligation; over the counter; sell short; spread; swap*.

credit default swap index (CDX) An index made up of credit default swaps. These indices are used to hedge or insure against default on a basket of corporate names, typically sub-investment grade. The cost of purchasing this basket protection is expressed as a spread, for example 0.20%. The spread is multiplied by the value insured to obtain the overall cost or premium to purchase the credit protection. For example, to insure against a $10 million exposure at 0.20%, it will cost $20 000 per annum.

CDS indices are liquid and well traded. They trade on small bid-offer spreads and so are cheaper instruments to purchase than a host of separate CDSs to hedge risk. When a CDS index spread increases, it is an indication that investors are more concerned about the chances of default.

There are two main CDS index products, namely iTraxx (European and world) and CDX (American and emerging markets). Also see *credit default swap; emerging market; liquid*.

credit derivative A derivative in which the payoff is related to the underlying entities' payment performance. A credit derivative is an over-the-counter instrument that separates the credit risk of an entity or instrument and transfers that risk to another party. Also see *credit risk; derivative*.

credit enhancement
1. Using multiple tranches to sell a debt asset. The tranches are structured with varying levels of seniority and offer a debt cushion. A debt asset is broken into a series of credit investments with different risk and reward characteristics usually manufactured through varying levels of subordination (seniority). The securitisation process uses features of credit enhancement. Also see *debt cushion; securitisation*.

2. Credit enhancement can also involve guarantees by third parties, letters of credit, debt reserve funds and contingent equity.

credit enhancement facility (CEF) A facility that is deeply subordinated and that acts as a first loss or second loss portion in a securitisation vehicle. The facility can be provided by a sponsor and be in the form of cash. Also see *liquidity facility; subordinate*.

credit event A bankruptcy, acceleration of a loan, default, failure to pay, a repudiation, moratorium or restructuring and a potential series of other factors. Also see *acceleration; bankruptcy; default; repudiation*.

credit extension See *private sector credit extension*.

credit line An arrangement between a lender and a borrower whereby unsecured credit is given or made available to the borrower for a specified period of time. Sometimes called a line of credit. Also see *credit line; revolving credit facility; unsecured*.

credit-linked note (CLN) A financial debt instrument that is created through a special-purpose vehicle (SPV). The SPV holds assets such as bonds or loans that are purchased through the proceeds of the issue of debt securities. The interest payments or coupons received from the debt are used to pay the coupons on the debt issued. At maturity the investors receive the par value of their assets unless there has been a default. The SPV will often purchase credit default swaps to mitigate this risk of default on the underlying debt. In the event of a default, investors receive the recovered value of the underlying debt assets. Also see *collateralised debt obligation; credit default swap; special-purpose vehicle*.

credit loss ratio A ratio used for banks or collateralised debt obligation (CDO) structures that indicates the credit-related losses to total debt book or par value of issued CDOs:

$$\text{credit loss ratio} = \frac{\text{credit losses}}{\text{total debt book}}$$

Sometimes the credit loss ratio is referred to as the default rate. Also see *collateralised debt obligation; cost to income ratio; default rate; non-performing loan*.

credit market A market in which debt instruments such as bonds and loans are sold.

creditor An entity that monies are due to as a result of services or goods delivered. Loan and bond providers are also classed as creditors. Creditors usually appear on the balance sheet under the current liabilities section. Often called trade creditors or accounts payable. Also see *creditor; balance sheet; current liability*.

creditors days See *creditor settlement*.

creditor settlement A measurement of the number of days on average that a company takes to settle its accounts, defined by:

$$\text{creditor settlement} = \frac{\text{accounts payable}}{\left[\frac{\text{cost of sales}}{365}\right]}$$

Companies always try to maximise this ratio to free up cash for other working capital purposes. Also called creditors days. Also see *debtors days; inventory days*.

credit rating Credit rating agencies such as Moody's assign long-term credit ratings of Aaa, Aa, A, Baa, Ba, B, Caa, Ca and C where Aaa is the lowest risk debt. Standard & Poor (S&P) and Fitch assign credit ratings of AAA, AA, A, BBB, BB, B, CCC, CC, C,

CI, R, SD and D where AAA is the lowest risk debt. Anything above BBB– or Baa3 is considered to be investment grade. Fitch and S&P use a + and – operator that gives further credit ranking layers where Moody's uses the 1, 2 and 3 operators.

Short-term rankings for Moody's are P1, P2 and P3 which are superior, medium risk and below prime respectively. Short-term ratings for S&P are A–1; A–2, A–3, B, C and D where A–1 is extremely strong and D in default. Fitch uses F1, F2, F3, B, C and D for short-term rankings.

The following table approximately equates the Moody's, S&P and Fitch long-term ranking metrics:

S&P and Fitch	Moody's
AAA	Aaa
AA	Aa2
AA–	Aa3
A	A2
A–	A3
BBB+	Baa1
BBB	Baa2
BBB–	Baa3
BB+	Ba1
BB	Ba2

S&P and Fitch	Moody's
BB–	Ba3
B+	B1
B	B2
B–	B3
CCC+	Caa1
CCC	Caa2
CCC–	Caa3
CC	Ca
C	C
D	D

The following table approximately equates short-term ratings:

S&P	Moody's	Fitch
A–1	P1	F1
A–2	P1	F2
A–3	P2	F3
B	P2	B
C	P3	C
D	P3	D

Companies obtain a credit rating because it:
- allows them to raise debt more cost effectively
- allows them access to wider international financial markets
- attracts investors with investment mandates for specific credit ratings
- gives the markets a degree of confidence in their creditworthiness
- makes complex financial transactions a little simpler
- can give them a competitive advantage.

Also see *default; investment grade*.

credit rating agency An institution that rates the creditworthiness of companies and corporations. Well-known agencies are Standard and Poor, Moody's and Fitch IBCA. Credit rating agencies are independent and charge the company being rated a fee to undertake the ratings process. Also see *credit rating*.

credit report The investigation into the history and financial position of an entity seeking a loan.

credit risk A credit risk arises from the risk that a counterparty that has entered into a credit agreement may default or not meet its obligations timeously. Also see *default; liquidity risk; operational risk; timeously*.

credit spread The difference between risk-free debt, such as government bonds, and more risky debt such as corporate debt. The credit spread between countries gives an indication of the country risk premium. Asset swap margins give a good measure of relative credit spreads. Also see *asset swap margin; country risk premium; government bond*.

credit spread option An option based on the credit spread of a particular entity. The option defines payment or payment profiles on the underlying credit spread. These instruments can be used to provide a degree of protection against credit risk although, unlike credit default swaps, they are not defined against specific credit events. They can be useful when credit spreads widen without specific credit events occurring. Also see *credit default swap; credit risk; credit spread*.

credit support annex (CSA) A form of credit protection used in interest rate swap contracts and other derivatives that sets the rules for the posting of collateral. A CSA formally documents the collateral arrangements between counterparties and is usually done through a master outline published by the International Settlement and Dealers Association (ISDA). Issuers of the derivative contracts must ensure that the contracts are legally binding and obtain credit approval from a bank. Also see *collateral; interest rate swap*.

credit support letter A letter drafted by a bank that is non-binding and that indicates potential financial support for a bid or particular financial transaction. The letter is indicative only and the transaction still has to go through the bank's internal approval process. The letter is effectively a statement of intent.

credit swap See *credit default swap*.

credit union A financial institution owned as a cooperative by its members. The owners of the union are effectively the account holders. Also see *cooperative; mutual bank; post bank*.

creditworthy An entity with a low probability of default (good credit quality) that can be extended credit.

critical region When hypothesis testing, the critical region is the rejection area where the null hypothesis will be rejected. Also see *hypothesis testing; null hypothesis*.

critical value The point or boundary at which a region becomes a critical region in hypothesis testing. Also see *critical region; hypothesis testing*.

cross acceleration If a borrower goes into default on any other debt obligation and the lenders of those loans choose to accelerate them, then cross-acceleration clauses in a separate loan agreement can force acceleration. Also see *acceleration; default*.

cross-border trading Trading between counterparties in different countries.

cross collateral Participants in a transaction pooling collateral. If there should be a default, the lender will have recourse to each of the individual collateral-providing counterparties. Also see *collateral; joint and several guarantee liability; recourse*.

cross-currency interest rate swap The combination of a currency swap and an interest rate swap. A specified amount of money bearing a floating interest rate in a particular currency is swapped for a specified amount of money bearing a fixed interest rate in another currency. Also see *currency swap; floating interest rate; interest rate swap; swap*.

cross default A clause in a debt agreement such as a loan document that indicates that if the borrower goes into default on any other debt obligation, then they automatically go into default on the debt agreement in question.

In the event of default on a loan, lenders can have significant influence and control over the borrower's affairs. Cross-default clauses are therefore included so that when loans go into default and certain lenders are given further influence over the borrower, all other lenders are afforded an equal degree of influence.

To reduce the impacts of cross-default clauses, borrowers may seek to address failures as mandatory prepayment events or negotiate grace periods in which to remedy events of default. Also see *cross acceleration; default; event of default*.

crossed cheque A cheque that has double lines drawn on it to indicate that the cheque cannot be cashed and must be paid into a bank account as opposed to an open cheque that can cashed. Also see *cheque; open cheque*.

cross elasticity Substitute products alter demand. For example, if DVD player prices go up, fewer players will be purchased and thus fewer DVD disks will be purchased. The elasticity of demand is positive if the goods are substitutes (more elastic) and negative if they are complementary (less elastic). Also see *elastic*.

cross listing See *dual listing*.

crossover credit An entity that has a credit rating just shy of investment grade. For example, a fallen angel may have a credit rating downgrade from investment grade to one notch below investment grade. Also see *credit rating; fallen angel; investment grade*.

crossover index A credit default swap index of crossover credit grade CDS instruments. Also see *credit default swap; credit default swap index; crossover credit*.

crossover rate The rate at which two mutually exclusive projects have equal net present value (NPV). When plotting the NPV versus the discount rate, the point at which the curves of the mutually exclusive projects cross over is the crossover point. The crossover point makes the NPV of both projects equal. Also see *discount rate; mutually exclusive; net present value*.

crossover refunded The revenue streams that are used to secure debt obligations are used to repay those debt obligations. Also see *general obligation bond*.

cross rate The exchange rate between two currencies, neither of which are in US dollars. Cross rates can be quoted directly or manufactured by using dollar-based rates of the constituent currencies.

cross security Security pledged in a financial transaction that has been pledged in another lending transaction.

crude oil Oil pumped out of the ground in unprocessed form. It is measured and sold in barrels. Also see *barrel*.

CSA See *credit support annex*.

CSC See *current service cost*.

CSCE Coffee, Sugar and Cocoa Exchange.

CSD See *central securities depository*.

CSFB Leveraged Loan Index A secondary market leveraged loan index used in the US. This index is created and published by Credit Suisse First Boston.

ct See *carat*.

CTC See *cost to company*.

CTD See *cheapest to deliver*.

CU Confidentiality undertaking. Also see *non-disclosure agreement*.

cubic spline A mathematic formulation of a spline of degree 3 with continuity C^2. The second derivatives of the spline polynomials are set equal to zero at the endpoints of the interval of interpolation. Also see *spline*.

cum dividend Shares trade cum dividend when the purchaser of the share is entitled to the next dividend payment. A share trades cum dividend between the dividend declaration date and before the record date. Also see *ex dividend; record date*.

cum interest The purchaser of a bond is entitled to the next coupon payment because the bond is traded between the last payment date and the register closing date for coupon payment. The seller therefore sells the bond with the accrued interest included in the sale price. All-in price = clean price + accrued interest. Also see *accrued interest; all-in price; bond; clean price; coupon; cum dividend; ex interest*.

cumulant In probability theory and statistics, a random variable X has an expected value $\mu = E(X)$ and a variance $\sigma^2 = E((X - i)^2)$. These are the first two cumulants: $\mu = \kappa_1$ and $\sigma^2 = \kappa_2$. The cumulants κ_n are defined by the cumulant-generating function:

$$g(t) = \log(E(\exp(tX))) = \sum_{n=1}^{\infty} \frac{K_n}{n!} = \mu t + \frac{\sigma^2 t^2}{2} + ...$$

Also see *variance*.

cumulative dividend If dividend payments on cumulative preference shares are missed, the payments accumulate and will be paid before ordinary shareholders when the company is able to do so. Also see *cumulative preference share; dividend*.

cumulative preference share A preference share whose dividend payments accumulate if the company is unable to make payments. The payment accumulates until such a time as payment can be made. Cumulative preference shareholders may be afforded voting rights in a company should the company miss a dividend payment. Also see *preference share*.

cure period The period under which a cure right is applicable. Also see *cure right*.

cure right An option in a loan agreement that allows specific remedies to avoid a breach of a covenant. Injecting shareholders funds into an EBITDA measure for leverage covenants and coverage covenants is a good example of cure rights. Often called an equity cure right when shareholders inject equity funds or subordinated loans. Also see *covenant; coverage covenant; EBITDA; equity cure; leverage covenant; shareholders capital*.

currency Money in public hands. Also see *M1; M2; M3*.

currency carry trade See *carry trade*.

currency convertibility The ability to exchange one currency for another. Not all currencies are equally convertible as governments have different levels of foreign reserves. Some large financial transactions, particularly in smaller markets such as in South Africa, may be affected by currency convertibility and may therefore require relevant exchange control approvals. Also see *foreign reserves*.

currency devaluation The decrease in the buying power of a local currency in foreign markets. The term is often used with reference to the process of monetary authorities actively devaluing the currency. Also see *currency revaluation*.

currency fluctuations Movements, usually in the short term, that are sharper than the overall trend in exchange rates. Also see *exchange rate*.

currency revaluation An increase in the buying power of a local currency on foreign markets. The term is often used with reference to the process of monetary authorities actively appreciating the currency. Also see *currency devaluation*.

currency risk See *exchange rate risk*.

currency swap Two parties agree to swap payments based on different currencies. For example, at the end of every year for five years one party agrees to pay €100 to a counterparty and the counterparty agrees to pay $700 in return. Exchange rate differences account for the profit and loss incurred. Currency swaps can be used to convert debt instrument cash flows into alternate currencies. Most often the currencies bear interest at fixed rates. If the interest rates are floating interest rates, then the currency swap is called a basis swap. If one is fixed and the other floating, it is called a cross-currency interest rate or basis swap. Currency swaps take the form of interest rate swaps where interest payment cash flows are swapped against one another in different currencies. Also see *basis swap; cross-currency interest rate swap; interest rate; floating interest rate; swap*.

current account
1. A national account that records the flow of money resulting from a country's international trade of goods and services:

   Balance on current account = trade balance + service receipts + income receipts − service payments − income payments + current transfers

   The current account has two subaccounts, the trade and service accounts. Also see *balance of payments; financial account; trade balance*.

2. A bank account, sometimes called a cheque account, that account holders use for day-to-day banking transactions. Current accounts attract low interest rates.

current asset An asset listed on a company's balance sheet which satisfies any of the following criteria:
- It is expected to be realised, or is intended for sale or consumption, in the entity's normal operating cycle.
- It is held primarily for the purpose of being traded.
- It is expected to be realised within 12 months of the balance sheet date.
- It is cash or a cash equivalent (as defined in IAS 7 cash flow statements) unless it is restricted from being exchanged or used to settle a liability for at least 12 months after the balance sheet date.
- It generally has a life of less than one year.

Also see *asset; balance sheet; current liability; liability*.

current assets ratio A ratio that measures the short-term liquidity of a company and is defined by:

$$\text{current assets ratio} = \frac{\text{current assets}}{\text{total liabilities}}$$

If the ratio is very low, the company in question may have difficulties in servicing debt obligations.

current cost
1. The amount of cash or cash equivalents that would have to be paid if the same or an equivalent asset was acquired to replace the existing asset.
2. The undiscounted amount of cash or cash equivalents that would be required to settle a debt obligation.

Also see *asset; cash equivalent*.

current liability A liability that appears on a company's balance sheet that is classified as current when it satisfies any of the following criteria:
- It is expected to be settled in the entity's normal operating cycle.
- It is held primarily for the purpose of being traded.
- It is due to be settled within 12 months of the balance sheet date.
- The entity does not have an unconditional right to defer settlement of the liability for at least 12 months after the balance sheet date.

Items such as creditors, overdrafts, tax liabilities, dividends declared and not yet paid and short-term loans are classified as current liabilities. All other liabilities are classified as non-current. Also see *balance sheet; creditor; current asset; dividend; liability; overdraft*.

current maturity The time between the current date and the date of maturity of a financial instrument.

current ratio A ratio that measures how the short-term debt claims on a business are covered by the most liquid part of the company's asset base. The current ratio is defined by:

$$\text{current ratio} = \frac{\text{current assets}}{\text{current liabilities}}$$

Inventory is excluded from current assets to give the popular acid test ratio. Also see *acid test (quick) ratio; cash ratio; current asset; inventory; short-term debt*.

current ratio covenant A financial covenant in a loan agreement that requires that the borrower maintain a current ratio of no less than a given value. Banks use this ratio to ensure the current liabilities of a company do not become excessive. Also see *current ratio; financial covenant*.

current service cost (CSC) The increase in present value of the defined benefit fund obligation resulting from an employee's service in the financial period under question. Also see *defined benefit fund*.

current tax The amount of income tax payable on the taxable profit for a period.

current yield (CY) The coupon returns from a bond expressed as a ratio of its current price:

$$\text{current yield (CY)} = \frac{\text{annual bond coupon}}{\text{bond current all-in price}} = \frac{C}{BV}$$

- For bonds trading at a premium to par or nominal value, the CY is greater than the yield to maturity.
- For discount bonds, the CY is less than the yield to maturity (YTM).
- For bonds trading at par value, the CY is equal to the YTM.

The current yield is also referred to as the running yield, earnings yield or flat yield.

With reference to equity markets, the term current yield is used to describe the earnings yield. Also see *all-in price; clean price; earnings yield; par value; total price; yield to maturity*.

curvilinear regression An expression sometimes used for non-linear regression models or polynomial regression models. Also see *non-linear*.

cushion bond A bond that trades at prices (i.e. at higher yields) below similar bonds because the bond is callable and the probability of being called is high. Also see *callable bond*.

custodian A depository institution that holds assets on behalf of others. Banks, brokers and other financial institutions are custodians of assets for depositors.

custody Safekeeping of assets or the protection of the integrity of assets.

customs duty A tax levied on goods imported into a country. Also see *excise tax*.

CVR See *contingent value right*.

cyclical company A firm that does well when overall economic conditions are positive and poorly in economic downturns. Automotive companies are good examples of cyclical companies. Cyclical companies may well have high beta values. Also see *beta; countercyclical; firm*.

cyclical share See *cyclical company*.

cyclical unemployment Unemployment that arises from periodic downswings in business cycles. Cyclical unemployment is subject to changes in aggregate demand. Also see *aggregate demand; cyclical company*.

cylinder option See *zero cost collar*.

CYP The Cypriot pound divided into 100 cents.

Czech koruna The unit of currency of Czechoslovakia prior to integration into the European Monetary Union and the adoption of the euro. Also see *euro*.

CZK The Czech koruna divided into 100 hellers (or haleru).

D A credit rating used by S&P, Moody's and Fitch that indicates that the company has defaulted on its debt obligations. Also see *credit rating*.

Daily Official List (DOL) A London Stock Exchange primary information provider for reporting trade data. Media companies such as Bloomberg and Reuters publish this information via their market information systems. SENS is the JSE equivalent. Also see *Bloomberg; JSE; London Stock Exchange; primary information provider; Reuters; SENS*.

dalasi The currency of Gambia divided into 100 bututs.

damages Money awarded by a court as compensation for the effects of wrongdoing or breach of contract by another party.

dark liquidity A transaction that occurs off exchanges and is not visible to investors until after it is complete. These transactions do not contribute to price discovery.

data room When doing a substantial transaction that requires significant due diligence, large amounts of confidential information need to be processed by the investors. Sponsors give the investors a secure room on their business premises where the investors and their affiliates can analyse various documents and perform a proper due diligence process. Also see *due diligence*.

day count A set of conventions that is used to calculate the time applicable to interest payments. The following conventions are used:
- **30/360:** Interest calculations are made using 30 days in a month and 360 days in the year. This method is widely used in Europe and came about because 360 is easily factored into 180, 90 and 60 days.
  - 30/360 US (or 30U/360) uses 30 days for the 28 or 29 days of February and 30 days for the 31st of any month.
  - 30E/360 changes the 31st of any month into 30.
  - 30E/360 ISDA changes the last day of the month to 30 and does not adjust for February. This method is sometimes called the Eurobond basis.
- **Actual/360:** The difference between dates is the actual number of Julian days and the year is assumed to be 360 days long. Financial transactions in US dollars, euros and yen use this day count convention.
- **Actual/Actual:** The difference between dates is the actual number of Julian days and the year is assumed to be 365 or 366 days long for a leap year.
- **Actual/365:** The difference between dates is the actual number of Julian days and the year is assumed to be 365 days long irrespective of whether or not it is a leap year. Financial transactions in pounds, rands and Australian dollars use this day count convention.

daylight facility See *daylight overdraft*.

daylight overdraft A banking facility that allows a client to go into overdraft during business hours as long as the balance outstanding is settled before the close of business on the same day.

Even though they are short term in nature, daylight overdraft facilities have a degree of default risk. Daylight overdrafts are said to provide bounce protection. Also see *swingline loan*.

day move The price change of a share in a single day. It is usually calculated by subtracting the current closing price from the closing price of the day before.

days conventions See *day count*.

days sales in inventory The number of trading days that a company can operate for on average until its current inventory is exhausted:

$$\text{days sales in inventory} = \frac{\text{inventory}}{\left[\frac{\text{cost of goods sold}}{365}\right]}$$

This ratio gives an indication of how efficiently a company manages its inventory. The ratio varies from industry to industry. Also see *inventory*.

DAX Index Top 30 companies by market capitalisation on the German Stock Exchange. Also see *market capitalisation index*.

DBSA Development Bank of South Africa.

DCF See *discounted cash flow valuation*.

DCM
 1. See *debt capital market*.
 2. See *Development Capital Market*.

dead capital See *idle capital*.

dead cat bounce A market that makes gains after a drastic fall. The gains after the fall are probably not reflective of market fundamentals but result from strategies where traders have to cover open positions and some investors are bargain hunting. Also see *fundamentals; open position*.

dealer An individual or institution that buys and sells on financial markets. Dealers are the principals in financial markets and profit from the spread between the bid (buy) and ask (sell) prices. Also see *ask price; bid price; spread*.

dealers market A security that is bought from a dealer over the counter. Also see *over the counter; security*.

debenture A loan or bond that is secured or unsecured. A debenture is a loan payable at a fixed date, generally with a tenor of more than ten years. When unsecured, it is often referred to as a loan stock or a naked debenture. The interest is charged at a fixed rate and must be paid before dividends are paid to shareholders. Holders of debentures have the same claim as other senior creditors on the underlying assets under liquidation unless the debenture is secured against an asset by a fixed or floating charge. Debentures are sometimes called corporate bonds.

Advantages of using debentures as a source of funds include:
- access to a large pool of investors
- restrictive financial covenants are not required
- no dilution of voting rights for equity shareholders.

Disadvantages of using debentures as a source of funds include:
- credit rating requirements
- interest rates and demand may be volatile
- minimum sizes of approximately $500 million are required on the international markets to cover the costs associated with the issue.

A debenture can also simply be a document which creates a security over all a company's business. Also see *credit rating; dividend; fixed charge; floating charge; liquidation; loan stock; secured loan; subordinated debenture; unsecured.*

debenture redemption reserve A reserve account that collects funds to pay off maturing debt obligations. These accounts are used to ensure that maturing debentures do not have adverse liquidity constraints on companies.

debit An accounting entry that is accompanied by a credit entry.

debt Any financing vehicle that is a contractual claim on the borrower (and not a function of its operating performance), creates tax deductible payments, has a fixed life and has priority claim on both operating cash flows and proceeds under bankruptcy.

If debt is raised and then used in the production of income, the interest on that debt is deductible from tax charges. The deductibility is usually equal to the tax rate multiplied by the interest charges. Operating environments subject to onerous tax regimes have highly debt leveraged businesses due to the taxation advantage. Also see *thin capitalisation.*

debt capacity The maximum amount of debt that a company can support from its earnings and equity base. The debt capacity can be derived from ratios such as the debt equity, interest cover and debt service cover ratio. Also see *debt to equity ratio; debt service cover ratio; interest cover.*

debt capital Money contributed to the establishment and operation of a business and raised through debt markets. Also see *debt; equity capital; share capital.*

debt capital market (DCM) The market where bonds, commercial paper and other debt instruments are issued and traded. Bilateral loans are not classified as debt capital market instruments. Also see *primary market; secondary market.*

debt consolidation Borrowing from a single institution to repay several separate creditors. Debt is consolidated to reduce the overall cost of debt and the amount of administrative work involved in managing all the separate debt obligations. Syndicated loans often constitute an opportunity for corporates to consolidate a set of bilateral facilities into a single, more easily manageable loan.

debt convertible
1. See *convertible debt/bond.*
2. A fixed income instrument such as a bond that can have interest rates convertible from fixed to floating interest rates or vice versa. The option to convert interest rates is open to the holder of the bond and not the issuer. Also see *bond; floating interest rate; interest rate.*

debt cost The cost of borrowing money. A tax benefit can be derived from debt service costs which lowers the effective service cost by tiD where t = the corporate tax rate; i = the interest rate; D = the value of the debt. Also see *weighted average cost of capital.*

debt cover See *interest cover.*

debt coverage A ratio that measures to what extent operational cash flows cover debt obligations:

$$\text{debt coverage} = \frac{\text{net debt}}{\text{EBITDA}}$$

Net debt to EBITDA ratios are used as financial covenants in loan agreements to ensure that borrowers do not become excessively indebted relative to earnings. Also see *EBITDA; interest cover.*

debt crisis Extremely poorly performing debt markets or debtors. Illiquidity in the banking market as a result of the subprime crisis in 2007/8 is an example of a debt crisis. A country or large corporation defaulting on debt obligations may also be termed a debt crisis. Also see *subprime crisis*.

debt cushion The amount of debt on the balance sheet contractually inferior to a particular debt instrument, i.e. how many people are behind one in the debt queue in the event of liquidation. In general, debt instruments with a higher debt cushion have a slightly higher average recovery than those with lower cushions and will therefore command a lower interest rate.

When arranging large syndicated loan transactions on highly leveraged deals, tranches of differing seniority are often structured with different fees and interest rates. The different tranches offer investors instruments with different risk and reward profiles and provide the investors in the senior tranches with a debt cushion. Also see *balance sheet; interest rate; securitisation*.

debt equity swap During times of financial crisis companies may wish to reorganise their debt and encourage lenders to exchange their current debt investments for equity considerations. Some debt instruments such as convertible bonds have equity swap provisions built into them at the start of the contract. Also see *convertible debt/bond*.

debtor An entity that owes the company money as a result of being supplied goods or services on credit. Sometimes called accounts receivable or trade receivables.

debtors collection period See *debtors days*.

debtors days The average length of time the company waits for debtors to pay their accounts defined by:

$$\text{debtors days} = \frac{\text{accounts receivable}}{\left[\frac{\text{sales}}{365}\right]}$$

A high debtors days number when compared to peers indicates that the company is ineffective at collecting monies owed to it and excessive cash is tied up in the working capital. Also see *creditor settlement; inventory days; working capital*.

debt ratio A ratio that gives the proportion of funds provided by creditors to the business:

$$\text{debt ratio} = \frac{\text{total debts}}{\text{total assets}} \text{ which is equivalent to } \frac{\text{total assets} - \text{total equity}}{\text{total assets}}$$

As more of the company is funded through debt, the debt ratio increases indicating an increase in financial risk.

debt ratios See *debt ratio; debt to equity ratio; times interest earned*.

debt relief An agreement to restructure the repayment of debt. Both the interest and principal payments can often be rescheduled.

debt rescheduling The adjustment of the term structure of debt to assist the borrower to meet payment obligations.

debt restructuring The process whereby a company restructures its debt obligations by modifying amounts, margins, tenors and amortisation profiles. Debt restructuring may also involve the exchange of debt for equity in a debt equity swap. Also see *debt consolidation; debt equity swap*.

debt security When companies or governmental organisations borrow money, they do so with the issue of debt securities. A debt security is a contractual obligation to the investor by the borrower to abide by the terms stipulated in the contract. Bonds and loans are both forms of debt securities. Also see *paper; security*.

debt service The payment of interest and principal on a debt obligation. Debt service is calculated by adding net finance charges to scheduled repayments of borrowings and financial lease obligations. In addition to finance leases and debt, one may choose, if appropriate, to include service obligations under hybrid instruments such as preference shares. Also see *capital lease; preference share*.

debt service cover ratio (DSCR) A ratio that defines the extent to which cash flows cover debt interest and principal payments:

$$\text{debt service cover ratio (DSCR)} = \frac{\text{cash available to service debt (typically EBITDA or FCF)}}{\text{interest expense} + \text{capital payments}}$$

Assigning a larger balloon portion to a debt amortisation schedule will result in the improvement of debt service coverage ratios. However, bullet repayments may increase the refinancing risk. Also see *bullet loan; interest cover; refinancing risk*.

debt service reserve account (DSRA) An account in which cash reserves are set aside by a borrower to be used should cash generated from operations not be sufficient to cover debt obligations. DSRA-related structures and covenants are included in loan agreements for project financing structures. DSRA minimum balances in project finance deals are usually about half a year's capital and interest payments. Also see *covenant; project finance*.

debt switching The act of restructuring the term profile of debt. Also see *debt consolidation; debt restructuring*.

debt to equity ratio The total debt invested in a company as a proportion of the owners equity:

$$\text{debt to equity ratio} = \frac{\text{total debt}}{\text{owners equity}}$$

In general, the debt obligation considered is the long-term debt unless a business has a large portion of the long-term capital structure in the form of short-term debt. Supermarket chains are examples of organisations which have large trade creditors books which are continually rolled over to form part of the long-term capital structure of the business.

Debt to equity ratios are used as covenants in loan agreements to ensure borrowers do not take on excessive levels of debt. Also see *capital structure; long-term debt; owners equity; short-term debt*.

debt to income ratio See *debt coverage*.

debt to net capital employed ratio A ratio that defines how much of the operating and non-operating capital of the business is financed through the use of debt:

$$\text{debt to net capital employed ratio} = \frac{\text{total debt}}{\text{net capital employed}}$$

Net capital employed is the sum of a company's fixed assets and its working capital. Also see *capital employed; gearing; leverage; working capital*.

debt to total assets ratio See *debt ratio*.

debt to total capital ratio A ratio used to indicate the overall capital structure of a business:

debt to total capital ratio = $\dfrac{\text{total debt}}{\text{total capital employed}}$

The information contained in this metric is the same as the information contained in the debt to equity ratio. Also see *capital structure*.

debt with warrants See *bond with warrants*.

decentralisation The process of shifting decision-making power from a centralised place to a wider group. For example, a large company may allow managers who are not in the head office wider ranging decision-making powers. Another example is when central governments move power to local or regional government structures.

declaration date
1. The date on which dividends are declared. Shares trade cum dividend between the declaration date and the record date. Also see *cum dividend; ex dividend; record date*.
2. The expiry date of an options contract.

decoupling The process of markets exhibiting less correlation. The opposite effect to contagion. For example, if the producer of a product is reliant on a single market for the sale of its goods, they would be coupled to that market. As the producer finds alternate markets for its goods, that process will effectively decouple the producer from its original market. Also see *contagion; correlation*.

dedicated portfolio A form of investment portfolio that seeks to match the flows of cash from assets generated in the future to the future liabilities of the portfolio. These may be used by pension funds to invest in low-risk long-dated assets. Also see *pension fund*.

deed A legal document that indicates the ownership of an asset. Sometimes called a title deed. Also see *title*.

deep discount bond A bond that is trading or issued at significantly less than par value. It generally has low coupons or is a zero coupon bond. The difference between the purchase or issue price and the redemption price at maturity provides investors with the returns they require. Also see *bond; zero coupon bond*.

deep in/out the money An option that is in/out the money by a long way and is highly unlikely to be in/out the money before maturity. Also see *option; out the money*.

default In general, a default occurs when one of the following transpires:
- A scheduled payment on debt or a financial transaction is not made.
- A credit loss event has occurred such as a charge off, specific provision or restructuring.
- The borrower is behind on any credit obligation.
- The borrower has filed for bankruptcy.

A series of additional default events that are business specific may be engineered into debt agreements.

Borrowers usually have a small time period in which they can rectify the default after which creditors take appropriate action. Sometimes called an event of default. Also see *arrears; event of default*.

default interest In the event of default, the applicable interest rate on the principal loan value is often increased. Also see *interest rate*.

default model A statistical model used by banks and other lenders to determine the default probability, loss given default and exposure at default. Also see *KMV; loss given default*.

default or credit risk premium The portion of the nominal interest rate or bond yield that represents compensation for the possibility of default. Other premiums are also included in lending margins, for example liquidity and statutory cost premiums. Also see *current yield; default; default risk spread; liquidity premium; nominal interest rate; statutory cost*.

default point The point at which the market value of a firm's assets render the firm unable to service its debt obligations. Also see *expected default frequency*.

default probability The probability that a default will occur within a specified time frame. Default probabilities are important in credit modelling. Also see *expected default frequency; KMV*.

default put option A put option used in preference share financial structures that becomes a valid put option in an event of default. Also see *event of default; preference share; put option*.

default rate The number of loans that default over a given period, usually one year, divided by the number of loans outstanding at the beginning of the period. The calculation can be adapted to use the principal value of the loans and losses. The default rate is sometimes referred to as the credit loss ratio. Also see *credit loss ratio; default*.

default risk The investment risk associated with changes in the creditworthiness of a firm. The default risk is the risk that the borrower is unable to repay interest or capital on loans or bonds. The default risk depends on a range of variables such as economic and industry conditions, levels of debt (gearing) and company management.

default risk spread The yield difference between country bonds issued in the same currency. For example, compare the yield on South African government US dollar Yankee bonds against similarly dated US government bonds. Default risk spreads effectively measure the default risk of one government against the other. Also see *country risk premium; government bond; Yankee bond*.

defeasance A financial structure that creates a certainty of payments. The payments in these structures are met by a source that is not the original debtor. For example, a financier issues a bond and then lends the proceeds to a corporate so that they can prepay their existing bond obligations. Under the repayment structure the corporate has a debt obligation to the financier and will pay an effective interest rate that is more favourable.

defensive company A company unlikely to be affected by economic downturns. It generally has a low beta value. Also see *beta; cyclical company*.

defensive investment See *defensive company*.

defensive share A share with a low beta, irrespective of its specific underlying business.

defensive strategy A low-risk investment strategy where a wide range of stocks is selected to diversify risk and obtain returns close to what the overall market would return. Also see *Satrix 40*.

deferment period The period for which a callable bond is not callable. Call provisions advantage the issuer of a bond and investors seek to invest for a period of time under which the exercising of a call option will not jeopardise their investment returns. Also see *callable bond; call option*.

deferral call option The right to delay the start of a project. Also see *option*.

deferral option An option to defer the start or end of a project. Also see *option*.

deferred call A call provision that stipulates that for a specified part of the initial life of the bond it cannot be called. Also see *convertible debt/bond*.

deferred compensation A mechanism usually used for highly paid employees to take advantage of alternative tax efficient salary increases by purchasing endowment policies. The policies can be surrendered on retirement and/or death benefits made attributable to nominated beneficiaries. Also see *endowment insurance policy*.

deferred interest The delay of interest payments on a loan. Banks may delay interest payments because an entity is unable to make payment but is highly likely to resolve its current difficulties. Also see *mezzanine debt; payment in kind; toggle note*.

deferred liability A payment obligation for services rendered during the current financial period but which will only be cash settled in future accounting periods. Deferred liabilities arise through the accrual basis of accounting. Also see *accrual basis of accounting; deferred taxation*.

deferred share A special kind of share where dividend payments on the shares are deferred. Also see *dividend*.

deferred taxation An accounting term meaning a future tax liability or asset, resulting from temporary differences between tax payment dates and accounting reporting dates or the difference between the accounting book value of an asset and its value calculated for tax purposes. For example, if an asset is depreciated by an accounting convention that is slower than permitted by formal tax deductions, the book value of the asset will be higher than the taxable value. To reconcile the two numbers if the asset were sold for book value, the gain over the tax value would be subject to taxation and that amount of taxation would be shown as a deferred tax liability.

When deferred tax appears as an asset, it effectively constitutes a loan at no cost from the relevant tax collection authority. Deferred tax is not considered to be part of the long-term capital of the business. Also see *asset; liability*.

deferred tax liability See *deferred taxation*.

deferred tax reserve A journal entry that balances tax expenses and tax payable.

deficiency agreement For some loan facilities, especially in project finance, a deficiency provision is set out if there is a limited ability for cash flows from the project to service debt obligations. The cash shortfall is made up by another party, most often the project sponsor. Also see *cash deficiency guarantee; debt service reserve account; project finance; sponsor*.

deficit When expenditure is greater than income. The term is used in the context of describing the difference between government income and expenditure. A deficit is the opposite of surplus. Also see *surplus*.

deficit spending When corporations or governments spend more than they earn. The cash in excess of income that is spent is raised through debt.

deficit unit A borrower of money. An entity that is effectively deficit spending. Also see *surplus unit*.

defined benefit fund The member of a defined benefit fund receives a guaranteed pension based on his/her final salary and number of years of employment (contribution to the fund). The name defined benefit is derived from the fact that the benefit amounts are defined in advance. Any pension fund liability is the responsibility of the employer. On resignation, employees are given their contributions plus a growth portion. There is a 10% corridor within which funds can run a deficit or surplus before the company has to start covering the liability or distributing the profits. The actuarial liability or surplus is calculated using a discounted future cash flow model that uses high-quality corporate debt rates (AA). Sometimes called a final salary scheme. Also see *defined contribution fund; liability; pension fund; surplus.*

defined contribution See *defined contribution fund.*

defined contribution fund The employer and employee contribute to the pension fund. On retirement, an employee is entitled to his/her contribution, the employer's contribution and any growth of the fund. Employers do not have any liability under defined contribution funds other than the agreed contributions. Under defined benefit funds, employers can have extensive pension fund liabilities as employees are guaranteed pension funds based on their final salary and number of years of employment. Also see *defined benefit fund; pension fund.*

defined event A defined event triggers compensation on an insurance policy.

deflation An environment in which the prices of goods consistently decline, i.e. negative inflation. Deflation has significant economic consequences so central banks set policy to avoid it. Also see *disinflation; inflation.*

deflator See *implicit price deflator.*

degree of operating leverage See *operating leverage.*

degrees of freedom The number of independent comparisons that can be made among the elements of a sample. The term is analogous to the number of degrees of freedom for an object in a dynamic system, which is the number of independent coordinates required to determine the physical state of the object.

deleverage Reducing the level of debt in a company. This can be done when the financial risk associated with having a high degree of leverage is too great and management takes a decision to reduce debt facilities. Deleverage may also result from companies finding the cost of debt excessive. Also see *debt to equity ratio.*

deleveraged floater A financial instrument with a floating interest rate that is calculated as a fraction b of a reference rate, for example LIBOR or JIBAR, and an added margin. The coupon rate is therefore given by:

rate = (b × reference rate) + margin

Investors use these instruments to match the cash flows from their assets and their liabilities. Also see *floating interest rate; JIBAR; LIBOR; reference rate.*

delisting The removal of a listed company from a stock exchange. After shares have been delisted, they are no longer tradable on the exchange where they were listed. Private equity companies often purchase listed companies and take them private by delisting them. Also see *floating a company.*

deliverable obligation A credit default swap (CDS) is settled by deliverable obligation when a triggering credit event occurs. The seller of the CDS protection has to purchase the defaulted debt instrument or contract for face value. Also see *credit default swap.*

delivery date The date at which delivery of an asset in a futures contract must be made. Also see *futures contract*.

delivery month See *contract month*.

delivery notice Notification to the buyer of a futures contract that the underlying asset will be delivered on the specified delivery date. Also see *delivery date*.

delivery point The designated location of delivery of an asset in a futures contract.

delta
1. The Greek letter Δ or δ. Also see *Greek alphabet*.
2. For options, delta measures the change in option premium C per unit change in the price of the underlying S:

$$\Delta = \frac{dC}{dS}$$

Delta defines how much of the underlying asset needs to be bought or sold to hedge the option. Sometimes called the hedge ratio. Also see *Black-Scholes options pricing model; gamma; Greeks; leverage factor; option premium*.

delta hedging Keeping the delta of an options portfolio to zero. This has the effect of reducing the options price risk to changes in the price of the underlying asset. This is achieved by positions with positive and negative deltas that cancel one another. Also see *delta*.

delta spread A spread designed using the purchase and sale of options to create a delta of zero. This has the effect of reducing the options price risk to changes in the price of the underlying asset. The deltas of the various options are calculated against one another as ratios. Sometimes called a calendar spread or neutral spread. Also see *delta*.

DEM The Deutschmark, former currency of Germany before the introduction of the euro. Also see *euro*.

demand The sales volumes that results when a product is offered at the defined price. In general, the demand for a product is inversely related to the price. In capitalist economies prices adjust to supply and demand dynamics. Also see *price elasticity of demand*.

demand deposit A deposit that can be withdrawn immediately. A current account from which funds can be drawn from an ATM or bank branch immediately is an example of a demand deposit. Also see *automated teller machine; M2*.

demand guarantee A guarantee that is payable by the issuer on receipt of a demand against the guarantee. The guarantor is not afforded the opportunity of checking that a default has occurred and the guarantee holder is not required or entitled to make a second demand.

demand pull inflation theory If aggregate demand exceeds aggregate supply, then the general level of prices in an economy will rise to accommodate the excess demand. A higher demand than supply pulls prices upwards. Also see *aggregate demand; aggregate supply; cost push inflation theory*.

dematerialisation When securities are issued in electronic form as a book entry security and there is no physical share certificate. The ownership of the share exists as a digital accounting record only. Also see *book entry security; immobilisation*.

demerger The process of large corporations splitting into smaller individual companies. Also see *merger*.

de minimus A threshold figure below which no action occurs. For example, in loan covenants de minimus amounts may be specified above which a breach of contract or event of default will occur. Often called a carve out. Also see *event of default*.

demonstrated reserves The sum of the measured mineral resources and the indicated mineral resources. Also see *indicated mineral resources; measured mineral resources*.

density function A name used by scientists for the probability density function.

Department of Trade and Industry (DTI) A South African ministry that has jurisdiction over all trade and industry in South Africa. (See www.dti.co.za.)

dependent variable A variable that responds to changes in another. For example, the actual returns received on an investment depend on the size of the investment.

depositor An individual or business that deposits cash into a bank or another deposit-taking institution.

deposit-taking institution An institution such as a bank or post office that accepts deposits from households and firms. Also see *firm*.

depreciable amount The cost of an asset less its residual value. Also see *asset*.

depreciation Depreciation reflects the economic principal that investments on long-term capital equipment cannot be allocated to a single period but must be allocated to all periods applicable to the working life of the particular asset. Depreciating an asset involves the systematic allocation of the depreciable amount of the asset over its useful life.

There are generally three methods of accounting for depreciation:

- The straight line method where the value of the asset changes by the same nominal amount over its useful life
- The diminishing or reducing balance method which deducts a decreasing amount from the value of the asset over its life, usually based on a geometric series
- The units of production method which diminishes the value of an asset with increasing amounts as the asset reaches the end of its useful life.

In the case of an intangible asset, the term amortisation is generally used instead of depreciation. Also see *geometric series; intangible asset; reducing balance depreciation; straight line method of depreciation*.

depreciation tax shield A tax saving that results from the deduction of depreciation from taxable profits. Calculated as the allowable depreciation multiplied by the tax rate. Also see *depreciation*.

depression A prolonged recession. Also see *recession*.

deregulation The process of the elimination or streamlining of laws that impose an unnecessary regulatory burden on companies.

derivative
1. A financial instrument or other contract with all three of the following characteristics:

designated investment exchange | developmental financial institution (DFI)

- Its value changes in response to the change in a specified interest rate, financial instrument price, commodity price, foreign exchange rate, index of prices or rates, credit rating, credit index or other variable, provided in the case of a non-financial variable, that it is not specific to a party to the contract, sometimes called the underlying. Also see *credit rating; foreign exchange rate.*
- It requires no initial net investment or an initial net investment that is smaller than would be required for other types of contracts that would be expected to have a similar response to changes in market factors.
- It is settled at a future date. Derivatives are traded on the SAFEX exchange in South Africa. Also see *South African Futures Exchange.*

2. The derivative in mathematics is the instantaneous rate of change of a function with respect to one of its variables. It can be thought of as the slope of a function at a given point. The mathematical derivative of a function is defined by the following equation:

$$\frac{df}{dx} = \lim_{\Delta x \to 0} \frac{f(x + \Delta x) - f(x)}{\Delta x}$$

designated investment exchange Any non-UK stock exchange recognised by financial services regulators (FSA) in the UK.

detachable security A security that is packaged with another security that can be traded separately from the original package it was sold in. Also see *non-detachable security.*

detachment point The maximum loss exposure (loss given default) of a tranche of debt securities issued by a collateralised debt obligation vehicle. Sometimes called the exhaustion point. Also see *attachment point; collateralised debt obligation; tranche.*

deterministic process Events that have no random or probabilistic aspects but proceed in a fixed predictable fashion. A deterministic function is a well-defined function in time. Also see *stochastic process.*

deterministic trend This involves a process that can be defined with an equation that is an exact function over time. For example, in the equation $Y_t = \alpha + \delta t + e_t$, the time variable quantity t is multiplied by a time invariant variable δ. The term δt is referred to as the deterministic trend since it is an exact function of time and is easily determined. Also see *stochastic trend.*

Deutschmark The former currency of Germany before the adoption of the euro. Also see *euro.*

devaluation The loss of value of an asset. The term devaluation is used in the markets with reference to foreign exchange. For example, if the rand-US dollar exchange rate moves from R9 to R10 per dollar, the rand has devalued. Some countries keep their currencies artificially devalued through fixed exchange rates to improve the competitiveness of their export industries. Also see *clean float; crawling peg; fixed exchange rate.*

developing country Developing countries are defined by the World Bank in terms of gross national income per capita as follows:

- **Low income:** US$755 or less
- **Lower-middle income:** from US$756 to US$2 995
- **Upper-middle income:** from US$2 996 to US$9 265.

Also see *emerging market; gross national income.*

developmental financial institution (DFI) A financial institution set up by government and used to provide finance and financial products to sectors of the economy not

widely covered by commercial financiers. The Development Bank of South Africa (DBSA) is an example in South Africa.

development bank See *developmental financial institution*.

Development Capital Market (DCM) A JSE listing category that caters for smaller companies and has fewer listing requirements than the main board. The DCM listing category has been created to assist smaller developing companies raise equity capital through the JSE. The Alternative Investment Market (AIM) on the LSE is a similar listing board. Also see *Alternative Investment Market; JSE; main board*.

DFI See *developmental financial institution*.

DFP Delivery free of payment.

DGM See *dividend growth model*.

DI900 A submission by South African banks to their regulator (SARB) that details their assets and liabilities. The DI900 is a useful source of information for the analysis of the South African banking industry and credit market. Also see *credit market; South African Reserve Bank*.

diagonal spread The purchase and sale of an option with different strike prices and expiration dates. Also see *horizontal spread; vertical spread*.

Dickey Fuller test A statistical test used to find a unit root. The method is based on the form of the time series being:

$$\Delta y_t = \phi y_{t-1} + \sum_{j=1}^{p-1} \alpha_j^* \Delta y_{t-j} + u_t$$

where Δ = the first difference operator; y_t = the variable of interest; ϕ = a coefficient; α_j^* = constant; u_t = an error term.

If $\phi = 0$, then the series has a unit root and is non-stationary. The null hypothesis used in Dickey Fuller tests is:

$H_0: \phi = 0$

Hence, if the *t* statistic is less than the critical value, then the null hypothesis is rejected and the system is stationary. Also see *null hypothesis; unit root*.

DIE See *designated investment exchange*.

difference equation A difference equation expresses a value of a variable as a function of its own lagged values. Also see *autoregressive*.

differential cost A cost that differs between alternatives. Also see *differentiation*.

differentiated A product that is suitably different from all other products in its class so that buyers are willing to pay more for it and are unable to substitute another product for it. Being differentiated is the opposite of a homogeneous product. Also see *homogeneous*.

differentiation
1. Making a product different from its substitutes. This may be done through brand building or research and development.
2. Calculating the derivative of a mathematical function. Also see *derivative*.

diffusion index

1. A measure of the percentage of stocks that have advanced in price or are showing a positive momentum over a defined period. The diffusion index is used in the technical analysis of stocks and is one of the many different tools used by technical analysts to increase the probability of picking winning stock. Also known as the advance/decline diffusion index. Sometimes called the dynamic factor.

2. A measure of the breadth of a move in any of the conference board's business cycle indicators (BCI), showing how many of an indicator's components are moving together with the overall indicator index. The diffusion index can help an economist or trader interpret any of the composite indices of the BCI more accurately. The diffusion index breaks down the indices and analyses the components separately, exhibiting the degree to which they are moving in agreement with the dominant direction of the index. Also see *conference board*.

DIFX Dubai International Financial Exchange.

diluted earnings per share The amount of profit for the period that is attributable to ordinary shareholders divided by the weighted average number of ordinary shares outstanding during the period, both adjusted for the effects of all dilutive potential ordinary shares to be issued through instruments such as employee share options or convertible bonds. Also see *fully diluted earnings per share; ordinary share; weighted average*.

dilution A reduction in earnings per share or an increase in loss per share resulting from the assumption that convertible instruments are converted, that options or warrants are exercised or that ordinary shares are issued on the satisfaction of specified conditions. For example, there will be a dilution of earnings when shares are issued to directors or BEE partners for less than what they are worth. Dilution is expressed at the time that the options are issued. Also see *diluted earnings per share; option; ordinary share; warrant*.

diminishing balance See *reducing balance depreciation*.

dinar The name of the currency of many countries, including Algeria (DZD), Jordan (JOD), Kuwait (KWD), Libya (LYD), Macedonia (MKD), Serbia (RSD), Tunisia (TND) and Iraq (IQD).

direct cost See *variable cost expense*.

direct finance Lenders (surplus units) and borrowers (deficit units) are matched without the use of a financial intermediary such as a bank. Sometimes called disintermediation. Also see *deficit unit; disintermediation; indirect finance; intermediary; surplus unit*.

direct investment See *foreign direct investment*.

directive A change made by a government to the financial system that is not made by an act of law. Directives are often made when loopholes in legislation need to be plugged quickly and the permanent changes to the law are then made at a later date.

direct lease When a manufacturer leases an asset to a customer directly. For example, Hewlett-Packard may lease computers it manufactures directly to customers. Also see *asset*.

direct method of reporting cash flows from operating activities A method which discloses major classes of gross cash receipts and gross cash payments. On the cash flow statement cash flows are derived from cash received from customers less cash paid to suppliers and employees. Also see *cash flow statement; indirect method of reporting cash flows*.

direct offer An advertisement in a newspaper, magazine or pamphlet that can be sent to the issuing firm accepting an investment opportunity in the advertisement.

director See *board of directors*.

directors report The portion of a company's annual financial statements compiled by the company's management that provides a summary and overview of the year's financial performance, future prospects and strategy. If substantial changes have occurred since the previous financial year, they are highlighted and explained in this section of the financial statements. Also see *financial statements*.

direct quotation The exchange rate quoted as the domestic price of a foreign currency against a single US dollar. For example, ZAR7.50 = US$1. Also see *indirect quotation*.

dirty float The foreign exchange rate of a country is termed a dirty float when it is allowed to fluctuate with the intervention of monetary authorities. Under a dirty float monetary authorities can manipulate the exchange rate. Also see *clean float; crawling peg; fixed exchange rate; foreign exchange rate; free float; managed float; pure float*.

dirty price The price of a bond including accrued interest. The dirty price is called the all-in price in South Africa. Also see *accrued interest; all-in price; bond*.

disbursement Drawdowns under a loan facility. Also see *drawdown*.

discontinued operation An operational asset that is held for near term sale or has already been disposed of. Income from discontinued operations for an accounting period is shown as a separate line item so that analysts have an idea of income prospects going forward.

discount The amount by which an asset is sold under the current, fair market or net asset value. Also see *discounting*.

discount bond A bond that pays small or no coupons and is issued at or trades at a price lower than par value. Investors are rewarded for holding the bond by the increase in value as the bond approaches the date of maturity (pull to par). Also see *discount security; par value*.

discounted cash flow valuation (DCF) Calculating the present value of future cash flow to determine the value today. The present value of the cash flow is calculated by using a discount factor. Also see *cash flow; discount factor; discount rate*.

discount factor To discount a stream of cash flows the following equation is used:

$$PV = \frac{FV}{(1+r)^t}$$

The discount factor in the above equation is:

$$\frac{1}{(1+r)^t}$$

Also see *present value*.

discount forward A currency trades at a forward discount when the forward price is lower than the spot price. This is unusual because financing and other charges can constitute cost of carry and the forward rate should theoretically be higher than the spot rate. Also see *contango; cost of carry; spot market; spot price*.

discount house A financial intermediary that buys and sells instruments such as bills of exchange, discount notes such as treasury bills, bankers acceptance notes and

discounting | disinflation

promissory notes and commercial paper. Also see *bankers acceptance; bill of exchange; commercial paper; promissory note; treasury bill.*

discounting
1. Calculating the present value of future cash flows. Also see *discount rate.*
2. The process of issuing securities below their par value or redemption value. Also see *discount security; par value; redemption value; rediscount.*

discount note See *discount security.*

discount rate The rate used to calculate the present value of future cash flows. It is used (as r) in the following calculation to discount future cash flows:

$$PV = \frac{FV}{(1+r)^t}$$

where PV = present value; FV = future value; t = number of time periods; r = discount rate.

The equation must be applied individually to each cash flow when discounting cash flows. Rearranging the above equation to solve for the discount rate the equation is:

$$r = \left(\frac{FV}{PV}\right)^{\frac{1}{t}} - 1$$

The investor decides what discount rate constitutes a suitable rate of return for him/her. The rate investors require is usually the risk-free rate plus a premium required by the investor for assuming additional risk, the risk premium. An example of the discount rate is an investor paying R90 for a discount security that matures in 45 days. The discount rate calculated by the above equation will be:

$$r = \left(\frac{100}{90}\right)^{1/(45/365)} - 1$$

The discount rate is sometimes used when referring to the central bank discount rate. Also see *cash flow; central bank discount rate; discount security; future value; geometric mean; risk-free rate; risk premium; security market line; weighted average cost of capital.*

discount security A security such as a treasury bill that is sold at a discount to face value and redeemed at face value. There are no coupon payments and the investor receives reward for holding the security from the difference between the discount price and the face value or par value at which the security is redeemed in the future (pull to par). Also see *discount rate; face value; par value; pull to par.*

discount window See *accommodation.*

discretionary account An account held with a stockbroker where the broker may trade on the client's behalf without obtaining explicit permission for the trades. Also see *client account; managed account; non-discretionary account; stockbroker.*

discretionary income Income available to an entity after all financial obligations have been met.

discretionary order See *market not held order.*

diseconomies of scale A situation where smaller firms can produce goods at lower costs than their larger counterparts. Diseconomies of scale is the opposite of economies of scale. Also see *economies of scale.*

disinflation A reduction in the rate of inflation with the resulting inflation rate remaining positive. If the inflation rate becomes negative, the term deflation is used. Also see *deflation; inflation.*

disintermediation The removal of an intermediary. In the disintermediation process banks are often replaced by institutional investors as the interest rates they offer become favourable over the bank rates. The market in which this occurs is called a grey market. Also see *institutional investor*.

disinvestment The process of foreign investors selling their investments in a country and moving their cash elsewhere. Also see *capital flight*.

dispersion The amount of variability in a data set. Also see *variance*.

distressed securities Securities in companies that are in or close to bankruptcy. In the loan market, loans are considered to be distressed when their value drops below 80% of par and/or is trading at a spread of over 1 000 bps. These securities are at or near default, or have been issued by companies that currently have poor creditworthiness. Also see *bankruptcy*.

distributable reserves A portion of accumulated shareholders equity (retained earnings) on a company's balance sheet that shows money that has been set aside to acquire assets or distribute cash to shareholders. Distributable reserves are the opposite of non-distributable reserves which are accumulated through revaluations and are difficult to distribute to shareholders. Also see *balance sheet; non-distributable reserves*.

distribution yield See *dividend payout ratio*.

diversifiable risk Unsystematic risk or risk that can be avoided by investing in a wider range of assets.

diversification Spreading an investment across asset classes to eliminate some, but not necessarily all, of a portfolio's risk. Diversification is the act of not putting all one's eggs in one basket. Also see *portfolio expected returns*.

dividend Distribution of profits to holders of equity (shares) investments in proportion to their holdings of equity. Also see *attributable profit; equity; retained earnings; special dividend*.

dividend cover The degree to which earnings exceed dividend payments:

$$\text{dividend cover} = \frac{\text{earnings per share}}{\text{dividends per share}}$$

If this ratio increases, the proportion of earnings that are being retained by the company is increasing. The ratio is usually set as policy by the company and constitutes a strong signal to the markets. Also see *market value ratios*.

dividend discount model See *dividend growth model*.

dividend equalisation reserve A reserve account set up to ensure that the company can keep dividend payouts stable into the future. The reserve is used so that dividend payouts will not have to be decreased in less profitable years.

dividend growth model (DGM) A model that assumes a firm's value is defined by the present value of its future dividend payments. The expected future cash flows are discounted using a simplified version of the sum of a geometric series mathematical formula:

$$P_t = \frac{D_{t+1}}{R - g}$$

where t = number of time periods; D = dividend returned; R = discount rate associated with the cash flows, usually the cost of equity; g = dividend growth rate.

The simplification of the formula assumes that the discount rate R is greater than the dividend growth rate g. The DGM assumes that the stock will be held in perpetuity, dividends will grow at constant rates in the future and discount rates will remain constant in the future. The dividend growth model is also called the Gordon growth model. Also see *cost of equity; discount rate; dividend; geometric series; perpetuity; valuation*.

dividend in specie A dividend payment made through the transfer of assets rather than in cash. When large corporates dispose of subsidiaries, they may prefer not to sell the subsidiary but instead issue shares in the newly listed company to shareholders (unbundled). Also see *dividend; script dividend*.

dividend payout ratio An indication of the proportion of income that is returned to shareholders as dividends:

$$\text{dividend payout ratio} = \frac{\text{cash paid to shareholders}}{\text{net profit after tax}}$$

dividend payout ratio = 1 − retention ratio

Also see *dividend; dividend cover; dividend yield; retention ratio*.

dividend policy A policy set by the management of a company that sets out what proportions of profits management aims to distribute to shareholders. The dividend policy is usually specified in annual financial statements and is often changed or set in such a manner to increase the share price. Also see *dividend cover; dividend payout ratio; retention ratio*.

dividend protection Dividend payouts can reduce the value of shares and hence the value of options on those shares. Shares or options that are dividend protected impose some form of restriction on the value of dividends that a company may pay out. Share options such as those built into convertible debt often have dividend protection to ensure that the value of the options is not excessively decreased. This protection can come in the form of an adjustment to the option strike price or cash payments to option holders should dividends be paid.

dividend pusher A feature built into hybrid instruments that ensures that dividends paid to ordinary shareholders or share buy-backs are limited until the obligations on the hybrid instrument in question are met. There may also be specifications that the instruments rank pari passu with other hybrid instruments and common equity. Also see *hybrid; pari passu*.

dividend strip The purchase of shares solely for returns in the form of dividends. The shares are sold after the record date which is the date on which the share register is closed and the holders of the shares on that day receive the dividends declared for that period. Also see *record date*.

dividend yield (DY) The ratio of the dividends paid on a share to the price of the share:

$$\text{dividend yield (DY)} = \frac{\text{dividend per share}}{\text{price per share}}$$

The dividend yield gives an indication of the cash-based returns owners have received for holding the share. The dividend is historical and is the total value of the dividend payments over the last 12 months. If a company is newly listed and does not have a history of declared dividends, the projected dividends that management anticipates declaring are used in the calculation to derive a forward dividend yield. A good dividend yield ratio acts as a sign of company health and shows the ability of the company to turn cash into returns for shareholders.

In the financial press the dividend yield is often indicated by DY%, where the dividend is the dividend paid during the financial year divided by the current ruling share price. The dividend yield added to the capital gains yield gives the total return on an equity investment. Also see *capital gains yield; dividend; earnings yield; financial year; forward dividend yield; market value ratios.*

division A part of a company that is not classified as a separate legal entity but is set up to perform specific functions or business and is often given a degree of management autonomy. Also see *affiliate; associate; joint venture; subsidiary.*

DKK The currency of Denmark, the Danish kroner divided into 100 øre.

D-loan A loan that has less seniority than a C-loan and subsequently has higher margins and often longer tenors. D-loans are aimed at investment funds such as hedge funds. Also see *A-loan; B-loan; C-loan; hedge fund; margin; seniority.*

DMTN Domestic medium-term note.

document agent The bank that handles all the documents in a syndicated loan. Also see *syndicated loan.*

documentary credit See *documentary letter of credit.*

documentary letter of credit A written undertaking by a bank issued on behalf of an importer to pay the exporter a given sum of money within a specified time providing all conditions in the document are met. Also see *bankers acceptance; letter of credit.*

dog
1. An underperforming asset.
2. See *Boston matrix.*

DOL See *Daily Official List.*

dollar The name given to the currency of many countries although it is used principally with reference to the United States. Countries that also use the dollar for a currency name include Australia, Barbados, Bahamas, Bermuda, Canada, Hong Kong, Namibia, New Zealand, Singapore and Zimbabwe.

dollar bond A bond that is expressed as the dollar price, i.e. as a cost per $100 of par value. Also see *dollar price.*

dollar duration Bond duration is a measure of changes in price in percentage points. Dollar duration gives absolute numbers. The ratio of change in bond price (ΔP) to change in bond yield is defined as:

$$\frac{\Delta P}{P} = -MD \times \Delta i$$

where MD is the modified duration and Δi is the change in bond yield.

If $\Delta V = -A \times MD \times \Delta i \times \frac{P}{100}$

where ΔV is the change in value, then for a one basis point change on a one million holding:

$$\Delta V = -1\,000\,000 \times MD \times 0.01 \times \frac{P}{100} = -MD \times P$$

Also see *basis point; bond; bond duration; duration; modified duration.*

dollar price The price of a bond when expressed as a cost per $100 par value. Also see *dollar bond; yield price*.

dollar roll A form of repurchase agreement where a security is sold at an early date and bought back for settlement at a later date. The benefits of owning the security in the roll window do not accrue although a profit is made because prices of the later dated security are cheaper. Also see *repurchase agreement*.

dollar value per basis point See *present value of a basis point*.

domestic absorption Total spending in an economy, including spending by households, government and investments made. Also see *gross domestic product*.

domestic bond A bond issued by a company in the jurisdiction of its incorporation and in the currency of that jurisdiction. Also see *bond; foreign bond*.

domicile The country or place of an entity's home or, in the case of a company, its country of registration. For people their domicile may differ from their nationality. For example, South Africans living in London are domiciled in England. The applicable domicile may have implications for tax treatments and obligations.

dominant firm When a firm is the only firm with a significant market share, it is termed the dominant firm. The prices that dominant firms set dictate the price trend in the market. Also see *monopoly*.

dong The currency of Vietnam divided into 100 hao.

doomsday call A call provision in a bond that can be triggered under certain conditions. Common conditions used in Canadian corporate bonds.

doorstep business A business that delivers products to households. Home milk delivery is a good example of a doorstep business.

doorstep lender A financial institution that lends to households.

double barrelled Debt instruments that have more than one form of security.

double dated bond A bond that is redeemable on two separate dates. Also see *callable bond*.

double default Default of both a borrower and guarantor.

double dip Tax depreciation allowances accessed simultaneously in two countries.

double entry A method in accounting that requires a transaction to be entered into the accounting books twice. The double-entry system specifies that payment is a credit and receipt is a debit.

double option The combination of a put option and call option into a single option, giving the holder the right to buy or sell the underlying asset at the predetermined price and time horizon. Also see *call option; put option*.

double taxation Investments made by entities in a foreign country may be technically subject to income tax in both the home and foreign country. Countries have double taxation agreements in place whereby foreign tax credits are given to investors to ensure that income is only taxed once. Also see *foreign tax credit*.

dovish In the context of interest rates, dovish means favouring a decrease in interest rates. Dovish remarks have a less aggressive tone. The converse of dovish is hawkish. Also see *hawkish*.

Dow Jones An index that tracks the top 30 closing prices of blue chip stocks on the New York Stock Exchange (NYSE). The index represents a large portion of the market capitalisation of the NYSE. The index is calculated as a price weighted arithmetic average. Also see *index; New York Stock Exchange; price weighted index*.

down payment The upfront deposit on the purchase of an asset. The balance of the purchase price is funded through financing facilities and paid off over a period of time after purchase.

downside Exposure to the possible decrease in the value of an asset. Also see *upside*.

downside protection A position created with the use of derivative instruments that limits the potential losses of an investor. Also see *position*.

downsizing The process of reducing the output and workforce of an organisation. The term is also used when higher performing assets are replaced with lesser performing assets. Also see *rationalisation; rightsizing*.

DPB Designated professional body.

dragon bond A bond that is issued in Asia but denominated in US dollars. Also see *bond*.

drawdown Borrowing of monies in a loan facility.

drawdown loan The drawing of funds against a credit line. These loans are similar to credit cards with a credit limit and where the client can spend at his/her discretion until that limit is reached. Revolving credit facilities are similar in nature. Also see *revolving credit facility*.

drawstop An action imposed by lenders, usually in an event of a default, where the borrower's loan account is effectively frozen and can no longer be drawn on. Also see *event of default*.

drift A process that moves with a particular long-term trend. The term drift is most often used to describe the process of random walk with drift. Also see *Brownian motion; random walk with drift*.

drop dead fee See *termination fee*.

DSCR See *debt service cover ratio*.

DSRA See *debt service reserve account*.

DTC Depository Trust Corporation.

DTI See *Department of Trade and Industry*.

dual capacity When a firm acts as both an agent trader and principal trader in stock market transactions. Also see *agent trader; principal trader*.

dual currency issue Bonds that pay coupons and principal in difference currencies. The principal usually has some room for appreciation in the stronger currency. These bonds are used by multinational corporations with needs for capital and payments in different currencies. Also see *multinational*.

dual listing The process of a company listing on stock exchanges in multiple jurisdictions. For example, SABMiller is listed on the London and Johannesburg Stock Exchange. Also see *inward listing*.

due bill repo See *hold in custody repo*.

due diligence Before lending money or purchasing a business, it is necessary to know more about an entity's risk profile and business operations. A due diligence exercise analyses the risk and business prospects. It differs considerably across business sectors and may involve various levels of detail. External companies, usually consulting companies, provide due diligence services.

duopoly A market or industry dominated by two companies. Also see *monopoly; oligopoly*.

Du Pont analysis A Du Pont analysis analyses the factors that drive return on equity (ROE). ROE is broken down as follows:

$$\text{ROE} = \frac{\text{sales}}{\text{assets}} \times \frac{\text{profit}}{\text{sales}} \times \frac{\text{assets}}{\text{equity}}$$

This can be broken down further into:

$$\text{ROE} = \frac{\text{sales}}{\text{total assets}} \times \frac{\text{PBIT}}{\text{sales}} \times \frac{\text{assets}}{\text{equity}} \times \frac{\text{PBT}}{\text{PBIT}} \times \frac{\text{NPAT}}{\text{PBT}} \times \frac{\text{total liabilities}}{\text{equity}-1}$$

where PBIT = profit before interest and taxation; PBT = profit before tax; NPAT = net profit after tax.

The above equation can be further refined to:

ROE = profit margin × asset turnover × interest effect × tax effect × equity multiplier

To boost ROE, managers may focus on one or more of the driving metrics in the Du Pont analysis. Also see *equity multiplier; profit margin; return on equity; sustainable growth rate*.

duration The duration of an asset or liability is a weighted maturity of the cash flow on that asset or liability, where the weights are based on both the timing and magnitude of the cash flow. Also see *asset; bond duration; cash flow; liability*.

duration asset The formula used is the same as that outlined in the Macaulay duration equation with the face value of the bond replaced by the salvage value of the asset. Also see *asset; bond; face value*.

Durbin-Watson test This statistical test is used to test if there is first order autocorrelation. Where residuals are defined by e_i; e_{i-1} the test statistic is defined as:

$$d = \frac{\sum_{i=2}^{n}(e_i - e_{i-1})^2}{\sum_{i=1}^{n} e_i^2}$$

The range of values for d is $0 \le d \le 4$. When $d < 2$ there is an indication of positive first order autocorrelation. When $d > 2$ there is negative first order correlation. Also see *autocorrelation*.

Dutch auction An auction where the price of an asset starts at a high value and is lowered until a participant is willing to pay the current price. In a Dutch auction of securities a series of bids from investors is received. The bids are then ranked from most to least favourable. The point at which the required liquidity can be reached dictates the clearing price. This has the implication that all winning bidders are compensated at the price point at which the required quantum is raised. The US Federal Reserve and Treasury use this style of auction to sell government bonds. Bonds are also commonly sold in this manner in South Africa. Also see *auction; auction rate security; English auction; government bond*.

Dutch disease syndrome A single dominant sector, often evident in commodity exporting countries, that can cause overvaluation of the currency and then can erode the competitiveness of other economic sectors. The name comes from the strengthening of the Dutch guilder in the 1970s due to the export of newly discovered natural gas. The exports strengthened the currency to such a point that the domestic economy became uncompetitive.

DWAF Department of Water Affairs and Forestry in South Africa.

DY See *dividend yield*.

dynamic factor See *diffusion index*.

DZD The Algerian dinar divided into 100 centimes.

EAD See *exposure at default*.

earmark Identify for alternative purposes. An investor may earmark specific shares for purchase or sale.

earnings Profits.

earnings per share (EPS) Earnings attributable to shareholders per share owned:

$$\text{earnings per share (EPS)} = \frac{\text{earnings after tax}}{\text{number of ordinary shares}}$$

The EPS ratio is used to derive company valuations. EPS is susceptible to changes if sizeable acquisitions were made during the year. Also see *acquisition; dilution*.

earnings yield A ratio that gives the market valuation of the company:

$$\text{earnings yield} = \frac{\text{earnings per share}}{\text{price per share}}$$

This is the inverse of the price earnings (PE) ratio. In published share tables this ratio is calculated by using earnings for the most recent financial year over the current market price. The current yield on a bond is sometimes called the earnings yield. Also see *current yield; dividend yield; market value ratios; price earnings ratio*.

earn out payment A further payment at a later date after defined financial goals have been met by a company that is the target of an acquisition. For example, a company may acquire another for a purchase consideration of R100 million. The purchaser may agree to pay a further R20 million in another 12 months after the acquisition if the target produces defined levels of profit or reaches other defined milestones. Sometimes called a profit warranty.

EBIT Earnings before interest and taxation. Also see *EBITDA*.

EBITDA Earnings before interest, taxation, depreciation and amortisation. This is the trading profit of a company, i.e. sales − cost of sales − other operational expenses. EBIDTA allows investors to compare companies in similar sectors with different asset structures.

Be careful when using EBITDA as capital expenditure is a cash flow item that is often not included. Alternatively, free cash flow can be used as a measure of trading profit as it includes the effects of cash flows associated with capital expenditure and investments. Also see *amortisation; asset; capital expenditure; depreciation; free cash flow; gross profit margin*.

EBITDA margin The EBITDA margin measures the extent to which cash operating expenses use up revenue:

$$\text{EBITDA margin} = \frac{\text{EBITDA}}{\text{total revenue}}$$

Also see *EBITDA; gross profit margin*.

EBITDAR EBIDTA adjusted for lease or rental expenses. The lease expense present in the earnings data is effectively reversed out of EBITDA. This is usually done by analysts who like to remove operating and financial leases which have different accounting treatments.

EBITDAR is also used in loan covenants (fixed charge cover ratio) to allow effective coverage monitoring for companies with substantial operating lease obligations. Also see *EBITDA; capital lease; fixed charge cover ratio; operating lease*.

EC See *economic capital*.

ECA See *export credit agency*.

ECB See *European Central Bank*.

ECH Equity clearing house. Also see *clearing house*.

ECM Economic capital markets.

econometrics Mathematical methods used for analysing causal relations among economic and financial variables. Also see *causality*.

economic capital (EC) The amount of capital that banks and other financial service providers have to put aside as a buffer against potential losses associated with their business activities. The measurement of economic capital requires complex stochastic modelling tools, where factors such as interest rate risk, pricing risk, credit risk, equity market risk, liquidity risk, operational risk correlations of portfolio assets, country risks, exposures and many other variables are taken into account. EC is calculated as the additional assets required to reduce the probability of ruin. EC targets are set by management or regulators and are key to defining a bank's credit rating. Also see *credit rating; credit risk; interest rate risk; operational risk; probability of ruin; return on economic capital; risk adjusted performance measurement; risk adjusted return on capital; stochastic process*.

economic debt Net financial debt plus various provisions for obligations such as pensions and operating leases. Also see *net debt*.

economic life
1. The period over which an asset is expected to be economically usable by one or more users. Also see *asset*.
2. The number of production or similar units expected to be obtained from the asset by one or more users. Also see *asset*.

economic profit The profit made by a company in excess of its cost of capital. Economic profit is the profit after tax and minority interests, less a capital charge. The capital charge is the average shareholders equity excluding minority interests multiplied by the cost of capital. Also see *average shareholders equity; cost of capital; minority interest; return on equity; weighted average cost of capital*.

economic rent In economic theory, economic rent is a payment to factors of production or input in excess of that which is needed to keep it employed in its current use. Returns above the risk adjusted required rate of return constitute the economic rent. Also see *factors of production*.

economic trend A pattern indicating trends in the economy measured with econometric techniques.

economic unit A participant in the economy. Economic units are categorised as financial and non-financial. Financial units are the financial intermediaries and non-financial units are households and businesses along with the foreign and government sector.

economic value added (EVA) A metric based on the concept of residual income that calculates the profit returned in excess of the cost of capital. EVA is calculated by:

$$EVA = NPAT - \text{cost of capital} \times \text{opening capital}_{@\text{year start}}$$

By rearranging the following equation is obtained:

$$\text{EVA} = \left(\frac{\text{NPAT}}{\text{sales}} \times \frac{\text{sales}}{\text{capital}} - \text{WACC}\right) \times \text{capital}$$

where NPAT = net profit after tax; capital = the total capital employed including both debt and equity.

The drivers of EVA are thus operating profit (net margin), fixed asset turnover and weighted average cost of capital (WACC). A positive EVA implies that value has been created and a negative EVA implies that value has been destroyed.

EVA is a registered trademark of its developer, Stern Stewart & Co. Also see *fixed asset turnover; residual income; weighted average cost of capital.*

economies of scale An increase in production associated with a less than proportional increase in costs. The benefits usually accrue from increased production capacity. Also see *diseconomies of scale.*

EDF
1. See *expected default frequency.*
2. European Development Fund.

EDSP See *exchange delivery settlement price.*

EEA See *European Economic Area.*

EEC European Economic Community.

EEK The Estonian kroon divided into 100 senti.

EFCF Estimated free cash flow. Also see *free cash flow.*

effective annual return (EAR) The annualised return or yield on an asset where all interim payments are expressed as an annual rate. The formula for converting from nominal compounding to an effective rate is given by:

$$i_{\textit{eff}} = \left(1 + \frac{i_{nom}}{m}\right)^m - 1$$

where m = the number of compounding operations; i_{nom} = the annual percentage rate.

Also see *annual percentage rate; continuous compounding; effective rate per period.*

effective duration A bond duration calculated for bonds with an embedded option. The Macaulay duration calculation does not work correctly for bonds with embedded options as the options adjust the sensitivity of the instrument to changes in interest rates. Effective duration is an approximation of the slope of a bond's value as a function of interest rate and is given by the following equation:

$$\text{effective duration (ED)} = \frac{V_{-\Delta y} - V_{\Delta y}}{2\,(V_0)\,\Delta y}$$

where $V_{\Delta y}$ = the values that the bond will take if the interest rate changes by y; Δy = the amount that the yield changes; V_0 = the value of the bond at the current point in time.

Also see *bond duration; dollar duration; embedded option; interest rate; modified duration; portfolio duration.*

effective exchange rate An overall measure of the movement of a currency against major currencies can be obtained by calculating an effective exchange rate. The effective exchange rate is a weighted average rate which is obtained by weighting the exchange

effective gearing (EG) The change in the price of an option with a 1% change in the price of the underlying asset:

$$\text{effective gearing (EG)} = \frac{dC}{dS} \times \frac{S}{C} = \Delta \times \frac{S}{C}$$

This is effectively the delta of the option multiplied by the simple gearing where C = the option premium; S = the price of the underlying asset. With an effective gearing of 4.0×, for every 1% the underlying asset price changes, the price of the option will move by 4%. Also see *delta; option premium; simple gearing*.

effective rate For a bond the effective rate includes the capital gain or loss and the bond's coupon payments. Also see *bond; current yield*.

effective rate per period To change an annual percentage rate into a rate per period, the following formula can be used:

$$\text{effective rate per period} = (1 + \text{annual rate})^{1/\text{\# of periods}} - 1$$

Also see *annual percentage rate*.

effective tax rate The tax paid by a company as a proportion of profit:

$$\text{effective tax rate} = \frac{\text{tax paid}}{\text{profit before tax}}$$

Due to specialist financial structures and the benefits of tax deductibility on interest the effective tax rate can be less than the corporate tax rate.

effective yield The yield on an investment that includes the effects of compound interest. For bonds this includes the assumption that all coupons are reinvested at the same coupon rate. Also see *compound interest*.

efficiency ratio See *cost to income ratio*.

efficient capital market Well-organised markets such as the New York and London Stock Exchanges are broadly classed as efficient markets. These markets have large numbers of profit maximising participants analysing and valuing securities. The timing of new information that the markets receive is random and market participants rapidly adjust security prices to reflect new information in an unbiased manner. Also see *efficient market; security*.

efficient capital market hypothesis See *efficient capital market*.

efficient market A market where the prices of financial securities adjust rapidly to the arrival of new information. The current price reflects all known public information about the security. In efficient markets, shares with higher returns are usually associated with higher levels of risk. Also see *efficient capital market*.

efficient market hypothesis (EMH) See *efficient capital market*.

EFT See *electronic funds transfer*.

EGM See *extraordinary general meeting*.

EGP The Egyptian pound.

eigen value or eigen vector In mathematics, an eigen vector of a transformation is a non-null vector that is unchanged by that transformation. A solution is obtained that is invariant under reference frame transformation.

Mathematically, v_λ is an eigen vector and λ the corresponding eigen value of a transformation T if the equation $T(v_\lambda) = \lambda v_\lambda$ is true, where $T(v_\lambda)$ is the vector obtained when applying the transformation T to v_λ.

For matrices, $(A - \lambda I)v = 0$ must be solved to obtain the eigen values. Solve for $det(A - \lambda I) = 0$ and substitute the λ back in to obtain the eigen vectors.

EIR Effective interest rate. Also see *effective annual return*.

elastic The change in quantity demanded for a product as a function of its price. Elasticity is defined by the following equation:

$$\text{elasticity} = \frac{\% \text{ change in quantity sold}}{\% \text{ change in price}}$$

If the price elasticity of demand is greater than one, then the product is labelled as a price elastic good and changes in quantity supplied do not influence the price sharply. Also see *elasticity coefficient; price elasticity of demand*.

elasticity A measure of responsiveness or sensitivity of demand to price changes. Also see *elastic; inelasticity; price elasticity of demand*.

elasticity coefficient

$$\text{elasticity coefficient} = \frac{\% \text{ change in quantity}}{\% \text{ change in price}}$$

Also see *elastic*.

elasticity of demand See *elastic*.

electronic funds transfer (EFT) The transfer of funds electronically through computer networks.

electronic money (e-money) A record of monies that is stored electronically. Accounts at most modern banks are e-money accounts.

electronic scrip register (ESR) The holder of securities is called a book entry security where evidence of the rights of the holder is stored in an electronic database called the electronic scrip register. Also see *book entry security; dematerialisation*.

elephant Very large.

eligible paper Securities accepted by central banks in repo or rediscounting transactions. The range of securities that central banks accept in repo or rediscounting operations is of great importance as repo transactions have significant effects on the liquidity of financial markets. Also see *central bank; rediscount; repurchase aggrement*.

eliminator In a segmented report, an eliminator is a line used to adjust for double accounting. For example, sales between divisions in a group could be double counted and so an eliminator will be used to reverse such effects.

Elliot wave A method of analysis that hypothesises that market prices move in a series phase or wave. Elliot wave theory is complex in nature and outside the scope of this publication.

EMA Exponential moving average. Also see *moving average*.

embedded derivative A derivative instrument that is a component of a financial contract that is itself not a dedicated derivative instrument. The cash flows and pricing of the host financial contract are modified by the presence of the embedded derivative. Embedded derivatives are accounted for separately from their host contracts if the cash flows associated with the derivative differ from those of the host contract. The derivative portion of the contract could stand up on its own as a derivative and the combined instrument is not recognised at fair value.

An example of an embedded derivative is financiers or service providers participating in the upside of profits delivered over and above interest or service charges. Other examples are a gold mine paying an additional fee to a loan provider over and above the interest at a rate determined by the gold price or a power company receiving an additional fee based on the aluminium price.

embedded option An option contained within another financial instrument. Good examples are conversion options written into convertible debt contracts. Also see *convertible debt/bond; option*.

EMBI (Emerging Market Bond Index) An index of emerging market bond yields published by JP Morgan. Also see *current yield; index*.

EMEA Europe, Middle East and Africa.

emergency window See *accommodation*.

emerging market Capital markets of developing or middle income countries that have been liberalised to promote capital flows and attract foreign capital. Also see *capital market*.

EMH Efficient market hypothesis. Also see *efficient capital market*.

emolument Monies and benefits paid to an employee by an employer. The term is used with reference to benefits and wages paid to directors of companies.

e-money See *electronic money*.

employee participation The participation by employees in the profits of an enterprise through share ownership.

employee share option See *share option*.

employment rate The percentage of people in a country that is in formal employment.

EMTN European medium-term note.

EMU European Monetary Union.

encumbrance A legal term used to describe claims on the title of a property or an asset. Mortgages, liens, pledges, assignments, hypothecation and deeds of cession are examples of encumbrances. Also see *assignment; cession; hypothecation; lien*.

endogenous Parameters within the scope of the model. Also see *exogenous*.

endowment insurance/policy A traditional long-term insurance vehicle combined with a long-term investment vehicle. Investors contribute monthly and receive a lump sum which is tax free after five years. Life cover is often added to the policy. All investment monies are invested in specific investment funds with a fee charged for administration. Also see *universal policy*.

endowment plan An investment that is made with monthly instalments and that pays out a lump sum on maturity.

English auction An auction format where the price of an asset is determined by a series of bids. The asset is sold at the highest bid price to all the bidders at or below that price. Most governments other than the US use this method to sell government bonds. Also see *auction; Dutch auction; government bond*.

enterprise value (EV) The total value of a company regardless of the way it is funded, i.e. the value independent of the capital structure of the enterprise. The enterprise value is given by:

enterprise value (EV) = equity value + net debt + minority interest

The enterprise value is often referred to as the total enterprise value, entity value, gross value, firm value, aggregate value or leveraged market capitalisation. The equity value is the market capitalisation. Also see *enterprise value; capital structure; equity; market capitalisation; Modigliani-Miller or M&M proposition; net debt*.

enterprise zone An area set up with favourable benefits to encourage a particular range of business activities. Benefits may include tax breaks and subsidised property.

entity value See *enterprise value*.

entry The entry into an industry by a company not previously involved in that sector. The new entrant will have to build new productive capacity and face a series of barriers to entry.

EOD See *event of default*.

EOM End of month.

EONIA See *European overnight index average*.

EPC Engineering, production/procurement and construction.

EPS See *earnings per share*.

Equalisation Fund A fund in South Africa administered by the Central Energy Fund that collects levies from the retail sale of petroleum products. The equalisation fund is used to pay subsidies, smooth fluctuations in the retail price of liquid fuel and afford tariff protection to the synthetic fuel industry. Also see *Central Energy Fund*.

equator principles A framework which lenders abide by on a voluntary basis guiding them to ethical and environmentally friendly financing activities.

equilibrium A price position in the market where demand and supply are matched at an equilibrium price. The market usually moves about this equilibrium price. Also see *equilibrium price level; static equilibrium*.

equilibrium price See *equilibrium price level*.

equilibrium price level The price at which aggregate supply and demand match. Also see *aggregate supply*.

equipment trust certificate (ETC) A financial security primarily used in aircraft finance. The mechanics involve a trust certificate that is sold to investors to raise funds to purchase the asset. The asset is managed through a trust on behalf of the investors and leased to an end user. On maturity of the ETC, the lessee receives title to the asset. Financing methods of this nature effectively create security over an asset through lenders having legal title.

equities Ordinary shares in a business. Also see *ordinary share*.

equity The ownership stake or share in a company. The equity in a company is defined as the residual interest in the assets of the entity after deducting all its liabilities. Equity has infinite life, no seniority in the event of bankruptcy and gives proportional management control to the owner, i.e. the owner has voting rights.

equity accounted An accounting method where a company owns a significant number of shares in another company and exerts a substantial degree of influence but does not control the company in which it invested. The income shown against the investment is booked as a proportion of the net profit after tax of the company invested in. The proportions are in line with the proportionate stake that is owned.

equity capital Funds supplied to establish and run a company raised through the issue of equity. Also see *debt capital; equity; share capital*.

equity claw A covenant in a particular bond issue that allows companies to redeem a portion of issued bonds if they issue new equity. Bond investors often accept these clauses because under an equity issue more cash will flow into the business and ultimately allow the company to service debt more easily. The equity issuers have a subordinate claim on the increased assets of the company under liquidation which implies less risk to the debt holders. Also see *bond; liquidation; subordinate*.

equity cure An arrangement where shareholders or sponsors in a financial transaction are afforded the opportunity to rectify the breach of financial covenants by injecting fresh equity or subordinated loans into the company. For example, if a net debt to EBITDA ratio was breached and R50 million is required to ensure the ratio passes the test, shareholders funds injected can be added to EBITDA. Lenders often resist these clauses, impose limitations on the numbers of cures allowed and whether or not they can be done consecutively.

equity derivative A derivative that is based on an underlying equity asset such as a share traded on a stock exchange. Also see *derivative; equity*.

equity equivalent In South Africa when attaining a BEE status, a company need not sell an equity component to black investors but can alternatively develop the skills of staff and new recruits. The skills development programme is passed by government as an equity equivalent consideration. Also see *black economic empowerment*.

equity financing The financing of a business by the issue of equity.

equity fund An investment fund that invests only in equity assets of listed companies on the stock exchange.

equity gearing Boosting the capital in a business by borrowing. Also see *gearing*.

equity instrument See *equity*.

equity kicker An addition to a financial contract that affords a lender an equity stake in the borrower in return for advancing finance on favourable terms. The equity stake usually takes the form of an option to buy equity. Also see *equity*.

equity-linked note A debt instrument that has its returns linked to equity market returns. These instruments are based on baskets of shares or indices. They have the advantage of giving equity-like returns while protecting the capital portion of an investment. They are created by the purchase of a call option together with the purchase of a zero

equity market The primary and secondary markets associated with the trade in shares of companies. The JSE is the principal equity market in South Africa for public equity investments. Also see *JSE; primary market; secondary market*.

equity method A method of accounting whereby an investment is initially recognised at cost and adjusted thereafter for the post-acquisition change in the investor's share of net assets. The profit or loss of the investor includes the share of the profit or loss of the asset. Also see *net asset*.

equity multiplier A term used in a Du Pont return on equity analysis, defined by:

$$\text{equity multiplier} = \frac{\text{total assets}}{\text{total equity}}$$

The ratio is often used to analyse banks. Also see *capital adequacy; Du Pont analysis; return on equity*.

equity option An option with an underlying equity share or a basket of shares. Also see *equity; option*.

equity repo A repurchase agreement (repo) transaction with the underlying collateral being an equity asset. Normally, repo collateral assets are bonds. Also see *bond; collateral; repurchase agreement*.

equity risk premium The premium over the risk-free rate of return that investors require when investing in riskier equity assets. Also see *equity; market risk premium; risk-free rate*.

equity share capital The share capital in a business. Also see *share capital*.

equity swap A financial contract whereby counterparties agree to exchange cash flows on a principal amount. The one party agrees to pay a rate of return on an equity asset or index and the other agrees to pay a floating or fixed rate of interest. Equity swaps can be in the form of funded equity swaps where a loan is made to a counterparty. Typical debt obligations are required from the borrower and the economic benefits of the shares are paid to the lender. Also see *hybrid; swap*.

equivalent annual cost (EAC) The present value of the costs of a project calculated on an annual basis. To calculate EAC, take the present value of all the costs and distribute them evenly across the life of the project using the annuity present value formula shown below. Also see *annuity present value*.

$$C = \frac{APV}{\left[\dfrac{1 - \dfrac{1}{(1+r)^t}}{r}\right]}$$

erasure guarantee A guarantee by an organisation such as an independent auditor that validates the legitimacy and accuracy of changes made to securities.

Erb-Harvey approach The Erb-Harvey-Viskanta model of determining the cost of equity is a method of determining the cost of equity for a particular market relative to a home market:

$$CS_{i,t+1} = \gamma_0 + \gamma_1 \ln(CCR_n) + \varepsilon_{i,t+1}$$

where $CS_{i,t+1}$ = semi-annual return (\$) for country i; CCR = country credit rating on a scale of 1–100, usually indexed from the Institutional Investor magazine; $\varepsilon_{i,t+1}$ = residual from regression equation.

This approach questionably assumes that all projects in the country have the same risk. There is no beta in the equation which would apply an adjustment for individual project risk. Also see *adjusted hybrid capital asset pricing model; beta approach; Bludgeon approach; Estrata downside risk model; global capital asset pricing model; Godfrey and Espinosa cost of equity model; Goldman Sachs model; lambda approach; Lessard's model; semi-annual.*

ergodic A system that is not evolving.

erosion The cash flows of a new project that come at the expense of a firm's existing projects, i.e. how much does the project or product that is being considered cannibalise existing projects? Also see *cannibalise; cash flow; firm*.

error correction model A model, usually of economic variables, where the movement of a variable depends on its divergence or gap from the long run equilibrium in the previous period. Also see *vector error correction model*.

error mean square The error sum of squares divided by its number of degrees of freedom. Also see *degrees of freedom*.

error of estimation The difference between estimated and actual value.

error sum of squares In the analysis of variance, this is the portion of total variability that is due to the random component in the data. It is based on the replication of observations at certain treatment combinations in the experiment. It is sometimes called the residual sum of squares, although this is really a better term to use only when the sum of squares is based on the remnants of a model fitting process and not on replication. Also see *variance*.

error variance The variance of the error term in a model. Also see *variance*.

escrow A legal arrangement where an asset is delivered into a trust pending further transaction obligations such as payments. Cash delivered into an escrow account is usually invested in short-term low-risk assets until the date at which it is paid to a counterparty. Share certificates are often placed in escrow accounts when used as security packages in loan transactions.

escrowed to maturity Debt obligations that are not callable or easily pre-payable can be synthetically netted off by depositing the cash necessary to fund the interest and principal payments into an escrow account. With such an arrangement there will be a negative carry on the cash balance, i.e. the interest received will be smaller than the interest payable. Also see *negative carry*.

ESOP Employee share/stock ownership programme.

ESP The peseta, the former currency of Spain before the introduction of the euro. Also see *euro*.

ESR See *electronic scrip register*.

ESS See *explained sum of squares*.

estate duty Tax levied on the assets of a deceased.

estimated default frequency (EDF) See *expected default frequency*.

estopped A legal principle which precludes a person from asserting something contrary to what is implied by a previous action or statement of that person. For example, if a lender promised not to charge interest for the first three months, the lender would subsequently not be entitled to sue for the three months' interest.

Estrata downside risk model A model used to determine the cost of equity capital in foreign markets:

$$CE = R_{f,US} + (R_{MG} - R_{fG})RM_i$$

where $R_{f,US}$ = US risk-free rate; R_{MG} = expected global market return; R_{fG} = global risk-free rate; RM_i = ratio of semi-standard deviations of returns of local and world markets (relative downside risk measure).

This method accounts for downside risk more heavily. Also see *adjusted hybrid capital asset pricing model; beta approach; Bludgeon approach; equity capital; Erb-Harvey approach; global capital asset pricing model; Godfrey and Espinosa cost of equity model; Goldman Sachs model; lambda approach; Lessard's model; semi-standard deviation.*

ETA Estimated time of arrival.

ETC See *equipment trust certificate.*

ETF See *exchange traded fund.*

ETN See *exchange traded note.*

EU See *European Union.*

EUR The euro currency. Also see *euro.*

EUREX A European derivatives exchange and clearing house.

EURIBOR Euro interbank offer rate. The interbank rate in the Eurozone. Also see *interbank rate; LIBOR.*

euro The common currency of some of the countries in the European Union. Divided into cents. Also see *European Union; Eurozone.*

Eurobond A bond that is issued in a country outside the domicile of the country of the issuer. For example, if a South African company issues bonds in dollars and sells them in Japan, they would be called Eurobonds. In general, if the currency and the market are different from the company's domestic market, then issued bonds are called Eurobonds. The terms international bond and global bond are increasingly being used. Eurobonds settle through Euroclear and Clearstream. Also see *domicile; Eurodollar bond.*

Eurobond basis See *day count: 30E/360.*

Euroclear A company in Belgium that operates as a clearing and settlement house. Also see *clearing.*

Eurocredit A bank loan given in a currency that is not the currency of domicile of the lender. Also see *Eurobond.*

Eurocurrency Currency held in a country by a non-resident of that country. Also see *Eurobond.*

Eurodeposit A deposit in a Eurocurrency. Also see *Eurocurrency.*

Eurodollar Dollars in existence outside the US.

Eurodollar bond A Eurobond that is issued in US dollars. A South African company issuing bonds in dollars and selling them in Japan is issuing Eurodollar bonds. Also see *Eurobond.*

Eurodollar time deposit A US dollar deposit outside the US. They can yield slightly higher interest rates than deposits in the US. Also see *interest rate.*

Euromarket The market for financial securities in Europe.

Euronote A debt instrument of short tenor (commercial paper) issued by companies in the Euromarket. Also see *commercial paper; Eurobond*.

European callable bond A bond that is callable only on predefined dates.

European Central Bank (ECB) The ECB is the central bank for Europe's single currency, the euro. The ECB's main task is to maintain the euro's purchasing power and thus price stability in the euro area, i.e. to control inflation etc. The euro area in 2007 comprised 12 European Union countries that have introduced the euro currency since 1999. Also see *central bank; euro; European Union; inflation*.

European Economic Area (EEA) EU countries, including Norway, Iceland and Lichtenstein. Also see *European Union*.

European option An option that may only be exercised on the expiry date. Also see *American option; option*.

European overnight index average (EONIA) The weighted average of the interest rates of all the overnight interbank lending transactions in the European Monetary Union. The rate is published by the European Banking Federation. EONIA differs from EURIBOR in tenor as it is an overnight rate. Also see *EURIBOR; interest rate; South African overnight index average; weighted average*.

European-style FX Foreign exchange rate quote where the US dollar is quoted as the base currency, for example US$1 = €0.7. Also see *American-style FX*.

European Union (EU) A union of European countries allied to advance the causes and economic benefits of the member countries. Countries included in 2007/8 are Austria, Belgium, Bulgaria, Cyprus, Czech Republic, Denmark, Estonia, Finland, Germany, Greece, Hungary, Ireland, Italy, Latvia, Lithuania, Luxembourg, Malta, Netherlands, Poland, Portugal, Romania, Slovakia, Slovenia, Spain, Sweden and the United Kingdom. Not all countries use the euro currency, only those in the Eurozone. Also see *euro; Eurozone*.

Eurowarrant A warrant traded in the European markets. Also see *warrant*.

Euroyen bond A bond issued in yen by a company that is not Japanese outside Japan. A Euroyen bond is a particular class of Eurobond. Also see *Eurobond; Eurodollar bond*.

Eurozone The European monetary area.

EVA See *economic value added*.

event of default (EOD) In loan agreements, a set of conditions is imposed on borrowers to protect the lenders from losing their money. If the borrower fails to meet the requirements set out in a loan agreement, an event of default occurs.

The key events of default include non-payment of interest or principal, breach of any financial covenants, breach of other stated obligations, misrepresentation of information, cross default, insolvency, cessation of business, unlawfulness of financial documents and material adverse changes.

When an event of default occurs, the borrower is required to notify lenders. Lenders put a drawstop in place and no more funds are advanced. The borrowers and lenders then meet to decide how to remedy the default and/or how the loan will be accelerated. Also see *cross default; drawstop; financial covenant*.

events after the balance sheet date Those events, favourable and unfavourable, that occur between the balance sheet date and the date when the financial statements are authorised for issue. Two types of events can be identified:

- Those that provide evidence of conditions that existed at the balance sheet date (adjusting events after the balance sheet date)
- Those that are indicative of conditions that arose after the balance sheet date (non-adjusting events after the balance sheet date).

Also see *balance sheet; financial statements*.

evergreen An agreement that renews at the end of a term. The term is used for loans which do not have a defined maturity date but are cancelled with a given numbers of days' notice. Evergreen repetition of representations is repetition of representations daily. Also see *representation*.

EVT See *extreme value theory*.

ex Without rights. Also see *ex dividend; ex interest; ex rights*.

excess reserves Banks and other financial institutions that have reserves in excess of their reserve requirements and clearing balance. Also see *capital adequacy; reserve requirement*.

excess spread The difference between the interest rate paid and interest received. The term is used with reference to a securitisation vehicle. For example, if the commercial paper issued to fund the securitisation of mortgage bonds is issued at LIBOR + 100 bp and the mortgage bonds pay LIBOR + 150 bp, then the excess spread is 50 bp. Also see *interest rate; LIBOR; securitisation*.

exchangeable bond The holder of a bond has the right or option to convert the bond to a specific predetermined number of shares in another company. These are used by holding companies when lending to their subsidiaries. Also see *bond; convertible debt/bond*.

exchange control The regulation and restriction of foreign exchange flows by authorities. Exchange controls are put in place to prevent the flight of cash from a country and the destabilisation of exchange rates. Central banks exercise exchange control by setting regulations and through open market operations. Also see *foreign exchange; managed float; open market operations*.

exchange delivery settlement price (EDSP) The price of the settlement of a futures contract decided by the clearing house that takes variation margins already paid into account. The final price of the underlying is calculated by averaging over a short period of time to prevent rogue traders cornering the market. Also see *clearing house; corner the market; variation margin*.

exchange offer Swapping of debt for equity.

exchange rate The cost or price of a unit of one currency in terms of another.

exchange rate parity The supply and demand for a currency is perfectly balanced. Also see *fixed exchange rate; interest rate parity; purchasing power parity; sterilisation*.

exchange rate points 1/10 000th of a currency unit, i.e. 10^{-4}.

exchange rate risk When buying or selling securities and debt in foreign markets or running operations, the investor needs to convert his/her home currency into foreign currency or vice versa. Fluctuations in the exchange rate expose the investor to additional risk.

Investors add on risk premiums to their required rate of return to compensate for assuming this risk or they enter into hedging contracts to minimise or eliminate this risk. Also see *hedge*.

exchange traded A financial instrument such as equities, derivatives or commodities futures that are traded on recognised financial exchanges like the LSE, JSE and NYSE. Also see *JSE; London Stock Exchange; New York Stock Exchange*.

exchange traded fund (ETF) A fund that tracks stock market indices and is passively managed. It can be bought or sold at any time during the day and can be sold short. An ETF is made up of the appropriate proportions of the underlying stocks that the particular index tracks. It is designed to track the performance of and gain broad exposure to the sector it tracks.

One of the nuances that should be considered when using ETFs is that using market capitalisation indices results in a fund that is overweight in the stocks that are overvalued by the market and vice versa for the undervalued stocks.

The SATRIX 40 is a popular South African ETF. Sometimes called a tracker fund. Also see *exchange traded note; market capitalisation; overweight; Satrix 40; sell short*.

exchange traded note (ETN) A publicly traded, index-linked debt instrument that acts like an exchange traded fund (ETF). Instead of buying a note with an underlying asset, basket of assets or commodity, a debt note is bought with the same returns as an underlying index. The principal risk the investor faces is the credit risk of the issuer of the note so the issuers are often set up as ring-fenced SPVs. Also see *exchange traded fund; ring fenced; special-purpose vehicle*.

Exchequer In the UK, the government department charged with the collection and management of national revenue. This department is called the National Treasury in South Africa. The South African Reserve Bank uses an account called the exchequer account to account for the inflow of government funds. Also see *exchequer account; South African Reserve Bank; treasury*.

exchequer account The South African Reserve Bank uses an account called the exchequer account to account for the inflow of government funds. Also see *paymaster general; South African Reserve Bank*.

excise duty See *excise tax*.

excise tax A special tax levied on particular goods produced in a country. Excise tax is usually charged on goods such as cigarettes and alcohol. Sometimes called a sin tax. Also see *customs duty*.

exco Executive committee.

excon Exchange control.

ex dividend Shares trade ex dividend when the purchaser of the share is not entitled to the next dividend payment. The shares go ex dividend shortly after the record date and before the date on which the dividend is paid. The dividend goes to the seller if shares are sold in the ex dividend period. The price of securities usually drops as shares become ex dividend as investors are not entitled to the dividend payout until the next dividend declaration date, i.e. the upcoming dividend payment is not factored into the share price. Also see *cum dividend; dividend; ex interest; record date*.

execution The performance of the mechanics of a financial transaction.

execution risk The risk that the issue of a financial instrument or syndicated loan will not be fully subscribed at the launch price.

exercise A term used to indicate that the holder of the option is exercising the right to buy or sell the underlying asset as per the option contract.

exercise price See *strike price*.

ex interest If a bond is traded when the register for payment is closed (record date), the coupon will be paid to the seller of the bond and hence all accrued interest will be included in the purchase price of the bond.

all-in price = clean price plus accrued interest

Also see *accrued interest; cum interest; ex dividend*.

exogenous In an economic model, an exogenous change is one that comes from outside the model and is unexplained by the model. For example, in the simple supply and demand model, a change in consumer tastes or preferences is unexplained by the model and leads to endogenous changes in demand that lead to changes in the equilibrium price. Also see *endogenous; equilibrium price level*.

exotic Financial instruments that are non-standard, i.e. not plain vanilla. These usually evolve from instruments or markets that are illiquid or underdeveloped. Also see *illiquid; vanilla*.

expansion option An option to expand an investment or asset. Also see *option*.

expectations Anticipation by investors of a particular result for a company. Share prices are driven by expectations of the revenue generation ability of a company and future prospects.

expectations theory See *adaptive expectations*.

expected default frequency (EDF) A measure of the probability that a firm will default on its debt obligations over a specified period of time. The time horizon is one year. An EDF value of 1.4 indicates that there is a 1.4% chance that the firm will default in the next year. The key metrics that determine an EDF are the current market value of a firm, the level of a firm's debt obligations and the vulnerability of the company value to changes in market valuations. EDF modelling includes historical market default data. Credit rating agencies such as Moody's supply EDF modelling resources and expertise. Also see *credit rating agency; KMV*.

expected exchange rate The expected value of the exchange rate at a date in the future.

expected loss The expected value of the losses associated with a loan or class of assets. More formally, this translates into the 50th percentile (mean value) of the loss probability distribution calculated from historic periods. The expected loss is supposed to be a forward-looking measure and is therefore adjusted for factors such as business changes and the business cycle. The expected loss combines factors such as the adjusted exposure and the expected default frequency. Also see *expected default frequency; expected value; unexpected loss*.

expected return The return that investors expect to receive when investing in a particular asset. The expected return is a weighted average of all the possible outcomes. It is therefore calculated by multiplying the probability of an occurrence of a state with its associated outcome:

$$R = \sum_{i=1}^{n} k_i \times P_i$$

where R = the expected return; k_i = the return in the particular state i; P_i = the probability of occurrence of that state i; n = the number of states.

The mean of a normal distribution is often considered to be the expected return. Also see *arithmetic mean; normal or Gaussian distribution*.

expected value The expected value is usually the mean value of a sample set. For time series data that has an insignificant degree of autocorrelation, at a point in time t the best estimate of the value at $t + 1$ is the population mean. The expected value at $t + 1$ is therefore also the mean. Also see *autocorrelation; arithmetic mean*.

expenditure
1. Money spent in the hope of generating revenue.
2. An economic indicator that consists of all government, private sector and parastatal expenditure. Also see *parastatal*.

expense ratio A cost to income ratio that is used to analyse banking or insurance companies where the income is measured as premiums received. Also see *cost to income ratio*.

expenses Decreases in economic benefits during the accounting period in the form of outflows or depletions of assets or incurrence of liabilities that result in decreases in equity. Cash flows relating to distributions to equity participants are not classed as expenses.

experienced volatility The actual fluctuation of market prices while running an options position. It is a backward-looking measure of actual fluctuations. Also see *historical volatility; implied volatility; volatility*.

expiration date The last day on which an option may be exercised. Also see *American option; European option; option*.

explained sum of squares (ESS) The sum of squared predicted value deviations in a standard regression model. For example, $y_i = a + bx_i + \varepsilon_i$ where y_i = the response variable; x_i = the explanatory variable; a and b = coefficients; i indexes the observations from 1 to n; ε_i = the error term.

If $\hat{a}$ and $\hat{b}$ are the estimated regression coefficients, then $\hat{y}_{i_1} = \hat{a} + \hat{b}x_i$ is the predicted variable. The ESS is the sum of the squares of the differences of the predicted values and the grand mean:

$$\text{explained sum of squares (ESS)} = \sum_{i=1}^{n}(\hat{y}_i - \bar{y})^2$$

In general, total sum of squares = explained sum of squares + residual sum of squares. Also see *regression; residual sum of squares*.

exponential moving average (EMA) See *moving average*.

export credit The provision of financial support in the form of a loan or guarantee by an export credit agency to a company that is exporting goods to countries that may carry some risk. Export credit finance usually attracts low rates due to the guarantees provided by institutions of strong creditworthiness. Also see *export credit agency*.

export credit agency (ECA) An agency set up by a domestic government that provides export credit guarantees, finance and insurance to companies in that country to support their business efforts abroad. They are set up to promote the export of goods from their home country. Also see *export credit*.

Export Credit Guarantee Department The official export credit agency of the UK. Also see *export credit agency*.

export deflator See *implicit price deflator*.

export parity pricing The world prices of goods multiplied by the exchange rate less costs associated with export such as transport and tariffs. The export parity price should constitute the floor for prices domestically as companies will start selling in the international markets if local prices trend below export parity pricing levels. Also see *import parity pricing*.

exposure The degree to which an investment is susceptible to a specific risk (unsystematic risk). For example, an investor holding shares in a gold mining company is exposed to the price of gold. Also see *unsystematic risk*.

exposure at default (EAD) The exposure or potential loss that a bank may have when a borrower defaults at the time that the borrower defaults. Basel II uses the EAD measure in the calculation of economic capital. The calculation of EAD is governed by the Basel approach (advanced or foundation approach). Also see *Basel; economic capital*.

expropriation The forced sale of an asset at a price dictated by government. The price for the asset may be substantially below market value. Investors who invest in markets that face risks of expropriation will demand premiums for assuming the additional risk.

ex rights When a share is selling without a recently declared right. The share sells ex rights after the record date of the rights issue. Also see *record date; rights issue offer*.

ex rights price The price of a share after a rights issue. Also see *ex dividend; nil price; subscription price*.

extendable bond A bond with an option that the issuer may exercise to extend the maturity of the bond. Companies use these bonds to lock in more favourable interest rates than would be available in the market to refinance the bonds at the point of the extension. Also see *bond; interest rate; option*.

extension fee A fee charged to extend the tenor of a loan agreement. When the option to extend is delivered, the decision to do so is the choice of the lender. This is different to term out provisions where lenders are obliged to extend. Also see *evergreen; term out fee*.

external debt Obligations to creditors outside a home country.

external value of a currency The buying power of a currency in a foreign market.

extra dividend See *special dividend*.

extraordinary general meeting (EGM) A general meeting that is not scheduled at an ordinary time. They are usually used to address issues that have arisen and cannot be addressed at an annual general meeting. Also see *annual general meeting; special general meeting*.

extraordinary item An item in a company's accounts that is not considered to be normal in the course of trading and is unlikely to occur again. It is often excluded when analysing revenue. Also see *act of God*.

extraordinary redemption A bond that can be called by an issuer under special conditions such as natural disasters, failed projects and other unanticipated events.

extraordinary resolution See *special resolution*.

extreme value theory (EVT) A branch in statistical analysis that is used to analyse extreme deviations from the expected value of a probability distribution. In the banking industry, EVT is used to derive probabilities associated with unexpected losses. Also see *unexpected loss*.

face value The value of a financial instrument when the instrument is issued or redeemed from the issuer at its date of maturity. The term is derived from the values printed on bond and share certificates in the past. The face value is not necessarily the price paid for the instrument. Sometimes called the nominal value or par value. Also see *nominal value; par value; share premium*.

facility A loan or financial support.

facility agreement Formal documentation that outlines the terms and conditions of a loan. Facility agreements are signed by borrowers and lenders and legally bind all parties to the terms and conditions contained in the agreements. Also see *Loan Market Association*.

facility fee A fee payable to participating banks in a syndicated loan calculated as a small percentage of the outstanding loan amount. In the US facility fees are charged on the whole facility amount irrespective of the level to which the facility is drawn. In the European market it is common for banks to charge a commitment fee on the balance of the undrawn facility and a margin on the drawn facility. Also see *administrative agent fee; commitment fee; margin; participation fee; prepayment fee; syndicated loan; upfront fee; usage fee*.

facility letter A letter that outlines banking facilities a lender is prepared to make available to a borrower and some of the key conditions associated with that availability. Facility letters are often used for vanilla loan agreements such as general banking facilities. Also see *vanilla*.

factor debtors (factoring) A company's debtors book (accounts receivable) is turned into cash by selling it to a financier who becomes the legal holder of the debt obligations. The financier assumes responsibility for collections as well as the credit risk of the debtors. Factoring is a useful method of raising cash if debt and equity are not accessible options. Factoring provides cash of between 60% and 80% of the value of the receivable accounts. Benefits of factoring include:

- turning credit sales into cash
- providing additional working capital to take advantage of immediate business opportunities
- increasing management administration time as debtors management is effectively outsourced
- gaining credit information from the factor
- benefiting from the wealth of knowledge and experience of the factor.

Also see *credit risk; debtor; invoice discounting facility; securitisation; working capital*.

factors of production Natural resources, labour, capital and entrepreneurship.

failed trade A trade that failed to settle because a party to the contract failed to meet one or all the conditions specified in the contract. The failure is usually caused by non-payment.

fair value The amount for which an asset can be exchanged or a liability settled between knowledgeable willing parties in an arms length transaction. Fair value is often calculated from the present value of future cash flows using an appropriate discount rate. Also see *arms length; asset; liability; present value*.

fairway bond A bond that capitalises or accrues interest when the underlying base interest rate is outside a predefined range or zone. It derives its name from golf. If the ball is on the fairway, the game is going well and if the ball is in the rough, the game is going poorly and the outlook is negative. Also see *interest rate*.

fallen angel A company that previously had an investment grade credit rating and has slid to sub-investment grade. Also see *credit rating; investment grade; sub-investment grade*.

false market A market where information is not transparent and reliable.

Fannie Mae Federal National Mortgage Association. Fannie Mae is an organisation in the US that invests in home loans and provides guarantees. Fannie Mae buys mortgages on the secondary market, pools them and sells them on in the form of collateralised debt obligations or agency bonds. Liquidity is injected into the primary home lending market by Fannie Mae investing in the secondary market. Also see *agency bond; collateralised debt obligation; Freddie Mac; secondary market*.

Farmer Mac Federal Agricultural Mortgage Corporation. Farmer Mac is an organisation in the US that invests in agricultural loans and provides guarantees. Farmer Mac buys agricultural mortgages on the secondary market, pools them and sells them on in the form of collateralised debt obligations or agency bonds. Also see *agency bond; collateralised debt obligation; Fannie Mae; Freddie Mac*.

FAS See *free alongside ship*.

FCF See *free cash flow*.

FCFE See *free cash flow to equity*.

FDI See *foreign direct investment*.

FEC See *forward exchange contract*.

Fed See *Federal Reserve*.

federal funds Funds placed on deposit with the Federal Reserve of the US by financial institutions.

Federal Reserve The central bank of the United States of America. Also see *central bank; South African Reserve Bank*.

Fed funds rate The rate at which depository institutions lend balances to other depository institutions through the US Federal Reserve (Fed). The Fed does not directly have the ability to change this rate as they do with the central bank discount rate, but they can influence the rate through open market operations such as the purchase and sale of government treasury bills. There are various published rates including the spot, average and target rates. LIBOR and EURIBOR are similar rates used in the European market. Also see *central bank discount rate; EURIBOR; Federal Reserve; LIBOR; open market operations; spot market; treasury bill*.

feedstock Raw materials to supply or feed a manufacturing plant.

fee income Income that banks generate for providing services not related to lending money. Arranging fees charged to manage a bond issue is considered fee income.

fee letter A letter in addition to other documentation such as term sheets that details fees to be paid to the arranger of a financial transaction. A fee letter is used when the general details of the fees are not to be released to a wider audience. Also see *term sheet*.

ferrous metal A metal that contains iron (Fe). Steel, stainless steel and many other materials are classed as ferrous metals.

FFO See *funds from operations*.

fiat currency A currency that is not backed by a precious metal such as gold. In modern economies just about all currencies are fiat currencies and their only intrinsic value is the trust that the holders have in the currency. Also see *gold standard*.

FIBOR Frankfurt interbank offered rate. Also see EURIBOR.

FICA See *Financial Intelligence Centre Act*.

fiduciary A person responsible for taking care of property in a trust agreement.

fiduciary duty A lawful responsibility to act in the best interest of another party. Also see *board of directors*.

FIFO First in first out. FIFO constitutes an accounting method for valuing inventory and thereby assigning cost of sales. A company using this method records the first units that were purchased as the first ones that are sold. FIFO has the effect of valuing the inventory of a company lower than the LIFO (last in first out) method. Switching from FIFO to LIFO has the effect of decreasing a company's earnings as new goods are effectively sold at old prices. Also see *inventory; LIFO*.

FIFSA Financial Intermediaries Federation of South Africa.

fill or kill order A fill or kill order requires that a buy and sell match the order identically or the order is not executed.

FIM The former currency of Finland, the markka. Finland now uses the euro. Also see *euro*.

final hold The final amount allocated to a bank in a syndicated loan. The final hold may be scaled back if total commitments exceed the facility amount, i.e. the deal is oversubscribed. Also see *commitment*.

final notice A notice issued to a debtor indicating that final payment is due.

final salary scheme See *defined benefit fund*.

final take See *final hold*.

finance vehicle See *special-purpose vehicle*.

financial account An account used in economics to calculate direct investment, portfolio investment and loans to a country from the outside world. Also see *current account*.

financial advisor A person or company that is employed to offer advice on investments in financial markets. They may also be employed to manage assets.

financial analyst A person employed by banks and fund managers to research specific companies, markets or market sectors. They produce reports, sometimes called broker reports, that recommend to their customers what stocks and markets to trade in and how to do so.

financial asset
1. An asset that is not physical such as stocks, bonds and other financial instruments.
2. For companies, a financial equity asset is an equity asset that represents less than 20% of the total ownership. Also see *equity*.

financial assistance The process of a company giving financial aid to another entity that is acquiring shares in it. In many jurisdictions supplying financial assistance is illegal. South Africa has limitations imposed on the provision of financial assistance which is covered by section 38 and subsequent amendments to the Income Tax Act.

financial capital Money or funds that can be used to acquire financial assets.

financial close The date on which all the conditions precedent have been met in a financial transaction. Also see *conditions precedent*.

financial condition The financial health of a company. The financial condition includes factors such as outstanding liabilities, assets and equity positions. The financial condition can be measured with ratios such as debt ratios and capital structure ratios and is often expressed as a formal credit rating published by a credit rating agency such as S&P, Fitch or Moody's. Also see *capital structure; debt ratio*.

financial cost ratio

$$\text{financial cost ratio} = \frac{\text{PBT}}{\text{PBIT}}$$

where PBT = profit before tax; PBIT = profit before interest and tax. Also see *Du Pont analysis*.

financial covenant A covenant on a loan that forces the borrower to maintain minimum levels of financial performance. Financial covenants include coverage covenants and leverage covenants as well as current ratio covenants, tangible net worth covenants, minimum net worth and maximum capital expenditure covenants, and loan to value and capital ratio covenants which are often used for financial institutions. Also see *affirmative covenant; capital ratio covenant; covenant; coverage covenant; current ratio covenant; leverage covenant; loan to value ratio; maximum capital expenditure covenant; minimum net worth; negative covenant; tangible net worth covenant*.

financial flexibility The capacity of a firm to meet any unforeseen contingencies that may arise and take advantage of unanticipated opportunities. The funds a company has on hand and credit lines (standby banking facilities) in place ultimately determine the financial flexibility of a firm. Also see *credit line; firm*.

financial futures Futures contracts that are based on financial instruments such as an equity share and not an underlying commodity. Also see *commodity; futures contract*.

financial institution An organisation that accepts funds from the public and invests them in financial assets. Banks, fund managers and insurance companies are financial institutions.

Financial Intelligence Centre Act (FICA) An Act passed by the South African government to receive, analyse and disseminate suspicious transaction reports. It also creates a range of anti-money laundering obligations for financial institutions, including customer identification and verification, record-keeping requirements and requirements governing internal controls. Also see *know your customer; money laundering*.

financial intermediary An entity such as a bank or other financial institution and brokers that match parties in financial transactions. Banks match depositors with lenders and assume some of the risks involved.

financial lease See *capital lease*.

financial leverage See *leverage*.

financial leverage equation The equation that relates return on equity to the level of debt or leverage in a company:

$$ROE = ROTC + [ROTC - k_d]\frac{D}{E}$$

The financial leverage equation can be derived from:

$$ROE = \frac{EAIAT}{E} \equiv \frac{EBIAT = k_d D}{E} \text{ and } ROTC = \frac{EBITA}{D+E}$$

where k_d = the interest payable to debt holders; ROE = return on equity; ROTC = return on total capital; D = debt; E = equity; EAIAT = earnings after interest after tax; EBITA = earnings before interest after tax.

Also see *leverage; return on equity*.

financial market A place where buyers and seller meet to exchange capital assets such as shares and bonds. Also see *bond*.

financial needs approach An approach used to determine the appropriate level of life insurance for a customer based on the future requirements of their beneficiaries.

financial rate agreement curve (FRAR) Swaps between banks to balance out interest rate risks. This curve is useful in determining what the market thinks is going to happen to interest rates in the future. If the curve moves, then the market is expecting interest rate changes. Also see *interest rate risk; swap*.

financial regulator In South Africa, the financial regulators are the Bank Supervision Department of the South African Reserve Bank and the Financial Services Board. In the UK the Financial Services Authority (FSA) is the financial sector regulatory authority. Most countries have financial regulatory authorities. Also see *Financial Services Authority; Financial Services Board; South African Reserve Bank*.

financial risk The risk of not being able to cover financial obligations. Financial risk is highly dependent on the debt levels in the business. Financial risk therefore depends on the capital structure, issued preference shares, lease obligations and economic cycle. Also see *business risk; capital structure; leverage; preference share; total risk*.

Financial Services Authority (FSA) Regulator of the financial services industry in the UK. The statutory objectives of the FSA include:

- maintaining confidence in the UK financial system
- promoting public understanding of the financial system
- securing protection for customers
- contributing to the reduction in financial crime.

Financial Services Board (FSB) A regulatory organisation in South Africa that regulates the financial services industry in the interest of the public. The main Acts that are administered by the FSB in 2007/8 include the:

- Financial Services Board Act (Act 97 of 1990)
- Pension Funds Act (Act 24 of 1956)
- Friendly Societies Act (Act 25 of 1956)
- Financial Institutions (Protection of Funds) Act (Act 28 of 2001)
- Financial Supervision of the Road Accident Fund Act (Act 8 of 1993)
- Supervision of the Financial Institutions Rationalisation Act (Act 32 of 1996)

- Long-term Insurance Act (Act 52 of 1998)
- Short-term Insurance Act (Act 53 of 1998)
- Inspection of Financial Institutions Act (Act 80 of 1998)
- Insider Trading Act (Act 135 of 1998)
- Financial Advisory and Intermediary Services (FAIS) Act (Act 37 of 2002)
- Collective Investment Schemes Control Act (Act 45 of 2002)
- The Securities Services Act (Act 36 of 2004).

Also see *collective investment scheme*.

financial services industry Includes banking, credit granting services, insurance, retirement funding and investment services.

financial stability The price stability and financial conditions in a country.

financial statements A complete set of financial statements comprises:
- a balance sheet
- an income statement
- a statement showing either:
  - all changes in equity or
  - changes in equity other than those arising from transactions with equity holders acting in their capacity as equity holders
- a cash flow statement
- notes containing a summary of significant accounting policies and other explanatory notes.

Also see *balance sheet; cash flow statement; consolidated accounts; income statement*.

financial structure The side of the balance sheet indicating the firm's equity and liabilities. Also see *balance sheet; capital structure*.

financial structure ratio A ratio that gives the user an idea of how the company is capitalising itself:

$$\text{financial structure ratio} = \frac{\text{assets}}{\text{equity}}$$

Also see *Du Pont analysis*.

Financial Times A highly regarded business newspaper published daily in the UK and distributed throughout the world.

Financial Times Industrial Index An unweighted index of the top 30 companies traded on the London Stock Exchange. This index has largely been replaced by the FTSE 100 Index. Sometimes called the FT 30 Index. Also see *FTSE 100*.

financial year A 12-month period which is considered to be a year in which financial transactions are recorded. Companies are required to produce a set of financial statements and have an annual general meeting (AGM) at the end of their financial year. Also see *annual general meeting; financial statements*.

financing cash flow Cash flow associated with the issuing of equity or debt and the associated payments of dividends and interest. Also see *dividend; investment cash flow; operating cash flow*.

finco A company set up as a special-purpose financing vehicle.

FINDI (Financial and Industrial Index) An index of financial and industrial stocks traded on the JSE. This index is traded through derivatives on SAFEX. Also see *ALSI; INDI; JSE; RESI; South African Futures Exchange*.

fine ounce A troy ounce of 99.5% pure gold. Also see *bullion; carat; troy ounce*.

fire sale value The value of the business if the business were liquidated and the assets were sold relatively quickly. Also see *liquidation*.

firm A legal person that is an individual, company, partnership or the trustee of a trust.

firm commitment See *commitment*.

firm offer An offer or quote that remains valid for a stated period.

firm order An order that remains valid for the stated period. The supplier or broker does not have to refer back to the customer in the firm offer window to execute a purchase or trade. Also see *discretionary account*.

firm price See *firm quote*.

firm quote A promise to trade at the quoted price. On stock exchanges market makers are required to provide firm quotes for a specified minimum transaction size. Also see *market maker*.

firm value See *enterprise value*.

first call date The first date at which a callable bond may be called. Also see *callable bond; call option; convertible debt/bond*.

first demand guarantee See *demand guarantee*.

first difference The first difference operator (Δ) is often used when analysing time series data such as stock market prices. It is calculated by differencing the current value of the time series by the previous value, i.e. $y_t - y_{t-1}$. Also see *derivative*.

first lien A claim or lien on an asset in a loan or alternate debt instrument that is senior to other claims on those assets in an event of default. A first lien loan is more senior to a second lien loan. Also see *lien; second lien*.

first order integrated The time series is of first order if the present value depends only on the previous value and not by more than one lag. If the elements of a time series are differenced, i.e. $t_{i+1} - t_i$, then stationary series is obtained. The series is said to be first order integrated. Also see *autocorrelation; unit root*.

fiscal A generic term used to describe borrowing and spending.

fiscal agent An agent that handles treasury-type fiscal operations on behalf of a company. These functions may include the payment of dividends and coupons on bonds. Also see *dividend; fiscal*.

fiscal balance The difference between revenue and expenses. If the balance is positive, the entity has a fiscal surplus; if negative, there is a fiscal deficit. The term fiscal balance is used most often with reference to government spending and revenue. In South Africa, data to calculate government fiscal balance is available from the South Africn Reserve Bank website. Also see *deficit; South African Reserve Bank; surplus*.

fiscal drag An increase in nominal income due to inflation-related wage increases can push people into higher tax brackets, effectively taxing them more heavily in real terms. Governments avoid this effect by adjusting the tax brackets for inflation by a method called bracket indexation. Sometimes called bracket creep. Also see *bracket indexation; inflation*.

fiscal policy Spending and borrowing policy. The term is usually used in the context of government spending and borrowing.

fiscal stimulus Government spending to boost the economy.

fiscal year A 12-month period defined for taxation purposes. In South Africa, the fiscal year is from 1 April to 31 March and in the UK, the fiscal year is from 6 April to 5 April the following year. Also see *financial year*.

Fisher effect/equation An equation that gives the relationship between real interest rates, nominal interest rates and inflation and is defined by:

$$1 + R = (1 + r)(1 + h)$$

where R = nominal return; r = real return and h = inflation.

Also see *inflation; nominal interest rate; real interest rate*.

Fitch A credit rating agency. Also see *credit rating; credit rating agency*.

fixed annuity An annuity that pays a fixed amount for the contracted period. Also see *annuity*.

fixed asset A long-term tangible asset held for business use and not expected to be converted to cash in the current or upcoming fiscal year. Items such as manufacturing equipment, real estate and furniture are fixed assets. Fixed assets are sometimes referred to as plant or PPE. Also see *property, plant and equipment; tangible asset*.

fixed asset turnover A ratio that measures how effectively assets are being used to generate sales:

$$\text{fixed asset turnover ratio} = \frac{\text{sales}}{\text{fixed assets}}$$

If the fixed asset turnover ratio increases, then assets are being managed more efficiently. Note that the fixed asset turnover ratio is sensitive to purchases of assets late in the year that have not as yet been used effectively for the full reporting period in the generation of additional sales. Also see *asset management ratios*.

fixed capital Cash tied up in the fixed assets of a business.

fixed charge A charge in which the creditor can have a specific asset sold to cover payments not made in the event of default. The debtor may not transact on the asset without the charge holder's consent. A charge is in place to prevent borrowers disposing of key assets without permission of the lenders. Also see *charge; event of default; floating charge*.

fixed charge cover ratio A ratio that measures the degree to which operational cash flows cover interest payments, preference shares and other medium- to long-term obligations such as rentals and leases. It has various forms as indicated by the following equations:

1. $$\frac{\text{operating cash flow}}{\text{preference share payments}}$$

2. $\dfrac{\text{operating cash flow}}{\text{long-term intrest charges}}$

(Sometimes called interest cover or times interest earned.)

3. $\dfrac{\text{EBITDA + rental and operational lease payments}}{\text{interest charges + rental and operational lease payments}}$

(This ratio is often used in loan covenants.)

fixed cost See *fixed expense*.

fixed exchange rate Monetary authorities of a country make a commitment to intervene in currency markets by buying and selling currency to prevent the exchange rate from deviating off predefined fixed levels. Also see *clean float; crawling peg; exchange rate parity; managed float; pure float; sterilisation*.

fixed expense A cost that is not affected directly by production volumes. Fixed expenses remain regardless of volumes produced. Examples of fixed expenses include building maintenance and administration staff.

fixed for fixed A cross-currency swap that has two fixed rate legs.

fixed for floating An interest rate swap where one leg is a fixed interest rate and the other is a floating rate. Also see *interest rate swap*.

fixed income Investments that maintain a principal amount and pay a predictable interest, coupon or dividend. Bonds, loans and preference shares are examples of fixed income investments. Also see *bond; dividend; preference share*.

fixed income arbitrage A trading strategy that makes arbitrage profits off differently priced, nearly identical bonds. Also see *arbitrage*.

fixed income equivalent A convertible bond whose conversion option is so far out the money that the bond trades as if it were a straight fixed income instrument. Also see *convertible bond; out the money*.

fixed income security See *fixed income*.

fixed interest market Debt markets are sometimes called fixed interest markets because the majority of instruments carry fixed rates of interest. In pure form the fixed interest market is the market for fixed income securities only.

fixed interest rate A financial instrument that pays a fixed rate of return over the life of the contracted agreement. This is in contrast with a floating interest rate where the rate paid on the principal varies with market movements from period to period, normally one, three or six months. Also see *floating interest rate; JIBAR; LIBOR; variable interest rate*.

fixed interest rate bond A bond that pays a fixed interest coupon until maturity. Also see *coupon*.

fixed payment coverage ratio This ratio is a variant of the interest cover ratio and indicates how the operating profits of a company cover its long-term debt liability service costs:

$$\text{fixed payment coverage ratio} = \dfrac{\text{leasing expenses + interest}}{\text{operating profit}}$$

Also see *fixed charge cover ratio; interest cover; long-term debt*.

fixed peg exchange rate See *fixed exchange rate*.

fixed rate | floating charge

fixed rate A rate of interest that does not change over the life of a financial instrument.

fixed rate bond A bond with a fixed coupon payment and a single maturity date.

fixed rate payer The entity in an interest rate swap that agrees to pay a fixed rate with reference to a principal at predefined dates. Also see *interest rate swap*.

fixed rate receiver The entity in an interest rate swap that receives a fixed rate with reference to a principal at predefined dates. Also see *interest rate swap*.

fixed term A defined period of time.

flat yield (FY) The yield of the coupons on a bond against its purchase or market price.

$$\text{flat yield (FY)} = \frac{\text{gross annual coupon}}{\text{market price}}$$

The flat yield metric is used by investors who buy long dated or perpetual bonds and are not concerned about redemption or selling before the date of maturity. Also see *bond; yield to maturity*.

flat yield curve A yield curve that has long-term and short-term bonds giving the same or similar yields. Also see *backwardation; contango; yield; yield curve*.

flex
1. To change the margins or spreads on loans to sell them in the debt or syndicated loan market. Also see *margin; reverse flex; upward flex*.
2. A change in assumptions in a financial model to determine how sensitive it is to particular parameters.

flexible forward See *zero cost collar*.

flex option An option traded on an exchange such as Euronext. LIFFE that has flexible conditions. Changes such as the date of maturity can be made in the option contract. Also see *London International Financial Futures and Options Exchange (LIFFE)*.

flex the budget Restate an obsolete budget at new activity levels or make adjustments to reflect new information. Also see *budget*.

flex up See *upward flex*.

flight to safety The process of investors divesting from risky assets and purchasing safe assets such as government bonds and treasury bills. Also see *government bond; treasury bill*.

floater See *floating rate note*.

floating a company The process of listing a company on a stock exchange. Also see *delisting*.

floating charge A charge or security over assets of a business by creditors that occurs in the instance of a default triggering event.

With a fixed charge, a company needs permission from the charge holder to sell an asset. Floating charges are usually over operational assets such as inventories. With a floating charge, borrowers can buy and sell assets without explicit permission and the charge will only be initiated in an event of default or winding up. Floating charges exist because assets such as inventories are logistically impossible to secure with a fixed charge. In the event of liquidation of a company, floating charge holders are paid before unsecured debt holders, but do not have a senior claim on assets that are under fixed charges.

The holders of floating charge security are not entitled to all the proceeds of the sale of the assets governed by that charge. Proceeds are shared with liquidators and unsecured creditors in a predefined manner that advantages, but does not necessarily fully cover, charge holders.

Floating charges have the advantage that they can offer security holders security over significant portions of the business. Floating charges are disadvantaged by the fact that assets can be sold before the charge holders have the option of exercising their security.

There is no formal concept of a floating charge in South Africa and financiers in this market use a general notarial bond which achieves a similar effect. Also see *charge; event of default; fixed charge; general notarial bond; liquidation; winding up.*

floating exchange rate An exchange rate that is freely traded without the interference of monetary authorities. The monetary authorities do not have set targets or bands of exchange rates that they actively manage and will intervene only under exceptional circumstances. Also see *exchange rate parity; fixed exchange rate; sterilisation.*

floating interest rate An interest rate that changes or potentially can change with time during a contract period. Floating interest rates vary from period to period, typically one, three or six months, with three months being the most common. A floating rate is different from a fixed interest rate where the interest rate stays fixed for the life of the contract. Also see *fixed interest rate; interest rate; JIBAR; LIBOR.*

floating rate See *floating interest rate.*

floating rate bond (FRB) See *floating rate note.*

floating rate certificate of deposit (FRCD) A certificate of deposit paying a variable interest rate that is usually linked to money market rates. These certificates are used in intermarket lending. Also see *certificate of deposit; interest rate; money market.*

floating rate note (FRN) A medium-term bond with a variable coupon rate. The rate is usually defined as a spread to a floating reference rate such as LIBOR or JIBAR. Most FRNs have quarterly coupons. Investors in FRNs face little interest rate risk because the interest rates rise and fall with the market rates, but they are subject to the credit risk of the issuer. FRNs are over-the-counter instruments generally issued by banks, building societies, credit unions and corporates. Investors in FRNs are sophisticated investors who understand the nature and risk profile of the issuer. Sometimes called a floater. Also see *credit union; interest rate; JIBAR; LIBOR; over the counter; reference rate; spread.*

floating rate payer The entity in an interest rate swap that agrees to pay a floating interest rate and receives a fixed interest rate at predefined dates with reference to a principal or nominal amount. Also see *floating interest rate; interest rate; interest rate swap.*

floating rate receiver The entity in an interest rate swap that receives a floating rate and pays a fixed interest rate at predefined dates with reference to a principal amount. Also see *floating interest rate; interest rate swap.*

floor
1. A low point in a pricing cycle.
2. A series of options that protects holders against drops in interest rates. These can be constructed by shorting interest rate guarantees. Also see *cap; interest rate; interest rate guarantee; short position.*

floortion An option on a floor. Also see *floor; option*.

floor trading See *open outcry*.

flotation See *initial public offer*.

flow equilibrium price The price at which supply and demand for goods is matched. Also see *demand; equilibrium*.

flow through share A type of ordinary share that allows a corporation to make a tax deduction on dividend payments on behalf of the investors. The investors can then deduct the tax paid from their personal tax liability when filing their tax returns. Also see *dividend*.

FOB See *free on board*.

FOF See *futures and options fund*.

FOK See *fill or kill order*.

forbearance Lenders not enforcing debt obligations as they fall due.

forced conversion The process where the issuer of a callable convertible bond calls the bond. The bond holder is given a period of time to respond, usually one month, and if no response is imminent, the bond holder is given the call price of the bond irrespective of the value of the underlying stock. Callable convertible bonds are often classed as hybrid securities because they have equity-like characteristics. Also see *callable bond; hybrid*.

force majeure A clause in a contract that frees parties of obligations in circumstances of an extraordinary event out of the control of the contracted parties. Force majeure clauses in loan agreements include terms governing material adverse changes in the borrower's business or financial condition and changes in the state of debt capital markets. Examples of events covered by force majeure provisions may include earthquakes, other natural disasters, terrorist attacks and political changes. Also see *act of God*.

foreclosure The legal action that follows a default on a loan. In property finance, a foreclosure indicates that the property will be sold to repay the outstanding amount on the loan. If a company cannot settle debts under the foreclosure of one of its loans, the lender may start liquidation proceedings.

foreign bond A bond that is issued in a domestic market in the domestic market's currency by a foreign entity. Foreign bonds are regulated by the domestic market authorities and are usually given nicknames such as bulldog bonds (UK), Matilda bonds (Australia), maple bonds (Canada) and samurai bonds (Japan).

Since investors in foreign bonds are usually the residents of the domestic country, investors find them attractive because they can add foreign content to their portfolios without the additional exchange rate exposure. Sometimes called Eurobonds. Also see *bulldog bond; Eurobond; maple bond; Matilda bond; samurai bond*.

foreign concessionary loan A loan given by the World Bank for development by the International Monetary Fund for economic stabilisation. Also see *International Monetary Fund; World Bank*.

foreign currency bond See *foreign bond*.

foreign currency effect The change in the value of investments in foreign markets associated with appreciation or depreciation in the exchange rate. Rising strength of the foreign currency means that investors lose value in their home currency and depreciation means that investors gain value. Investors in foreign markets demand a premium for assuming exchange rate risk. Also see *exchange rate risk*.

foreign direct investment (FDI) Investment in the productive assets of a county. These investments are usually long term and are often called bricks and mortar investments. The investments are associated with significant ownership stakes and carry an equity stake of 10% or more. Also see *capital movement*.

foreign exchange Foreign currencies traded in a currency market. Also see *American-style FX; European-style FX*.

foreign exchange rate The rate at which a currency can be exchanged against other foreign currencies.

foreign exchange requirement A capital adequacy requirement that dictates that financial institutions hedge their exposure to changes in foreign exchange rates. Also see *capital adequacy; foreign exchange rate*.

foreign exchange risk See *exchange rate risk*.

foreign exchange swap See *FX swap*.

foreign investment See *foreign direct investment; foreign portfolio investment*.

foreign investment restrictions Restrictions designed to control foreign investment, usually with the intention of protecting a country's financial system.

foreign portfolio investment (FPI) Stocks and bonds bought by foreigners. These cash flows are usually prospective in nature and are not as long term as foreign direct investment. Also see *foreign direct investment*.

foreign reserves A country's holdings of foreign currencies and gold. If a country's international receipts are smaller than payments, the foreign reserves will decrease. The sum of the current account balance, the capital transfer balance, the financial account balance and unrecorded transactions affects changes in the foreign reserves. Gold reserves can be sold to obtain foreign currency and are therefore included in foreign reserve accounting. Foreign reserves are held by central banks and the stock of foreign reserves affects the country's currency convertibility. Central banks use their foreign reserves to smooth under- and overshoots of exchange rates caused by large financial transactions. Also see *central bank; currency convertibility; gold reserves*.

foreign sector Persons or companies acting as investors or lenders resident anywhere outside the country in question.

foreign tax credit When countries have double taxation treaties in place, an entity is given foreign tax credits in its home country for taxes paid to the foreign government party to the treaty. Also see *double taxation*.

FOREX See *foreign exchange*.

form 20F Financial statements and formal documentation submitted to the Securities and Exchange Commission (SEC). These filings are publicly available to investors for the purpose of evaluating investments. The 20F is required for the registration of securities of foreign private issuers on US exchanges. Also see *Securities and Exchange Commission*.

forward See *forward contract/dealing*.

forwardation See *contango*.

forward band See *zero cost collar*.

forward book Various net exposures for forward contracts which a bank has incurred as a result of dealing activities. For a central bank to reduce its currency forward book exposure, it needs to buy the underlying currencies, therefore increasing the country's net foreign reserves and potentially devaluing the currency in the process. Also see *central bank; forward contract/dealing*.

forward commitment See *forward contract/dealing*.

forward contract/dealing Dealing in commodities or securities for delivery at a date in the future. This allows dealers and manufacturers to cover their future requirements by hedging their more immediate requirements. These are similar to futures contracts but are not sold over the counter between investors. Also see *break forward; futures contract; over the counter*.

forward cover The purchase of the physical underlying asset in a forward contract to cover against potential future losses. In South Africa, the term is usually used with reference to protection against adverse changes in future exchange rates. Also see *forward contract/dealing*.

forward delivery Goods that are purchased for a delivery date in the future. Also see *futures contract*.

forward differential The difference between the forward and spot exchange rate usually quoted as point differences (basis points). The differences can be a discount or a premium. Sometimes the forward differential is called the swap rate. Also see *backwardation; basis point; contango; spot market; swap rate*.

forward discount See *discount forward*.

forward dividend yield A dividend yield calculated using projected rather than historic dividends. Forward dividend yields are used when a company is newly listed and does not have publicly available historic dividend information. Also see *dividend yield; historical dividend yield*.

forward exchange A contract to exchange one quantity of a currency for another at a predetermined date in the future. The rate of the exchange is specified as the contract is written.

forward exchange contract (FEC) The formal contract that governs a forward exchange transaction. Also see *forward exchange*.

forward exchange rate Rates determined in the forward exchange market. Also see *forward exchange*.

forward integration The process of suppliers venturing into front end business ventures to offer more direct service to the public or end consumer. Also see *backward integration; horizontal integration; vertical integration*.

forward interest rate The interest rate for a loan over a specific period starting at a specified date in the future. Also see *forward rate agreement; interest rate*.

forward margin The difference between the spot and forward exchange rate. Also see *forward exchange rate; spot market*.

forward PE The price earnings ratio calculated using future earnings estimates. Also see *historic PE; price earnings ratio*.

forward price The fixed price at which an asset will be purchased in a futures contract. Also see *asset; futures contract*.

forward rate agreement (FRA) An agreement that enables users to hedge against unfavourable movements in interest rates. FRAs are over-the-counter products and are not traded on exchanges. FRAs fix interest rates at dates in the future. For example, a 2×3 FRA is a two-month forward agreement on a three-month loan, i.e. a loan for three months that starts in two months' time. The interest rate on the loan, called the FRA rate, is set when the contract is first entered into. Because FRAs are cash settled, no loan is ever actually extended. Instead, contracts settle with a single cash payment made on the first day of the transaction called the settlement date. Also see *hedge; interest rate; over the counter; short-term interest rate futures*.

forward start An agreement to enter into contractual conditions at a predetermined date or range of dates in the future.

forward start swap A swap that is a commitment to enter into a swap at a predetermined date in the future. To construct the swap, two swap agreements of differing lengths are entered into. For example, an investor could enter a three-year and two-year swap. The two-year swap cancels the cash flows of the three-year swap in the first two years and the investor is left with the swap exposure for year three only. Sometimes called a deferred swap. Also see *forward rate agreement; swap*.

FOS Financial Ombudsman Service.

fourth market Buyers and sellers that trade equities without the intermediation of brokers. Large financial institutions often trade with one another without the use of an intermediary.

FP Future price.

FPI Financial Planning Institute.

FRA See *forward rate agreement*.

fractional share A fraction of a share. Fractional shares can arise when shareholders elect to purchase more shares with dividends and do not have a whole number of dividends to purchase the last share.

fractional warrant A warrant that is an option on a fraction of a share. These need to be combined to purchase a new share. Also see *warrant*.

franchise A business arrangement where a franchise sets up a business using the name, trademarks and proprietary technology of the franchisor. Franchisors supply inventories, advertising and many other services to assist the franchisee.

frank/franc The currency of Switzerland and former currency of France and Belgium before they joined the euro. Some West African countries use the franc as a unit of currency. Also see *CFA franc; euro*.

franked dividend A dividend payment that has already been taxed. Tax is not payable by the dividend receiver. Also see *dividend*.

franked income Income that has already been taxed. Tax is not payable by the income receiver.

fraud Illegal misrepresentation of information to make a monetary gain.

FRB Floating rate bond. Also see *floating rate note*.

FRCD See *floating rate certificate of deposit*.

Freddie Mac Federal Home Loan Mortgage Corporation of the United States. Freddie Mac is an organisation that invests in home loans and provides loan guarantees. Freddie Mac buys mortgages in the secondary market, pools them and sells them on in the form of collateralised debt obligations or agency bonds. By investing in the secondary home loan market Freddie Mac provides liquidity to the primary market makers. Also see *agency bond; collateralised debt obligation; Fannie Mae; mortgage; primary market*.

free alongside ship (FAS) A requirement that the seller of goods has to deliver them alongside a ship on a quay. Also see *free on board*.

free asset ratio The ratio of the assets of an insurance company to its liabilities. Also see *solvency ratio*.

free capital
1. Capital assets such as cash and cash equivalents. Also see *cash equivalent*.
2. Shares in a company available for purchase on open markets. Often called the free float. Also see *free float*.

free cash flow (FCF) Net cash after capital expenditure:

free cash flow (FCF) = NI + D&A − CI ± ΔWC

where NI = net income; D&A = depreciation and amortisation; ΔWC = the changes in working capital.

FCF measures may also make adjustments for items such as dividends received, provisions made and exceptional items.

FCF represents the cash that a company can generate after laying out the money required to maintain or expand its asset base (stay in business capital). Free cash flow is an important measure because it indicates whether a company is in a position to pursue opportunities that enhance shareholder value. Without cash, it is difficult to develop new products, make acquisitions, pay dividends and reduce debt.

Banks often use FCF to debt service obligation measures as covenants in lending agreements and to assess the ability of the business to service debt. Also see *acquisition; asset; capital expenditure; cash flow; debt service cover ratio; out the money; stay in business capital*.

free cash flow to equity (FCFE) A measure of the cash available to equity holders in a business after creditors have been paid. FCFE is therefore free cash flow (FCF) adjusted for debts paid and received. FCFE is calculated by:

free cash flow to equity (FCFE) = FCF + new debt proceeds − debt repaid

Also see *free cash flow*.

free dealing security/stock A liquid share. Also see *liquid*.

free float
1. The sector of the market that is liquid. These are the shares available for purchase by the general public on exchanges such as the JSE or LSE. Shares held strategically by long-term investors that are not traded frequently are excluded from the free

float measure. The availability or liquidity of the shares is translated into a weighting for the construction of an index. Sometimes called free capital. Also see *index; liquid*.

2. With reference to currencies, see *pure float*.

3. Money in the form of cash.

freely usable currency A currency that is widely accepted for payments on international transactions. The IMF in 2007/8 classified the Japanese yen, pound sterling, euro and US dollar as freely usable currencies.

free market A market in which there is little or no interference by regulators. Prices in free markets adjust according to the dynamics of supply and demand. Also see *command economy*.

free on board (FOB) This is the price that includes delivery onto a specified vessel. The exporter's liability ends once the goods are loaded onto the ship. Also see *free alongside ship*.

free trade zone A geographic area, usually in the form of a combination of member countries, where goods may be traded between trade zone members free of import and export duties.

freight derivative A derivative instrument that is based on an underlying shipping capacity. A forward contract to lock in a fee on renting a ship or capacity on a ship is a good example of a freight derivative. It is common for manufacturers and ship owners to use these instruments. More recently, banks and hedge funds have been trading in these instruments on a speculative basis. Also see *forward contract/dealing; hedge fund*.

frequency The number of occurrences of a particular event over a period of time.

FRF The former currency of France, the frank. France now uses the euro. Also see *euro*.

frictional unemployment People who remain voluntarily unemployed.

fringe benefits See *perk*.

FRN See *floating rate note*.

front end fee A once-off amount payable upfront to banks for arranging loans, bonds or equity issues. If there is more than one bank involved in the issue, the fee is shared by the banks according to their level of commitment or their respective roles. Sometimes called an arrangement or upfront fee.

front running Dealing for own account before releasing key information or research notes to the market. Front running is an illegal activity.

frozen asset An asset that is not accessible for any number of reasons. Assets are frozen when legal actions are pending or when sanctions have been imposed.

FSA See *Financial Services Authority*.

FSB See *Financial Services Board*.

FSCS Financial service compensation scheme.

FSG Financial services group.

FT 30 Index See *Financial Times Industrial Index*.

FTE Full-time equivalent, a metric used to indicate income per employee. Also see *income per employee*.

FTSE A British company that produces stock market indices and provides a range of services to the financial sector.

FTSE 100 The top 100 companies by market capitalisation on the London Stock Exchange. Also see *FTSE 250; market capitalisation index*.

FTSE 250 The top 250 companies by market capitalisation on the London Stock Exchange after the FTSE 100. Company number one in the FTSE 250 Index is the 101st largest company by market capitalisation on the LSE. Also see *market capitalisation index*.

FTSE 350 An aggregation of the FTSE 100 and FTSE 250. Also see *FTSE 100; FTSE 250*.

FTSE Eurofirst 50/80/100 Market capitalisation index of the top European companies usually quoted in euros. Also see *market capitalisation index*.

full cover Insurance or guarantees that provide compensation for a wide range of eventualities usually covering commercial, political and environmental events.

full recourse Lending where the borrower is obligated to repay the debt regardless of circumstances and eventualities.

fully diluted earnings per share A diluted earnings per share calculation that assumes all convertible instruments such as convertible debt, convertible preference shares and warrants have already been converted irrespective of whether their conversion is compulsory or not. Also see *convertible debt/bond; convertible preference share; diluted earnings per share; warrant*.

fundamental analysis A top-down approach to determine the long-term macroeconomic fundamentals, business conditions and the gains and losses associated with them. When conducting a fundamental analysis of a company, its economic environment, past history, future prospects, present environment and results are all considered. Also see *technical analysis*.

fundamental equilibrium exchange rate (FEER) The equilibrium exchange rate is determined by the current account balance target, which depends on the underlying sustainable equilibrium for international assets as well as national income based on full employment. Also see *current account*.

fundamentals Markets or price trends that are driven by a sound economic rationale and not by speculative activity.

funded debt See *long-term debt*.

funded participation Participation in the economics of a loan or other debt instrument by a third party purchasing a participation from the original lender with a physical cash advance in consideration of the debt notional. The third-party lender has no recourse to or relationship with the borrower and has limited recourse to the original lender. Sometimes called a subparticipation. Also see *recourse; risk participation*.

funded scheme A funded retirement or pension scheme where asset allocations today are made against future anticipated drawings or liabilities. A fully funded scheme has sufficient assets to cover all future obligations. These schemes are opposite to pay as you go or unfunded schemes. Also see *pay as you go*.

funding agreement A fixed income contract that provides principal and interest for a period of time.

fund manager A fund manager invests funds on behalf of individuals or institutions. In South Africa, pension and provident funds often outsource their fund management to separate fund management companies. These fund management companies are required to be capitalised separately from those intermediaries whose funds they invest. Companies such as Alan Gray, Coronation and Investec Asset Management are well-known South African fund managers. Also see *intermediary; pension fund; provident fund*.

fund of funds An investment fund that invests many other unit trusts or mutual funds. These funds are ultimately more diverse than the funds they invest in. Funds of funds are often prone to excessive overall charges and fees. Also see *mutual fund; unit trust*.

funds from operations (FFO) The funds generated by a company from normal operations. When evaluating credit ratings, S&P calculate this metric by taking the cash flow from operating activities (from the cash flow statement) with dividends paid and changes in working capital added back. Also see *cash flow statement; credit rating; dividend; EBIDTA; free cash flow; Standard and Poor; working capital*.

fungible An instrument or asset that can easily be exchanged or traded for another. Cash in the form of a freely tradable currency is the most fungible asset.

fungible issue A bond that is issued with exactly the same terms and conditions present in a previous bond issue. This is done to save on legal and administration costs. The process is sometimes referred to as an additional tranche or tapping. Also see *bond*.

fungible securities Financial instruments that are exactly or nearly the same. They are issued by the same issuer and are generally interchangeable. Also see *fungible issue*.

furtherest month The month with the latest delivery (furtherest away) date in a futures contract.

future economic benefit The potential to contribute, directly or indirectly, to the flow of cash and cash equivalents in an entity. The potential may be a productive one that is part of the operating activities of the entity. It may also take the form of convertibility into cash or cash equivalents or a capability to reduce cash outflows, such as when an alternative manufacturing process that lowers the costs of production is developed. Also see *cash equivalent*.

future price (FP) The price of an asset when traded on the futures market. The price is usually in line with the following equations:

future price (FP) = spot price + carry cost − carry return

which leads to the formal mathematical definition:

$FP = Se^{((r-q) \times t)}$

where r = carry cost in log returns; q = carry return in log terms; t = term; S = spot price.

Also see *spot price*.

futures See *futures contract*.

futures and options fund (FOF) A fund that can invest in options and futures for speculation purposes. These funds are used in the UK. Also see *geared futures and options fund*.

futures contract An agreement to buy and sell a fixed quantity of a commodity at a fixed date in the future at a priced fixed today. It is effectively a bet on the future price. Unlike an option it involves a definite purchase or sale of an underlying asset. Futures provide a mechanism for purchasers to mitigate the risk of changing asset or commodity prices. When applied to a currency, this is called a forward exchange contract. They are traded on exchanges and involve the use of clearing houses. Currencies are widely traded in the futures market. Also see *clearing house; forward contract/dealing; futures exchange; option; variation margin.*

futures driven When the spot market prices are being driven by the prices of futures contracts. Also see *cost of carry model; spot market.*

futures exchange An organised futures exchange such as SAFEX where futures and options are traded. A clearing house is used on these exchanges to ensure the proper fulfilment of contracts. Also see *clearing house; South African Futures Exchange.*

futures option An option on a futures contract. Also see *futures contract; option.*

future value (*FV*) The amount an investment is worth after one or more interest or return periods. The *FV* is calculated by the following equation:

future value $(FV) = PV(1 - r)^t$

where r = interest rate; t = number of periods; PV = present value.

Also see present value.

future value interest factor The $(1 - r)^t$ term in the future value calculation. Also see *future value.*

FV See *future value.*

FX See *foreign exchange.*

FX rate The amount of the second currency exchanged per unit of the first currency. For example, the rate quoted for the dollar-rand is usually expressed in rands per dollar as R7 per US dollar.

FX requirement See *foreign exchange requirement.*

FX swap A combination of a spot and forward transaction in the foreign exchange market. Two parties effectively exchange currencies for a certain length of time and agree to reverse the transaction at a later date. For example, a party could sell euros against dollars today and then buy euros with dollars in the future. Also see *spot market; swap.*

G3 The world's three leading currencies, the US dollar, the euro and the Japanese yen. Also see *euro; yen*.

G7 Economic forum of leading world economies. The six countries at the first economic summit were France, Germany, Italy, Japan, the UK and the US. They were joined by Canada in 1976. The roots of the G7 economic forum and membership lie in the 1973 oil crisis.

G8 The G7 plus Russia which joined in 1994. The heads of state of the G8 meet annually to discuss economic issues. Also see *G7*.

G10 The nations that met in 1961 to arrange the special drawing rights of the International Monetary Fund. These were Belgium, Canada, France, Germany, Italy, Japan, Netherlands, Sweden, the UK and the US. Also see *International Monetary Fund; special drawing right*.

G15 Established in 1989, the G15 is made up of countries from Latin America, Africa and Asia. Its main focus is to foster codevelopment in developing nations.

G20 A committee of finance ministers and central bank governors of the G8 and 12 other key countries. Also see *G8*.

G30 A group of financiers and academics whose objective is to maintain world economic awareness and understanding of financial issues. Members include central bankers, heads of international banks and key academics.

G77 The largest coalition of developing nations in the UN. It was established in 1964 to promote members' collective economic interests and create an enhanced joint negotiating capacity in the UN.

GAAP See *Generally Accepted Accounting Principles*.

gains Increases in economic benefits or revenue.

gamma
1. The Greek letter Γ or γ. Also see *Greek alphabet*.
2. A measure of the change in an options delta per unit of change in the price of the underlying asset:

$$\gamma = \frac{d\Delta}{dS} = \frac{d}{dS}\left(\frac{dC}{dS}\right) = \frac{d^2C}{dS^2}$$

Sometimes called the hedge risk ratio. Also see *Black-Scholes options pricing model; delta*.

3. A mathematical distribution defined by the equation:

$$f(x, k, \theta) = x^{k-1}\frac{e^{-x/\theta}}{\theta^k \Gamma(k)} \text{ for } x > 0$$

where $k > 0$ = the shape parameter, sometimes indicated by a γ; $\theta > 0$ = the scale parameter, sometimes indicated as a β. A graph of the gamma distribution is shown alongside. Also see *Greeks*.

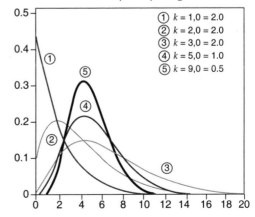

① $k = 1, \theta = 2.0$
② $k = 2, \theta = 2.0$
③ $k = 3, \theta = 2.0$
④ $k = 5, \theta = 1.0$
⑤ $k = 9, \theta = 0.5$

gap See *interest rate risk*.

gap risk The risk that the price of securities will not change continuously but will exhibit a large jump. In illiquid markets this happens frequently as single trades induce this effect.

Garman/Kolhagen An option pricing model for currency options. Also see *Black-Scholes options pricing model; option*.

gas oil An oil formed from the distillation of petroleum with a range of intermediate boiling temperatures and viscosity.

GATT See *General Agreement on Tariffs and Trade*.

Gaullism A French political ideology whose main component advocates independence from foreign powers.

Gaussian distribution A term used by scientists to describe a normal distribution. Also see *normal or Gaussian distribution*.

GBF See *general banking facility*.

GCC See *general credit committee*.

GCM See *general clearing member*.

GDE See *gross domestic expenditure*.

GDFI Gross domestic fixed investment.

GDP See *gross domestic product*.

GDP deflator The price of a basket of newly produced goods today versus the price of an identical basket a year ago. This is a variable basket measure of inflation, unlike CPI which is a fixed basket. The deflator adjusts for new expenditure and investment patterns. Inflation is often measured with this deflator.

In most systems of national accounts, the GDP deflator measures the difference between the real or chain volume measure GDP and the nominal or current price GDP. The formula used to calculate the deflator is:

$$\text{GDP deflator} = \frac{\text{nominal GDP}}{\text{real GDP}} \times 100$$

The GDP deflator effectively takes into account the behavioural changes in consumer spending as well as the changes in prices. Also see *gross domestic product; implicit price deflator; inflation*.

GDP expenditure approach A method of determining GDP that uses the actual expenditure on goods:

$$\text{GDP} = C + I + G + X - M$$

where C = consumption; I = investment; G = government spending; X = exports; M = imports. This method of calculating GDP is prone to double counting. Also see *GDP income approach; GDP value added approach*.

GDP income approach A method of determining GDP that uses returns to the owners of factors of production. Wages, salaries, interest received, dividends received and rental profit are used in the determination of GDP. Tax collection agencies such as SARS in South Africa provide the necessary data so this measurement approach is therefore accurate. Also see *dividend; factors of production; GDP expenditure approach; GDP value added approach; South African Revenue Service*.

GDP inflation A measure of all the prices in an economy. Unlike CPI, this is not based on a basket of goods and does not exclude imported and intermediate goods. Also see *consumer price index*.

GDP multiplier A measure of how much GDP increases as autonomous expenditure increases:

$$\text{GDP multiplier} = \frac{1}{(1 - b(1 - t))}$$

where b = the marginal propensity to consume; t = the taxation rate.

Also see *autonomous expenditure; marginal propensity to consume*.

GDP real growth GDP adjusted for changes in prices or inflation. This has the effect that prices are specified with respect to a particular base year. To obtain the time series of real GDP data, the prices today are discounted at the prevailing inflation rate for each successive year. Also see *base year; gross domestic product; inflation*.

GDP value added approach A method of determining GDP that accumulates value added at each part of the value chain. The data for this method is collected from tax revenue collection agencies such as SARS in South Africa. The method is the most reliable method as the underlying data comes from companies that have been audited. Also see *GDP expenditure approach; GDP income approach; South African Revenue Service; value chain*.

GDR See *global depository receipt*.

geared futures and options fund A futures and options fund in the UK that is allowed to expose 20% of the value of the fund to uncovered derivative positions. These funds are not permitted to borrow. Also see *futures and options fund*.

gearing The ratio of long-term debt funding to total long-term business funding, i.e. debt and equity. As a company becomes more highly geared, it becomes a more risky investment. Gearing a business with debt is often called leverage. Financiers refer to the net debt to EBITDA ratio as the gearing of a business. Also see *debt ratio; leverage; long-term debt*.

gearing ratio

$$\text{gearing ratio} = \frac{\text{debt}}{\text{equity}}$$

Also see *leverage ratios*.

GEMM Gilt edged market maker. A market maker in UK government gilt securities. Also see *gilt; market maker*.

General Agreement on Tariffs and Trade (GATT) A treaty that reduces trade tariffs and trade barriers between treaty signatories. South Africa is a signatory to this treaty. The functions of GATT have been replaced by the World Trade Organisation (WTO). Also see *trade barrier; World Trade Organisation*.

general banking facility (GBF) A banking facility used by companies for general banking requirements. The facility may consist of various subcategories such as overdraft, settlement, daylight, foreign exchange, bonding and letter of credit facilities. Monies drawn from GBFs are short-term borrowings and should ideally not form part of the long-term capital structure of a business. Also see *capital structure; revolving credit facility*.

general clearing member (GCM) A member of a clearing house that can clear as a principal, agent or on behalf of a non-clearing member. Also see *clearing house; individual clearing member; non-clearing member.*

general collateral Securities offered as collateral in the repo market that are not special, can generally be interchanged and have no onerous restrictions on them. Also see *collateral; special collateral.*

general credit committee (GCC) A committee in a bank that makes decisions on whether credit will be extended to a client or not. GCCs are usually high level and apply only to large transactions.

Generally Accepted Accounting Principles (GAAP) Procedures and standards followed by accountants in the US that stipulate accounting and financial reporting. South Africa now follows the IFRS. Also see *International Financial Reporting Standards.*

general meeting See *annual general meeting; extraordinary general meeting; special general meeting.*

general notarial bond (GNB) A notarial bond (hypothecation) in favour of a creditor over the movable assets of a business. These assets can include debtors books and inventory. The holder of a GNB is not a secured creditor, is subordinated to creditors who hold special notarial bonds (fixed charges) and does not have any power to take possession of assets subject to the bond unless the bond contract explicitly caters for this. In the UK, a floating charge is the equivalent of a general notarial bond. Also see *fixed charge; floating charge; notarial bond; special notarial bond.*

general obligation bond A bond issued that has cash flows backed by the general cash flows from an entity that is usually a municipality rather than by a specific revenue stream. Also see *crossover refunded.*

general offer An offer for the purchase of shares made to all company shareholders. General offers happen after a single entity acquires a majority stake and makes an offer for the balance. Also see *mandatory offer; squeeze out; whitewash.*

general partner A partner in a project with unlimited liability.

general prohibition The FSA in the UK states, 'No person may carry out a regulated activity in the United Kingdom unless they are an authorised person or an exempt person.' Also see *Financial Services Authority.*

general proxy A proxy transferring the vote from one shareholder to another at a company general meeting without any special instruction attached to the vote. Also see *annual general meeting; extraordinary general meeting; proxy; special general meeting; special proxy.*

genussschein See *profit participation certificate.*

geometric Brownian motion (GBM) A geometric Brownian motion (GBM) is a continuous-time stochastic process in which the logarithm of the randomly varying quantity follows Brownian motion.

A stochastic process S_t is said to follow a GBM if it satisfies the following stochastic differential equation:

$$dS_t = uS_t dt + vS_t dW_t$$

where W_t = a Wiener process or Brownian motion; u = the percentage drift and v = the percentage volatility are constants.

The equation has an analytic solution:

$S_t = S_0 \exp((u - v^2/2) t + vW_t)$

for an arbitrary initial value S_0.

Sometimes called exponential Brownian motion. Also see *Brownian motion; random walk with drift; stochastic process; volatility.*

geometric mean The basis used to find the discount rate of a present value-future value calculation. As an arithmetic mean of a geometric series where the variable as a growth rate of the multiplicative factor is not appropriate, the geometric mean can be used. For example, to calculate the average mean return of a series of compounding variable interest rates:

$(1 + R)^n = (1 + R_1) (1 + R_2) (1 + R_3) \ldots (1 + R_n)$

where R is the average annual interest rate over the entire period. This reduces to:

$R = \sqrt[n]{(1 + R_1)(1 + R_2)(1 + R_3) \ldots 1 + R_n} - 1$

The formal definition of a geometric mean of a set $\{a_1, a_2, \ldots, a_n\}$ is therefore:

$\text{mean} = (a_1 \times a_2 \times a_3 \ldots a_n)^{\frac{1}{n}} = \sqrt[n]{a_1 \times a_2 \times a_3 \ldots a_n}$

For calculation purposes logs and their properties can be used to do the calculation:

$\log(\text{mean}) = \dfrac{\sum \log(x)}{n}$

$\therefore \text{mean} = \exp\left(\dfrac{\sum \log(x)}{n}\right)$

A well-used notation convention when indicating products in geometric means is:

$a_1 \times a_2 \times a_3 \ldots a_n = \prod_{i=1}^{n} a_i$

Also see *arithmetic mean; discount rate; future value; geometric series; interest rate; present value.*

geometric mean return

geometric mean return $= \sqrt[n]{(1 + R_1)(1 + R_2) \ldots (1 + R_{n-1})(1 + R_n)} - 1$

geometric series The following equation defines the terms in the geometric series:

$ar^0; ar; ar^2; ar^3 \ldots ar^{n-1}$

where $a^n = ar^{n-1}$

The sum of a geometric series is defined mathematically by:

$\text{SUM} = \dfrac{a(1 - r^n)}{1 - r}$

Present value calculations and the dividend discount model (Gordon model) are based on geometric series sums. Also see *dividend growth model; geometric mean.*

geometric series sum See *geometric series.*

gharar Financial speculation in the Islamic world. Also see *Islamic finance.*

GIC See *guarantee investment contract.*

Giffen good An unusual price, supply and demand relationship for goods that is evidenced by price increases increasing the quantity demanded. The usual relationship is for demand to decrease as the price of the goods increases. This relationship is sometimes evidenced in the supply demand dynamics of staple foods such as bread where demand is driven by poor households that are unable to afford superior foodstuffs. As the price of the cheap staple rises, they can no longer afford to supplement their diet with better foods and must consume more of the staple food.

gift tax A tax levied on gifts between individuals. These taxes are levied to close inheritance tax and other loopholes.

gilt (GLT)

1. The British term for a UK government bond. Sometimes South African and Irish government bonds are also called gilts. Also see *government bond*.
2. A thin covering of gold. The term gilt used for debt securities comes about because the original debt certificates were gold edged and hence the term gilt edged evolved.

gilt edged See *gilt*.

gilt fund An investment fund that invests in debt instruments, usually in the form of government bonds and treasury bills. Also see *government bond; treasury bill*.

gilt option An option on a gilt (bond) security.

giro A bank funds payment and clearing system used in Europe.

glamour stock A share or business that is currently popular with investors.

global bond See *Eurobond*.

global capital asset pricing model An approach used to determine the cost of equity in a foreign market by investors.

For a South African investor investing in Nigeria, then local = SA and foreign = Nigeria and the cost of equity is given by:

cost of equity = $Rf_{global\ market} + \beta_{local\ against\ world}\ (Rm_{global\ market} - Rf_{global\ market}) \times 0.6$

where $Rf_{global\ market}$ = risk-free rate in the global market; $Rm_{global\ market}$ = rate of return in the global market; β is measured by the local against global markets.

This method of pricing assets assumes that the investors have a diversified portfolio of global assets and that the portion of non-systematic risk is minimised through diversification. Also see *adjusted hybrid capital asset pricing model; beta; beta approach; Bludgeon approach; Erb-Harvey approach; Estrata downside risk model; Godfrey and Espinosa global capital asset pricing model; Goldman Sachs model; lambda approach; Lessard's model*.

global depository receipt (GDR) A certificate similar to an American depository receipt (ADR) issued by a bank that represents an investment in an underlying equity share. GDRs can be traded separately from the underlying equity shares and are used to invest in emerging market companies. Sometimes called a participatory note or P-note. Also see *American depository receipt; participatory note*.

globalisation The process of a free flow of business, ideas and labour across the globe. The increasingly open world trade markets and developments in communications technology are advancing globalisation.

global facility A banking facility that can be used in various forms such as cash advances, letters of credit, bankers acceptances and swingline loans. Sometimes called a general banking facility. Also see *bankers acceptance; general banking facility; letter of credit; swingline loan*.

global master repurchase agreement (GMRA) A standard document used globally in non-US dollar markets that outlines the formalities of a repurchase agreement (repo) transaction. Also see *repurchase agreement*.

GLOBEX A 24-hour electronic platform developed by Reuters for trading derivatives. Also see *Reuters*.

glossies A company's financial statements in a physical format. The name is derived from the glossy paper on which they are printed.

GLT See *gilt*.

GmbH Abbreviation used in the title of German companies that indicates the company is a limited liability company. Also see *BV; limited liability; NV; PLC*.

GMRA See *global master repurchase agreement*.

GNB See *general notarial bond*.

G-note A cash note with a nominal value of 1 000. The name comes from the use of the slang term 'one G' meaning a thousand. Also see *nominal value*.

GNP See *gross national product*.

Godfrey and Espinosa cost of equity model This is an approach used to determine the cost of equity in a foreign market by investors. For a South African investor investing in Nigeria, then local = SA and foreign = Nigeria:

$$\text{cost of equity} = Rf_{\text{local market}} + CRP + \frac{\sigma_{\text{foreign}}}{\sigma_{\text{local}}} (Rm_{\text{local market}} - Rf_{\text{local market}}) \times 0.6$$

where CRP = country risk premium; $Rf_{\text{local market}}$ = risk-free rate in the local market; $Rm_{\text{local market}}$ = rate of return in the local market; σ_{foreign} = standard deviation of returns on the foreign market; σ_{local} = standard deviation of returns on the local market.

The use of $\beta = \frac{\sigma_{\text{foreign}}}{\sigma_{\text{local}}}$ is simply assuming the correlation coefficient in the determination of β is 1. Remember $\beta = \frac{\rho_{\text{foreign, local}} \sigma_{\text{foreign}}}{\sigma_{\text{local}}}$. The factor of 0.6 is a double counting adjustment factor. Removing the correlation effect contained in beta adjusts for inconsistencies in the markets that are contained in the beta variable.

Also see *adjusted hybrid capital asset pricing model; beta; beta approach; Bludgeon approach; country risk premium; Erb-Harvey approach; Estrata downside risk model; global capital asset pricing model; Goldman Sachs model; lambda approach; Lessard's model; Pereiro's adjusted CAPM model*.

go firm Do the deal.

going concern A business that is viewed as a going concern is viewed as a continuing operation for the near future and can operate with no external assistance. It is assumed that the entity has neither the intention nor the necessity of liquidation or of curtailing materially the scale of its operations. Also see *liquidation*.

going long See *long position*.

going public Taking the necessary steps to an initial public offer. Also see *initial public offer*.

going short See *short position*.

golden handshake The retrenchment or firing of an employee while offering them a substantial retrenchment package. Also see *golden hello*.

golden hello The payment of a significant amount of money for an employee to join a firm. Sometimes called a sign-on bonus. Also see *golden handshake*.

golden shares Nominal shares that may outvote ordinary shares in special circumstances. These shares are often used by governments when holding stakes in companies of national importance.

Goldex FTSE or JSE index of gold mining stocks. Also see *FTSE; index; JSE*.

Goldman Sachs model An approach used to determine the cost of equity in a foreign market by investors.

For a South African investor investing in Nigeria, then local = SA and foreign = Nigeria:

$$\text{cost of equity}_{\text{local market}} = Rf_{\text{local}} + \text{CRP} + \frac{\sigma_{\text{foreign}}}{\sigma_{\text{local}}} \beta (Rm_{\text{global}} - Rf_{\text{local}})(1 - R) + R_p$$

where Rf_{local} = risk-free rate in the local market; $Rm_{\text{global market}}$ = rate of return in the global market; β (beta) is measured by the local asset against local markets; R = correlation of local returns and sovereign bond; $\sigma_{\text{foreign \& local}}$ = standard deviation of local and foreign; R_p = project-specific risk premium.

Also see *adjusted hybrid capital asset pricing model; asset; beta; beta approach; Bludgeon approach; bond; Erb-Harvey approach; Estrata downside risk model; Godfrey and Espinosa global capital asset pricing model; lambda approach; Lessard's model; Pereiro's adjusted CAPM model*.

gold reserves Gold bullion held by central banks that can be bought or sold to decrease or increase holdings of foreign currencies. When referring to a mining company, the term may be used with reference to measured mineral resources or inferred mineral resources. Also see *bullion; central bank; foreign reserves; inferred mineral resources; measured mineral resources*.

gold shares/stocks Equity shares in gold mining companies.

gold standard A monetary system used prior to 1971. Currencies had fixed conversion rates against the US dollar and had a par value fixed to a quantity of gold. Balance of payments deficits were settled in gold under the gold standard. The gold standard was implemented after World War II and is also called the Bretton Woods system. Also see *balance of payments*.

go long See *long position*.

good delivery A status flag on a security that indicates that it is fit to be delivered to the purchaser. If a share has a specific feature that restricts transfer, the share would not be of good delivery.

good standing certificate See *certificate of good standing*.

good till cancel (GTC) A buy or sell order in the market that remains live until cancelled. Sometimes called an open order.

good till day A buy or sell order in the market that remains live until the end of the day on which it was placed.

goodwill Future economic benefits arising from assets that cannot be individually identified and separately valued or recognised. The purchase price of the business less net asset value is classed as goodwill. Goodwill is not amortised under IFRS and is impaired annually. Goodwill appears as an asset in a company's balance sheet and is sometimes called an intangible asset. Also see *asset; International Financial Reporting Standards*.

go public To list a company on a recognised stock exchange such as the JSE. Also see *initial public offer; JSE*.

Gordon growth model See *dividend growth model*.

go short See *short position*.

governing law The legal jurisdiction or legal system under which a financial contract is binding. With loan agreements, the law under which security is posted is the local law of the borrower or security holder and the governing law of finance documentation is usually that of the lender's domicile. Also see *domicile*.

government bond A debt instrument issued by the government for a period of more than one year with the purpose of raising capital by borrowing. When an invester buys government bonds, he/she is effectively lending money to the government. They have different structures and interest payment systems. Also see *bond; treasury bill*.

government deficit See *deficit*.

government deposits Deposits of a government's treasury. These usually include deposits from tax collection authorities and commission from customs and excise tax. Also see *excise tax; treasury*.

government sector Central and provincial governments as well as local authorities.

government securities Securities issued by the government treasury. Also see *treasury*.

Govi Government security or bond.

GOVI Index An index published by the Bond Exchange of South Africa that contains the top ten government bonds (by liquidity) of the All Bond Index (ALBI). Also see *All Bond Index; OTHI Index*.

grace period The number of days after the due date that an entity has to fulfil an obligation under a financial contract. For example, in the event of default on a loan there will sometimes be a grace period during which the borrower may rectify the event of default.

grade
1. The quality or purity of a raw material. The term is used with reference to physical commodities such as metals and oil. Also see *Brent North Sea crude oil; carat*.
2. The credit rating of an entity. Also see *credit rating*.
3. The score attained in an examination.

graft
1. Informal term for hard work.
2. Informal term for bribery and other corrupt practices pursued for gain in politics or business.

Granger causality Variable X Granger causes Y if past values of X can help explain Y. The existence of Granger causality does not guarantee that X causes Y. Also see *causality; causal variable*.

grantor A seller of options or other financial contracts.

granular Providing detail.

GRD The former currency of Greece, the drachma. Greece now uses the euro. Also see *euro*.

Greek alphabet

alpha	eta	nu	tau
A α	H η	N ν	T τ
beta	theta	xi	upsilon
B β	Θ θ	Ξ ξ	Y υ
gamma	iota	omicron	phi
Γ γ	I ι	O ο	Φ φ
delta	kappa	pi	chi
Δ δ	K κ	Π π	X χ
epsilon	lambda	rho	psi
E ε	Λ λ	P ρ	Ψ ψ
zeta	mu	sigma	omega
Z ζ	M μ	Σ σ ς	Ω ϖ

Greeks (the) For options, the Greek letters, delta (Δ), gamma (γ), rho (ρ), theta (θ) and vega (V), constitute various sensitivities of the option to underlying variables. Also see *Black-Scholes options pricing model; delta; gamma; rho; theta; vega*.

greenback A United States dollar.

green chip A top performing company that is environmentally friendly.

greenfield A project or venture that will be developed from scratch. In the mining industry greenfield refers to a mining company that is developing a mine from an untouched piece of ground. Also see *brownfield*.

green shoe provision A provision or option allowing the underwriters of a share or bond issue to purchase additional securities at the original price. Traditionally for equities, the option is to purchase 15% of the number of shares in the issue. The provision gives underwriters market clout to stabilise market activities after the issue of the securities. The option also gives underwriters the ability to cover short positions more cheaply.

Underwriters may use green shoe provisions to profit if there is exceptional demand or to extend favours to their top clients. The name green shoe provision came about because a company bearing that name was the first to use this type of option. Sometimes called an over allotment option. Also see *option; underwriter*.

grey market See *disintermediation*.

gross debt All the interest-bearing debt or long-term and short-term loans of a company. Gross debt includes the following:
- Borrowings from financial institutions

- Acceptance credits and bill discounting facilities
- Bonds, notes such as commercial paper, debentures, loan stock and similar instruments
- Capital leases (finance leases)
- Trade receivables (debtors) sold with recourse to the reference entity
- Guarantees, letters of credit and other indemnity-type obligations
- Repurchase agreement (repo) transactions used with the purpose of raising finance
- Other transactions having the commercial effect of borrowing such as sale and leaseback.

Also see *acceptance credit; bond; capital lease; commercial paper; debenture; gross gearing ratio; guarantee; letter of credit; net debt; repurchase agreement; sale and leaseback; term loan.*

gross domestic expenditure (GDE) The value of all expenditure on goods and services in a country in a specified period of time, usually a single year. Also see *gross domestic product.*

gross domestic product (GDP) The value of all final goods produced in a country in a specified period of time, usually a single year. There are different methods of measuring GDP that include the GDP income approach and GDP expenditure approach. Also see *GDP deflator; GDP expenditure approach; GDP income approach; gross domestic expenditure.*

gross fixed capital formation The addition to the fixed capital stock in a country before capital consumption (depreciation). Also see *capital consumption; depreciation; net national product.*

gross gearing ratio A ratio used by banks to analyse a company's creditworthiness:

$$\text{gross gearing ratio} = \frac{\text{gross debt}}{\text{net tangible assets}}$$

The ratio measures the ability of the company to pay off its debt with the proceeds of the liquidation. Also see *gross debt; liquidation; net gearing ratio.*

gross income Revenue less costs of sales.

gross interest Interest income before the deduction of any tax benefits.

gross investment See *net investment.*

gross margin See *gross profit margin.*

gross national income (GNI) The value of all final goods produced in a country in a specified period of time, usually a year, less payments plus income received from other countries:

gross national income (GNI) = GDP + foreign factor receipts − foreign factor payments

gross national product (GNP) A widely used measure of a country's economic activity. GNP is equal to GDP less compensation of employees and property income payable to the rest of the world plus the corresponding items receivable from the rest of the world. Also see *gross domestic product.*

gross premium Premiums received by an insurer less reinsurance premiums paid. Also see *reinsurance ratio; solvency ratio*.

gross profit margin Gross profit expressed as a proportion of sales:

$$\text{gross profit margin} = \frac{\text{gross profit}}{\text{sales}}$$

A declining gross profit margin means the cost of sales is increasing or mark-ups are down. The gross profit margin is measured before interest charges and taxation. Also see *EBITDA margin*.

gross revenue pledge A pledge that the issuers of a bond will use revenue received to pay the bond's debt servicing costs before using the cash flows for operations. These bonds are highly restrictive on issuers, safer for investors and therefore attract lower rates of interest.

gross up See *tax gross up*.

gross value See *enterprise value*.

gross yield The return on an instrument before tax.

group A parent company and all its subsidiaries. A group produces a set of consolidated financial statements. Also see *consolidated accounts*.

group 1, 2 and 3 projects Group 1 projects are EVA positive, group 2 projects are EVA neutral and group 3 projects are EVA negative. Also see *economic value added*.

group accounts See *consolidated accounts*.

group of See *G3; G7; G8; G10; G15; G20; G30; G77*.

group taxed profits The profit of a group including all subsidiaries after tax with an adjustment for minority shareholders.

growing annuity A regular cash flow over a period of time that grows at a fixed constant rate.

$$\text{present value } (PV) = \frac{C}{r-g}\left[1 - \left(\frac{1+g}{1+r}\right)^t\right]$$

where C = payment; r = rate of return; g = payment growth rate; PV = the present value.

The formula is derived using the sum of a geometric sequence. Also see *cash flow; geometric series; growing perpetuity*.

growing perpetuity A perpetuity whose regular cash payments increase with time.

$$D_t = D_0 \times (1+g)^t$$

is similar to the future value formula:

$$FV_t = PV(1+r)^t$$

where t = number of periods; D_t = dividend returned at time t; D_0 = dividend just paid; g = perpetuity growth rate.

Also see *future value; growing annuity; perpetuity*.

growth company A company that has projects capable of exceeding the cost of capital. Also see *cost of capital; weighted average cost of capital*.

growth fund A fund that invests in growth shares. Also see *growth share*.

growth share A share that gives above average returns for its given risk levels. It is usually an undervalued share that undergoes price adjustments in the short to medium term. Also see *growth company*.

GSE Government sponsored enterprise.

guarantee An agreement whereby one party undertakes to pay any losses suffered by another party associated with a breach of a contract or legal obligation. Also see *surety bond*.

guarantee debt/bond Debt issued by one company and guaranteed by a third party. The credit risk of the debt therefore depends on the risk associated with both the issuer and the guarantor. Parastatals often use these instruments guaranteed by government. Guarantees are difficult to realise and are the subject of more litigation than any other security. Also see *credit risk; initial margin; variation margin*.

guarantee fee A fee accrued by guaranteeing debt. Also see *guaranteed debt/bond*.

guarantee fund A fund maintained by an exchange or clearing house that is used in the event of one of its members defaulting on a financial obligation. Also see *clearing house*.

guarantee investment contract/certificate (GIC) A deposit taken by highly rated banks that is low risk and therefore provides a low rate of return.

guarantor A person or entity that guarantees the debt obligations of another.

guarantor test A test of the ability of guarantors or guarantee providers to meet the obligations of the guarantee. Compliance with a guarantor test is often evidenced as a covenant in loan agreements. For example, a 75% compliance with a guarantor test implies that 75% of the loan obligation amount should be the minimum aggregate level of all the assets of the guarantor. Also see *covenant*.

guilder (NGL) The former currency of the Netherlands. The Netherlands now uses the euro. Also see *euro*.

gun jumping See *insider trading*.

haircut
1. Lenders often require a margin to limit their exposure when trading in markets. When trading in the repo market, the value of securities posted against the borrowing of cash must exceed the cash amount by a margin called the haircut. Also see *margin; repurchase agreement*.
2. A discount applied to security that is provided as collateral for a loan. For example, if government bonds are used as security, banks may discount their value by 15% and then provide a loan that is no greater than the value of the bonds less the 15% discount.

half life The time it takes to halve the principal outstanding in a financial transaction. Also see *average life*.

Hamada equation The Hamada equation relates the betas of firms to their gearing through a linear mathematical relationship:

$$\beta_l = \beta_U \left(1 + \frac{D}{E}(1 - T_C)\right)$$

where β_l = beta of a leveraged firm in the same line of business or the equity beta; β_U = beta of an unleveraged firm or asset beta; D/E = debt/equity; T_C = tax rate.
Also see *asset; beta; firm; gearing; Modigliani-Miller or M&M proposition*.

handling fee A fee charged for processing a financial transaction.

Hang Seng Index A market capitalisation index of the top 33 companies on the Hong Kong Stock Exchange. Also see *market capitalisation index*.

hard asset An asset with physical form. These can be commodities such as precious metals or oil, or property, plant and equipment such as buildings and motor vehicles.

hard call protection See *call protected debt; soft call protection*.

hard commodity A non-perishable commodity such as a precious metal.

hard copy A copy of a document that is in a physical printed format. A soft copy is the digital version.

hard currency
1. Physical money in the form of notes and coins.
2. A currency that is not likely to lose value against other currencies over time. The loss of value usually occurs through inflationary effects. Also see *purchasing power parity; soft currency*.

hardening period The period of time which needs to expire before security posted in a financial transaction becomes enforceable. Hardening period regulations are put in place to prevent companies that are nearly or technically insolvent from entering into transactions where they post security and effectively prejudice other creditors.

hard loan A loan paid in a hard currency. An example of a hard currency loan is a loan between a South African bank and a Kenyan borrower denominated and paid in US dollars. Also see *hard currency*.

hard number A South African business cycle leading (index) indicator that is composed of cash supply and the motor vehicle sale variable. Cash supply and vehicle sales are supplied sufficiently frequently and ahead of other economic indicators. Money supply and vehicle sales are smoothed (Henderson smoothing) and equally weighted in the hard number. The hard number trend correlates well with the coinciding indicator issued by central banks. The advantage of the hard number is that the variables that constitute this index are available sooner. The hard number cycle is measured as the smoothed growth or contraction in the hard number index. The hard number was developed by Brian Kantor of Investec Securities. Also see *central bank; coinciding indicator; Henderson smoothing process; index; leading indicator; money supply*.

harmonic mean A mean that is the reciprocal of the arithmetic mean of the reciprocals of the data values. The measure is used as a measure of central tendency.

$$\bar{h} = \left(\frac{1}{n}\sum_{i=1}^{n}\frac{1}{x_i}\right)^{-1}$$

Also see *arithmetic mean; geometric mean*.

harmonised index of consumer prices (HICP) An indicator of inflation used in Europe and monitored by the ECB to set monetary policy. It is a weighted average of CPI measures of each member state in the Eurozone. Also see *consumer price index; European Central Bank; Eurozone; inflation; monetary policy*.

hawkish In the context of interest rates, hawkish means favouring an increase in interest rates. Hawkish statements have a more aggressive tone. The converse of hawkish is dovish. Also see *dovish; interest rate*.

HDSA Historically disadvantaged South African individuals and groups. Also see *black economic empowerment*.

head grade The grade of ore, often expressed in grams or kilograms per ton of ore, leaving a mine and entering the processing plant. The expression comes from the headgear above the shafts that is used to lift the ore from underground.

headline earnings per share (HEPS) Trade earnings per share adjusted for transactions not of a capital nature:

$$\text{headline earnings per share (HEPS)} = \frac{\text{trade earnings}}{\text{number of shares}}$$

Trade earnings exclude items such as profit on the sale of buildings, amortisation of goodwill and profit or loss on the sale of an asset or investment. This is a measure put in place by the JSE and not a stipulation of accounting regulations such as GAAP and IFRS. HEPS is not really a good measure of earnings because it can be difficult to distinguish exactly which transactions are of a capital nature. It is preferable to be given a list of the unusual items and investors can then decide what should be omitted from HEPS. Also see *asset; Generally Accepted Accounting Principles; International Financial Reporting Standards; JSE*.

headline inflation The rate of change of the consumer price index (CPI). Headline inflation is a key measure for households as it indicates the rate at which the cost of living is rising. Headline inflation does not exclude volatile items in the way that core inflation does and the measure is thus susceptible to supply and other inflationary shocks. Also see *consumer price index; core inflation; inflation*.

headroom
1. Spare capacity. If a production facility has 20 units of headroom, it can easily produce an extra 20 units without the need for further investment in productive capacity.
2. In finance, the level of funds accessible to a company at any given time.

heat rate The fuel required to generate a single unit of electricity, usually a KW/h.

hedge A transaction or an investment position designed to mitigate risk of other financial exposures. For example, a manufacturer may conclude a contract to sell a product for delivery over the next six months. If the price of the raw materials fluctuates and the manufacturer does not have enough stock, an open position will result. The open position can be hedged by buying raw materials through a futures contract and matching certainty of income with expenditure. It is possible to reduce vulnerability substantially by hedging. Also see *futures contract; open position*.

hedge bond Futures contracts can be used to hedge bonds. For example, if investors want to hedge a portfolio of bonds, they can sell futures contracts that give the right to sell the bond asset at a future date at the specified price. If yields go up, then the bond price goes down and the investors lose on the bond asset held. However, they have the right to sell bonds at a higher future price than the underlying asset and hence minimise the loss through the profit achieved on the futures contract. Due to bonds and futures contract pricing not changing in direct proportion, losses do not match gains perfectly. Also see *bond*.

hedge fund A fund, usually invested in by wealthy individuals and institutions, which is allowed to use aggressive strategies that are unavailable to mutual funds (unit trusts). These strategies include selling short debt, leverage, programme trading, swaps, arbitrage and other derivative instruments. Hedge funds are exempt from many of the rules and regulations governing other mutual funds, which allows them to accomplish their investing goals. Due to their aggressive investment strategies, they accept funds only from sophisticated individuals and not from the wider public. Hedge funds are restricted by law to no more than 100 investors per fund. As a result, most hedge funds set extremely high minimum investment amounts, ranging from $250 000 to over $1 million. As with traditional mutual funds, investors in hedge funds pay a management fee. Hedge fund managers also collect a percentage of the profits, usually 20%. Also see *absolute return fund; arbitrage; derivative; mutual fund; short position; swap*.

hedge ratio See *delta*.

hedge risk ratio See *gamma*.

hedging See *hedge*.

held to maturity A financial instrument that is held to the date of maturity and not bought and sold beforehand.

Henderson smoothing process Henderson smoothing acts as a trend filter and is commonly used in time series analysis to smooth seasonally adjusted estimates to generate a trend estimate. They are used in preference to simpler moving averages because they can reproduce polynomials of up to degree 3, thereby increasing the chances of capturing trend turning points. The general form of a Henderson filter of term $2m + 1$ is given by:

$$w_j = \frac{315\,[(m+1)^2 - j^2]\,[(m+2)^2 - j^2]\,[(m+3)^2 - j^2]\,[3\,(m+2)^2 - 11j^2 - 16]}{8\,(m+2)\,[(m+2)^2 - 1]\,[4\,(m+2)^2 - 1]\,[4\,(m+2)^2 - 9]\,[4\,(m+2)^2 - 25]}$$

for $j = -m, \ldots, m$

Herfindahl-Hirschman Index A measure of the size of a firm to the size of an industry. A value of 100% implies that the firm is a monopoly. Also see *monopoly*.

Hermes A German export credit agency. Also see *export credit agency*.

Herstatt risk The risk that a counterparty does not deliver a security after payment has already been made for that security. Sometimes called settlement risk. Also see *counterparty risk*.

HIBOR Hong Kong interbank offered rate. Also see *JIBAR; LIBOR; SHIBOR*.

HICP See *harmonised index of consumer prices*.

hidden reserve See *off balance sheet reserve*.

high The maximum value, usually the maximum price, at which a share was traded over a day, week, month or year. In the share tables published in financial newspapers, high indicates the highest trade price for the day.

high net worth individual An individual with large amounts of net assets.

high-water mark Investment funds are often measured by their own prior performance. High-water marks are the highest net asset values previously attained at the end of a defined period. Some fund managers are only compensated for managing funds if the current value exceeds the high-water mark. Also see *net asset value*.

high-yield bond A bond that is sub-investment grade, usually with a credit rating of BB+ and below. Sometimes called junk bonds. Also see *bond; credit rating; junk bond; sub-investment grade*.

hire purchase (HP) A method of financing an asset where possession is taken on payment of a deposit and ownership is taken when the last scheduled payment is made. Hire purchase agreements are often extended by retailers selling assets to finance companies and the finance companies in turn entering a hire purchase agreement with the consumer. Sometimes called a suspensive sale or a lease purchase. Also see *consumer credit*.

historic Based on past data. Historic data is often difficult to use as a predictor of future trends because the data may come from periods of significant volatility and structural differences and consequently have a high standard error. Also see *volatility*.

historical cost Assets are recorded at the amount of cash paid or the fair value of the consideration given to acquire them at the time of their acquisition. Liabilities are recorded at the amount of proceeds received in exchange for the obligation or, in some circumstances such as income tax, at the amount of cash expected to be paid to satisfy the liability incurred in the normal course of business. Also see *fair value; liability*.

historical dividend yield A dividend yield based on actual past dividends declared and not forecast dividends. Also see *dividend yield; forward dividend yield*.

historical volatility Standard deviation or the percentage change in the value of an asset over a historic period of time. It is a backward-looking measure of actual fluctuations. Also see *asset; experienced volatility; implied volatility; standard deviation; volatility*.

historic PE The price earnings ratio calculated using past earnings numbers. Also see *price earnings ratio*.

historic volatility See *volatility*.

HK Hong Kong.

HKD Hong Kong dollar.

HLT Highly leveraged transaction.

HMRC Her Majesty's Revenue Customs. SARS is the South African equivalent of this UK tax collection agency. Also see *South African Revenue Service*.

Hodrick-Prescott filter The Hodrick-Prescott filter is a tool often used in the analysis of business cycles. It is used to obtain a smoothed representation of a time series that indicates a long-term trend. The filter can be made more sensitive to short-term trends by using a modifier (λ) similar in concept to using a smaller moving average for moving average smoothing. The formula is defined as follows:

y_t for $t = 1, 2, \ldots T$ denotes the logarithms of a time series variable. τ is a trend component that is used to minimise:

$$\sum_{t=1}^{T}(y_t - \tau_t)^2 + \lambda \sum_{t=2}^{T-1} [(\tau_{t+1} - \tau_t) - (\tau_t - \tau_{t-1})]^2$$

The first term of the equation is the sum of the squared deviations $d_t = y_t - \tau_t$. The second term is a multiple λ of the sum of the squares of the trend component's second differences. This second term has the effect of penalising variations in the growth rate of the trend component. The larger the value of λ is, the higher the penalty of variation. A value of $\lambda = 1\,600$ is considered to be reasonable.

holder The purchaser of a security or option. Also see *option holder; security*.

hold in custody repo (due bill repo) A repo in which the party who receives the cash does not deliver the securities to the counterparty but segregates them by means of an internal account for the benefit of the cash provider.

holding company A company that has a controlling stake in another company, usually called a subsidiary. Holding companies do not have any operational assets. Sometimes called the parent.

holding period The period for which a financial instrument or position is held.

hold position The investor's final investment position with respect to the total transaction launch size. For example, when syndicating a loan, the hold position is the amount of debt each bank is taking on. Also see *syndicated loan*.

hole in the wall A British term for an ATM. Also see *automated teller machine*.

holiday period A time window in which payment of interest or capital on debt is not required.

homogeneous
1. A term indicating that objects being compared are the same.
2. Products produced by different manufacturers that are essentially indistinguishable. It is difficult for the producers of homogeneous products to convince the purchaser to pay any more for their product. A homogeneous product is the opposite of a differentiated product. Also see *differentiated*.

horizontal integration The process of a business expanding its range of products and services in the same part of a value chain. Also see *backward integration; forward integration; vertical integration*.

horizontal merger A merger between firms that sell similar products in the same markets.

horizontal spread The combination of the purchase and sale of an option with the same strike price but with different expiration dates. Also see *diagonal spread; vertical spread*.

hostile takeover bid A bid from a company to acquire the ownership of another company against the wishes of the target's shareholders and management. Also see *agreed bid; poison pill*.

hot money
1. Money that has been made through illegal activities.
2. Cash that moves rapidly to and from financial centres in response to news, arbitrage opportunities and changes in rates.

house broker See *brokerage house*.

housekeeping period The period at the end of the day's trading on certain stock exchanges where orders that have not been executed are removed from the trading system. Also see *auction period*.

housing bond A bond that is secured by a portfolio of mortgage bonds on houses. Also see *collateralised mortgage obligation*.

how's your father A British term sometimes used to describe a bribe.

HP See *hire purchase*.

HRK The Croatian kruna divided into 100 lipa.

HUF The Hungarian forint divided into 100 fillér.

hurdle rate The rate of return which forms a benchmark against which asset or project returns are measured. For example, if an investor were seeking a 10% return on investment, then 10% would constitute the hurdle rate. Any investment made would be expected to return more than the required minimum hurdle rate. Also see *asset; return on investment*.

hybrid A financial instrument that has features of more than one other financial instrument. Hybrids are most often non-dilutive fixed income instruments that incorporate equity with features such as deep subordination, payment deferral and long dated tenors. Features such as mandatory conversion on convertible debt may class it as a hybrid security. The issuers of hybrid capital often have discretion on coupon deferral and deferrals do not constitute an event of default.

Hybrids are created to take advantage of tax structures and give debt equity similar cash flows. Hybrids can be advantageous to credit ratings as debt can often be reclassified as equity, thereby reducing financial risk. Hybrids are generally used in M&A finance, share repurchases, equity substitutions and to fund pension fund liabilities.

Certain classes of hybrid capital are accounted for as though they are equity and the coupon payments are tax deductible by the issuer. Sometimes hybrids are termed quasi equity. Also see *credit rating; event of default; quasi equity; tenor*.

hybrid scheme A retirement fund that offers both defined benefit and defined contribution features. The selection is made according to whichever is most advantageous at the time.

hyperinflation Excessive levels of inflation. The equation derives from the quantity theory of money where $MV = PY$ indicates that as the money supply (M) increases, the velocity (V) at which money changes hands increases and prices (P) increase in a cyclical fashion. From 2006 Zimbabwe has experienced a hyperinflationary environment where price increases are in excess of 1 000% per annum. Also see *inflation; money supply; quantity theory of money.*

hypothecation The pledge of assets as a form of security against a loan and granting of authority for the assets to be sold in the event of default. Also see *encumbrance; rehypothecation.*

hypothesis testing A statistical test of a scenario. There is typically a null and alternative hypothesis. Also see *alternative hypothesis; null hypothesis.*

IBD
1. Interest-bearing debt.
2. Investment banking division.

IBOR Interbank offer rate. Also see *interbank rate; LIBOR*.

IBRD International Bank for Reconstruction and Development.

ICE See *Intercontinental Exchange*.

iceberg order A big buy and sell order on a stock market that is released as smaller chunks to the market so that market prices are not driven adversely. The name comes from the fact that an iceberg's visible component is only a fraction of the entire iceberg.

ICM See *individual clearing member*.

ICMA International Capital Markets Association. The ICMA is an organisation that regulates Eurobonds and the global master repurchase agreement. Also see *Eurobond; global master repurchase agreement*.

ICR Interest cover ration. See *interest cover*.

ICVC Investment company with variable capital.

IDB See *interdealer broker*.

idiosyncratic risk See *unsystematic risk*.

idle capital Capital that is not being put to profitable use. The money the banks need to keep aside for capital adequacy requirements is often called idle capital. Idle capital is sometimes called dead capital. Also see *capital adequacy*.

IDR
1. International depository receipt. Also see *global depository receipt*.
2. The Indonesian rupiah.

IFA Independent financial adviser.

IFC See *International Finance Corporation*.

IFRS See *International Financial Reporting Standards*.

IHT Inheritance tax.

IISA Insurance Institute of South Africa.

illiquid When trading volumes are low and the availability of underlying stocks or assets is limited, a market is deemed to be illiquid. There are often price under and overshoots in illiquid markets and valuing assets in illiquid markets is difficult.

ILS The Israeli shekel divided into 100 agorot.

ILT The former currency of Italy, the lire. Italy has now adopted the euro. Also see *euro*.

IM See *information memorandum*.

IMF See *International Monetary Fund*.

immobilisation When excess capital in the company is used to buy shares and distribute those shares to remaining shareholders (scrip or bonus issue), the shares are immobilised in a central securities depository to facilitate subsequent book entry transfers. Also see *bonus issue; central securities depository; dematerialisation.*

immunisation See *contingent immunisation.*

impact day The day on which securities may be traded in the secondary market after being issued in the primary market. Also see *primary market; secondary market.*

impairment Writing down the value of an asset with sufficient regularity. Although the value of the asset can be written up or down, it is considered to be more risky to write an asset up in value. An impairment loss should be recognised as an expense in the income statement for assets carried at cost and treated as a revaluation decrease for assets carried at revalued amounts. Impairment is an estimation of value. Also see *asset; depreciation; income statement.*

impairment loss The amount by which the value of an asset recorded in a company's books exceeds the price for which the asset can be sold in the market. Also see *asset.*

imperfect market A market that is not considered to be an efficient capital market. An imperfect market is illiquid and can be dominated by a monopoly, duopoly or oligopoly. South African markets are generally not considered to be perfectly efficient. Also see *duopoly; efficient capital market; monopoly; oligopoly.*

implicit price deflator A broad measure of prices derived from separate estimates of real and nominal expenditures for gross domestic product (GDP) or a subcategory of GDP. Without qualification the term refers to the GDP deflator and is effectively an index of prices for everything that a country produces. The implicit price deflator, unlike CPI which is restricted to consumption, includes prices of a limited basket of goods as well as imported goods and services. Also see *consumer price index; GDP deflator; gross domestic product; implicit price deflator.*

implied loss given default (LGD) A loss given default calculated using a fixed asset pricing model on risky but not yet defaulted loan obligations. Also see *market loss given default; workout loss given default.*

implied volatility The volatility implied by option prices for a given security. The implied volatility effectively illustrates what the market is factoring into their option pricing models to obtain the option prices observed. It is a forward-looking measure of expected fluctuations over the future life of an option. To calculate the implied volatility, the current market prices are put into an option pricing model such as Black-Scholes. Also see *Black-Scholes options pricing model; experienced volatility; historical volatility; option; volatility.*

import deflator See *implicit price deflator.*

import parity pricing (IPP) Products produced locally that are priced as if they included transport costs, customs costs, insurance and other costs that would have been incurred had they been imported. Import parity pricing is often exploited by companies or industries that constitute a monopoly or oligopoly where local cost advantages allow them to profit from high importation costs. Also see *export parity pricing; monopoly; oligopoly.*

import quota A limitation on the quantity of imported goods allowed to enter a domestic market. Import quotas are used as policy tools by governments to advantage local companies. Their efficacy is questioned by economists.

import substitution The attempt to replace imported commodities with locally manufactured ones. Import substitution is managed through mechanisms such as import quotas, tariffs and artificial overvaluation of currencies.

INCA See *Infrastructure Finance Corporation.*

incipient default A default that is beginning to happen.

income Increases in economic benefits during an accounting period in the form of cash inflows, enhancements of assets or the decrease of liabilities. Income effectively constitutes the inflows that result in the increase of equity in a business but are not the proceeds of the issue of new equity.

income and expenditure account See *profit and loss account.*

income bond A bond that earns interest only when the issuing company has sufficient cash resources to service it. Holders of income bonds have a right to funds before shareholders and sometimes before subordinate debt holders. Also see *subordinate.*

income from discontinued operations A line item that appears in the income statement of a company indicating that the particular income generated was from operations that ceased during the reporting period or will cease to operate in the next reporting period.

income fund An investment fund that aims to give good periodic income from coupons or dividends rather than from returns in the form of capital gains. Also see *capital gains.*

income per employee A metric often used by analysts to evaluate how effectively companies use their human resources. The income per employee ratio is defined by:

$$\text{income per employee} = \frac{\text{income}}{\text{number of employees}}$$

The metric is widely used for analysing financial institutions. Income per employee is often called the full-time equivalent number of employees.

income smoothing The process of a company acting within accounting rules to state earnings at levels not reflective of its underlying economic reality. There may be many reasons why a company's management smooths earnings but the prime reason is usually to shift income from good years to less profitable years to manage investors' expectations. Also see *cookie jarring.*

income statement An accounting statement that shows the income and expenses of a company. The income statement effectively tracks the changes in opening and closing balances of retained earnings on the balance sheet. Also see *balance sheet.*

income stock A security that is bought for the income it provides and not capital gains. Also see *bond fund; widow and orphans fund.*

income tax Tax revenue collected by the government from the incomes of companies and individuals. There are various income tax philosophies and systems that are beyond the scope of this text.

inconvertibility The inability to exchange one currency for another.

incoterm A standard definition that is used in international trade contracts. Incoterms are protected by copyright by The International Chamber of Commerce. Also see *copyright.*

incremental cash flow The difference between a firm's future cash flow with or without the project that is currently being evaluated. Also see *cash flow; firm*.

incremental cost of capital See *marginal cost of capital*.

incurrence covenant A covenant in a debt contract that is activated under specific events or conditions. Also see *covenant; maintenance covenant*.

indemnity An obligation from an indemnifier to a creditor. An indemnity is an agreement by which one party makes good losses incurred by another. It is an independent payment obligation unaffected by the invalidity of a debtor's payment obligation. In other words, an indemnity is an agreement to hold a party harmless against another's loss. Also see *guarantee*.

indemnity insurance An insurance policy that compensates for a loss. The payments and repairs under the policy are designed to place the policy holder in the same position as before the loss event occurred.

indenture A document stating the terms and conditions of a securities issue. For example, the indenture on a bond lists the obligations of the issuer to the holder, including the payment schedule and features such as call option provisions and sinking funds. Also see *call option; sinking fund*.

independent financial adviser (IFA) A firm that acts independently and has no formal ties with any particular provider of financial services or products. These firms recommend the purchase and sale of assets to clients and charge a fee for advice given. Also see *firm*.

independent guarantee A type of guarantee that is undertaken by a clearing house. In the event of a default by a clearing member, initial cover is provided by liquidation of the member's assets and then from the asset pool of the clearing house itself. The clearing house has no separate guarantee fund as with a mutual guarantee. Also see *clearing house; mutual guarantee*.

index A grouping of a set of financial instruments to give a performance measure of the collective. Indices are used for:

- benchmarks of performance for professional portfolio managers
- the creation and monitoring of index funds
- the economic measure of market rates and returns
- predictors in technical analyses of markets
- determining the systematic risk of an asset.

The JSE ALSI is an example of an index that is a collective measure of the entire market of listed equities on the JSE. Also see *ALSI; index fund; JSE; systematic risk; technical analysis*.

index arbitrage The process of buying and selling instruments based on indices and making a corresponding buy or sell on the underlying assets to make a risk-free return. The process of profiting off an arbitrage opportunity adjusts supply and demand and subsequently changes prices in the market, closing down the opportunity.

indexation The adjustment of a financial or economic variable for the effects of inflation. Wages and taxes are often linked to inflation measures such as the consumer price index (CPI) and retail price index (RPI) to ensure that they keep constant real relative values. Also see *consumer price index; inflation; real price; retail price index*.

indexation allowance An adjustment made to capital gains tax that accounts for the time value of money. This has the effect that capital gains tax is only paid on the real gains made from investments and not gains that are inflationary. Also see *capital gains tax; time value of money*.

indexed loan A loan whose repayment is linked to an index, usually an inflationary or foreign currency index to protect the lender against inflationary or exchange rate risk. Also see *index-linked bond*.

indexed rate Interest rates linked to an index. The index is usually an inflation-related index such as the consumer price index (CPI). Also see *consumer price index; index; index-linked bond; inflation*.

indexed statement A standardised financial statement presenting all items relative to a certain base year amount. Also known as a common base year financial statement. Also see *base year; common base year financial statement*.

index fund A fund that invests in assets to replicate the returns on an index. Satrix 40 is a good South African example that replicates the top 40 companies listed on the JSE ALSI. Also see *ALSI; JSE; Satrix 40*.

index future A futures contract to buy or sell a derivative instrument based on an index. Also see *futures contract; index*.

index-linked bond A bond whose cash flows are linked to an index. Inflation-linked bonds are a good example where the issuer uses an index such as the consumer price index (CPI) to protect against inflationary effects. Also see *consumer price index; indexed loan; inflation-linked bond*.

index-linked loan See *indexed loan*.

index number See *base year*.

index option An option that has an index such as the JSE ALSI or FTSE 100 as its underlying reference asset. Also see *option*.

index tracking See *index fund; passive management*.

INDI An index of resources and mining shares traded on the South African JSE. The INDI is traded as a derivative on SAFEX. Also see *ALSI; derivative; FINDI; index; JSE; RESI; South African Futures Exchange*.

indicated mineral resources An estimate of mineral resources based on geological exploration and sampling data that is close enough for geological continuity and grade to be reasonably assumed. Indicated resources cannot be fully trusted until confirmation has been received that they have become measured resources. Also see *inferred mineral resources; measured mineral resources*.

indication of interest The expression by investors of their level of appetite for the issue of a security. These processes are used to establish market dynamics and prices when undergoing primary issuance of financial securities.

indicative pricing A price that is not a firm quote but rather an indication of a possible price for a transaction. They are usually given by stockbrokers when they do not want to give an exact binding quote on a stock in a volatile market. Bankers often give indicative pricing on loans subject to full approval by credit committees. Also see *firm quote; stockbroker*.

indicative terms The terms of a loan that are an indication only of what conditions a bank is prepared to lend against. Indicative terms and pricing are not legally binding and are usually subject to credit committee approval. Also see *credit committee; indicative pricing*.

indicator A metric that indicates a pattern or trend in data. For example, the consumer price index (CPI) is an indicator of inflation. Also see *consumer price index; inflation*.

indirect cost See *fixed expense*.

indirect finance Financing that is facilitated by an intermediary such as a bank. Indirect finance takes the form of households (surplus units) making deposits into a deposit-taking institution who in turn lends to firms or other households (deficit units) who have a cash requirement. The deposit-taking institutions bear the risk of the credit extension. The investor does not have direct contact with the borrower. Also see *deficit unit; direct finance; firm; surplus unit*.

indirect financial transaction See *indirect finance*.

indirect method of reporting cash flows from operating activities With this method of determining cash flows, profit or loss is adjusted for the effects of transactions of a non-cash nature, any deferrals or accruals of past or future operating cash receipts or payments and items of income or expense associated with investing or financing cash flows. In the cash flow statement:

cash generated from activities = net profit +/− non-cash items such as depreciation and amortisation +/− changes in operating working capital (debtors, creditors, inventory).

For changes in working capital:

- increases in debtors imply an increase in cash
- increases in creditors imply a decrease in cash
- increases in inventory imply a decrease in cash.

Also see *cash flow; cash flow statement; creditor; debtor; depreciation; EBITDA; inventory; net profit; working capital*.

indirect quotation An exchange rate quoted as the foreign price of a local currency, for example the rand euro rate quoted as ZAR1 = 0.1EUR. Also see *direct quotation*.

indirect securities Money market securities issued by financial intermediaries such as banks. Also see *commercial paper; intermediary; money market*.

individual clearing member (ICM) A member of a clearing house that can clear as a principal or agent. Also see *clearing house; general clearing member; non-clearing member*.

individual savings account (ISA) A form of tax-free savings account in the UK that was created to encourage the public to save. ISAs have a cash and securities component. There are strict limits on these accounts and investors can invest in a range of approved securities such as equities, government bonds and derivatives.

industrials The industrial sector of the economy. There are a range of indices worldwide that track the industrial sector such as the Indi (FTSE/JSE Industrial 25 Index) in South Africa.

industry risk Risk associated with the changes in returns from companies relating to events that affect the industry as a whole. Also see *beta*.

inelasticity A situation where there is a low price elasticity of demand. Inelasticity implies that $\frac{\text{\% change in quantity}}{\text{\% change in price}}$ lies between [0, 1].
Also see *elasticity; price elasticity of demand*.

inferred mineral resources A part of a mineral resource that is estimated using limited sampling and reasonable geological assumptions. The US Securities and Exchange Commission does not recognise inferred resources as they have an amount of uncertainty to their existence and it cannot be assumed that they will ever be upgraded into measured or indicated mineral resources. Also see *indicated mineral resources; measured mineral resources*.

inflation A persistent rise in the general level of prices or a persistent decrease in the quantity and quality of goods and services that can be purchased with a single currency unit. Also see *cost push inflation theory; demand pull inflation theory*.

inflation-linked bond A bond that is usually issued by governments and that offers investors protection against inflation. In South Africa, they are indexed to headline inflation with the interest adjusted after a three-month lag. A key inflation-linked South African bond is the R189. In the US, treasury inflation protected securities (TIPS) are the key inflation-linked bonds. Also see *bond; headline inflation; inflation; R189; treasury inflation-protected security*.

inflation-linked certificate of deposit A certificate of deposit with returns adjusted for inflation, i.e. index linked. Also see *certificate of deposit; inflation; inflation-linked bond*.

inflation-linked swap A swap where one of the cash flows is linked to a recognised inflation index such as the CPI, RPI or HICP and the other cash flow is linked to a fixed or floating interest rate. Inflation swaps transfer the risk of inflation from one counterparty to another.

Inflation-linked swaps are used to hedge liabilities of pension funds and other long-term debt provisions. Inflation swaps are over-the-counter instruments. Also see *consumer price index; floating interest rate; harmonised index of consumer prices; inflation; long-term debt; over the counter; pension fund; retail price index; swap; treasury inflation-protected security*.

inflation premium The portion of a return rate that represents compensation for expected future inflation. Also see *inflation*.

inflation proofing Increasing the nominal amount of an investment so that its real value is maintained and value is effectively not lost through inflation. Also see *real price*.

inflation rate The rate at which the general level of prices increases in a country. Normally expressed as an annualised number. Also see *headline inflation*.

inflation swap See *inflation-linked swap*.

inflation targeting A policy set by monetary authorities to keep inflation rates at targeted levels. The authorities achieve this with macroeconomic policy and changes in interest rates. The target levels are usually set as a band within which inflation can vary. Also see *inflation; interest rate*.

information memorandum (IM) A document produced by lead banks at the start of the loan syndication process that gives key information on the borrower. Possible participants in the transaction use the IM to assist in getting the deal passed by credit and other relevant committees. IMs need to be signed off by the borrower before wider distribution. Also see *credit committee*.

information ratio (IR) A ratio used to measure the returns produced by an investment manager relative to a benchmark after accounting for the risk taken to deliver the performance. The ratio is defined as:

$$\text{information ratio (IR)} = \frac{\text{annualised return of fund} - \text{annualised return of benchmark}}{\text{standard deviation of [fund} - \text{benchmark]}_{\text{calculated at all points i}}}$$

Information ratios are based on historic data and are not necessarily a good indicator for future performance. Also see *Sharpe ratio*.

Infrastructure Finance Corporation (INCA) A private-sector corporation that provides long-term loans to finance infrastructure provided by local government. The INCA's main source of funding is bonds.

ingot A bar of precious metal. Also see *precious metals*.

inheritance tax A tax levied on a deceased estate.

initial margin Derivative exchanges (clearing houses) reduce the risk of counterparties defaulting through a margining system. A cash payment (initial margin) must be made before a client is allowed to deal in a particular derivative. In the event of a default on the transaction, the margin posted can be used to settle claims. Also see *clearing house; maintenance margin; variation margin*.

initial public offer (IPO) The first sale of shares in a company or a mutual fund to the public. IPOs give the issuer the opportunity to change the equity ownership profile of the business in addition to raising cash. Sometimes called a flotation. Also see *mutual fund; preferential offer*.

injunction order A legal order that states that an entity is not allowed to undertake a particular activity. For example, a mine may receive an injunction to discontinue mining operations due to health and safety risks.

INR The Indian rupee divided into 100 paise.

inside information Price-sensitive information that is not accessible to the wider market. Trading with inside information is generally illegal and termed insider trading. Also see *insider trading*.

insider See *insider trading*.

insider trading An illegal activity involving the trading in securities armed with information that will have an effect on the market price of an asset and that has not yet been made public. Insider trading is sometimes referred to as front running. Also see *front running*.

inside the fence See *behind the fence*.

insolvency A financial position where a company's liabilities exceed its assets (balance sheet insolvency) or when cash flows generated cannot meet debt service obligations (cash flow insolvency). The term insolvency does not necessarily imply that a company is being wound up. Also see *winding up*.

instalment credit See *instalment debt*.

instalment debt Debt that has the capital portion paid by equal instalments over the life of the loan. Although the interest rate may be floating and so can change over time, instalment debt typically, but not always, carries a fixed rate of interest. Sometimes the term amortised is used.

instalment sale The sale of an asset where a minimum of one instalment payment is received after the close of the financial year in which the asset was sold.

instant auction A trading system where buy and sell orders are instantly matched up. Sometimes called a continuous auction.

institutional investor An institution that invests the collective investments of the public. Insurance companies and fund managers are examples of institutional investors.

instrument A general term used for stocks, debt securities, derivatives and many other financial products.

insurance option An option on an insurance index. Also see *option*.

insurer A financial institution that covers individuals or organisations against particular losses. These losses include theft, fire, natural disasters and many other potential loss events. Insurers are classed as short-term insurers and long-term insurers as well as reinsurers. Also see *long-term insurer; reinsurer; short-term insurer.*

intangible asset An identifiable non-monetary asset without physical substance. If intangible assets are acquired, they are amortised and impaired if necessary or not amortised but impaired annually. Intangible assets include intellectual property (IP), trademarks, deferred charges and share or bond premiums. Goodwill is also an intangible asset on a company's balance sheet. Also see *asset; goodwill.*

integer Any whole number, i.e. a number with no decimal places. The numbers 1, 2, 3 and 4 are integers.

integration The process of combining operations of companies under merger and acquisition scenarios. Mergers and acquisitions often make business sense as the integration process yields synergies. Also see *backward integration; forward integration; horizontal integration; synergy; vertical integration.*

intellectual property (IP) Assets such as software, patents, manufacturing processes and other pieces of knowledge that are key to running an operation and/or provide a competitive advantage. IP is often difficult to value and account for.

inter alia Among other things or among others.

interbank Transactions that occur between banking institutions. These transactions are often in the form of interbank lending. Also see *interbank rate; JIBAR; LIBOR.*

interbank deposits Deposits of monies in the wholesale market between banks.

interbank market Banks fund themselves from many sources including borrowing money from one another. When borrowing in the interbank market, banks borrow for defined interest periods and at an interbank rate such as LIBOR in London or JIBAR in Johannesburg. Also see *interbank rate; JIBAR; LIBOR.*

interbank rate The rate at which bankers lend money to one another in the interbank market to adjust their liquidity positions. Also see *EURIBOR; Fed funds rate; LIBOR.*

intercept
1. The constant value in a linear regression.
2. The place at which a line crosses the y-axis on a two-dimensional graph.

intercommodity risk The risk associated with intermonth and intermarket spread positions. Also see *clearing house; position; standard portfolio analysis of risk*.

Intercontinental Exchange (ICE) An electronic marketplace for trading futures and over-the-counter contracts. General participants may trade for their own account and as agents. Natural gas, Brent North Sea crude oil and gas oil futures can be traded on the ICE. Also see *Brent North Sea crude oil; gas oil; natural gas; over the counter*.

intercreditor agreement An agreement between creditors that regulates the seniority of debt, the rights and obligations of the creditors and what should occur in the event that the borrower defaults. Borrowers can be parties to intercreditor agreements.

interdealer broker (IDB) A broker that acts as an intermediary between market makers. They take on riskless principal transactions and provide anonymity for the market makers. Also see *market maker; riskless principal transaction*.

interest The returns paid to lenders for the privilege of borrowing money. The returns are specified as a percentage of the sum advanced under the loan. Also see *interest rate*.

interest add on An instrument or security that is bought with an interest payment made at the date of maturity. Also see *security*.

interest arbitrage See *carry trade*.

interest bearing A financial instrument or contract that pays interest.

interest cost With respect to pension funds, the interest cost is the increase during a period in the present value of the defined benefit obligation which arises because the benefits are one period closer to settlement. Also see *defined benefit fund; pension fund*.

interest cover (IC) A ratio that indicates how easily a company can meet the interest payment obligations on its interest-bearing debt. The ratio is typically defined as:

$$\text{interest cover (IC)} = \frac{\text{profit before finance charges and tax}}{\text{total finance charges}} \text{ or by } \frac{\text{EBITDA}}{\text{total finance charges}}$$

If a company can cover interest expense easily, it can probably cover dividend payments easily. The lower the IC ratio is, the more the company is burdened by debt expense. When a company's interest coverage ratio is 1.5 or lower, its ability to meet interest expenses may be questionable. An interest coverage ratio below 1 indicates the company is not generating sufficient revenues to satisfy interest expenses.

Interest cover ratios are used as covenants in loans. If a company has significant lease obligations, for example retail companies, a fixed charge cover ratio is often used. Also called times interest earned. Also see *covenant; debt service cover ratio; EBITDA; fixed charge cover ratio*.

interest-only loan A loan that does not pay any of the capital off, i.e. there is no amortisation. The entire capital portion of the loan is due at the date of maturity. Interest-only loans are often called bullet loans. Also see *amortisation; balloon loan; bullet loan*.

interest-only strip A security issued out of a mortgage-backed securitisation whose cash flows are determined by the interest received from the underlying portfolio of mortgage bonds.

interest rate The rate of charge or return for borrowing and lending money or making an investment. Interest rates are usually expressed as a percentage of the value of the amount borrowed. The interest rate effectively constitutes the value of money for a unit of time.

interest rate anticipation swap A swap used to take advantage of interest rate changes. For example, under a bullish view, as rates fall, bond prices rise and longer dated bonds will rise more in value than shorter dated bonds. Under a bearish view, as rates rise, bond prices go down and short-term bonds will be affected less than longer dated bonds. If investors expect interest rates to go down, they may swap shorter for longer tenor bonds as the longer dated instruments are more sensitive to changes in interest rates. Also see *bond; interest rate*.

interest rate cap A series of interest rate guarantees (caplets) that provide protection against rate hikes over a single interest period in the future. Also see *interest rate guarantee*.

interest rate ceiling The maximum interest rate that can be charged or return that will result from the use of options. The interest rate ceiling is synthesised through the use of a cap. Also see *cap; interest rate; interest rate floor*.

interest rate collar Protection against rising interest rates using a cap combined with the use of a floor giving a combination with limited upside or downside should interest rates fall or rise. Interest rate collars are constructed using a long position in an interest rate cap at one strike rate and a short position in an interest rate floor at a lower rate. Also see *cap; floor; interest rate; short position*.

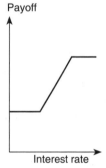

interest rate cycle A theory that postulates that interest rates move up and down in cycles, generally in conjunction with changes in the business cycle. Also see *business cycle*.

interest rate effect The rate of investment in an economy increases as interest rates decrease. The cost of capital (WACC) is lowered through lower interest rates and lesser performing projects are more readily accepted through lower hurdle rates. Also see *cost of capital; hurdle rate; interest rate; weighted average cost of capital*.

interest rate exposure See *interest rate risk*.

interest rate floor The minimum interest that can be charged or the resultant rate from the use of options. Also see *interest rate ceiling*.

interest rate futures Futures contracts on interest rates. The contracts allow investors to hedge or bet on future interest rates.

interest rate guarantee (IRG) The option to exercise a forward rate agreement. IRGs provide protection against adverse movements in interest rates. IRGs are priced with an adaptation of the Black-Scholes option pricing model. Also see *forward rate agreement; interest rate; Black-Scholes options pricing model.*

interest rate margin The difference between the rates at which banks borrow and lend money. For some corporate loans, banks will charge a margin above the relevant interbank rate such as JIBAR or LIBOR. Also see *JIBAR; LIBOR; margin.*

interest rate option An option whose underlying reference is the returns from an interest-bearing financial instrument such as a treasury bill. Also see *treasury bill.*

interest rate parity The basic theoretical identity that relates interest rates and exchange rates:

$$(1 + i_\$) = \frac{F}{S}(1 + i_c)$$

where $i_\$$ = the domestic interest rate; i_c = the interest rate in the foreign country; F = the forward exchange rate between domestic currency ($) and foreign currency (C).

Also see *covered interest rate parity; interest rate.*

interest rate product A financial contract in which the borrower is obligated to pay interest to the lender at the specified dates.

interest rate risk The risk that value will be lost in an asset portfolio with a change in interest rates. For example, the price of a bond goes down if interest rates go up and a portfolio of bonds will lock value in this situation. Bonds with different time horizons and coupon structures have different sensitivities to changes in interest rates. To reduce the interest rate risk of a portfolio, an investor selects a range of different bonds and may enter into swaps such as interest rate anticipation swaps to manage the interest rate risk. Also see *interest rate anticipation swap.*

interest rate swap Counterparties swap payments in the same currency based on an interest rate. For example, one party specifies a position against a fixed interest rate and the other a floating interest rate. The differences between the two rates account for the flow of cash associated with the swap. There is no exchange of principal in an interest rate swap. Principal amounts are used as a basis for calculation only and are usually termed the notional principal.

The floating interest rates are usually with reference to money market rates such as LIBOR or returns on commercial paper, bankers acceptances, certificates of deposits, Fed funds rate or the prime rate.

Interest rate swaps are used to manage the views and risks associated with fixed and floating interest rates and are over-the-counter instruments. Interest rate swap obligations can be senior to debt on a company's balance sheet. However, by default, they will be pari passu to senior debt.

Also see *balance sheet; bankers acceptance; certificate of deposit; commercial paper; Fed funds rate; fixed interest rate; floating interest rate; interest rate; LIBOR; money market; notional principal; over the counter; pari passu; prime rate; seniority; swap.*

interim dividend A dividend paid to shareholders halfway through a financial year, usually based on the half-yearly results. The final dividend is paid when the full year's financial results are released. Also see *dividend*.

interim financial report A financial report containing either a complete set of financial statements as described in IAS 1 or a set of condensed financial statements as described in IAS 34 for an interim period. Also see *financial statements*.

interim loan A loan used as short-term finance, effectively a form of bridging finance. Also see *bridging finance*.

interim report See *interim financial report*.

intermarket spread The combination of a purchase and sale of the same asset or instrument on different exchanges to take advantage of price differentials. The instruments are typically futures contracts with the same date of maturity. Also see *futures contract; intramarket spread*.

intermediaries offer When trying to raise capital in the form of equity or bonds, companies under an intermediaries offer approach different lead managers who offer the financial instrument to preferential customers. The offer is therefore not available to the wider public. Also see *lead manager; placing*.

intermediary Intermediaries match supply and demand for capital. They attract savings from surplus units and lend to deficit units. They include institutions such as banks and make their money from price differentials between borrowing through deposits and lending. Intermediaries such as banks obtain returns by taking on the risks associated with the counterparties. Also see *deficit unit; surplus unit*.

intermediate customer A customer who is knowledgeable and experienced, but not considered to be as sophisticated as market counterparties. When dealing with intermediate customers, less legal protection is required through financial regulations than when dealing with private customers. Also see *market counterparty; private customer*.

intermediate goods Semi-processed raw materials such as steel which will be transformed into another form.

intermediate target A variable such as money supply that is not under the direct control of a central bank but responds quickly to changes in monetary and macroeconomic policy. Also see *money supply*.

intermediation The process of acting as an intermediary. Also see *intermediary*.

intermonth charge The margin charged by options clearing houses associated with positions that are intramonth and intramarket. Also see *clearing house; initial margin; margin; variation margin*.

internal audit An audit undertaken by a company itself to ensure that internal procedures and controls are effective and that the business is being run properly. External auditors are normally required to sign off on a company's annual financial statements.

internal growth See *organic growth*.

internal growth rate (IGR) The maximum achievable growth rate without external financing being injected into the business or project:

internal growth rate (IGR) = $\dfrac{\text{RONA} \times b}{1 - (\text{RONA} \times b)}$

where RONA × b = the percentage return of net assets retained; 1 − (RONA × b) = the percentage return of net assets not retained.

RONA is the return on net assets defined by:

$$\text{RONA} = \frac{\text{net profit after tax and interest}}{\text{total assets} - \text{current liabilities}}$$ and

$$b = \frac{\text{addition to retained profit}}{\text{net profit}}$$

The last formula is commonly referred to as the plough-back ratio.

The factors that affect b, i.e. RONA, profit margins, asset turnover and dividends are the drivers of IGR. A business that funds itself exclusively with internally generated cash flows and reserves is termed a self-financing business. Also see *fixed asset turnover; profit margin; retention ratio; return on net assets; sustainable growth rate.*

internal measure A measure of how long a business would run if all cash flows were to dry up.

$$\text{internal measure} = \frac{\text{current assets}}{\text{average daily operating costs}}$$

Also see *cash flow.*

internal rate of return (IRR) The discount rate at which a project's net present value (NPV) is zero. The discount rate at which the NPV is zero must be compared to a hurdle rate for meaningful analysis. To solve the following equation, the NPV is set to zero and the discount rate r is determined:

$$\text{NPV} = \sum_{n=0}^{t} \frac{\text{NOCF}}{(1+r)^n} - \sum_{n=0}^{t} \frac{\text{NICF}}{(1+r)^n}$$

where NOCF = net operating cash flows; NICF = net investment cash flows; r = the discount rate determined.

If the IRR is greater than the required hurdle rate, then there is a potential value achievable by investing in the project or asset. Note that there are multiple solutions for determining r in the above equation when cash flows are irregular. Another disadvantage of the IRR method is that the NPV for one project may be higher than another at specific discount rates. Also see *cash flow; discount rate; hurdle rate; net present value.*

internal value The purchasing power of a currency in its domestic market.

international bond See *Eurobond.*

international bulletin board (ITBB) A trading platform on the London Stock Exchange used for trading international equities. The system has multicurrency capability and has market makers buying and selling. Also see *market maker.*

international depository receipt See *global depository receipt.*

International Finance Corporation (IFC) An organisation that is a member of the World Bank and that provides loans, structured finance, risk management products and advisory services to build the private sector in the developing world. Also see *structured product; World Bank.*

International Financial Reporting Standards (IFRS) Standards and interpretations adopted by the International Accounting Standards Board (IASB). They comprise:

- International Financial Reporting Standards

- International Accounting Standards
- interpretations originating from the International Financial Reporting Interpretations Committee (IFRIC) or the former Standing Interpretations Committee (SIC).

International Monetary Fund (IMF) The IMF is an international organisation of 184 member countries. It was established to promote international monetary cooperation, exchange stability and orderly exchange arrangements, to foster economic growth and high levels of employment and to provide temporary financial assistance to countries to help ease balance of payments adjustments. See www.imf.org for further details.

international order book (IOB) An order book for American depository receipts (ADRs). Also see *American depository receipt; global depository receipt*.

international reserves See *foreign reserves*.

International Swaps and Derivatives Association (ISDA) A trade association for swaps and derivatives traders. The association addresses a number of issues associated with the derivatives industry and aims to reduce risk. The ISDA also produces standard documentation for various financial contracts. The term ISDA is most often used with reference to the standard contract or master agreement that the association has produced on behalf of its members.

international unit trust A fund that invests in companies listed on overseas stock exchanges.

interpolation The process of using mathematical techniques to form continuous data sets from discrete data points, i.e. sophisticated methods for joining the dots on a graph. There are many techniques to interpolate data which are beyond the scope of this text. Also see *spline*.

intertemporal budget constraint The limits of expenditure at each point in time and the links between spending, borrowing and lending. This boils down to what a party borrows now is what it will have to pay back later. For example, for a country the discounted values of future trade balances must be zero.

interval measure A ratio that gives an indication of how long the business can last without any further operational or investment cash inflows:

$$\text{interval measure} = \frac{\text{current assets}}{\text{average daily operations costs}}$$

Also see *cash ratio*.

in the money (ITM) The exercise price of an option is in the money if a profit will be made if the option is exercised at the current market price of its underlying asset. Also see *at the money; option*.

intraday margin The additional margin required by clearing houses if markets start to become excessively volatile. This is payable immediately and can be drawn from the variation margin account. Also see *clearing house; initial margin; margin; variation margin*.

intramarket spread Buying and selling options with the same underlying assets on the same market with different times to maturity. Also see *intermarket spread*.

intrinsic value
1. The lower bound of an options value or what the option would be worth if it were about to expire. It is measured by calculating the profit that would be made if the

option were exercised. The intrinsic value is therefore a measure of how deep the option is in the money. Also see *call option; strike price; in the money; option; put option; time premium.*

2. The price of a real object or the perceived value at a point in time.

introduction A company obtaining a listing without issuing more shares but by moving shares off one stock exchange and onto another.

inventory Assets:
- held for sale in the ordinary course of business
- in the process of production for such sale
- in the form of materials or supplies to be consumed in the production process or in the rendering of services.

An inventory includes goods purchased and held for resale such as merchandise purchased by a retailer and held for resale, or land and other property held for resale. It also includes finished goods produced or work in progress being produced by an entity as well as materials and supplies awaiting use in the production process. The costs of a holding inventory include overheads, wastage, theft, write downs or reversal of write downs. Sometimes called stock.

In the case of a service provider, an inventory includes the costs of the service for which the entity has not yet recognised the related revenue.

inventory days (ID) A ratio used to determine the number of days' worth of inventory at average sales levels defined as follows:

$$\text{inventory days (ID)} = \frac{\text{inventory}}{\left[\frac{\text{cost of sales}}{365}\right]}$$

Also see *creditor settlement; debtors days.*

inventory turnover (IT) A ratio that measures how efficiently an inventory is managed. The ratio is defined as:

$$\text{inventory turnover (IT)} = \frac{\text{cost of sales}}{\text{inventory}}$$

An increased inventory turnover ratio indicates that there is a more efficient management of inventory and no build-up. The number effectively gives the number of times a year the current inventory turns over. Sometimes called a stock turnover ratio. Also see *asset management ratios.*

inverse order With reference to a loan, inverse order refers to capital payments from the date of maturity backwards.

inverted market A futures market in which the longer term futures contracts are less expensive than the shorter term contracts. Also see *backwardation; inverted yield curve.*

inverted spread When a yield curve is inverted or in backwardation, short dated instruments trade at higher yields than the longer dated instruments. The difference between the yields forms the spread. Also see *backwardation.*

inverted yield curve A yield curve that is in backwardation. The South African yield curve pictured below is inverted. Also see *backwardation; yield curve.*

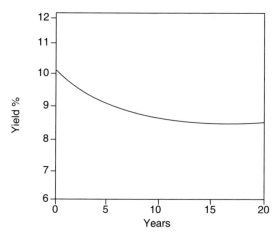

investment Expenditure on capital goods that are expected to generate a return.

investment analyst See *analyst*.

investment bank A bank whose customers include corporations and high net worth individuals. Its services include corporate finance, corporate lending, investment management, derivative markets, stockbroking services, international services, property investments, making markets in financial assets and trading in money and capital markets. Often called merchant banks in the UK and South Africa. Also see *capital market*.

investment cash flow Cash used for capital expenditure. Also see *capital expenditure; financing cash flow; operating cash flow*.

investment grade Companies or debt instruments with credit ratings better than and including BBB– (S&P and Fitch) or Baa3 (Moody's) are considered to be investment grade. Anything below these ratings is considered to be sub-investment grade or junk. Also see *BBB; credit rating; sub-investment grade*.

investment grade bond An investment grade bond with a credit rating better than and including BBB– (S&P and Fitch) or Baa3 (Moody's). Companies issue these bonds to obtain fixed, relatively cheap, long-term finance and use them to optimise the term of their debt. Investment grade bonds are unsecured. Also see *credit rating; investment grade; junk bond; unsecured debt*.

investment holding company A holding company set up to make investments in other companies. Investment holding companies do not have any cash-generating operational assets of their own. Also see *holding company*.

investment property Property (land or a building, or part of a building or both) held by the owner or by the lessee under a finance lease to earn rentals, for capital appreciation or both, rather than for:

- use in the production or supply of goods or services or for administrative purposes
- sale in the ordinary course of business.

Investment property is valued at fair value or cost. Also see *fair value*.

Investment Services Directive (ISD) The ability to operate under a different country's financial regulator in Europe. The ISD allows investment services firms to be passported into the UK and through the European Economic Area. Also see *European Economic Area*.

investment trust A company that is capitalised with investors' funds. Shares are issued and the proceeds are invested on behalf of the shareholders. The difference between investment trusts and unit trusts is that investors in investment trusts are shareholders.

invisible asset See *intangible asset*.

invisible import The flow of cash into a country by non-physical means. Tourism and the services industry are examples of invisible imports.

invoice The bill for a purchase or service provided.

invoice discounting facility A credit facility that allows a business with a large proportion of sales to clients on credit terms to borrow against its debtors book. A bank provides a loan based on the credit profile of the underlying debtors book for a value generally less than the total value of the debtors book. The credit risk of the debtors still lies with the holder of the debtors book and not the bank providing the facility. As the debtors accounts are repaid, the discounting facility is repaid. Also see *debtor; factor debtors*.

inward listing A foreign entity listing on a local exchange. Also see *dual listing*.

IOB See *international order book*.

IP See *intellectual property*.

IPE International Petroleum Exchange.

IPO See *initial public offer*.

IQD The currency of Iraq, the dinar divided into 100 cents.

IR See *information ratio*.

IRG See *interest rate guarantee*.

IRM Interest rate market.

IRO In respect of.

iron butterfly See *butterfly spread*.

IRR See *internal rate of return*.

irredeemable securities See *perpetual bond*.

irrelevant cost
1. Does not differ between alternatives.
2. A cost that does not depend on future cash flow. Also see *cash flow*.

irrevocable letter of credit A letter of credit that cannot be changed without the consents of all parties to the letter. Also see *letter of credit*.

IRS
1. Inland Revenue Service.
2. International Retail Service, a system on the London Stock Exchange (LSE) that gives international brokers access to the LSE. Also see *London Stock Exchange*.

ISA See *individual savings account*.

ISD See *Investment Services Directive*.

ISDA
1. See *International Swaps and Derivatives Association*.
2. International Settlement and Dealers Association.

iShare An exchange traded fund or aggregation of a set of shares into one instrument. Each iShare represents a proportionate ownership of the fund.

ISIN International Securities Identification Number.

ISK Iceland krona divided into 100 aurar.

Islamic bond See *sukuk*.

Islamic finance Muslims believe that the Koran prohibits the payment of interest (*riba*) and further prohibits financial speculation (*gharar*). These beliefs therefore make many Western financial instruments inaccessible to Muslim investors. Investment products tailored for compliance with Islamic law such as *sukuks* have thus been created to satisfy Islamic investors' needs. These Islamic financial instruments are structured using discounts, sale or lease structures, profit shares and repurchase agreements. Also see *repurchase agreement; sukuk*.

issue See *shares in issue*.

issued share capital The number of shares of a company currently in issue. Companies may have authorised share capital in excess of the issued share capital. Also see *authorised share capital*.

issued value The number of shares in an issue multiplied by the par value (the price at which they were issued). This number should correspond to the sum of the share capital and share premium accounts on the balance sheet. Also see *par value; share capital; share premium*.

issuer The entity that offers a financial instrument for sale on a primary market. Also see *primary market*.

IT
1. Information technology.
2. See *inventory turnover*.

ITBB See *international bulletin board*.

ITC Investment trust company.

ITM See *in the money*.

Ito The calculus of stochastic difference equations. Also see *stochastic difference equation*.

iTraxx See *credit default swap index*.

Jarque-Bera test In statistics, the Jarque-Bera test is a goodness-of-fit measure of departure from normality based on the sample kurtosis and skewness. The test statistic *JB* is defined as:

$$JB = \frac{n}{6}\left(g_1^2 + \frac{g_2^2}{4}\right)$$

where g_1 = the sample skewness; g_2 = the sample kurtosis; n = the number of observations or degrees of freedom in general.

The statistic has an asymptotic chi-squared distribution with two degrees of freedom and can be used to test the null hypothesis that the data is from a normal distribution since samples from a normal distribution have an expected skewness of 0 and an expected excess kurtosis of 0. As the equation shows, any deviation from this increases the *JB* statistic.

The reported probability of a Jarque-Bera test is that the test statistic exceeds the observed value under the null hypothesis. A small probability value will lead to the rejection of the null hypothesis that the distribution is normal (H_0: normal distribution). Also see *degrees of freedom; kurtosis; null hypothesis; skewness*.

JBIC Japan Bank for International Cooperation. This Japanese bank provides financial services to the developing world.

JET Johannesburg Equities Trading System.

JGB Japanese government bond. The Japanese bond market is very liquid for 10-year bond instruments. JGBs come in long dated 10-year and super long dated 20-year bonds. Also see *government bond; liquid*.

JIBAR The Johannesburg interbank acceptance rate is a South African money market rate updated daily as indicated by a number of local and international banks. The banks are polled daily at approximately 10:30 and asked for their mid-point (between bid and offer) deposit bankers acceptance rate, quoted as a yield. The highest two and lowest two rates are eliminated and the remaining rates are averaged and rounded to three decimal places.

The rate quoted is in yield form and is quoted as the JIBAR rate. Rates are quoted for a series of months, namely one, three, six and 12 months. For the one month or 1M JIBAR, the quoted yield is effectively an NACM rate, 3M is NACQ, 6M is NACS and 12M is NACA.

JIBAR rates are published by the South African Futures Exchange (SAFEX). Also see *HIBOR; interbank rate; LIBOR; money market; NACA; NACM; NACQ; NACSA; SHIBOR; South African Futures Exchange; yield*.

JIBOR Term sometimes incorrectly used to describe JIBAR. Also see *JIBAR*.

JMD Jamaican dollar divided into 100 cents.

jobber A dealer who buys and sells securities and holds positions for short time periods in an attempt to profit.

jobbers turn The difference between the bid price and ask price that jobbers profit off. Also see *ask price; bid price; jobber*.

jobless growth Growth in an economy that does not translate into an improvement in the employment rate. Also see *employment rate*.

JOD Jordanian dinar divided into 100 piasters.

Johannesburg interbank acceptance rate (JIBAR) See *JIBAR*.

Johannesburg Securities Exchange (JSE) See *JSE*.

Johannesburg Stock Exchange (JSE) See *JSE*.

Johansen test A statistical test for the cointegration of variables. Also see *cointegration*.

joint account An account with a bank or a securities broker that is owned by more than one party.

joint and several guarantee/liability A joint and several guarantee is a combination of a joint obligation and a several obligation. In a joint and several guarantee the liability for default is enforceable against all the guarantors and/or borrowers in the borrowing group. The enforcing party or lender can call the entire obligation on a pro rata proportional basis or call on an individual obligor in the lending structure at their sole discretion. Ultimately, a guarantor signing into a joint and several guarantee is potentially responsible for the whole amount of the loan irrespective of the existence of other guarantees. Lenders seek joint and several guarantees as first prize because it allows them to choose whom they pursue. Their decisions to pursue may be influenced by geography, strategy and economics. Also see *joint obligation; several obligation*.

joint bid A bid prepared by two or more financial institutions for the provision of services or finance on a single transaction.

joint bond A bond that is guaranteed by a party other than the issuer.

joint guarantee See *joint obligation*.

joint obligation An obligation where more than one party owes jointly. For example, if two parties borrow R2 million and undertake to repay it jointly, the lender will join the obligors under any claims. If one of the obligors is unable to service its obligations, the lender may deem the other obligor liable. Also see *joint and several guarantee liability; several obligation*.

joint profit maximisation A situation where a range of small companies in a market realises their collective power and succeeds in raising the prices in the market to maximise profit. This type of collusion is often illegal. Also see *corner the market*.

joint stock A company that issues shares and that is not a company or corporation with limited liability status. The stockholders are liable for the company's activities and financial risk. The shares in these companies can be traded on secondary markets. Companies incorporated in this manner are extremely rare. Also see *financial risk*.

joint venture (JV) A contractual arrangement whereby two or more parties undertake an economic activity which is subject to joint control. Also see *associate; division; subsidiary*.

JPY Japanese yen.

JSE South Africa and Africa's principal financial stock and securities exchange. Many financial instruments such as equity, derivatives and debt instruments can be traded on the JSE. The JSE is Africa's largest trading exchange. The name has been changed initially from the Johannesburg Stock Exchange to the Johannesburg Securities Exchange and again to simply the JSE. Also see *South African Futures Exchange*.

JSE ALSI See *ALSI*.

judicial management When a company is on the verge of going out of business, a court may appoint new managers to rescue the company before it goes into liquidation. There is usually an associated reprieve with respect to debt obligations. Judicial management is a term used in South Africa. It is called administration in the UK and Chapter 11 in the US. Also see *Chapter 11*.

jumbo CD A certificate of deposit with a very large denomination. Also see *negotiable certificate of deposit*.

jump A sudden change in prices.

junior creditor A creditor to a borrower who is subordinate to other creditors, has a junior or lesser claim on the assets of a business under liquidation and can have lesser claims on cash flows for debt servicing. In intercreditor agreements junior creditors are generally restricted from demanding repayment, accelerating, enforcing by court action and taking action to put obligors into insolvency. Also see *intercreditor agreement; liquidation; subordinate*.

junior debt See *subordinated debenture*.

junk bond A bond with a rating below Moody's Baa3 or S&P's and Fitch's BBB–. Sometimes called a high yield bond or sub-investment grade bond. Junk bonds are typically 10-year loans and have published ratings. They usually have call protection and make whole covenants. Junk bonds are high yield credit and are often speculative in nature. The borrower's ability to repay is subject to economic and business-specific forces. The value of junk bonds is therefore volatile and often displays equity-like returns. Covenants on junk bonds include limitations on restricted repayments, limits on incurrence of additional debt, granting of security to third parties, dividend payments or share buy-backs and limits on the sale of substantial assets. Also see *call protected debt; covenant; dividend; high-yield bond; make whole clause; sub-investment grade*.

junta A Spanish word describing a board of directors or committee. Often military coups install a ruling committee referred to as a junta. Also see *board of directors*.

jurisdiction clause A clause in a financial agreement whereby one or more of the parties subject themselves to a legal jurisdiction and waive any immunities they may have.

JV See *joint venture*.

Kangaroo bond See *Matilda bond*.

keep-well agreement An agreement whereby a party guarantees to cover another party, often a subsidiary, by injecting capital as needed.

kerb trading
1. Transactions done outside trading hours. The term is usually used on derivative exchanges.
2. The time during the day on the London Metals Exchange (LME) when the floor is open to trading on all contracts. The LME trading floor is extremely busy during these periods. Also see *London Metals Exchange*.

KES The Kenyan shilling divided into 100 cents.

Keynesian dictum Demand creates its own supply.

key reversal A sharp change in a pattern or trend. Technical analysts have many different methods for spotting and analysing key reversals.

KIBOR Kuwait interbank offer rate.

kicker Something additional that has a potential upside in a financial contract. Equity kickers are used in debt contracts to give lenders an equity stake in the borrower in return for advancing finance on favourable terms. The equity exposure usually takes the form of an option to buy equity shares. Also see *equity*.

kilo- 1 000 or 10^3.

kina The currency of Papua New Guinea divided into 100 toea.

kJ Kilojoule, a unit of measure of energy equalling 1 000 joules.

KLIBOR Kuala Lumpur interbank offered rate. Also see *JIBAR; LIBOR*.

KLSE Kuala Lumpur Stock Exchange.

KMV A division of the Moody's credit rating agency that provides credit analysis tools and expertise to lenders. KMV has developed a model that attempts to estimate the probability of default for a firm over a given period of time. The KMV model uses the following factors when calculating default probabilities:
- Current market capitalisation
- Volatility of market capitalisation over a three-year period
- Current on balance sheet leverage and debt maturity profile.

The KMV model outputs an estimated default frequency. Also see *balance sheet; credit rating agency; expected default frequency*.

Knaggs Law The more complex a plan is, the larger the chance of failure is.

knock in option A barrier option triggered when the price of the underlying asset triggers the option on the way up. Also see *barrier option*.

knock out option A barrier option triggered when the price of the underlying asset triggers the option on the way down. Also see *barrier option*.

know your customer (KYC) A set of rules and procedures that must be followed by banks and investment advisers when lending money to or transacting with a client.

These procedures are principally aimed at minimising any fraudulent activity and at ensuring that money laundering is not taking place. Also see *Financial Intelligence Centre Act; money laundering*.

KOSPI Korean Composite Stock Price Index. The index is a market capitalisation index based on all equities traded on the Korean Stock Exchange. The base value of 100 was set on 4 January 1980. Also see *market capitalisation index*.

Korean won (KRW) The currency of South Korea, divided into 100 chon.

KRI Key risk indicator.

krona Independent currency of Sweden, Norway and Denmark.

Kruger Rand South African gold bullion coins often used as a form of physical gold investment. A Kruger Rand is a troy ounce of gold. The British equivalent is a Britannia Coin. Also see *bullion; troy ounce*.

KRW The Korean won divided into 100 chon.

kt See *carat*.

kurtosis A measure of the degree to which a unimodal distribution is peaked. Higher kurtosis means more of the variance is due to infrequent extreme deviations as opposed to frequent modestly-sized deviations.

A high kurtosis distribution has a sharp peak with more substantial tails, while a low kurtosis distribution has a rounded peak with wide shoulders. A high kurtosis implies there are more extreme infrequent variations and a low kurtosis implies less frequent deviations from the mean.

Kurtosis is more commonly defined as the fourth cumulant divided by the square of the variance of the probability distribution which is known as excess kurtosis:

$$\gamma_2 = \frac{\kappa_4}{\kappa_2^2} = \frac{\mu_4}{\sigma^4} - 3$$

Also see *cumulant; leptokurtic; mesokurtic; platykurtic; skewness; unimodal; variance*.

kwacha
1. The currency of Malawi divided into 100 tambala.
2. The currency of Zambia divided into 100 ngwee.

kwanza The currency of Angola divided into 100 lwei.

KWD The Kuwait dinar divided into 1 000 fils.

kWh A unit of electricity, 1 000 watts supplied for a single hour.

KYC See *know your customer*.

KYD Cayman Islands dollar.

KZR The currency of Angola, the kwanza divided into 100 lwei.

Laffer curve A curve that shows the relationship between tax rates and tax collection. The curve is a plot of the tax rate versus tax revenue collected as indicated below:

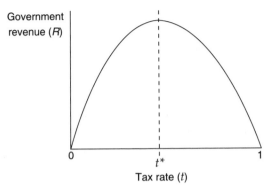

The curve indicates that if taxes are raised beyond a critical point, tax revenue collected will decline as taxpayers increase efforts to pay less taxes or the tax burden incentivises them not to produce an extra income. (*Source*: wikipedia.org)

lagging indicator An economic variable that historically shows changes in trends after the economy as a whole exhibits changes. A moving average is a typical example of a lagging indicator. Also see *leading indicator; moving average*.

lag operator The lag operator is defined to be a linear L^i operator such that $L^i y_t \equiv y_{t-i}$ The lag operator has the following properties:

- Lag of a constant is a constant $Lc = c$
- Distributive law holds $(L^i + L^j)y_t = L^i y_t + L^j y_t = y_{t-i} + y_{t-j}$
- Associative law holds $(L^i L^j)y_t = L^i(L^j y_t) = L^i(y_{t-j}) = y_{t-i-j}$
- L raised to a negative power is a lead operator $L^{-i} y_t = y_{t+i}$
- For $|a| < 1$ the infinite sum $(1 + aL + a^2L^2 + a^3L^3 + \ldots + a^n L^n)y_t = \dfrac{y_t}{1 - aL}$
- For $|a| > 1$ the infinite sum $(1 + a^{-1}L^{-1} + a^{-2}L^{-2} + a^{-3}L^{-3} + \ldots + a^{-n} - n)y_t = \dfrac{-aLy_t}{1 - aL}$

Also see *linear*.

lambda approach A method of determining the cost of capital in foreign markets. It is an extension of the beta approach with the country risk premium being adjusted by a parameter lambda (λ) so that the project itself has an adjustment for its degree of country risk.

The country risk (λ) and systematic risks (β) are separated in this model.

For a South African investor investing in Nigeria, then local = SA and foreign = Nigeria:

cost of equity = $(Rf_{\text{local market}}) + \beta(Rm_{\text{local market}} - Rf_{\text{local market}}) + \lambda CRP$

where CRP = country risk premium; $Rf_{\text{local market}}$ = risk-free rate in the local market; $Rm_{\text{local market}}$ = rate of return in the local market; β = beta value of the project with respect to the project's market returns.

The CRP can be measured with a variety of methods including default risk spreads and relative equity marked standard deviations.

If $\lambda = 1$, then the project contains average country risk.

If $\lambda > 1$, then the project contains above average country risk.

If $\lambda < 1$, then the project contains less than average country risk.

Lambda is measured by one of the following three approaches:
- Adjust for the proportion of revenues of the project from the foreign market:

$$\frac{\text{\% of total revenue in the foreign market of the foreign asset that you are purchasing}}{\text{\% revenues in the foreign market for average company in that foreign market}}$$

- Adjust for the proportion of earnings of the project from the foreign market:

$$\frac{\text{\% of total earnings in the foreign market of the foreign asset that you are purchasing}}{\text{\% earnings in the foreign market for average company in that foreign market}}$$

- Regression of returns on a stock against the returns of a country bond yields a slope = λ. This method effectively measures the sensitivity of the stock price to the country risk.

Some challenges of using this method include revenues and earnings that are often published intermittently while stock prices and bond yield data need to be available.

Also see *adjusted hybrid capital asset pricing model; beta approach; Bludgeon approach; bond; cost of capital; country risk premium; Erb-Harvey approach; Estrata downside risk model; global capital asset pricing model; Godfrey and Espinosa cost of equity model; Goldman Sachs model; Lessard's model; Pereiro's adjusted CAPM model.*

Land Bank The Land and Agricultural Bank of South Africa. The Land Bank intermediates between investors, usually pension funds and insurance companies, and farmers. The Land Bank sells debt securities to raise the money to lend to farmers. Also see *pension fund*.

Land Bank bill A short-term discount security issued by the Land Bank. The bank issues Land Bank bills to fund short-term agricultural financing. Land Bank bills, if issued according to specific conditions, will qualify as liquid assets for the liquid asset reserve requirements for banks. Also see *discount security; Land Bank*.

large exposure requirement A capital adequacy requirement for financial services institutions that requires them to hedge their exposure to a limited customer. Also see *DI900*.

lari The currency of Georgia divided into 100 thetri.

last day to register (LDR) The date on which existing shareholders on company records are designated as the recipient of rights, dividends and other corporate actions. Sometimes called the record date. Also see *record date*.

launch The date on which a bond issue, syndicated loan or a range of other financial instruments is offered to primary market participants. Also see *primary market*.

laundering See *money laundering*.

law of demand The lower the price is, the higher the demand for a product will be. Prices and quantity are inversely related. Also see *Giffen good*.

law of diminishing marginal utility Each unit of a good consumed adds less utility than the unit consumed before it. Marginal utility decreases the more a product is consumed. An everyday example is the consumption of a cup of coffee or tea. The consumption of the first cup leads to a decreased desire to consume a second cup. The marginal propensity to consume more coffee or tea has thus reduced. Also see *law of demand*.

law of iterated expectations The law of iterated expectations is often indicated by $E_t E_{t+1}(x) = E_t(x)$. One cannot use limited information at time t to predict the forecast error one would make if one had superior information at $t + 1$. Also see *adaptive expectations*.

law of one price If the price of identical assets is different, an arbitrage opportunity exists whereby a market participant can simply buy the asset at the lower price and sell it at the higher price. As markets are efficient, investors will immediately capitalise on arbitrage opportunities and the process of capitalising on these opportunities drives prices in the direction of equalisation.

law of supply The higher the price is, the greater the supply is. As more and more profit can be made, more and more producers chase the profit opportunities and supply in the market increases. As a result, supply of the goods or services increases and prices should subsequently start to drop. Also see *law of demand*.

lb See *pound*.

LBMA London Bullion Market Association.

LBO See *leveraged buyout*.

LBP The Lebanese pound.

LC See *letter of credit*.

LCDS See *loan credit default swap*.

LDC Less developed country.

LDR See *last day to register*.

lead arranger See *mandated lead arranger*.

lead bank See *lead manager*.

leading indicator An economic variable that historically has changes in trends before the economy as a whole exhibits changes. Data such as unemployment numbers, new vehicle sales, approved building and housing permits, money supply and changes to inventories are leading indicators. Also see *hard number; lagging indicator*.

lead manager
1. New issues of bonds or securities are underwritten by a lead manager. The lead manager may syndicate underwriting to co-managers. Also see *mandated lead arranger*.
2. In syndicated lending, the lead manager is a second-tier bank that has a lesser role to the mandated lead arranger and book runner. Also see *book runner; mandated lead arranger; subordinate*.

league tables Rankings of lenders or service providers. These rankings can be done by region, product class and lending parameters such as underwriting commitments, amounts book run, participations and advisory mandates. Banks take league tables seriously and use them to benchmark market share and refine strategy. For the loan market these league tables are published in journals such as *Euromoney*.

learning option A set of compound rainbow options. Also see *option; rainbow option*.

lease An agreement whereby the lessor conveys to the lessee the right to use an asset for an agreed period of time in return for a payment or series of payments. This is an alternative to buying the asset. The beneficial use of the asset is important and not who has legal title to it.

The asset must go onto the lessee's balance sheet as a capital or finance lease if the lessee has control over it and the present value of the lease obligation covers more than 90% of the purchase price. When booked on the balance sheet the asset is shown as both an asset and liability entry.

The following are some potential advantages of leasing:
- There may be a reduction in taxes.
- There may be a reduction in uncertainty.
- It may be cheaper than purchasing.
- It may require fewer restrictive covenants and other terms and conditions such as securities on debt.
- It may encumber fewer assets than borrowing to purchase.

Leasing may make income statements and balance sheets look more positive and therefore boost parameters such as return on assets (ROA). Also see *balance sheet; capital lease; covenant; income statement; liability; net lease; operating lease; return on assets; title*.

lease adjusted net debt Operating leases have the effect of moving debt off the balance sheet. There are significant obligations related to these leases and, when analysed, it is common for analysts to adjust the net debt for operating leases. There are two widely used methods for making the adjustment – cash flows related to the leases can be discounted or the multiple method can be used. Also see *balance sheet; multiple method of lease adjustment; net debt*.

lease purchase agreement See *hire purchase*.

lease rate An equivalent interest rate calculated off a series of lease payments. Also see *interest rate; lease*.

lease term The lifespan of a lease. Also see *lease*.

least squares regression (OLS – ordinary least squares) It is recommended that you read through the entry on regression before reading the text below.

Assume that the data set consists of the points (x_i, y_i, z_i) with $i = 1, 2, ..., n$. Assume also that the function f is of a particular form containing some parameters which need to be determined. For instance, suppose that it is quadratic, meaning that $z = a + bx + cy$, where a, b and c are not yet known. One now seeks the values of a, b and c that minimise the sum of the squares of the residuals:

$$\Pi = \sum_{t=1}^{n}[z_i - f(x_i, y_t)]^2 = \sum_{t=1}^{n}[z_i - (a + bx_i + cy_i)]^2 = \min$$

In classical OLS the variables being regressed need to be independent of one another. Also see *regression*.

leg A component of a financial transaction or structure.

legal opinion Opinions from legal professionals, usually in written form, that comment on the enforceability and validity of the terms and conditions in a financial contract.

legal persona By law, companies, in addition to actual people, are recognised as natural persons independent of their owners or shareholders.

legal reserve See *reserve requirement.*

legal risk The risk a party incurs with respect to the enforceability of a contract. Legal opinions are sought on key transactions to minimise the legal risk. Also see *legal opinion.*

lekgotla A South African word used for an offsite or a town hall to mean a widely inclusive and open meeting. The term bosberaad is used with similar meaning. Also see *offsite; town hall.*

lender An entity that lends money in return for interest payments. Also see *interest.*

lender of last resort Central banks are lenders of last resort. They lend funds to depository institutions such as banks when the banks are unable to borrow from other sources. Central banks are set up as lenders of last resort to safeguard the financial system from systemic risk. Central banks also lend funds to other entities in unusual circumstances involving national or regional emergencies or if failure to attain credit would adversely affect the economy. Also see *central bank.*

lending office The branch of a bank from which the funds of a loan are disbursed.

leone The currency of Sierra Leone divided into 100 cents.

leptokurtic A distribution with positive kurtosis is called leptokurtic. In terms of shape, a leptokurtic distribution has a more acute peak around the mean and fatter tails. Also see *kurtosis; mesokurtic; platykurtic.*

Lessard's model A method of determining the cost of capital in foreign markets.

cost of equity = $(Rf_{US}) + CRP + \beta_1 \beta_2 (Rm_{US} + Rf_{US})$

where CRP = country risk premium; Rf_{US} = risk-free rate of the US; Rm_{US} = market rate of return in the US; β_1 = beta value of the foreign market versus US market; β_2 = beta value of similar US project calculated against the US market.

Lessard's approach assumes that the US market is a good proxy for the global market. Lessard's approach ignores possible double counting of country risk through CRP and β_1, the beta value of the foreign market versus the US market.

Also see *beta approach; Bludgeon approach; cost of capital; country risk premium; Erb-Harvey approach; Estrata downside risk model; global capital asset pricing model; Godfrey and Espinosa cost of equity model; Pereiro's adjusted CAPM model.*

lessee The entity that uses a leased asset.

lessor The entity that leases out an asset to another for a fee.

letter of acceptance A temporary document that indicates how many shares have been issued under a new share issue.

letter of allocation Under a rights issue, a company will distribute information, usually in a letter, to all shareholders giving them an indication of their allocated rights. Also see *rights issue/offer.*

letter of comfort A letter issued by an entity, often the parent company, to lenders indicating that the issuer of the letter will in principal support the debt obligations of the borrower. Letters of comfort do not constitute guarantees and have no legal binding. Also see *moral obligation bond.*

letter of credit (LOC/LC) A guarantee issued by a bank to pay off debt obligations if the borrower is unable to. LCs work by virtue of the fact that the entity issuing the guarantee is more creditworthy than the borrower. Banks charge a fee for issuing a letter of credit but cash other than the fees does not change hands unless there is a default under the terms and conditions of the LC. LCs are often provided by banks under LC facilities that borrowers can use freely within the facilities' bounds. These LC facilities can be used as a bonding facility to finance imports and exports and as guarantees to borrow money from other lenders that satisfy particular currency and legal requirements. LC facilities are often syndicated and can appear in facility agreements as part of a wider financing structure. Also see *bankers acceptance; bonding facility; syndicated loan*.

letter of intent A formal letter from one party to another indicating willingness to undertake a financial or business transaction.

level coupon bond A bond whose interest payments or coupons are fixed over the life of the bond.

leverage
1. When leveraging a business, the business takes on more interest-bearing debt (increased gearing). The business should be in a position to generate a return in excess of the costs of the debt. Sometimes called gearing. Also see *gearing*.
2. The ratio of debt to equity in a business.
3. Banks sometimes use leverage to describe the ratio of net debt to EBITDA. Also see *EBITDA; net debt*.

leverage buyout (LBO) All the shares of a public firm are bought by a group, usually management or a private equity company, who buy the shares with the proceeds from the issuing of debt. The firm is often delisted if a publicly listed company. Sometimes called a management buyout. Also see *firm; management buyout*.

leverage covenant A financial covenant agreement on a loan that limits the levels of debt that a borrower may take on relative to cash flow. This is usually measured as the ratio of total debt or net debt to EBITDA. Also see *cure right; financial covenant*.

leveraged lease A leveraged lease is a tax-oriented lease in which the lessor borrows a substantial portion of the purchase price of the leased asset on a non-recourse basis. This means that if the lessee stops making lease payments, the lessor does not have to keep making the full loan payments. The financier therefore has financial exposure to the lessee. Also see *asset; non-recourse*.

leveraged loan A leveraged loan is usually defined in two different ways. The first way is to define the loan against the credit rating of the borrower and the second is to define it against a margin over an interbank rate such as LIBOR. The second way uses a credit rating where a leveraged loan is a loan with a credit rating of BB or lower. S&P use the margin method and define a leveraged loan as a loan that has a margin of 125 bp over LIBOR while Bloomberg defines a leveraged loan as a loan that has a margin of over 250 bp over the LIBOR rate. Leveraged loans are usually in the form of senior bank syndicated debt and make up the majority of the secondary syndicated loans market. Also see *credit rating; interbank rate; LIBOR; margin*.

leveraged market capitalisation See *enterprise value*.

leverage factor The change in value of a derivative such as an option expressed as a function of the change in value of the underlying reference. Also see *delta*.

leverage ratios In banking the term leverage ratio is often used as follows:

$$\text{leverage ratio} = \frac{\text{net debt}}{\text{EBITDA}}$$

Other ratios that indicate the degree of leverage include the debt to equity ratio, debt to total assets ratio and the equity multiplier. Also see *debt to equity ratio; debt ratio; equity multiplier; gearing*.

Lev-X A European leveraged loan credit default swap index. The Lev-X index is composed of 35 subordinated LCD obligations. Investors can use indices such as these to hedge exposure or take a long or short position on a basket of loan obligations. Also see *credit default swap index; loan credit default swap*.

LGD See *loss given default*.

LGF Long gilt future.

liability A present obligation of an entity arising from past events. The settlement of a liability is expected to result in an outflow from the entity of resources such as cash.

libertarianism A liberal philosophy that espouses the removal of onerous regulations and restrictions on an economy and politics.

LIBID The London interbank bid rate at which UK banks borrow money from their counterparts (the buy or bid rate). LIBID is calculated at 11h00 daily (London time) by the British Bankers Association (BBA). Also see *interbank rate; LIBOR*.

LIBOR The London interbank offered rate at which UK banks lend to their counterparts (the sell or offer rate). LIBOR is calculated at 11h00 daily (London time) by the British Bankers Association (BBA).

LIBOR is often used as the basis for the pricing of floating interest rate loans, interest rate swaps, FRAs, interest caps and floors. LIBOR rates are available off the BBA website at www.bba.org.uk. Also see *floating interest rate; forward rate agreement; interbank rate; JIBAR; LIBID*.

lien A claim against an asset to secure a loan. A lien generally gives the power of retention but not the power of sale. A good example is a motor mechanic who has repaired a car and retains the vehicle until full payment for the services has been received. The mechanic will not take legal ownership of the car and is obliged to take care of the asset. Also see *encumbrance; first lien; pledge; second lien*.

life assurance See *life insurance*.

life insurance An insurance policy that pays a lump sum to the dependents or nominees of the policy holder in the event of the death of the policy holder.

life of mine (LOM) The remaining life of a mining asset. The ore body, mining technology and commodities prices have a significant influence on the life of mine.

lifestyle business Small businesses that are set up not with the aim of growth and profits but rather in pursuit of the owner's interests. Retail businesses such as hobby shops, camping stores and speciality sports stores often fall into this category.

LIFFE See *London International Financial Futures and Options Exchange*.

LIFO (last in first out) Last in first out is a method of valuing inventory. A company using this method records the last units that were purchased as the first ones that are sold. The LIFO valuation method has the effect of valuing the inventory of a company highly, especially in an economic environment with high inflation. Switching from the LIFO to FIFO method increases a company's earnings. The effect of a change results from old goods purchased at lower prices being sold at new higher prices. Also see *average cost; FIFO*.

lignite Low-grade coal generally used to fire power stations. Sometimes called brown coal.

like for like sales Retailers often publish their sales growth for a current period against like operations from the previous period. The results therefore exclude results from acquired and discontinued operations. Investors want to see like for like sales growing as it shows organic growth resulting from management driving operations and not simply from acquisitions. Like for like sales illustrate management's ability to gain efficiency. Also see *acquisition; common base year financial statement; organic growth*.

LIMEAN The average of LIBOR and LIBID. Also see *LIBID; LIBOR*.

limit buyer The entity that places a limit order.

limit down See *price limit*.

limited liability (Ltd) An investment where the investors are not liable for losses accrued to the investment. For limited liability companies, the shareholders are not responsible for any liability or loss incurred by the company. The only loss investors in a limited liability company can incur is the initial cash invested. In South Africa limited liability is signalled by the letters Ltd at the end of the company's name. Also see *GmbH; unlimited company*.

limited partnership A partnership where the liability of the partners does not extend beyond the initial investment made. The term limited liability is most often used. Also see *general partner; limited liability; partnership*.

limited recourse The borrowing of monies where the lender has limited claims (recourse) against the borrower or guarantor in the event of default. Limited recourse debt is often used in project finance. Also see *event of default; project finance; recourse*.

limit order An order for a purchase or sale on a stock exchange that states a maximum or minimum price for the transaction. Also see *market order*.

limit up See *price limit*.

linear When a relationship between variables is directly proportional. Linear relationships can be determined through the use of a linear regression and can be described by an equation such as the two-variable straight line equation:

$y = mx + c$

or the higher order $y = a_1 + a_2 x_1 + a_3 x_2 + \ldots + a_n x_{n-1}$

where a_1 is known as the intercept and a's are the parameters of the independent variables.

Linear regressions are not necessarily characterised by a straight line. For example, $y = a_1 + a_2 x^2 + a_3 x$ is a linear combination of variables that does not necessarily plot as a straight line. However, when the term linear is used in finance, a straight line is usually being referred to.

In the two-dimensional straight line $y = mx + c$, the slope of the straight line plot is given by m and c is the intercept.

Also see *linear regression; non-linear*.

linear regression A model that relates the relationship between variables, a dependent variable and independent variables, with a random error term. The model can be expressed as a linear function:

$$y = a_1 + a_2 x_1 + a_3 x_2 + \ldots + a_n x_{n-1}$$

where a_1 is known as the intercept and a's are the parameters of the independent variables.

Linear regressions are not necessarily characterised by a straight line, but most often when the term is used in finance, reference is being made to a straight line. Linear regressions are determined computationally by methods such as the least squares regression. Also see *least squares regression*.

line chart A chart of the price of a security or share over time.

line item A single item, usually a separate line, reported in a company's financial statements. Also see *financial statements*.

line manager A person that has immediate authority over an employee at work. A line manager is generally the person to whom the employee reports directly.

line of credit See *credit line*.

linked policy An investment policy that is linked to the value of the underlying investment assets and not predetermined amounts such as with endowment policies. Also see *endowment insurance policy*.

liquid The volumes of trade in a particular security or asset. A liquid asset is one that can be converted to cash or another asset rapidly for fair value. Also see *fair value*.

liquid asset
1. An asset that can be converted to cash or to another asset rapidly for fair value. Also see *fair value*.
2. Assets such as government bonds, treasury bills and Land Bank bills held by banks as part of their regulatory liquidity requirements. Banks are forced to hold a predetermined portion of their assets in low-risk liquid instruments to ensure they do not take on excessive risk and possibly lose depositors' money.

liquid asset requirements A term used in South Africa to describe the legal requirements that banks have to hold liquid assets. Banks are forced by regulators to hold a predetermined portion of their assets in low-risk instruments such as key government bonds, treasury bills and Land Bank bills. These requirements are designed to protect the banks' depositors. Also see *statutory cost*.

liquidated damages A remedy for which parties have contracted, specifying amounts due for breach of contract.

liquidation The process of selling off a company and turning its underlying assets into cash. Liquidation often occurs when a company is bankrupt and creditors seek monies owed to them. A liquidator is appointed to manage the sale of the company's assets to pay creditors.

liquidation preference The process of assigning the proceeds of a liquidation to debt holders according to the seniority of the debt. Also see *liquidation*.

liquidation value The value received by the shareholders when a firm is liquidated. Also see *firm; liquidation*.

liquidity
1. The speed and ease with which assets can be converted into cash.
2. The liquidity of a security can be measured by how often it is bought and sold. For stocks this is known as the volume of trades. A liquid stock is one that is bought and sold frequently on a market.
3. The ability of a company to service its debt obligations. Also see *cash ratio*.

liquidity facility A facility in a securitisation or loan structure that is usually in the form of a cash account or a revolving credit facility (RCF) that can provide cash to cover timing differences in interest income and expenses. Also see *credit enhancement facility; revolving credit facility; securitisation; swingline loan*.

liquidity preference theory The theory postulates that yield curves are theoretically meant to slope upwards because longer maturity bonds are more risky than shorter term bonds and more sensitive to interest rate changes. Investors therefore require higher rates of return or a premium. Yield curves can often diverge from this theory and can be inverted when investors expect future interest rates to be lower than the current short-term rates. Also see *yield curve*.

liquidity premium The premium associated with the liquidity of a financial instrument. If there is an active market for securities, investors can easily buy and sell and thereby alter their positions. If markets are illiquid, this may not be the case. In an illiquid market investors demand a premium for holding securities due to the additional risk associated with not being able to sell easily. Also see *yield to maturity*.

liquidity ratio See *cash ratio*.

liquidity ratios Acid test (quick ratio), cash ratio, current ratio and interval measure. These are classed as liquidity ratios and are used to analyse the primary concerns of a firm's ability to meet its short-term debts without undue stress. Also see *acid test (quick) ratio; cash ratio; current ratio; firm; interval measure; short-term debt*.

liquidity risk
1. Liquidity risk arises from the lack of marketability of an investment. If a financial instrument that is illiquid is purchased, a liquidity risk premium is required by the investor. Also see *credit risk; illiquid; operational risk*.
2. The risk that a company does not have sufficient cash and readily available credit lines to meet operational cash requirements over a period of time.

liquidity shortage The total cash resources a bank has to borrow each day from the SARB to cover cash reserve deficits. Sometimes called the money market shortage. Also see *repo rate; South African Reserve Bank*.

liquid market See *liquid*.

liquid ratio See *acid test (quick) ratio*.

liquid yield option note (LYON) A zero coupon convertible bond. Also see *zero coupon convertible*.

lira The name of the currency of Turkey and former currency of Italy, Malta and San Marino before adoption of the euro. Also see *euro*.

listed share A share that is traded on a recognised stock exchange. Brokers have seats on exchanges and buy and sell listed shares on behalf of their clients who can be members of the public.

listing The granting of permission by a stock exchange for a company to list its shares on that exchange.

listing requirements Rules and regulations set by stock exchanges that have to be fulfilled before a company can list on the exchange.

litigation Legal action or proceedings.

living standards measure (LSM) A set of measures that indicates the quality of life of individuals. The World Bank introduced LSMs to measure social wellbeing. In South Africa, the South African Advertising Research Foundation (www.saarf.co.za) produces living standards measures and research where LSM1 (poorest) is the lowest and LSM10 the highest category (richest). LSMs use a scoring system that scores users on whether they have access to running water, appliances, electricity and many other services and material goods.

LKR The Sri Lankan rupee.

LLCR See *loan life cover ratio*.

Lloyds member A member of a Lloyds syndicate. Also see *Lloyds of London; Lloyds syndicate*.

Lloyds of London An insurance market meeting place in London where members come together to form syndicates to pool the risk of significant insurance exposures. Historically, Lloyds members have participated in syndicates that insure ships and other marine assets but they are not restricted to these types of high-value assets. Lloyds is an exchange and not an insurance underwriter itself.

Lloyds syndicate A member, or a group of members, of Lloyds of London who underwrites insurance through Lloyds of London. Also see *Lloyds of London*.

LMA See *Loan Market Association*.

LME See *London Metals Exchange*.

loan amortisation See *amortised loan*.

loan average life See *average life*.

loan credit default swap (LCDS) A credit default swap (CDS) that has settlement linked to loans of a company. The instrument allows investors or banks to change their long only positions in the loan markets to a short position or allows them to take on credit risk synthetically. LCDSs can be settled physically, by delivery of a loan or can be cash settled. The spread on these assets usually follows the loan and not the bond markets. The underlying loans are often secured. Also see *bond; credit default swap; credit risk; syndicated loan*.

loaned up A bank that has lent out as much money as its reserve requirement allows it to. Also see *capital adequacy; reserve requirement*.

loan life cover ratio (LLCR) A ratio that measures the net present value of cash available to service debt obligations divided by the principal debt outstanding. The cash flows used are usually those applicable over the life of the debt obligation.

$$\text{loan life cover ratio (LLCR)} = \frac{\sum \text{discounted cash flows available for financing}}{\text{principal outstanding}}$$

The LLCR gives the user a good idea of how the cash flows can cover the outstanding debt balance. It is in essence an assets to liabilities ratio, where the asset is the future cash flows of the project. The cost of debt (reference rate and margin) is used to discount the cash flows. Loan life cover ratios are sometimes used as covenants in loan agreements, especially in the field of project finance. Also see *covenant; reference rate*.

Loan Market Association (LMA) A UK-based trade association of banks. The LMA, among other things, develops standard agreements and templates for loans. The leadership structure of the LMA rotates and the organisation forms a useful collaborative environment for bank debt providers. See www.loan-market-assoc.com for more details.

loan participation note (LPN) Loan participation notes allow investors to participate in the economic investment of a loan without having legal title to the loan. With LPNs, investors participate on a pro rata basis in the loans and collect both interest and principal payments. Also see *global depository receipt; participatory note; pro rata; syndicated loan*.

loan price ratio See *loan to value ratio*.

loans and receivables Financial assets with fixed or determinable payments that are not quoted in an active market other than:

- those that the entity intends to sell immediately or in the near term, which are classified as held for trading, and those that the entity upon initial recognition designates as at fair value through profit or loss
- those that the entity upon initial recognition designates as available for sale
- those for which the holder may not recover substantially all its initial investment, other than because of credit deterioration, which shall be classified as available for sale.

An interest acquired in a pool of assets that are not loans or receivables, for example an interest in a mutual fund or a similar fund, is not considered to be a loan or receivable. Also see *fair value; mutual fund*.

loan stock A form of unsecured debenture. Also see *debenture; unsecured*.

loan syndication See *syndicated loan*.

loan to value ratio A ratio that measures the proportion of a loan facility to the total value of a company.

$$\text{loan to value ratio} = \frac{\text{loan principal}}{\text{value of asset}}$$

The value of the asset is usually determined by market norms. For example, a property asset will be valued by a recognised professional. Loan to value ratios are sometimes used as covenants in loan agreements, especially when lending is against property assets that are posted as security. Also see *covenant*.

LOC See *letter of credit*.

location swap Dealers exchange quantities of assets, usually precious metals, in one location for the same assets in a different location. This is done to reduce transportation expense. Also see *precious metals; swap*.

locked in
1. A contract with no exit.
2. A financial position that cannot be closed.
3. A fixed rate of interest.

lockup A lockup is a feature of a loan agreement that limits the borrower's ability to disburse funds to equity shareholders. The lockup clause inserted in loan agreements usually matches operational cash flows with debt service requirements.

If a company is doing badly and only has enough cash to cover senior debt obligations, it is likely that lockup levels have been reached. With a lockup, holders of the senior debt can then force the company not to pay dividends to equity shareholders and accumulate funds until they are out of lockup. Often when deep into lockup, a cash sweep provision kicks in so that lenders can forcibly extract cash from the business.

Lockups are defined against ratios such as the debt service cover ratio and the net debt to EBITDA ratio. They are set at levels above those set for an event of default. Lenders want the lockup levels to be as high as possible while borrowers want them as low as possible. It is common for lockup ratios to be 10 to 20% above the default ratios. Also see *cash sweep; debt service cover ratio; dividend; event of default; seniority.*

lockup agreement An agreement that limits the ability of shareholders who are usually company insiders, connected persons, venture capitalists and large investors from selling their shares for a period of time after a financial transaction. This agreement applies when an unlisted company is listed under an initial public offer (IPO). Shares are locked up during the IPO as the company and the underwriter of the share issue want to ensure that no single existing investor can jeopardise or profit excessively from the share issue. Also see *initial public offer; venture capital.*

loco
1. Most commonly form of traded gold in London.
2. A locomotive.

lodgement date The last date on which shares are lodged to be eligible for corporate actions such as rights issues, dividends and bonuses. Also see *rights issue offer.*

logarithmic return

$$\text{return} = \ln\left(\frac{FV}{PV}\right)$$

where FV = future value; PV = present value; $\ln$ = the natural log.

Sometimes called the continuously compounding return. Also see *continuous compounding.*

log normal A probability distribution where the logarithm of a number is normally distributed. The log provision implies that values of the probability can never be negative. Many financial variables are modelled as log normally distributed as they do not have negative losses. Log normal distributions have the following equation form:

$$f(x, \mu, \sigma) = \frac{1}{\sigma\sqrt{2\pi}} \exp\left(-\frac{(x-\mu)^2}{2\sigma^2}\right)$$

where μ = the mean; σ^2 = the variance.

The diagram alongside illustrates log normal distributions with differing parameters.

If a random variable X has this distribution, then $X \sim N(\mu, \sigma^2)$. If $\mu = 0$ and $\sigma = 1$, the distribution is called the standard log normal distribution. Also see *arthmetic mean; normal or Gaussian distribution; variance.*

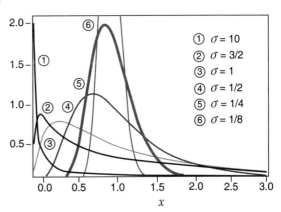

① $\sigma = 10$
② $\sigma = 3/2$
③ $\sigma = 1$
④ $\sigma = 1/2$
⑤ $\sigma = 1/4$
⑥ $\sigma = 1/8$

LOM See *life of mine*.

London Clearing House (LCH) A central clearing house in London used to clear government bonds in financial markets. The LCH acts on behalf of the International Petroleum Exchange and London Metals Exchange. More recently the name has been changed to LCH.Clearnet. Also see *clearing house; government bond; London Metals Exchange*.

London interbank bid rate See *LIBID*.

London interbank offered rate See *LIBOR*.

London International Financial Futures and Options Exchange (LIFFE) An exchange in London where futures and options are traded. It has recently been renamed Euronext.LIFFE.

London Metals Exchange (LME) An exchange in London where non-ferrous metals are traded.

London Stock Exchange (LSE) The stock exchange in London which is one of the largest financial exchanges in the world. There are many British and international companies listed on this exchange. The main requirements for listing on the LSE main board are that the company:

- is public
- is older than three years
- has a 25% free float
- has derivative instruments in issue not greater than 20% of the issued share capital.

Also see *free float; issued share capital; main board*.

long A term used to indicate that an actual security or asset is owned. For example, if an investor is long on a share, the investor actually has that share in his/her possession and seeks to benefit through price appreciation over time and dividend receipts. Also see *long position; short position*.

long bond A bond that has a maturity date far into the future. Long bonds are usually issued to finance projects that have a long period of generating returns on the investment. Infrastructural assets such as dams and water pipelines are financed with long bonds.

long call The purchase of a call option. The payoff relationship of purchasing a call option is illustrated below. Also see *call option; short call*.

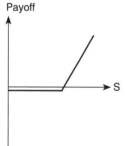

long dated Financial instruments that have dates of maturity longer than 10 years.

long funded When the liabilities of a bank are of longer maturity than the obligations of the bank. This type of situation is rare as banks fund themselves short and lend long. Also see *mismatch*.

long hedge Taking a long position in a futures contract to hedge against the price of a commodity moving upwards. A commodity user will take a long position to ensure that he/she pays the desired price at the future date, thereby hedging input costs. Also see *long position; short hedge.*

long liquidation A reduction in the number of assets or stocks currently held. Also see *long position.*

long position An investment strategy that involves purchasing a security such as a share in the anticipation that the value of the investment will rise. Long positions are also applicable to investments in many other financial instruments such as derivatives and options. For all these financial instruments a long position is one that results in profit should there be a rise in prices of the underlying assets or instruments themselves. A long position is created by being in possession of the security. Sometimes called a bull position. Also see *option; short position.*

long put The sale of a put option. The payoff diagram is illustrated below. Also see *put option; short put.*

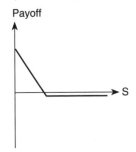

long stop date The date at which a final commitment or obligation is due.

long straddle See *straddle.*

long term Usually one or more years.

long-term debt Debt such as debentures, bonds and bank loans that have a maturity of longer than one year. Long-term debt appears on a company's balance sheet as a source of capital. Also see *balance sheet; bond; debenture; debt.*

long-term insurer A long-term insurer performs a similar intermediation function to the short-term insurer. However, the nature of the loss covered is longer term and is usually in the form of life insurance policies. Also see *reinsurer; short-term insurer.*

lookalike An over-the-counter financial instrument that is constructed off the back of the specification of an exchange listed contract. It is essentially a private copy of a public contract. These synthetic instruments are created when the liquidity of trade in the reference asset is low. Also see *over the counter; synthetic instrument security.*

look back option See *path dependent.*

loss A decrease in economic benefits. It is no different in nature from other expenses.

loss given default (LGD) How much lenders will lose if a borrower defaults. The loss includes principal, fees and coupons. The loss given default is equal to (1 − recovery rate). LGD is measured as market LGD, implied LGD and workout LGD and is sensitive to factors such as whether or not the debt is secured, unsecured or collateralised. Also see *default; implied loss given default; market loss given default; recovery; recovery rate; workout loss given default.*

loss of profits policy See *business interruption policy or insurance*.

loss ratio The claims payouts or losses by an insurance company as a proportion of the premiums received.

lottery A method of assigning shares and other securities that are oversubscribed. Also see *lottery bond*.

lottery bond A government bond with a unique serial number. Serial numbers are drawn randomly and the bonds that match those serial numbers are prepaid. The issuing government therefore has a decreasing total notional outstanding. Some of the bonds are redeemed at a face value greater than notional thus benefiting the holder who effectively wins the lottery. Also see *government bond*.

low In published share tables, low indicates the lowest price traded for the day.

LSE See *London Stock Exchange*.

LSM See *living standards measure*.

LSTA Loan Syndications and Trading Association. This is an American equivalent of the Loan Market Association. Also see *Loan Market Association*.

LTL
1. Long-term liabilities.
2. The Lithuanian litas.

LTM Last twelve months.

LTV See *loan to value ratio*.

LUASA Life Underwriters Association of South Africa.

lucite A physical version of a tombstone, usually cast in Perspex. Also see *tombstone*.

LUF The currency of Luxembourg, the franc divided into 100 centimes.

lump sum A single payment rather than a series of instalments.

LVL The currency of Latvia, the lat divided into 100 santims.

LYD The currency of Libya, the dinar divided into 100 piastres or 1 000 dirhams.

LYON See *liquid yield option note*.

M0 A measure of money supply in South Africa that consists of coins and notes only. All coins and notes in the bank system are included. Also see *money supply*.

M1A A measure of money supply in South Africa that consists of coins and notes (M0) plus cheque and transmission accounts. Also see *monetary base; money supply*.

M1 A measure of money supply in South Africa that consists of M1A plus demand deposits other than cheque and transmission accounts. Also see *demand deposit; M1A; monetary base; money supply*.

M2 A measure of money supply in South Africa that consists of M1 plus short- and medium-term deposits. Also see *M1; monetary base; money supply*.

M3 A measure of money supply in South Africa that consists of M2 plus long-term deposits. Also see *M2; monetary base; money supply*.

M&A Merger and acquisition. Also see *acquisition; merger*.

Maastricht Treaty The treaty that created the European Union. Also see *European Union*.

Macaulay duration See *bond duration*.

MACD See *moving average convergence divergence*.

macroeconomic equilibrium The equilibrium of the economy as a whole.

macroeconomics Economic theory that deals with wider national and international economic issues. Also see *microeconomics*.

MAD The Moroccan dirham divided into 100 centimes.

MAE See *material adverse effect*.

maiden dividend The first dividend declared by a company. Also see *dividend*.

main board Most companies are listed on the main board of stock exchanges. Some stock exchanges such as the JSE in South Africa can list companies on alternative boards such as the VCM, DCM or AltX boards. On the London Stock Exchange, companies are listed on the main board and can also be listed on the Alternative Investment Market (AIM) board. Also see *Alternative Investment Market; Development Capital Market; London Stock Exchange; venture capital market*.

main market See *main board*.

maintenance bond A bond issued to provide funding for the maintenance of an asset.

maintenance covenant A covenant that depends on the maintenance of cash flows, debt cover and other key financial tests of a business's ability to service its debt. It is often tested every quarter and is stricter than an incurrence covenant. For example, a company may be required to maintain a net debt to EBITDA return of less than 3:1 or may be required to maintain sufficient insurance cover. Also see *covenant; interest cover; EBITDA; financial covenant; incurrence covenant; net debt*.

maintenance margin The minimum level specified by the exchange by which an investor's derivative position may fall as a result of an unfavourable price movement before the investor is required to deposit an additional variation margin. The maintenance margin is typically a lower level of about 75% than the initial margin posted when the derivatives transaction was entered into. Also see *initial margin; variation margin*.

maintenance reserve account A reserve account used to fund the future expenses related to anticipated maintenance of an asset.

majority A 50% + 1 vote usually constitutes a majority. In syndicated lending agreements, the majority can be defined by a number such as 66% of the facility commitments. In South Africa, majority for control of public companies is defined as 35%. The 35% majority is set forth by the Securities Regulation Panel (SRP). Also see *Securities Regulation Panel*.

make whole clause A clause in a loan agreement, often private placement loans, that penalises the borrower for early prepayment. The prepayment premium is significant for private placements as the termination fee is calculated by discounting future cash flows, the margin income, at the risk-free rate. Also see *private placing placement*.

making a market The purchase and sale of securities regardless of market conditions. Market makers quote buy (bid) and sell prices (ask), purchase and sell assets quickly and profit from the differential in the bid and ask price.

malpractice insurance See *professional indemnity insurance*.

managed account An account held by a broker on behalf of a client. The mandate on these accounts is the maximisation of profit and the minimisation of risk. Managed accounts take the form of a discretionary account or a non-discretionary account. Discretionary accounts require consultation with the client before trading while non-discretionary accounts allow the brokers to trade as, when and on what assets they like. Also see *discretionary account; non-discretionary account*.

managed currency See *managed float*.

managed float With a managed float foreign exchange rates are allowed to fluctuate under market conditions within predetermined limits. When exchange rate limits are exceeded, monetary authorities intervene by buying or selling foreign exchange reserves. When monetary authorities do not intervene, the exchange rate is classed as a clean float. Also see *clean float; crawling peg; dirty float; fixed exchange rate; foreign exchange rate; free float*.

managed portfolio A portfolio managed by institutional investors who invest funds on behalf of the public. Portfolio managers have varying mandates and seek specific returns at accepted risk levels. Also see *institutional investor*.

management accounting Accounting procedures used internally by companies to manage costs and various other aspects of the business. The accounting reports are not subject to accounting rules and regulations, are not audited and are only used by management.

management buy-in A group of external managers, who believe they can do a better job of running a company without the existing shareholders, buy the company in the hope of turning it around to make a profit.

management buyout (MBO) Company managers buy equity in the business they run. MBO transactions are usually financed with a significant portion of debt.

management company A company that makes profits by supplying services under management contracts.

management contract A contract to manage the assets of a company. Mine owners may give management contracts to companies that physically run the mining operations for them. Asset management companies may be given contracts to manage unit trusts and other funds.

management fee A term sometimes used for an arrangement fee or other fee on a financial transaction. Also see *arrangement fee*.

management risk The investment risk associated with losses that can be incurred by managers potentially doing harm to the firm. Also see *firm*.

managing agent See *co-agent*.

manat The currency of Turkmenistan divided into 100 tenga.

mandate
1. A written authority giving mandatory power for one entity to act on behalf of another. Mandates usually come to an end on death, bankruptcy or diseases such as mental illness.
2. A formal signing by a client giving exclusivity to a financial service provider to undertake a deal.

mandated arranger See *mandated lead arranger*.

mandated bank A bank that is given the authority to approach the market on behalf of the borrower. Also see *mandated lead arranger*.

mandated lead arranger (MLA) An investment bank that has been given the authority by a client to lead the provision of finance and syndication or sell down of that finance. The MLA title is important for industry league tables. Also see *investment bank; lead manager; syndicated loan*.

mandatory bid See *mandatory offer*.

mandatory convertible Convertible debt where convertibility is obligatory, not optional. Also see *convertible debt/bond*.

mandatory costs See *statutory costs*.

mandatory offer Under takeover bids in the UK and many other countries with similar laws, when an acquirer acquires more than 30% of the voting rights of the target, they have to make a mandatory offer for the rest of the share capital at the highest price paid for the share by the acquirer over the past 12 months. The rules governing this code in the UK are published in the blue book. Also see *blue book; general offer; squeeze out; whitewash*.

mandatory prepayment A covenant in debt agreements that covers clauses such as change of control and credit ratings and that allows lenders to declare all outstanding loans and accrued interest due and payable. Mandatory prepayment events do not cause cross defaults. Also see *accrued interest; covenant; credit rating*.

mandatory quote period (MQP) The period during which market makers must provide two-way quotes. Also see *market maker*.

maple bond A bond issued in Canada by companies that are not Canadian and denominated in Canadian dollars. Also see *bulldog bond; Eurobond; Matilda bond; samurai bond; Yankee bond*.

margin

1. A measure of a financial variable against the turnover of the business, for example the EBITDA margin. Also see *EBITDA margin*.
2. Another term for spread. Also see *spread*.
3. The difference between the rate that banks borrow and lend money. For some corporate loans banks charge a margin above the relevant interbank rate such as JIBAR or LIBOR. Also see *JIBAR; LIBOR*.
4. The payment to or receipt of cash or collateral from a derivatives exchange based on losses or gains incurred in holding a particular position. Also see *collateral*.
5. When trading in the repo market, the value of securities posted against the borrowing of cash must exceed the cash amount by a margin sometimes called the haircut. Also see *haircut; repurchase agreement*.
6. The amount that a client borrows from a stockbroker to purchase shares. Also see *stockbroker*.

Also see *collateral margin; initial margin; maintenance margin; variation margin*.

marginal cost The price of producing one extra unit or raising one extra unit of finance. Also see *break-even contribution margin per unit; margin per unit*.

marginal cost of capital The incremental financing cost associated with the provision of new capital.

marginal efficiency of capital The extra profit or yield per unit of investment into productive capacity. Businesses will continue investing capital if their projects are expected to give returns in excess of the cost of capital. Also see *cost of capital*.

marginal firm A company that has a high cost base and is exposed to small fluctuations in the sale price of their product. Mining companies with ore bodies that are not particularly profitable fall into this class. When commodities prices are high, they make profits. As commodities prices decline, they scale back or shut down. Share prices for marginal gold mining companies are highly dependent on the gold price.

marginal lending facility See *marginal lending rate*.

marginal lending rate The rate at which central banks lend to illiquid financial institutions. The lending is short term and fully secured. Financial institutions borrow against assets such as treasury bills and other short-term securities. The lending against security is in the form of a repurchase agreement (repo).

In the US the term central bank discount rate or discount rate is used. The term emergency lending rate is also used. In South Africa the marginal lending rate is often called the repo rate. Also see *central bank discount rate; repo rate; repurchase agreement; treasury bill*.

marginal producer See *marginal firm*.

marginal propensity to consume (MPC) A change in consumption resulting from a change in income:

$$\text{marginal propensity to consume (MPC)} = \frac{\text{change in consumption}}{\text{change in income}} = \frac{\Delta C}{\Delta Y_d}$$

For example, if MPC = 90%, then for a 100 unit change in income, 90 extra units are consumed and 10 are saved. MPC and the marginal propensity to save (MPS) are related, where MPC = 1 − MPS. Also see *marginal propensity to save; utility theory*.

marginal propensity to import (MPI) A change in imports resulting from a change in income:

$$\text{marginal propensity to import (MPI)} = \frac{\text{change in imports}}{\text{change in income}} = \frac{\Delta M}{\Delta Y_d}$$

For example, if MPI = 90%, then for a 100 unit change in income, 90 extra units of goods are imported.

marginal propensity to save (MPS) A change in savings resulting from a change in income:

$$\text{marginal propensity to save (MPS)} = \frac{\text{change in savings}}{\text{change in income}} = \frac{\Delta S}{\Delta Y_d}$$

For example, if MPS = 10%, then for 100 units extra income, 10 are saved and 90 are consumed. MPS and marginal propensity to consume (MPC) are related by MPS = 1 – MPC. Also see *marginal propensity to consume*.

marginal propensity to withdraw (MPW)

marginal propensity to withdraw (MPW) = MPS – MPI

where MPS = the marginal propensity to save; MPI = the marginal propensity to import.

marginal revenue See *margin per unit*.

marginal tax The extra tax T paid for extra income earned Y:

$$\text{marginal tax} = \frac{\Delta T}{\Delta Y}$$

Marginal tax is usually applicable only over a particular tax threshold. Also see *average tax rate; fiscal drag*.

marginal utility An additional utility derived from the consumption of a further good. Also see *marginal propensity to consume*.

margin build The improvement of profits by increasing cost efficiency rather than growing revenues. Also see *like for like sales*.

margin call The process of calling in margin in the form of cash or collateral to cover positions in derivative trades and on margin loans. Also see *collateral; initial margin; margin loan; variation margin*.

margin grid See *pricing grid*.

margin loan A loan extended against a pool of assets, usually a pool of equity shares. The conditions on the loan are such that if the value of the pool of assets falls below a certain level, usually expressed as a loan to value ratio, a margin has to be posted. Posting a margin involves the posting of more security in the form of shares or cash to ensure that the security cover is adequate. Many drivers affect these loans such as the share or asset volatility, volumes traded and current valuation multiples.

margin of safety The amount that sales can drop from an existing sales level before the company no longer makes a profit. The margin of safety can be expressed as sales volumes by:

existing sales volume – break-even sales volume

or as units:

existing sales units – break-even sales units

margin per unit The additional revenue contributed to a firm from the sale of an extra unit of output. It is calculated by:

$$\text{margin per unit} = \frac{\text{revenue} - \text{variable expenses}}{\text{number of units produced}}$$

Sometimes called marginal revenue.

margin ratchet The change of margins in a loan agreement according to changes in the risk profile of a business. The risk changes can be measured in the form of leverage and interest cover or as changes to credit ratings. Also see *credit rating; interest cover; leverage*.

mark down Reduce the price of a security or good. This is usually done in anticipation of excess supply over demand.

market A physical or virtual area where purchasers and sellers buy and sell goods, securities and services.

marketable parcel A parcel of shares of a particular company that trades in a certain size as set by an exchange. Sometimes called a marketable lot or a board lot or parcel.

market appreciation The current higher market price of an asset less the price paid for the asset. This is not a realised profit and is only realised when the asset is sold. Sometimes called a paper profit. Also see *market depreciation*.

market asset disclaimer assumption The present value of future cash flows without real option or flexibility is the best unbiased estimate of the market value of the project were it a traded or marketable asset. Also see *asset; cash flow; real option*.

market breadth A parameter that measures the degree of overall market participation in a market trend. It effectively measures the market sentiment. Market breadth is measured by the number of overall shares that advanced or declined.

market cap

1. See *market capitalisation*.
2. In published share tables market cap indicates the number of shares in the market multiplied by the closing price on the day.

market capitalisation The share price of a company multiplied by the number of fully paid for and issued shares on the market. Market capitalisation gives the total market value of a company.

market capitalisation index A stock market index calculated by a simple averaging of market capitalisations. The index gives the average valuation of all companies in the market being analysed:

$$\text{market capitalisation index} = \frac{\sum \text{number of shares} \times \text{market prices}}{\text{number of companies in index}}$$

market clearing price or level The price at which a primary market's security issue will be fully taken up in the market. Sometimes called a clearing rate in bond auctions. Also see *auction; primary market*.

market counterparty A knowledgeable and financially sophisticated customer. These customers include financial institutions, government departments and central banks. The rules governing transactions with market counterparties are more lenient than for dealings with private and intermediate customers who are less educated in financial dealings. Also see *intermediate customer; private customer*.

market depreciation The current low market price of an asset less the price paid for the asset. This is not a realised loss and is only realised when the asset is sold. Sometimes called a paper loss. Also see *market appreciation; mark to market*.

market disruption An event or series of events that causes abnormal price movement in the market. Trading on exchanges can be suspended when market disruption events occur.

market dysfunction A situation where a lender's cost of borrowing exceeds its revenue from lending. There are often clauses in loans protecting lenders from market dysfunction.

market economy An economy in which consumers and producers have the freedom to produce, sell and spend. In a market economy there are few onerous government controls and supply and demand dynamics control the market. Also see *command economy*.

market expectation pricing theory The shape of the yield curve is dominated by the demand for bonds of specific tenors. The yield curves are humped and the demand comes from investors such as pension funds with specific investment mandates or investors choosing more liquid instruments. Also see *pension fund; yield curve*.

market flex When syndicating a loan or issuing a bond, market flex indicates that margins, fees and structures have been changed because sales targets have not been met or the underlying credit risk has changed. Market flex agreements are often put in place to ensure that the borrower adopts a proactive approach to the distribution process. Market flex indicates pricing has increased while reverse flex indicates that pricing has decreased. Borrowers are sensitive to market flex provisions. Also see *credit risk; reverse flex; structural flex*.

market forces The buying and selling dynamics in markets that match supply and demand.

market if touched The triggering of a trade when the price of an underlying asset reaches a particular level. Sometimes called a board order. Also see *stop loss*.

market interest rate The interest rate determined in the market by the matching of the purchase and sale of debt securities. Also see *interest rate; yield curve*.

Market Loan Association (MLA) See *Loan Market Association*.

market loss given default (LGD) The loss given default calculated after a default event. It is calculated using the price at which the debt instrument trades after default. Also see *credit default swap; implied loss given default; loss given default; workout loss given default*.

market maker An intermediary who is willing to quote buy and sell prices to participants. Sometimes called a price maker or committed principal.

market neutral When derivatives or long and short positions in the market combine in such a manner as to reduce the exposure to the overall direction of the market to near zero.

market not held order An instruction to a broker that is an order to trade allowing the broker to delay execution in an attempt to get a better price. Sometimes called a discretionary order.

market order When executing a transaction on a stock exchange, a market order states that the price should be at the best possible price in the auction period.

market rate The rate at which money is borrowed from banks.

market regulator A body appointed by a government to regulate financial markets. Also see *Financial Services Authority*.

market risk A risk that influences a large number of assets. A global economic slowdown would constitute a market risk. Sometimes called non-diversifiable risk as diversification of a portfolio does not minimise this risk. Also see *systematic risk*.

market risk of a share The risk of the market adjusted for the degree to which a share tracks the market defined by:

market risk share = $\beta_S \sigma_M$

where β_S = beta of the share; σ_M = standard deviation of the market.

The measure becomes relevant in small markets dominated by a few large companies. For example, in South Africa the JSE is dominated by large mining companies and so the overall market is highly influenced by the performance of these mining shares. Also see *beta*.

market risk premium (MRP) The premium over the risk-free rate of return that investors require to invest in a particular market or asset. Usually defined mathematically as:

market risk premium (MRP) = $(E(R_m) - R_f)$

where $E(R_m)$ = the estimated return of the market; R_f = risk-free rate of return.

The risk-free rate of return is normally measured by government bonds or treasury bills. The MRP can be adjusted for volatility in the equity markets by the relative equity market standard deviations approach or by default risk spreads. Also see *beta; capital asset pricing model; combined market risk premium approach; default risk spread; government bond; relative equity market standard deviation; risk-free rate; security market line; treasury bill; volatility*.

Markets in Financial Instruments Directive (MiFID) A directive to open up European capital markets by improving price transparency of financial instruments and making it easier to trade across borders in Europe. Also see *capital market*.

market to book value The market value of a company expressed as a ratio of its net asset value. Also see *net asset value*.

market value Once traded in the secondary market, buyers and sellers of shares determine the price at which they are traded. Through this buying and selling, the market sets the market value of the securities. The total market value is therefore equal to the total number of shares multiplied by the share price giving the market capitalisation. The difference between the market value and the book value shows the market view of the future potential of the business. Also see *book value; market capitalisation; secondary market*.

market value added (MVA) Shareholders' wealth is maximised only when the difference between the market value of a company and the capital employed is at a maximum.

market value added (MVA) = total value − total capital

The total value is the adjusted value of the assets on the balance sheet. Also see *balance sheet; economic value added*.

market value of debt When an entity issues a bond, that bond can be traded in a secondary market. Due to alternate views on returns, the yield to maturity in that secondary market can vary from the coupon payments on the date of issue. There can thus be a difference between how the market values the debt and the value of the debt

market value ratios Dividend yield or dividends per share; earnings yield or earnings per share; price earnings; dividend cover; price to book value. Also see *book value; dividend cover; dividend yield; earnings yield; price earnings ratio.*

market volatility index (VIX) An index calculated by the Chicago Board Options Exchange that tracks market volatility. Also see *South African Volatility Index; volatility.*

marking to market See *mark to market.*

Markov process or property In probability theory, a stochastic process has the Markov property. The Markov property is defined if the conditional probability distribution of future states of the process, given the present state, depends only on the current state, i.e. it is conditionally independent of the past states (the path of the process) given the present state. A process with the Markov property is usually called a Markov process and may be described by the term, Markovian. Also see *stochastic process.*

Markowitz efficient frontier Representation of a set of portfolios that has the maximum return for a given level of risk, or alternately, the maximum risk for the given return.

mark to market The process of recognising all securities in a portfolio at their current market value. Marking to market is used when instruments such as options can only realise profits at future dates and their current valuation is most easily ascribed to the current market price. Also see *variation margin.*

mark-up
1. Charges in excess of the costs of producing goods or services.
2. The update of documentation to adapt to more specific conditions and for feedback from counterparties. Also see *boiler plate document.*

master agreement An overall agreement under which a smaller series of transactions takes place.

master note A negotiated low-risk debt instrument issued by the Federal Farm Credit Banks in the US. The investor may have the ability to vary the principal amount and exercise a put option for early maturity. Conversely, the issuer may have the ability to exercise a call option for early redemption. Also see *call option.*

matador bond A bond issued by a foreign firm, denominated in euros and traded in the Spanish foreign bond market. Also see *bond; bulldog bond; Eurobond; firm; foreign bond; maple bond; Matilda bond; samurai bond; Yankee bond.*

match funding The process of a financier matching the terms, typically the tenor, of the funding provided to the corresponding funds raised. For example, banks seek to match five-year loans with five-year deposits. Also see *match rate funds; tenor.*

matching
1. Participants in a transaction agreeing the terms and conditions before settlement of the transaction.
2. Matching of the maturity profile of assets and liabilities of banks. Also see *mismatch.*

matching concept See *matching of costs with revenues*.

matching of costs with revenues Expenses are recognised in the income statement on the basis of a direct association between the costs incurred and earnings of specific portions of income. This process involves the simultaneous recognition of revenues and expenses that result directly and jointly from the same transactions or other events. Also see *income statement*.

matching principle An accounting principle where expenses are offset against income for the same accounting period. Also see *accounting period*.

match rate funds Matching the cost of providing a loan with the cost of funds. For example, on a three-month loan a South African bank may fund itself at 3M JIBAR + 10 bp and then loan the funds out to a top credit quality client at JIBAR + 15 bp. The funding of the trades in this case is closely matched. Also see *JIBAR*.

material Of significance or influencial.

material adverse effect (MAE) An event or effect that is detrimental to a company and that affects its ability to remain a going concern and pay its creditors. Banks use MAE clauses in covenants in loan agreements that usually refer to:

- the business prospect as a whole
- the ability of a borrower to fulfil its obligations
- the validity or enforceability of the finance document
- the right or remedy of a lender in respect of a finance document.

Also see *covenant; going concern*.

material adverse event An event that has a material adverse effect on a transaction or business. Also see *material adverse effect*.

material subsidiary A subsidiary of a company that forms a substantial part of the company's business. It is classed as material by virtue of the fact that it makes significant contributions to profit or constitutes a significant portion of the consolidated assets. Also see *subsidiary*.

Matilda bond A bond issued by a foreign company in the Australian market denominated in Australian dollars. Also called a kangaroo bond.

maturity The specified date at which a bond, loan or financial contract will expire and the date on which the issuer will repay the outstanding principal amount. Also see *principal*.

maturity guarantee A guarantee over the obligations of a securitisation vehicle on redemption.

maturity structure The time structure of the maturing obligations of a company. Analysis of the maturity structure of debt is important for companies to allow them to manage their cash flows and match their obligations.

maturity value See *nominal value; redemption value*.

maximum capital expenditure covenant A financial covenant in a loan agreement that requires that the borrower limit capital expenditure to a predefined amount or ratio, usually specified as a percentage of cash flow. Also see *financial covenant*.

MBO See *management buyout*.

MBS Mortgage-backed security. Also see *collateralised mortgage obligation*.

McJob A low paid boring job with little or no future prospects.

mean See *arithmetic mean*.

mean reversion The mean reversion is a tendency for a stochastic process to remain near, or tend to return over time, to a long-run average value. For example, interest rates and implied volatilities tend to exhibit mean reversion while exchange rates and stock prices tend not to. Stock market returns, however, do tend to exhibit mean reversion. The following stochastic equation illustrates how mean reversion can be defined:

$$X_{t+1} = X_t - b[X_t - E(X)] + \varepsilon_t$$

The term $b[X_t - E(X)]$ effectively pulls the series to the mean value.

Also see *central tendency; interest rate; stochastic process*.

mean reversion trading rule If mean reversion exists, then a trading rule based on an above or below average discount on the share can be used. A below average discount on the share provides a sell opportunity and an above average discount provides a buy opportunity.

measured mineral resources A mineral resource or ore body that has been explored and sampled to a sufficient degree that there is confidence that the ore body can be economically developed. The grade and continuity of the ore body is known with a high degree of certainty. Also see *indicated mineral resources; inferred mineral resources*.

measurement The process of determining the monetary amounts at which the elements of the financial statements are to be recognised and carried in the balance sheet and income statement. Also see *balance sheet; financial statements; income statement*.

median The median of a data set is the number that divides the data set into two equal halves. If the number of observations in the set is an even number, then the mean value of $\frac{n}{2}$ and $\frac{n}{2} + 1$ observations is classed the median value.

Also see *arithmetic mean; mode; quartile*.

medium dated note A security that has maturities of between three and seven years.

medium-term note program (MTN) Unsecured debt instruments offered to investors on a continuous basis. The notes have terms of five to ten years and attract floating interest rates. They are often called Euronotes or domestic medium-term notes if issued outside the US. The infrastructure for MTNs is such that they can be held back from the market and released in such a way as to acquire funds as and when the borrower requires them. An advantage of MTNs is that only one listing and documentation procedure is undertaken to access funds at a number of points in time. Also see *floating interest rate; unsecured*.

MEFF Spanish futures and options exchange. MEFF clears and trades options and futures on bonds, interest rates and the IBEX-35 Index as well as futures and options on the leading Spanish stocks. Also see *interest rate*.

Mei Moses Index A financial index that tracks the price of artworks.

member
1. A person who has been allowed membership of a pension scheme or is entitled to benefits under the scheme.

2. A stockbroker who is a member of a stock exchange and is allowed to trade on the exchange. Also see *stockbroker*.

member firm A stockbroker who is a member of a stock exchange. Also see *member; stockbroker*.

memorandum A company's memorandum gives information about its relations with the outside world and market. The information includes its name, country of domicile, objectives, liability status and authorised share capital. Also see *articles of association; authorised share capital; domicile*.

memorandum of satisfaction A legal document that indicates that obligations under mortgage bonds have been released.

merchandise exports Exports of goods (and not services) from a country.

merchant bank A term used in the UK for an investment bank. Also see *investment bank*.

merger The process whereby two similarly sized companies form a single entity. There is no dominant control of the new entity by one single party and the shareholders share the risks and rewards of the new company more or less equally. Also see *acquisition*.

mesokurtic Distributions with zero kurtosis (skew). The most prominent example of a mesokurtic distribution is the normal distribution. Also see *kurtosis; leptokurtic; platykurtic*.

metical (MT) The currency of Mozambique divided into 100 centavos.

mezz See *mezzanine debt*.

mezzanine debt Floating interest rate debt with a mix of cash coupons and increases in the principal amount of the debt (PIK). Mezzanine debt is neither pure debt nor pure equity, but has cash flow characteristics of both and is a second or third ranking security. Mezzanine debt can give capital growth on the asset through the PIK. Mezzanine debt is generally high yield debt as the credit risk is increased by having to wait longer for cash returns and being subordinated in the event of default. Mezzanine debt is usually subordinate to senior debt and can sometimes be secured. Also see *capital gains; floating interest rate; payment in kind; secured; seniority; subordinate*.

MFRC See *Micro Finance Regulatory Council*.

MIBOR Madrid interbank offered rate. Also see *JIBAR; LIBOR*.

microcredit See *microloan*.

microeconomic equilibrium The equilibrium levels in a single market.

microeconomics The study of the economics of individual firms, industries and customers. Also see *macroeconomics*.

Micro Finance Regulatory Council (MFRC) A South African regulatory body that regulates the microlending industry. The Department of Trade and Industry (DTI) obliges all lenders that are exempt from the Usury Act to register with the MFRC. Also see *Department of Trade and Industry; Usury Act*.

microlender An entity that advances microloans. Also see *microloan*.

microloan A loan that falls into the category of money lending transactions exempt under the Usury Act exemption notice. These are small personal loans to individuals that do not have access to conventional credit from commercial banks. Also see *Usury Act*.

middleman An entity that makes a profit by trading goods between producers and consumers.

middle market A market that is medium sized.

middle market price The mid price of a security between the highest and lowest price for the day. Also see *mid price*.

middle price See *mid price*.

mid price The price midway between the bid price and ask price:

$$\text{mid price} = \frac{\text{bid price} + \text{ask price}}{2}$$

Also see *ask price; bid price*.

mid swap The arithmetic mean of the bid and offer swap rate. Bond spreads are quoted over mid swaps in the European markets, whereas in South Africa they are quoted over the government yield curve. Also see *swap rate; yield curve*.

MiFID See *Markets in Financial Instruments Directive*.

minimum net worth A covenant specified in loan agreements that indicates the borrower must maintain a net worth greater than the amount specified. The net worth is usually specified through a measure called the tangible net worth. Net worth covenants give lenders comfort that shareholders will not extract excessive levels of cash from the business. Also see *net worth; tangible net worth*.

minimum variance portfolio When obtaining a portfolio's expected return and standard deviation, there is a point at which a particular set of portfolio weights will have a minimum standard deviation or risk. Also see *Markowitz efficient frontier; portfolio expected returns; standard deviation*.

mining fund An investment fund that holds underlying mining assets. In South Africa, the bulk of these funds is made up of gold, platinum, coal and iron ore related stocks.

mining house A company that owns a series of mining assets.

minority See *minority shareholder*.

minority interest The portion of the profit or loss and net assets of a subsidiary attributable to equity interests that are not owned, directly or indirectly, through subsidiaries by the parent. Also called the outside shareholders interest or OSHI. Also see *net assets*.

minority protection Regulatory protection that ensures minority shareholders in companies are not taken advantage of.

minority shareholder A shareholder who has a small stake or minority interest in a company and does not have substantial control or influence.

mismatch
1. When the liabilities of a bank are shorter term than the exposures of its loans advanced. To fund the long-term loans, banks must roll over short-term debt obligations. Most banks are run on this basis and rely on rolling over short-term debt obligations.

2. A financial position that is not perfectly offset.

misrepresentation A misleading statement or information provided when negotiating a financial contract.

mission statement A statement of the high-level objectives and purpose of a company.

mixed economic system Private individuals and businesses make some economic decisions and governments also make some commercial decisions. Socialism is a good example of a mixed economic system. Also see *command economy; market economy*.

MKD The currency of Macedonia, the dinar divided into 100 deni.

MLA

1. See *mandated lead arranger*.
2. Market Loan Association. Also see *Loan Market Association*.

MLR Minimum lending rate.

MLRO Money laundering reporting officer.

mode The observed value in a data set that occurs most frequently. For example, in the data set {1, 2, 3, 4, 5, 6, 7, 1, 2, 3, 4, 5, 5, 5, 8, 9, 5} the number 5 appears most frequently and is hence the mode.

In a continuous probability density function which has a first derivative, the mode is usually defined as the value at which the first derivative is equal to zero and the second derivative is less than zero. Also see *arithmetic mean; median*.

model risk Risks associated with the assumptions and inaccuracy of underlying mathematics of modelling financial markets.

modified duration (*MD*) Modified duration measures the sensitivity of a bond's price to changes in the yield to maturity:

$$\text{modified duration } (MD) = \frac{D}{1+\frac{i}{k}}$$

where D = duration; i = interest rate; k = the number of coupon payments (discounting periods in a year).

A % change in bond price = $-MD \times \Delta$ yield change which can be expressed as:

$$\frac{\Delta P}{P} = -MD \times \Delta i$$

where P = the price of the bond.

Also see *bond duration; dollar duration; duration; effective duration; yield to maturity*.

modified following convention If the date of maturity of an instrument is on a weekend or holiday, then delivery is made on the next working day unless it is at month end when the delivery is made on the previous day.

Modigliani-Miller or M&M proposition

1. The value of a firm is independent of the capital structure. By analogy, if the total value were a pie, the value is not dependent on the way the pie is sliced. The value of the firm according to this theory depends on the operating cash flows:

$$\text{value} = \sum_t \frac{OCF}{(1+r)^t}$$

where *OCF* = operational cash flow at each point in time *t*; *r* = the applicable discount rate.

2. A firm's cost of equity capital is a positive linear function of its capital structure. It is dependent on the required rate of return on assets (R_A), the cost of debt (R_D) and the debt to equity ratio. The equation can be rearranged for calculating the weighted average cost of capital (WACC) to obtain:

$$R_E = R_A + (R_A - R_D)\frac{D}{E}$$

where R_A = weighted average cost of capital (WACC); R_E = the return on equity.

M&M argued that in a world of no taxes, the benefit from the cost of debt being lower than the cost of equity is offset by the fact that as debt is added, the cost of equity rises to compensate for the increased risk borne by the shareholders. Thus the overall WACC remains unchanged.

In a world of taxes, because interest is typically a tax-deductible expense, as more debt is added, more tax saving is realised. The operating cash flow and hence the value of the firm is increased by the amount of the tax shield [$Tc \times D$] and the WACC subsequently falls as debt is added.

At high levels of debt, however, the possibility of bankruptcy becomes real. The cost of equity, and perhaps even the cost of debt, will rise sharply at high debt levels, causing the WACC to increase and hence corporate value to fall.

Also see *capital structure; cost of debt; cost of equity; debt to equity ratio; firm; linear; return on assets; weighted average cost of capital*.

momentum A number or variable that is derived from a mathematical formula and that measures the impetus or energy behind the price movement of a security compared to the initial boost that set the trend in motion.

momentum indicator A variable which measures the rate at which prices rise and fall. It gives an indication of the latent strength or weakness of a trend. It is also called an oscillator because values oscillate between defined levels or about a longer term trend.

monetary base The sum of a central bank's liabilities. These include notes in circulation and other reserves. Also see *central bank; M0*.

monetary inflation An increase in money supply is a driver of inflation.

monetary policy A policy that exercises control in an economy by setting interest rates and reserve requirements to change money supply and inflation. Also see *fiscal policy; inflation; interest rate; money supply; reserve requirement*.

monetary policy committee (MPC) A committee chaired by a central bank governor that makes all decisions with respect to monetary policy set by the central bank. Interest rate changes are the most frequent monetary policy decisions made by the MPC. MPCs sit a number of times a year to review economic conditions, analyse forecasts and set monetary policy such as interest rates. Also see *central bank; interest rate; monetary policy*.

monetary union A set of countries that uses the same currency. The euro and CFA franc are examples of such currencies. Also see *CFA franc; euro*.

monetisation Converting an asset into cash by financial engineering that does not result in loss of control of the asset. Securitisation is a process whereby monetisation can be engineered. Also see *securitisation*.

money Coins and notes as well as deposits in deposit-taking institutions such as banks. There are different classes of money that include:

- **M1**: M1A (notes and coins) + demand deposits (deposits that can be withdrawn immediately)
- **M2**: M1 + short-term savings + medium-term deposits (60-day deposits)
- **M3**: M2 + long-term deposits (> 90 days).

Also see *demand deposit; deposit-taking institution; M1; M2; M3; monetary base*.

money fund A unit trust where investors' funds are pooled and used to buy a range of money market products and minimise risk through diversity in the portfolio. Money funds are actively managed by fund managers. Money funds give higher returns than money market deposits (money market investment accounts), but are not as liquid and flexible. Also see *money market; unit trust*.

money laundering Activities designed to obscure the source of illegally obtained money.

money machine See *automated teller machine*.

money market Short-term debt and securities are sold and traded in the money markets. Money market securities are issued by banks, discount houses and governments. Instruments with a maturity date of less than one year make up the money market. Principal instruments used on money markets include treasury bills, commercial paper and bankers acceptance notes. The money market is controlled by central banks changing interest rates. Users of the market include government, mutual funds and pension funds. Also see *bankers acceptance note; central bank; commercial paper; discount house; interest rate; mutual fund; pension fund; short-term debt; treasury bill*.

money market investment account Money market investment accounts are retail banking deposit products. The funds attracted from these accounts appear on the balance sheets of banks and make up an important part of their funding structure. Money market accounts have the following properties:

- Interest rates are more conservative than money funds.
- Cleared funds can be drawn immediately with a card from an ATM.
- Interest rates are tiered according to the balance in the account.
- No service fees are charged if the balance remains above a certain level.

Also see *automated teller machine; interest rate; money fund*.

money market shortage The extent to which banks are indebted to a central bank. Sometimes called the liquidity shortage. Also see *central bank*.

money market unit trust A unit trust that has underlying investments in money market instruments. Also see *money market*.

money multiplier (MM) The proportion by which money supply will increase in response to a change in deposits. The money multiplier is defined mathematically by:

$$\text{money multiplier (MM)} = \frac{1}{\text{reserve requirement}}$$

Also see *money supply; multiplier; reserve requirement*.

money purchase pension scheme See *defined contribution fund*.

money supply The total value of money in circulation. M1, M2 and M3 are included in the measure and broader forms of money supply including M4 and M5 can also be used. Also see *M1; M2; M3; monetary policy*.

money transfer The movement of money from one entity to another through routes such as cheques, physical delivery, accounting entries in the books of financial intermediaries and settlement of trades through specialised transfer systems. Also see *Society for Worldwide Interbank Transactions*.

monoline insurer An insurer with a good credit rating that guarantees debt. Having monoline insurance can give companies access to capital at rates and levels of liquidity they ordinarily would not achieve on a standalone basis. Also see *credit rating; wrapped bond*.

monopoly A business that has such dominant market share that it controls prices in the market. Most countries have regulations in place to limit the formation or power of monopolies. SABMiller is an example of a company that has a monopoly over the South African beer market. Also see *duopoly; oligopoly*.

monopoly price A price that a monopoly business charges to maximise profit through a balance of price and volume.

monopoly profit Profit that is above normal competitive rates due to a company being in a monopolistic market position. Sometimes called economic profit or excess profit. Also see *monopoly; monopoly price*.

monopsony A market with only a single buyer. The opposite of a monopoly. These entities can restrict the volume of purchases in an industry to control and depress prices to below competitive levels. Also see *monopoly*.

Monte Carlo Monte Carlo methods are a widely used class of computational algorithms for simulating the behaviour of various physical, financial and mathematical systems. They are distinguished from other simulation methods such as molecular dynamics by being stochastic. Monte Carlo methods use random numbers as opposed to deterministic algorithms. Because of the iterative nature of algorithms and the large number of calculations involved, the method is suited to calculation using a computer. Also see *stochastic process*.

Moody's A credit rating agency. Also see *credit rating agency*.

moonlighting Having more than one job. The second job may result in a conflict of interest with the first job.

moral hazard When the provision of insurance increases the probability of the event being insured against. This usually occurs because the party involved has less incentive to take protective or preventative action. For example, people may be less careful drivers knowing their cars are fully insured.

moral obligation bond A bond issued by government organisations such as municipalities that has the tax benefits associated with these investments and often has further credit risk mitigation through a moral indication that the bond will be protected from default. Reserve funds are often set up to ensure that debt service obligations can be met. The moral pledge is not legally binding and is similar in concept to a letter of comfort. Also see *letter of comfort*.

moral suasion An economic term used to indicate when central banks and other market participants politely ask banks to implement changes and do not forcibly make changes to regulations or monetary policy. Sometimes called open mouth operations.

moratorium
1. A period of time that a defaulter under a debt obligation has to rectify the default. Sometimes called a grace period.
2. The suspension of a particular activity. For example, governments may place moratoriums on the development of property if it comes to light that such developments may have damaging social or environmental consequences.

mortgage The process of offering up an asset as a form of security against a loan. Houses and other forms of fixed property are usually financed on this basis. The bank offers a loan and the borrower offers the title deeds as security against him/her defaulting on the loan payments. The bank can take legal ownership of the asset in the event of default under the loan. Also see *default; encumbrance; event of default; mortgage bond; title*.

mortgage backed security See *collateralised mortgage obligation*.

mortgage bond A bond secured by a mortgage on a property or asset. Mortgage bonds are held over real estate or physical immovable equipment that can be liquidated. On liquidation of the entity that holds title to the asset, the mortgage bond holder has first ranking claim on the proceeds of the sale of that asset as a secured creditor. Mortgage bonds are created by conveyancers and are registered in a deeds registry.

Debt investors usually consider mortgage bonds as high-grade, safe investments. If an issuer of a mortgage bond goes into default and has both secured and unsecured bonds outstanding, the secured bondholders are paid off first. Naturally, because unsecured bonds carry a greater risk than secured bonds, they pay higher yields.

A mortgage bond is similar to a special notarial bond with the key difference being that mortgage bonds are usually secured against fixed property while the special notarial bond is secured against movable assets. Also see *bond; default; liquidation; secured; special notarial bond; unsecured*.

mortgage debenture See *mortgage bond*.

mortgage equity withdrawal (MEW) The change in the outstanding levels of mortgage debt owed on current housing stock. Rising MEW indicates that bigger mortgages are being taken out, reducing the amount of equity homeowners have in their homes.

mothballed A factory or facility such as a power station that has been shut down to reduce capacity but is left in working condition to be reused at another point in time.

MOU Memorandum of understanding.

moving average A time series that has each value adjusted (smoothed) from its original values. A simple moving average is constructed by adjusting each data value in the series to the average value of a specified number of neighbours. A simple moving average is given by the equation below:

$$\text{moving average}_t = \frac{F_t + F_{t-1} + F_{t-2} \ldots + F_{t-n}}{n}$$

where F_t = the value of the data set at point t; n = the number of data points used in the averaging process.

Weighted moving averages use multiplicative factors to place more importance or weight on particular data points. The weights decrease down to zero the further one gets away from the data point in question.

moving average convergence divergence (MACD) | multilateral agency

$$\text{weighted moving average}_t = \frac{W_n F_t + W_{n-1} F_{t-1} + W_{n-2} F_{t-2} \ldots + W_{n-n} F_{t-n}}{n}$$

where F_t = the value of the data set at point t; n = the number of data points used in the averaging process; W_n = the weight to be applied to the respective neighbour.

A variety of weighting functions can be used to tailor the moving average. An exponential moving average applies stronger weights to more recent data in the series. Exponential moving averages therefore react more quickly to short-term fluctuations in prices. The weighting function used can be something like:

$f(x) = e^{Ax}$

where A = a constant.

Moving averages are typically lagging indicators. Also see *lagging indicator*.

moving average convergence divergence (MACD) The creation of a momentum oscillator by subtracting a longer moving average indicator from a shorter one. The standard form of the MACD is the difference between a 26-day and 12-day exponential moving average. Using shorter moving averages creates a more responsive indicator.

A positive standard MACD indicates the gap between the 12-day and 26-day average is widening and the rate of change of the shorter average is higher than the longer average. This indicates positive momentum and a bull period. If the difference is negative, the security being analysed is experiencing a bear trend. Also see *bear; bull*.

MPC
1. See *marginal propensity to consume*.
2. See *monetary policy committee*.

MPI See *marginal propensity to import*.

MPS See *marginal propensity to save*.

MPW See *marginal propensity to withdraw*.

MQP See *mandatory quote period*.

MRP See *market risk premium*.

MSCI Index (Morgan Stanley Capital International) A series of indices constructed by Morgan Stanley to help institutional investors benchmark their returns. These indices are also used for investment purposes in the form of exchange traded funds by many different types of investors. There is a wide range of indices created by Morgan Stanley, covering developed and emerging economies and economic sectors. Also see *index; institutional investor*.

MT The currency of Mozambique, the metical, divided into 100 centavos.

MTN Medium-term note. Also see *medium-term note program*.

Mulligan A reattempt with the consequences of the previous error or default erased. The concept is used in loans where defaults are waived and borrowers are afforded the opportunity to comply at the next applicable date.

multicurrency loan A loan that has embedded cross-currency swaps to allow funds to be provided in multiple currencies. Also see *currency swap*.

multilateral agency An organisation such as the World Bank, the IFC and others that are created by a wide range of international members. These organisations are usually established to promote economic development. Also see *World Bank*.

multilateral development bank See *multilateral agency*.

multilateral real exchange rate When analysing exchange rates it is sometimes desirable to formulate an exchange rate based on baskets of currencies. To calculate the multilateral rate, a geometric weighted average of bilateral rates is used as follows:

$$ex_{multi} = w_1 r_1 \times w_2 r_2 \times \ldots \times w_n r_n = \prod_{i=1}^{n} w_i r_i$$

The weights are usually chosen in accordance with the levels of trade in the particular currencies and sum to 1. When using trade weights the rate is then referred to as a trade weighted exchange rate.

Do not use this methodology if the compositions of the weightings change over time as specific mathematical adaptations are required. Also see *bilateral real exchange rate; trade weighted exchange rate; weighted average*.

multinational A company that operates in multiple countries. Sometimes called a transnational company.

multiple method of lease adjustment When adjusting net debt for operating leases, a rough adjustment is made by multiplying the operating lease expense by a predetermined factor. The predetermined factor usually ranges between five and eight and is industry specific. The basis of the factor used is a discount factor. Also see *lease adjusted net debt*.

multiple valuation The process of valuing a business by applying a multiple to its earnings. This is a crude valuation approach and gives a ballpark valuation only. For example, if companies in a sector have a market capitalisation of 10× EBITDA, then using a 10× multiple on another company in the sector will give an approximate valuation.

multiplier When investment occurs in an economy, or other economic variables are influenced, a feedback mechanism can result. For example, if R100 million is invested in a new football stadium, the contractor may spend R90 million on the project and extract R10 million in profit. The subcontractors or suppliers that are paid the R90 million may extract R9 million and pay the rest to other suppliers or labourers. This cycle may continue and the original R100 million may be cycled through various parts of the economy a number of times constituting the multiplier effect. Also see *marginal propensity to consume; money multiplier*.

multiplier bond See *bunny bond*.

multivariate distribution In probability theory and statistics, a multivariate normal distribution, also sometimes called a multivariate Gaussian distribution, is a specific probability distribution that can be thought of as a generalisation to higher dimensions of the one-dimensional normal distribution.

A random vector $X = [X_1, \ldots, X_n]$ follows a multivariate normal distribution if it satisfies the following equivalent conditions:

- Every linear combination $Y = a_1 X_1 + k + a_n X_n$ is normally distributed.
- There is a random vector $Z = [Z_1, k, Z_n]$ whose components are independent standard normal random variables, a vector $\mu = [\mu_1, k, \mu_n]$ and an N by M matrix A such that $X = AZ + \mu$.
- There is a vector μ and a symmetric, positive semi-definite matrix Σ such that the characteristic function of X is $\phi_x(u; \mu, \Sigma) = \exp\left(i\mu^T u - \frac{1}{2} u^T \Sigma u\right)$.

Also see *linear*.

multiyear tranche An issue or tranche of debt that is longer than a single year.

municipal bond A bond issued by a local governmental authority that is usually a municipality or council. Municipal bonds have favourable tax treatments to incentivise investors to provide finance to local government authorities. Also see *moral obligation bond; yield equivalence*.

municipal convertible A zero coupon municipal bond that can be converted into a coupon-bearing bond under predefined conditions. Also see *convertible debt*.

municipal inflation-linked bond An inflation-linked bond issued by a municipality. Also see *inflation-linked bond*.

municipal notes A short-term commercial paper programme used by municipalities to cover expenses in anticipation of taxation and other revenue. Also see *commercial paper; medium-term note program*.

munifacts An information service that provides information on municipal bonds.

MUR The Mauritian rupee divided into 100 cents.

murabah A transaction that is compliant with Islamic laws (shariah) where the seller of a product must expressly state the costs that they incurred. Transactions of this nature are used in the provision of finance from Islamic banks.

mutatis mutandis A term used in legal documents when comparing two or more cases, meaning making necessary alterations while not affecting the main point.

mutual A business or fund that is collectively owned by its investors (depositors) or customers.

mutual bank Mutual banks intermediate almost exclusively between surplus and deficit households. There is a strong element of government and banking sector debt as the mutual banks hold investments in many of their respective bonds and other financial instruments. Also see *credit union; post bank*.

mutual fund An American term for unit trust. Also see *unit trust*.

mutual guarantee A type of guarantee that is used or operated by a clearing house. In the case of default by a member, initial cover is provided by the member's assets, then from a guarantee fund contributed to by the clearing house members and then finally by the clearing house itself. Also see *clearing house; default; independent guarantee*.

mutual life insurance company A life insurance company that is not owned by shareholders. Any profits or benefits made by the company are distributed to shareholders.

mutually exclusive If two options or projects are mutually exclusive, they cannot be exercised simultaneously. One or the other must be selected.

MVA See *market value added*.

MXN The Mexican peso divided into 100 centavos.

MYR The Malaysian ringgit divided into 100 sen.

NACA Nominal annual compounded annually. Also see *effective rate per period*.

NACD Nominal annual compounded daily. Also see *effective rate per period*.

NACH Nominal annual compounded half-yearly (semi-annually). Also see *effective rate per period*.

NACM Nominal annual compounded monthly. Also see *effective rate per period*.

NACQ Nominal annual compounded quarterly. Also see *effective rate per period*.

NACSA Nominal annual compounded semi-annually. Also see *effective rate per period*.

NAD The Namibian dollar.

nafca The currency of Eritrea divided into 100 cents.

NAFTA See *North American Free Trade Agreement*.

NAIC See *National Association of Insurance Commissioners*.

NAIC credit rating The National Association of Insurance Commissioners in the US has a credit rating system used for the US private placement market. The rating system has four levels, NAIC 1 to NAIC 4. NAIC 1 is the top credit rating and is equivalent to the S&P AAA to A– band. NAIC 2 corresponds to the BBB+ to BBB– band. NAIC 3 corresponds to the BB+ to BB– band. NAIC 4 corresponds to the B+ to B– band. If the company being rated already has a credit rating from a credit rating agency, it is translated directly into its NAIC equivalent. Also see *credit rating; credit rating agency; National Association of Insurance Commissioners; private placing placement*.

naira (NGN) The currency of Nigeria divided into 100 kobo.

naked An unhedged long or short position.

naked debenture A debenture with no security against the borrower's assets. Also see *debenture*.

naked option See *uncovered option*.

name lending Lending to investment grade clients based on their good name (and often strong credit rating) rather than detailed credit analysis. Also see *investment grade*.

narrow market An illiquid market. Also see *illiquid*.

narrow money Coins and notes measured by M1A. Also see *broad money; M1A*.

NASAAC North American Special Aluminium Alloy.

NASDAQ See *National Association of Securities Dealers Automated Quotation System*.

NASDAQ Index A market value weighted index of securities traded on the NASDAQ exchange. Also see *index; NASDAQ*.

National Association of Insurance Commissioners (NAIC) An association in the US that represents member insurance companies. They have an internal credit rating system used for US private placements. Also see *NAIC credit rating; private placement*.

National Association of Securities Dealers Automated Quotation System (NASDAQ) A securities trading system in the US. The system enables trades in over-the-counter securities.

national debt The net borrowings of a government, both domestically and internationally.

nationalisation A process where a government acquires assets held in private hands or assets belonging to other levels of government such as municipalities. The nationalisation process usually takes place as a compulsory sale of an asset to the government but this is not always the case. Some rogue governments nationalise assets by simply taking them or not paying a fair value for them. Also see *fair value*.

National Loan Register (NLR) All microloans that are granted in South Africa have to be registered with the NLR. All registered members have access to the list and use it to evaluate the credit profile of potential customers.

national scale rating (NSR) A credit rating that measures credit risk in a narrowly defined peer group, usually companies in a single country or geographic zone, compared to the whole world. Also see *credit rating*.

natural gas A gaseous fossil fuel consisting mainly of methane found in oil fields, natural gas fields and in coal beds. Also see *Btu*.

natural hedge A cash flow that offsets other risks. For example, a company with a cash-generating subsidiary in another currency zone has a natural hedge against currency fluctuations.

NAV See *net asset value*.

NCD See *negotiable certificate of deposit*.

NCM See *non-clearing member*.

NDA See *non-disclosure agreement*.

NDF See *non-deliverable forward*.

NDP Net domestic product. Also see *net national product*.

NDR See *non-distributable reserves*.

near cash A non-cash asset that enjoys a highly liquid market and can easily and quickly be converted into cash. US treasury bills are a good example.

near money See *near cash*.

NEDO Index See *Baxter's Index or adjustment*.

NEER See *nominal effective exchange rate*.

negative amortisation loan The increase in the balance of a loan caused by interest charges being larger than the repayments made to service the loan. If the monthly payments on adjustable-rate mortgages are not enough to cover both the interest and principal payments on the loan, the shortage is added to the principal. This situation occurs when the mortgage payments reach the maximum as defined by the loan agreement while the interest rate on the loan increases. Also see *interest rate*.

negative arbitrage A situation where the proceeds of a loan or bond issue are placed on deposit at a lower interest rate than payable on the debt instrument. Also see *negative carry*.

negative basis trade A trading strategy where a bond is bought and a credit default swap (CDS) on the bond is purchased at the same time. If the basis is negative, then the credit default swap spread will be smaller than the bond spread. The trader locks in a risk-free profit called an arbitrage profit. Also see *arbitrage; bond; credit default swap; positive basis trade.*

negative butterfly A yield curve that has long- and short-term interest rates lower than mid-term rates. The yield curve is shaped like a negative parabola. Also see *backwardation; contango; interest rate; normal yield curve; positive butterfly; yield curve.*

negative carry When borrowed funds are deposited at an interest rate that is less than the rate due on the borrowings. Negative carry provides an incentive for borrowers to repay their borrowings. Also see *negative arbitrage; positive carry.*

negative cash flow Cash outflows exceed cash inflows.

negative convexity Bonds that have built-in call options exhibit negative convexity at certain combinations of price and yield. The broader concepts of negative convexity are beyond the scope of this text. Also see *call option; convexity.*

negative covenant A covenant that limits the borrower's activities in some way. These covenants govern new investments, new debt, liens, asset sales, acquisitions and guarantees. Sometimes called a restrictive covenant. Also see *acquisition; affirmative covenant; covenant; financial covenant; positive covenant.*

negative equity When the value of an asset is less than the money borrowed to purchase the asset. A good example is when housing prices drop shortly after purchase and the mortgage on the property is higher than the realisable value.

negative pledge A term in a debt agreement that limits the borrower's ability to offer assets as security to other lenders. There are often some exclusions called carve outs to the clause in debt agreements. The reasons that lenders seek the negative pledge clauses are:

- to preserve equality among creditors. In unsecured lending, under the negative pledge new lenders cannot seek security and thereby rank ahead of existing creditors under liquidation. In secured lending, lenders require a negative pledge to ensure that the assets over which they have security are not dissipated.
- to provide an early trigger or warning system. If borrowers seek to have this clause waived, they may well be finding it difficult to raise finance on an unsecured basis and are therefore offering assets as security.
- to protect and keep in place the pool of assets the borrower had when the original debt was advanced.

negative risk The combined purchase of a cyclical and countercyclical asset. The trade effectively allows the introduction of negative risk into the portfolio through the introduction of the countercyclical asset. Also see *countercyclical.*

negative yield curve A yield curve that is in backwardation. Also see *backwardation.*

negotiable certificate of deposit (NCD) A certificate of deposit issued by banks that acknowledges the deposit of a specific sum of money for a fixed period of time at a defined interest rate. These are guaranteed by the deposit-taking bank, can be sold in a highly liquid secondary market and cannot usually be cashed in before maturity. The

negotiated sale | net foreign assets (NFA)

purchase of NCDs is limited to large institutional investors. They are of bearer type and have large minimum face values. In South Africa, the NCD rate is normally quoted as a discount rate on a nominal annual compound annually basis. Also see *bearer; discount rate; interest rate; institutional investor; liquid; secondary market.*

negotiated sale The process of a single underwriter of the issue of a bond determining the price along with the issuer. The negotiated sale process often results in bond issues being more successful in the market.

net advance See *advance ratio.*

net assets net assets = total assets − total liabilities

net asset value (NAV) net asset value (NAV) = total assets − total liabilities

This number is often calculated on a per share basis by dividing the net assets of a business by the number of shares in issue. Also see *book value.*

net book value See *book value.*

net cash flow The actual cash flow of a company after tax and payment of dividends. See the definition of *cash flow* for notes on how to derive the cash flow numbers.

net current assets net current assets = current assets − current liabilities

The net current assets should be a positive number for a healthy, liquid company. Also see *current asset; current liability.*

net decline See *advance ratio.*

net debt Net debt gives an indication of the company's overall indebtedness. Net debt is the debt of a firm less cash balances:

net debt = gross debt − cash and cash equivalents

where gross debt = all the interest-bearing long- and short-term liabilities of the firm.

Net debt is often adjusted for pension fund liabilities and operational lease commitments. Preference shares are often treated as long-term debt in the net debt calculation. Net debt to EBITDA is a ratio used by banks to determine appropriate levels of debt when lending to a company and are included in financial covenants. Also see *covenant; gross debt; lease adjusted net debt; long-term debt; net debt.*

net debt per capita The net financial indebtedness of a country divided by its population.

net domestic product See *net national product.*

net earnings See *net profit.*

net foreign assets (NFA) The net holdings of a country's foreign investments in debt, equity, currency and gold or foreign reserves:

net foreign assets (NFA) = FDIA + EQA + DEBTA + FX − FDIL − EQL − DEBTL

where FDI = foreign direct investment; EQA = equity portfolio investment; DEBT = foreign stocks of debt instruments. The suffix A indicates assets and L indicates liabilities.

Also see *balance of public finance; foreign direct investment; foreign reserves.*

net forward position The extent to which a central bank's forward sales of foreign currency exceeds its forward purchases. An oversold forward book exposes the government to the risk of losses associated with the exchange rate. Also see *net open forward position*.

net gearing ratio A ratio used by banks when analysing a company's creditworthiness:

$$\text{net gearing ratio} = \frac{\text{net debt}}{\text{net tangible assets}}$$

The tangible assets measure is used because tangible assets are easy to ascribe a value to and are easier to sell if the company goes into liquidation. The net gearing ratio may not be an appropriate ratio to analyse industries with significant intellectual property such as pharmaceuticals or information technology. Also see *gross gearing ratio; net debt*.

net income See *net profit*.

net interest
1. Interest expenses less interest received.
2. Interest income less tax paid.

net investment Investment (capital expenditure) in a business less capital consumption (depreciation). Also see *capital consumption; depreciation*.

net lease A lease where the lessee is required to maintain and insure the asset. The lease payments with this arrangement are usually reduced. Also see *capital lease; operating lease*.

net national product (NNP) The gross domestic product (GDP) or gross national product (GNP) of a country less capital consumption (depreciation). Also called net domestic product. Also see *capital consumption; depreciation; gross domestic product; gross national product*.

net open foreign currency position See *net open forward position*.

net open forward position (NOFP) The sum of a central bank's gross gold and foreign exchange reserves less foreign loans and its oversold forward book. This is effectively the extent to which the reserve bank's future obligations to deliver foreign currency, usually US dollars, are not covered by the net reserves. Also see *central bank; net forward position*.

net operating income The sales (turnover or revenue) less the variable expenses of a company. Analysts often focus on the net operating income data of companies as tax and extraordinary items do not offer much information about a company's ability to generate income. Also see *extraordinary item; variable cost expense*.

net position The position that results when looking at all an investor's long and short positions against a particular asset or market.

net present value (NPV) The present value of the cash flows of a project. NPV is given by the following formula:

$$\text{net present value (NPV)} = \sum_{n=0}^{t} \frac{\text{net operating cash flows}}{(1+r)^n} - \sum_{n=0}^{t} \frac{\text{net investment cash flows}}{(1+r)^n}$$

where r = the applicable discount rate; t = the date of the last anticipated cash flow.

If NPV is greater than zero, then the project is a good investment. If NPV is less than 0, then the project is potentially a poor investment.

NPV has the advantage over the internal rate of return (IRR) measure because the mathematics of the IRR method can return multiple solutions. Also see *internal rate of return*.

net profit The total revenue of a company less all expenses:

net profit = sales − variable expenses − fixed expenses

Sometimes called net income or net earnings. Also see *fixed expense; variable cost expense*.

net profit margin

$$\text{net profit margin} = \frac{\text{net profit (earnings after income tax)}}{\text{sales}}$$

If the ratio goes down, costs have risen relative to sales. Also see *profitability ratios*.

net profit ratio See *net profit margin*.

net realisable value (NRV) The net amount that an entity expects to realise from the sale of inventory in the ordinary course of business. Fair value reflects the amount for which the same inventory could be exchanged between knowledgeable and willing buyers and sellers in the marketplace. The former is an entity-specific value; the latter is not. Net realisable value for inventories may not necessarily equal fair value less the costs to sell. Inventories are usually valued at the lower of cost price and net realisable value. Also see *fair value*.

net selling price The amount recoverable from the sale of an asset in an arm's length transaction between knowledgeable willing parties less the costs of disposal. When impairing an asset, the net selling price or the value in use can be used. Also see *asset; impairment*.

net settlement The offsetting of balances and payment of the difference only.

net tangible assets net tangible assets = total assets − intangible assets

Also see *tangible asset*.

netting off Subtracting liabilities from assets or subtracting costs from revenues. Also see *accounting equation*.

net working capital (NWC) net working capital = current assets − current liabilities

Also see *current asset; current liability*.

net working capital to total assets

$$\text{net working capital to total assets ratio} = \frac{\text{current assets} - \text{current liabilities}}{\text{total assets}}$$

net working capital turnover A ratio that measures the sales output obtained from cash resources that are tied up in working capital.

$$\text{net working capital turnover ratio} = \frac{\text{sales}}{\text{net working capital}}$$

Also see *asset management ratios; working capital*.

net worth The net value of a business which is calculated by subtracting the value of the liabilities from the assets. Net worth is usually measured as owners equity. Also see *accounting equation*.

newco A term broadly used to name a new company set up as a special-purpose entity for a particular transaction, often an acquisition.

new issue An initial offer of shares made available to the public through an initial public offer. Also see *initial public offer*.

new money Money made by the current generation and not inherited from previous generations. Also see *old money*.

New York Mercantile Exchange (NYMEX) 'The New York Mercantile Exchange, Inc., is the world's largest physical commodity futures exchange and the pre-eminent trading forum for energy and precious metals.' See www.nymex.com. Also see *precious metals*.

New York Stock Exchange (NYSE) The stock exchange on Wall Street in New York is one of the largest in the world. See www.nyse.com. Also see *Wall Street*.

NGN The Nigerian naira divided into 100 kobo.

NIFO (next in first out) This method of valuing inventory is the same as the last in first out (LIFO) method. Also see *LIFO*.

Nikkei The main index on the Tokyo Stock Exchange in Japan. Calculated as a price weighted arithmetic average of the top 225 companies on the Tokyo Exchange. The Dow Jones Index is similarly calculated as a price weighted arithmetic average. Also see *Dow Jones; price weighted index*.

nil coupon bond See *zero coupon bond*.

nil paid letter (NPL) A letter which represents a shareholder's entitlements under a rights issue. Nil paid letters can be traded on exchanges before the actual rights issue. After the record date of the rights issue the shares trade ex rights and nil paid letters are issued to shareholders who were on the register immediately prior to the record date. Also see *ex rights; record date; rights issue/offer*.

nil price When accepting a rights issue, a portion of the rights can be sold and the proceeds used to purchase shares. The nil price, or nil cost, is an indication of how many rights must be sold to purchase shares with the remaining rights. The number of rights sold is calculated by the following equation:

$$\text{number of rights sold} = \frac{\text{number of rights available} \times \text{subscription price}}{\text{theoretical ex rights price}}$$

nil sum game See *zero sum game*.

NIR See *nominal interest rate*.

NL
1. No liability, the Australian equivalent of the South African Ltd or British PLC.
2. The Netherlands.

NLG The former currency of the Netherlands, the guilder. The Netherlands has now adopted the euro. Also see *euro*.

NLR See *National Loan Register*.

NMS See *normal market size*.

NNP See *net national product*.

no-arbitrage condition See *arbitrage free condition*.

NOHC Non-operating holding company.

NOIBOR Norway interbank offer rate. Also see *JIBAR; LIBOR*.

noise Random fluctuations of an observable variable. Also see *random walk with drift*.

NOK The Norwegian krone divided into 100 ore.

nomad See *nominated adviser*.

nominal annual return (NAR) The annualised return or yield earned without taking into account interest that is earned off the interim payments. Also see *effective rate per period*.

nominal capital See *authorised share capital*.

nominal effective exchange rate (NEER) A measure of the exchange rate in terms of the exchange rates of a group of currencies. It is calculated for a particular country's currency as a weighted average of the bilateral exchange rates of the currencies of that country's main trading partners and is normally presented as an index number. Also see *multilateral real exchange rate; trade weighted exchange rate; weighted average*.

nominal exchange rate The exchange rate quoted at a particular point in time, valid at the time of the quote. Often called the spot rate. Also see *real exchange rate*.

nominal interest rate (NIR) The interest rate expressed in terms of the interest payment made each period. The NIR is not adjusted for the effects of inflation. Also see *effective rate per period; Fisher effect/equation; inflation*.

nominal principal A quantity of the underlying reference or asset that a derivatives contract is based on.

nominal value The principal value of a financial instrument on the date of issue:
- In the bond markets, the nominal value is the price at which the security was issued. For example, a single bond may be issued for a price of R1 million and may then trade at values above or below R1 million. The nominal value of the bond is the price at which it was issued, i.e. R1 million. At redemption of a bond the nominal value is paid back to the investor and so it is sometimes called the redemption value or maturity value. For bonds, the term par value is often used for nominal value.
- For equity shares, the nominal value is the minimum price of a share on the date of issue. This is an arbitrary number the issuing company decides on and is much lower than the actual market value of the share. The nominal value is the legal capital of the business and is set low to protect the shareholders from liability in the event that the liabilities of the company exceed its assets. The par value is often R1 per share so that the company can easily track the number of shares in issue by means of a share capital account. To determine the actual value at which shares were issued, the share capital and share premium accounts must be added. Sometimes called the par value. Also see *par value; share capital; share premium*.

nominal yield The coupon rate on a bond expressed as a percentage of the par or nominal value. Also see *yield*.

nominal yield spread The return on a bond expressed as a spread over the appropriate government bond or swap curve. Also see *swap curve*.

nominated adviser A person employed by an Alternative Investment Market (AIM) listed company, who advises directors on the responsibilities of the company regarding listing requirements. Also see *Alternative Investment Market*.

nominee An entity or person with the authority to register shares or securities on behalf of other people. Also see *nominee account*.

nominee account When small numbers of shares are bought by a number of clients through a broker, the shares are pooled into a nominee account. The nominee is the registered owner of the shares in the company's register and the cash flows associated with the shares are directed to the purchaser through the nominee account.

non-arbitrage price A price that does not allow the generation of risk-free profits. Also see *arbitrage; arbitrage free condition*.

non-callable bond A bond that does not have call provisions.

non-clearing member (NCM) A member of a clearing house that cannot perform clearing transactions but must transact through general clearing members. Also see *clearing; clearing house; general clearing member; individual clearing member*.

non-competitive tender Prices obtained by small to medium investors when they are assigned a price in a bidding process that is an average of all the bids received. The bidding process is usually for debt securities such as government bonds and treasury bills. Also see *government bond; treasury bill*.

non-contributory fund A pension fund where only the employer contributes. Also see *pension fund*.

non-cumulative preference share A holder of this class of preference shares forgoes the dividend payments if the issuer is unable to make payment. Also see *cumulative preference share; dividend; preference share*.

non-current asset An asset that does not meet the definition of a current asset. Generally, these are assets retained for long-term use. Property, plant and equipment (PPE) are examples of non-current assets. Also see *current asset; fixed asset*.

non-deliverable forward (NDF) A forward contract that is settled in cash and not by physical delivery. Also see *contract for difference; forward contract/dealing; physical delivery*.

non-detachable security A security that is packaged with another security that cannot be traded separately from the original package it was sold in. Convertible debt is often non-detachable. Also see *convertible debt/bond; detachable security*.

non-disclosure agreement (NDA) A legal agreement that is signed by parties to a transaction that states that they will not disclose information about the deal to any other counterparty without explicit written permission. These are used when disclosing sensitive information in information memorandums in syndicated loan transactions. Also see *information memorandum; syndicated loan*.

non-discretionary account A trading account held with a stockbroker that requires the stockbroker to gain permission for any trade he/she undertakes. Also see *discretionary account; managed account; stockbroker*.

non-distributable reserves (NDR) A portion of accumulated shareholders equity (retained earnings) that are not distributable to shareholders and are usually in the form of dividends or other shareholder returns. NDRs are reserves that are attributable through revaluations of assets, are not in the form of cash and so are difficult to distribute. A share premium is classed as a non-distributable reserve. Also see *distributable reserves; reserves; share premium*.

non-executive director A director who sits on the board of a company and who is appointed to provide expertise and independent judgement on key company matters rather than to become involved in the day-to-day running of the business.

non-linear The relationship between a set of variables is not in direct proportion. Also see *linear*.

non-marketable securities Securities that are sold over the counter and not on recognised exchanges. Also see *over the counter*.

non-participating preference share A preference share that does not have additional rights. Holders receive the mandated dividend and do not receive any residual profits in the business. Also see *dividend; participating preference share; preference share*.

non-performing loan A loan that is in default, usually through non-payment of interest or capital. Analysts often look at a bank's non-performing loans to the total loan book to analyse the quality and credit profile of the bank's loan book. Banks seek to minimise their non-performing loans. Also see *credit loss ratio*.

non-recourse Debt structures where lenders do not have the ability to seek compensation from the asset owners (sponsors) in the event of default. Lenders in non-recourse financing structures rely only on the cash flows from the underlying asset or guarantees provided to service the debt. Project financing structures are often non-recourse or limited recourse in nature. Also see *project financing; sponsor*.

non-recurring item An extraordinary item in the financial statements of a company. Also see *extraordinary item*.

non-repudiation Ensuring that once a contract is entered into, neither of the parties may revoke the agreement. Also see *repudiation*.

non-revolving facility A term loan with a long availability period. Also see *term loan*.

non-stationary process A data series whose statistical properties such as standard deviations change over time. For example, in financial markets, the daily volatility is time dependent and hence a non-stationary process. Also see *stationary process; unit root; volatility*.

non-systematic risk See *unsystematic risk*.

non-tariff barrier A trade barrier that does not involve a customs tariff. An example of this is restrictions on agricultural products through disease control measures. Also see *trade barrier*.

non-taxable income Income that is not subject to taxation. Many governments encourage individuals to save by allowing the income from such investments to be non-taxable. In South Africa dividend income is non-taxable as at 2008. Also see *individual savings account*.

non-voting ordinary share An ordinary share with no voting rights. In South Africa, they are called N-shares. Also see *B-share; N-share; ordinary share*.

NOPAT Net operating profit after tax. Also see *EBITDA*.

normal cost See *fixed cost*.

normal market size (NMS) The number of shares that constitute the most common transaction for a company's shares on a stock exchange.

normal or Gaussian distribution A symmetric bell-shaped frequency distribution that is completely defined by its standard deviation and mean. The distribution is defined by the following equation:

$$f(x, \mu, \sigma) = \frac{1}{\sigma\sqrt{2\pi}} e^{-\frac{(x-\mu)^2}{2\sigma^2}}$$

where σ = the standard deviation; μ = the mean. A graph of a few examples of the functions indicated by the equation is shown below.

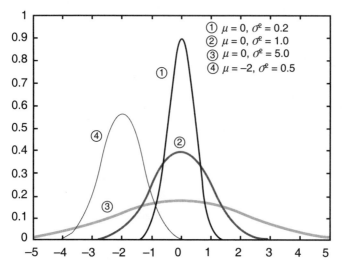

For a normal distribution, 68.3% of the population in a normal distribution lies within one standard deviation and 95.5% of the population lies within two standard deviations. Also see *Bernoulli distribution; log normal; arithmetic mean; standard deviation.*

normal random variable A random variable with a normal distribution. The normal random variable results in the central limit theorem. Also see *central limit theorem; continuous random variable; normal or Gaussian distribution.*

normal yield curve A yield curve that obeys the liquidity preference theory and is in contango and not backwardation by default. The graph below illustrates a normal yield curve. Also see *backwardation; contango; forward differential; liquidity preference theory.*

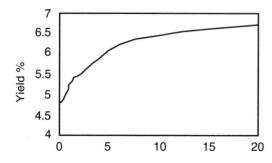

North American Free Trade Agreement (NAFTA) An agreement that allows for free trade with no duties and tariffs between the United States, Canada and Mexico.

NOSH Number of shares.

nostro account An account held by a foreign bank in the UK denominated in the home currency of the foreign bank. Also see *vostro account.*

notarial bond A bond over assets that has been attested by a notary. Also see *general notarial bond; special notarial bond*.

notary A person who has the authority to attest legal documents. Also see *attest*.

notch An incremental change in the credit rating of a firm. For example, the upgrade from BBB to BBB+ is a change of a single notch. Also see *credit rating; firm*.

note A financial instrument, usually a debt instrument in the form of a bond or treasury bill. Notes can also include promissory notes and banknotes. Also see *bond; promissory note; treasury bill*.

note issuance facility A commercial paper programme to issue Eurocurrency notes. Also see *commercial paper; Eurocurrency*.

note of default A notice issued to a borrower that they are in default on debt obligations and legal action may be taken.

notes to financial statements The notes to financial statements contain information in addition to that presented in the balance sheet, income statement, statement of changes in equity and cash flow statement. Notes provide narrative descriptions or disaggregations of items disclosed in the statements and information about items that do not qualify for recognition in the statements. Also see *balance sheet; cash flow statement; income statement*.

notional See *notional principal*.

notional principal The principal amount on which a swap and other financial transactions are based. For example, in an interest rate swap the counterparties swap cash flows against different interest rates and calculate the cash flows against a notional principal rather than a physical principal amount. Also see *interest rate; interest rate swap; swap*.

novation
1. The replacement of a legal obligation with another legal obligation with the consent of all the parties involved. Novation often allows loans to be transferred between companies in merger and acquisition activities. Also see *acquisition; merger*.
2. The process whereby the clearing house of a derivatives exchange interposes itself as an intermediary between the buyer and seller. One contract is created by the buyer and another is created by the seller. Also see *clearing house*.

NPL See *nil paid letter*.

NPV See *net present value*.

NR Not rated.

NRST Non-resident shareholders tax.

NRV See *net realisable value*.

NSE Nairobi Stock Exchange.

N-share A type of equity share used in the South African market that has fewer voting rights than ordinary shares. Although the JSE no longer allows listing of N-shares, those N-shares in existence are still traded on the exchange. If a company already has N-shares that are listed, it may issue more of them. Also see *A-share; B-share; JSE; ordinary share; profit participation certificate*.

NSR See *national scale rating*.

null hypothesis $H_0 : \mu = 50$ centimetres per second, i.e. the hypothesis is that the mean value of the population is 50 centimetres per second.

$H_1 : \mu \neq 50$ centimetres per second is the alternate hypothesis that will be true if the null hypothesis is false.

The statement $H_0 : \mu = 50$ is called the null hypothesis. The second equation constitutes the alternative hypothesis. Also see *alternative hypothesis*.

NV Naamloze vennootschap, which implies that a Netherlands registered company is a limited liability public company that may be traded on a stock exchange. The shares in NV companies are not necessarily registered to particular owners and are easily transferable. Also see *BV; limited liability; GmbH; PLC*.

NWC See *net working capital*.

NYMEX See *New York Mercantile Exchange*.

NYSE See *New York Stock Exchange*.

NZD The New Zealand dollar divided into 100 cents.

OAT A French government bond of term seven to thirty years. These bonds can carry fixed or floating interest rates. Also see *BTAN; government bond*.

obligation The duty of a borrower against the claims of a lender. This is the duty to pay back monies borrowed.

obligor An entity that is indebted to another entity.

occupational pension scheme (OPS) A pension scheme that is contributed to under an employee's conditions of employment. Occupational pension schemes may be open to people in the same or similar professions across a range of different employers. These schemes consist of defined benefit or defined contribution schemes. Also see *defined benefit fund; defined contribution fund*.

OCF Operational cash flow.

odd lot A transaction on a stock exchange when securities are sold in numbers that are not in multiples of 100. Whole number trades are called round lots.

OECD See *Organisation for Economic Cooperation and Development*.

OECD country rating A country risk rating system used by the Organisation for Economic Cooperation and Development (OECD) and called the country risk classification method. The risk classification is a similar concept to credit ratings issued by credit rating agencies such as S&P or Moody's. The ratings give an indication of the ability of a country to service its external debt obligations. The details of the OECD ratings system are confidential and not published. Also see *credit rating; credit rating agency; Organisation for Economic Cooperation and Development*.

OEICS Open-ended investment company, which is the same as an investment company with variable capital (ICVC).

OFAC See *Office for Foreign Assets Control*.

OFEX An investment exchange in London that is not recognised by the FSA as an investment exchange. There are a limited number of companies listed on OFEX and it is considered a cheap method of acquiring a listing for smaller companies. Also see *Financial Services Authority*.

off balance sheet A financial instrument or an obligation that does not appear as an asset or liability on the balance sheet of a company. Operating leases and securitisations can move items off balance sheet. Also see *balance sheet; liability; operating lease; securitisation*.

off balance sheet liability A liability that may be attributable to a company in the future but does not have to be shown on the balance sheet in financial statements because of accounting rules or standards. Lease obligations are often considered to be off balance sheet liabilities. The off balance sheet liabilities are stated as a contingent liability in a company's financial statements. Also see *contingent liability; operating lease*.

off balance sheet reserve Funds held in the reserves of a company that are not stated on the balance sheet. The effect may be achieved by deliberately undervaluing company assets. Companies use such mechanisms in good years to smooth earnings and improve balance sheets in less profitable years. Sometimes called hidden or secret reserves. Also see *cookie jarring*.

offer See *bid price*.

offer by tender A method of the auction of securities where bids are made by potential buyers on lots of securities. The highest bidders receive all the securities that they have bid for, the next highest bidders receive their allocation and so on until all the securities available have been sold. Also see *auction*.

offer for subscription The direct sale of shares to the public.

offering circular or memorandum A legal document that offers shares or securities for sale. Also see *information memorandum; rights issue*.

offer of sale The sale of shares by an investment bank to the investor public by a process called underwriting. The banks acquire the shares for less than they sell them to the public. Also see *green shoe provision; investment bank; underwrite*.

offer period When purchasing a significant amount of shares in a business, usually a controlling stake, the offer period is the period for which the offer remains valid.

offer price The lowest price at which a dealer or issuer of an asset or bond is willing to sell. Also see *asset; bond*.

offer to purchase A takeover bid. Also see *takeover*.

Office for Foreign Assets Control (OFAC) A department of the US Treasury that enforces economic and trade sanctions based on United States government foreign policy and national security goals. The office ensures that financial services are not provided to countries or persons under sanction or terrorist or criminal organisations.

official list See *main board*.

official rate
1. The rate of exchange of currencies officially stated and supported by a government.
2. The rate at which bank employees borrow from their employers in South Africa. The rate is a little lower than rates available to the public and is set by the Minister of Finance.

official reserves and liabilities An account that records a country's holdings of gold and foreign reserves. It serves as the means of correcting imbalances between inflows and outflows of foreign currencies.

official settlements balance An overall measurement of a country's private financial and economic transactions with the rest of the world.

off market swap A swap that has a non-zero value at the start of the trade. An initial payment must be made from one party to another as compensation. Also see *swap*.

off market transfer A transfer of securities that are listed on an exchange that takes place outside the exchange. Also see *over the counter*.

offset
1. The process of a bank netting off the debit and credit balances of a single client. Also see *set off*.
2. Entering into a transaction to close a position. This may be done through options and futures contracts.

offshore An entity or transaction that is conducted outside the domicile of the country in question. Transactions, banking and many other financial services are often done offshore to take advantage of favourable tax treatments in other jurisdictions.

offsite A meeting that takes place away from the office in which participants, usually upper levels of management, focus on strategy and improvement. In South Africa these meetings are sometimes called a bosberaad or a lekgotla. Also see *bosberaad; lekgotla*.

off-take agreement
1. A private negotiation between a producer and a consumer to trade a quantity of goods or services at a predetermined price at future dates.
2. An agreement whereby productive output, usually from mining operations or refining, is sold to a customer over a specified time frame at predetermined prices. Also see *toll manufacturing concern*.

off-taker The purchaser in an off-take agreement.

off the run A security that has enjoyed price appreciation for some time and is no longer enjoying the same significant gains.

off the shelf See *shelf company*.

old money Money or wealth generated by past generations and passed down to the next through inheritance. Also see *new money*.

oligarchy A form of government where a country is ruled by a small number of elite persons.

oligopoly A market whose dynamics are determined by a few participants who can act collectively and control prices. Also see *duopoly; monopoly*.

omnibus account An account used by brokers through which trades of people who are not the account holder are settled.

OMR The Oman rial divided into 1 000 baizas.

on demand Debt that is callable at any point in time by the lender. For example, overdraft accounts are on demand accounts.

one sided When quotes for only a purchase (bid) or sell (offer) are quoted in the market. Such markets are said to be illiquid. Also see *illiquid*.

one-way price A price quoted only for the purchase or the sale of an asset. Market makers are usually forced by exchange rules to quote two-way prices. Also see *two-way price*.

onlending See *relending*.

on market trade A trade that occurs on recognised exchanges. Also see *off market transfer; over the counter*.

opco An operational subsidiary or asset in a company group structure.

OPEC See *Organisation of Petroleum Exporting Countries*.

open The price at which a security was traded on the first trade of the day. Also see *security*.

open auction See *auction*.

open cheque A cheque that can be cashed at the bank of origin. Also see *cheque; crossed cheque*.

open economy See *openness of market*.

open-ended A fund that can contract and expand in size.

open-ended indenture A bond contract where collateral backing the contract may be used as collateral in the issue of other bonds. Due to decreased access to security, open-ended indentures trade at a premium to their closed counterparts. Also see *closed-ended indenture; collateral*.

opening price The price of securities at the start of a trading day. Due to the release of new information and trading on other exchanges in different time zones, the opening prices of securities may not be the same or near the closing prices of the securities on the previous day.

open interest The number of outstanding futures contracts that a holder or collective of holders is obliged to deliver to a futures exchange. Also see *futures contract*.

open market dealing See *open market operations*.

open market operations The process of central banks buying and selling government bonds and other financial instruments to influence the money supply base and therefore the money supply in a country. Central banks manipulate exchange and inflation rates through open market operations. Also see *central bank; government bond; inflation; money supply; sterilisation*.

open mouth operation A statement by a governor of a central bank that is made to influence markets. Open mouth operations are often undertaken before changes to monetary policy are made. Also see *central bank; open market operations*.

openness of market The degree to which an economy is dependent on exports and imports. The openness of a market is defined by:

$$\text{openness of a market} = \frac{\text{exports} + \text{imports}}{\text{GDP}}$$

or in shorthand: $\frac{X + M}{Y}$

Large degrees of openness, i.e. high levels of exports and imports, make a country vulnerable to exchange rate fluctuations. The composition of imports and exports is also significant economically. For example, South Africa exports a large proportion of metal minerals so the price of metals has a substantial effect on the welfare of the South African economy which is an open economy.

open order On securities exchanges, an order to buy or sell that is open to be executed at any price until the close of trading. Sometimes called a good till executed order.

open outcry A trading market where bids, acceptances and conclusions of transactions are made on an open floor by physical word of mouth. Also called floor trading.

open position

1. A position that results when a manufacturer or dealer is locked into a futures contract. The manufacturer or dealer is then vulnerable to changes in prices of raw materials or underlying securities.

2. An investor or dealer who has an investment position, a long position or a short position, that is open to losses or gains associated with movements in the market. Also see *long position; short position*.

open repo A repo trade with no fixed maturity date. It is possible that an open repo will be terminated, terms changed and collateral substituted. Also see *collateral; repo; term repo*.

operating activities The principal revenue-producing activities of an entity and other activities that are not classed as investing or financing activities. Operating activities are typically those operations that will continue into the future.

operating cash flow (OCF) Cash flow received during the course of normal business. This is the cash received from the sales of goods or services less the costs incurred in obtaining or delivering them.

There are a number of methods used to determine cash flow:

- The tax shield approach

    operating cash flow (OCF) = [(sales − costs) × (1 − T)] + [depreciation × T]

- The top down or direct method

    operating cash flow (OCF) = sales − costs − taxes

- The bottom up or indirect approach

    operating cash flow (OCF) = NPAT + depreciation

Also see *financing cash flow; investment cash flow.*

operating cycle The time between the acquisition of raw materials for processing and their ultimate realisation in the form of cash.

operating income See *net operating income.*

operating lease An operating lease has a term shorter than the useful life of the asset. An operating lease is effectively a rental, is not treated as a capitalised asset/liability on the balance sheet and is expensed through the income statement. The present value of the lease payments is lower than 90% of the value of the underlying asset and the lessor usually has to maintain the asset. There are often terms in the lease contract that give the lessee the option to cancel the lease before the expiration date. Operating leases are classed as off balance sheet obligations. Also see *capital lease; lease; net lease.*

operating leverage The operating leverage defines the extent to which a company or project has a fixed cost component. Companies with significant operational leverage have high proportions of fixed to variable costs. The operational leveraged asset or business essentially has a greater beta:

$$\beta_{asset} = \beta_{revenue} \left[1 + \frac{PV \text{ (fixed costs)}}{PV \text{ (variable costs)}} \right]$$

Operational gearing imposes significant risk as business cycle downturns cannot easily be matched with a lowering of the cost base. Conversely, when economic and business conditions are strong, then highly operationally geared companies benefit as they can generate additional revenue at little extra cost.

Operating leverage is defined by a ratio that measures the sensitivity of net operating income to changes in sales volumes:

$$\text{operating leverage} = \frac{\text{NPAT}}{\text{sales}}$$

Businesses such as hotels have significant operational gearing as infrastructure and staff levels need to be maintained even when the hotels are not fully occupied.

Financial leverage is something quite different and is defined as the extent to which a company is financed through debt which has a fixed repayment commitment. Also see *beta; fixed expense.*

operating margin The operating profit margin of a company defined as a portion of sales:

$$\text{operating margin} = \frac{\text{operating profit}}{\text{sales}}$$

Also see *cost to income ratio; profit margin*.

operating profit The operating profit of a business is the profit made from the day-to-day trading of the company:

operating profit = gross profit − operating expenses − depreciation − amortisation

Also see *depreciation; EBIT*.

operating target The sets of variables such as money supply that central banks target and influence with monetary policy tools. Also see *central bank; monetary policy; money supply; open market operations*.

operational gearing See *operating leverage*.

operational risk The risk or loss associated with internal business processes. Operational risk is one of the factors used when setting capital adequacy requirements for banks under Basel II. Also see *Basel; capital adequacy; credit risk; liquidity risk*.

opportunity cost The cost of the best alternative forgone, i.e. the benefit forgone. For example, if there are two mutually exclusive projects or investment opportunities, A and B, and A is selected, then the opportunity cost is the return achievable from B. B is the best opportunity forgone. Also see *mutually exclusive*.

OPS See *occupational pension scheme*.

option In finance, an option is a contract whereby one party, the holder or buyer, has the right but not the obligation to exercise a feature of the contract, the option, on or before a future date, the exercise date. The other party, the writer or seller, has the obligation to honour the specified feature of the contract on the day it is exercised. Since the option gives the buyer a right and the seller an obligation, the buyer has received something of value. The amount the buyer pays the seller for the option is called the option premium.

Share options where the holder may purchase shares at a predefined price are often given to management to encourage them to drive the future price of the shares and ultimately realise gains for shareholders.

Options are derivative instruments that are widely used to manage the risks of many financial transactions. Also see *abandon option; American option; average price option; bandwidth contract; barrier option; Bermuda option; call option; compound option; contract option; deferral call option; embedded option; European option; expansion option; flex option; green shoe provision; index option; learning option; option premium; put option; rainbow option; real option; share option; strike price; switching option; vanilla option*.

option adjusted spread If a bond has an embedded option, it will trade at a different spread to bonds without embedded options. The option therefore adjusts the spread of the bond. Also see *convertible debt/bond; convexity; embedded option*.

option fence See *zero cost collar*.

option holder A person who buys an option. Also see *option*.

option-linked bond or debt A bond that has returns linked to commodity or other asset prices. These instruments tailor the cash flow on the bonds to the cash flow of the issuing firm using embedded options. Option-linked bonds reduce the likelihood of default as the lender's obligations can be adjusted for periods of weak cash flows. Option-linked bonds are structured as a combination of a straight bond and a call option on an underlying asset or commodity. Also see *bond; call option; default; firm*.

option margin See *initial margin; variation margin*.

option premium The price that the buyer pays the seller when purchasing an option. The option premium is the sum of the intrinsic value and the time value of an option. The premium is affected by the option's expiry date, the volatility, price and cash flow of the underlying asset and the strike price. Also see *intrinsic value; option; time premium*.

option price The amount per share that an option buyer pays. Also see *option premium*.

option pricing curve A graph indicating the option price at a series of points in time. Also see *Black-Scholes options pricing model; option*.

option to purchase An option to purchase an asset or commodity at some date in the future.

option writer A person who sells an option.

order The offer to purchase or sell a security at a predetermined price.

order cheque A cheque that can be transferred to a third party. Also see *cheque*.

order driven A trading system that requires a match of a buy and sell order. There is no market maker taking positions in an order-driven system. Also see *market maker; SEETS*.

ordinary annuity A series of fixed payments made at the end of each period over a fixed amount of time. Also see *annuity due; annuity present value*.

ordinary share An equity instrument that is subordinate to all other classes of equity instruments. The holders of these shares have the right to vote on issues that affect the company. Ordinary shareholders have no special rights with respect to either dividends or insolvency claims. Also see *dividend; subordinate*.

ords Ordinary shares.

organic growth Growth in a company that results from investment with own funds in existing processes and businesses. If analysts were looking at organic growth in a company, they would reverse the results attributable to any acquisitions made. Sometimes called internal growth. Also see *internal growth rate*.

Organisation for Economic Cooperation and Development (OECD) An organisation that provides a collaborative environment where governments compare policy, seek answers to common problems, identify best practice and coordinate domestic and international policies. The mandate of the OECD is broad as it covers all economic, environmental and social issues.

Organisation of Petroleum Exporting Countries (OPEC) A cartel-type organisation that adjusts the prices of crude oil by controlling supply to the market. Also see *cartel; crude oil*.

origin
1. The vertex point on a graph, i.e. the position where both axes have a zero value.
2. The country in which a product is produced.

orphan trust A trust with no parent. Also see *trust*.

orthogonal
1. Perpendicular lines.
2. Variables are orthogonal to one another if they are statistically independent.

Osborne Index See *Baxter's Index or adjustment*.

oscillator A price indicator used by traders to analyse patterns that cycle or oscillate between bands or in a limited range about a longer term trend. Oscillators deduce information such as whether prices are moving strongly in a particular direction (momentum) or whether they are overbought or oversold. A commonly used simple oscillator is the use of a moving average and a price trend. A buy signal is indicated when the price trend is below the moving average and a sell signal is indicated when the trend is above the moving average. Also see *momentum indicator; moving average; overbought; oversold*.

OSHI See *outside shareholders interest*.

OTB See *out the box*.

OTC See *over the counter*.

OTHI Index An index published by the Bond Exchange of South Africa that contains all the bonds in the All Bond Index (ALBI) not contained in the GOVI Index. Also see *All Bond Index; GOVI Index*.

OTM See *out the money*.

ounce (oz) See *troy ounce*.

outlier Observations from a data set that lie so far outside the main body of observations that they are considered to be from another population or of erroneous values. Outliers are often eliminated before further statistical analysis is performed on a data set.

outside shareholders interest (OSHI) A portion of equity or profit attributable to co-owners of a subsidiary. Sometimes called a minority interest. Also see *minority interest*.

out the box (OTB) The price of a security as it is launched onto a market.

out the money (OTM) An option that will not return a profit if exercised. Also see *option*.

overactive Shares that are trading in excessive volumes with prices that are not increasing. It is probable that overactive shares may soon experience price acceleration. Also see *active stock*.

overall balance See *official settlements balance*.

over allotment option See *green shoe provision*.

overbought An indicator that signals that due to substantial trading volumes and movements in share prices, the indicator has hit its upper bound. The indicators used are oscillators. It is probable that the price of an overbought security is at a peak. Also see *oscillator; oversold*.

overcollateralise Offering collateral valued at slightly higher than the value of the debt with the aim of lowering the cost of funds. For example, banks may require more than 2× the value of a loan when the loan is secured through a pledge of listed equity shares. Also see *collateral; collateralised debt obligation*.

overdraft A facility for a bank account to go into debit so that the account holder owes the bank money, up to a predefined limit for a short period of time. Overdrafts are provided on a demand basis, meaning that the bank can demand immediate repayment at any point in time. Also see *overdraft rate*.

overdraft cheque account An account that allows the holder to write cheques in excess of the positive balance of the account. Also see *overdraft rate*.

overdraft rate The rate at which banks negotiate overdraft facilities depending on the risk profile of the borrower. Overdraft rates are semi-fixed floating interest rates and usually attract high interest rate charges. Also see *floating interest rate; interest rate*.

overfitting Adding more parameters to a model than is necessary.

overfunding The process where a central bank influences money supply by issuing government securities in excess of what is needed to finance a deficit. The excessive issue drains cash from the financial system. These issues are often called open market operations. Also see *central bank; open market operations*.

overgeared A company that has taken on excessive levels of debt. Also see *gearing*.

overhead See *fixed expense*.

overheating A growth in demand in excess of supply (capacity) in an economy. Overheating leads to inflation and subsequent rises in interest rates which cool demand in the economy.

overinvestment Excessive investment in the productive capacity of a firm. This usually occurs when managers become overly bullish about economic conditions and increase capacity excessively.

overlapping debt The overlapping of tax bases. For example, a municipality may change taxes in a jurisdiction that is also governed by national government tax laws.

overnight call rate The interest rate that banks charge one another for lending funds overnight. Overnight call rates are quoted as annualised rates. Also see *interest rate; South African overnight index average*.

overnight indexed swap A swap carried out where a fixed rate is swapped against a series of overnight rates. For example, a fixed one-week rate can be swapped against a compound of overnight rates. Settlements are usually done at maturity rather then daily. Also see *swap*.

overreaction The market is said to overreact when prices are temporarily driven off reasonable levels in response to a particular piece of news or information. Prices are said not to obey fundamentals when they overreact. Also see *fundamentals*.

overrun
1. Production in excess of the initial order.
2. The amount of spending above initial budgets for a project.

overshoot Pricing in the market that has overshot (above or below) the securities' long-run value.

oversold

1. An indicator that has hit its lower bound due to movements in share prices. The indicators used are normally oscillators. It is probable that the price of an oversold security is at a low. Also see *oscillator*.
2. Excessive selling in a market in excess of the demand. The price of oversold securities plummets rapidly.
3. The sale of goods or services that cannot be delivered or produced. Also see *overbought*.

oversold forward book See *net forward position*.

oversubscribed When the applications to purchase a new issue of a security or shares exceed the number of securities available for sale. Oversubscription usually results when the price of the security on offer is below what the wider market thinks is a fair price. Also see *green shoe provision*.

over the counter (OTC) Markets or transactions that take place outside the jurisdiction of a recognised financial market. OTC instruments are usually used for the trading of specialised derivative products. OTC transactions have associated default risk and often have limited price transparency. Also see *default risk; derivative*.

overtrading Trading beyond the capital base of a firm. Firms that overtrade, trade on credit and run significant liquidity risk. Also see *liquidity risk*.

overweight A portfolio with significant levels of a particular asset or class of assets. If a portfolio has too much invested in mining assets, the portfolio is overweight mining. Also see *underweight*.

owner financing A transaction in which the seller of an asset provides finance to the owner. Motor vehicle companies often finance the cars they sell through financing subsidiaries. Also see *captive finance company*.

owners equity The funds in a company that have been provided by the owners or are attributable to owners. Funds attributable to shareholders include retained income and share capital. Sometimes owners equity is called shareholders capital. Also see *accounting equation; retained earnings/income; share capital; shareholders capital*.

Oyj Finland's equivalent of a PLC. Also see *PLC*.

oz See *troy ounce*.

P2P
1. Public to private. Also see *private equity*.
2. Peer to peer.

PA See *power of attorney*.

PAB See *private activity bond*.

packaged product A standardised low-risk financial product such as an authorised unit trust, life policy or stakeholder pension.

pac man bid A bid where a target turns on the predator.

paid-up share capital The capital injected into a business by the shareholders. The paid-up capital is measured in the accounts through the share premium and share capital accounts. Also see *share capital; share premium*.

pan-European Across Europe.

paper A generic term usually used in the context of the purchase of debt securities or equity. In the past when investors purchased a debt or equity investment they were issued with a physical paper certificate to verify that they owned the investment. Also see *debt security; equity*.

paper bid See *paper transaction*.

paper loss See *market depreciation*.

paper money Banknotes.

paper profit See *market appreciation*.

paper trail See *audit trail*.

paper transaction A transaction such as the purchase of an asset that is settled through the issue of financial securities such as shares rather than in cash. Acquisitions are often settled on this basis or through a combination of cash and shares.

paper value See *nominal value*.

par See *par value*.

paradox A situation where two seemingly mutually exclusive factors appear to be true at the same time. Also see *mutually exclusive*.

parallel shift A shift of the entire yield curve in a particular direction. The yield curve maintains its shape and therefore mathematically its first derivative. The curve simply moves up or down.

parametric statistics Parametric inferential statistical methods are mathematical procedures for statistical hypothesis testing which assume that the distributions of the variables being assessed belong to known parameterised families of probability distributions. For example, in the analysis of variance it is assumed that the underlying distributions are normally distributed and that the variances of the distributions being compared are similar. The Pearson product-moment correlation coefficient assumes normality of the underlying distribution. Also see *analysis of variance; correlation coefficient; normal or Gaussian distribution*.

parastatal A company or corporation which has government as one of the major and usually controlling shareholders. Transnet, Telkom and Eskom are good examples in South Africa.

parent A company that has a controlling stake in another company, the subsidiary. Parent companies do not usually have any operational assets. Sometimes called a holding company. Also see *subsidiary*.

pari passu Debt or equity that is of equal seniority. Pari passu covenants in loan agreements are used to ensure that lenders do not become subordinated to existing or new debt investors. Lenders want to be pari passu to ensure they receive the same treatment as other lenders in the event of bankruptcy. Also see *seniority; subordinate*.

pari passu bond A bond that ranks pari passu with one or more bonds. Sometimes called a parity bond. Also see *pari passu; parity bond*.

parity
1. The parity of convertible debt is defined as the value of the equity component of the debt. This can be higher or lower than the current price of the bond. The parity is defined as the conversion ratio or the number of shares an investor can convert into multiplied by the current equity price. If investors were using a convertible bond to invest in equity, then this would be the key variable to track. Also see *conversion ratio; convertible debt/bond*.
2. In economics, the term is used with reference to equality or consistency, typically between commodities and currencies. Also see *exchange rate parity; interest rate parity; purchasing power parity*.
3. A term used for par value. Also see *par value*.

parity bond A bond that ranks pari passu with one or more bonds. Sometimes called a pari passu bond. Also see *pari passu*.

parking
1. The storage of goods or holding of assets for a short period of time.
2. Placing a financial transaction on hold.

parsimonious model A simple model that has a great deal of explanatory power.

partial credit guarantee A guarantee that effectively promises to guarantee debt up to a predefined limit that is usually less than the entire debt package.

partial redemption The payment of a portion of an investment or a portion of the value of a particular security to the investor before the final date of maturity.

partial risk guarantee A guarantee issued by organisations such as the World Bank that covers part of the risks associated with financing a project. For example, the World Bank issues partial risk guarantees to mitigate political and regulatory risks and cover off deteriorating investment environments. These guarantees enable commercial lenders to provide finance more effectively as many of their risks are mitigated. Also see *World Bank*.

participant A participant in the purchase of a loan asset is afforded the loan payment rights only and no legal title. If the loan is sold as an assignment, the buyer is set up as the lender on record. A participation involves a greater degree of risk because there is no direct claim on the original borrower of the loan.

participating bank A bank that participates in a syndicated loan.

participating loan A syndicated loan. Also see *club deal*.

participating option (call or put) An option that affords purchasers some, but not all, of the up- or downside.

participating preference share A preference share with additional rights. Holders receive the mandated dividend plus any residual profits after a specified dividend payment to ordinary shareholders. Preference shares are less risky than ordinary shares as their dividend payments rank senior to the dividend payments on ordinary shares. They also offer investors further profit should the company do well and may carry voting rights. Also see *dividend; ordinary share; preference share; priority percentage*.

participation bond A bond that has coupon payments that are linked to the issuer's income.

participation bond scheme An investment fund where monies invested are lent out in the form of loans, typically first mortgage bonds over commercial and industrial properties. Sometimes called a participation mortgage scheme. Also see *mortgage bond*.

participation fee A fee payable to participating banks in a syndicated loan. A participation fee is an upfront once-off fee with the lion's share allocated to the senior banks which take large participations. Also see *administrative agent fee; commitment fee; facility fee; participating bank; syndicated loan; upfront fee; usage fee*.

participatory note (PN or P-note) A derivative instrument issued by investment banks linked to underlying equity securities. P-note investors receive exposure to equities they ordinarily would not be able to invest in due to logistic or regulatory constraints. Sometimes called a global depository receipt (GDR). Also see *American depository receipt; global depository receipt*.

partnership A business ownership structure that is similar to a sole proprietorship with the key difference being that the business is owned by between two and 20 individuals. The partners agree to share the profits of the business but have unlimited liability for the obligations of the business. Also see *sole proprietorship; unlimited liability*.

partnership agreement A form of shareholder agreement between the partners in a business that is registered as a partnership. Also see *partnership; shareholder agreement*.

par value The principal value of a financial instrument on the date of issue:

- In the bond or loan markets, the par value is the price at which the security was issued. For example, a single bond may be issued for a price of R1 million and then may trade at values above or below R1 million. The par value of the bond is the price at which it was issued, i.e. R1 million. At redemption of a bond, the par value is paid back to the investor and so is sometimes called the redemption value or maturity value. If the instrument trades above par value after the primary issue of the bond or loan, the purchasing investor is prepared to accept an all-in return that is less than the present value of the coupon or interest payments.

- For equity shares, the par value is the minimum price of a share on the date of issue. The issuing company decides on an arbitrary number that is much lower than the actual market value of the share. The par value is the legal capital of the business and is set low to protect the shareholders from liability in the event that the liabilities of the company exceeds its assets. The par value is often R1 per share so that the company can track the number of shares in issue easily by means of a share capital account. Also see *face value; nominal value; share capital; share premium*.

passing a dividend The failure of a company to declare dividends. Also see *dividend*.

passive management A fund management strategy that seeks not to beat the market but rather to emulate the average returns of the market. Sometimes called index tracking. Also see *iShare; Satrix 40*.

path dependent A process that is dependent on the series of prior states. There are options written in the financial markets that have path dependent payoffs such as an average price option (Asian option). Also see *average price option*.

pay as you earn (PAYE) A form of personal taxation levied on salaries and wages. The tax is deducted from employees' monthly income by employers on behalf of a tax revenue collection agency.

pay as you go
1. An arrangement whereby funds are distributed as they are made. Pay as you go pension funds pay retired people with the funds collected from current contributors. Sometimes called unfunded schemes. Also see *funded scheme; pension fund*.
2. Payment in advance for a service or goods. Cell phone contracts can be pay as you go when users pay in advance of using the service.

payback See *payback period*.

payback period The time that it takes to recover the initial investment. The investment is a good one if the payback period is less than a number of years prescribed by the investor. The calculation of the payback period is done by simply adding the cash flows generated by the asset with no discounting.

The advantages of analysing investments using the payback period approach are that it is easy to understand, it adjusts for the uncertainty of future cash flows and is biased towards liquidity.

The disadvantages of using the payback period approach are that it ignores the time value of money and has an arbitrary cut-off point. Cash flows beyond the cut-off point are ignored and the method is biased towards shorter term projects. Also see *cash flow; time value of money*.

PAYE See *pay as you earn*.

paymaster general The SARB uses an account called the paymaster general account to account for the expenses of government. Also see *exchequer account*.

payment agent An entity that acts on behalf of the issuer of securities and performs the necessary payments to the holders.

payment cascade See *cash waterfall*.

payment in kind (PIK) A payment not made in cash. These may be made in the form of discounts on products or increases in the principal amounts on debt investments, for example an interest rollup, instead of coupons. Also see *mezzanine debt; toggle note*.

payments system A system used in the settlement of financial transactions.

payment terms The terms and conditions under which payment is made for goods delivered or services rendered. For example, payment can be made as cash on delivery or within 14 days or even within 90 days.

payout ratio See *dividend payout ratio*.

PCE See *private consumption expenditure*.

PCH Payment clearing house.

peak size The part of an iceberg order visible to the market. Also see *iceberg order*.

pegging The process of fixing exchange rates. Also see *clean float; crawling peg; fixed exchange rate; free float; managed float*.

PEN The Peruvian soles divided into 100 centimos.

penny share
1. In the UK, a penny share is defined as a share not in the FTSE 100 with a market capitalisation less than £100 million and shares that are trading with a bid price ask price spread of greater than 10% of the bid price. Also see *ask price; bid price; FTSE; spread*.
2. A share with a value of less than R1 in South Africa.

pension Funds paid to people when they reach a predefined age, usually 60 or 65 years old, or when they retire. These funds are provided from various forms of pension funds. Also see *pension fund*.

pension fund A fund that invests pension contributions by individuals and pays the funds back to those individuals on retirement or termination of their employment. In South Africa, there is legislation that governs pension funds (Pensions Fund Act). The funds are invested in private and public sector debt as well as equity. Pension funds are large and wield considerable power in South African financial markets. Also see *defined contribution fund; provident fund; Public Investment Corporation*.

people pill A people pill is a variation of the poison pill whereby the current management of a company that is subject to a takeover bid threatens to quit en masse in the event of a successful bid. Also see *poison pill*.

PEP See *personal equity plan*.

per diem interest A clause in a home loan agreement that states the borrower must pay the interest accrued from closing or signing off the loan to the first formal interest payment date.

Pereiro's adjusted CAPM model A method of determining the price of equity in foreign markets. For a South African investor investing in Nigeria, then local = SA and foreign = Nigeria:

cost of equity = $Rf_{global\ market} + \beta_{local\ against\ global} (Rm_{global\ market} - Rf_{global\ market})(1 - R_i^2)$

where $Rf_{global\ market}$ = risk-free rate in the global market; $Rm_{global\ market}$ = rate of return in the global market; β is measured by the local against global markets; R_i^2 = the amount of variance in project i's volatility explained by country risk (to avoid double counting of country risk).

The method assumes that investors hold a locally diversified portfolio. Also see *adjusted hybrid capital asset pricing model; beta; beta approach; Bludgeon approach;*

perfect hedge | perpetuity

Erb-Harvey approach; Estrata downside risk model; Godfrey and Espinosa cost of equity model; Goldman Sachs model; lambda approach; Lessard's model; volatility.

perfect hedge A hedge position that completely eliminates risk. Also see *hedge*.

perfectly elastic demand A product of which consumers demand an infinite amount at a given price. However, if the price is raised, the propensity to purchase will be significantly reduced to near zero demand for the goods. Perfectly elastic demand implies that the price elasticity of demand equals zero, i.e. demand P versus Q plots as a horizontal line. A banknote is a good example of an item with perfect elasticity of demand. If R51 is charged for a R50 banknote, the demand for the purchase of the banknotes would instantly drop to zero. Also see *price elasticity of demand*.

perfectly inelastic demand A product of which consumers will demand the same quantity irrespective of the price. Perfectly inelastic demand implies that the price elasticity of demand equals infinity, i.e. demand P versus Q plots as a vertical line. For example, the price of chemical gas masks in times of war is perfectly inelastic. Also see *price elasticity of demand*.

performance bond A type of surety bond which provides for compensation in a situation where a contractor or developer does not perform under contracted obligations. Also see *letter of credit; surety bond*.

period of grace See *grace period*.

perk A non-monetary benefit associated with part of an employment package. A company car is an example of a perk. Sometimes called a fringe benefit.

perpetual See *perpetual bond*.

perpetual annuity See *perpetuity*.

perpetual bond A bond with regular coupons and a principal that never matures. Perpetual bonds are often classed as equity and not debt. A value can be ascribed to the value of a perpetual bond using the following bond value formula:

$$\text{bond value} = C \left[\frac{1 - \frac{1}{(1+r)^t}}{r} \right] + \frac{FV^t}{(1+r)^t}$$

where C = the coupon payment; r = the discount rate; FV = the future value; t = time.

Due to t being infinite in the equation, $\frac{1}{(1+r)^t}$ reduces to a value of 0 and the whole equation above reduces to:

perpetual bond value = $\frac{C}{r}$

Sometimes called an undated bond, a consol or simply a perpetual.

perpetual preference share A preference share that is owned forever and is not redeemed.

perpetuity An annuity whose cash flows continue forever. It is often called a console in the UK. The present value is given by the following equation:

$$PV = \frac{C}{r}$$

where r = discount rate; C = annuity payment.

See *perpetual bond* for details on how the above equation is derived. Also see *cash flow; discount rate*.

personal equity plan (PEP) A form of tax relief in the UK used to encourage UK nationals to invest in the equity share markets. A general PEP, which includes investments in unit trusts, allows £6 000 to be invested tax free while a single company PEP carries a £3 000 allowance.

personal loan A loan granted to individuals by banks or microlenders that is not secured against an asset. Also see *asset; bank; microlender; secured*.

peseta The former currency of Spain before the introduction of the euro. Also see *euro*.

peso The name of the currency of Argentina, Chile, Columbia, Cuba, Dominican Republic, Mexico, Philippines and Uruguay.

potentially except transfer (PET) A transfer of monies between people exempt from taxes.

petro dollars A generic term used to describe the cash and significant investment capacity that oil-producing nations and corporates have in economic environments when oil prices are high.

petty cash Small amounts of cash held by businesses for sundry purchases such as tea and coffee and other miscellaneous items for office use.

pfandbrief A collateralised bond issued by German banks that is securitised by long-term assets such as mortgage bonds. These instruments are widely traded, are highly liquid and considered to be one of the safest forms of European private sector investment. Due to their strong credit quality they consequently trade on thin margins. Pfandbriefe are collateralised debt obligation instruments. Also see *bond; collateralised debt obligation; liquid*.

PFE
1. Peak funding exposure.
2. Potential future exposure.

PFI
1. See *private finance initiative*.
2. Project finance initiative.

PGK The currency of Papua New Guinea, the kina divided into 100 toea.

PGM See *platinum group metals*.

PHLX The Philadelphia Exchange. One of the important sets of instruments traded on this exchange are FX currency options.

PHP The Philippine peso divided into 100 centavos or centimo.

physical book runner An entity that actually undertakes the process of book running and is not simply awarded the title. Sometimes called the coordinator. Also see *book runner*.

physical delivery Under a forward contract the underlying assets are required to be delivered physically on the date of maturity of the contract. Also see *forward contract*.

physicals See *actuals*.

physical settlement The underlying asset is delivered to the purchaser at maturity of the contract.

PIB Public information book.

PIBOR Paris interbank offer rate.

PIC See *Public Investment Corporation*.

pickup An increase in returns or margin related to the occurrence of a specific and often predefined event. For example, a margin pickup stepup may apply on certain loans after certain periods of time to encourage borrowers to refinance. Pickups on margins in the event of credit rating downgrades are commonly used. Also see *credit rating*.

PIK See *payment in kind*.

pip The minimum price movement in a financial market. The term is mainly used in foreign exchange markets where a pip is a single basis point. Also see *basis point*.

PIP See *primary information provider*.

pit An area of an exchange where trading takes place by open outcry. Also see *open outcry*.

PIT Point in time.

PKR The Pakistan rupee divided into 100 paise.

placement See *placing*.

placement ratio (PR) A ratio that indicates how successful or how much demand there is for the placement of a bond in the market. The ratio is defined as:

$$\text{placement ratio (PR)} = \frac{\text{number of bonds sold in a week}}{\text{number of bonds available for sale in the same week}}$$

Sometimes called an acceptance ratio.

placing Companies attempting to raise capital approach selected institutions and high net worth individuals to purchase securities, i.e. the securities are placed with selected individuals. Sometimes called selective marketing. Also see *intermediaries offer; net worth; private placing/placement*.

plain vanilla See *vanilla*.

planning horizon The time period on which a financial planning process focuses. The planning horizon is usually two to five years.

plant See *property, plant and equipment*.

plastic money Money spent using bank or credit cards.

platinum A precious metal mined in South Africa and other countries. It is one of the world's heaviest and rarest metals. It is a transition element in the periodic table with chemical symbol Pt. It is used in jewellery and as a catalyst in many chemical processes. Also see *precious metals*.

platinum group metals (PGM) The six metallic elements of platinum, palladium, rhodium, ruthenium, iridium and osmium. These are transition metals in the periodic table and are usually found together in ore bodies. Uses of platinum group metals include catalytic converters in motor cars and industrial processes, and jewellery. South Africa has a large proportion of about 79% of the world's proven platinum reserves which are mainly found in the Bushveld Complex. Also see *Bushveld Complex*.

platykurtic A distribution with negative kurtosis or 'peakness' is called platykurtic. In terms of shape, a platykurtic distribution has a smaller peak around the mean, i.e. a lower probability than a normally distributed variable of values near the mean, and thin tails. The most platykurtic distribution of all is the Bernoulli distribution with $p = 0.5$ (for example, the number of times one obtains heads when flipping a coin), for which the kurtosis is -2. Also see *Bernoulli distribution; kurtosis; leptokurtic; mesokurtic*.

PLC An abbreviation used in the UK for public limited company. The South African equivalent is Ltd. Also see *limited liability*.

PLCR See *project life coverage ratio*.

plea bargain A legal process generally used in America, in which a defendant pleads guilty to a lesser charge in return for a prosecutor dropping more serious charges. The bargaining process usually involves the handing over of key information that enables prosecutors to convict other criminals involved.

pledge An asset given by a borrower to a lender as a form of security against a loan. The asset technically remains under the ownership of the borrower until the loan has been repaid. A pawnbroker is an example of an entity that accepts pledges of goods and issues loans against these goods. Banks often lend against pledges of shares and government securities. Also see *security; share cover*.

pledged asset See *pledge*.

pledge debt Debt that has goods attached as security. Also see *pledge*.

PLN The currency of Poland, the zloty divided into 100 groszy.

plough-back ratio See *retention ratio*.

PLUS See *OFEX*.

PMI See *purchasing managers index*.

PN See *participatory note*.

P-note See *participatory note*.

POCA See *Proceeds of Crime Act*.

point See *basis point*.

point elasticity The price elasticity at any particular point on the price-quantity demand curve. Also see *price elasticity demand*.

point of satiety Saturation point. Consumers have reached the point of satiety when they cannot purchase any more of a product.

points upfront For credit default swaps, when the default risk of the underlying company is high, the issuer of the CDS will require a premium upfront expressed in basis points. Also see *basis point; credit default swap; default risk*.

poison pill A clause or option in a company's articles of association that will effectively place the company in a dire financial position in the event of a takeover bid. For example, Peoplesoft guaranteed its customers in June 2003 that if it were acquired within two years, presumably by its rival Oracle Corporation, and product support was reduced within four years, its customers would receive a refund of between two and five times the fees they had paid for their Peoplesoft software licences. Also see *people pill*.

policy-based guarantee A guarantee issued by the World Bank that extends beyond partial risk guarantees on specific projects to sovereign borrowing. These guarantees are designed to support developing nations in raising debt and thereby support growth and development. Also see *World Bank*.

political risk See *country risk*.

pool
1. When syndicating a loan, the lead bank pays participation fees to participating banks from an arrangement fee paid by the client. Participation fees are structured to various ticket levels so that they do not add up to the total arrangement fee. The cash left over is called the pool and is sometimes called the book runner's skim. Also see *book runner*.
2. An aggregation of something.
3. Joining together for the purposes of investing.

pool factor In a collateralised debt obligation (CDO) structure, the pool factor is the level of underlying loan assets that remain expressed as a function of the original CDO principal value:

$$\text{pool factor} = \frac{\text{value of remaining assets}}{\text{original value of assets}}$$

For example, in collateralised mortgage obligations, as the number of underlying mortgage prepayments increase, the pool factor will decrease. Also see *collateralised debt obligation*.

Porter's five forces Five market forces used when analysing the competitiveness of an industry. They are:
1. the threat of new entrants
2. the bargaining power of buyers
3. the threat of substitutes
4. the bargaining power of suppliers
5. barriers to entry.

portfolio A group of assets such as shares and bonds held by an investor. Portfolios are usually assembled to reduce unique or unsystematic risk. Also see *unsystematic risk*.

portfolio beta The beta value of a portfolio. The portfolio beta is made up of the weighted average betas of the individual components of the portfolio:

$$\beta_p = \sum_{i=1}^{n} \varpi_i \beta_i$$

where β_i = the beta of individual components with respect to the wider market; ω_i = individual weight in portfolio.

Also see *beta*.

portfolio covariance and correlation terms The covariance and correlation of a portfolio is a measure of the risk associated with the portfolio. To calculate the risk of a portfolio the covariance (Cov) and correlation ($\rho_{i,j}$) of each security with every other security is calculated by:

$$Cov(r_i, r_j) = \sum_s Pr(s)[r_i - E(r_i)][r_j - E(r_j)]$$

and

$$\rho_{i,j} = \frac{Cov(r_i, r_j)}{\sigma_i \sigma_j}$$

where $Pr(s)$ = probability of state s; r_i = return of investment i; r_j = return of investment j; $E(r)$ = expected return; σ_i and σ_j = the standard deviations on securities i and j respectively.

Once the correlations and covariances have been calculated, the standard deviation of the portfolio can be calculated using:

$$\text{variance} = \sum_{\text{all } i} \sum_{\text{all } j} E(r_i) \times E(r_j) \times Cov(i, j)$$

and

$$\text{std deviation } (\sigma) = \sqrt{\text{variance}}$$

Also see *expected return*.

portfolio duration Duration is additive and so the duration of a portfolio is the weighted average of the duration of each component:

$$\text{portfolio duration} = \frac{\sum_{i=1}^{n} w_i \, \text{duration}_i}{n}$$

Also see *duration; weighted average*.

portfolio effect The reduction of risk due to increasing diversity in a portfolio of assets.

portfolio enhancement See *covered call*.

portfolio expected returns The expected return on a portfolio calculated by the return on a portfolio in a single state, usually a single point in an economic cycle:

$$r(s) = \sum_{\text{all assets}} w_{is} \times r_i$$

combined with the probability of being in an expected state and defining that probability over a range of economic conditions giving:

$$E(R_p) = \sum_{s} Pr(s) r(s)$$

where w_i = weight in portfolio; r_i = expected return of asset i; $Pr(s)$ = probability of state s; $r(s)$ = return in a single state.

Also see *expected return*.

portfolio insurance The use of derivatives and futures contracts to close out the returns and protect the invested capital in a portfolio. Also see *close out*.

portfolio manager A professional who invests a portfolio of assets on behalf of a group of investors.

portfolio structure A breakdown, usually by percentages, of the assets in a portfolio.

portfolio variance The variance on a total number of n shares in a portfolio is given by:

$$\sigma_p^2 = \sum_{i=1}^{n} \sum_{j=1}^{n} \omega_i \omega_j \rho_{i,j} \sigma_i \sigma_j$$

where ω_i and ω_j = the portfolio weights for shares i and j; σ_i^2 and σ_j^2 = the variances; $\rho_{i,j}$ = the correlation coefficient between the two shares.

Also see *variance*.

portfolio weight The percentage of a particular asset expressed as a fraction of the total portfolio.

position The purchase of assets or futures contracts in such a manner that benefits can be gained if there is net movement in the price of the assets or market. The movement can be up or down. Also see *close out*.

positional risk The risk associated with taking a position in the market. Also see *position*.

position limit A limit imposed by derivatives exchanges to stop dominant positions in the market. They are in place to stop traders cornering the market. Also see *corner the market*.

position risk requirement A capital adequacy requirement that requires market participants to hedge their positional risk significantly with derivative products or have a cash reserve to cover possible losses. Also see *capital adequacy; positional risk*.

positive basis trade A positive basis trade can result when a trader takes a short position on a bond, sells a credit default swap (CDS) on that bond at the same time and the CDS spread is larger than the bond spread. Under these conditions an arbitrage profit is made. Also see *arbitrage; bond; credit default swap; negative basis trade; short position*.

positive butterfly A yield curve that has long- and short-term interest rates higher than mid-term rates. The yield curve is shaped like a positive parabola. Also see *backwardation; contango; interest rate; negative butterfly; normal yield curve; yield curve*.

positive carry When borrowed funds are deposited at an interest rate that is higher than the rate due on the borrowings. A positive carry implies a profit can be made by borrowing money and lending it on to someone else. Also see *interest rate; negative carry*.

positive covenant A covenant that limits the lender's activities in some way. It is usually designed to ensure that lenders undertake certain actions. Also see *affirmative covenant; covenant; financial covenant; negative covenant*.

positive yield curve A yield curve that is in contango. Also see *contango*.

post bank A post bank is mainly a deposit-receiving institution. There is a strong element of government and banking sector debt in the investment activities that post banks hold. Also see *credit union; mutual bank*.

post date The date to which a financial document is set some time in the future.

pound
1. The currency of the United Kingdom and other countries such as Cyprus, Egypt, Lebanon, the Sudan and Syria.
2. A unit of mass (lb). 1 lb = 0.45359237 kg

power of attorney (PA) A legal document that indicates the right of one person to act on behalf of another.

power of sale A right given to lenders in a mortgage-backed loan agreement whereby they are given the power to sell the asset subject to the mortgage in an event of default. Also see *event of default*.

PPA Power purchasing agreement.

PPE See *property, plant and equipment*.

PPP
1. See *purchasing power parity*.
2. See *public private partnership*.

praecipium The front-end fee paid to an arranger of financing facilities to compensate for human resources and skills employed to undertake the transaction. Sometimes called a skim. Also see *skim*.

precious metal lease rate The rate charged for borrowing precious metals. Also see *precious metals*.

precious metals Gold, silver and the platinum group metals. Also see *platinum group metals; troy ounce*.

pre-emptive right A stipulation in the articles of association of a company that gives the shareholders the right to maintain their proportion of ownership in the business. Pre-emptive rights are evidenced through rights issues when further equity capital is raised. Also see *articles of association; equity; rights issue*.

pref share See *preference share*.

preference share An equity investment in a company whereby the holder of a preference share is promised a fixed dividend on preference shares for a stipulated or infinite period. Preference shares are thus regarded as fixed income securities.

Preference shares normally enjoy preference in payment of dividends and distribution of assets over ordinary shareholders if the company should become insolvent. Preference shares are thus less risky than normal equity investments. Preference shares are often classified as an intermediate form of security as their cash entitlements rank between ordinary shares and debt.

Voting rights on preference shares are usually restricted and are only afforded if dividends are in arrears.

Preference shares offer a lower risk of insolvency to the issuer as dividends can be deferred in times of low profitability avoiding the insolvency proceedings that would be associated with issuing debt if interest payments are missed.

Preference shares may be redeemable or convertible at a fixed or variable date. A preference share may be callable through cash payment or the issue of ordinary shares. Americans call preference shares preferred stock.

Also see *callable bond; dividend; fixed income; N-share; ordinary share; participating preference share; priority percentage; profit participation certificate; security*.

preferential debt See *seniority*.

preferential offer Shares offered preferentially to directors, employees, associates of a company or selected institutions in conjunction with a public offer. In South Africa, BEE transactions are often characterised by preferential offers to selected individuals and company staff. Also see *black economic empowerment; initial public offer; public offer*.

preferential payment A payment made to senior creditors.

preferred ordinary share An equity share with preferred rights such as fixed and/or cumulative dividends. They rank ahead of ordinary shares for cash flows and capital distributions. Once the preferred ordinary shareholders have been paid, the ordinary shareholders are paid. After the obligatory distributions have been made on preferred and ordinary shares, the two classes of equity holders then rank pari passu (equally) in sharing any surplus capital. Preferred ordinary shares may have variable or no voting rights. Also see *preference share*.

preferred stock An American term for a preference share. Also see *preference share*.

pre-hedge A futures position that is established before the underlying asset or commodity is acquired.

prelisting statement A statement issued by a company not immediately needing to raise capital, but seeking a listing on a stock exchange. Also see *prospectus*.

premium
1. An amount in excess of the face value of an instrument. Also see *face value; share premium*.
2. An amount in excess of the issue share price. Also see *stag*.
3. The price a buyer pays to a seller of an option to exercise that option. Also see *option*.
4. The price in excess of the intrinsic value that the market is willing to pay for an option. Also see *intrinsic value*.
5. The difference between spot and forward prices of assets. Also see *spot market; spread*.

premium bond A bond selling for a value higher than par value. Bonds sell at values above par when the rates of return required by investors are lower than the coupons. Also see *par value*.

premium income Income, usually paid monthly, that is received by insurance companies from their range of clients.

prepaid Expenses or assets that have been paid for in advance of the date at which the benefit is going to be received. Prepaid expenses are indicated as current assets on a company's balance sheet. Also see *accrual*.

prepayment
1. Expenses or assets that have been paid for in advance of the date at which the benefit is going to be received. Prepaid expenses are indicated as current assets on a company's balance sheet.
2. A payment on a loan facility or bond that is made before the scheduled date of maturity. A prepayment need not be payment on the entire facility but can be made on individual utilisations.

prepayment fee A fee charged by a bank or institutional investor that requires the borrower to pay a once-off fee for prepaying a loan. The private placement loan market is sensitive to prepayment and consequently insists on punitive prepayment penalties. Also see *administrative agent fee; commitment fee; facility fee; institutional investor; participation fee; upfront fee; usage fee*.

prepayment risk The risk that a debt instrument is paid before maturity and the investor will have to invest the proceeds in a lower yielding investment.

prescribed assets Specific assets assigned by government and/or other regulators that banks and other financial institutions are required to hold. For example, in South Africa pension funds are required to hold particular proportions of government securities in their portfolios. Banks are required to hold portions of their asset portfolios in prescribed liquid assets. Also see *liquid asset; pension fund*.

present value (PV) An estimate of the current value of an asset calculated by discounting its future cash flows. The present value calculated in today's money of a single future cash flow is given by the following formula:

$$\text{present value } (PV) = \frac{FV_t}{(1+r)^t}$$

where FV_t = future value at point in time t; r = interest or discount rate.

To calculate the value of an asset, the above formula is adapted to cover the range of cash flows produced over the life of an asset:

$$\text{present value } (PV) = \sum_{all\ i} \frac{CF_{@i}}{(1+r)^i}$$

where $CF_{@i}$ = the cash flow produced by the asset at point in time i.

Also see *annuity present value; cash flow; discount rate; future value*.

present value factor A factor used to calculate the present value of a cash flow. It is a component of the present value formula and is defined as:

$$\frac{1}{(1+r)^t}$$

where t = the number of time periods elapsed; r = the applicable discount rate.

Also see *discount rate; present value*.

present value of a basis point How much the value of a bond will change if the yield shifts by one basis point. Also see *basis point; bond; bond value*.

present value of growth opportunities (PVGO) The current value of a firm is made up of the present value of the current operations and the present value of future growth opportunities expected to be taken. The valuations of innovative companies in growth sectors are significantly influenced by the market perception of future growth. Also see *firm*.

preservation of capital An investment strategy that is designed not to lose any capital invested. The downside is that the returns are not as good as strategies that involve higher levels of risk.

preserved benefit The funds former pension fund contributors are entitled to if they cease to be contributors to a scheme before retirement.

PRI Political risks insurance.

price control The process of an organisation, usually a government, setting prices of goods and/or services. Also see *command economy; price fixing*.

price discovery The process of the market reaching price levels based on the dynamics of supply and demand.

priced out A share has been priced out to a piece of news or information when the market has already adjusted the price of the asset fully to the information.

price earnings ratio (PE) The price of a share expressed as a proportion of its earnings:

$$\text{price earnings (PE)} = \frac{\text{share price}}{\text{earnings per share (EPS)}}$$

PE ratios give the market valuation of the company by an indication of the price investors are willing to pay per unit of reported profits/earnings. High PE ratios indicate that investors see potential growth in earnings. The use of PE ratios as an analysis tool is often open to distortions in irrational movements of share prices.

There are two PE calculations that are employed. Future earnings estimates can be used indicating a forward PE or historical earnings can be used to indicate a historical PE. The media usually quote the historical PE, reporting last year's earnings relative to the current share price.

The following equations illustrate how the PE ratio and dividend discount model are related:

$$P_0 = \frac{E_1}{R_E - g} = \frac{E_0(1+g)}{R_E - g}$$

$$\frac{P_0}{E_0} = \frac{1+g}{R_E - g}$$

$$P_0 = \frac{D_1}{R_E - g} \text{ but } D_1 = E_1 \times (1-b) \text{ and } g = ROE \times b$$

$$\frac{P_0}{E_1} = \frac{1-b}{R_E - (ROE \times b)}$$

where ROE = required return on equity; b = retention ratio; E_1 = earnings next time period; R_E = discount rate; D_1 = dividend declared next time period.

The earnings number used is usually the net profit of the business, i.e. the profit attributable to equity shareholders.

From the equation:

$$P_0 = \frac{E_1}{R_E - g} = \frac{E_0(1+g)}{R_E - g}$$

one can see that the PE ratio can also be considered a payback period for buying a share for price P_0 and earning E_0 growing at g per annum.

According to the above argument and assumptions that govern that argument, the current PE ratio can be seen as containing the expected future growth in earnings and capital costs.

In the JSE share tables published in the South African business media, the PE ratio is indicated as the closing price divided by the annualised rolling headline earnings per share. Also see *dividend growth model; market value ratios; net profit; return on equity*.

price efficiency The degree to which the current market prices reflect current information. Also see *efficient capital market*.

price elastic If the price elasticity of demand for a product is greater than one, then the good is said to be price elastic. A price elastic product has a significant change in quantity demanded with a corresponding change in price. Goods that are not differentiated and are easily interchangeable are price elastic. Also see *elasticity; inelasticity; price elasticity of demand*.

price elasticity of demand A measure of the responsiveness of quantity demanded of a product to the change in its sale price:

$$\text{price elasticity of demand} = \frac{\% \text{ change in quantity}}{\% \text{ change in price}}$$

A product is termed price elastic if the ratio is less than one and inelastic if greater than one. Also see *elasticity; inelasticity*.

price fixing The forced stipulation of a price by a manufacturer or supplier. Price fixing implies that a price is forced on the buyer without prices in the market being reached by competitive supply and demand dynamics. Price fixing is usually an illegal activity if not imposed by governments. Sometimes called price control. Also see *command economy; price control.*

price gap A price gap results when trading stops for a period. For example, trading usually stops overnight and the price of the asset on resumption of trade can be a distance away from the previous closing price creating a price gap. Also see *opening price.*

price index An index comprising a basket of goods that tracks price changes of goods or inflation. The consumer price index (CPI), retail price index (RPI) and horizontal index of consumer prices (HICP) are such measures. Also see *consumer price index; inflation; retail price index.*

price leadership The process whereby a powerful entity in a market sets a price and competitors in the market are forced to follow a similar pricing strategy.

price limit A limit imposed on exchanges, in particular derivative exchanges, that prevents prices moving too fast during a trading session. When the price goes up by the limit, it is said to be limit up and when it has moved down by the limit it is said to be limit down. Trading can be suspended when price limits are hit.

price maker See *market maker.*

price persistence The price changes of a share over time relative to the changes in price of an overall index. Also see *beta; elasticity.*

price range The lowest and highest prices of an asset traded over the last specified period.

price risk
1. For bonds, price risk describes the change in the price of a bond due to a change in interest rates. Bonds with longer dated tenors are more sensitive to changes in interest. Also see *bond; interest rate.*
2. In general, the potential loss resulting from changes in prices of an asset.

price-sensitive information Private information on the prospects of a business that will have an influence on price if released to the market. Also see *insider trading.*

price skimming The process of charging as much as possible from customers for a product. This is achieved by starting at a high price and dropping the price until it reaches a point at which the goods clear.

price spread See *vertical spread.*

price stickiness Price stickiness is the phenomenon where prices do not change freely but instead stick in disequilibrium, often due to imperfect information. For example, nominal wages are said to be sticky as they do not ever go down as easily as they go up.

price support The support of the prices of particular products. Governments often perform market operations or give subsidies particularly in the agricultural sector to ensure the profitability of farmers and hence food supply.

price taker A client who accepts the prices quoted by a price maker for financial securities. Also see *market maker.*

price tension Maintaining or encouraging competitive forces in a market to ensure prices remain competitive.

price to book ratio The price of a share as traded on the market compared to the book value of the company's asset:

$$\text{price to book ratio} = \frac{\text{share price}}{\text{book value per share}}$$

The ratio is used to determine if a share is cheap. It could be considered cheap if the market values the company less than its net asset value. For companies with substantial intangible assets such as intellectual property, the ratio is relatively meaningless as the book value of the assets does not reflect the value of the intangible assets. Also see *book value; intangible asset*.

price to cash flow ratio

$$\text{price to cash flow ratio} = \frac{\text{share price}}{\text{cash flow for the period per share}}$$

price to sales ratio A ratio used to determine if share prices are expensive or cheap and that uses the turnover or sales of a business as a function of its share price:

$$\text{price to sales ratio} = \frac{\text{share price}}{\text{sales for the period per share}}$$

A low ratio may indicate that the share is cheap. This ratio must be used with caution because it does not take the actual profitability of the company into account. Also, sales revenue is not fully attributable to equity shareholders like net profit is so companies with high levels of debt or lower profit margins will appear underpriced. Also see *net profit*.

price value of a basis point The change in price of a bond given a change in interest rates of one basis point. Also see *basis point; bond; bond value; interest rate*.

price weighted index A stock index such as the Dow Jones that is weighted by the price of each share. The implication of this is that the higher the price of a share is, the more influence it has on the index. Also see *Dow Jones; market capitalisation index*.

pricing grid A grid that changes loan pricing, usually the margin, according to parameters such as leverage or credit rating. Pricing grids are used to compensate banks with higher interest income when the credit risk of a company changes. Pricing grids can also advantage borrowers with cheaper interest rates and fees if they can keep their credit risk profiles indicated by metrics such as credit ratings low. Also see *credit rating; leverage; margin*.

prima facie A Latin term for on the face of it.

primary capital See *tier 1 capital*.

primary dealer An institution such as a bank that can trade with the central bank. Also see *central bank*.

primary goods Raw unprocessed goods such as raw metals that have not been beneficiated in the manufacturing cycle and raw agricultural products. Also see *commodity*.

primary information provider (PIP) A system on exchanges whereby companies release information to the markets through the information system on the exchange. The information is then distributed to the public by secondary information providers such as Bloomberg and Reuters. SENS is the JSE primary information system. Also see *JSE; secondary information provider; SENS*.

primary issue An initial placement of securities by government or a business. These are often in the form of a public offer or private placements. Also see *initial public offer; private placing/placement; public offer.*

primary market The market for the original issue of securities or loans by government or a business. The sale of securities in the primary market is called a public offer or a private placement. Primary markets are in contrast with the secondary markets where shares and securities already owned by the public are traded between members of the public. Also see *private placing/placement; public offer; secondary market.*

primary securities Money market securities that are issued by ultimate borrowers. Also see *indirect securities; money market.*

primary surplus Revenue less expenditure excluding interest expense.

primary trend An overall trend in price evolution that lasts for a sustained period of time, usually for a period longer than a year. Upward and downward fluctuations about the primary trend can occur. Also see *super cycle.*

prime brokerage A generic term for many different products offered by an investment bank to a hedge fund. Also see *hedge fund; investment bank.*

prime cost See *variable cost/expense.*

prime lending rate See *prime rate.*

prime paper High-quality short-term debt. Prime paper is usually issued by a top-class company or is guaranteed by one of the top banks. Also see *short-term debt.*

prime rate The benchmark interest rate that banks charge their customers. In South Africa, the prime lending rate is a benchmark rate published by commercial banks. The SA prime rate is a few per cent higher than the marginal lending rate or repo rate. Banks often lend to their key high-quality clients at rates below the prime lending rate. The prime lending rate is expressed as a nominal annual compound monthly rate. Also see *interest rate; marginal lending rate; NACM; repo rate.*

principal The amount that the issuer will pay the holder when a financial instrument matures. Sometimes called the face value, redemption or par value. Also see *face value; par value.*

principal trader A trader who trades for his/her own account and takes positions in the market. Also see *position.*

print Publicly printed numbers.

printing a deal The price or spread at which a deal is struck.

priority percentage The share of profits of a business that must be paid to holders of preference shares before holders of ordinary shares can be paid dividends. Also see *preference share.*

private activity bond (PAB) A bond issued by a public entity, typically a municipality, where a significant portion of the proceeds are used by one or more private entities. They are classed as PABs because they have different tax treatments to public bonds. Also see *private purpose bond.*

private company An unlisted company with a minimum of one director and one shareholder. There is usually a limit on the maximum number of shareholders and there are often restrictions on the transfer of shares in the company. Also see *public company*.

private consumption expenditure (PCE) An economic variable that tracks the spending on goods and services of the private sector.

private customer A customer who is not classed as experienced or knowledgeable about financial markets. Private customers are afforded extensive protection under regulatory regimes when dealing with financial service providers. Also see *intermediate customer; market counterparty*.

private equity The process of wealthy individuals or specialised funds seeking extra returns by buying undervalued assets which are often public companies, delisting them if they are listed and then holding on to them for a period before selling them at significant profits in the future. Private equity firms usually use substantial amounts of debt to capitalise the companies they buy. Private equity firms often take active management roles in the firms they purchase. Pension funds do not allocate investment resources to private equity companies or funds as they are risky in nature. Also see *pension fund*.

private finance initiative (PFI) The provision of funding for major capital government projects from the private sector. Private firms complete and manage the capital projects on behalf of government. Governments introduce PFIs to improve efficiency in areas of public service where governments are not effective. Sometimes called a public private partnership (PPP).

private placing/placement (PP/USPP) An unregistered, unlisted and often unrated borrowing or equity security sold to a select group of sophisticated institutional investors. The sale and trade of these securities is governed by the key Rule 144A in the US. The entity issuing the securities identifies a list of entities that they consider to be suitable investors and offers the securities to them only. Private placement investors are typically insurance companies and other investment funds.

Companies that borrow money (issue security) on a private placement basis are not able or willing to tap the public bond market but seek to diversify their investor base away from their traditional sources of funding. Companies use PPs for debt because no credit ratings are required, the deals are private, issue sizes are smaller, banking fees are lower and no registration with regulatory bodies is applicable.

There is not as much liquidity in the private placement loans market compared to the bond market and loans are capped to US$1 billion in the PP market. The PP market does not require debt to be rated as they use their own rating system (NAIC).

PPs are term loans, have tenors of five to 15 years and are often used to enhance capital structure by extending the maturity profile of a company's debt. PP investors are sensitive to prepayment and impose significant penalties on borrowers that wish to prepay before maturity.

The advantages of a PP market include:
- access to a deep pool of institutional investors
- less susceptibility to market volatility
- privacy within the group of investors
- no ratings requirement
- longer tenors.

The disadvantages are the following:
- For debt, the loans are term in nature and are therefore less flexible than revolving credit facilities.
- Covenants required are similar in nature to bilateral loans and syndicated loans.

Also see *bilateral; bond; capital structure; covenant; credit rating; initial public offer; institutional investor; National Association of Insurance Commissioners; revolving credit facility; Rule 144A; schuldschein; syndicated loan; term loan.*

private purpose bond A bond issued by a public enterprise, typically municipalities, to fund private projects such as ports. They are classed as private purpose bonds because they have different tax treatments. Also see *private activity bond*.

private sector Companies and corporations that are not part of government and that are set up for the creation of profit. Governments sometimes maintain ownership stakes in private sector companies, especially when they are key strategic assets. Eskom, Transnet and Telkom are good examples in South Africa.

private sector credit extension (PSCE) An economic term used to describe the total loans and advances to the private sector of the economy. Credit extension data is a key variable in the determination of reserve or central bank monetary policy. South African credit extension data can be obtained from the SARB Quarterly Bulletin. Also see *central bank; monetary policy; South African Reserve Bank.*

privatisation The process of government-owned enterprises being sold to the private sector, i.e. a transfer of assets from the public to the private sector. Privatisation is undertaken because market participants are more adept at the profitable delivery of goods and services than governments are. Private companies are more competitive than government-owned ones and privatisation results in lower prices, better quality and less red tape. Sometimes called corporatisation. Also see *golden shares.*

probability A number that lies between 0 and 1 assigned to events in the sample space that expresses the likelihood that an event will occur. Probability values closer to 1 indicate events which are more likely to occur.

probability density function A function used to calculate probabilities and to specify the probability distribution of a continuous random variable. Also see *normal or Gaussian distribution.*

probability distribution For every measurable value a probability can be assigned to the likely outcome. Probabilities are assignable over a sample space and collectively make up a probability distribution. A probability distribution extends beyond a sample space and becomes a probability distribution over s state space. Also see *normal or Gaussian distribution.*

probability of ruin Where the present value of future liabilities exceeds the present value of assets. Also see *economic capital.*

probable More likely than not. Probable implies we are more than 51% sure.

probate
1. The legal process of dealing with the terms of a will in a deceased estate.
2. The application for the right to deal with a deceased person's estate.

proceeds account An account into which banks pay the proceeds of a loan, equity, bond or any other security issue.

Proceeds of Crime Act (POCA) An act passed by the UK government that sets out laws on financing and the investing of the proceeds of criminal activity including money laundering. Also see *money laundering*.

procyclical Cycles that rise and fall together. For example, the strength of the economy and interest rates usually rise and fall together. Also see *interest rate*.

producer price index (PPI) A measure of the price of a basket of goods and services at wholesale level. PPI is effectively a measure at the factory gate as opposed to the consumer price index (CPI) which is measured at the shop counter. CPI and PPI may differ through variables such as taxes, subsidies and transport. PPI indices come in a host of formats and are a leading indicator of CPI. PPI is a measure of output while CPI is a measure of the ultimate cost of living. Sometimes PPI is known as the wholesale price index. PPI data for South Africa can be obtained from www.statssa.gov.za. Also see *consumer price index; leading indicator*.

product Multiplication of a set of numbers or variables. A well used notation convention when indicating a product is:

$$a_1 \times a_2 \times a_3 ... a_n \equiv \prod_{i=1}^{n} a_i$$

Also see *geometric mean*.

product differentiation See *differentiation*.

product homogeneity See *homogeneous*.

production price index (PPI) See *producer price index*.

productivity The measure of the amount of output for the amount of input used in generating the unit of output. This is considered to be one of the key indicators of economic health.

professional indemnity insurance The provision of insurance to professionals such as engineers, lawyers, doctors and various business managers that covers them in the event that they are sued for negligence. Sometimes called malpractice insurance.

Professional Securities Market (PSM) A stock market segment or board that falls under the London Stock Exchange that enables companies to raise capital through the issue of debt, convertible debt and depository receipts to professional and institutional investors. Also see *convertible debt/bond; global depository receipt; institutional investor; Rule 144A*.

profit The residual amount that remains after expenses, including capital maintenance adjustments, have been deducted from income.

profitability index (PI) A method of evaluating the profitability of a company calculated by:

$$\text{profitability index (PI)} = \frac{\sum \text{discounted future net operating cash flows}}{\sum \text{present value of initial investment}}$$

A decision must be made on how to choose the investment cash flows, for example whether to account for investment cash outflows at the beginning of a project or later on.

Advantages of using the PI method of evaluating a company's profitability include the following:

- It has a close relation to net present value (NPV).

- It is easily understandable.
- It is useful when funds are limited.

Disadvantages are the following:

- It is problematic when comparing mutually exclusive investments.
- By dividing, the scale of profits is ignored.

The PI method is not considered to be as useful as the net present value (NPV) method. Also see *cash flow; mutually exclusive; net present value.*

profitability ratios See *gross profit margin; net profit margin; return on equity; return on total assets.*

profit and loss account An account of the income and expenses of a company. Also called an income statement or sometimes an income and expenditure account.

profit loss policy See *business interruption policy or insurance.*

profit margin

1. Gross profit margin is the gross profit of a company expressed as a portion of sales:
$$\text{gross profit} = \frac{\text{earnings before interest and taxation}}{\text{sales}}$$
2. Net profit margin is the net profit of a company expressed as a portion of sales:
$$\text{net profit} = \frac{\text{earnings after interest, tax and other expenses}}{\text{sales}}$$

Also see *profitability ratios.*

profit participation certificate (genussschein) A security, usually of German companies, giving the holder the right to participate in the net profits or liquidation proceeds of a company. The holder has no voting rights and the shares have junior subordination under liquidation. Unlike debt, they have no maturity, no fixed payments or payment dates. They are similar in concept to preference shares and N-shares in South Africa. Also see *liquidation; N-share; preference share.*

profit sharing ratio The ratio at which various stakeholders share in the profits of a company. Partnerships use ratios where each partner is allocated a portion of the company's profit. Companies may have ratios where management, shareholders and employees split profits.

profit taking The selling of securities to lock in realised profit. Also see *realised gain; unrealised loss/profit.*

profit warning A statement issued by a listed company indicating that profits in the near future will be below expectations.

profit warranty When selling a business, the seller may have to provide a warranty of profit levels into the future. A portion of the payment of the purchase price may be deferred for a period of time to ensure that profit levels are maintained. A profit warranty is often called an earn out provision in documentation.

pro forma Projection of the future.

pro forma statement Projection of future anticipated financial statements.

progress payment A payment made when a project such as a construction project reaches a defined milestone.

prohibition order A regulatory authority order barring a firm or person from undertaking particular activities.

project finance The provision of finance to complete standalone projects. These projects are usually infrastructural projects and long term in nature. The financing relies on the cash flows the asset will generate and the debt package is non-recourse to the project sponsors. See financial ratios widely used in project finance including *debt service coverage ratio; loan life cover ratio; project life coverage ratio; reserve life coverage ratio; reserve tail ratio*. Also see *non-recourse; sponsor*.

project holding company A company that owns several projects. These holding companies are put in place so that different sets of liabilities can be secured against a host of assets. The project holding company is usually ring fenced from the sponsors. Also see *ring fenced; sponsor*.

project life coverage ratio (PLCR) A loan life coverage ratio used for project financing:

$$\text{project life coverage ratio (PLCR)} = \frac{\sum \text{present value of the project's cash available for financing}}{\text{principal outstanding}}$$

Also see *debt service coverage ratio; loan life cover ratio; reserve life coverage ratio; reserve tail ratio*.

project note A financial instrument issued to finance projects. Project notes are usually short term in nature and are used to get projects to particular milestones or finance small projects. These notes are often issued by municipalities and other public organisations.

proletarian shopping A technical term given by economists to benefits received from the proceeds of crime, i.e. stealing.

promissory note A contract that details the promise of a payment from one party to another at a date in the future. These arise from loan obligations and other forms of debt. The contract specifies the principal amount, interest rate, maturity and other formal clauses. Promissory notes are used in trade finance where a supplier of goods or a service is issued with a promissory note for cash payment at a date in the future. The receiver of the promissory note can sell or discount the note in a secondary market for immediate cash realisation. Also see *interest rate*.

prompt date
1. A term used on the London Metals Exchange for delivery date.
2. The date on which payments are due for the purchase of goods.

propco A subsidiary of a company that holds property assets. These companies may be ring fenced and used for raising finance against property assets. Also see *ring fenced*.

property bond A bond issued by vehicles such as collateralised mortgage obligations.

property finance The provision of funds through a loan to develop or purchase physical property.

property loan stock An investment fund that can use more debt than a property unit trust to purchase physical assets. Using debt in this manner is sometimes called gearing. Also see *gearing; property unit trust*.

property, plant and equipment (PPE) The assets of a company used in the generation of profit. PPE includes land, buildings, vehicles, machines and other assets that have

property trust | provident fund

an economic life of longer than a year. The value of PPE on a company's books is reduced by depreciation. Also see *depreciation*.

property trust A company that issues equity shares, pools the proceeds of the share issue and purchases or constructs a portfolio of diversified physical property assets. The property assets are usually rented out to tenants. Also see *property loan stock; property unit trust*.

property unit trust (PUT) An investment fund that invests in physical property. There are limitations placed on these unit trusts such as the amount of debt that the unit trust may use. PUTs are limited to using no more than 30% of the asset value of their portfolio in the form of debt. Also see *property loan stock*.

proportionate consolidation A method of accounting and reporting whereby a company's share of each of the assets, liabilities, income and expenses of a jointly controlled entity is combined line by line with similar items in the company's financial statements or reported as separate line items. Also see *financial statements; line item*.

proprietary Information or assets used for the benefit of an individual organisation.

pro rata

1. The assignment of cost or income to a non-integer period. For example, if a person is paid R10 per hour and works for only half an hour, he/she will be paid R5 on a pro rata basis.

2. For loans there may be multiple tranches of differently structured debt in a single facility. Pro rata refers to a slice of the facilities sold to an investor in proportion to their original size.

prospectus A statement by a company seeking to raise equity capital and obtain a stock market listing. The prospectus contains a fair presentation of the affairs of the company. Sometimes called an offering circular or offer for sale. Also see *equity; prelisting statement*.

protection buyer A counterparty that wishes to reduce exposure to a risk, usually credit risk, and pays another party to take on the risk. In the case of credit risk, protection is purchased through a credit default swap. Also see *credit default swap; credit risk; protection seller*.

protection seller A counterparty that wishes to increase exposure to a risk, usually credit risk, and assumes the risk usually through derivative instruments such as credit default swaps. Also see *credit default swap; credit risk; protection buyer*.

protective covenant A covenant in a loan agreement that restricts the borrower's ability to raise further debt. Protective covenants are used so that the issuer does not become overextended, thereby increasing the risk of default for the original lenders. Also see *covenant*.

protective put The purchase of a put option when the investor is in possession of the underlying asset effectively limiting excessive loss. A protective put has similar economic rewards to the creation of a call option. Also see *call option; put option*.

proven mineral reserves See *measured mineral resources*.

provident fund Retirement savings in the form of a defined contribution scheme. Being a member of a provident fund may be mandatory for employees. Contributions to these schemes are made up of equal contributions by the employee and employer. Also see *defined contribution fund; pension fund*.

provision A possible future liability of uncertain timing or quantum. A company reports these when it has incurred an expense for the period in question but does not yet know the actual full amount or is not sure that the full liability will arise. Also see *liability*.

provisional allotment letter A temporary letter issued under a rights issue, indicating the rights due to the shareholder. Also see *nil paid letter; rights issue/offer*.

provisional call A quasi call feature on convertible debt instruments which is applicable in the non-callable period if the underlying asset price attains specified predefined levels. These features are built in to protect convertible issuers from exceptional adverse movements in the price of the share into which the instrument is converted.

proxy A person who is nominated to vote on behalf of a shareholder at a company general meeting. Also see *annual general meeting; extraordinary general meeting; general proxy; proxy form; special general meeting; special proxy*.

proxy fight Unhappy shareholders act on their dissatisfaction and move to replace management.

proxy form A notification form sent to a company indicating that the shareholder wishes to nominate a proxy representative at a general meeting. Also see *annual general meeting; extraordinary general meeting; proxy; special general meeting*.

proxy vote A vote taken by a proxy at a shareholders meeting. Also see *proxy*.

prudent A word that indicates caution or a conservative approach. Normally the least bold option is labelled the prudent option.

prudential limits or requirements Regulations that apply to financial intermediaries such as banks that ensure that their businesses are managed in a cautious or prudent manner and that liquidity in markets is assured. Also see *liquid asset; prudent*.

PSCE See *private sector credit extension*.

PSM See *Professional Securities Market*.

PSNCR See *public sector net cash requirement*.

Pt Symbol used for platinum. Also see *platinum*.

PTE The former currency of Portugal, the escudos. Portugal now uses the euro. Also see *euro*.

Pty Ltd When this is attached to the end of a company's name in South Africa or Australia, it indicates a private company with limited liability. Also see *limited liability*.

public company A listed or unlisted company that has a minimum of two shareholders and two directors. Also see *private company; Securities Regulation Panel*.

public debt management The management of all outstanding government debt including changes in the size, composition, type and maturity structure of all debt of the public sector.

Public Investment Corporation (PIC) An organisation that invests money on behalf of public sector entities in South Africa. These entities include the Government Employees Pension Fund, the Associated Institution Pension Fund, the Compensation Commissioner and the Unemployment Insurance Fund. The corporation is wholly

public offer | **purchasing power parity (PPP)**

owned by the government and is one of the largest investment managers in the country. See their website for more details: www.pic.gov.za. Also see *pension fund; Unemployment Insurance Fund.*

public offer The sale of a security that is open to the general public. Public offers usually take the place of offering the securities for sale on recognised stock exchanges. Also see *private placing/placement; security.*

public private partnership (PPP) A financial partnership between the private sector and government. A private company assumes a government function, bears the risks associated with performing that function and is paid a fee for doing so. Governments undertake PPPs when they are unable to undertake the project effectively themselves. Sometimes called a private finance initiative (PFI).

public sector The government itself and all government-owned enterprises. Public sector companies are set up for motives other than profit.

public sector net cash requirement A British term for government deficit.

public spread When there is a sufficient number of a company's shares available to the public to ensure that there is a liquid market in the shares. Also see *liquid.*

public works Infrastructural development activities undertaken by governments. The South African government has a separate ministry to oversee these development activities.

pula (BWP) The currency of Botswana divided into 100 thebe.

pull to par When a bond approaches maturity its price converges to its par value. Also see *bond; bond value.*

pull to redemption See *pull to par.*

punter A gambler.

purchase on margin The purchase of securities through the use of credit facilities afforded by a broker.

purchasing managers index (PMI) A weighted index that contains variables such as new orders, inventories, deliveries, production and employment data. The data is collected from purchasing managers throughout industry. The PMI is considered to be a reliable barometer for manufacturing activity across industry and tends to be a good leading indicator of inflation and the producer price index. The key strength of the data is its timing as it comes out before other key data and gives a good measure of the strength of the manufacturing sector. Also see *inflation; leading indicator; producer price index.*

purchasing power The ability to purchase goods and services with a unit of currency, i.e. the amount of goods or services received for actual cash paid. Under inflationary conditions, the purchasing power of a currency erodes as goods become more and more expensive. The theory of purchasing power parity proposes that differences in inflation rates between currencies is ultimately a predictor of long-term exchange rates between the countries. Also see *purchasing power parity.*

purchasing power parity (PPP) A theory that proposes that differences in inflation rates between currencies are ultimately a predictor of long-term exchange rates between the countries. The rationale underlying the theory is that most goods can be traded internationally at negligible cost. Arbitrage opportunities dictate that prices of goods in different countries must obey the law of one price. If goods are cheaper in one country, residents from other countries will purchase goods in that cheaper market. Hence the price unit of currency A with respect to currency B will in the long run tend to equal the ratio of price levels in country A with respect to the price levels in country B. PPP is expressed quantitatively by the following formula:

$$e = \frac{P}{P_w}$$

where e = exchange rate in foreign currency per unit domestic currency; P = domestic price level; P_w = world price level.

The real exchange rate (r) is often represented as $r = n\frac{P}{P_w}$

where n = the nominal rate in units of foreign currency per unit home currency.

PPP does not make any general assertion about the direction of causation between exchange rates and price levels. Also see *arbitrage; law of one price*.

purchasing power risk The investment risk associated with the impact of inflation on the price of the asset. Also see *inflation*.

pure expectation pricing theory A theory that postulates that the shape of the yield curve is explained by market expectations of future interest rates. Also see *adaptive expectations; interest rate; liquidity preference theory; market expectation pricing theory; yield curve*.

pure float The exchange rate is classed as a pure float when foreign exchange currency markets are left entirely to private market forces and monetary authorities do not intervene. Sometimes called a free float. Also see *clean float; crawling peg; fixed exchange rate; managed float*.

pure play approach A pure play is a company that focuses on a single line of business. To analyse independent projects, comparison with these focused companies constitutes a pure play approach.

pure yield pickup swap Debt instruments, usually bonds, with low yields are swapped for instruments with higher yields. The trade-off of the swap is that the higher yielding instruments are riskier and the potential for default is higher. Asset managers may use these instruments to balance the risk profiles of their portfolios without the need to buy and sell underlying instruments directly. Also see *swap*.

put See *put option*.

PUT See *property unit trust*.

put bond See *puttable bond*.

put-call parity The price of put and call options is normally directly proportional due to conversion arbitrage. The equation between put and call options with the same strike price and exercise dates that defines put-call parity is expressed as follows:

$$C - P = S_0 - PV(X)$$

where C = the price of a call; P = the price of a put; S_0 = the price of the security at the date the option is written; $PV(X)$ = the present value of the exercise price.

The equation is modelled on the cash flows associated with selling a call, buying a put and funding the exercise with a loan. Also see *call option; conversion arbitrage; strike price; put option*.

put call ratio

$$\text{put call ratio} = \frac{\text{volume of put options sold}}{\text{volume of call options sold}}$$

put option The right to sell an asset at a fixed price during a particular period in time. The opposite of a call option. If an investor expects the price of an asset to drop, an option can be bought to give the holder the right to sell the asset at a fixed price at a future date. When the price of the underlying asset drops, the asset can be bought on the market at the discounted price and sold at the higher price through the put option. The price of puts and calls is linked through put-call parity. The payoff relationships of purchasing and selling a put option are illustrated below. Also see *call option; put-call parity*.

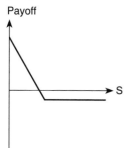

Purchasing a put (long)

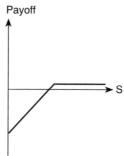

Selling a put (short)

put or pay agreement A supply agreement whereby the supplier agrees to supply a particular quantity of goods at predefined times. If the supplier fails to meet the delivery obligations, it is required to compensate the purchaser for any production or revenue losses or costs associated with finding a new supplier. Also see *take or pay contract*.

put provision This is an option built into a bond that allows the holder of the bond to redeem the bond at par value at specific or a range of dates. Bond instruments with these provisions are issued in the market infrequently and are often called puttable bonds. Also see *puttable bond*.

put ratio back spread A trading strategy created with options that profits from falling prices but limits losses if prices rise. It is constructed by combining put options of different strike prices. Also see *bear; put option*.

puttable bond The holder of these bonds has the right to sell the bonds back to the issuer at par value at predetermined dates. The bond is said to have a put provision. Also see *par value; put provision*.

put through A stock market transaction where a broker has a matched buy and sell order for the same share from two separate clients. If the transaction value is greater than a threshold amount, then the transaction can be concluded at any price irrespective of the prevailing market prices, provided both parties agree. Also see *broker; special bargain*.

p-value The p-value of a test statistic is the probability of observing a test statistic at least as extreme as the one computed given that the null hypothesis is true. For example, if there is a population with a normal distribution and a mean of 50, the probability of getting a sample with a mean value of 58 can be worked out.
- If the p-value is less than 0.01, the test is highly significant and there is overwhelming evidence that the alternative hypothesis is true.
- If p lies between 0.01 and 0.05, there is strong evidence that the alternative hypothesis is true.
- If p exceeds 0.1, then there is no evidence that the alternative hypothesis is true.

Also see *acceptance region; null hypothesis*.

PVT Private.

pyramid An ownership structure that is set up to sell portions of companies off and maintain ultimate control of the cash-generating asset. For example, a holding company A may own 100% of company B. Company A may sell off 49% of company B thereby realising cash and maintaining control over the company. In a similar fashion company B may have a 100% stake in another company C of which it sells 49%. In this way company A maintains control of B and C even though it has only a 26% economic interest.

QAR The Qatar rial divided into 100 dirhams.

Q-ratio A method of looking at investment decisions by comparing the market value of an asset to the cost of reproducing such an asset:

$$Q = \frac{\text{cost of existing}}{\text{cost of new}}$$

This ratio shows competitiveness in the property industry where it answers the key question, what does it cost to build a new building versus buying an existing building? The question is important to the economy. If the market values assets more highly than the cost of replacing them, businesses start building and developing new assets. On average, the ratio should be equal to one and the time series of the ratio should show mean reversion characteristics. This ratio is sometimes referred to as Tobin's Q. Also see *mean reversion*.

qualified institutional investor A purchaser who can buy unregistered securities in the US governed by Rule 144A. Also see *private placing/placement; Rule 144A*.

qualifying lender A lender that qualifies to participate in a syndicated loan transaction. To qualify, lenders may need, for example, branches in the jurisdiction of the borrower to gain tax benefits.

quality shares Shares issued by top companies that have proven records of earning profits and distributing dividends.

quality spread The difference in yield of two financial instruments reflecting the underlying credit risk differentials.

quality swap A swap from government bonds to corporate bonds. Investors often enter into these swaps if credit spreads are expected to narrow. Also see *credit spread; government bond; swap*.

quantity theory of money A theory that relates money supply to prices and income levels in an economy. Simplistically, the quantity theory of money is defined by:

$$MV = PY$$

where M = money supply; V = velocity of circulation; P = the price level; Y = the income.

Also see *money supply*.

quarterly Financial statements published by a company every three months.

quartile The three values of a variable that partition the data set the variable may assume into four equal parts. The central value is usually called the median. The values below and above the median are called the upper and lower quartiles. Also see *median*.

quasi equity A hybrid security that is usually a deeply subordinated debt instrument or a senior equity-type security such as a preference share. Quasi equity shareholders are entitled to cash flows or liquidation proceeds after more senior debt holders and before ordinary equity shareholders. Sometimes called a hybrid instrument because they have features of both debt and equity. Also see *hybrid; preference share; seniority; subordinate*.

quick ratio See *acid test (quick) ratio*.

quid pro quo A trade-off. Something gained for something conceded. Also see *reciprocity*.

quorum The minimum number of people required to be present at a company meeting for the meeting or decisions made at the meeting to be formally recognised.

quote (quotation)
1. An indication of the price and other terms and conditions at which a seller of goods or services is prepared to trade at.
2. A term used to indicate that a security is traded on an exchange.

quoted price For a bond the quoted price is the clean price. Also see *clean price*.

quote driven A system of trading that requires a market maker to quote two-way prices for people to buy and sell shares. Also see *ask price; bid price; market maker; order driven*.

R A credit rating that indicates that the company is under regulatory supervision due to it not meeting its financial obligations. An R rating is worse than a CI rating. Also see *credit rating*.

R153 A South African government bond with the following key variables:
- Issue date: 22 June 1989
- Fixed coupon rate: 13% p.a. (semi-annual payments)
- Maturity date: 31 August 2011

R157 A South African government bond with the following key variables:
- Issue date: 18 January 1991
- Fixed coupon rate: 13.5% p.a. (semi-annual payments)
- Maturity date: 15 September 2016

R186 A South African government bond with the following key variables:
- Issue date: 01 April 1998
- Fixed coupon rate: 10.5% p.a. (semi-annual payments)
- Maturity date: 21 December 2027

R189 A South African government bond with the following key variables:
- Issue date: 20 March 2000
- Fixed coupon rate – inflation-linked principal: 6.25% p.a. (semi-annual payments)
- Maturity date: 31 November 2013

R196 A South African government bond with the following key variables:
- Issue date: 22 November 2005
- Fixed coupon rate: 10% p.a. (semi-annual payments)
- Maturity date: 28 February 2009

R197 A South African government bond with the following key variables:
- Issue date: 30 May 2001
- Fixed coupon rate – inflation-linked principal: 5.5% p.a. (semi-annual payments)
- Maturity date: 07 December 2023

R201 A South African government bond with the following key variables:
- Issue date: 27 May 2003
- Fixed coupon rate: 8.75% p.a. (semi-annual payments)
- Maturity date: 21 December 2014

R202 A South African government bond with the following key variables:
- Issue date: 20 August 2003
- Fixed coupon rate – inflation-linked principal: 3.45% p.a. (semi-annual payments)
- Maturity date: 07 December 2033

R203 A South African government bond with the following key variables:
- Issue date: 07 May 2004
- Fixed coupon rate: 8.25% p.a. (semi-annual payments)
- Maturity date: 15 September 2017

R204 A South African government bond with the following key variables:
- Issue date: 11 August 2004
- Fixed coupon rate: 8% p.a. (semi-annual payments)
- Maturity date: 21 December 2018

R206 A South African government bond with the following key variables:
- Issue date: 11 August 2005
- Fixed coupon rate: 7.5% p.a. (semi-annual payments)
- Maturity date: 15 January 2014

R207 A South African government bond with the following key variables:
- Issue date: 17 June 2005
- Fixed coupon rate: 7.25% p.a. (semi-annual payments)
- Maturity date: 15 January 2020

R^2 **coefficient of determination (R-squared)** The proportion of the variance of a response variable that is explained by the predictor variables when a linear regression is performed. R^2 indicates how much of the total variance is contained or explained by the linear regression. The formula for R^2 is:

$$R^2 = \frac{E_{SS}}{T_{SS}} = 1 - \frac{R_{SS}}{T_{SS}}$$

where E_{SS} and T_{SS} are given by:

$$E_{SS} = \sum_{i=1}^{n}(\hat{y}_i - \bar{y})^2 \text{ and } T_{SS} = \sum_{i=1}^{n}(y_i - \bar{y})^2$$

where E_{SS} = the explained sum of squares; R_{SS} = the residual sum of squares; T_{SS} = the total sum of squares.

Also see *explained sum of squares; linear regression; variance*.

raider An entity that specialises in purchasing undervalued assets through hostile takeovers. Also see *vulture fund*.

rainbow option An option that is driven by multiple sources of uncertainty. Also see *compound option; option*.

rally A period of substantial upward short-term price activity in a generally downward trending market. A rally is the opposite of a correction where there is a brief downward price movement in an upward trending market. Also see *correction*.

rand (ZAR) The currency of the Republic of South Africa divided into 100 cents.

rand hedge South African stocks that benefit from rand weakness and tend not to be negatively influenced by rand strength. These stocks have predominantly foreign currency costs and foreign currency income. Companies such as SAB, Richemont and even Sasol are considered to be rand hedges. They tend to be more risky due to their exposure to the volatility in the exchange rates. Also see *rand leverage; rand neutral; rand play; volatility*.

rand leverage South African stocks that benefit from rand weakness. These companies have foreign income and rand-based costs. Mining and tourism companies are examples of rand leveraged stocks. Also see *rand hedge; rand neutral; rand play*.

rand neutral South African stocks that neither benefit nor gain from rand strength or weakness. These companies have approximately half their income in rands and half in international currencies such as the US dollar, for example Old Mutual. Also see *rand hedge; rand leverage; rand play*.

random walk with drift A process that is a random walk with drift is defined by the following formula:

$$Y_t = \alpha + Y_{t-1} + e_t$$

where e_t = the random variable; α = the drift and must be non-zero.

With α non-zero, this allows for changes in variables to be on average non-zero. Also see *Brownian motion; drift; geometric Brownian motion; mean reversion; stochastic difference equation; unit root*.

rand play South African stocks that have costs in dollars and revenue in rands are negatively correlated with rand weakness and benefit from rand strength. In South Africa, companies like Edcon, Woolworths and other importers are generally considered to be rand plays as they import large quantities of goods which they ultimately sell in rands. Also see *rand hedge; rand leverage; rand neutral*.

Rand Refinery A refinery in South Africa that specialises in the refinement, transport and sale of newly mined gold. Gold from mining operations that is not of required purity is sent to the Rand Refinery where it is refined to a purity suitable for bullion and jewellery. The Rand Refinery also provides other services including storage, sales and distribution. Also see *bullion*.

range The largest less the smallest value of a data set.

range forward contract See *zero cost collar*.

rank A number assigned to an observation according to some criterion.

RAPM See *risk adjusted performance measure*.

RAROC See *risk adjusted return on capital*.

RARORAC Risk adjusted return on risk adjusted capital. Also see *risk adjusted return on capital*.

RAS Russian accounting standards.

ratchet effect The process of variables such as wages undergoing increases and not undergoing decreases. These economic variables are often called sticky downwards. Also see *sticky*.

rate anticipation swap See *interest rate anticipation swap*.

rate of exchange See *exchange rate*.

rate of interest See *interest rate*.

rate of turnover The rate at which assets are turned over. Also see *inventory turnover*.

rate trigger A trigger in a bond contract that allows the bonds to be called if interest rates fall by predefined amounts or levels. Calling in the bonds in a low interest rate environment enables the company to refinance the bonds at more favourable current market rates. Also see *interest rate*.

rating See *credit rating*.

rating agency See *credit rating agency*.

ratings grid See *pricing grid*.

ratings service See *credit rating agency*.

ratio analysis The use of financial ratios to assess the performance and financial condition of a company. There are hundreds of different ratios used across many industries to perform these analyses. Also see the more commonly used ratios including *acid test (quick) ratio; cash ratio; current ratio; interval measure; return on assets; return on equity*.

rationalisation The process where a company reorganises to increase efficiency and refocus on its target markets. Rationalisation may involve the retrenchment of workers and the closure of business units. Also see *downsizing; rightsizing*.

ratio Q See *Q-ratio*.

RBZ Reserve Bank of New Zealand.

RCF See *revolving credit facility*.

RCH See *recognised clearing house*.

RD See *record date*.

RDC See *Regulations and Decisions Committee*.

real The currency of Brazil divided into 100 centavos.

real asset An asset of tangible form.

real cash flow Real cash flow is the nominal cash flow discounted by the appropriate inflation rates so that it can be expressed in real terms:

$$\text{real cash flow} = \frac{\text{nominal cash flow}}{(1 + \text{inflation rate})^n}$$

where n = number of years.

Also see *Fisher effect/equation; inflation*.

real effective exchange rate A broad measure of the prices of one country's goods and services relative to the prices of goods and services in the country's trading partners. It is calculated as a weighted average of the ratios of a country's domestic price index to the price indices of its foreign trading partners, where the indices are expressed in the same currency units. Also see *purchasing power parity; real exchange rate; weighted average*.

real estate swap A swap where money is exchanged against a real estate property index. Also see *swap*.

real exchange rate The exchange rate quoted in money terms at any particular time is the nominal exchange rate. For analytical purposes a real exchange rate can also be calculated by taking price movements into account. The real exchange rate is therefore a measure of the nominal exchange rate adjusted for differences in the inflation between countries:

$$e_r = e \frac{P_w}{P}$$

where $\frac{P_w}{P}$ = the inflationary differential; P = the price level (CPI) in the country of interest; P_w = the price level in the foreign country or world; e = the nominal exchange rate.

The real exchange rate is important because it measures a country's economic competitiveness. Also see *bilateral real exchange rate; consumer price index; inflation; nominal exchange rate.*

real interest rate The interest rate or rate of return that has been adjusted for inflation. This is the amount by which the actual/nominal interest rate exceeds the rate of inflation. Real interest rates are the effective rate investors demand for forgoing the use of their money. The rate is calculated using the Fisher equation. Also see *Fisher effect/equation; inflation; interest rate; nominal interest rate.*

realisable asset See *liquidity.*

realised gain The gain that is made when physical profits are actually taken. For example, an investor may have bought shares for R80, sold them for R100 and has therefore realised a gain of R20. However, if the investor is still holding the shares and has not sold, then the gain has not been realised. Also see *mark to market.*

realised profit See *realised gain.*

realised yield The return already earned from a bond. The return includes coupons already paid. The realised yield is different from the concept of yield to maturity which is the rate required by investors to invest in a bond and receive future earnings from that bond. Also see *yield to maturity.*

real option The right, but not the obligation, to take a particular action such as deferring, expanding, contracting or abandoning at a predetermined cost for a predetermined time. The value of the option is contingent on the uncertain value of a real asset, for example an irreversible investment opportunity in a new project. Management can affect the value of the underlying asset. Also see *asset; option.*

real option analysis (ROA) An analysis based on sets of options on fixed assets. Also see *fixed asset.*

real price The price discounted to a base year to account for inflation. To do the calculation the current price is discounted by the previous year's inflation measure and then the year before that.

$$\text{real price}_{\text{year x}} = \text{current price} \times \frac{1}{(1+\text{CPI}_{n-1})} \times \frac{1}{(1+\text{CPI}_{n-2})} \times ... \times \frac{1}{(1+\text{CPI}_{n-x})}$$

$$\text{real price}_{\text{year x}} = \text{current price} \prod_{i=1}^{x} \frac{1}{(1+\text{CPI}_{n-i})}$$

The real price is sometimes referred to as the constant dollar, pound or rand price. Also see *base year; inflation; real cash flow.*

real rate See *real return.*

real return The return of an investment adjusted for inflation. Also see *inflation; real interest rate.*

real terms Financial data adjusted for the effects of inflation. Also see *inflation.*

real time Information that is available immediately.

real value See *real price.*

rebalancing Portfolios are rebalanced when the prices of assets change relative to one another and the portfolio is adjusted to account for these price differentials.

rebate
1. The income stream from the holder of a security to the party that has been lent a security under stock or other security lending arrangements. Also see *stock lending*.
2. A discount given on a product or service that is returned to the purchaser after payment has been received for the initial purchase.
3. A tax payment returned to the taxpayer after completion of a tax evaluation.
4. A discount on a bill of exchange before the final date of maturity of the bill.

recapitalisation Changing the financial mix (capitalisation) of a firm either by raising equity to reduce debt or raising debt to reduce the proportion of equity. Also see *firm*.

receivables See *creditor*.

receivable securities Securities that are to be received by a purchaser or depositor for a transaction that will be settled at a future date. Also see *futures contract; option*.

receivables turnover A ratio that measures how quickly or efficiently a company can collect monies from clients on sales made. The ratio is defined by:

$$\text{receivables turnover} = \frac{\text{net credit sales}}{\text{accounts receivable}}$$

Sometimes companies may report the ratio as a proportion of sales which may distort the metric somewhat if a significant portion of sales are in cash. Also see *asset management ratios*.

receiver
1. A person appointed to administer the assets of another entity.
2. See *receiver of revenue*.

receiver of revenue A government department tasked with collecting tax revenue. In South Africa, the receiver is the South African Revenue Service (SARS).

receivership The legal process of creditors forcing security against assets of a company or forcing a change of management. Also see *event of default*.

recession A decline in economic activity over a period of time. Technically, a recession is defined as two successive quarters of negative GDP growth. Recessions are associated with a downturn in the business cycle, lower employment, decreasing inflation and falling levels of investment. A prolonged recession is called a depression. Also see *depression; inflation*.

reciprocity A term derived from the word reciprocal that indicates that one party concedes on a particular condition if the other party makes concessions elsewhere. Golf clubs often have a system of reciprocity whereby a member of club A is afforded member privileges at club B and members at B are afforded privileges at A. Also see *quid pro quo*.

recognised clearing house (RCH) A clearing house recognised by the UK financial regulator, the FSA. Also see *clearing house; Financial Services Authority*.

recognition The process of incorporating in the balance sheet or income statement an item that meets the definition of an accounting element and satisfies the following criteria for recognition:
- It is probable that any future economic benefit associated with the item will flow to or from the entity.
- The item has a cost or value that can be measured with a strong degree of reliability.

Also see *balance sheet; income statement*.

record date (RD) The date at which a company's securities ownership register is checked and dividend or coupon payments are allocated against that register. Sometimes called a books closed date. Also see *cum dividend; cum interest; declaration date; dividend; ex dividend.*

recourse If a borrower should default on a debt obligation, the lenders have the ability to claim for damages from the borrower's parent, sponsor or guarantor. This is the opposite of non-recourse lending where lenders cannot seek higher level compensation for damages. Also see *non-recourse; sponsor.*

recourse agreement An agreement under a lease where the retailer or agent is tasked with recovering monies due under lease or rental agreements.

recoverable amount The higher of an asset's net selling price and its net present value. Also see *net present value; net selling price.*

recovery The amount a creditor receives when a borrower defaults. Also see *default; loss given default.*

recovery rate The proportion of the face value of debt that a debt holder can recover for a given credit event. These numbers are often quoted as the number of cents in a dollar, pence in a pound or cents in a rand. Also see *face value; loss given default.*

redeemable bond A bond that can be redeemed, i.e. the capital is repaid to the holder of the bond by the issuer before the maturity date at certain future intervals or dates specified in the contract. Sometimes called a callable bond. Also see *puttable bond.*

redeemable preference share A preference share that is redeemable, i.e. the capital will be repaid to the holder of the preference share by the issuing company at a specified future date or over a given future period of time. Also see *convertible preference share; participating preference share; preference share.*

redemption The process of paying the principal value of a bond or outstanding utilisations on a loan, prior to or at the date of maturity. Also see *bond.*

redemption date See *maturity.*

redemption price See *redemption value.*

redemption value The value or price of a financial instrument at maturity. The redemption value is often called the face value, par value or nominal value of the instrument. Also see *face value; nominal value; par value.*

rediscount The process of discounting short-term financial instruments such as bills of exchange or treasury bills a second or further time. Central banks often purchase discounted securities in exchange for cash at a rate lower than the initial discount rate. The central banks rediscount in lieu of interest payments for the cash handed over. The effect of central banks rediscounting is a release of cash into the financial system. The securities used in these operations are often referred to as eligible paper. Also see *bill of exchange; central bank; discounting; eligible paper; treasury bill.*

rediscount rate The rate at which a central bank rediscounts, or sometimes discounts, short-term financial instruments such as bills of exchange or treasury bills. Also see *bill of exchange; central bank; marginal lending rate; treasury bill.*

reduced form equation An equation that expresses the value of a variable in terms of its own lags, lags of other endogenous variables, current and past values of exogenous variables and disturbance terms. Also see *autocorrelation.*

reducing balance depreciation The reduction rate in the value of an asset on a company's books is applied to the current book value of the asset annually. The value is reduced by smaller and smaller nominal amounts each year. For example, an asset may be depreciated by 20% of its current book value each year. Also see *asset; book value; straight line method of depreciation*.

reduction of capital The reduction in the authorised share capital of a company. A motion to do this is usually passed as a resolution at a company general meeting. Also see *annual general meeting; resolution; special general meeting*.

redundant
1. Information that has become null and void due to the release of new information.
2. To be made redundant is to lose one's job.

reference entity The issuer of a debt obligation with respect to a credit derivative. For example, an investor may purchase a credit default swap (CDS) instrument from a bank written against a debt obligation of a reference entity such as a corporate. If the corporate defaults on its debt obligations, the bank would compensate the investor under the terms of the CDS. Also see *credit derivative*.

reference index The index that a derivative is referenced against.

reference rate
1. The base rate at which banks benchmark lending. Also see *base rate*.
2. The interest rate against which various swaps and derivatives are referenced.

refinancing The replacement of existing debt with new debt.

refinancing risk The risk that the refinancing of maturing loans will be more costly than current debt or the risk that lenders will not be willing to advance further loans at all. Refinancing risk has the possible implication that the cost of borrowing in the future may exceed the predicted costs today. If a company uses short-term debt as part of the long-term capital structure of the business, then this risk will be particularly prevalent. For example, a three-year project is initially financed with a one-year loan at 6%. When that loan matures at the end of year 1, there is a risk that the new rate on the new loan will be higher than the first loan's rate of 6%, thus jeopardising the financeability of the project. Also see *capital structure; reinvestment risk; short-term debt*.

refunded bond A bond that has its principal and coupon cash flows set aside in an escrow account or investment so that it can be paid off on the date of maturity. Also see *escrow*.

refunding See *refinancing*.

registered capital See *authorised share capital*.

registered form The ownership of a bond is registered by the issuer and payment is made directly to the owner on record. Also see *bearer; bond*.

registered office An office where a register of the company's shares is kept and is the official address of the company that appears on company stationery.

registered owner The shareholder in the register of members. Also see *register of members*.

registered security An electronic database entry recording who owns a security and who is entitled to the cash flows associated with it. Also see *electronic scrip register*.

register of members
1. A list of members in a nominee account held by a broker. Also see *nominee account*.
2. A list of shareholders and their respective shareholdings maintained by a company.

registrar The entity responsible for handling a company's register of members. Also see *register of members*.

registration The recording of the title to securities. The record is held by the company secretary.

regression The method by which a linear relationship is derived from a data set. The value of one variable is described as a linear combination of the other variables. As an example in two dimensions, a regression can be viewed as plotting a best fit straight line to a scatter plot of data points. Applying the equation $y = mx + c$ where m is the slope and c is the intercept to the best fit line is a crude method of determining the linear regression. Regression can be used for prediction, hypothesis testing and determining causality. Also see *causality; least squares regression*.

regression model A mathematical model of the form:

$$Y = \alpha + \beta X + e$$

where Y = the dependent variable; X = the independent variable; e = a set of errors.

The above model can be of higher dimensions by making β an $n \times 1$ matrix and making X and Y n length vectors. Also see *least squares regression; regression*.

Regulations and Decisions Committee (RDC) The financial authority in the UK that undertakes prosecuting and disciplinary actions in conjunction with the FSA. Also see *Financial Services Authority*.

regulatory capital See *capital adequacy*.

rehypothecation Securities held by a lender that are in the lender's possession because they have been hypothecated as security in lending operations. The process of rehypothecation is when the lender uses those securities in its possession (which it does not technically own) as security to borrow money from other parties. Also see *hypothecation*.

reinsurance The process of insurance companies minimising their risk on large insurance exposures through selling down or reinsuring that exposure to other insurance companies and reinsurers.

reinsurance ratio A ratio that roughly indicates the degree of risk an insurance company is exposed to. It is generally calculated by the following:

$$\text{reinsurance ratio} = \frac{\text{gross premium income} - \text{reinsurance premium paid}}{\text{reinsurance premium}}$$

Also see *reinsurance*.

reinsurer A reinsurance company that takes on some of the risk that other insurance companies are exposed to, thereby assisting in adjusting the risk exposure profile of those companies. Also see *long-term insurer; short-term insurer; underwriter*.

reinvestment protection swap A switch from high coupon bonds to zero coupon bonds. This is done to eliminate reinvestment risk. Also see *bond; swap; zero coupon bond*.

reinvestment rate risk The uncertainty concerning rates at which intermediate cash flows can be reinvested. A zero coupon bond does not have these risks because there is no intermediate flow in the form of coupons. Short-term bonds are less risky because there is no significant amount of time to recover returns. Also see *cash flow; coupon*.

reinvestment risk The risk that interest rates will be lower at a future date when an interest-bearing instrument matures. Also see *refinancing risk*.

REIT Real estate investment trust.

related party A business or person that does business with another and has a vested interest. An example is the spouse of a director or an intercompany transaction in a group. Sometimes called a connected person. Also see *connected person; vested interest*.

relationship banking The formation of relationships between banks and clients. The relationships allow the banks to understand their clients' businesses and to offer a suite of appropriate products at appropriate costs in the most efficient manner.

relative equity market standard deviation A method by which the country risk premium (CRP), as determined by a method such as the default risk spread, is adjusted for the volatility in the equity markets.

$$CRP_{country\ x} = MRP_{home\ country} \times \text{relative standard deviation}_{country\ x}$$

where $\text{relative standard deviation}_{country\ x} = \dfrac{\sigma_{country\ x}}{\sigma_{home\ country}}$

This approach is based on historical data and is often biased by a lack of liquidity in developing markets giving artificially low risk measures. The standard deviations must be calculated in the same currencies. Also see *beta approach; combined market risk premium approach; country risk premium; default risk spread; market risk premium; volatility*.

relative strength The price of a share relative to that of the market. Relative strength is calculated by dividing a specific share price by the market index for the day. If the relative strength is going up, the share in question is rising faster than the overall market.

relative volatility The volatility of one asset compared to another. Usually calculated by dividing the volatility of the asset in question by the reference asset. Also see *volatility*.

relative yield The yield of a single bond against another bond.

relending The process of one financial institution, usually a multilateral agency such as the World Bank, lending to another financial institution who then lends to the ultimate borrower. Sometimes called onlending. Also see *World Bank*.

relevant cost Future cash flows that differ between alternatives. Relevant costs and revenues that will be changed by entering a business. Also see *cash flow*.

releveraging The process of introducing debt into the capital structure of a business generally after debt has been paid down. Also see *capital structure*.

reliance letter A letter issued by a consultant or firm producing a report such as a due diligence study indicating that a third party can rely on the information contained in the report. Also see *due diligence*.

remaining life How long an asset such as a mine will be in operation before it becomes unprofitable to run. For a mine, the term life of mine may be used.

remittance The process of workers earning money in foreign countries transferring that money to their home country.

remuneration The payment paid to employees for services provided. Car and housing allowances are included in addition to the salary or wages. The total package is expressed as a cost to company. Also see *cost to company*.

renminbi A term sometimes used to describe the currency of China. It is usually used together with the word yuan. Also see *yuan*.

renounceable right See *rights issue*.

rent Monies paid for the use of an asset. The term rent is normally associated with the lease of land or buildings. Also see *capital lease*.

renting back See *sale and leaseback*.

renunciation The surrender or transfer of rights and/or obligations. An example of renunciation is the transfer of rights in a rights issue. Also see *rights issue*.

reoffer spread The spread at which corporate bonds trade over risk-free securities such as government bonds. Also see *yield curve*.

repatriation The process of liquidating a foreign investment and taking the proceeds back to the investor's home country.

repayment schedule The plan or schedule of repayments put in place that borrowers must follow to pay back a loan in full.

replacement capital covenant A covenant used in hybrid capital instruments that sets outs the terms and conditions under which hybrids can be redeemed and what financial instruments such as cash and shares can be used in the redemption process. Also see *hybrid*.

replacement cost The costs associated with the replacement of an asset. Also see *value to business*.

replicating portfolio A method of determining valuations and characteristics by comparison to similar entities. An everyday example is selling a second-hand car. To determine the value, the seller may look at newspaper ads and the Internet to determine the price at which similar cars are selling. Based on this data, the seller determines a price at which to sell the car.

repo See *repurchase agreement*.

repo rate
1. The interest rate charged under a repurchase agreement. Also see *interest rate; repurchase agreement*.
2. In South Africa, the rate at which the South African Reserve Bank (SARB) lends money to banking institutions. The SARB lends to banks through the accommodation or discount window and lends against securities such as government bonds and treasury bills. The accommodation lending against securities takes the form of a repurchase agreement (repo). Also see *bank rate; marginal lending rate; repurchase agreement; South African Reserve Bank*.

reporting date The last day of the accounting period covered by financial statements or by an interim financial report. Also see *financial statements*.

reporting deadline The time deadline after a transaction in which the relevant details of the transaction must be reported to an exchange or relevant authority.

reporting period The period for which a company's financial statements are reported. Also see *reporting date*.

repossession The act of seizing a borrower's assets if they have defaulted on debt obligations such as payments.

representation
1. In a loan agreement, a representation clause covers details on how borrowers communicate and signal compliance with the terms of the loan agreement. Representations cover aspects such as legal status, binding obligations, non-conflict with other obligations, power and authority, validity of documentation, governing law, tax issues, no default, financial statements and pari passu ranking of debt. Representations usually repeat periodically. Also see *pari passu*.
2. A statement of fact, not a promise. Also see *warranty*.

repudiate To reject something, state that it is untrue or that a party disagrees with or does not accept a term or condition.

repudiation The process of backing out of a contract once entered into. Also see *non-repudiation*.

repurchase See *repurchase agreement*.

repurchase agreement A repurchase agreement (RP or repo) is a financial transaction often used in money markets and through central bank accommodation. A more accurate and descriptive term is sale and repurchase agreement, since what transpires is the sale of securities now for cash by party A, the cash borrower, to party B, the cash lender, with the promise made by A to B to repurchase the securities later. Party A pays the requisite implicit interest to B at the time of repurchase. The implicit interest rate is known as the repo rate. The difference between the selling and repurchase price represents the interest on the funds advanced. Repo transactions are essentially a form of secured lending as possession and title of securities change hands with the exchange of cash.

Repurchase agreements are normally treated as secured lending in economic statistics. The economic benefits on the securities such as coupons on bonds accrue to the cash borrower and are retained on the borrower's balance sheet. They generally attract lower interest charges due to lower risk associated with the security backing.

The repo market is valuable in times of financial stress as it enables the flow of cash between central banks and financial institutions that ultimately provides the liquidity to keep financial markets functioning. Also see *accommodation; bond; interest rate; money market; repo rate; reverse repurchase repo; secured*.

required reserves See *reserve requirement*.

rescheduling The renegotiation of the terms of a debt package. Rescheduling often extends the tenor of the debt and takes place when borrowers are finding it difficult to comply with the original conditions.

reserve account
1. Effectively a 'vault' of money in the form of foreign currency and gold that is held by a central bank. Central banks use the reserve accounts to manage and influence exchange rates. Also see *central bank; foreign reserves*.

2. A company account that sets funds aside for a particular purpose or contingency.

reserve asset An asset such as gold and foreign exchange, typically widely traded currencies such as US dollars, pounds or euros, kept by central banks. Also see *central bank; reserve account*.

reserve bank accommodation Financial institutions borrow from central banks when they are illiquid. They do so through an accommodation window or discount window. Also see *accommodation; central bank; illiquid*.

reserve bank bill See *reserve bank debenture*.

reserve bank debenture A short-term transferable discount security that is issued by central banks for banking institutions to invest short-term excess funds. The discount nature of the security implies that the central bank pays the principal plus the interest at the redemption date. Also see *central bank; discount security; security*.

reserve capital Part of the issued share capital of a company that will only be called upon if the company is wound up. Also see *issued share capital*.

reserve currency See *reserve asset*.

reserve life coverage ratio (RLCR) A loan life cover ratio tailored for mining or oil and gas projects:

$$\text{reserve life coverage ratio (RLCR)} = \frac{\sum \text{discounted cash flows available for financing}}{\text{principle outstanding}}$$

Also see *debt service cover ratio; loan life cover ratio; project life coverage ratio; reserve tail ratio*.

reserve money The note and coin liability of a central bank plus domestic currency deposits of banks and mutual banks with the central bank. Also see *central bank; liability; reserve account*.

reserve price The minimum price a seller is willing to accept in an auction. Should bids above the reserve price not be received, the sale will not be executed.

reserve requirement The amount of money banks must hold in cash and other liquid assets versus the level of their deposits. For example, if the reserve requirement or cash reserve ratio is 10% and a deposit of R100 is made, then the bank may lend out R90 and keep the remaining R10 in reserve. Central banks set reserve requirements and use the vehicle as a policy tool to control inflation through effective control of money supply. Also see *capital adequacy; central bank; inflation; liquid asset; money supply*.

reserves
1. Funds that constitute an asset other than share capital of a company acquired through retained profit or through the issue of share capital at a premium over issue price. The retained and undistributed profits of a company that form part of the shareholders' capital in the business or reserves can be used for expansion of the business in the future or can be distributed to shareholders if distributable. Also see *distributable reserves; non-distributable reserves*.
2. Funds that deposit-taking institutions are required to maintain on deposit at central banks. The amount varies with set policy and the liabilities of the deposit-taking institutions. Also see *central bank; liquid asset*.
3. The economically mineable portion of a mineral resource.

reserve tail The reserves that remain after the payment of the project financing on a mining or oil and gas project.

reserve tail ratio The percentage of reserves that financiers ignore when sizing debt and evaluating resource project financing such as mining or oil and gas. The ratio offsets the risk of fluctuating reserves and other technical risks associated with extracting the mineral. The ratio is indicated as a percentage of the total measured mineral resources. Also see *debt service cover ratio; loan life cover ratio; measured mineral resources; project life coverage ratio; reserve life coverage ratio.*

reset margin The margin above an index. For example, if a company enters into a loan agreement and pays an interest rate of JIBAR + 30 bps, then the reset margin is 30 bps. Also see *interest rate; JIBAR.*

RESI Index of resources or mining shares traded on the JSE. The RESI can be traded as a derivative on SAFEX. Also see *ALSI; derivative; FINDI; index; INDI; JSE; South African Futures Exchange.*

resident-based income tax A system of taxation where residents of a country are subject to the taxation system of that country.

residual The difference between the observed and predicted value of a particular variable. In a linear regression, the residual is the difference between the observed variable and the predicted variable by application of the regression coefficients. Also see *linear regression.*

residual asset value
1. The value of an asset after the completion of a lease term.
2. The value of an asset in excess of the financing secured against that asset.

residual cover The cash flows from a project after settlement of debt financing. The residual cover is expressed as a percentage of the original loan. Also see *loan life cover ratio.*

residual cushion The amount of cash flow after debt financing.

residual income (RI) The economic benefit in excess of the required return on investment:

residual income (RI) = $NPAT + (I) \times (1 - T_c) - WACC \times (T_A - CL)$

where $NPAT$ = net profit after tax; I = the cost of debt; T_c = the corporate tax rate; $WACC$ = the weighted average cost of capital; T_A = the total assets; CL = the current liabilities.

Current liabilities are usually subtracted because they are not part of the permanent capital structure of the business. Identify whether some of the short-term liabilities are a current payment of long-term debt. If they are, then they should probably be excluded from current liabilities. Finance charges are reverse added to income (reversed) because net profit is compared to WACC which already includes the measure of finance charges.

Advantages of using residual income as an analysis technique are the following:
- Users tend to invest in anything that provides significant returns in excess of WACC.
- The method encourages investments aimed at growth.

Disadvantages are the following:
- Different WACCs are used for different divisions of a company with different associated risks. The method does not account for this.
- The method forms a short-term view.
- RI produces an absolute number so divisional comparison is difficult.
- It is not a good measure to use if one does not have control over investment decisions.

- RI uses financial accounting measures as a means of evaluating cash flows and is thus not always measured accurately. Adjustments to accounting statements to reflect the underlying economic reality are often needed.

Economic value added (EVA) is an adaptation of the residual income method. Also see *capital structure; cash flow; current liability; economic value added; long-term debt; net profit; return on investment; weighted average cost of capital*.

residuals (linear regression) When doing a linear regression, the deviations of the data points from the best fit line are termed the residuals:

$$e_i = y_i - \hat{y}_i$$

where $\hat{y}_i$ = the values associated with the least squares (best) fit line. Also see *least squares regression; linear regression*.

residual sum of squares (RSS) The sum of squares of residuals. In a standard regression model where the equation $y_i = a + bx_i + \varepsilon_i$ applies, y and x are the regressand and the regressor respectively, and ε is the error term. The sum of squares of residuals is the sum of squares of estimates of ε_i. Also see *error sum of squares; regression; residuals*.

residual value guarantee A guarantee from a party, typically a third party, that an asset will have a minimum value at a predefined date in the future. For example, a manufacturer of an aircraft guarantees to financiers that in five years the aircraft asset can be sold for a minimum of 25% of its original value.

resistance If the price of a security is rising as a result of the dominance of buyers, a point will be reached where sell orders are triggered effectively lowering the price and thereby maintaining the price at or below the resistance level. Also see *security; support*.

resolution A decision made by the shareholders of a company or their representatives. Resolutions are taken in a democratic voting process where decisions take effect only upon a majority or supermajority vote. Also see *proxy; special resolution*.

restitution See *restitution order*.

restitution order A legal judgement that compensation must be paid by the defendant who is the entity responsible for the loss incurred by the complainant.

restrictive covenant See *negative covenant*.

restructure
1. Adjusting the capital structure of a business. Also see *capital structure*.
2. The process of changing the structure of debt or equities to suit a company's cash flows or needs more effectively.

retail bank A bank that provides financial products and services to and takes deposits from individuals and small businesses. Also see *investment bank*.

retail bond See *retail note*.

retail investor An investor who deals in smaller numbers of shares for private purposes.

retail market Companies and industries directly involved with selling products to end consumers.

retail note A bond issued by a corporation of medium term, typically longer than a single year. The notes pay a fixed rate of interest over the early part of their life (up to nine months) and then pay a floating interest rate thereafter. Most retail notes are callable. Sometimes called a retail bond. Also see *callable bond; floating interest rate*.

retail price index (RPI) A measure of inflation used in the UK. It is measured as the cost of a weighted average basket of goods consumed by an average household. It is a more realistic measure of the cost of living than the CPI because it includes owner-occupied living costs and local property taxes. See www.statistics.gov.uk for more details. Also see *consumer price index; inflation*.

retail tender An offer to purchase shares in a private placement. The tender can specify the desired quantum and the price at which the offer is made.

retained earnings/income Attributable profit not paid out to shareholders as dividends, but rather reinvested in the core business. Also called earned surplus of accumulated earnings or unappropriated profit. Also see *attributable profit; dividend*.

retention of title A transaction where the seller of an asset transfers legal title of the asset only after payment has been received in full. A hire purchase agreement in vehicle finance is an example of such a contract. Also see *hire purchase; repurchase agreement*.

retention ratio A ratio that indicates how much of the profit generated by a company is retained for the future. The retention ratio is given by:

$$b = \frac{\text{addition to retained profit}}{\text{net profit}}$$

The dividend payout ratio is equal to $(1 - b)$. Also see *dividend payout ratio; internal rate of return*.

retirement annuity An annuity investment used to fund the retirement needs of an investor. These annuities often pay a lump sum on retirement and a fixed monthly amount for a specified period thereafter. Also see *annuity*.

retractable bond A bond that has an option the holder can exercise forcing the issuer to call the bond.

return The profit an asset provides quoted as a percentage of the purchase price of the asset:

$$\text{return} = \frac{\text{profit}}{\text{purchase price}}$$

return on assets (ROA) The profit made per unit of invested capital:

$$\text{return on assets (ROA)} = \frac{\text{net profit after tax}}{\text{total assets}}$$

Also see *profitability ratios*.

return on capital employed (ROCE) A ratio that is used to analyse the profitability of a company before tax and interest charges:

$$(\text{ROCE}) = \frac{\text{operating profit}}{\text{capital employed}} = \frac{\text{EBIT}}{\text{shareholders funds} + \text{LT debt}} = \frac{\text{EBIT}}{\text{assets} - \text{current liabilities}}$$

Analysts use this measure to compare the returns of a business against the capital employed regardless of how the capital has been employed. If ROCE is less than a hurdle rate, then the company has destroyed value for shareholders. Approximately equal to return on investment. Also see *capital rationing; hurdle rate; internal rate of return; net present value; residual income; return on investment; weighted average cost of capital*.

return on economic capital (ROEC) The return in excess of the economic capital set aside by a bank or a financial institution. ROEC is measured against a hurdle rate which investment returns must exceed. A more sophisticated measure of return is the risk adjusted return on capital (RAROC). Also see *economic capital; weighted average cost of capital*.

return on equity (ROE) The earnings of a company expressed as a ratio of equity capital:

$$\text{return on equity (ROE)} = \frac{NPAT}{TA - TL}$$

where $NPAT$ = net profit after tax; TA = total assets; TL = total liabilities.

Disadvantages of using ROE as a performance measure are the following:

- It discourages investment that returns under preset return on investment (ROI) and not all projects give WACC beating returns.
- It is not a good measure to use if there is no control over investment decisions.
- It discourages investment with growth outlooks.

A Du Pont analysis breaks down the ROE measure into a series of other metrics and gives more insight into the individual drivers. Average shareholders equity over the course of a reporting period is used in the ROE calculation. Also see *average shareholders equity; du Pont analysis; return on investment; weighted average cost of capital*.

return on investment (ROI) The returns on an equity investment defined by:

$$\text{return on investment (ROI)} = \frac{NPAT + (1 - T_c) \times I}{TA - CL}$$

where $NPAT$ = net profit after tax; T_c = the corporate tax rate; I = the interest rate; TA = total assets; CL = current liabilities.

Current liabilities are subtracted because they are not part of the permanent capital structure of the business. Identify whether some of the short-term liabilities are a current payment of long-term debt. If they are, then they should potentially be excluded from current liabilities. ROI encourages managers to invest in projects that attain returns in excess of the weighted average cost of capital (WACC). Also see *capital structure; current liability; long-term debt; residual income; weighted average cost of capital*.

return on net assets (RONA) After tax and interest return on net assets:

$$\text{return on net assets (RONA)} = \frac{\text{net profit after tax and interest (NPATI)}}{\text{total assets} - \text{current liabilities}}$$

Also see *internal growth rate; net assets; residual income; sustainable growth rate*.

return on shareholders funds See *return on equity*.

return on total assets (ROA) A ratio that measures returns on the assets employed in generating a profit, defined by:

$$\text{return on total assets (ROA)} = \frac{NPBT}{TA}$$

where $NPBT$ = net profit before tax and finance charges; TA = total assets.

ROA is not a good indicator of performance in companies that have large values of embedded unrecognised intellectual property. When applied to suitable companies, the ROA method gives a good measure of how management has been performing in generating turnover from assets. Asset bases do differ from year to year so it is best to look at this ratio over a series of years. Also see *profitability ratios*.

Reuters A company that provides market-related information to the market participants. Also see *Bloomberg; secondary information provider*.

revaluation The restatement of assets and liabilities. Under IFRS revaluations are permissible. Under GAAP they are not permitted. Revaluation of assets has an effect on some performance measures such as ROA and can be used to boost the balance sheet. Also see *balance sheet; Generally Accepted Accounting Principles; International Financial Reporting Standards; return on total assets*.

revaluation model Property, plant and equipment (PPE) is revalued with sufficient regularity. This can strengthen the balance sheet, but metrics such as return on assets can be negatively affected. Also see *balance sheet; property, plant and equipment; return on assets*.

revaluation reserve See *revaluation surplus*.

revaluation surplus An equity account used for increasing the value of an asset. The asset account is debited and the revaluation reserve is credited when revaluing assets upwards. Also see *asset*.

revalued amount of an asset The fair value of an asset at the date of a revaluation less any subsequent accumulated depreciation and accumulated impairment losses. Also see *depreciation; impairment*.

revenue The gross inflow of economic benefits during the period of the ordinary activities of a business. Revenue is usually the equivalent of sales.

revenue anticipation note A bond that is issued with a varying payment profile. The bond may have no or limited coupon payments for a period and then coupon payments can kick in as the issuer is receiving revenue at a future date. These bonds are used for financing projects that may take some development time before they start producing income. Also see *tax anticipation note*.

revenue bond A bond issued to finance a specific project with the revenue from that completed project being used to service the obligations on the bond.

revenue reserve Profits that are set aside and allocated to meet financial obligations that a company has in the future that may or may not arise.

reverse arbitrage The sale of an asset and the purchase of a futures contract on that asset to gain a risk-free profit from mispricing in the market.

reverse cash and carry The opposite of a cash and carry strategy. Also see *cash and carry strategy*.

reverse convertible Convertible debt where the right of conversion lies with the issuer of the bond, i.e. the issuer can force the bond holder to convert the debt to equity. Reverse convertibles are not common instruments. Also see *convertible debt*.

reverse enquiry When an entity not invited to participate in a deal hears about the deal and approaches the arrangers of the deal with a request to participate.

reverse flex A decrease in the margin or fees associated with a syndicated loan or a debt capital market issue. Reverse flex usually occurs when the loan or security issue is oversubscribed when sold in the market and the borrower is effectively in a position to reduce the price to the point where the quantum desired is subscribed at the lower price. Also see *debt capital market; margin; upward flex*.

reverse privatisation See *nationalisation*.

reverse repurchase/repo An entity that needs a security for a particular transaction borrows the security in exchange for cash. When the borrower has finished using the security, they return it, pay an interest charge and receive their original cash back. A reverse repo is simply a normal repo seen from the counterparty's point of view. Also see *repurchase agreement*.

reverse takeover A takeover where the acquirer is the party whose equity has been obtained by the acquiree.

reverse yield gap The difference between the returns offered by equity shares and long dated risk-free government debt where the equities' returns are lower than the returns on government debt. If the bonds are yielding lower returns than the equities, the term yield gap is used. Also see *yield*.

revocable A commitment from a bank to provide funds under a facility that can be removed at the choice of the bank concerned at any point in time. These facilities are often called uncommitted. Also see *committed facility*.

revolver See *revolving credit facility*.

revolving bank facility See *revolving credit facility*.

revolving credit facility (RCF) A loan facility that is available over a period of time from which the borrower can draw on and pay back a series of smaller loans (utilisations) in that period entirely at their discretion. Borrowers have the right and not the obligation to draw the funds as and when needed. Borrowers can effectively fully draw the funds and roll over utilisations for the period of the facility so that the RCF approximates a term loan. At the end of the period all outstanding advances and interest must be paid in the form of a bullet payment. An overdraft on a cheque account or a credit card are good everyday examples of revolving credit facilities with the key difference being that they are revocable and are not fully committed like an RCF.

RCFs are used by companies to fund general working capital requirements and are often secured against inventories and accounts receivable.

RCFs carry a commitment fee charged on the undrawn balance to compensate banks for the regulatory capital that they have to put aside under their capital adequacy requirements.

Advantages of an RCF include the following:

- Flexible self-managed repayment schedules
- Flexible self-managed drawing schedules
- Savings on interest if used appropriately
- Possible additional features such as letters of credit and swingline facilities.

Also see *capital adequacy; commitment fee; letter of credit; swingline loan; term loan; working capital*.

revolving underwrite facility (RUF) A medium- or long-term financial instrument issuance programme underwritten by banks. The underwriting banks' obligation is to purchase any of the issued notes if they are not purchased in the open market. The underwrite commitment is open for a much longer period of time than an underwrite would be on a standalone basis. RUFs closely resemble commercial paper programmes. RUFs have staggered maturities. Also see *commercial paper*.

RFP
1. Request for proposal.
2. Received free of payment.

rho
1. The Greek letter ρ or P. Also see *Greek alphabet*.
2. A measure of the sensitivity of the price of an option to interest rates. The measure is per unit change in interest rates:

$$\rho = \frac{dC}{dr_f}$$

Also see *Black-Scholes options pricing model; Greeks; interest rate; option*.

rial The currency of Iran, Oman and Qatar. Also see *riyal*.

riba The term used in Islamic countries for interest. Also see *Islamic finance*.

riding the yield curve Trading securities of different maturities and hence different positions on the yield curve. Traders rely on yield curve shape, changes and shifts to make a profit. Also see *yield curve*.

RIE Recognised investment exchange.

rigging the market See *corner the market*.

rights issue/offer The offer of the sale of new shares to existing shareholders at a specified price (take-up price) and date. Rights issues are used to raise equity capital for the company without forcing a dilution of shareholder rights. Shareholders are informed of their entitlements under a rights issue through a nil paid letter.

Rights issues have a degree of time value associated with them and have to be executed within a certain time frame. They therefore effectively constitute an option on purchasing a share.

Valuing the rights and calculating the new share price can be done with the two equations below:

$$P_x = \frac{(N \times P_0) + P_S}{N + 1}$$

$$R = P_0 - P_x$$

where P_x = new share price; N = number of rights needed to buy a share (the subscription ratio); P_S = subscription price of a new share; P_0 = share price of share carrying right; R = price of a right.

When a shareholder is not obliged to subscribe for shares under a rights issue, the term used to describe the rights issue is renounceable rights. Also see *equity capital; nil paid letter; subscription price; subscription ratio; take-up price*.

rightsizing The restructuring of an organisation to improve efficiency and profitability. Rightsizing often involves fewer retrenchments than downsizing and can even be associated with an increase in the size of the workforce. Also see *downsizing; rationalisation*.

rights letter See *nil paid letter*.

ring fenced An entity that is allowed full autonomy and is not directly influenced by external entities. Ring fencing is undertaken to abstract liability and ensure that the structure put in place is not influenced by other obligations the sponsor or owner may have in any other field of business. Financing structures that are non-recourse in nature are said to be ring fenced. Various forms of project finance structures are ring fenced. Also see *special-purpose vehicle*.

ringgit (MYR) The currency of Malaysia divided into 100 sen.

RIS Regulatory information service. Also see *secondary information provider*.

risk
1. The chance that an investment will be lost.
2. With an individual equity share, the standard deviation of returns is associated with risk. Also see *standard deviation*.
3. For banks, the following risks are the key material risks – operating risk, liquidity risk and credit risk. Also see *credit risk*.

risk adjusted asset An asset on the balance sheet of a financial institution that has been adjusted for the risk associated with it. The calculation of the risk adjusted assets of a company is done by applying a risk weight to each asset and summing them up. Risk adjustments are also made to off balance sheet assets such as committed available loan facilities, guarantees and letters of credit.

risk adjusted discount rate (RADR) A premium added to the discount rate to account for the risk of uncertain cash flows. Also see *discount rate*.

risk adjusted performance measure (RAPM) The returns on an asset or project adjusted for the risk involved in participating in the project or making the investment:

$$\text{risk adjusted performance measure (RAPM)} = \frac{\text{revenues} - \text{cost} - \text{expected loss}}{\text{value at risk}}$$

The value at risk is the amount of operating capital needed to cushion the investor, typically a bank, against operating losses, market and other risks. The value at risk is interpreted as the risk capital or economic capital.

The RAPM measure allows the measurement of returns in terms of the balance between risk and reward. Also see *economic capital; return on economic capital; return on equity; risk adjusted return on capital*.

risk adjusted return on capital (RAROC) A measure used by banks to gauge returns on capital employed:

$$\text{risk adjusted return on capital (RAROC)} = \frac{\text{risk adjusted return}}{\text{risk or economic capital}}$$

thereby

$$\text{RAROC} = \frac{\text{revenue} \pm \text{treasury transfer prices} - \text{expenses} - \text{expected loss}}{\text{capital required for unexpected loss}}$$

The capital for unexpected losses must include capital for credit risk, market risk, operational and other risks. The capital for unexpected losses is often called economic capital and is the capital that needs to be put aside to sustain desired risk profiles and credit ratings. Also see *economic capital; return on economic capital*.

risk capital See *venture capital*.

risk contamination The risk that a failing asset will drag another asset that is performing well into default.

risk-free rate The rate of return investors would receive if they invested in a risk-free asset that is guaranteed to return their original investment. High-quality government debt is usually considered to be a risk-free investment. Also see *discount rate*.

riskless principal transaction A broker who matches a buy and sell identically, does not take a position and essentially executes a riskless transaction. The broker makes profits off fees or a mismatch in the buy and sell pricing. Also see *interdealer broker*.

risk management
1. Procedures and rules enforced in an organisation to control financial and other risks.

2. The purchase of derivative instruments to hedge financial risks that a company faces.

risk participation The process of a subparticipant in a loan or other credit security guaranteeing the obligations of the borrower for a fee. This is done through an instrument such as a credit default swap (CDS). The participation is unfunded because no cash flows of principal take place unless a credit event covered in the CDS contract occurs. Sometimes called a subparticipation. Also see *credit default swap; funded participation*.

risk premium The excess return required by investors for investing in a risky asset. The premium is expressed over a risk-free asset. The risk premium on small companies' shares is greater than for larger companies and even greater than the risk premium for corporate bonds which are more senior instruments.

risk premium = expected return – risk-free rate

Sometimes called the market risk premium.

risk shifting The tendency of stockholders in firms and their agents (managers) to take on much riskier projects than bond or equity holders expect them to. Because debt investors do not have voting rights in a company, the debt contracts often place limitations on the company to ensure it does not take an excessive risk or change its primary business. Also see *bond; firm*.

risk spread The difference in yield of government and corporate bonds. The difference gives the market's perception of the riskiness associated with holding the debt of that particular company. In South Africa, the spread on bonds is usually quoted over the relevant government bond rate.

risk warning notice (RWN) Notice given to investors indicating the risk associated with financial products and transactions. These are sent when advice on purchases is given and when purchases of derivative products are made. Also see *derivative*.

riyal (SAR) The currency of Qatar divided into 100 dirhams and Saudi Arabia divided into 100 halalas. Also see *rial*.

RLCR See *reserve life coverage ratio*.

RMBS Residential mortgage backed securities.

ROA See *return on assets*.

road show A presentation by corporations to potential investors to educate them about the investment being offered.

ROCE See *return on capital employed*.

ROD Record of depositors.

RODR Rand overnight deposit rate.

ROI See *return on investment*.

ROIE Recognised overseas investment exchange.

rollercoaster swap A swap where the principle of the cash flow calculation changes over time. This gives flexibility of payments and is used to meet the demands of cyclical financing. Also see *swap*.

rolling
1. A term often used to indicate that a window of analysis has a fixed span in time and as analyses on different dates are made, the window keeps its span and rolls along in time.

2. The process of refinancing maturing debt with new debt.

rolling settlement The settlement of a financial trade a number of days after the trade occurred.

rollover
1. The process of refinancing maturing debt with new debt. Sometimes called rolling.
2. The process of resetting interest rates in a swap or loan.

roll up loan A loan where interest is not paid but capitalised. Also see *payment in kind; toggle note*.

ROM Record of members.

RON The Romanian leu divided into 100 bani.

RONA See *return on net assets*.

RORAC Return on risk adjusted capital. Also see *risk adjusted return on capital*.

rouble The currency of Russia divided into 100 kopeks. Also called a ruble.

round lot A transaction on a stock exchange when securities are sold in numbers that are in multiples of 100. Trades not in these rounded numbers of securities are called odd lots.

round tripping The process of an entity borrowing money from one party and lending it on at a higher rate to make a profit. These financial structures are constructed in different tax regimes and are used to profit off mismatches in legislation.

royalty A fee paid to the issuer of a concession or licence. Mining companies usually pay royalties to governments for mineral rights. Technology companies often pay or charge royalties for the lease of intellectual property or proprietary pieces of information.

RPI See *retail price index*.

RPIX The retail price index (RPI) less interest rate charges on home loans. Also see *CPIX; interest rate; retail price index*.

RSD The currency of Serbia, the dinar divided into 100 para.

RUB See *rouble*.

rubber cheque A cheque that has had payment or encashment rejected because there are insufficient funds in the underlying bank account. These cheques are said to bounce. Also see *cheque*.

ruble See *rouble*.

RUF See *revolving underwrite facility*.

Rule 144A A US Securities and Exchange Commission (SEC) rule that permits suitably qualified institutional investors to buy and sell restricted securities. Restricted securities are not tradable on public markets and are only available to select investors. Rule 144A is the key driver behind the US private placement market.

Bonds issued by corporates under Rule 144A are referred to as 144A bonds. 144A bonds give the issuer access to major US institutional investors and substantial investor capacity. 144A bonds require an onerous due diligence process with higher legal costs and a rather extensive marketing process for successful subscription. Also see *due diligence; institutional investor; private placing/placement; qualified institutional investor; Securities and Exchange Commission*.

Rule of 72 The time it takes to double one's money on a compound interest investment can be approximated by:

$$\frac{72}{r\%}$$

A 10% investment will therefore take approximately seven years to double. Also see *compound interest*.

ruling price The last recorded price at which a security was bought and sold.

run
1. A series of investors or depositors trying to withdraw funds from a financial institution simultaneously. Often called a run on the bank.
2. A change in the value of a currency due to a lack of confidence.
3. See *rally*.

running the books See *book runner*.

running yield See *current yield*.

rupee The name of the currency of India, Mauritius, Nepal, Pakistan, the Seychelles and Sri Lanka.

rupiah The currency of Indonesia divided into 100 satang.

Russell 2000 The Russell 2000 Index offers investors access to the small-cap segment of the US equity market. The Russell 2000 is constructed to provide a comprehensive and unbiased small-cap barometer and is completely reconstituted annually to ensure larger stocks do not distort the performance and characteristics of the true small-cap opportunity set. The Russell 2000 includes the smallest 2000 securities in the Russell 3000. Also see *index*. (*Source*: http://www.russell.com)

RWN See *risk warning notice*.

RWA Risk weighted asset. Also see *capital ratio*.

S&P See *Standard and Poor*.

S&P 500 An index of top 500 companies by market capitalisation on the New York Stock Exchange. Also see *market capitalisation index*.

SA
1. South Africa
2. Société anonyme, a French term for a legal corporate.

SABOR See *South African benchmark overnight rate*.

SACCI South African Chamber of Commerce and Industry, formerly called SACOB, the South African Chamber of Business.

SACU Southern African Customs Union.

SADC Southern African Development Community.

safe custody The protective care by a custodian of securities or even physical goods for another entity.

safe investment A capital investment that has little or no risk of being lost. Government securities of reputable governments are considered to be the safest form of investment possible.

SAFEX See *South African Futures Exchange*.

SAIA See *South African Insurance Association*.

sale and leaseback A sale and leaseback occurs when a company sells an asset it owns to another party and immediately leases it back. In a sale and leaseback, two things happen:
- The lessee receives cash from the sale of the asset.
- The lessee continues to be the beneficial user of the asset.

With a sale and leaseback, the lessee often has the option of repurchasing the leased asset at the end of the lease. Sale and leasebacks are used to move assets off the balance sheet. Also see *asset; balance sheet; capital lease; operating lease*.

salvage value The value of an asset once it has been used or fully depreciated. Also see *fire sale value*.

same day funds The settlement of a financial transaction that occurs on the same day that the trade is made.

SAMOS See *South African multiple option settlement system*.

sample space The set of all possible outcomes of a random experiment.

samurai bond A yen-denominated bond issued in Tokyo by a non-Japanese company and subject to Japanese regulations. Other types of yen-denominated bonds are Euroyens issued in countries other than Japan. Also see *Eurobond; risk spread; shogun bond*.

sanctions Legal restrictions on countries or individuals that limit financial transactions and other business dealings with them. Sanctions are usually imposed by bodies such as governments and the United Nations. Also see *Office for Foreign Assets Control*.

SAONIA See *South African overnight index average*.

SAR The Saudi Arabian riyal divided into 100 halalas.

SARB See *South African Reserve Bank*.

Sarbanes-Oxley An Act passed by the United States congress that aims to protect investors from fraudulent reporting of company accounts.

SARS See *South African Revenue Service*.

SASRIA See *South African Special Risks Insurance Association*.

SASWITCH Electronic interbank payment system used for ATMs and point-of-sale payments. Also see *automated teller machine*.

Satrix 40 The Satrix 40 is a popular JSE exchange traded fund. The Satrix 40 tracks the FTSE/JSE Top 40 index. This index comprises the 40 largest companies by market capitalisation on the JSE.

Satrix 40 accurately replicates the FTSE/JSE Top 40 index by holding the exact weighting and number of shares that constitute this index. Any dividends that are paid by the top forty companies are paid out to Satrix 40 shareholders at the end of each quarter. In this way the holders of Satrix 40 securities replicate the total performance (capital plus dividend yield) of the top 40 companies listed on the JSE.

Satrix is a company that holds the underlying assets for investors. In addition to Satrix 40, there are many other index-based funds such as the Fini (FTSE/JSE Financial 15 index), Indi (FTSE/JSE Industrial 25 index), Resi (FTSE/JSE Top 40 index) and Swix (FTSE/JSE Swix Top 40 index). Also see *basket price; dividend; dividend yield; exchange traded fund; FTSE; index; JSE*.

SAVI See *South African Volatility Index*.

saving The difference between income and expenditure where income exceeds expenditure. Savings are put aside by individuals for future purchases and to fund retirement.

savings and loan organisation An American term for a building society.

savings bank A bank set up to accept as deposits relatively small sums of savings from households. The Post Office Bank in South Africa is a good example.

SBLI Stock borrowing and lending intermediary.

scanning risk A component of SPAN where an algorithm uses various probabilities to determine the risks of a portfolio. The highest risk is usually assumed. Also see *standard portfolio analysis of risk*.

schatz A two-year German government bond. Also see *bobl; bund; government bond*.

scheme of arrangement An arrangement between the shareholders or creditors of a company with the company. The arrangements are approved by courts and are used to reschedule debt, for takeovers or acquisitions and for return of capital. In an acquisition, a scheme of arrangement can be used to reorganise shares in the target. Also see *acquisition*.

schuldschein A German debt instrument that is similar to a US private placement. A schuldschein is effectively a bond or loan-type instrument that is placed with a series of private investors rather than listed on a bond or stock exchange. Investors are banks, savings banks and insurance companies and the tenors of the instruments vary between two and five years. Schuldschein instruments are quick to execute, ratings are not an absolute requirement and the structure can be adjusted to suit an issuer's needs more closely than a bond would allow. Also see *private placing/placement*.

SCM Structured capital market.

scope economies Benefits gained from marketing and selling a range of products instead of a single product. For example, Coca Cola distributors often sell a range of similar beverages and achieve efficiencies through packaging, transport, distribution and marketing.

screen rate A rate, typically a base interest rate such as LIBOR or JIBAR, that is quoted on a secondary information provider such as Reuters and Bloomberg. Also see *Bloomberg; interest rate; JIBAR; LIBOR; Reuters*.

scrip
1. Abbreviation for subscription or securities receipt.
2. A scrip issue is another term for a bonus issue. Also see *bonus issue*.

scrip bid A bid or takeover offer for a company predominantly in the form of shares. There may be a cash element to a scrip bid. The shareholders of the target company will hold shares in the merged entity after the transaction. There may be capital gains tax advantages to a scrip bid over a cash offer. Also see *capital gains tax*.

scrip borrowing The borrowing of securities for a fee. Brokers often loan securities between one another to facilitate short selling. Also see *short position*.

scrip issue See *bonus issue*.

scrip loan See *scrip borrowing*.

script dividend The payment of a dividend through the issues of shares. There is usually a small premium on the value of the shares offered over a cash dividend. Also see *dividend in specie*.

scriptless trading Electronic trading where share certificates are not delivered.

SD A credit rating that indicates that the company has defaulted on selective debt obligations. An SD rating is worse than an R rating. Also see *credit rating*.

SDR See *special drawing right*.

SDRT Stamp duty reserve tax, a tax on electronic share trades.

SEAQ A quote-driven system that trades small companies on the London Stock Exchange and the Alternative Investment Market. Also see *Alternative Investment Market; London Stock Exchange; quote driven*.

seasonal The variance of an economic variable over short periods of time. For example, retail sales pick up over the Christmas period.

seat Permission to trade on a stock exchange. Also see *member*.

SEATS The trading system on the London Stock Exchange. The system is a quote and order driven system that trades medium-sized companies. Also see *London Stock Exchange; order driven; quote driven; SEAQ*.

SEC See *Securities and Exchange Commission*.

SEC issuance An issue of a security that is registered with the Securities and Exchange Commission. This is as opposed to a Rule 144A issuance that is not registered. Also see *Rule 144A; Securities and Exchange Commission*.

secondary information provider (SIP) A company such as Reuters or Bloomberg that provides information to the markets from primary information systems on stock exchanges. Also see *Bloomberg; Daily Official List; primary information provider; Reuters*.

secondary market An owner or lender of securities sells or lends to another investor without the original issuer of the security being involved in the transaction. There are two types of secondary markets:

- The dealer market where a security is bought from a dealer over the counter
- The auction market where buyers and sellers meet.

Also see *primary market; security*.

secondary mortgage market The market for mortgage securities bought and sold between financial institutions and investors after the original primary sale.

secondary shares/stock Performing stocks that are not yet considered to be blue chip shares. Also see *blue chip*.

secondary tax on companies (STC) A tax paid by companies on dividends declared. In South Africa, it was 12.5% until October 2007 when it was set to 10% of the value of the dividend payment. The dividends received by shareholders are then not taxed as STC taxes the revenue at company level. The following example illustrates STC:

Company A owns 100% of company B and company B declares a R10 dividend. R10 will be paid over to Company A and R1 will be paid over to SARS. If Company A now declares a dividend of R20, they will have to pay STC of 10% of the additional dividend added, i.e. (R20 – R10) × 10%. This is often called an STC credit.

Also see *dividend*.

second-hand policy Policy holders can sell endowment or universal policies by taking a lump sum from an investor. The investor then waits for the surrender of the policy at a future date. Also see *endowment insurance/policy; universal policy*.

second lien A claim or lien on an asset in a secured loan agreement that is subordinated to more senior debt secured against the same asset. An example is a second mortgage on a house where the second lender has a subordinate claim to the first lender on the asset in the event of default. Also see *default; first lien; mortgage; pari passu; secured; seniority; subordinate*.

second mortgage A second loan that is secured against an asset with an existing mortgage. A second mortgage is usually subordinate to the first mortgage. Also see *mortgage; secured; subordinate*.

second tier market An alternative market for securities not listed on the main boards of stock exchanges. The Alternative Investment Market (AIM) in the UK and the AltX market on the JSE are examples of second tier markets. Also see *Alternative Investment Market; Development Capital Market; JSE; main board*.

secret reserve See *off balance sheet reserve*.

section 21 A South African company set up under section 21 of the Companies Act that is a not-for-profit company and cannot distribute profits to its members. Organisations such as political parties, religious groups, charities, social and community groups are set up as section 21 companies. In the UK similar non-profit organisations are set up as companies limited by guarantee. Also see *Companies Act; company limited by guarantee*.

sector A group of businesses that are in a similar or the same industry. For example, the mining sector refers to all companies that are involved in mining.

secular change A movement over time, generally a long period of time rather than seasonally. Sometimes called temporal change.

secured Financial instruments, usually in the form of debt instruments, that have an asset attached to them. For debt, title to the asset offers the lenders the opportunity to recover more of their money in the event of default. Also see *event of default*.

secured loan (secured debt) A loan that has an asset attached to it. In the case of default on the debt, the asset is liquidated to compensate the issuer of the debt. Security for short-term loans includes accounts receivable and/or inventories. Directors of small companies often secure business loans against private assets. Also see *default; liquidation; unsecured debt*.

secured note An agreement that verifies that one entity will lend to another at a predetermined rate.

securitatem debiti A Latin phrase used in legal documents that indicates security for debt.

securities Tradable financial instruments such as bonds. See *security*.

Securities and Exchange Commission (SEC) The authority in the US that is responsible for securities trading, stock options, stock index options, currency transactions on exchanges and the Chicago Board Of Trade (CBOT). Their mission is to 'protect investors, maintain fair, orderly, and efficient markets, and facilitate capital formation'.

securities lending The borrowing of a security for purposes of covering or creating an investment position (typically a short position). Securities are normally lent out for a fee and the lending process often takes the form of a repurchase agreement (repo). Also see *repurchase agreement; short position*.

Securities Regulation Panel (SRP) The regulatory panel in South Africa set up under the Companies Act that monitors transactions in company shares to ensure that all dealings are fair, to ensure good business practice and to promote an orderly market. Company control, the number of shares that can be acquired in a calendar year and what those acquisitions are subject to are covered by the SRP. A significant focus of the SRP is the protection of minority shareholders. See www.srpanel.co.za for more details. Also see *acquisition; Companies Act*.

securitisation The process of converting a non-tradable asset into a tradable asset. For example, a bank may take home loans on its books, create a debt instrument such as a bond securitised against the home loans and sell the bonds to investors. The process of securitisation is usually done through a special-purpose vehicle sometimes called a conduit. The advantage of banks securitising their assets is that they can move assets off the balance sheet into an SPV and balance the risks of their credit portfolios. After securitising assets, banks are then free to lend more funds against their capital bases defined by capital adequacy requirements. The banks also remove operational risk by using an SPV. Securitisation uses multiple tranches with differing seniorities or subordination to provide varying degrees of debt cushion and hence a series of credit investments with different risk and reward characteristics to appeal to a wide range of investors off the back of a single pool of assets. The process of using different levels of subordination is called credit enhancement. Also see *balance sheet; capital adequacy; conduit; credit enhancement; debt cushion; mortgage; securitised bond; special-purpose vehicle; true sale*.

securitised bond Repackaging a set of existing cash flows into a tradable asset. For example, by issuing a series of bonds against a book of home loans, the home loan interest payments are used to finance the bond coupons. Also see *securitisation*.

securitised mortgage A mortgage that is converted into a tradable asset. Also see *asset; mortgage*.

security
1. A generic term for an investment such as a bond or a share. A security is a paper certificate or electronic record that is evidence of ownership of the financial instrument.
2. The issuer of debt secures part of the value of the debt against an asset. The borrower is legally given claim to the secured asset if the lender defaults. Security is offered to gain access to and reduce the cost of debt and needs to be registered formally. Debt that is secured is often called pledge debt. Also see *default; fixed charge; floating charge; secured*.

security market line (SML) A positively sloped straight line that shows the relationship between expected return and beta. It forms the basis of the capital asset pricing model (CAPM) and describes the risk or return trade-off in the capital markets. The equation for the line is:

$$E(R_i) = R_f + [E(R_m) - R_f] \times \beta$$

where $E(R_m) - R_f$ = the risk premium of the market; R_m = the return of the market; R_f = the risk-free rate (usually the yield on treasury bills); R_i = the expected return on the investment.

The slope of the graph of returns on the investment $E(R_i)$ versus β gives the market risk premium. It enables an estimate of the cost of equity capital which is the required rate of return by shareholders. Also see *beta; capital asset pricing model; capital market; cost of equity; expected return; market risk premium; treasury bill*.

security trust A trust set up to hold security against which lenders can provide funds to borrowers.

seed capital The initial capital used to launch a project or business. Venture capitalists often provide such finance. Also see *venture capital*.

SEETS A trading system on the London Stock Exchange that is order driven. The system trades share in companies with large market capitalisations. The system operates from 08h00 to 16h30 daily and trades are reported immediately. Also see *London Stock Exchange; order driven; market capitalisation; SEAQ*.

segregated account A separate account, usually used in securities trading brokerages, that portions an investor's securities and does not use a set of records maintained by the broker.

SEHK Stock Exchange of Hong Kong.

SEK Swedish krona divided into 100 ore.

self-financing A company that can finance expansion and growth through cash flows and internal reserves and does not require external debt or equity finance. Also see *internal growth rate*.

self-liquidating A security is self-liquidating when it is secured and repaid from the proceeds of the sale of the underlying asset or is repaid from the income generated by that asset. Also see *secured; security*.

self-regulatory organisation (SFO) An organisation that is not subject to oversight by a regulator. These organisations should observe standards of fairness and confidentiality.

self-tender A form of share buy-back where a company tries to purchase back its own shares. Also see *share buy-back*.

sellers market A market that enables sellers to elevate prices due to demand exceeding supply.

sellers price The price at which a dealer is prepared to sell. Also called the ask price. Also see *ask price; bid price*.

selling out The sale of securities by a broker because the client is unable to effect payment or post a margin call. The client will be liable for the difference between the price paid and sold.

selling pressure A downward moving price in trading conditions characterised by significant trading volumes. Also see *buying pressure*.

sell off The market selling shares or securities en masse.

sell short The sale of shares or securities that are not owned by the seller. The trader takes the view that the price of the asset being sold will go down and at a future date the securities can be purchased for a lower price and returned to the securities lender. The short seller will need to borrow the securities sold from a stock lender. Also see *short position; stock lending*.

sell signal A signal arising from the use of an indicator that a security must be sold. Also see *oscillator*.

semi-annual Twice annually. Usually refers to the payment of interest on a bond or loan.

semi-gilt A gilt or bond issued by quasi government institutions such as parastatals and municipalities.

semi-standard deviation The square root of the semi-variance. Semi-standard deviation is effectively the standard deviation of the loss. Semi-standard deviation is calculated the same way as standard deviation, except only samples below mean are used in the calculation. Semi-standard deviation can be used as a risk function in generating an efficient frontier. See *Estrata downside risk model* for an example of the application. Also see *semi-variance; standard deviation*.

semi-strong efficient market Not all company information is contained in the share price. The information contained is at minimum the publicly available information.

semi-variance The mean of the squared negative deviations from the expected value of a distribution. Semi-variance can be used as a risk function in generating an efficient frontier. It is effectively calculated in the same way as the variance, but only for values below the target value which may or may not be the mean. Also see *semi-standard deviation; variance*.

senior bank debt Debt issued by banks to companies. The debt is subordinated only to secured debt. It is a relatively cheap form of debt for strong corporations and the

senior debt | settlement facility

potential pool of funds can be significant. It is also possible to form syndicates for these loans. Also see *revolving credit facility; subordinate; term loan*.

senior debt See *seniority*.

seniority The first claim on assets when a company goes insolvent or the first claim on cash flows for servicing of debt. Debt often has a seniority ranking and debt holders are entitled to the proceeds of liquidation ahead of equity investors. The order of seniority is usually:

1. senior secured loans
2. senior unsecured loans
3. senior subordinated loans
4. subordinated loans
5. hybrid debt such as preference shares
6. equity.

Also see *liquidation*.

SENS The Stock Exchange News Service. SENS is an information service provided by the JSE which broadcasts company announcements and price-sensitive information to data subscribers. The aim of SENS is to deliver information to the investor community quickly, reliably and transparently. Also see *Daily Official List; JSE; primary information provider*.

SENSEX The Bombay Stock Exchange Sensitive Index, sometimes called the BSE 30 Index. Also see *BSE 30*.

sensitivity The effect on the overall result from changes in a single input variable.

sentiment The mood of the market. Also see *bear market; bull market*.

serial bond Bonds issued on the same date but with different tenors forming a series. One can view these bonds as a single bond with different tranches.

serial correlation See *autocorrelation*.

service company A company that provides services to clients and does not provide physical goods.

service cost See *current service cost*.

SET Securities Exchange of Thailand.

set off The processing of applying an asset against a liability or a loss against a gain. Bankers often set off a positive balance on one account against a negative balance on another. Also see *offset*.

SETS See *SEETS*.

settlement The fulfilment of the conditions of a contract. This is normally associated with the delivery of assets and/or payment of cash in financial markets. Also see *asset*.

settlement date The date after the issue of a security when payment is made.

settlement facility A credit facility put in place that allows companies to access funds for very short periods of time, for example one or two days. The facilities are used to cover mismatches in the timing of payment obligations and funds received. Also see *settlement*.

settlement price See *exchange delivery settlement price*.

settlement risk See *Herstatt risk*.

seven S framework Strategy; structure; systems; skills; shared values; style; staff.

several guarantee See *several obligation*.

several obligation Obligations that are unaffected by the presence of other parties. For example, if two parties each have a liability of R1 million to a lender, then the total liability to the lender is R2 million. The obligations are independent of one another and non-payment by one party does not give the lender the right to seek compensation from the other obligors. In a syndicated loan the lenders' obligations are several. For example, should a single lender in a syndicated loan not advance funds, the other lenders will not be obliged to make up the shortfall. Also see *joint and several guarantee/liability; joint obligation*.

SGD Singapore dollar.

SGT Abbreviation for sterling. Also see *sterling*.

SGX Singapore Stock Exchange.

shadow director A party that instructs a director sitting on the board of a company and that seat holder follows the instruction of the shadow director. Shadow directors are often majority shareholders who instruct their representatives to undertake certain actions. If the directors that hold the board positions do not effectively execute those instructions, they are normally replaced. Also see *connected person; related party*.

shadow rating A credit rating given by a credit rating agency that is not made available to the wider public. The shadow rating is made available at the company's discretion to selected investors. Sometimes called a silent rating. Also see *credit rating; credit rating agency*.

shadow revenue Departments in an organisation that do not directly book revenue but assist in the generation of revenue have shadow revenue attributable to them. Usually used as a measure of performance.

shadow toll A toll based on the use of an asset but not paid by the user. The toll is usually paid by the government or contracting authority.

share Part ownership of a company. Owning a share gives the right to share in the profits and residual assets under liquidation. Shares carry voting rights that effectively give the shareholders influence in the decision-making processes in companies. Also see *liquidation; ordinary share; preference share; seniority*.

share buy-back The repurchase by a firm of its existing shares, either via the market or by a tender to all shareholders. This may be done instead of declaring dividends because:
- dividend increases may negatively affect future expectations
- specific shareholders can be removed by targeting the buy-back
- the negative dilution effect boosts the share price
- if share options are exercised they will dilute earnings.

The shares bought back appear as treasury shares on the balance sheet. Also see *balance sheet; dividend; firm; share option; tender; treasury shares*.

share capital The price of the share stated on the share certificate (nominal value or par value) multiplied by the number of shares in issue. This number can be added to the share premium to obtain the total value of shares issued by the company at the average price at which the company issued the shares over the company's lifetime and not at the current share price. Also see *asset base; authorised share capital; market capitalisation; nominal value; par value; share premium*.

share certificate A physical document that is issued to the holder of shares, proving that he/she is the rightful title holder. Also see *title*.

share code The code, usually three letters long, assigned to a specific share on stock exchange information systems.

share cover An asset cover ratio where the asset provided as security for a loan is in the form of shares. The ratio is calculated as:

$$\text{share cover} = \frac{\text{market value of shares}}{\text{total debt secured by the shares}}$$

Share cover is often a metric used by banks when they are ceded shares in companies as collateral for loans. The share cover that banks require is usually well in excess of the loan value because share prices are subject to crashes and volatility in equity markets. Also see *asset cover; collateral; security*.

shareholder agreement An agreement between shareholders of a company that governs the business interactions between the shareholders and the business that they own.

shareholder loan A loan to a company from an equity holder. Shareholder loans may be issued instead of raising capital through equity issues to take advantage of differing tax treatments as interest payments on loans are often tax deductible.

shareholders The owners of a company. They are often called equity holders and have shares in the company. Also see *equity*.

shareholders capital Share capital and retained income (reserves). Sometimes called owners equity. Also see *owners equity; retained earnings/income; share capital*.

shareholders equity See *shareholders capital*.

shareholders funds See *shareholders capital*.

shareholder value analysis (SVA) A technique that is similar to the economic value added (EVA) method that defines how management decisions affect the present value of future cash flows. Also see *economic value added; present value*.

share index An index based on the prices of shares. These indices can be constructed in a variety of ways such as by market capitalisation. Also see *ALSI; market capitalisation index*.

share loan See *stock lending*.

share option These are options offered today to purchase shares in a company at a future date at the price specified today. If at the future date the value of the shares on the open market is greater than the price specified in the option, the holder will exercise the option to purchase the shares at the lower price. The holder of the option can then profit by purchasing the shares below market value through the option and then sell them at market value. Share options are given to management in companies to provide them with an incentive to drive the share price upwards and realise higher gains for shareholders.

share pledge The use of equity shares as security against a debt obligation. Also see *margin loan; share cover*.

share premium The premium at which the share was issued by the company over the par value. To obtain the total value of shares issued by the company, the share premium must be added to the share capital. Note that these numbers are calculated at the price at which they were issued by the company and not the current market price. Also see *par value; share capital*.

share price The cost of the purchase of equity shares in a company. Finance theory postulates that the share price is the present value of future dividends and the present value of future price:

$$P_0 = \frac{P_t}{(1+r)^t} + \sum_{k=1}^{t} \frac{D_k}{(1+R)^k}$$

where through the dividend growth model

$$P_t = \frac{D_t \times (1+g)}{R-g} \text{ or } P_t = \frac{D_{t+1}}{R-g}$$

where g = the dividend growth rate; D_t = the dividend returned at time t; D_k = the dividend paid at time k; R = the discount rate; P_t = the price of share at time t.

Also see *discount rate; dividend growth model; equity*.

share register A record of all the shares of a company and the owners of those shares along with the owners' relevant details. Entry in the record is evidence of ownership of the shares. Also see *electronic scrip register; record date*.

share retention agreement An agreement by parties not to dispose of their shares in a company. This is often required in finance agreements where sponsors of a project have experience and expertise that the lenders do not want leaving the project before the end of the financing agreements.

shares in issue The actual number of shares that have been issued by a company and have been taken up by equity investors. Companies may have more authorised share capital than evidenced through shares in issue. Also see *authorised share capital*.

share split When share prices go too high, companies sometimes collect individual shares and issue multiples in return. For example, one share can be converted into five. The price should then drop by the multiple of the swap. Companies split shares to keep their shares liquid in the market. Sometimes share splits constitute a positive signal to markets as it is an indication that management is expecting the price to rise in the future. Also see *consolidation of shares; liquid*.

share warehousing See *warehousing*.

Sharpe ratio A ratio that measures the expected returns over the risk-free rate of an index per unit risk of that asset:

$$S = \frac{E[R_m - R_f]}{\sigma}$$

where R_m = the market return; R_f = the risk-free rate; σ = the standard deviation of the excess return.

High Sharpe ratios imply that the investor is obtaining good returns for the amount of risk taken. The S&P equity market index has a Sharpe ratio of approximately 0.3. Secondary market term loan indices have Sharpe ratios as high as 0.9. Sharpe ratios are often used to measure the performance of fund managers. Also see *information ratio; Standard and Poor*.

shelf company A business entity that is created through a process that does not involve incorporation. Shelf companies are often established because it can take some time to set up a company and establish a history and credit profile. These companies are put on the shelf and used as and when they are needed. They do not hold operational assets and are used to hold other vehicles.

shell operation See *cash shell*.

sheqel/shekel The currency of Israel divided into 100 agorot.

SHIBOR Shanghai interbank offered rate. Also see *HIBOR; JIBAR; LIBOR*.

shilling
1. Currency of Kenya, Uganda, Tanzania and Somalia divided into 100 cents.
2. Former currency of Austria which now uses the euro. Also see *euro*.

shipper The term a carrier uses to indicate who booked shipping capacity with them to move goods. The shipper is not necessarily the seller. Also see *carrier*.

shogun bond A foreign currency denominated bond issued in Tokyo by a non-Japanese company and subject to Japanese regulations. Also see *bond; samurai bond; risk spread*.

short See *short position*.

short call The sale of a call option. The payoff relationship of selling a call option is illustrated below. Also see *call option; long call*.

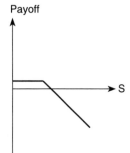

short cover The purchase of options or securities to close a short position. If an investor has sold short options such as a call option, the underlying asset or call option would be purchased and held until the call option sold was exercised. Sometimes called a buy-back. Also see *call option*.

short dated A security that has a redemption or maturity date of generally less than a year although the term can be used for periods as long as three years.

short hedge Taking a short position in a futures contract to hedge against the possible downward movement of the price of a commodity. For example, commodity producers take a short position to ensure that the price they receive at the future date is locked in. Also see *long hedge; short position*.

short option minimum charge The minimum initial margin required by clearing houses to parties writing deeply out the money options. Also see *clearing house; initial margin; out the money*.

short position A position that will gain in the event of a fall in the value of the underlying asset. A short position is entered into by selling a security that is not owned (short sale).

Entering into a put option where the underlying asset is not owned also constitutes a short position. Also see *long position; put option; sell short*.

short put The sale of a put option. Sellers of these options give the right to the purchasers to sell an asset to them at the stipulated price at a future date. The payoff diagram of a short put is illustrated below. Also see *long put; put option*.

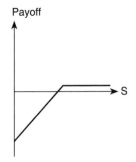

short run A brief period of increased activity that is too small to sustain increasing volumes or capacity permanently.

short sell See *short position*.

short straddle See *straddle*.

short strangle See *strangle*.

short term A period of less than a year.

short-term debt Debt due and payable within a year, typically in the following financial reporting period. Short-term debt is indicated in the current liabilities section of a company's balance sheet.

short-term debt ratio A ratio used to analyse the risk that a company may have cash flow problems servicing debt obligations in the short term. The ratio is defined by:

$$\text{short-term debt ratio} = \frac{\text{short-term debt}}{\text{long-term debt}}$$

Companies with high short-term debt ratios are exposed to significant refinancing risk. Also see *refinancing risk*.

short-term insurer Short-term insurers cover households and businesses against losses. They intermediate between households by accepting cash as premiums and paying out cash in the event of losses. These losses usually include fire, theft and accidental damage. They use the premiums paid to invest in equity as well as private and government-sector debt. Also see *debt; equity; long-term insurer; reinsurer*.

short-term interest rate The interest rate on short-term instruments such as treasury bills that usually have a maturity of less than a year. Also see *forward rate agreement; interest rate; treasury bill*.

short-term interest rate futures An instrument that allows a user to lock into a short-term interest rate at a date in the future. These are exchange traded instruments unlike forward rate agreements (FRAs) which are over the counter. They generally have inflexible terms and conditions and are cash settled. Also see *forward rate agreement; interest rate*.

short-term loan A loan that is used for purposes similar to an overdraft. They are used for working capital financing and must be repaid on a specific date. They are based on the lender's base cost of funds and are priced at a premium above an interbank rate.

Sometimes called a cash advance bridge loan or a revolving credit facility. Also see *interbank rate; overdraft; working capital*.

short-term rating See *credit rating*.

side deal A deal struck off the record between parties that substantially advantages one party. Side deals sometimes occur in takeovers and acquisitions where the management of the target is offered incentives offline to advantage the bidder. These incentives may be in the form of cash or job offers. Side deals may be illegal and are almost always of questionable ethics. Also see *acquisition*.

sideways movement A small movement of share prices up and down with no definite trend. The share price effectively remains constant for a period of time. Also see *mean reversion*.

significant influence The power to participate in the financial and operating policy decisions of an entity, but not control these policies. Significant influence may be gained by share ownership, statute or agreement. Also see *Securities Regulation Panel*.

silent rating See *shadow rating*.

SIMEX Singapore International Monetary Exchange.

simple gearing The price of an asset divided by an option price on that asset:

$$\text{simple gearing} = \frac{\text{underlying asset price}}{\text{option price}}$$

Also see *effective gearing*.

simple interest Interest earned on the original principal amount. There is no compounding and the interest payment is defined by:

$$\text{interest} = P \times i \times \frac{D}{B}$$

where P = the principal invested; i = the annual rate of interest; D = the number of days in the interest period; B = the basis which is usually the number of days per year. Also see *compound interest*.

simple rate See *simple interest*.

simulation A financial model that runs through a series of scenarios and tests the likely outcomes. Also see *Monte Carlo*.

single stock future The obligation to buy or sell a stock at a predetermined price and date in the future, i.e. a futures contract on shares in a specific company. Single stock futures give geared exposure to shares in the market. In South Africa, single stock futures are traded on SAFEX. They are traded internationally on Euronext.LIFFE, MEFF and One Chicago. Also see *contract for difference; futures contract; gearing; option; South African Futures Exchange*.

sinker A bond whose cash flows are paid from a sinking fund. Also see *sinking fund*.

sinking fund A bond trustee holds a reserve fund for payment of capital on the debt to lenders. A fund can also be set up into which deposits are made so that on maturation of the bond cash flow of the bond issuer is not adversely affected.

sinking fund bond A bond with more than one maturity date. The whole of the principal is therefore not paid at once but over a series of predefined dates.

sin tax Excise tax levied on goods such as alcohol and cigarettes and activities such as gambling. Also see *excise tax*.

SIP See *secondary information provider*.

SIT The Slovenian tolar divided into 100 stotins.

SIV See *structured investment vehicle*.

skewness In probability theory and statistics, skewness is a measure of the asymmetry of the probability distribution of a real-valued random variable. A distribution has positive skew (right-skewed) if the right or higher value tail is longer or fatter and negative skew (left-skewed) if the left or lower value tail is longer or fatter. Skewness is defined mathematically as the third standardised moment and is written as:

$$\gamma_1 \gamma_1 = \frac{\mu_3}{\sigma^3}$$

where μ_3 = the third moment about the mean; σ^3 = the standard deviation. Also see *kurtosis; standard deviation*.

skim A term used in the banking world indicating that fees charged are in excess of the costs of providing a financial product. For example, with a syndicated loan the borrower pays an arrangement fee to the banks. The mandated lead arranger (MLA) in the deal then sells down the loan to a syndicate of debt investors. In the sell-down process banks are each allocated a portion of the arrangement fee according to their level of commitment in the syndicate. When the monies allocated to the participant banks for arrangement is less than the fee paid by the client, the book runner or MLA makes a skim on the syndicated loan participation. Sometimes called a praecipium. Also see *arrangement fee; mandated lead arranger; syndicated loan*.

SKK Slovakian koruna divided into 100 hellers.

SLA Service level agreement.

SLB Scrip lending and borrowing.

sleeping partner A partner in a business who has contributed capital but does not take an active role in the day-to-day running of the business. The sleeping partner benefits from being entitled to a share in the company's profit.

sliding peg A term used for crawling peg. Also see *crawling peg*.

slush fund Cash set aside for payments to individuals to further the benefits of the company. The payments can be, but are not necessarily, bribes.

small country assumption The assumption in an economic model that a country is too small to affect wider world prices, incomes or interest rates. Also see *interest rate*.

smart money Funds invested by sophisticated and intelligent investors who have a good understanding of financial markets.

SNB See *special notarial bond*.

snooze you lose In a syndicated loan agreement, if a member of the lending syndicate does not signal intent or submit a vote in issues related to the facility, then the voting right will be transferred to the loan agent. Also see *yank the bank*.

SOCA Serious and Organised Crime Agency. An agency in the UK dedicated to eliminating organised crime.

social security A government-funded scheme that gives financial assistance to the unemployed, including retirement benefits.

Society for Worldwide Interbank Financial Transactions (SWIFT) An organisation that is owned by international banks. SWIFT is based in Belgium and runs a worldwide network of financial messaging services between banks.

SOFFEX Swiss Options and Financial Futures Exchange.

soft call protection A premium that the issuer of a bond has to pay to call a bond. The premium is usually a few basis points and can only be exercised after the period of call protection. Soft call protection is similar to the concept of a prepayment penalty in loan agreements. Also see *call protected debt*.

soft commodities Agricultural products traded in the commodities market, for example wheat, maize, cocoa, sugar and coffee.

soft copy The digital version of a document. The hard copy is a printed version.

soft currency A currency that loses value against other currencies through inflationary and other economic effects. Also see *hard currency; purchasing power parity*.

soft loan A loan advanced under conditions more favourable than available on the open market. Soft loans are often given to companies for political reasons as governments try to boost particular industrial sectors or provide favours to friends. Soft loans may, in addition to favourable pricing, have less onerous covenants and other obligations. Also see *covenant*.

soft underwrite
1. For share issues, when an underwriter agrees to buy shares at a later stage after the pricing process is complete. The shares are then placed with institutional investors. Also see *institutional investor*.
2. For a loan syndication, a commitment to underwrite the portion of debt not taken up by the bank market after an initial round of commitments. Borrowers may often expect the lead banks to take up larger holds in the event that the loan is undersubscribed. It is often called a free underwrite because underwrite fees are not charged.

sole proprietorship A business owned by a singe person who bears unlimited liability for the business operations. Also see *partnership; unlimited liability*.

solvency The ability of an entity to meet its debt obligations. The solvency of a company is measured by a number of different ratios such as the current ratio, quick or acid test ratio, cash ratio and interval measure. Also see *acid test (quick) ratio; cash ratio; current ratio; interval measure*.

solvency margin A ratio similar to the capital adequacy ratio used in banking that determines the solvency of an insurance company. It is calculated by dividing the insurance company's assets by its liabilities. It is also common to see a solvency margin calculated by shareholders funds being expressed as a percentage of net premiums, i.e. gross premiums less reinsurance premiums paid. Solvency margins are set for the insurance industry by regulators. Also see *capital adequacy; shareholders funds*.

solvency ratio A ratio that measures a company's ability to meet its long-term obligations. It can take several forms and is often measured by:

$$\text{solvency ratio} = \frac{\text{net worth}}{\text{total liabilities}}$$

Also see *free asset ratio*.

solvent See *solvency*.

sort code A set of numbers on a cheque or other money transfer instrument that identifies the branch where a bank account is held.

SOTP Sum of the parts. Also see *sum of the parts valuation*.

source and application of funds statement A cash flow statement.

sources and uses A statement whereby a borrower signals to the lenders where it intends to spend the proceeds of a loan or bond issue.

South African benchmark overnight rate (SABOR) The weighted average of the interest rates of all the overnight interbank lending transactions and wholesale funding. SABOR replaced the South African overnight index average (SAONIA). Also see *interest rate; JIBAR; weighted average*.

South African Futures Exchange (SAFEX) A South African exchange that trades in financial and agricultural futures. SAFEX is a division of the JSE. Also see *futures contract; JSE*.

South African Insurance Association (SAIA) An association that represents its member short-term insurance companies in South Africa. The SAIA represents its members at all levels, acts as a spokesperson, lobbies, negotiates and communicates with stakeholders.

South African multiple option settlement system (SAMOS) A system operated by the SARB that facilitates the transfer of funds in lieu of payments between financial institutions. Also see *South African Reserve Bank*.

South African overnight index average (SAONIA) The weighted average of the interest rates of all the overnight interbank lending transactions. Used to be published by the SARB until March 2007 when it was replaced by the South African benchmark overnight rate on deposits (SABOR). Also see *European overnight index average; interest rate; South African benchmark overnight rate; South African Reserve Bank; weighted average*.

South African Reserve Bank (SARB) The central bank of the Republic of South Africa. See http://www.reservebank.co.za for more details. Also see *central bank*.

South African Revenue Service (SARS) The tax collection agency of the government of South Africa.

South African Special Risks Insurance Association (SASRIA) An organisation that is backed by government and that covers losses associated with riots, civil commotion, strikes, lockouts and uprising.

South African Volatility Index (SAVI) A measure of volatility (short-term risk) in the South African equity market. The index was developed by Cadiz and the Johannesburg Stock Exchange. Also see *JSE; volatility*.

sovereign bond See *government bond*.

sovereign debt Debt instruments, usually bonds and treasury bills, issued by a sovereign government. Also see *bond; treasury bill*.

sovereign guarantee A guarantee from a government.

sovereign immunity A situation where it is not possible to sue or seize the assets of a company due to the legal jurisdiction of incorporation of that company.

sovereign risk The risk of never getting one's money back due to factors associated with country risk. This risk can be measured in the difference between inflation-linked bonds in the US which is considered to be one of the safest investments in the world and inflation-linked bonds in other countries. Also see *inflation-linked bond*.

sovereign risk premium The risk for which an investor expects to be compensated for the chance of never seeing his/her money again. For example, the total South African sovereign risk premium is measured as the difference in SA government bond yields paid in rands and the US government equivalent yields paid in US dollars. Also see *current yield; sovereign risk*.

sovereign wealth fund (SWF) A fund set up by a government to invest monies from trade surplus accounts. These funds vary in strategic nature and the asset classes in which they are invested. Countries that have strong surpluses from oil revenues have such funds. Also see *trade surplus*.

SPA Sale and purchase agreement.

SpA The abbreviation used in Italy to indicate that a company is a public limited company. The term Limited (Ltd) is used in South Africa, and PLC is used in the UK. SpA officially stands for Societa per Azioni.

SPAN See *standard portfolio analysis of risk*.

SPC Special-purpose company, a term used in the UK for a special-purpose vehicle. Also see *special-purpose vehicle*.

SPE Special-purpose entity, a word used to describe a special-purpose vehicle. Also see *special-purpose vehicle*.

special assessment bond A form of special tax bond used to fund a development project and secured through taxes levied on the community that is the beneficiary of the particular project. Also see *special assessment tax; special tax bond*.

special assessment tax A tax levied on the community that is the beneficiary of a project. Also see *special assessment bond*.

special bargain A stock market transaction that is above or below market prices where buyers and sellers are represented by different brokerage firms. Special bargains are used when the deals involved require volumes beyond the capacity of the market. Also see *firm; iceberg order; put through*.

special bond See *special notarial bond*.

special collateral Securities that are highly sought after in the repo market. Substitution of collateral is not allowed when the collateral is of special form. Also see *collateral; general collateral; repurchase agreement*.

special cum The period after the date that a share goes ex dividend where the share is technically meant to trade ex dividend but can be traded as cum dividend. Also see *cum dividend; ex dividend; special ex*.

special dividend A dividend declared that is irregular in nature and usually follows an exceptionally profitable year or is paid from the proceeds of the sale of an asset. Sometimes called an extra or a bonus dividend. Also see *dividend*.

special drawing right (SDR) The SDR was originally intended as a reserve asset for countries under the auspices of the IMF. SDRs now have only limited use as reserve assets and their main function is to serve as the unit of account of the IMF and some other international organisations.

SDRs are defined in terms of a basket of major currencies used in international trade and finance. At present (2009), the currencies in the basket are the euro, the pound sterling, the Japanese yen and the US dollar. The amounts of each currency making up one SDR are chosen in accordance with the relative importance of the currency in international trade and finance.

SDRs are a form of money used by the IMF and its members, are allocated in line with quotas, can be drawn at will and interest is charged and paid. The value of an SDR is calculated against a basket of key currencies and quoted daily on the major exchanges. Also see *asset*.

special ex The period before the date that a share goes ex dividend where the share is technically meant to trade cum dividend but can be traded ex dividend. This special ex option is usually only available ten days before the ex dividend date. Also see *cum dividend; ex dividend; special cum*.

special general meeting A general meeting called by a company to communicate information to shareholders or make decisions in the form of special resolutions. Also see *annual general meeting; extraordinary general meeting; special resolution*.

specialised finance Finance tailored to a specific need by a company or corporate.

special notarial bond (SNB) A notarial bond that gives the holder perfect security under insolvency proceedings. An SNB bond specifically prescribes movable assets, for example valuable mining equipment or aircraft. In the event of insolvency, the bond holder has first rights over other creditors to the proceeds of the sale of the specific asset. SNBs are registered in deeds registries. A mortgage bond is conceptually an SNB over an immovable asset. Called a fixed charge in the UK. Also see *fixed charge; general notarial bond; mortgage bond; notarial bond*.

special proxy A proxy given the power to vote on a shareholder's behalf with special instructions to vote for or against resolutions. Also see *general proxy; proxy; resolution*.

special-purpose company (SPC) See *special-purpose vehicle*.

special-purpose entity (SPE) See *special-purpose vehicle*.

special-purpose institution (SPI) A company that is put together for a securitisation operation. Also see *securitisation*.

special-purpose vehicle (SPV) An entity or company that is set up to hold or manage a particular asset or project. The cash flows, risks and liabilities are contained in the SPV. SPVs are typically ring fenced. Also see *ring fenced*.

special resolution A resolution that must be passed by the board of directors of a company authorising a company to undertake a particular and substantial transaction such as an acquisition, disposal or liquidation. Also see *resolution; special general meeting*.

special tax bond A bond issued by a government or local authority that is secured against the proceeds of a designated tax, usually a form of excise tax, special assessment tax or ad valorem duty. An example is the issue of a bond to fund the building of healthcare facilities secured against the taxes collected on cigarettes and alcohol. Also see *ad valorem duty; excise tax; special assessment tax*.

specific risk See *unsystematic risk*.

speculation The purchase of assets with the objective of profiting from changes in the price of the asset not attributable to economic logic or drivers.

speculative position Taking an unhedged position in a market to profit potentially from market movements.

spike A temporary swing in the price of a security, quickly followed by a correction to the prevailing trend.

spin off The process of making a subsidiary of a company a separate company on its own. The shares in the separate company are distributed to the shareholders of the parent. Sometimes called unbundling.

spline A function defined by piecewise polynomials used for interpolating point data. They are used extensively for a range of interpolation purposes. Also see *cubic spline*.

split See *share split*.

split rights The process of selling some rights under a rights issue and then using the proceeds to buy shares with the remaining rights options. Also see *rights issue*.

sponsor
1. An entity that is raising finance to acquire an asset or company.
2. An entity that provides cash to a counterparty to be associated with that counterparty's business or performance, for example when a company sponsors a sportsperson.
3. A broker that assists in listing or puts their name to a new company listing on a stock exchange.

sponsoring broker See *sponsor*.

spot See *spot market*.

spot commodity A commodity traded on the spot market for immediate delivery. Also see *spot market*.

spot market The trade in goods for immediate settlement of the terms of trade and delivery. Immediate implies within two days ($t + 2$) for currency exchanges.

spot month See *contract month*.

spot month charge The margin charged by an options clearing house for options in their delivery months. The charge is to ensure that there is cash available to settle the delivery. Also see *clearing house; contract month*.

spot price The price of a commodity on the spot market. A spot transaction is usually for delivery of the underlying asset in two days ($t + 2$). Also see *spot market*.

spot rate The interest or exchange rate for a trade that occurs in the market immediately.

spot trading Selling for immediate delivery.

spread
1. The difference between the bid price and offer or ask price. Also see *ask price; agio; bid price; choice price*.
2. The difference between the yield on a bond and a benchmark yield such as a government bond or treasury bill. For example, a bond may be trading at a yield of 7.0% and a US treasury bill may be trading at 6.5%. The bond is trading at a 0.5% or 50 basis points spread. Also see *basis point; government bond; treasury bill*.

spread bet A form of gambling against the movement in the price of shares. The bet is usually against a range of upper and lower values. If the price goes outside this range, the punter wins a multiple plus a set of points above or below the defined range.

spread margin An options clearing house offers lower margin requirements to entities that carry out spread trades only using options because there is less risk associated with spread trading than other options trades. Also see *clearing house; spread trade*.

spread option See *credit spread option*.

spread trade The process of purchasing and selling financial contracts such as futures contracts to profit from the price differential between their prices. Also see *arbitrage*.

springing subordination The subordination of a group of creditors where all creditors rank pari passu until an event of default occurs. Also see *event of default; pari passu*.

spurious correlation A spurious correlation between data exists because of a statistical fluke rather than true causality. Also see *causality*.

SPV See *special-purpose vehicle*.

squeeze out When a company acquires the majority of another company's share capital, there is a level at which it can effect a squeeze out. Under the squeeze out and relevant regulatory authority, the remaining minority shareholders can be forced to sell their existing shares to the acquiring company. Section 440K of the Companies Act in South Africa governs the squeeze out of shareholders.

Under finance provided for bids, banks often insist that the squeeze out be undertaken so that minority objections can be excluded, that no leakage of dividends to minorities occurs and that the acquirer fully controls the target.

Sometimes called a mandatory offer. Also see *Companies Act; dividend; general offer; mandatory offer*.

SRO See *self-regulatory organisation*.

SRP See *Securities Regulation Panel*.

stabilisation When the lead manager in an underwriting issue purchases the security in the secondary markets to support the issue price. The letter S is displayed on trading screens when a lead manager is performing a stabilisation operation. Also see *lead manager*.

stag The process of applying for the issue of new securities in anticipation that the price of the security shortly after having been issued will be higher in the secondary market. Staging is speculative and often drives prices upwards. Lead arrangers have to manage the issue carefully and ensure that the same investors have not applied for the share issue a number of times.

stagflation When interest rates rise in tandem with economic growth, central bankers focus on controlling the inflation usually associated with strong economic growth. Under certain conditions economic growth can slow or become negative in an environment where interest rates and inflation are on the increase. The scenario of slowing economic growth, rising interest rates and inflation is called stagflation. Stagflation is often the result of slowing economies being subjected to excessive commodity prices and economic conditions that do not respond effectively to monetary policy set by central banks. Also see *central bank; inflation; interest rate; monetary policy*.

staggered directorship A form of poison pill whereby directors of a company are appointed for a significant period of time and cannot be removed unduly. The implication of this approach is that the purchaser of such a company will not be in a position to change the board of directors. Also see *poison pill*.

staging profit When issuing shares in a new equity issue, the shares are underpriced so that the investors make a small profit. Underpricing boosts relations with new investors but may also aggravate existing shareholders.

stake building The process of an entity acquiring shares in a company at a reasonably slow rate to build a significant stake for strategic reasons. Also see *mandatory offer; squeeze out*.

stakeholder Someone other than a shareholder or lender that has a direct or indirect claim on the cash flow of a business, for example an employee or tax collection agency.

stakeholder lock-in Contracts with buyers and warranties are some parameters that can restrict the formulation and implementation of strategy.

stale cheque A cheque that has been written, not cashed and has been outstanding for so long that the bank where the relevant account is held will not cash it. Stale cheques are usually older than six months.

stamp duty A levy or tax imposed by government on financial transactions.

Standard and Poor (S&P) A company that is principally a credit rating agency. S&P also provides other financial products such as indices. Also see *credit rating agency*.

standard deviation A statistical term used to describe a parameter of a probability distribution. It is calculated by means of the following equation:

$$\sigma = \sqrt{\frac{\sum_{i=0}^{n}(x_i - \bar{x})}{n}} \text{ where } \bar{x} = \frac{\sum_{i=0}^{n} x_i}{n}$$

The standard deviation is the most common measure of price volatility in finance. Standard deviations cannot be added while variances can be. Also see *normal distribution; variance; volatility*.

standard portfolio analysis of risk (SPAN) SPAN evaluates the risk of an entire options trading account's futures/options portfolio. SPAN assesses a margin requirement based on such calculated risks. It accomplishes this by establishing reasonable movements in futures prices over a one-day period.

standby letter of credit A letter of credit that is issued and only used as a last resort should a financial transaction fail. Also see *letter of credit*.

standby liquidity facility A loan facility that companies use in exceptional circumstances. These facilities are often used to back up bond issuance programmes and are structured in the form of revolving credit facilities. Sometimes called a back-up facility. Also see *backstop facility; revolving credit facility*.

standby loan See *standby liquidity facility*.

standing order A stop order off a bank account. Also see *stop order*.

standstill agreement
1. An agreement in a hostile takeover where the target is afforded the opportunity of halting the takeover attempt. The target often purchases the shares already bought at a premium.
2. An agreement between multiple lenders and a borrower where debt is restructured instead of the lenders acting independently and calling for the winding up or liquidation of the borrower.

staple financing A financing agreement 'stapled onto' an acquisition offer. It is an indication of how the takeover firm plans to fund the deal and forms a guideline for how the eventual finance will be negotiated.

star An asset or product with great potential. Also see *Boston matrix*.

start up A newly formed business or venture. Also see *venture capital*.

start-up costs The costs associated with the start of a new venture.

state The government.

stated capital An accounting system where there is no par value and share premium for a share. The share is stated in the accounts at the price at which it was issued. Also see *par value; share premium*.

static equilibrium The equilibrium position that brings supply and demand into perfect balance. Also see *equilibrium*.

stationary process A random process where all its statistical properties do not vary with time. For example, the heights of a group of grown adults form a stationary data set. Also see *non-stationary process; unit root*.

statutory Required by law.

statutory accounts Accounts or financial statements that are required by law, usually a companies act. Also see *Companies Act*.

statutory company A company formed by an act of parliament.

statutory cost Statutory or mandatory costs are incurred by banking institutions when lending to clients as a result of the capital adequacy and cash reserves required by law. Statutory costs are passed on to lenders as a rate in addition to the interest rate and are usually included in the credit margin.

Statutory costs in different countries are generally a function of diversification of risk in their markets. Statutory costs are higher in markets with a high degree of systemic risk such as the smaller capital-poor emerging markets. For example, South Africa has significantly higher statutory costs than the UK.

Central banks set and monitor monetary and other policies that ultimately determine the markets' statutory cost requirements. Sometimes called associated costs, mandatory costs or liquid asset requirements. Also see *capital adequacy; central bank; emerging market; interest rate; liquid asset requirements; reserve requirement; systemic*.

statutory meeting See *annual general meeting*.

stay in business capital Capital expenditure to maintain existing productive assets. This includes the replacement of vehicles, plant and machinery and capital expenditure related to safety, health and the environment. Also see *capital expenditure; depreciation; free cash flow*.

STC See *secondary tax on companies*.

STEF Structured trade and export finance.

step-in rights The ability of lenders to take management control of a borrower to ensure that all the conditions of the financing facility are met.

step-up bond A bond with coupon payments stepping up over time. An example is a five-year bond with a 4% coupon for the first two years and a 6% coupon for the remaining three years. Companies may issue these bonds when they anticipate strong earnings growth in the future and will be able to afford higher future payments, thus effectively subsidising the nearer term obligations.

step-up cap An interest rate cap strategy where the strike price of the interest rate cap increases. These caps may be used to match financing with inflation-linked cash flows. Also see *accreting cap; inflation; interest rate*.

step-up margin A margin that increases over the life a loan. Margin step-ups are often used to encourage borrowers to refinance existing facilities.

stepwise regression A method of selecting variables for inclusion in a regression model. It operates by introducing the candidate variables one at a time as in forward selection and then attempting to remove variables following each forward step.

sterilisation The objective of sterilisation is to control money supply. It is done by central banks through open market operations. Sterilisation is a form of monetary action in which a central bank or federal reserve attempts to insulate itself from the foreign exchange market to counteract the effects of a changing monetary base. The sterilisation process is used to manipulate the value of one domestic currency relative to another and is initiated in the forex market. For example, to keep a currency undervalued against the US dollar, a central bank can purchase a large proportion of the dollars coming into the country and issue local currency into the market. The excess local currency is then mopped up in the domestic market by the sale of central bank or government securities. Another example is the US Federal Reserve (Fed) weakening the US dollar against another currency by selling dollars and purchasing foreign currency. The increased supply of the US dollar lowers the dollar value per unit foreign currency. Also see *central bank; exchange rate parity; fixed exchange rate; money supply; open market operations*.

sterling The currency of the UK, officially called the pound sterling, divided into 100 pence.

stet A Latin word meaning let it stand.

STI See *Straits Times Index*.

STIBOR Stockholm interbank offer rate.

sticky Economic variables that are resistant to change. Prices and wages are often sticky downwards, i.e. they go up easily but do not come down easily.

sticky money Funds invested that are long term in nature and not speculative.

sticky price A price that easily moves upwards but is less willing to go downwards. Wages usually fall into this category.

STIR future See *short-term interest rate futures*.

stochastic See *stochastic process*.

stochastic difference equation A stochastic difference equation is a linear difference equation with random forcing variables on the right-hand side. Here is a stochastic difference equation in k:

$$k_{t+1} + k_t = w_t$$

where k and w are scalars and time t goes from 0 to infinity. The w is an exogenous forcing variable.

$$Ak_{t+1} + Bk_t + Ck_{t-1} = Dw_t + e_t$$

where k is a vector, w and e are exogenous vectors and A, B, C and D are constant matrices.

Also see *Brownian motion; random walk with drift*.

stochastic process A stochastic process is a random function. In the most common applications, the domain over which the function is defined is a time interval. Familiar examples of processes modelled as stochastic time series include stock market and exchange rate fluctuations. Also see *deterministic process*.

stochastic trend A time series that contains a unit root. Also see *deterministic trend; unit root*.

stock
1. A term usually used in the US for an equity share.
2. A series of assets held by a company for sale, sometimes called inventories. Also see *inventory*.

stockbroker An intermediary or agent who facilitates the buying and selling of listed shares or securities. Stockbrokers need to be members of a stock exchange and in possession of a seat.

stock equilibrium price The price at which demand and supply of stocks match.

stockholder See *shareholder*.

stock lending The process of lending securities for a fee to an entity that needs them for a particular purpose. For example, the borrower may have shorted a share and needs the underlying shares to create his/her short position. The lending of the shares is often collateralised and can be undertaken to enhance the returns of a portfolio. Also see *rebate; sell short*.

stock option See *equity option*.

stock split See *share split*.

stock turnover The number of times a company turns over its inventory in a single year. The ratio is defined by:

$$\text{stock turnover ratio} = \frac{\text{cost of sales}}{\text{inventory}}$$

The higher the ratio is, the more efficiently a company is managing its inventory and effectively making more sales off a lower inventory base thereby releasing working capital. Sometimes called an inventory turnover ratio. Also see *inventory turnover*.

stop limit An order not to trade beyond a predefined limit.

stop loss A sell order that is executed when the price of the underlying asset declines to a predefined level at which the investor wants to discontinue owning the asset and losing value. Stop losses are specified at the time of purchase of a security as a percentage of the initial purchase price. A stop loss is a form of conditional order. Also see *conditional order*.

stop order
1. See *stop loss*.
2. If a client makes a payment by stop order, the bank is instructed to debit the account with a set amount regularly. The contract in this case is therefore between the client and the bank. To cancel or amend a stop order, the client must notify the bank. Sometimes called a standing order.

STP See *straight through processing*.

straddle The purchase of a combination of equal numbers of call options and put options with the same strike prices and expiration dates. Volatility in the market is required to profit off a straddle. A long straddle is when both options are bought and a short straddle is when both options are sold. The diagram below illustrates the payoffs for both long and short straddle positions. Also see *call option; put option; strangle; strike price; volatility*.

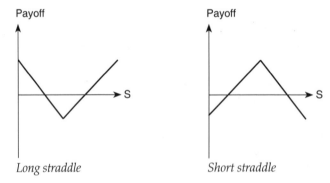

Long straddle   Short straddle

straight bond A bond with no embedded options or derivatives that pays coupons annually or semi-annually. Also see *bond*.

straight line method of depreciation The depreciation of an asset by a fixed amount, usually calculated at cost, per year down to zero over a defined number of years. For example, if an asset cost R12 and is depreciated over four years, its value is R12 in year 1; R9 in year 2; R6 in year 3; R3 in year 4 and R0 in year 5. This method is preferred as it allows for larger deductions earlier in the project than other methods such as the diminishing balance method. Also see *asset; depreciation*.

straight through processing (STP) The automated settlement of financial transactions to increase the speed and efficiency at which it is done.

Straits Times Index (STI) A market capitalisation index of the top 30 companies on the Singapore stock market. Also see *market capitalisation index*.

strangle The purchase of a combination of equal numbers of call and put options with different strike prices and expiration dates. Volatility is required in the market to profit off a strangle. A long strangle is when both options are bought and a short strangle is when both options are sold. The payoff diagram of a strangle is shown below. Also see *call option; put option; straddle; strike price; volatility.*

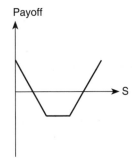

strap A trading strategy that involves the purchase (long) of two call options and one put option at the same strike price and expiration date. A strip involves one call and two puts. The diagram below shows the payoff relationship of this trading strategy. Also see *strike price; strip.*

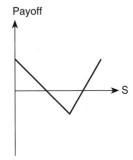

strike price The fixed price in an option contract at which the holder can buy or sell the underlying asset. Also called the exercise price. Also see *asset; option.*

STRIP Separate trading of registered interest and principal. Also see *stripping bonds.*

strip A trading strategy that involves the purchase (long) of one call and two put options at the same strike price. A strap involves two calls and a single put. The diagram below shows the payoff relationship of this trading strategy. Also see *strap; strike price.*

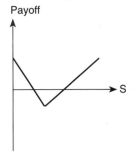

stripping bonds The cash flow payments or coupons from bonds are issued as a series of zero coupon bonds. The principal value of the bond is then left over as a remaining zero coupon bond. The separate bonds can be traded. The process of stripping often makes the market for the debt more liquid. The term C-strip refers to coupon strips while a P-strip is a principal value strip. Also see *bond; liquid; STRIP; zero coupon bond.*

strong holder A long-term investor who does not actively buy and sell a stock but holds onto it. The shares are said to be tightly held. Also see *sticky money; tightly held.*

strongly efficient market All information of every kind is contained in the share price. All market information is instantly impounded into the share price. The purchase of securities cannot be timed, books cannot be cooked and all investors have access to the same information at the same time. Having efficient markets is important so that investors obtain fair value and capital can be raised in the market at fair value. Also see *unbiased forward rate hypothesis.*

structural adjustment Changes made in an economy to raise productive capacity. Reforms associated with structural adjustments promote free and more open markets, liberalisation of exchange controls and tax reforms.

structural equation An endogenous variable is dependent on the current realisation of another endogenous variable.

structural flex When the structure of a syndicated loan is changed to ensure that the loan is fully subscribed in the syndication sell down process. Also see *market flex.*

structural subordination When a holding company has many subsidiaries, debt holders that hold parent company debt are effectively subordinated to lenders who have lent money to the subsidiaries. The parent company has an equity stake in the subsidiaries and so will receive the last proceeds of liquidated subsidiaries. The parent company debt holders therefore effectively only have claim on the equity assets of the parent company. The subsidiary debt holders receive any cash proceeds from the liquidation of subsidiaries before lenders to the parent. For these reasons, lenders do not like to lend to holding companies and tend to lend closest to the money or require cross-guarantee structures. Also see *concurrent creditor; holding company; subordinate.*

structural unemployment Unemployment that is not sensitive to cyclical demand but results when workers' skills do not match employers' needs.

structured finance See *structured product.*

structured investment vehicle (SIV) An investment company usually set up as a special-purpose vehicle that takes advantage of differences in the yields of long-term and short-term debt. SIVs purchase long dated AAA and AA debt using the proceeds from the issue of shorter term asset-backed commercial paper. SIVs are essentially a special type of collateralised debt obligation used for leveraged riding of the yield curve.

SIVs can become risky if there is significant volatility in the credit markets and the yield curve changes shape or shifts. If liquidity in the market begins to dry up, the ability of the SIV to roll over short-term commercial paper may become compromised thereby threatening the structure. Also see *collateralised debt obligation; commercial paper; securitisation; short-term debt; special-purpose vehicle; yield curve.*

structured note An instrument that is customised to the required risk profile of the investor. The structuring usually occurs through embedding options and other derivative contracts. Also see *structured product.*

structured product A synthetic investment instrument created to fill a specific need in the market. They are used to reduce the risk of a portfolio and use derivative products.

They can take the form of products that guarantee capital preservation or partial capital preservation. An example is an investor investing 100 units in a structured product. The structured product fund then purchases a zero coupon bond with nominal value of 100 at a price of 90 units and uses the remaining 10 units to purchase a derivative instrument such as an option to gain more risky exposure. At maturity, the capital portion is guaranteed. Securitisation is a method of structuring the risk of an underlying product and is often classed as a structured product. Also see *capital at risk product; capital secure product; equity-linked note; securitisation; zero coupon bond.*

subdivision See *share split.*

sub-investment grade A company or financial instrument with a credit rating below Moody's Baa3 or S&P's BBB–. Also see *credit rating; investment grade; junk bond.*

subordinate The level of claim that creditors have over the assets of an entity in liquidation. Subordinate lenders only receive proceeds from the liquidation after the claims of senior creditors have been settled. Also see *liquidation.*

subordinated debenture A debenture that has a claim on assets under liquidation only once senior creditors such as the holders of normal secured debt (pledge debt) have been paid. Also see *debenture; liquidation; pledge debt; seniority.*

subordination See *subordinate.*

subparticipation Participation in a loan through a funded participation or a risk participation. Also see *funded participation; risk participation.*

subprime See *subprime crisis; subprime loan.*

subprime crisis In 2007 a debt crisis resulted from subprime loans defaulting. The loans had been wrapped into collateralised mortgage obligations and many banks and other financial institutions that had invested in these suffered substantial write downs. Due to a lack of transparency in the collateralised mortgage obligation market, banks and other institutions became nervous and stopped lending to one another, creating significant liquidity constraints in the interbank markets. Also see *collateralised mortgage obligation; money market; subprime loan.*

subprime loan A loan that is offered to individuals for rates higher than the prime rate. These individuals do not qualify for loans at prime rates and constitute higher risk lending. Also see *prime rate.*

subrogation A legal concept usually used in the context of insurance or guarantees where one party is afforded the right to step into another's shoes. For example, should a person be in a car accident that was the fault of another party, the insurance company can step in, post payment for the repairs of the vehicle and then demand payment from the responsible party (or their insurer).

subscriber
1. An entity that purchases shares in a company.
2. An entity that signs up for a service or product delivery. Cell phone and pay TV consumers are called subscribers.

subscription price The price of a share when offered in a rights issue. Also see *ex rights price; nil price; rights issue offer.*

subscription privilege See *pre-emptive right*.

subscription ratio
1. The number of rights needed to acquire a share in a rights issue. Also see *rights issue offer*.
2. The total number of bids received for the issue of a bond over the final allocation.

subscription right See *pre-emptive right*.

subsidiary An entity, including an unincorporated entity such as a partnership, that is controlled by another entity known as the parent. Also see *affiliate; associate; division; joint venture*.

subsidy Payments from one party to another to make a product or service more competitive. Governments often provide subsidies to particular sectors to boost their performance, aid in creating or sustaining employment and for various other political objectives.

substance over form The principal that transactions and other events are accounted for and presented in accordance with their substance and economic reality and not merely their legal form.

substitute product A product that can be interchanged with little difference to the consumer. Substitute products influence the price of one another and are price elastic. Also see *price elastic*.

substitution swap A bond swap where bonds of different yields are swapped. Also see *yield pickup swap*.

sub-underwrite The process where underwriters minimise their underwriting obligations by selling down their underwriting commitments to other parties willing to take on the risk for a fee.

succession plan A human resources plan that ensures that key personnel can be replaced in the event of their leaving.

sukuk A form of Islamic bond that effectively has coupons, maturity dates and yields. Charging interest is not allowed under Islamic law and the bonds therefore have to have an underlying transaction such as the sale and leaseback on a property. Islamic investors must focus on an underlying asset and viability of a project, rather than the creditworthiness of the issuer. They are not allowed to receive interest payments on cash and are compensated by cash generated from business activities. Also see *bond*.

sum of the parts valuation (SOTP) An approach used to value a company by calculating the value of each of the operational units using a discounted cash flow valuation or multiple valuation techniques. The value of the company is then calculated by summing all its components. Also see *discounted cash flow valuation; multiple valuation*.

sunk cost A cost already incurred that does not affect future cash flows. These cash outlays should ideally not be considered as part of an investment decision. Also see *cash flow*.

supersede To replace with higher levels of authority or importance.

super cycle An extended period of high prices. The extended period of high prices in a super cycle is usually significantly longer than in ordinary economic cycles.

superdot Super designated order turnaround system. A system used on the New York Stock Exchange to trade equities.

supermajority Voting dynamics where more than a simple majority of 50% + 1 vote is required for a decision to be taken. Supermajorities are required for extraordinary resolutions and possibly special resolutions. A supermajority typically constitutes a 75% majority. Also see *special resolution*.

super sinker A short-term bond that has long-term coupons.

supervisory board An independent board appointed to guide and oversee the executive directors of a company.

supply or pay agreement See *put or pay agreement*.

supply risk The risk that the raw materials required for a production facility or to complete a building project become unavailable.

support Price levels for which there is purchasing support in the market. For example, if prices of a security fall from R11 to R10 and at R10 there are enough investors willing to purchase the share so that the price remains above R10, then there is support for the share at the R10 level. Also see *resistance*.

support letter See *credit support letter*.

support level See *support*.

supranational An organisation such as the World Bank that is set up by a number of nations. Also see *World Bank*.

surety A form of guarantee where one party stands for the obligations of another. The key difference between a surety and a guarantee is that with a guarantee the claimant can immediately call on the guarantor to remedy losses whereas with a surety, the claimant must first claim from the borrower. Only after the winding up of that claim can the claimant call on the surety to make whole any outstanding losses. Also see *surety bond*.

surety bond A guarantee whereby one party undertakes to pay any losses suffered by another party associated with a breach of a contract or legal obligation. The bond transfers risk from one party to another. These types of bonds are used in infrastructure projects and protect against failed delivery by contractors or contractors going insolvent. Banks and insurance companies often extend a bonding facility to companies under which they can issue surety bonds.

Sometimes called a performance bond. Also see *bond; bonding facility; guarantee*.

surplus When income or revenue is greater than expenditure, the surplus is the profit made. The term surplus is usually used with reference to non-profit organisations such as the government. Also see *deficit*.

surplus unit A lender of money. An entity with income greater than expenditure.

sushi bond A Eurobond issued by a Japanese company. Sushi bonds are taken up by financial investors in the Japanese market. Also see *Eurobond; samurai bond*.

suspended share A share that is not traded on a stock exchange because exchange regulators have found reason to suspend the share. Reasons may include the company entering into negotiations that can have a significant influence on the share price or events that can cause abnormal price movements.

suspense account An account used to process financial transactions that have not yet been finalised.

suspension of trading The suspension of trading on or outside the relevant trading exchange's order book. Also see *circuit breaker; trading halt*.

suspensive conditions Another phrase for *conditions precedent*.

suspensive sale A method of financing an asset where possession is taken on payment of a deposit and ownership is taken when the last scheduled payment has been made or when a set of suspensive conditions is fully met. A hire purchase agreement is a form of suspensive sale. Also see *hire purchase*.

sustainable growth rate (SGR) The maximum growth rate a firm can achieve without external equity financing while maintaining the same debt to equity ratio, dividend payout ratio, profit margin ratio and assets to turnover ratio. SGR is defined by:

$$\text{sustainable growth rate (SGR)} = \frac{\text{ROE} \times b}{1 - \text{ROE} \times b}$$

where ROE = the return on equity; b = the plough-back or retention ratio.

When analysing SGR look at what factors affect the plough-back ratio such as profit margins and dividends paid. Also see *Du Pont analysis; firm; internal growth rate; profit margin; return on equity; retention ratio*.

SVA See *shareholder value analysis*.

swap A derivative instrument where counterparties exchange one set of cash flows for another at predefined dates. Swaps such as interest rate swaps can be used to hedge risk. Swaps are over the counter and are negotiated outside exchanges. Swaps are valued by netting the present value of all the future cash flows. Also see *accreting swap; amortising swap; asset swap; backwardation swap; basis swap; bond swap; borrowers swap; commodity swap; constant maturity swap; contango swap; credit default swap; currency swap; equity swap; forward start swap; FX swap; hedge; inflation-linked swap; interest rate anticipation swap; interest rate swap; location swap; off market swap; overnight indexed swap; reinvestment protection swap; quality swap; real estate swap; rollercoaster swap; swap rate; total return swap; yield curve swap; yield pickup swap; zero coupon swap*.

swap curve When swapping fixed for floating rates in an interest rate swap, the fixed rates at which this is done can be plotted as a swap curve. For example, the fixed rate applicable for swapping a 10-year fixed rate bond into a floating interest rate will constitute a single data point on the swap curve. The South African swap curve rates are quoted on a nominal annual compound quarterly (NACQ) basis by default. The ask (offer) rate quoted is the rate the trader is willing to receive the floating rate and pay the fixed rate. The bid rate is the rate the trader is willing to receive the fixed and pay the floating rate. Also see *floating interest rate; interest rate swap; yield curve*.

swap points The difference between the exchange rate of the forward transaction and the exchange rate of the spot transaction in a foreign exchange swap. The swap points are normally a result of interest rate differentials between countries. Also see *interest rate; spot market*.

swap rate
1. For American-style FX, see *forward differential*.
2. The swap rate on an interest rate swap is the quoted fixed rate leg of the swap. The

rate can be arrived at by creating a swap using a fixed rate instrument as one set of cash flows and a floating interest rate for the other set of cash flows. Given the zero coupon rates for the fixed income instrument, the discount rates can be used in a bond valuation calculation (trading at par) to calculate the fixed rate of payment. Also see *bond; floating interest rate; interest rate swap; swap.*

swap spread A commonly used measure of the difference between the swap curve and government debt yield curve. The swap spread is commonly used by corporates in South Africa when analysing the cost of bond issuance and commercial paper programmes. Also see *swap curve; yield curve.*

swaption The purchaser of a swaption has the right, but not the obligation, to enter into a swap at a future date, i.e. it is an option on a swap. The swap will be entered into at a given rate, for a given maturity, on or before a specific future date. Swaption premiums are quoted as a percentage of a notional and are due upfront. A modified Black-Scholes model can be used to price a swaption. Also see *Black-Scholes options pricing model; swap.*

sweat money See *equity.*

sweep In a loan agreement there are sometimes provisions that allow for the borrower's cash to be used to pay off or service debt. These provisions are sometimes called a cash sweep. In personal finance, a cash sweep can be put on a current account to service outstanding credit card debt. The cash sweep effectively takes the form of the bank automatically deducting the appropriate credit card payment off the current account.

sweetener A transaction where additional elements such as options are thrown in to make the deal more attractive for investors. Also see *convertible debt.*

SWF See *sovereign wealth fund.*

SWIFT See *Society for Worldwide Interbank Financial Transactions.*

swingline loan A loan that is granted to a corporate that provides accessibility to strong cash flows and that can be used to fund debt payments. These are often short term and vary between one and ten days. Swingline loans are used as a support for a commercial paper (CP) programme and are used to cover timing differences in cash being received and paid. An example of the use of a swingline facility is a situation where a CP programme is refinanced with a revolving credit facility bank loan and the settlement of the CP notes does not coincide with the timing on the first drawdown on the RCF. Also see *commercial paper; daylight overdraft; revolving credit facility.*

switch One asset is sold and another purchased shortly thereafter.

switching option American call and put options that allow the owner to switch projects or operations at a fixed cost. Also see *fixed expense.*

sword A trading platform used on the London Metals Exchange (LME). Also see *London Metals Exchange.*

syndicate A generic term describing the process of a group of entities entering a financial agreement such as a loan or an investment as a collective. Syndicated products usually have an agent who manages the facility for the collective. Also see *syndicated loan.*

syndicated loan A large loan taken up by corporations that are financed by multiple banks usually with a single or small set of lead banks or book runners. These loans are made on reasonably low margins and are often in the form of revolving credit facilities or term loans. Banks syndicate loans to manage credit risk. Syndicated loans can be secured or unsecured debt, are nearly always senior debt and attract floating interest rates. Syndicated loans are callable by the borrower at par value without penalty unless prepayment provisions are expressly stipulated.

Advantages of a syndicated loan are the following:

- A large pool of credit is available.
- It can be cost efficient as lenders often anticipate relationship-based ancillary business.
- Standard terms and conditions make it easier to manage than a series of bilateral agreements.
- Borrowers can form relationships with a wide range of banks.
- It is confidential within the bank group.
- Credit ratings are not required.
- It has a flexible cash flow as borrowers can access term loans and revolving credit facilities as well as letter of credit facilities.

A disadvantage of a syndicated loan is that it has a limited tenor of anything up to seven years.

Also see *book runner; credit rating; credit risk; floating interest rate; letter of credit; margin; revolving credit facility; secured debt; seniority; tenor; term loan; unsecured debt*.

syndication agent The entity, usually an investment bank, that handles the syndication of a loan. The term book runner is used more frequently. Also see *agent; investment bank*.

synergy Similarities or compatible expertise or capabilities that give combined entities a competitive advantage. The management of companies use synergies in mergers and acquisitions to the advantage of the newly formed company. Also see *merger*.

synthetic collatralised loan obligation (CLO) A form of collateralised loan obligation where a true sale of assets from the originator does not occur. The credit risk is transferred to the special-purpose vehicle (SPV) by the SPV selling the originator a credit default swap (CDS) or loan guarantee instrument. The SPV issues bonds to the market and invests the proceeds of those bonds to collateralise the CDS instruments. Also see *credit default swap; credit risk; special-purpose vehicle; true sale*.

synthetic instrument/security A combination of alternate financial instruments to replicate the behaviour of another instrument. The word synthetic implies that it is artificially manufactured. Also see *lookalike*.

synthetic lease A synthetic lease places the ownership of an asset in a special-purpose vehicle (SPV) and leases the asset under an operating lease back to the company. The structure of this lease effectively moves the asset off the company's balance sheet. The depreciation of the asset is run through the SPV and not through the income statement of the company. Also see *capital lease*.

synthetic position A combination of options to give the same return cash streams of a long or short position in another underlying asset.

systematic risk A risk that influences a large number of assets such as the risks that affect the wider market. Also called market risk. All assets are exposed to a systematic risk and risks unique to the particular assets. The relationships between them can be described by:

$\sigma_s^2 \equiv R^2 \sigma_s^2 + (1 - R^2) \sigma_s^2$ = market risk² + unique risk²

market risk = $\sqrt{R^2 \sigma_s^2}$

unique risk = $\sqrt{(1 - R^2) \sigma_s^2}$

where R^2 = ANOVA parameter for the linear combination of the share versus the market and in this case represents the proportion of systematic risk; σ^2 = total risk² = share risk².

Also see *unsystematic risk*.

systematic risk principal The expected return on a risky asset depends only on the asset's systematic risk. Since unsystematic risk can be avoided by diversifying, then there is theoretically no reward for bearing it. Also see *asset; beta; expected return*.

system dependency ratio The percentage of contributors currently in a retirement fund that supports pensioners. The pension schemes where this ratio applies are the unfunded or pay as you go schemes. Also see *pay as you go*.

systemic How economic effects, usually negative effects, pass through a system. Also see *contagion*.

systemic risk The risk that an entire system will fail. The failure of a few large dominant banks constitutes systemic risk.

system lock-in Once a standard system has been adopted such as information technology platforms Windows or SAP, it is difficult and costly to transfer to another platform or product.

T+2 A convention that dictates delivery of cash two days after maturity of the underlying instrument.

T-day See *trade date*.

tail See *residual*.

taka The currency of Bangladesh divided into 100 paisa.

take and hold A purchased instrument that may not be sold on or that the investor has no intention of selling.

take delivery The process of actually taking delivery of the underlying assets under an options or futures contract.

take or pay contract An agreement where a party contracts to purchase a set number of goods for a specified period. If the purchaser is unable to take the goods it is contracted to purchase, it will still be liable to pay for the goods not taken. Take or pay contracts are common when arranging project finance. Also see *project finance; put or pay agreement*.

take out finance Finance raised with the aim of restructuring or taking out existing debt.

takeover The process of acquiring shares in a company to gain voting control. There are regulations in place governing takeovers aimed at protecting minority investors. The regulations include mandatory offers where the minority shareholders must be offered the same price as those sold in the takeover bid. Also see *acquisition; mandatory offer*.

taker The purchaser of an option. A taker is the opposite of a writer.

take up The holder of rights under a rights issue exercises the right and hands over the cash as well as the rights certificate in exchange for shares under the new issue. Also see *nil paid letter; rights issue/offer*.

take-up price Under a rights issue which is the offer of the sale of new shares to existing shareholders, the sale is offered at a specified price called the take-up price. Also see *rights issue/offer*.

taking a view
1. An opinion on which way the price of a share or market is going to move.
2. The length of time that one expects to hold a share before selling it.

tala The currency of Samoa divided into 100 sene.

tangible asset An asset generally physical in nature whose value is easily calculable. There should be an open active market with two-way prices quoted or established and accepted valuation models to determine the asset's value. Also see *intangible asset*.

tangible net worth Net worth, i.e. assets less liabilities and less intangible assets such as goodwill and intellectual property. A defined tangible net worth is often used as a financial covenant in loan agreements. For technology and other companies with significant intellectual property, the tangible net worth measure may not reflect the value of the business. Also see *financial covenant; goodwill; intangible asset; minimum net worth; net worth*.

tangible net worth covenant A financial covenant in a loan agreement that requires that the borrower maintain a specified level of tangible net worth. This ratio is used for loans to financial institutions, sometimes with the capital ratio covenant. This covenant is not useful for technology companies and others with significant intellectual property as the substantial value of the intangible assets is not captured in the measure of tangible net worth. Also see *capital ratio covenant; financial covenant*.

tap
1. A form of sale of government securities where smaller lots are made available to market makers. Also see *market maker*.
2. Tapping a bond is the process of raising funds in the bond market by using existing tradable bonds. The additional funding is acquired using the same documentation, terms and conditions as the previous issue.

taper relief The adjustment of capital gains tax rates according to whether the asset that is sold and potentially subject to capital gains tax is a business asset or not. Also see *capital gains tax*.

tapping See *tap*.

TARGET Trans-European real time gross settlement express transfer system.

target company A company that is subject to a takeover bid.

TARGET day A day when the TARGET system is operating for payment in euros. Also see *TARGET*.

target number of units The number of units to be sold to achieve a target net profit. The metric is defined by:

$$\text{target number of units} = \frac{\text{fixed costs} + \text{target profit}}{\text{contributed margin per unit}}$$

Also see *net profit*.

tariff
1. A taxation levied on imported goods. Tariffs can be flat rate charges or charged as a percentage of the cost.
2. A list of prices.

tau
1. The Greek letter T or τ.
2. The Greek letter sometimes used instead of vega. Also see *vega*.

tax A charge levied by governments on income.

taxable bond A bond whose coupons are taxable.

tax and loan account An account of the government with major commercial banks for loaning money and receiving tax payments.

tax anticipation note A bond that is issued by a government that will be serviced in the future with anticipated tax revenue. Also see *revenue anticipation note*.

tax base The income on which taxes are levied. The income is usually the aggregate income of a country.

tax break A tax allowance used by a government to encourage a particular activity or behaviour.

tax credit When payments such as dividends are made that have already had tax levied on them, recipients of the payment are given a tax credit so that they are not taxed twice.

tax deferred Financial instruments where tax is due on the date of maturity.

tax exempt Income from instruments that is free of taxation. Sometimes governments issue tax exempt bonds to provide incentives for investors to purchase the bonds.

tax free Goods or services that have not had taxes levied on them.

tax gross up When interest payments are subject to withholding tax or a similar deduction, the tax payable is added to or included in the interest due. This is done so that the lender receives the payment that they expected irrespective of whether or not withholding tax is levied. Also see *withholding tax*.

tax haven A country with a low tax rate. These countries use low tax rates to attract foreign investment. There are many small islands around the world that are considered to be tax havens.

tax holiday A period for which taxation has been waived for a particular transaction or project. Countries often give investors tax holidays for a defined period after completion of a project to attract investors.

tax incidence The division of taxes between buyers and sellers.

tax loss See *assessed loss*.

tax oriented lease A financial lease in which the lessor is the owner for tax purposes. Tax-oriented leases make the most sense when the lessee is not in a position to use tax credits or depreciation deductions that come with owning the asset. Also called a true lease or a tax lease. Also see *asset; financial lease*.

tax rebate A repayment to a taxpayer of excess taxes already paid.

tax return The documentation provided by income earners to tax authorities that enables the authorities to collect the appropriate tax due.

tax shield A deduction such as depreciation or interest on debt from taxable profits that has the effect of reducing the tax liability. Also see *depreciation*.

tax treaty A treaty between countries to ensure that income earners and investors are not taxed more than once.

Taylor expansion A mathematical concept that allows practitioners to obtain linear approximations to non-linear functions. If a function $f(x)$ has continuous derivatives up to $(n + 1)^{th}$ order, then this function can be expanded according to the following formula:

$$f(x) = f(a) + f'(a)(x-a) + \frac{f''(a)(x-a)^2}{2!} + \ldots + \frac{f^{(n)}(a)(x-a)^n}{n!} + R_n$$

where R_n, called the remainder after $n+1$ terms, is given by:

$$R_n = \int_a^x f^{(n+1)}(u) \frac{(x-u)^n}{n!} du = \frac{f^{(n+1)}(\xi)(x-a)^{n+1}}{(n+1)!} \quad a < \xi < x$$

When this expansion converges over a certain range of x, i.e. $\lim_{n \to \infty} R_n = 0$, then the expansion is called the Taylor series of $f(x)$ expanded about a.

Taylor's rule A monetary policy equation that relates what central banks should move interest rates to in response to divergences in inflation rates and GDP from potential GDP. Taylor's rule is defined by:

$$i_t = \pi_i + r_t^* + a_\pi(\pi_t - \pi_t^*) + a_y(y_t + \bar{y}_t)$$

where i_t = the target interest rate; r_t^* = the real equilibrium interest rate; a_π and a_y = constants, both typically set to 0.5; π_t = the rate of inflation; π_t^* = the target rate of inflation; y_t = the log of real GDP; $\bar{y}_t$ = the log of potential GDP.

Taylor's rule works well in large economies with efficient markets such as Europe and the US. In countries like South Africa, structural rigidities in markets and external shocks to the economy result in Taylor's rule generally predicting lower than required interest rates. Central banks used Taylor's rule as a guideline only. Also see *interest rate*.

TB See *treasury bill*.

TBA To be announced.

TBMA The Bond Market Association.

T-bond contract A bond futures contract on the CBOT exchange that uses a US treasury bill as the underlying asset. The treasury bill has a face value of $100 000, 6% coupon and a minimum time to maturity of 15 years. Also see *bond future; Chicago Board of Trade; face value; treasury bill*.

teaser The offer of a security to an investor to attract responses and gauge investor appetite at the offered levels.

technical analysis An analysis that is used to detect the best buy and sell timing in the marketplace. Also see *fundamental analysis*.

technical completion See *completion*.

technical default The issuer of a bond or borrower of a bank loan who violates a provision in the debt contract. A technical default does not involve payment and is often subject to renegotiation of the terms of the loans. Also see *default*.

technical reserves The assets held by insurance companies against their future liabilities.

TED spread The difference, or spread, between the rate on a government treasury bill and the corresponding interbank lending rate such as LIBOR or JIBAR. The three-month treasury bill and three-month interbank rates are typically used. The TED spread gives an indication of the risk premium the banking market is subject to. Also see *JIBAR; LIBOR; spread; treasury bill*.

telco A telecommunications company.

tender
1. An offer to purchase.
2. South African treasury bills and bonds are sometimes called tenders. Also see *bond; treasury bill*.

tenement
1. A legal term indicating the rights to a property. This term is used in the mining industry to indicate the ownership of mineral rights on land.
2. A building used for human habitation that is usually rented.

tenge The currency of Kazakhstan divided into 100 tiyn.

tenor The time between issuing a security and the date of its maturity. Also see *match funding*.

term
1. The time period of a loan agreement. Also see *tenor*.
2. The period of time before a financial security matures.
3. The conditions in a financial contract.

term bond A series of bonds that have the same date of maturity.

term deposit A deposit of funds over a fixed term. This investment carries a fixed interest rate. Sometimes called a fixed deposit.

terminal value The value of an investment at the final date of maturity or end of life. The terminal value is calculated using the present value formula. Also see *par value; present value*.

termination fee A fee paid to the purchaser of an asset or arranger of a financial transaction if the transaction is unsuccessful due to a predefined event. The reasons for termination may include the acceptance of a competing bid. The fee is paid to the bidder to compensate them for the time and costs associated with due diligence and other processes involved in the analysis of the target asset. Sometimes called a break-up fee, break fee or drop dead fee. Also see *due diligence*.

term loan A direct business loan of term one to five years that has an immediate or specified drawdown schedule. Term loans are repaid quarterly, semi-annually (amortising term loan) or at the end of the facility and capital payments made cannot normally be redrawn. These loans can have different tranches with variants such as tenor pricing and even levels of subordination. Term loans are used to finance capital assets such as property and equipment and can often be drawn down shortly after signing. Also see *amortising term loan; revolving credit facility; tranche*.

term out The ability to extend the period of a loan or turn a current set of borrowings, usually a revolving credit facility, into a term loan. There is a fee involved in opting for a term out and these options are generally available only to investment grade borrowers. Term out options are at the option of the borrower. Also see *revolving credit facility*.

term out fee The fee applicable in loan agreements if a term out option is exercised. Also see *extension fee; participation fee; term out*.

term repo A repo trade with a fixed maturity date. Usually done over one day. Also see *open repo*.

term sheet An outline that is not legally binding and that indicates the key points, conditions and terms of a deal, usually a loan. Even though not legally binding, term sheets constitute a moral obligation and further formal agreements and contracts are structured against the term sheets. Term sheets are useful because they focus both the borrower and the lender on the key points and fundamental issues of a deal. Also see *confirmation; facility letter*.

terms of trade (TOT) The ratio between export and import price indices:

$$\text{terms of trade} = \frac{\text{export price index}}{\text{import price index}}$$

Changes in the terms of trade signal changes in the welfare of the country. For example, if the terms of trade improve, i.e. increase, it means that a greater volume of imports can be purchased with an unchanged volume of exports, or that the same volume of imports can be purchased with fewer exports than before. This means in effect that the country has become richer than before, assuming all other things remained the same.

South Africa's terms of trade, including and excluding gold exports, are regularly published in the Quarterly Bulletin of the South African Reserve Bank (www.reservebank.co.za).

term structure
1. The time dependence of a variable.
2. The time schedule of payments for a loan.

term structure of interest rates A set of discount rates applicable to the date of maturity of fixed income securities such as government bonds. The term structure of interest rates constitutes a similar concept to the yield curve. Also see *government bond; yield curve*.

term to maturity The time from the present until the date of maturity of a bond or other financial instrument.

terrorism The use or threat of illegal and usually violent action designed to influence a government or the public for reasons of advancing a political, religious or ideological cause.

tertiary sector When referring to GDP this term indicates the trade and services sector. Activities such as transport, communication, trade, education, financial, personal and government are included in the tertiary sector. Also see *gross domestic product*.

Texas hedge A financial transaction that is not a hedge but rather the brave purchase of a number of the same securities or derivatives creating an open position. Also see *open position*.

THB Thailand baht divided into 100 stang.

The Greeks See *Greeks*.

theta
1. The Greek letter θ or Θ. Also see *Greek alphabet*.
2. A measure of the sensitivity of an option to time. As the time to maturity of an option decreases, the value of the option will decrease due to the likelihood of the option being in the money diminishing:

$$\theta = \frac{dC}{dT}$$

Also see *Black-Scholes options pricing model; in the money; Greeks; time decay*.

thickly traded market High volumes traded in the market.

thin capitalisation Tax benefits can be gained by multinational companies financing overseas operations with large amounts of debt due to interest expenses being tax deductible. The regulations apply when a non-resident controlling a company in South Africa extends funds through loans to the SA company.

In 2008, interest charges that are in excess of what is deemed to be reasonable, at 3× gearing with an interest rate of 15.5%, are disallowed as tax deductions under thin cap regulations.

Many countries have thin capitalisation legislation in place that limits the amount of debt relative to equity that a company may have to limit excessive gearing of companies, thereby protecting local economies from distortions of credit markets. In South Africa, in addition to thin cap regulations, there are restrictions (local borrowings restrictions) imposed on the maximum debt that a foreign-held company may have relative to shareholders capital. The local borrowing restriction is 300% of shareholders funds subject to approved exceptions. Also see *shareholders capital*.

thinly traded market Small trade volumes in the market.

third market The informal market where listed bonds are traded outside an exchange, usually between institutional investors. Also see *bond; institutional investor*.

throughput agreement A contract that obliges a party to deliver a product to a facility and pay for its processing. Also see *take or pay contract; toll manufacturing concern*.

through the cycle (TTC) A term used in credit markets that indicates the variable being referenced is referenced under a series of longer term credit conditions and not simply the current conditions. TTC indicates a long-term credit view.

TIBOR Tokyo interbank offered rate. Also see *interbank rate; JIBAR; LIBOR*.

tick The minimum price at which a security can move up or down:
- In the international bond futures market, a tick is defined as 1/64th of a point.
- In the international bond market, a tick is defined as 1/32nd of a point.

Also see *bond*.

ticket The level of commitment to which banks are invited when being offered participation in a syndicated loan. Also see *bracket; syndicated loan*.

ticking fee A fee used by financiers that are funding an acquisition. The borrower pays the financiers a fee from the date on which the deal is accepted until the date of closing of the acquisition and cash provision. Ticking fees are introduced because acquisitions may take a long time to receive approval and financiers are committed for the full period. Also see *commitment fee*.

tied agent An appointed representative that has authorisation to act for another company. Similar to a franchise. The tied agent operates in financial markets through the organisation to which it is tied.

tied loan A loan made between countries where a condition of the loan is that the borrower must use the proceeds to purchase goods in the lender's country. Export credit finance is an example of this type of lending. Also see *export credit*.

tier 1 capital The capital adequacy of a bank. Tier 1 capital is core capital and includes equity capital, disclosed reserves, some types of preference shares and certain forms of hybrid capital. Banking regulatory regimes require that banks have minimum levels of tier capital to total credit exposure. Sometimes called primary capital. Also see *capital adequacy; equity capital; hybrid; preference share*.

tier 2 capital A measure of the second most reliable form of capital for financial institutions and banks. It includes retained earnings, revaluation reserves, general loan loss reserves, hybrid capital instruments and subordinated debt. Banking regulatory regimes require that banks have minimum levels of tier capital to total credit exposure. Also see *hybrid; revaluation surplus; subordinate*.

tier 3 capital Short-term subordinated debt of banks and financial institutions. Also see *subordinate*.

tiger See *Asian tigers*.

tight knit A small or closed market. A tight knit oligopoly describes a situation where there are few producers supplying lower volumes and charging higher prices than would be charged and supplied in a competitive market. Also see *oligopoly*.

tightly held Shares held by investors who are reluctant to sell (strong holders). Volumes of shares traded for tightly held companies are low. Also see *free float*.

till money Physical cash held by banks. Sometimes called vault money.

time decay The decreasing value of an option as it approaches maturity. Theta is the measure of time decay for an option. Also see *theta*.

time draft An alternative term for *bill of exchange*.

timeously A term used in South Africa that refers to sufficient notice being given or meeting a deadline on time or with sufficient time to spare.

time premium The premium over the intrinsic value of an option associated with the time to the exercise date. There is some time value associated with an option because if there is time left to the exercise date, there is a lower probability that the option will be in the money. The period of the time premium is therefore a function of the probability that the option will be in the money. The closer the option is to expiry, the smaller the time premium is.

To calculate the time premium, subtract the intrinsic value off the market price. The call premium or price on the market is the sum of the intrinsic and time value. As interest rates rise, the time value of a call option rises and the time value of a put option falls. Also see *call option; interest rate; in the money; intrinsic value; option*.

times interest earned (interest cover) A ratio that measures how effectively income covers debt expenses:

$$\text{times interest earned} = \frac{\text{EBITDA or free cash flow}}{\text{net interest charges}}$$

where EBITDA = earnings before interest, taxation, depreciation and amortisation.

The lower the times interest earned ratio is, the more the company is burdened by debt expense. When a company's interest coverage ratio is 1.5 or lower, its ability to meet interest expenses may be questionable. An interest coverage ratio below 1 indicates the company is not generating sufficient revenues to satisfy interest expenses. Times interest earned ratios are often used as covenants by lenders in loan agreements. Sometimes called interest cover. Also see *covenant*.

time value For options, see *time premium*.

time value of money Due to inflation the buying power of a unit of currency diminishes over time. For example, R100 in a year from now will not buy you the same number of goods R100 will today. The value of cash flows is therefore adjusted or discounted to a particular date to compare purchasing power. Also see *discount; discount rate; inflation; real cash flow*.

TIMS Theoretical intermarket margining system. This is the Eurex equivalent of SPAN. Also see *EUREX; standard portfolio analysis of risk*.

TIPS See *treasury inflation-protected security*.

tip sheet An information document composed by researchers that gives subscribers recommendations on the buying and selling of shares. Also see *analyst*.

title A document that proves ownership of an asset. Also see *deed*.

Tla Amortising term loan.

TMC Target market criteria.

TND The Tunisian dinar divided into 1 000 millimes.

TNY Turkish lira.

TOCOM See *Tokyo Commodity Exchange*.

toe hold The purchase of an initial stake in a company with the aim of making a full acquisition at a later date.

toggle note A form of debt instrument that gives the issuer the discretion to pay interest or the option to convert interest into payment in kind (PIK). The accrued interest is effectively added as new debt securities. The PIK option is only applicable over the first half of the instrument's life. These instruments are useful to businesses that are cyclical because cash can be freed up when critically needed. Toggle notes are often used by highly leveraged companies and are priced at a premium to other debt instruments. Investors see them as lowering the risk of default because the company can defer interest payments. Investors usually require an increased margin when the toggle note issuer exercises the option to capitalise the interest. Toggle notes effectively give debt equity-like cash flows and can be classed as hybrid securities. Also see *adjustment bond; bunny bond; hybrid; leverage; payment in kind*.

Tokyo Commodity Exchange (TOCOM) Japanese futures commodity exchange.

tolar The currency of Slovenia divided into 100 stotin.

tolling agreement An agreement that states the obligations of and payments due to parties that use a toll manufacturing concern. Also see *toll manufacturing concern*.

toll manufacturing concern A manufacturing operation that charges customers in proportion to its operating expenses with the addition of a fixed margin. Toll manufacturing operations are usually owned by the companies that use their services. Also see *cost centre*.

toll revenue bond A bond issued to pay for the construction of a toll road, tunnel or similar piece of infrastructure. The fares collected from the asset when operational are used to service the bonds.

tombstone An advertisement published by financiers that outlines the transaction, the participants and the roles played by the participants. Tombstones are really a published bragging right by the banks. Sometimes called a lucite when in physical format. Also see *lucite*.

top The highest price of a security for the time window under evaluation.

top down Determining the operating cash flow by the direct method:

operating cash flow = sales − cost of sales − taxes

Also see *direct method of reporting cash flows*.

to redemption The holding of a security, usually a debt instrument, until the date of maturity. Also see *maturity*.

tort An obligation that a court imposes on a party as a result of damages caused to another party.

TOT See *terms of trade*.

total asset turnover A ratio that measures how effectively operational assets generate revenue:

$$\text{total asset turnover} = \frac{\text{sales}}{\text{operating assets}}$$

If the ratio increases, the firm is using its operating assets more efficiently. Also see *asset management ratios*.

total enterprise value See *enterprise value*.

total leverage A ratio that indicates how much debt a company has with respect to its EBIDTA.

$$\text{total leverage} = \frac{\text{total debt}}{\text{EBIDTA}}$$

Also see *EBITDA; leverage*.

total price The sum of the clean price and the accrued interest of a bond instrument. Also see *accrued interest; clean price; yield to maturity*.

total profit Profits before tax and interest charges.

total profits ratio

$$\text{total profits ratio} = \frac{\text{total profits}}{\text{total capital employed}}$$

total return swap (TRS) A derivative contract that conveys the up- and downside risk and rewards of an asset but does not attribute the legal ownership of the asset. The mechanics of these transactions are similar to entering into a contract with a bank where they purchase an asset, charge the client the finance fee for the principal and construct the swap cash and capital flows to match the underlying asset. Effectively one party pays interest payments and receives the cash flows, i.e. interest or dividends, and capital gains from the reference asset.

An example of a total return swap is a participant taking a R10 million position in a loan paying JIBAR + 100 bp. The participant is required to place collateral of R1 million in a collateral account and pay a finance cost of JIBAR + 50 bp on the R9 million remaining balance. The participant thus earns JIBAR + 100 on the entire R10 million and pays JIBAR + 50 on the R9 million balance over the collateral amount.

The returns are associated with significant risk. Should the issuer of the loan default and the value drop to R6 million, the participant will lose R4 million.

There is also counterparty risk associated with these swaps, especially if the writer of the swap is of low credit quality. Also see *collateral; counterparty; derivative; downside; upside*.

total risk total risk = financial risk + business risk

Total risk is normally measured quantitatively using the standard deviation on the returns. Also see *business risk; financial risk; standard deviation*.

total shareholder return (TR) The total shareholder return on an equity investment is defined by the following equation:

$$TR = s \times 100 \times \left(\log\left(\frac{p_t}{p_{t-1}}\right) \right) + dy_t$$

where p_t = the current price; p_{t-1} = the price at the end of the previous period; dy_t = the dividend yield expressed as a percentage of the current price; s = the number of periods in question.

Also see *dividend yield*.

total sum of squares The sum of the squares of the difference of the independent variable from its mean:

$$\sum_{i=1}^{n}(y_i - \bar{y})^2$$

Furthermore:

total sum of squares = explained sum of squares + residual sum of squares

total utility The sum of all utilities derived from units consumed.

town hall A meeting or presentation where the CEO or executive management of a company addresses all or most of its employees. The format of the meeting is usually open and participatory. Sometimes called a lekgotla in South Africa. Also see *lekgotla*.

tracker fund See *exchange traded fund*.

tradability The ease with which particular shares can be traded. Also see *liquidity*.

trade The purchase and sale of an asset or security.

trade balance (balance of trade) The difference between exports (X) and imports (M) into and out of a country. The trade balance constitutes the largest portion of a country's balance of payments and is used when calculating the balance on a country's current account. If imports exceed exports, then a trade deficit results. Sometimes called balance of trade. Also see *balance of payments; current account; trade deficit*.

trade barrier A restriction to trade set up by a government to inhibit trade and protect domestic industry. These barriers are usually set up in the form of customs tariffs, quotas and a range of other non-tariff barriers. Also see *non-tariff barrier*.

trade bill See *bill of exchange*.

trade creditor See *creditor*.

trade date The date on which financial contracts are concluded. Sometimes called the T-day.

trade debtor See *debtor*.

trade deficit The amount by which imports (M) from a country exceed exports (X). Also see *trade balance; trade surplus*.

trade gap See *trade balance*.

trademark A symbol, icon, picture or phrase that identifies a particular product or service. Trademarks need to be registered with patent offices and are owned and used exclusively by the registering party.

trader An entity that buys and sells securities in anticipation of making a profit from the difference between the purchase (bid) and sell (ask) price. Traders aim to turn the stock over quickly and do not take long-term positions in the shares that they trade. Also see *ask price; bid price*.

trade surplus The amount by which exports (X) from a country exceed imports (M). Also see *trade balance; trade deficit*.

trade weighted dollar A representation of the foreign currency price of the US dollar or the export value of the US dollar. Also see *purchasing power parity*.

trade weighted exchange rate This measure of the overall value of one currency against a basket of currencies is called a trade-weighted exchange rate. The rate is a weighted geometric average rate which is obtained by weighting the exchange rates between the country in question and its main trading partners' currencies. See *multilateral real exchange rate* for information on how to calculate trade weighted exchange rates. Also see *effective exchange rate; geometric mean*.

trading book
1. The mandate held by a dealer in a financial market as to what instruments he/she can trade.
2. A record of trading activities.

trading halt When trading on a financial exchange is halted. On the London Stock Exchange automatic execution is halted when a price moves by more than 5% from the last trade although trading is still permitted outside the exchange's order book. The trading of the share is halted after the triggering trade has been executed. Halting trading on shares gives exchange authorities time to investigate the reason behind the sharp move in prices. Also see *circuit breaker; suspension of trading*.

trading profit Gross profit less operating expenses. This is the profit that results from trading activities and not from unusual income or expenses. Depreciation, amortisation, dividend payments, exceptional items and tax are not included because they are not cash flows associated with day-to-day trading. Also see *depreciation; EBIDTA*.

tranche Slice or segment. Credit or shares are usually made available over a period of time in slices or tranches. Some loan facilities may have more than one tranche where tranches have different maturity, pricing and levels of subordination.

transaction cost The cost associated with purchasing or selling a financial instrument. Costs include fees, commissions and stamp duties. Also see *commission; discount security; stamp duty*.

transfer
1. The transfer of ownership of an asset.
2. The movement of cash from one entity to another.

transfer certificate
1. A means of transferring participation in a syndicated loan from one bank to another.
2. A document that transfers the rights of one party to another. Also see *novation*.

transfer deed A legal document that transfers ownership of an asset from one party to another.

transfer office A securities exchange office that handles the transfer of shares from one owner to the next.

transfer payment A transaction between households that is not included in the calculation of GDP. For example, when a person sells a second-hand good privately to another person there is no official record of the transaction. Monies paid for goods or services rendered such as the payment of retirement funds are also considered to be transfer payments. Also see *gross domestic product*.

transfer pricing The pricing at which transactions between units of a multinational firm take place, in particular cross-border transactions. These include intercompany transfer of goods, property, services and loans. Multinational companies select transfer pricing regimes that enable them to shift profits into countries with lower tax rates. As a response, countries impose arms length pricing-based tax laws to ensure that the appropriate proportions of profits are taxed where they are economically generated. Also see *arms length*.

transfer problem The relationship between international payments and the real exchange rate.

transfer risk The risk associated with the international trade on goods not being settled correctly through exchange controls.

transition matrix A matrix produced by credit rating agencies that gives probabilities of credit rating changes for companies. Also see *credit rating agency*.

transmuted listing statement A statement issued to the markets by a listed company when it changes the character of its core business. Companies that have undergone reverse takeovers, mergers, made significant acquisitions or undergone a change in control need to publish a transmuted listing statement. Also see *offering circular or memorandum; primary information provider*.

transnational See *multinational*.

transparency Openness, honesty and accountability. Transparency is key for the proper functioning of financial markets, where information on prices and volumes is instrumental in ensuring optimal and fair trade.

TRAX The trade reporting system for Eurobonds. Also see *Eurobond*.

treasurer A person that handles the financial affairs of an organisation and processes that entity's dealings with the financial markets. A treasurer works in a company's treasury.

treasury The name for the centre of financial operations in a company or government. The treasury is the department where funds are received, kept, managed and disbursed. Treasuries manage financial risks which include liquidity, counterparty, foreign exchange, commodity, interest rate and price risk. Also see *exchequer; interest rate*.

treasury bill (T-bill) A short-term obligation or debt instrument issued by a country's treasury having a maturity period of one year or less and sold at a discount from face value. T-bills do not carry coupon payments and the investor collects the reward for holding them by the discount from face value. Also see *discount security; face value; zero coupon bond*.

treasury bill rate The discount rate for which a treasury bill is sold. Also see *discount rate*.

treasury bill yield The yield on a treasury bill calculated by the following equation:

$$\text{yield} = \frac{\text{discount rate}}{1 - \frac{91}{365} \times \text{discount rate}}$$

The quoted discount rate R is given by:

$$R = \frac{\text{nominal value} - \text{market value}}{\text{nominal value}}$$

Also see *discount rate*.

treasury bond A bond issued by a government with a maturity of more than ten years with periodic coupon payments. Also see *bond*.

treasury index An index composed of a series of treasury bills and bonds. Also see *treasury bill*.

treasury inflation-protected security (TIPS) A security whose principal is tied to the consumer price index. With increasing inflation, the principal increases. With deflation, the principal decreases. When the security matures, the original or adjusted principal is paid to the holder, whichever is greater. The interest paid to the holder of the TIP is calculated by multiplying the inflation-adjusted principal by a fixed interest rate. If the yield of a normal treasury bill is subtracted from the yield of a TIP, the premium the market demands for being exposed to inflation is given. TIPS are instruments issued by the treasury of the United States. Other countries such as South Africa have similar inflation-linked bonds such as the R189 and R202. Also see *consumer price index; inflation; R189; R202; security; treasury bill*.

treasury lock A derivative instrument used to lock in the yield of a treasury bill. They are structured in such a manner that one party makes a fixed set of payments at the locked yield and receives the market rate in excess of the lock level. Also see *treasury bill*.

treasury management The process of a clearing house paying interest on margin accounts. The London Clearing House (LCH) pays account holders a base LIBID rate less a small margin. Also see *clearing house; LIBID; margin*.

treasury note A bond issued by a government treasury that has a maturity of two, five or ten years and that pays coupons. Also see *treasury bill*.

treasury shares Shares in a company owned by the company and appearing on the balance sheet. These shares were once traded in the market and have been purchased in the secondary market through a share buy-back. They are not used when calculating dividends or earnings per share. Sometimes called a treasury stock. Also see *balance sheet; dividend; secondary market; share buy-back*.

treasury stock See *treasury shares*.

treasury STRIP See *STRIP*.

treaty An agreement between parties, usually countries.

treaty lender A lender who is registered in a jurisdiction that is governed by a double taxation treaty. Also see *double taxation*.

trend line A line drawn between peaks and troughs on a time series chart that indicates movement in price.

triangular arbitrage An arbitrage opportunity that exists when cross rates between currencies allow speculators to purchase one currency, a second currency and then the home currency again at a profit. Also see *arbitrage*.

trigger option See *barrier option*.

trillion One million million or 10^{12}.

tri-party repo A custodian bank or clearing house that acts as an intermediary in a repo transaction. The tri-party agent is responsible for the administration of the transaction including collateral allocation, marking to market and substitution of collateral. Also see *clearing house; collateral; repurchase agreement*.

troy ounce (oz) The traditional unit of measure for a precious metal. One troy ounce = 31.1034807 grams. Also see *bullion; fine ounce; precious metals*.

TRS See *total return swap*.

true sale A securitisation structure where the asset being securitised is legally sold to the SPV used in the securitisation operation. When the legal ownership of assets is not transferred, the securitisation structure is sometimes called a covered bond or synthetic securitisation/CLO. Also see *covered bond; securitisation; special-purpose vehicle; synthetic collateralised loan obligation*.

trust A legal entity where assets are held by one or more persons (trustees) for the benefit of others. The benefits are specified in a trust deed. Trustees may also be beneficiaries of a trust. Also see *orphan trust; trust deed; trustee*.

trust deed
1. A written agreement between the issuer of debt and the lender detailing the terms of the bond. Also see *bond*.
2. A written agreement specifying the rules and regulations that govern a trust. Also see *trust*.

trustee The custodian of the assets of a trust. A trustee holds property or assets for the benefit of someone else. Also see *trust*.

trust fund A portfolio of assets held by a trust. Also see *trust*.

trust indenture The contract between the issuer of the bond and the party that is holding the instrument for investors.

trust letter A security document that banks hold over goods that allows the borrower to sell the goods and repay the debt obligations.

TSE Tokyo Stock Exchange.

TT Telegraphic transfer.

TTC See *through the cycle*.

turn The profit or spread that a trader makes by purchasing (bid price) and selling (ask price) a security. Also see *ask price; bid price; spread*.

turnkey
1. A start-up business that includes everything needed to start running it immediately.
2. A product that can just be inserted and functions properly right away. Plug and play computer devices are turnkey devices.

turnkey contract A construction contract that requires the asset being constructed to be delivered at a predefined date in full working order and at guaranteed performance levels.

turnover
1. The total revenue or sales of a business.
2. The number of times an asset is sold or replaced.
3. The total value of securities traded for a period.

turnover clause A clause in the retail sector where landlords base rentals on the turnover of the business.

turnover ratio See *inventory turnover*.

TV Theoretical value.

TWD Taiwan dollar divided into 100 cents.

two-tier offer An offer strategy in acquisition transactions where an initial offer is made at a premium price to gain control and thereafter the remaining minority shareholders are offered a lesser price. There are rules and regulations governing these types of activities. Also see *mandatory offer*.

two-way price The simultaneous quote of the buying and selling price of an asset. Also see *one-way price*.

type 1 error
1. Rejecting the null hypothesis H_0 when it is true is defined as a type 1 error. Also see *null hypothesis*.
2. Investing when there are no good hurdle-beating investments.
3. See *weighted average cost of capital*.

type 2 error
1. Failing to reject the null hypothesis when it is false is defined as a type 2 error. Also see *null hypothesis*.
2. Not investing when there are good hurdle-beating investments.
3. See *weighted average cost of capital*.

ubuntu An African philosophy of openness, sharing and affirmation.

UCITS *Undertakings for Collective Investment in Transferable Securities.*

UIF See *Unemployment Insurance Fund.*

UK See *United Kingdom.*

UKLA United Kingdom Listing Authority.

ULS Unsecured loan stock.

umbrella fund A fund of funds, often held offshore. Also see *fund of funds.*

unbalanced growth The situation in the world where countries such as the US run large current account deficits while poorer countries such as China and other developing nations are running surpluses. This has the effect that poorer, less developed countries are lending to wealthier developed nations.

unbiased forward rate hypothesis This is a form of the efficient market hypothesis. It states that the forward or future price of an asset is the expected value of the price of that asset's spot price in the future. If the spot price today is s_t and the future price f_t, then at $t + 1$ the purchaser pays f_t. Since the spot rate at $t + 1$ is s_t, the profit or loss realised is $s_{t+1} - f_t$. The unbiased forward rate hypothesis states that the profit from this operation should be zero. Also see *asset; efficient market; spot price; strongly efficient market.*

unbundling The process of a company disposing of a subsidiary by distributing shares to shareholders in proportion to their holding in the parent company. Also see *spin off.*

uncommitted facility A facility where the lender has the discretion to advance credit and call for repayment. These facilities are uncommon in the marketplace. Also see *committed facility; credit support letter.*

unconditional A bid or the provision of finance that is guaranteed to succeed. Also see *underwrite.*

uncovered interest rate parity The uncovered interest rate parity theory postulates that the interest rate difference between two countries' currencies is equal to the percentage difference between the expected spot exchange rate and the spot exchange rate.

$$\left(1 + i^{\$}_{t,t+1}\right) = \frac{E_t\left[S_{t+1}\right]}{S_t} \left(1 + i^{c}_{t,t+1}\right)$$

Essentially, when an investor has not covered him/herself against differences in countries' interest rates by buying forward, the forward rate in the covered interest rate parity equation is replaced by the expected future spot rate $E_t[S_{t+1}]$. There is now a degree of risk built into the uncovered position by using an expected value rather than a known quoted spot rate. Also see *cost of carry model; covered interest rate parity; interest rate; spot market.*

uncovered option An option written without any of the risk associated with the option being hedged. Also see *hedge.*

uncrossing price Matching price.

undated bond/security See *perpetual bond.*

underlying The asset on which a derivative instrument is based. Also see *derivative.*

undersubscription
1. The issue of a bond, equity or other security that is not fully taken up by the market (undersubscribed).
2. The commitments from banks in a syndicated loan facility do not total the amount sought by the borrower.
3. Underwriting commitments from banks do not total the amount sought by the borrower.

undertaking See *covenant*.

Undertakings for Collective Investment in Transferable Securities (UCITS) A European Union directive that aims to give collective investment schemes the ability to operate throughout Europe under authorisation from a single European state. Also see *collective investment scheme; European Union*.

undervalued
1. A share may trade at a price indicating a market value that is less than the net asset value of the business. Businesses in this position often unbundle. Also see *net asset value*.
2. A share may be considered to be undervalued if it trades at earnings multiples (PE ratios) less than that of its peers. Also see *price earnings ratio*.

underwater A financial position that results when the current price of a security is lower than the purchase price. The term is also used to describe conditions where the provision of a service or product costs more than the sales revenue received. When the securities are sold, the loss will be realised.

underweight A portfolio when it has a shortage of a particular asset or asset class. Sometimes the term underweight can refer to a sell recommendation. Also see *overweight*.

underwrite
1. In an initial public offer of shares or debt, an underwriter, usually an investment bank, guarantees for a fee to take up any securities not bought by the public. This achieves collection of all the capital sought. There is a cost associated with the service called an underwrite fee of about 2%. Also see *initial public offer; investment bank; underwriter*.
2. In the process of a loan syndication, the underwriters legally guarantee the deal for a minimum amount and then syndicate the loan out to the market. The arranging syndicate often agrees to place the entire amount of the loan or a significant portion of it. Also see *syndicate*.
3. The process of selling risk or exposure to other financial institutions. For example, insurance companies underwrite risk associated with insurance policies to other insurance companies.

underwriter
1. An entity that provides a guarantee for a financial transaction.
2. A person who examines risk and decides what fee should be charged to insure an asset.
3. A financial institution that guarantees to take up any securities not bought in a public offer or private placement. Also see *private placing/placement*.

Also see *underwrite*.

underwriting fee
1. An upfront fee charged by a bank to underwrite a loan. Also see *underwrite*.
2. A fee charged by an underwriter of a share issue to underwrite the issue. Also see *underwrite*.

undisclosed bear sale A bear sale that is undisclosed to stockbrokers and exchanges. These are strictly illegal. Also see *bear sale; stockbroker*.

undisclosed factoring A factoring operation where the identity of the factor is kept from the debtors. The seller of the debtors book in these circumstances is appointed as the agent to collect payments from the individual debtors and these debtors are unaware of the factoring process. Also see *factor debtors*.

undistributable profit See *non-distributable reserves*.

unearned revenue Revenue paid for which services and goods have not been delivered as yet. Pay as you go cellular phone contracts are a good example of this.

Unemployment Insurance Fund (UIF) A fund to which contributions by employees and employers are made for the provision of unemployment payouts in the event of an employee being retrenched.

unexpected loss The expected loss is defined as the expected value of a loss probability distribution, typically the mean value if there is a normal distribution. The unexpected loss is defined by the tails of the loss probability distribution. Expected and unexpected losses for a portfolio of assets are calculated in a similar manner to how portfolio expected returns are calculated. Also see *expected loss; portfolio expected returns*.

unfunded scheme See *pay as you go*.

unilaterally An agreement struck without the agreement of a court.

unilateral relief Double taxation relief between countries that do not have formal double taxation treaties.

unimodal A distribution that has only a single peak. A normal distribution is an example of a unimodal distribution. The graph below shows a series of normal distributions that are all unimodal. A distribution with two peaks is called a bimodal distribution. Also see *bimodal distribution; normal or Gaussian distribution*.

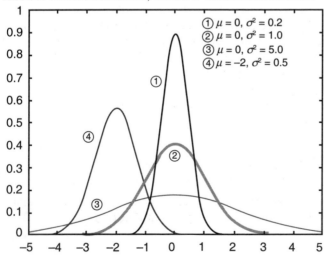

unissued share capital See *shares in issue*.

United Kingdom (UK) A country comprising England, Scotland, Wales and Northern Ireland.

unit elastic demand The price elasticity of demand equals one. This is at the midpoint of the demand curve on a price versus quantity graph.

unit holder An entity that is the owner of a unit trust. Also see *unit trust*.

unit labour cost The cost of labour per unit of output. For macroeconomic calculations this is calculated by dividing the average wage by the output per worker per hour.

unit normal A unit normal variable has mean equal to zero and a variance of one. Also see *variance*.

unit of account The currency of a country.

unit root In autoregressive econometric models a unit root is present if the coefficient $|b| \geq 1$ in $y_t = a + by_{t-1} + \varepsilon_t$
where y_t = the variable of interest at time t; b = the slope coefficient; ε_t = the error component. In general, $b = 1$.

If the unit root is present, the time series is said to have a stochastic trend or is integrated of order one or $I(1)$. The statistical test for a unit root is the Dickey Fuller test. If a time series has a unit root, then the best predictor of the $t + 1$ value is the value at t. If a unit root is present, the data set is non-stationary. If the elements of a time series are differenced, $t_{i+1} - t_i$, then a stationary series is obtained and the series is said to be first order integrated. Also see *cointegration; Dickey Fuller test; first order integrated; non-stationary process; stationary process; stochastic trend*.

unit trust A fund that receives monies, issues sub-shares or units to investors and then pools and invests the monies on behalf of the investing public. Unit trusts are managed by investment professionals who charge a management fee. Americans call unit trusts mutual funds. Also see *mutual fund*.

univariate time series The time variable in question is related to only one other variable.

universal policy An insurance policy that combines an endowment with life and disability cover. These policies become useful when a lump cash sum is needed in the future. They ensure the lump sum is available to a nominated beneficiary in the event of death or disability. Also see *endowment insurance/policy*.

unlimited company A company in which the liability of the member is not limited. This is as opposed to limited liability companies where members are not liable for the actions of the company. Also see *limited liability*.

unlimited liability The liability for the obligations of a business in excess of the amount invested. Also see *sole proprietorship*.

unlimited risk An investment in which the potential loss is not limited. Selling short and selling call options are such investments. Also see *call option*.

unlisted A company that is not listed and traded on a securities exchange. Holders of shares in these companies are not protected by the various rulings and compliance levels that listed companies are subject to under exchange rules and regulations.

unquoted An instrument that is not traded on an exchange but traded in an over-the-counter market. Also see *over the counter*.

unrealised actuarial loss/gain Defined benefit retirement funds have a 10% corridor in which value adjustments do not have to be made. The values of funds outside these corridors are the unrealised actuarial gains or losses. There are a number of different methods of modelling and determining unrealised gains or losses. When looking at valuations, attention must be paid to the method used and its pitfalls.

unrealised loss/profit A profit or loss associated with a change in the price of a security but not realised until that security is sold.

unsecured A financial instrument usually in the form of debt that is not backed by a physical asset. These are subordinate to secured debt, the holders of which have first rights on the proceeds of the sale of the asset securing the debt. Also see *subordinate*.

unsecured debt Debt that is not secured against a fixed asset such as property. Also see *secured*.

unsecured loan stock A form of debt issued by a company that is unsecured by any assets and is subordinate to claims on assets that have been used in securing other debt. Also see *debenture; subordinate*.

unsubordinated debt A debt instrument that ranks equal in seniority, i.e. pari passu, to other debt. Also see *pari passu*.

unsystematic risk A unique or asset-specific risk. This is the unique risks a company faces and is in addition to systematic or market risk. All assets are exposed to systematic risk and risks unsystematic or unique to the particular assets. The relationships between them can be described by:

$$\sigma_s^2 \equiv R^2 \sigma_s^2 + (1 - R^2) \sigma_s^2 = \text{market risk}^2 + \text{unique risk}^2$$
$$\therefore \text{market risk} = \sqrt{R^2 \sigma_s^2}$$
$$\therefore \text{unique risk} = \sqrt{(1 - R^2) \sigma_s^2}$$

where R^2 = ANOVA parameter for the linear combination of the share versus the market, remembering that R^2 in this case represents the proportion of the systematic risk; σ_s^2 = total risk^2 = share risk^2.

Also called diversifiable risk, unique risk or specific risk. Also see *systematic risk*.

unwind To reverse a financial position. The term is usually used with reference to a swap or hedge position. Also see *hedge; position; swap*.

upfront fee A fee charged by the mandated lead arranger for structuring and/or underwriting a syndicated loan. The upfront fee usually includes arrangement fees and participation fees. Also see *administrative agent fee; commitment fee; facility fee; mandated lead arranger; participation fee; prepayment fee; syndicated loan; usage fee*.

upfronting revenue An accounting treatment of earnings that apportions earnings that are meant to be apportioned equally over a series of years in a non-equal manner and loaded to the nearer term. For example, if a two-year gym contract is signed and paid for on day 1, 50% of the revenue should be recognised in year 1 and 50% in year 2. Revenue is upfronted when more than 50% of the revenue is recognised in year 1.

upside Exposure to the potential profit an asset can possibly deliver. Also see *asset; downside*.

upstairs trading Trading outside stock exchanges. Also see *dark liquidity*.

upstream The flow of funds from a subsidiary to a parent. The term is used with reference to loans that may be undertaken between subsidiary and parent.

uptrend A trend in a pricing pattern that has prices rising on average.

upward flex The increase in margin, spread and fees on a debt security. This usually occurs when the initial margin on the loan is too low and the market for the debt is undersubscribed in the market. The margin and/or fees are increased to encourage more investors to invest and get the debt to clear the market. Also see *margin; reverse flex*.

Ural crude Crude oil that comes from the Russian Federation.

uridashi bond A Japanese bond denominated in other currencies, often in Australian or New Zealand dollars. Also see *Eurobond*.

US United States.

US 144A See *Rule 144A*.

US$ United States dollar.

usage fee (utilisation fee) An annual fee payable when the balance on a revolving credit facility (RCF) falls below or above a predefined level. These fees are designed to encourage lenders to use or not to use the facility. It is most common for utilisation fees to kick in when the facility is drawn on to act as an incentive for the borrower not to use the RCF as a form of long-term capital. The introduction of usage fees often gives lenders lower margins which then have the effect of lowering commitment fees. Also see *administrative agent fee; commitment fee; facility fee; participation fee; prepayment fee; revolving credit facility; upfront fee*.

USD United States dollar.

useful life
1. The period over which an asset is expected to be available for use by an entity. Also see *asset*.
2. The number of production units expected to be obtained from an asset by an entity.

USM Unlisted securities market.

USPP See *private placing/placement*.

usury Charging excessive interest rates. Also see *interest rate*.

Usury Act An act of law of the South African government that regulates lending activities. The Act sets forth, among others, the maximum rates lenders may charge, disclosure of charges, recovery and many other parameters related to the provision of debt finance.

utilisation fee See *usage fee*.

utilisation request A request submitted by a borrower to a bank to obtain funds from a loan agreement.

utility theory A theory in economics that analyses the benefit gained from the consumption of goods or services. Also see *marginal propensity to consume*.

valuation The process of determining the value of an asset. The two main forces that drive valuations are the:
- future benefits such as earnings, rental and savings
- risk-free discount rate or next best alternative forgone, the opportunity cost.

Also see *asset; discount rate; opportunity cost*.

valuation football pitch The pooling of different valuation methodologies, plotting the range of valuations on a graph and making comparisons between them.

value added The additional value added to a product, firm or service by the addition of something extra. Value added processes are followed by an increase in profitability.

value added tax (VAT) A tax levied on goods at each stage of production according to the value added at that stage in the cycle and at final consumption.

value at risk (VAR) The mathematical or statistical modelling of the potential losses in the market.

value chain The series of activities from the starting point of manufacture for a product to the final consumption of that asset. Value chain analysis enables companies to focus on areas of the production cycle that can deliver the best margins and profitability and optimise the performance of product delivery. The concept of value chain analysis was popularised by Michael Porter.

value date The date at which an asset or security is delivered to an account and the date that payment is due. For example, on the foreign exchange spot market, the value date is two days ($t + 2$) after the completion of the transaction. Also see *asset; spot market*.

valued policy An insurance policy that stipulates the value of the insurance payout under a claim before the inception of the policy.

value in use The profit obtainable from the use of an asset until the end of its useful life and from its subsequent disposal. Value in use is calculated as the present value of estimated future cash flows. The discount rate should be a pre-tax rate that reflects current market assessments of the time value of money and the risks specific to the asset. Also see *asset; cash flow; discount rate; fair value; net selling price; time value of money*.

value to business The value of an asset held by a business. There are various ways the value can be calculated such as the lower of realisable value under sale, replacement value or the net present value of the future cash flows that the asset may generate.

value traded In published share tables value traded indicates the value traded on the day.

vanilla A straightforward financial instrument with no customised or exotic components. Also see *vanilla bond; vanilla option*.

vanilla bond A fixed interest rate bond. Also see *fixed interest rate bond; vanilla*.

vanilla option A normal option with no special or unusual features. Also see *option; vanilla*.

vanilla swap A straightforward fixed for floating interest rate swap. Also see *floating interest rate*.

VAR

1. See *vector autoregression*.
2. See *value at risk*.

variable annuity An annuity that has a variable payment profile. As with ordinary annuities, variable annuities pay monies at periodic intervals. However, the payments are not always equal and may vary according to a predefined pattern or with an underlying index such as the CPI. Also see *consumer price index*.

variable cost/expense A cost that increases with increasing levels of production. Raw materials and direct inputs into the manufacturing process are classed as variable expenses. Variable costs are therefore total costs less fixed costs. They are the costs associated with output volumes. Sometimes called direct costs or prime costs. Also see *fixed cost*.

variable interest rate The rate of interest on a loan or investment that varies. Also see *fixed interest rate; floating interest rate*.

variable rate bond See *floating rate note*.

variance The average squared difference between the actual return and the average return, i.e. the square of the standard deviation. Variance is defined by the following equation:

$$VAR = \frac{\sum_{i=0}^{n}(x_i - \bar{x})^2}{n} = \sigma^2 \text{ where } \bar{x} = \frac{\sum_{i=0}^{n} x_i}{n}$$

Variance ignores other dimensions of the distribution of probabilities around the mean such as skewness and kurtosis.

Variance operations:

$Var[A - B] = Var[A] + Var[B] - 2 \times Var[A; B]$

$Var[A + B] = Var[A] + Var[B] + 2 \times Var[A; B]$

Also see *kurtosis; standard deviation*.

variation margin Once an open position exists in a futures market, a daily valuation (mark to market) is done by the exchange to determine gains or losses. If there are losses, the exchange calls for additional cash or a variation margin from the client. The monies paid from one variation margin account will end up in the option counterparty's account. The process is sometimes referred to as continuous net settlement. Also see *initial margin; mark to market; open position*.

VAT See *value added tax*.

vault cash Physical notes and coins kept in vaults by banks and other financial institutions to be used in daily transactions.

VCM See *venture capital market*.

VCT See *venture capital trust*.

VEB The Venezuelan bolivar divided into 100 céntimos.

vector autoregression (VAR) Vector autoregression is an econometric analysis method where many variables are tested as predictors all at once. Econometricians regress these variables against a deterministic variable such as GDP to see what correlates and what does not.

More specifically, in a vector autoregression, many variables are put into the same autoregressive model. A VAR(1) model is defined by the following equation:

$Y_t = A + BY_{t-1} + \varepsilon_t$

where Y_t = a vector of several variables measured over the same sample period $(t = 1, ..., T)$; A = a vector of slope coefficients; B = a vector of autoregressive coefficients; ε_t = a vector of error terms.

Also see *autoregressive; gross domestic product; unit root*.

vector error correction model (VECM) An error correction model that is used for deriving a cointegration relationship between a vector of variables. Also see *cointegration; error correction model*.

vega A measure of the sensitivity of the price of an option to the volatility in the price of the underlying asset the option is written against. The measure is calculated per percentage point of change in volatility:

$$v = \frac{dC}{d\sigma}$$

Also see *Greeks; volatility*.

velocity of circulation See *velocity of money*.

velocity of money A measure of the number of times the average unit of currency changes hands in the form of cash or demand deposits in a given period of time. Velocity of money can be an indicator of inflation or increased inflationary pressure as the velocity tends to increase because holders of cash prefer not to hold cash due to the loss of value through inflation. Also see *demand deposit; quantity theory of money*.

vendor finance Finance supplied by the seller of goods. Automotive companies often supply finance to their customers through captive finance companies.

vendor placement The purchase of a business by issuing shares to the shareholders of the target. The target shareholders now holding shares in the purchaser's company will sell those shares to the market through a placement to institutional investors soon after the transaction.

venture capital The provision of equity capital, usually seed capital, to non-listed firms. Venture capitalists help to develop new products, expand working capital, strengthen balance sheets and make new acquisitions. They seek high returns because they take on significant levels of risk as the probability of the businesses in which they invest going bankrupt is high. Up to 40% returns are often required by VCs. Sometimes called risk capital. Also see *balance sheet; equity capital; firm; working capital*.

venture capital market (VCM) A share category on the JSE that is applicable to companies undertaking untested or greenfield ventures. Also see *greenfield; JSE*.

venture capital trust (VCT) An investment fund that invests in venture capital projects and assets.

vertical integration The process of a company expanding across the range of its manufacturing activities or businesses to achieve a wider portion of the value chain. Also see *backward integration; forward integration; horizontal integration*.

vertical spread An options trading strategy where two options with the same expiration dates but different strike prices are purchased and sold. Often called a price spread. Also see *bear spread; bull spread; diagonal spread; horizontal spread*.

vested interest
1. In a legal sense, an interest, usually in land or money held in trust, recognised as belonging to a particular person.
2. A personal stake in an undertaking, especially one with an expectation of a financial gain.

vesting period The period over which a share option is exercised. Also see *share option*.

vet To make a careful and critical evaluation of someone.

vintage The age of an object or investment. The word vintage is used when referring to something very old.

VIRT-X A competitor exchange to the London Stock Exchange in the UK. Pan-European blue chip stocks are traded on VIRT-X. The Financial Services Authority officially recognises VIRT-X as an investment exchange. Also see *pan-European*.

visible import A physical good that is imported.

VIX See *market volatility index*.

VOIP Voice over internet protocol. The use of computer networks for the transmission of audio signals or data. Skype is a leading VOIP software provider.

VOL Volatility.

volatile Securities with rapidly changing prices. Also see *volatility*.

volatility A measure of the variability of returns on an asset. Volatility is calculated by using variance or annualised standard deviation of the price or return. The historic volatility is the standard deviation of the past returns. Also see *South African Volatility Index; standard deviation; variance*.

volatility risk The risk to which the holder of an option is exposed due to the volatility in price of the underlying asset.

volume The number of shares traded on an exchange in a day's trading.

volume traded In published share tables this indicates the volumes in shares traded daily, usually shown in thousands of shares.

volume weighted average price (VWAP) A measure that effectively indicates the price at which the majority of the shares were traded for the period in question:

$$\text{volume weighted average price (VWAP)} = \frac{\sum_{\text{for each trade}} \text{share price} \times \text{number of shares}}{\text{total number of shares traded}}$$

This measure allows smoothing of the data to remove the effects of spurious trades or spikes in prices.

voluntary liquidation When a company liquidates or winds up on a voluntary basis and is not forced to do so by legal authority.

voluntary prepayment The settlement of a debt obligation before maturity of the particular debt instrument. Prepayment can sometimes incur prepayment fees. Also see *prepayment fee*.

vostro account An account held by a foreign bank in the UK denominated in pounds. Also see *nostro account*.

voting shares Ordinary shares that have voting rights. These voting rights allow the holder of the share to vote on key issues at company general meetings. Also see *annual general meeting*.

VRN Variable rate note. Also see *floating rate note*.

vulture fund A fund that specialises in buying discounted, distressed or defaulting bonds or loans with the aim of recovering the debt.

VWAP See *volume weighted average price*.

WACC See *weighted average cost of capital*.

waiver The relinquishment of rights or privileges, usually voluntarily. Sometimes actions or legal mechanics can result in the waiving of rights.

Wall Street A street in New York that is home to large and important financial institutions. The New York Stock Exchange and others are located on Wall Street.

war bond A bond issued by a government to fund a war effort. They are very long dated and are seldom issued into the market.

war chest A cash or credit facility that can be accessed quickly to finance a business opportunity such as an acquisition. War chest credit facilities are often in the form of revolving credit facilities. Also see *revolving credit facility*.

warehouse lending See *commercial loan selling*.

warehousing
1. The process of a company purchasing a small number of shares in another company through a series of nominees, thus ensuring anonymity.
2. The physical storage of goods.

WARF See *weighted average rating factor*.

warrant The holder of a warrant has the right, but not the obligation, to buy new shares directly from the company issuing them at a fixed price over a given period of time. Each warrant specifies the number of shares, the exercise price and the expiration date. Warrants cause the number of shares in issue to increase, creating earnings dilution and a decrease in earnings per share (EPS). A business often quotes an EPS and a diluted EPS so that investors can see what influence warrants will have on EPS if exercised. Warrant prices are based on the underlying stock prices and are therefore considered to be a form of equity. They do not carry voting rights or entitle the holder to dividend payments. Also see *call option; dividend; earnings per share*.

warranty
1. The promise by manufacturers of goods that they will fix or replace goods that are defective or faulty due to poor workmanship.
2. A promise that a fact is true. Also see *representation*.

wasting asset An asset whose value diminishes over time. Mines are examples of wasting assets that diminish in value over time as the mineral resource that they mine runs out.

weak holder A weak holder of a security as opposed to a strong holder is an investor who is not looking to hold for a long term and will sell the security quickly when pressured. Also see *sticky money; strong holder*.

weakly efficient market The current share price at minimum reflects its past prices. News and information is not fully reflected in prices and volumes of securities traded are quite small. Also see *semi-strong efficient market; strongly efficient market*.

wealth The net resources (assets – liabilities) owned by an individual.

wear and tear allowance An allowance for wear and tear on equipment that is tax deductible. Sometimes called depreciation. Also see *depreciation*.

weighted average (WA) An averaging process that takes into account differing levels of importance of particular components in calculating the average. For example, the average return of a market may be calculated by obtaining the average of each stock, weighting that stock by its market capitalisation and then calculating an overall average. The weighted average is described mathematically by:

$$\text{weighted average (WA)} = \frac{\sum_{i=1}^{n} w_i x_i}{n}$$

Also see *arithmetic mean; geometric mean; market capitalisation*.

weighted average cost of capital (WACC) WACC represents the minimum rate of return at which a company produces returns for both equity and debt investors. WACC is defined by the following equation:

$$WACC = W_{PE} \times R_{PE} \times W_{CE} \times R_{CE} + W_D \times R_D \times (1 - T_C).$$

where W_{PE} = the weight of preferred equity (preference shares); W_{CE} = the weight of common equity (normal shares); R_{PE} = the required return of preferred equity (preference shares); R_{CE} = the required return of common equity (normal shares); R_D = the required return on debt; W_D = the weight of debt; T_C = the tax rate and is included because interest payments on debt are tax deductible.

The return on equity and debt is calculated using market valuations because the next portion of capital that will be raised, will be raised at current market rates. Also see *debt; equity; preference share; security market line*.

weighted average credit rating The weighted average credit rating of a fund is the weighted average of the credit ratings of the debt instruments in which the fund has invested. Also see *credit rating*.

weighted average life See *average life*.

weighted average maturity The weighted average of all the maturities of the loans in a mortgage bond pool. This metric is often used by investors when looking at collateralised mortgage obligations. Also see *collateralised mortgage obligation*.

weighted average rating factor (WARF) A factor used by a credit rating agency that assigns credit risk to a portfolio of assets. WARFs are used in the process of securitisation and rating collateralised debt obligations (CDOs). To calculate the risk of a portfolio, the agency obtains a risk measure of each of the assets in the portfolio and calculates a single number by weighting each and summing them. Also see *collateralised debt obligation; credit rating agency; credit risk*.

weighted average shares in issue The number of shares issued before the period added to the shares issued in the accounting period adjusted for the length of time the new shares have been in existence.

weighted index An index of securities that has weights applied to the prices of those securities. Also see *market capitalisation index*.

West Texas Intermediate (WTI) A grade of crude oil named after the region from which it comes in the US. The price is measured in US dollars per barrel. Also see *barrel; Brent North Sea crude oil*.

whistle blower A person who reports criminal or improper business conduct to the relevant regulatory authorities.

white knight An acquirer of a business that is seen more favourably and is presenting more favourable terms and conditions than the other bidder, the black knight. Also see *black knight*.

white noise Errors in a function that are not autocorrelated. Being uncorrelated in time does not restrict the values a series can take. Any distribution of values is possible as long as the next value in the series is not significantly influenced by the previous value.

whitewash A term used in the UK to describe the process whereby shareholders in a company waive the need for a mandatory offer under an acquisition. Also see *mandatory offer; squeeze out*.

whole loan An original loan, not the loan obligation sold on. Also see *collateralised mortgage obligation*.

wholesale market The market for large financial transactions such as interbank lending in the money markets. Also see *money market*.

wholesale price index See *producer price index*.

wholly owned A subsidiary of a company that is held 100% by that company.

WIBOR Warsaw interbank offered rate.

widening of prices The increase in spread of the bid price and ask price. Also see *ask price; bid price; spread*.

widow and orphans fund A fund that has the aim of generating regular income rather than capital growth. Also see *capital growth*.

will A legally enforceable document outlining the distribution of the assets of a deceased.

winding up A term used to describe how a company dies. Companies are wound up when creditors seek forced payments on debt in the event of default. The assets of the company are sold and various economic stakeholders are paid with the proceeds.

window An opportunity to be taken or a period of time in which a transaction can take place.

window dressing Trying to make a situation, service or product appear better than it really is. The accounts of companies are often adjusted near year end to ensure that annual financial statements are presented in a positive manner.

WIP Work in progress.

withdrawal benefit Benefits payable when an employee leaves employment.

withholding tax The tax levied on dividends or interest payments to non-residents. If the two countries in question have double taxation agreements, tax will not be levied twice. Withholding tax is deducted from interest or dividend payments by the entity making the payments and ultimately paid over to the country's tax collection authority.

Currently (2008) withholding tax is not charged in South Africa but government is considering introducing withholding tax in favour of reducing secondary tax on companies. Also see *dividend; double taxation; secondary tax on companies*.

without recourse See *non-recourse*.

with profits Investment annuities and other instruments that have added benefits if the underlying investment funds return profits in excess of expectations.

with recourse See *recourse*.

won The Korean won, both North and South Korea, divided into 100 chon.

working capital The short-term assets and liabilities of a company. Working capital constitutes monies tied up in the operations of the company. Debtors, creditors and inventories constitute working capital. Changes in working capital = changes in debtors + changes in inventory − changes in creditors. Also see *cash conversion cycle; creditor; debtor; inventory*.

workout The rescue plans put in place to assist a defaulting lender to remedy the default.

workout loss given default (LGD) The loss given default calculated using discounted cash flows from the workout or liquidation process. Also see *implied loss given default; liquidation; market loss given default*.

workout period A period in which a company that has gone into default on a loan is afforded the opportunity to rectify the default, usually in consultation with its lenders. Also see *event of default*.

work system A purposeful definition of the real world in which people spend effort in more or less coherent activities to mutually influence each other and their environment.

World Bank 'The World Bank is a vital source of financial and technical assistance to developing countries around the world. We are not a bank in the common sense. We are made up of two unique development institutions owned by 184 member countries – the International Bank for Reconstruction and Development (IBRD) and the International Development Association (IDA). Each institution plays a different but supportive role in our mission of global poverty reduction and the improvement of living standards.' (*Source*: www.worldbank.org)

World Trade Organisation (WTO) 'The World Trade Organisation (WTO) is the only global international organisation dealing with the rules of trade between nations. At its heart are the WTO agreements, negotiated and signed by the bulk of the world's trading nations and ratified in their parliaments. The goal is to help producers of goods and services, exporters and importers conduct their business.' (*Source*: www.wto.org)

wrapped bond A bond whose issuance is backed by a monoline insurer. The support of the monoline reduces the credit risk of the bond and can change the debt rating and effective rate or spread of the issuance. Also see *bond; credit risk; monoline insurer*.

writ An order or legal document issued by a court. Writs can include instructions to carry out a judgement, seize assets or summons a person into court.

write To underwrite. Also see *underwrite*.

write down The process of adjusting the value of an asset downwards.

write off The process of adjusting the value of an asset to zero or nil value.

writer The original seller of an options contract. Also see *option; option writer*.

written down value See *book value*.

wrongful trading Trading by a company during a period in which it had no ability to avoid insolvency. Directors of companies engaged in wrongful trading may be prosecuted for the activity.

WTI See *West Texas Intermediate*.

WTO See *World Trade Organisation*.

XD See *ex dividend*.

Yankee bond A bond issued by a foreign firm, denominated in US currency and traded on the US foreign bond market. There is an exemption from registration requirements for resale of restricted securities to certain institutional investors under the assumption that they are sophisticated enough not to require protection by the Securities and Exchange Commission (SEC). This has led to non-US companies listing more easily and the market becoming more liquid. Also see *bulldog bond; Eurobond; firm; foreign bond; institutional investor; liquid; maple bond; Matilda bond; Rule 144A; samurai bond; Securities and Exchange Commission*.

yank the bank A clause in a syndicated loan agreement that allows the elimination or replacement of a bank from a syndicated loan. The bank is yanked when it refuses a waiver or request to which the majority of lenders in the syndicate have agreed. The remaining syndicate members can upscale their commitments to compensate or the facility can be downsized. Yank the bank provisions are typical in investment grade transactions. Also see *investment grade; snooze you lose*.

yard Informal term used for a billion. Also see *billion*.

years move In published share tables this indicates the price percentage move in the last 12 months.

yen (JPY) The currency of Japan divided into 100 sen.

yield The return gained for investing in a security. The return is normally expressed as an annualised percentage of the value of the asset. The yield on a financial instrument can be expressed in a variety of ways. The current yield expresses the coupon returns from a bond as a ratio of its current price. The yield to maturity expresses the yield as the rate required in the marketplace for investors to purchase a bond. Also see *bond; current yield; security; yield to maturity*.

yield curve A plot of the yields on government treasury bills or bonds of similar credit quality with various times to maturity. The shape of the yield curve is a function of the underlying variables that affect the term structure, real interest rates, expected future inflation and the interest rate risk premium. Movement of the curve up or down indicates changes in inflationary pressure. Flat yield curves reflect falling interest rates and possible economic slowdown.

Yield curves capture the market's view on interest rates. The shape of a yield curve is explained through the concepts of backwardation and contango. The South African government yield curve is quoted by default on Bloomberg as a nominal annual compounded half yearly (NACH) basis. Also see *backwardation; bond; contango; inflation; interest rate; interest rate risk; liquidity preference theory; market expectation pricing theory; pure expectation pricing theory; real interest rate; treasury bill*.

yield curve risk The risk associated with trades that are transacted at different points on the yield curve. These trades or positions face risks associated with movements or change in the shape of the yield curve. Also see *yield curve*.

yield curve swap A floating for floating interest rate swap where the rates are at different points on the yield curve. They can be called contango or backwardation swaps depending on the shape of the yield curve. Also see *backwardation; contango; interest rate swap; swap; yield curve*.

yield elbow The point on the yield curve where interest rates are highest. Also see *interest rate; yield curve*.

yield equivalence The yield on a taxable investment that would return the equivalent yield on a non-taxable security. Also see *municipal bond*.

yield gap The difference between the returns offered by equity shares and long dated risk-free government debt where the equities returns are higher than the returns on government debt. If the bonds are yielding better returns than the equities, the term reverse yield gap is used. Also see *reverse yield gap*.

yield maintenance Compensation paid to a lender when a debt obligation is repaid to compensate the lender for yield they could otherwise have earned. Also see *termination fee*.

yield pickup The yield gained by switching from a lower yielding bond to a higher yielding bond. Also see *bond; yield pickup swap*.

yield pickup swap A trade that involves the switching from a lower yielding bond to a higher yielding bond. Traders may do this to take advantage of greater liquidity in one bond over another or to take on more risk in their portfolios. The trade-off of yield pickup swaps is that the higher yielding instruments are riskier assets and the potential of default is increased. Also see *bond; swap*.

yield price The price of a bond expressed as a yield. Sometimes called the basis price. Also see *yield*.

yield spread The difference in yields between bonds of different terms, usually a ten-year bond and a treasury bill. The spread is thus the difference in rates between bonds placed on different parts of the yield curve. Also see *bond; treasury bill; yield curve*.

yield to call The yield from a bond if an investor were to hold onto the bond until such time as it is called. Also see *callable bond*.

yield to maturity (YTM) The rate required in the marketplace for investors to purchase a bond. The YTM rate is affected by:
- the market risk-free rate of return
- a premium over inflation
- interest rate premium
- credit risk premium
- liquidity premium.

To calculate the YTM on a bond, calculate the required rate of return for the discounted future cash flows to equal the current price. The YTM is often used as the opportunity cost variable in discounted cash flow calculations as a nominal annual interest rate. Sometimes called the yield to redemption. Also see *nominal annual return; bond value; clean price; credit risk; inflation; liquidity premium; bond yield; total price; yield*.

Yield-X Bond Exchange The JSE bond exchange. A competitor of The Bond Exchange of South Africa. Also see *bond; Bond Exchange of South Africa; JSE*.

young company The definition of a young company for the Alternative Investment Market (AIM) listing is a company less than two years old. Also see *Alternative Investment Market*.

YTR Yield to redemption. Also see *yield to maturity*.

yuan The currency of the People's Republic of China, sometimes called the renminbi, divided into 100 fen.

YUM The Yugoslavian dinar divided into 100 para.

ZAr South African cents, i.e. one hundredth of a ZAR.

ZAR The South African rand divided into 100 cents.

zero cost collar A put option purchased at a higher strike price with the proceeds from writing a call option at a lower strike price, or a call option purchased with the proceeds from writing a put option at a lower strike price. A combination of these options limits the up and downside risks of an investment over a collar portion. Sometimes called a range forward contract, flexible forward, cylinder option, option fence, min-max and forward band. Also see *call option; collar; downside; put option*.

zero coupon bond A bond that does not have a coupon. There are thus no intermediate cash flows in the form of coupons and zero coupon bonds trade at a discount to face value so investors are rewarded for holding them. These bonds are more sensitive to changes in interest rates than their coupon-paying counterparts. Also see *cash flow; discount security; face value*.

zero coupon convertible A zero coupon bond convertible into equity. Sometimes called a liquid yield option note. Also see *convertible debt; equity; liquid yield option note; zero coupon bond*.

zero coupon rate The rate that will be earned on a bond if the bond made no coupon payments. Zero coupon rates are widespread and exist for all major currencies. They can be used to derive discount factors for interest rate swap pricing. Also see *bond; discount factor; interest rate swap*.

zero coupon swap An interest rate swap agreement where payments are made at the maturity of the swap. Also see *interest rate swap; swap*.

zero coupon yield The yield on a zero coupon bond. Also see *yield; zero coupon bond*.

zero coupon yield curve A yield curve composed of zero coupon bonds. The zero coupon yield curve is often used to determine discount rates. Also known as the spot yield curve. Also see *spot market; yield curve*.

zero sum game One person's gain is another's loss. The net sum is zero. Sometimes called a nil sum game.

zero volatility spread The spread that an investor would earn if there were no changes (i.e. zero volatility) in interest rates. Also see *interest rate*.

ZK The currency of Zambia, the kwacha, divided into 100 ngwee.

zloty (ZL) The currency of Poland, the zloty, divided into 100 groszy.

Z score A statistical measure based on regression modelling that indicates the financial health of a company.

ZWD Zimbabwe dollar.